MOVEMENTS FOR ECONOMIC REFORM

MOVEMENTS
FOR
ECONOMIC REFORM

BY

PHILIP TAFT

Professor of Economics
Brown University

New York
RINEHART & CO., INC., *Publishers*

18119

To the memory of Otto Franklin Branstetter

PREFACE

The present work is an outgrowth of an undergraduate course in theories and programs of economic reform given for several years at Brown University. A course in this subject should give the student a background in ideas of reform, the movements that developed to promote them, and the institutions developed by these movements in the course of their activity. A student ought to be made aware that plans for reconstructing society are as old as written history and probably older. He ought to be introduced to the views of such writers as Plato, More, and Winstanley, so that he can appreciate that programs of reform may be based on a desire to achieve ends other than material plenty, and that the dream of a perfect society has haunted men in all ages.

A student should be able to place the ideas he encounters in historical perspective. It is important for him to realize that the varieties of modern socialism are not wild and rank growths, but are largely the extensions of the concepts of equality and progress developed in the age of the Enlightenment. The views of several of the eighteenth-century socialists should be examined with that in mind. He should also note the gradual emergence of modern socialist views with respect to history, class, and wealth in the first decades of the nineteenth century. Thus he will be able to appreciate later views that fought for dominance over the reform movements of the world. He will see for example, the ideas of Marx in better perspective, for he will note that many of them are an elaboration or a sharpening of earlier opinions.

It is important that the student become acquainted not only with Marxism, but with other philosophies of reform. The latter frequently contain trenchant criticisms both of the Marxist system and of capitalism and are even now competing for the suffrage of the people of different countries.

A course cannot stop with an analysis of abstract ideas. We know that the reaction of all countries to a body of doctrines is not the same. Only by examining the customs, traditions, and history of a country can we account for its acceptance, rejection, or modification of a doctrine. The same body of ideas may stimulate a party devoted to moderate reform in one country, or a group of totalitarian communists in another, or revolutionaries inspired by a theory of heroic violence in a third. Therefore we must examine how programs of reform are transformed in particular national environments. Such an approach also enables us to deal with writers and leaders whose ideas lack insight or originality, but, because of heroism, capacity for inspiring masses of people, or ability to evolve new political tactics, are important figures in revolutionary movements. Certainly Bakunin and Blanqui were mediocre theoreticians, but they are of considerable importance as improvisers of tactics.

The movements for economic reform have achieved limited or absolute power in a number of countries. A student ought to examine the institutions that have been created, so that he can estimate to what extent the hopes of the founders have been realized. How have these movements solved the age-old problems of scarcity and allocation of resources? Do these "new societies" dry up incentives, endanger technical progress, and threaten human freedom? Is there an attempt to dominate the reform movements of all countries by one power, and have certain governments been able to subvert institutions, originally founded to promote peace and understanding among the peoples of the world, into power instruments for national aggrandizement? A course in economic reform can help the student to begin to answer these questions, and it is my hope that this volume will partially smooth the student's way over this terrain.

A number of friends and colleagues have been kind enough to suggest changes and improvements. I am particularly grateful to Professor M. M. Bober of Lawrence College, who was kind enough to read the manuscript and has made available to me his wide learning in the field. His many suggestions for improvements and changes have been of great aid to me, as have those of Professor Robert Dahl of Yale University, Professor Howard Guy Dodge of Brown University, Professor Henry Spiegel of The Catholic University, and my colleagues, Professors Penelope Clair Hartland and James M. Morgan and Mr. Harlan Smith. Mrs. Evelyn

Uhlendorf, secretary of the Department of Economics, University of Michigan, has helped me with editorial problems. Not only has Theresa Taft typed most of the manuscript but I have profited from her knowledge of radical social movements. The John Hay Library of Brown University, the Widener Library at Harvard University, and the main branch of the New York Public Library have made their resources freely available to me. Finally I must record my indebtedness to my former teacher, Professor Selig Perlman, whose insight and understanding of social movements have been of lasting aid to me. Of course, I alone am responsible for whatever errors may have been committed.

Brown University   Philip Taft
Providence, Rhode Island
January, 1950

CONTENTS

MOVEMENTS FOR ECONOMIC REFORM

1. INTRODUCTION

Programs of reform and revolution have been presented in almost every age. Poets, philosophers, statesmen, and politicians are among those who have been inspired with visions of a brave new world—a world free from evil and devoted to beauty and justice. As expressed by Omar Khayyám:

> Ah Love! could you and I with Him conspire
> To grasp this sorry Scheme of Things entire,
> Would not we shatter it to bits—and then
> Re-mold it nearer to the Heart's Desire!

Men have not only dreamed, but have determined to make their dreams a reality. Some have planned flawless societies which could easily be attained once mankind perceived the proper principles of living. Others, while convinced that the future would be better and nobler than the past, insisted that man had to pass through a series of less fortunate stages before he could reach the best. A wide variety of plans and programs has been presented since Plato formulated his scheme in the *Republic*. Some of the formulators have gained an army of devoted followers and have thus been able, at least in part, to remake the world.

Practical people have derided the intellectual pretensions of revolutionaries, calling them unrealistic and visionary. Yet few men have influenced society as much as Plato, Owen, or Marx. One must not ignore those in whose names great causes have been born and upon whose words vast and powerful empires have been built. It may be comforting to regard social innovators as idle dreamers, and there is perhaps an element of folly and even arrogance in the readiness of man to offer a final and complete answer to life and living. Yet only a hopeless Philistine would end the characterization at this point. Many revolutionaries were men of

1

character, selflessness, and wisdom, and have left an indelible imprint upon society.

One must also avoid, in considering programs of reform, the smugness of the logician who believes that proof of a logical contradiction or inadequacy is fatal. It is easy to demonstrate numerous contradictions in the work of social innovators, but while this is important and necessary, an assumption of devastating superiority is scarcely warranted. We must bear in mind that these programs are set up in answer to some vital need. The desire for greater perfection in social relations is one aspect of the urge for the improvement and elevation of the human race. Though the road may be long and devious, and perhaps even a wrong road, the influence of these programs in stirring masses of followers and in evoking innumerable sacrifices should make it incumbent upon all of us to examine them carefully and without prejudice.

Classifying social innovators and their programs is difficult. Utopian and scientific elements, in varying combinations, enter into all programs of basic social change. Programs of social reorganization and the practical policies elaborated to carry them out seem to have been influenced by a number of conditions. The economic, political, and intellectual history of the period in which the views were evolved, the purpose toward which the programs were directed, and national and individual characteristics all seem to play a part. Certainly the history of the European revolutionary movement would have been different without Karl Marx; and had Lenin been born in England, the Bolshevik Revolution might have taken a different turn. There are great "ifs" in history, and they do not carry us much forward in our understanding; yet they do point to the importance of the several factors that shape the history of events and ideas. For that reason not only the ideas but the principal exponents, the leaders, tacticians, and statesmen, may shed light on the history of the movements for social reform.

Although they exercised a significant influence upon thinking, many writers did not themselves directly inspire a social movement. Many of the pre-Marxist writers fall in this category. As used in this volume, a social movement refers to a widely held desire to change political, social, or economic relations, not primarily for the advantage of the participants, but for the benefit of all people. These movements have a diverse origin and are inspired by many types of ideas, some of which seem of no significance when first formulated. It is perhaps not altogether accurate to describe social criticism before the late eighteenth century as a movement. As a rule, these critics were moralists and philosophers who attacked existing conditions on the basis of some moral or social principle. It is, however, useful to examine the views of such critics because of their influence upon later generations and because they demonstrate the eternal striving for the perfect and unattainable society.

With the growth of democracy and popular government, there appear true social movements that seek to rally a mass of people to their standards. These movements first manifested themselves in the different types of early nineteenth-century socialism. By the last third of the nineteenth century, Marxism or as Engels called it, scientific socialism was accepted by most of the more militant social reformers. Marxism is, however, more than a program of economic reform. It is virtually a complete philosophy of life; and while many agreed with the Marxist criticism of economic affairs, they rejected its views on philosophy and religion. Within the latter group were the ethical socialists who regarded a collectivist economy as a more desirable mechanism for distributing goods and services. They usually placed more emphasis upon moderate reforms than the Marxists, who regarded the ultimate displacement of capitalism as the primary goal.

Closely resembling the ethical socialists, but basing their criticism upon other grounds, are those Christian writers and preachers who attack capitalism as immoral and materialistic. In common with ethical socialists, they reject the subordination of the individual to economic processes. But the Christian writers also reacted to the spreading influences of Marxism, with its emphasis upon material advantage. Christian Socialism sought a return to an earlier form of economic life which had been obliterated by modern industralism.

Both Marxists and ethical socialists were cosmopolitan and internationalist in outlook and were concerned with the common interest of all people. The former's internationalism was based upon economic and class interpretation of phenomena, and, while the latter's was in part influenced by pacifist humanitarianism, this group also tended to ascribe international conflict to economic causes. There also arose, in part as a reaction to the Marxist and ethical socialists, and in part because of opposition to some aspects of capitalist society, a "socialist" movement which rejected humanitarianism and internationalism. Militantly nationalistic, it regarded capitalism as undesirable—and the more traditional forms of socialism as alien to the true spirit of the nation-state. Although this reactionary socialism represented a reversal of the humanitarian and internationalistic tendencies of the last two centuries, it has attracted a large following and has at times exercised a decisive influence over events.

An understanding of modern social movements requires more than an examination of abstract doctrines and principles, for in many countries groups espousing collectivist views influenced and directed policy. Marxism, which became the dominant creed of those advocating a drastic reorganization of society on the European continent, was unable to impose a common policy upon its followers in all countries. Under the impact of diverse social, political, and economic environments, Marxist ideology was either modified in theory or ignored in practice.

The movements that accepted a Marxist ideology developed a number of forms. Thus Marxism in Germany led to reformism; in Austria, to reformism plus a vigorous and democratic movement; and in Russia, to a totalitarian regime and the evolution of the doctrines of communism. In turn the proponents of Marxist communism have from the beginning maintained a militant campaign to transform the social movements of the world into a replica of their own. England and Spain showed themselves inhospitable to Marxism; socialist ideas in these countries have an ethical and religious origin and their socialist movements thus differed from the variety prevalent elsewhere. France developed a variant of Marxism called syndicalism, whose doctrines later became a source of inspiration for fascism. The United States has never had a strong or widely dispersed socialist movement, but it has developed several forms of agrarian radicalism. Several of these movements have gained either a partial or a complete influence over the policies of their governments and have thus been able to shape and devise new institutions.

The student of modern social movements faces a dual task: he require a knowledge of the concepts and systems which have been elaborated by one man or by groups of writers; he must learn how the movements themselves behaved and developed—the practical solutions they offered, and the problems they faced as actual operating governments or as responsible oppositions seeking to achieve or to exercise power. It is therefore my purpose to describe the views of Plato and several other early Utopians, largely to show how their approach to the ideal society differs from that of later writers and also as an example of the eternal search for perfection. Likewise, eighteenth-century writers on socialism are important to this study because of their emphasis upon equalitarian ideas which play such a dominant role in the work of later thinkers. In addition, the eighteenth century witnessed the first popular uprising, one which came to occupy an important place in socialist mythology. The chapters on early nineteenth-century socialists deal with forerunners of Marx, whose views came to dominate the movement. We must not only deal with Marxism and its predecessors but with such rival social movements as anarchism, which, while critical of capitalism, recognized the dangers of concentrated state power. Christian socialism is described, for it was an alternative to Marxism and arose out of the same general conditions. The chapters on developments within specific countries are intended to show how special histories and environments have influenced changes in ideas, and how they affected practice.

We can also examine alternatives to the Continental socialist systems as they appeared in English "laborism" and in this country's "New Deal." These movements are also attempts to rectify the evils of industrial capitalism, but in general their approach is more pragmatic and moderate than that of the Continental socialist schools. The description of their origin and operation will help us to see a different approach to modern social problems, an approach which is less ambitious, but which may ultimately be less costly in terms of human freedom and economic welfare.

2. THE FIRST UTOPIANS

In common with modern reformers, the early creators of ideal commonwealths emphasized the importance of social institutions in shaping the character of man. They also believed in the possibility of constructing an ideal society which would guarantee happiness. Although they did not seek to inspire or arouse large masses, their work has value not only as social criticism, but as an example of an approach different from that of modern critics. The writers to be dealt with in this chapter wrote at different times and in response to diverse circumstances. All of them, however, were of the opinion that justice could be obtained by reorganizing society on some communal principle, and their views resemble the modern versions in that they believed a large measure of social control was desirable.

PLATO (428–348 B.C.)

One of the earliest programs for social reorganization was devised by Plato, "the most influential of all philosophers, ancient, medieval and modern." [1] He was born during the Peloponnesian War, a time of trial and turbulence, and although Athens felt insecure and uncertain, its intellectual and spiritual life was in full vigor.

Plato came under the influence of Socrates, and after traveling outside his native country he founded the Academy, a school of philosophy. He presented his views in the form of dialogues, a literary form designed to stimulate thought. As a starting point some individual offers the ordinary or popularly held view on a subject: this view is then examined step by step, its falsity or limitations are exposed, and a view founded on true principles is developed.

[1] Bertrand Russell, *A History of Western Philosophy* (New York: Simon and Schuster, 1945), p. 104.

The philosophy of Plato centered in his theory of ideas. Plato believed that there exist eternal and unchanging forms or ideas, such as absolute beauty, truth, or justice from which particular qualities are derived. Particular objects are in a constant state of flux, and there must exist some eternal and immutable realities, or ideas, which particulars reflect. For example, particular tables were, for Plato, unreal, and they were only a reflection or copy of the real table which exists in the mind of God. Plato pursued philosophy because of his belief that the acquisition of knowledge is ennobling and that wisdom will enable man to live the good life.

THE REPUBLIC

The *Republic* is devoted to an investigation of justice and the good life. As a good man is a member of a state, it is necessary to determine how a good state is formed. Plato, as a philosopher, recognized that to be a good man requires knowledge. He therefore outlines a system of education which will enable man to pursue the good life. If the system of education is to work satisfactorily, a social and economic reorganization of society upon different principles is necessary.

Justice   In the dialogue in the *Republic,* Thrasymachus presents the popular view that "justice is nothing else than the interest of the stronger"; that the strong are justified in dominating the weak. Because power is the basis of political authority, the action of a ruler is always just. Might is right, and he who holds the might has justice on his side.

Plato rejects this view and instead defines government as an art which, similar to other arts, seeks to perfect the material with which it deals. "No science or art considers or enjoins the interest of the stronger or superior, but only the interest of the subject and weaker." The physician, as physician, is interested in the patient's welfare; the pilot is concerned with the welfare of the sailors under him and not with his own. Therefore, "no one as far as he is a ruler, considers or enjoins what is for his own interest, but always what is for the interest of his subject or suitable to his art." Consequently the ruler as ruler acts unselfishly and seeks only the well-being of his subjects. Moreover, in seeking the welfare of his subjects, the ruler will be following not only a more just but a wiser course. The ruler recognizes the need to set a limit to his actions, to avoid blindly rushing at every pleasure. Instead, the ruler walks firmly on his road toward a definite object. Because he recognizes the principles imposed by reason, the just man is the wiser, and, being wiser, he is also the better and the stronger.

Having disposed of the view that justice is the will of the stronger, Plato next examines the thesis that justice is the result of an artificial convention, a social compact based upon mutual fear. According to Glaucon, "When men have both done and suffered injustice and have had experience of both, not being able to avoid the one and obtain the other, they think that they had better agree among themselves to have neither; hence there arise laws and mutual covenants; and that which is ordained by law is termed by them lawful and just." Plato refuses to admit that justice is the result of mere convention. On the contrary it expresses the inner nature of man, something that is basic and everlasting. To illustrate the true nature of justice, he traces the origin of the state and then sets up an imaginary society free from the imperfections of existing ones.

The State   The State arises out of the needs of mankind; for no one is self-sufficing, and all of us have many wants. The outcome is specialization and the division of labor which increases with time. Economic activity is thus based upon the reciprocal advantage that accrues to all the participants as each gains by the increased efficiency of the other. Therefore, mutual interest is superior to self-seeking, and an exchange of services between ruler and ruled is superior to selfish individualism which aims at maximum personal advantage.

However, men are not everlastingly satisfied with the simple pleasures. In time, their tastes are refined—and improved, and a greater area and a larger population are needed for their support. To acquire more territory, war must be waged. Consequently, the state has need of an army, a specialized soldiery must be raised from those possessing an abundance of fighting spirit. A true soldier is like a good watchdog, fierce to strangers and enemies and gentle to those he knows and loves.

Guardians   The rulers or guardians of the State are to be a specialized class selected by a series of tests and trials from the ranks of the soldiers. Rulers should be philosophers, capable of recognizing the essence of truth, beauty, and justice; and masters of the special art of ruling, an art which they alone possess. In addition to being a master of the soldier's art, the ruler can be distinguished by his broad philosophic nature, capable of grasping truth. Plato has thus set up two dominant classes—the guardians and the military caste.

Commoners   In addition to the above two classes, a third, fitted for neither war nor government, will devote itself to supplying the economic needs of the community. Similar to the others, it will be specialized in function. Society will thus be divided into three classes: guardians or rulers, auxiliaries or soldiers, and commoners—artisans, traders, and farmers. Each group has special endowments and is obligated to discharge a special service.

Education   Education is a means of realizing justice and the good life, and is designed to provide for the development of every aspect of man throughout his life. The individual is to be trained in gymnastics and music. Gymnastics train the body and develop courage, strength and endurance; music, which includes literature, trains and encourages proper thinking. The arts will aid in the formation of right opinions; and as poetry, music, and the plastic arts exercise a strong attraction for youth, they could be used to stimulate love of virtue. Those who have shown the greatest aptitude during their period of artistic education will be trained in science, so as to perform more important state duties. The most adept in science will, in turn, receive an education in dialectics; and those who attain the highest skills in the latter discipline will be given the more important offices of the state. Those who have successfully met the tests given at every stage of a man's life, will be allowed time, after the age of fifty, for pure contemplation. They will, however, be required to remain in the service of the state.

Communism   As individual interest hinders the achieving of justice and the good life, Plato proposed that guardians and soldiers, the upper classes, live under a system of complete communism. Guardians and soldiers are to live in simple houses and eat plain food in common dining halls. They are to own neither gold nor silver and to possess only the most necessary elements of private property. Communism is extended from property to women and children. Plato expects this aspect of the program to encounter difficulties, but he believes they can be overcome by education. Both sexes are to have the same education and the same rights and obligations. Plato did not believe that the differences between the sexes had any effect on the ability of some women to be guardians.

Marriage of the guardians is to be conducted under the direction of the guardians, and they will arrange it so that the best men have the most offspring. Children are to be reared by the state and are not to be known to their parents. Consequently, all guardians of a certain age are to be regarded as parents, and the women called mother, the men to be called father. The inability to identify one's own child will lead to the strengthening of the bonds of union between members of the group, for no longer is anyone concerned with his own interest but only with the welfare of the corporate body. He hoped to force men to organize their lives differently and thereby to produce a different spirit and changed attitude of mind.

> [Plato's society] must be regarded as a pattern which cannot be perfectly realized under actual conditions but none the less determines the degree of excellence and happiness to which humanity can aspire.[2] The philosopher or sage is best fitted to recognize the true nature of the ideal and the means of its realization. The harmony or health of the individual soul and of the community can be secured only if reason and those possessed of reason control the lower faculties and the lower classes, each of which will find a measure of freedom and happiness by subordination to an authority which is superior in the nature of things.[3]

Political intelligence arises from the superior levels of the community and not from the masses. It is the philosopher who is most clearly able to distinguish between appearance and reality.

The difference between appearance and reality is illustrated by Plato in the allegory of the cave. A number of prisoners are sitting in a cave, chained with their backs to the light. To them, the mere shadows thrown on the wall by the fire burning near the entrance seem to have substance. A prisoner is released, and as he walks toward the light he fails to distinguish between the real objects and their shadows. Blinded by the light, he wants to turn back, but is forced outside, where the glare of the light dazzles and blinds him. After a time he becomes habituated to his new surroundings and he is able to gaze upon reality and the sun itself—the giver of light. Should this man now be forced to return to the cave, he will at first be as confused by the shadows as he had been by the real objects. Should he attempt to inform his companions on the difference between appearance and reality, he will be scorned and jeered at. Nevertheless, being imbued with true knowledge, he will become the natural leader because now he is able to contemplate the pure idea of good.

Thus philosophers, after initial confusion, achieve pure knowledge. "And now, being possessed of wisdom, they will not be allowed to spend their life in contemplation, but must return to the cave to rule the City, since it is the happiness of the whole community with which we are concerned, and this depends on the due performance by each citizen of that work for which he is naturally fitted."

[2] Roger Chase, *Until Philosophers Are Kings* (New York: Oxford University Press, 1929), p. 89.
[3] *Ibid.*, p. 91.

REASONS FOR COMMUNISM

Plato's system is only partially communistic, designed only for the upper classes. Those who are destined to participate must share a Spartan life. Goodness and justice are sought, not economic well-being. Plato's communism is ascetic and aristocratic; it does not lead to greater economic abundance, and it does not include more than a small segment of the population. It is a system of half-communism, and not an institution of all society. A small superior class submits itself to a rigid discipline for the benefit of all.

The entire system is authoritarian, with an élite class standing at the top of the social pyramid. Presumably, rulers will know what is good for those of baser mold, and will impose their will upon the masses. Plato's *Republic* is really a form of ascetic fascism, as the ordinary man is allowed to own property. The spirit is reactionary, anti-individual, and statist. In Plato's society the individual does not count; he exists only for the benefit of the state. It is assumed that those of superior merit will be recognized and trained and that a selfless attitude will be inculcated by training; the leaders would have to recognize talent almost at birth, a task not easily achieved even in our "aptitude-testing" world.

Despite the idealistic character of Plato's philosophy, the Platonic political system seems to be based on an implicit economic determinism. It is assumed that men either accumulate riches for their own profit or for the benefit of their offspring; eliminate the reasons for accumulating wealth, and men will cease to have reason for unjust acts, and selfless service to the community will be assured. This narrow economic determinism neglects the "power drives" of ascetics and others uninterested in the fleshpots or in storing up worldly goods. The illusion that economic resources are the chief or sole source of power is one especially attractive to our town times. Events have shown that oppression and injustice need not be based on economic factors, and certainly the communizing of property and family does not necessarily remove the power urges of man. Throughout most of his career, the greatest oppressor of modern times, Adolf Hitler, had no legal family and sought little property, although he was not averse to earning large royalties on *Mein Kampf*. He sought and attained power to use for his own emotional aggrandizement and not to initiate a dynasty. Like Marx, Plato seems to overstress economic factors in political life.

SIR THOMAS MORE (1478–1535)

More's Utopia is closely related to the character of the author and to the conditions of his time. The sixteenth century was an age of unrest and of religious, social, and economic change. The increase in the size of the farm, brought about by the enclosure movement (enclosure of open fields and conversion of arable land into pasture), the encroachment of pasture at the expense of arable land, the expulsion of the surplus population, and their transformation into destitute nomads were characteristic of More's time. The commutation of labor service and its replacement by monetary rent led to the growth of a "cash nexus" between man and man. Men were driven from the land by the enclosures of the arable and common land and formed a large body of propertyless workers. In an economic sense, the enclosure movement was progressive, as it wiped out the inefficient strip system, substituted the more lucrative sheep raising, and created a proletariat ready to sell its labor for wages. Nevertheless, More was among those who were outraged by the misery and suffering that followed, and his Utopia is a commentary upon conditions prevalent at that time.

Sir Thomas More was born in London of a distinguished family, his father being a judge of the King's Bench. He attended St. Anthony's School in London and at the age of fourteen became a page in the household of the Archbishop of Canterbury. After two years he was sent to Oxford, where he studied Latin and the classics. At Oxford, More came into contact with the revival of learning then in full force. He became acquainted with Erasmus and the two were close friends. In 1501, More was appointed reader at Furnival's Inn and in the spring of 1504 he was elected to Parliament. For some time More thought he might join a monastic order and became austere and ascetic, mortifying his body by fasting and by wearing a hair shirt. This phase passed, however, and he again occupied himself with legal studies and literary translations.

HENRY VIII

At the accession of Henry VIII to the throne, More rapidly gained in favor and fortune. He was appointed to responsible posts and had entrusted to him the more subtle tasks of diplomacy. Honors came to him in profusion. In 1518 he became master of requests and a little later a member of the Privy Council. In 1521 he was knighted and appointed under secretary of the Treasury. Successively, he became speaker of the House of Commons, chancellor of the Duchy of Lancaster, and in 1529 chancellor, succeeding Wolsey. At first his relations with his king were good, but Henry's rupture with Rome led More to give up the seals. More refused to accept the Act of Succession of 1534, which repudiated the pope as the head of the church. He was tried in July, 1534, and sentenced to death. On the scaffold he said to his nervous executioner, "Be not afraid to do thine office."

CRITICISM OF SOCIETY

While busy with other tasks, More composed his *Utopia,* or the country of nowhere, in 1516. The title has given us the word "utopian," a designation for the visionary and impractical.[4]

The *Utopia* is devoted to a criticism of existing social conditions and contains a plan for a more perfect society. More attacks the wide use of capital punishment, which went beyond the limits of justice and was harmful to the public welfare. "Simple theft is not so great an offense that it ought to be punished by death. Neither is there any punishment so horrible that it can keep them from stealing which have no other craft whereby to get their living." [5] He felt that the interests of society can best be served by providing opportunities for people so that they will not be driven to steal.

He also decried the indolence of the rich who rob the poor: "There is a great number of gentlemen among you, that are themselves as idle as drones, that subsist on other men's labour, on the labour of their tenants, whose rents are raised and pared to the quick."

Large standing armies and sheep raising came in for critical attention: "Your sheep that were wont to be so meek and tame, and so small eaters, now, as I hear it said, have become so great devourers, and so wild, that they eat and swallow down the very men themselves. They consume, destroy and devour whole fields, houses and cities." Prices of food had risen and despite the large increase in the number of sheep, the price of wool remained high. This he attributed to monopoly. "Suffer not these rich men to buy up all, to engross and to forestall, and with their monopoly to keep the market alone as please them."

---

4 R. W. Chambers, *Thomas More* (New York: Harcourt, Brace and Company, 1935), is a modern standard biography.

5 Sir Thomas More, *Utopia* (Oxford: The Clarendon Press, 1936), p. 12. The following quotations from More are from this source, pp. 13, 15–16, 18, 110.

More then depicted in detail his Utopia as an island cut off from the mainland, the center of a perfect commonwealth. In harmony with More's dislike of luxury, the inhabitants of Utopia shun ostentation. The cities are surrounded by thick, turreted walls. The streets are broad and open, but the houses stand close together. Their doors are never locked or bolted—anyone may enter, as there is nothing privately owned inside. Each town must contain six thousand families, and these form the basis of an electorate and government.

Every thirty families choose annually an officer called the phylarche, and every two hundred phylarches thus chosen select a prince who holds his office for life, unless deposed for tyranny. He is assisted by a council. All officers except the prince are chosen annually.

Industry Life in the perfect commonwealth is reduced to the most simple terms. Farming is the common occupation of all men and women. In addition, each learns a special trade, the lighter trades being learned by the women. There is a tendency for crafts to be hereditary although choice in selection is allowed. The blacksmith, clothing maker, carpenter, and mason represent the four chief trades. Officers see that each applies himself to his work with diligence and industry, and guard the inhabitants against overwork. Utopians work only six hours, three before noon, followed by a break for a meal and a nap, and three late in the afternoon. The evening meal comes after six hours of labor have been completed, and a period of leisure ends the day.

Social Practice The short workday is sufficient to supply the Utopians with all goods and services. At a given time the stewards, each representing thirty families, collect the goods needed by those he represents. The families are then summoned by a trumpet to a public hall to partake of their meal. Private eating is allowed, but regarded as poor taste. Bondsmen recruited from the prisoners of Utopia and the surrounding areas prepare the food. The Utopians take pleasure in the use of their minds and from the contemplation of virtue, but they are not opposed to the mundane enjoyments of eating and drinking. Simple dress is the rule; garments are varied only to distinguish the male from the female and the married from the single. The Utopians refuse to permit coercion in matters of religion, but all who deny the immortality of the soul or the rule of the creator are excluded from public position. They do not, however, insist upon the acceptance of a dogmatic creed. Utopians place no great value on money or on the precious metals. In Utopia "of gold and silver they make commonly chamber pots and other like vessels that serve for most vile uses."

While very solicitous of the ill, the Utopians preach self-destruction to those painfully and incurably sick. However, they do not order suicide but urge it only as an escape from incurable pain.

Women can marry when they reach the age of eighteen, and men when they are twenty-one. Sexual relations before marriage are punished by celibacy for the remainder of the offender's life, unless he is pardoned by the prince. Husbands and wives may divorce their adulterous partners. Habitual adultery is punishable by bondage. Bondsmen can be reprieved if they show that they are sorrier for their offenses than for their punishment.

Punishment as a deterrent to crime is only slightly used, for people are "lured to virtue with rewards and honors." Inordinately ambitious men do not rise to greatness easily. Few laws are placed on the statute books, for Utopians do not cherish an abundance of laws, nor do they deeply respect lawyers.

Inhabitants of Utopia place great stress upon peace, for "they count nothing so much against glory, as glory gotten in war."

"More had no desire to turn the world upside down, but rather a wish, in the quiet of a library, to turn the problem of wealth and poverty inside out and see what would come of it." [6] Another student believes that More took for his model the Inca civilization of Peru: "The great Utopia of Thomas More was not a product of his imagination, but a generally representative account of an actual country and its social system." [7] Whatever its origin, More's respect for manual work and his desire to make available the cultural heritage to all people show him to be a forerunner of modern social movements despite his belief in absolute monarchy.

TOMMASO CAMPANELLA (1568–1639)

Campanella was born at Stilo in Calabria. He entered the Dominican order as a youth and soon showed a strong interest in literary and philosophical studies. He was attracted to the work of Telesio, who

6 Algernon Cecil, *A Portrait of Thomas More* (London: Eyre and Spottiswoode, 1937), p. 121.

7 Arthur E. Morgan, *Nowhere Was Somewhere* (Chapel Hill, N .C.: The University of North Carolina Press, 1946), p. 17.

taught him to cast off the prejudices of tradition. His open adherence to these doctrines led to his trial for heresy at which he received a mild sentence. In his first philosophical work, published in 1589, he revealed an attitude toward physical phenomena which resembles that of the modern scientist and reflects the spirit of the Renaissance as mirrored by Pico della Mirandola and Bruno.[8] He was a transitional figure, an innovator in the use of scientific methods but a believer in the mystic and the occult.

His view of the universe was pantheistic. For him there existed a universal soul, broken up into individual parts and manifesting itself through the individual. In Campanella's universe there is no death, only mutation of being.

But he was more than a philosophic speculator. He took part in a conspiracy against the Spanish authorities and as a result was imprisoned and tried for civil disobedience and heresy. He escaped death by feigning madness and was condemned to perpetual imprisonment. He was incarcerated for twenty-seven years. After his release he settled in France, where he was befriended by Cardinal Richlieu.

IDEAS OF REFORM

Campanella's ideas of reform sprang from his philosophic and practical outlook. In *The City of the Sun* he developed his socialist views, describing a community organized on the city-state principle. The ruler is a priest—Hoh—who is chief of all temporal and spiritual affairs. He is assisted by three princes of equal authority, named Power, Wisdom, and Love. Power handles all matters respecting war and peace; all military affairs also are in his jurisdiction, and he is subordinate in this respect only to Hoh. Liberal and mechanical arts are ruled by Wisdom. Love is charged with matters affecting the race: marriage, the raising of children, the harvesting of crops. "He sees that men and women are so joined together that they begat the best offspring. Indeed, they laugh at us who exhibit a studious care for our breed of horses and dogs, but neglect the breeding of human beings."[9]

[8] C. Dentice Di Accadia, *Tommaso Campanella* (Florence: Vallecchi Editore, 1921), pp. 7–13.

[9] "The City of the Sun" in *Ideal Commonwealths* (London: Routledge and Kegan Paul Ltd., 1890), p. 224. The immediately following quotations from Campanella are from this source, p. 225.

COMMUNISM

"All things are common with them, and their dispensation is by the authority of the magistrates. Arts and honors and pleasures are common and are held in such a manner that no one can appropriate anything to himself." Community of wives is practiced, for "all private property is acquired and improved for that reason that each one of us by himself has his own home and wife and children. For when we raise a son to riches and dignities, and leave an heir too much wealth, we become . . . ready to grasp at the property of the state." Those without rank or wealth are likely to become avaricious and sly.

The family lies at the base of private property, for without the family, riches, dignity, and honor would not be important. To eliminate that self-love which is the basis of the family, Campanella would create a community of wives and children. "For . . . children are bred for the preservation of the species and not for individual pleasure." Once the family is abolished, the citizen could devote his entire time to the interests of the state. "In brief but unmistakable terms the celibate monk advises the Platonic theory of community of wives." [10]

LABOR

Occupations are alloted to both men and women, with men receiving the more difficult tasks. Sedentary work is usually given to women, who are excluded from working in wood or in arms manufacture. Young people are required to wait on their elders. Campanella advocated labor for all, and perpetual leisure for none. He feels that if all the able-bodied population engage in useful work, the workday can be shortened and the burden lightened for the worker. While he would provide for the aged, the healthy and able-bodied beggar would be forced to work. As all are compelled to labor, Campanella's commonwealth has no need of slaves. Slavery is objectionable on other grounds: a society that allows slavery naturally creates a leisure class which has too much time on its hands. All work, the carrying out of duty, is equally honorable, and no class division can be based upon the type of labor performed. Labor is a civic duty, and who performs the most burdensome and difficult tasks is worthy of the highest honor. Idleness is frowned upon, for it leads to

[10] William B. Guthrie, *Socialism before the French Revolution* (New York: The Macmillan Company, 1907), pp. 136, 235.

"avarice, ill-health, lasciviousness, usury and other vices and contaminates and corrups many families by holding them in servitude for their own use, by keeping them in poverty and slavishness, and by imparting to them their own vices." As everyone in the City of the Sun works a few hours a day, the people avoid both the vices of the idle and the vices of the poor. For "grinding proverty renders men worthless, cunning, sulky, thievish, insidious; vagabonds, liars, false witnesses . . . and wealth makes them insolent, proud, ignorant, traitors . . . boasters." [11] In the ideal commonwealth, people are "rich because they want nothing and poor because they possess nothing."

EDUCATION

All important knowledge is taught in the City of the Sun, and taught in a manner which makes learning an enjoyable pleasure rather than a wearisome burden. Children of both sexes are instructed together and by men of approved worth. In their education, gymnastic exercise is not neglected, and an effort is made to strengthen the body as well as the mind. At seven years of age, the teachers begin to discover the predilections of each child, and they direct his interests according to his bent. An attempt is always made to train each child in the skills for which he is best fitted and in which he will be most useful.

JAMES HARRINGTON (1611–1677)

Harrington's *Oceana* is one of the great works of political science written in the seventeenth century. Its author attended Trinity College, Oxford, where he studied under the theologian Chillingworth. He then traveled abroad, observing the different forms of Continental government, and was attracted by the political institutions of Venice. He became a republican, but because of his friendship for Charles I he avoided participation in the struggle between the king and Parliament. After the execution of Charles, Harrington devoted himself to framing a code of rules to resolve the social and political confusion of his time. The result was *Oceana*, published in 1656. His work occasioned a number of comments, and in answer to his critics Harrington published a summary of his principles, *Art of Law Giving and Systems of Politics*.

Although *Oceana* was written in the form of a political romance, the author had England in mind. The hero of the tale is Olphaus Megaltor

11 *Ideal Commonwealths*, pp. 237, 238.

(Cromwell), who, seeking to imitate the Spartan Lycurgus, devised a new constitution and retired when his nation was prosperous and happy.

GOVERNMENT

Harrington proposed to divide the country into a number of parishes and to teach the inhabitants the use of the ballot. Parishes would be combined into hundreds, and hundreds into tribes. Two elections would be held: first, one fifth of the voters would be chosen on a popular basis as an electoral college; then this group would choose the actual members of parliament, which would consist of senators and representatives. The senators would be charged with debating issues, and the representative would decide the issues placed before them by the senate. Executive power would be divided among four separate councils—state, war, trade, and religion. Religious differences would be tolerated, although a national church would be set up.

SOURCE OF POWER

Harrington held that power in government derives from wealth in the form of property. Restricted possession of wealth produces oligarchy, while widespread ownership of property will assure democracy. He pointed out that since the first Tudor the most important form of wealth —land—had been increasingly transferred from the gentry to the middle class; therefore, transfer of political power must follow. His proposals limited the ownership of land by an individual in England and Ireland to a value of two thousand pounds. However, he wanted the estates broken up gradually. To prevent future concentration of ownership of landed property, he would not allow those who owned property above two thousand pounds to acquire more by purchase, and he would restrict inheritance to one thousand, five hundred pounds. Harrington had before him as a model "the agricultural democracy which Aristotle had commended." [12]

He also held that in nations where commerce is more extensively developed, power would be distributed in accordance with the possession of capital. In relating political power to means of production, Harrington—as did Plato—gave prominence to economic considerations.

Harrington's socialistic division of property is designed to make a republic possible, but he hoped that a large landowning class would avoid

[12] H. R. Russel Smith, *Harrington and His Oceana* (Cambridge: Cambridge University Press, 1914), p. 32.

the extreme forms of democracy. His suggestions with respect to the ballot in direct election and rotation in office are to that end. Voting by ballot would eliminate the possibility of violence and fraud. Rotation or alternation in office is as important to government as is the circulation of blood to the individual; it makes possible more widespread participation in government, assures continuity, and prevents tyranny. Rotation would be achieved by annual election to triennial offices. The government would be composed of a senate of 300 members, and a representative assembly of 1,050, which reflected the interest of the people. Under this arrangement the senate could propose but only the assembly had the power to dispose or reject.

EQUALITY

The basis of the Oceanic commonwealth would be equality. Because of the law limiting property, high position could be achieved only by social service and intelligence and not by material possessions. Consequently, wealth would exercise a less important role in society, and the desire for accumulation would diminish.

Harrington's idea of distribution of power exercised a marked influence upon subsequent constitutional development, especially in the United states in the system of checks and balances and the separation of powers. At the Massachusetts Constitutional Convention in 1799, the acceptance of the doctrine of the separation of powers showed Harrington's influence upon the thinking of John Adams and other political leaders. A suggestion that Oceana be substituted for Massachusetts in the preamble to the constitution was made and rejected.[13] Harrington's ideas aided in the creation of republican sentiment and contributed to the belief that widely diffused landownership is the guarantee of freedom.

Harrington was writing in the midst of a great struggle between monarchic and popular rights. He sought largely to point out that power follows wealth, and that a system of checks and balances was essential to the preservation of a democratic society. In his emphasis upon economic considerations he is an intellectual forerunner of nineteenth-century socialism.

13 *Ibid.*, p. 194.

GERRARD WINSTANLEY (FL. 1609)

The views of Gerrard Winstanley were developed in the midst of the great revolutionary conflict between Charles I and Parliament. Monarchic absolutism, religious freedom, and arbitrary taxation were the issues that divided king and Parliament. The opposition was, however, not united. At one extreme were the Presbyterians, who sought to substitute their form of authoritarian rule for that of the Church of England. At the other extreme, the Independents stood for freedom of conscience and individual rights, but they themselves were divided into "gentlemen," Independents, and Levellers.[14] The Levellers were politically radical and individualistic; they sought reforms that would safeguard personal and civil liberties, which were conceived as "inalienable rights inherent in every human being and inseparable from the idea of freely acting personality. The critical points in a political program were . . . . suffrage and the bill of rights; the first to insure that government should be responsive to the popular will, the second to keep even a popular government from intruding upon the inviolable domain of individual right." [15]

At the extreme of the Leveller movement was a communist faction led by Gerrard Winstanley. As a young man, Winstanley settled in London and entered trade. The Civil War ruined his business and he turned to farming, at which he made a precarious living. He underwent a profound religious experience and finally " . . . he arrived at tranquility in the consciousness of a personal revelation—an 'experimental' knowledge of God within him, which supersedes the 'imaginary' knowledge of the letter and the external law of ordinances and ceremonial, and which he conceived to be the cause of a complete moral transfiguration." It was this personal revelation which induced him to organize a communist group to cultivate the common land. The plan had been announced earlier in "The New Law of Righteousness." Winstanley and his followers expected "the physical realization of the Kingdom of God upon earth." His view of life and his motivations were religious, for Winstanley believed that the inner life glows in all men, that God is in every creature, that Christ will rule the earth, and that all men are equal in the sight of God. The communist movement he inspired was based on religious principles.

14 Eduard Bernstein, *Cromwell and Communism.* Translated by H. J. Stenning (London: George Allen & Unwin, Ltd., 1930), p. 66.

15 *The Works of Gerrard Winstanley.* Edited by George H. Sabine (Ithaca, N.Y.: Cornell University Press, 1941), pp. 3–4. The following quotations from Winstanley are from this source, pp. 9, 38, 145–149, 269–271.

In the "New Law of Righteousness" he tells of being in a trance and hearing the words "Worke together, Eat bread together; declare this all abroad. . . . *Whosoever it is that . . . doth not look upon themselves equal to others,* The hand of the Lord shall be upon the labourer . . . . All tears, occasioned through bondage cannot be wiped away till the earth become in use to all a Common Treasurie." Winstanley regarded his experience as a command for him to establish a communistic society.

DIGGING

He preached to all who would listen to him. He and his followers issued "A Declaration of the Poor Oppressed People of England" in which the ownership by landlords is attacked.

We . . . declare unto you, that call yourself Lords of Manors, and Lords of the Land, That in regard the King of Righteousness, our Maker, hath inlightened our hearts so far, as to see That the earth was not made purposely for you, . . . but it was made to be a common Livelihood to all . . . . We finde Resolutions in us, grounded upon the inward law of Love, one towards another, To Dig and Plow up the Commons, and waste Lands through *England,* and that our conversation shall be unblameable, That your laws will not reach to oppress us any longer. . . . For though you and your Ancestors got your propriety by murther and theft, and you keep it by the same power from us, that have equal right to the land with you.

They declared they would cut down the trees in the woods for their private use.

On April 1, 1649, a small group of men appeared at an uncultivated spot at the side of St. George's Hill on the Commons in the County of Surrey and began to "dig." They explained their purpose of plowing and planting upon the Commons without the payment of rent. In the first days of their experiment, the Diggers—as this group of Levellers was called—worked and sang. They expected to be joined in their enterprise by thousands of others. Instead, they aroused the local population, who attacked the Diggers and burned one of their houses.[16] Undeterred, they continued their work, despite continued hostility. Apprised of the action of the Diggers, the Council of State ordered General Fairfax to intervene. Winstanley and his closest co-worker, William Everead, were brought before the general and fined. The Diggers continued but they were con-

[16] David W. Petegorsky, *Left Wing Democracy in the English Civil War* (London: Victor Gollancz, Ltd., 1940), p. 161.

tinually harassed by the local population. In July, Winstanley and a group of his followers were arrested, and heavy fines were imposed upon them for trespassing. The small band was prevented from resuming its project elsewhere. Despite the failure of this effort, attempts to seize the commons for purposes of joint cooperative labor were at the time made in other parts of England.[17]

After the collapse of the communist experiment, Winstanley gave a detailed statement of his views in "The Law of Freedom in a Platform." True freedom he finds in the free enjoyment of the earth. Man can be liberated from the bondage of kings and landlords, and the external forms of his enslavement—buying and selling—abolished. Instead of bartering their wares, men ought to work at their trades and deposit the fruit of their labor in public warehouses, so that "every family as they want such things as they cannot make . . . shall go to these shops, and fetch without money, even as now they fetch with money." [18] Such a state would, according to Winstanley, restore peace and freedom, and make provision for the weak and oppressed.

Winstanley enunciated the principles that determine the two forms of government—that of common preservation in which the strong help the weak, and that of self-preservation in which the rich and powerful are favored. The former is a true commonwealth, and frequent elections and short tenure are requirements for its achievement.[19] He also outlined a detailed plan of government. The first officer is the father of the family who is to train his children in the arts and sciences—secular education is favored. Above the family stand the local, county, and national officers. Local officers are of two kinds, overseers of the peace and of the trades. The former maintain order, the latter supervise the apprenticeship in and practice of the trades as well as the warehouses where goods are stored. Men over sixty years of age are charged with general supervision of affairs. Parliament has the task to "give out orders for the free planting and reaping of the Commonwealth's land." [20] Such arrangements, Winstanley believed, would end poverty, as each would have enough and none more than he needed. While opposed to buying and selling, Winstanley would allow them in trade with foreigners. In the relations between the

[17] Margaret James, *Social Problems and Policy during the Puritan Revolution* (London: Routledge and Kegan Paul, Ltd., 1930), pp. 103–152.
[18] *The Works of Gerrard Winstanley*, p. 526.
[19] *Ibid.*, pp. 538–542.
[20] *Ibid.*, p. 557.

sexes, Winstanley was conservative. He believed in monogamy and the sanctity of the family, and he would punish severely violators of the moral law.

Winstanley provided a link in the chain of development of revolutionary doctrines, for in his time he proposed and attempted to carry out drastic reforms. The religious sources for his inspiration and his emphasis upon the sovereignty of the individual place him apart from most modern revolutionaries. His capacity to combine revolutionary thought with action places him, however, closer to the moderns than to earlier formulators of ideal commonwealths.

3. SOCIALIST IDEAS IN THE EIGHTEENTH CENTURY

Although most of the socialist theories developed during the eighteenth century seem, by modern standards, quite primitive, a number of these ideas occupy a significant place in later socialist systems.

The eighteenth century witnessed a critical examination of ancient creeds and shibboleths. Happiness of the individual was held to be the main purpose of society. Moreover, happiness could be most effectively achieved by destroying the feudal restrictions upon economic and political activity. Man should be allowed freedom to choose his governors and to conduct his economic affairs without the restraints and limitations imposed by the old social controls.[1]

Human institutions, regardless of their age, had to justify themselves before the bar of reason, and an attempt was made to apply the methods of science to moral and political questions. The eighteenth century was not content to study man in his historical environment; it sought, on the contrary, to discover the natural man behind the conventions, customs, and traditions that had been built up in the past centuries.[2]

Against the conventional and the artificial in urban life was juxtaposed the innocent rustic tranquillity of an old society. Thus arose the concept of the beauty of the primitive and the nobility of the savage, uncorrupted by civilization. From the abstraction of a state of nature and the noble savage, it was easy to deduce that man has been corrupted by law and civilization. In the blissful state of nature, private property—it

[1] Kingsley Martin, *French Liberal Thought in the Eighteenth Century* (London: Ernest Benn, Ltd., 1929), p. 220.

[2] André Lichtenberger, *Le Socialisme au XVIII siècle* (Paris: Ancienne Librairie Germer Bailliere et Cie., 1895), pp. 2–6.

was assumed—did not exist, and equality was the rule. The desire for equality and happiness for all made a deep impression upon writers and thinkers of that time. They were critical of the inequality they found around them, especially the inequality of wealth. The entire complex of ideas was favorable to the development of socialism.

The eighteenth century also accepted the view that infinite and unending progress and "the indefinite malleability of human nature by education and institutions" were possible.[3] Some of the writers, notably Helvetius, tried to show that in a well-organized society, all men could attain the highest level of mental and moral development. The belief that man was capable of infinite development if surrounded by proper institutions was an important factor in the systems of early nineteenth-century socialism and appears in Marxism and its variants. However, in the eighteenth century the idea of progress "had been a vague optimistic doctrine which encouraged the idealism of reformers and revolutionaries but could not guide them."[4]

The doctrines of socialism were the fruit of the speculations of literary men and philosophers who believed in infinite progress and in the ability of all men to achieve happiness by changing and controlling human institutions. The idea of equality also played a role in the formation of subsequent opinion. Some writers limited their ideas of equality to equal political rights and equal opportunity—without restriction—to buy and sell labor and commodities; another school interpreted equality to mean the abandonment of private property and the establishment of some type of communist utopia. Exponents of the latter views believed that private property had been forcibly and fraudulently appropriated and some felt that as "private property had been unjustly acquired and was upheld by class legislation, it must be abolished."[5]

JEAN-JACQUES ROUSSEAU (1712–1778)

Leading the attack upon inequality and private property was Jean-Jacques Rousseau, the man who mirrored most closely the tone and temper of his time. He was born at Geneva, where his forefathers had settled after having been driven from France during the religious wars. At an early age, Jean-Jacques showed his love of reading and knowledge and

[3] J. B. Bury, *The Idea of Progress* (London: Macmillan & Co., 1921), pp. 165–166.
[4] *Ibid.*, p. 278.
[5] Martin, *op. cit.*, p. 239.

devoured the good and bad books in his father's library. As a youth he was apprenticed to an uncle who ran a watchmaking shop, but he found travel and vagabondage more to his taste. He exercised a significant influence upon subsequent generations as the inspirer of the romantic movement with its emphasis upon nature and uninhibited man. His ideas developed slowly, and he was almost forty years old when he attracted attention by an attack upon civilization. He then produced a series of works, the most important being *Émile* and the *Social Contract,* both of which appeared in 1762.

His *Discourse on the Origin of Inequality,* published in 1755, is the work in which the modern equalitarian can find the most ammunition. Rousseau claimed that, in order to discover the true nature of mankind or the conditions of its original existence, it is necessary to set aside the changes that have been imposed by social institutions. He appealed to sentiment and imagination more than to science and experience.[6]

HUMAN NATURE

According to Rousseau, human nature is governed by principles that antedate reason. We have a concern for ourselves and our own preservation; and because we are repelled by pain, we are determined to prevent the suffering of others. In his capacity for sensation, man resembles other animals; he differs from them in possessing the power to choose, in not being a slave to impulse. Man's capacity to choose is the basis of progress but also the cause of his vices.

INEQUALITY

Rousseau thought that progress has led to inequality. There is one kind of inequality which "consists in a difference in age, health, bodily strength, and the qualities of the mind or soul: and another, which may be called moral or political inequality, because it depends on a kind of convention and is established, or at least authorized, by the consent of man. The latter consists of the different privileges which some men enjoy to the prejudice of others; such as that of being rich, more honored, more powerful, or even in a position to exact obedience." [7]

6 Charles William Hendel, *Jean-Jacques Rousseau* (New York: Oxford University Press, 1934), I, 47–48.

7 Rousseau, *The Social Contract and Discourses* (New York: E. P. Dutton & Co., 1946), p. 160. The following quotations from Rousseau are from this source, pp. 142, 202, 203, 205, 219. Reprinted by permission of the publishers.

Inequality can be traced to the "first man who, having enclosed a piece of ground, bethought himself of saying 'This is mine' and found people simple enough to believe him." In other words, the establishment of property is the cause of inequality. It might have been possible to maintain equality had men been of equal strength and skill. However, men are differently endowed with these attributes, skill and strength, and these differences lead to natural inequality which, once developed, "becomes more sensible and permanent in its effects, and begins to have an influence in the same proportion over the lot of individuals."

Inequality is strongly resisted and "the destruction of equality was attended by the most terrible disorders. Usurpations by the rich, robbery by the poor, and the unbridled passions of both suppressed the cries of natural compassion and the still, feeble voice of justice, and filled men with avarice, ambition and vice. Between the title of the strongest and that of the first occupier, there arose perpetual conflicts, which never ended but in battles and bloodshed." Property leads also to the creation of political society with the consequence that a usurpation is transformed into an irrevocable right. By plausible argument, the rich have created a social organization and law to protect their titles. These have "bound new fetters on the poor, and given new powers to the rich; which irretrievably destroyed natural liberty, eternally fixed the law of property and inequality, converted clever usurpation into unalterable right and, for the advantage of a few ambitious individuals, subjected all mankind to perpetual labor, slavery and wretchedness."

Rousseau concluded that inequality in property is the principal cause of the multitude of evils which beset mankind. The law of the strongest appears again, its difference in being that in a state of nature it manifests itself in a pure form, while now it arises as a consequence of excessive corruption. However, "the despot is master only so long as he remains the strongest; as soon as he can be expelled, he has no right to complain of violence. The popular insurrection that ends in the death or deposition of a sultan is as lawful an act as those by which he disposed, the day before, of the lives and fortunes of his subjects." Thus, inequality, the promoter of despotism, leads eventually to revolution.

Rousseau was motivated by a desire to complete the political revolution which had abolished feudal privilege. He envisaged the perfect society as one of small middle-class proprietors, for "laws," he said, "are equally powerless against the treasures of the rich and the misery of the poor." [8] In common with a number of other writers, he had in mind a small equalitarian republic. *The Discourse on the Origin of Inequality* is a strong attack upon property and property holding and furnished a powerful weapon to subsequent critics of individual ownership.

MORELLY (?–?)

Nothing is known of Morelly's life, and his works have also been attributed to others. *Le Code de la Nature, ou Le Véritable Eprit de ses Loix de tout temps négligé ou méconnu,* published in 1775, presents the eighteenth-century thesis of the natural goodness of man. Man decays and becomes aggressive and wicked as a result of the pressure of social institutions. Society and private property transform the harmony of nature into social antangonism.

THE CODE OF NATURE

Morelly criticized the errors of moralists and legislators. He believed that they have misunderstood human nature in their assumption that man is vicious and wicked. Rather, Morelly argued, moralists should provide a situation in which it would be impossible for man to be evil and depraved—man is created for happiness.

PROPERTY

Legislators fail to recognize that the world has enough for all. In contradiction to the natural law of communality, property has been made the basis of all institutions; thus property is the cause of all crime, the frequent begetter of evil. The solution Morelly proposed is the abolition of property, which would enable man to establish a perfect government modeled on the laws of nature.

PERFECT SOCIETY

Morelly's final plan, which he believed would assure the virtue and happiness of man, advocates the abolition of private property except for those goods that are used personally by the individual; the division of the nation into cities, tribes, and families; the maintenance of every citizen at public expense, each one contributing according to his ability; and the requirement that all between the ages of twenty-one to twenty-five work

8 Alfred Cobban, *Rousseau and the Modern State* (London: George Allen & Unwin, Ltd., 1934), p. 203.

on farms. Under the plan, professions and trades would have the number of workers proportionate to the undesirability of the work, a master watching over each profession to see that the work is efficiently performed. The ascetic Morelly advocates the suppression of all vanity and adornment, with simple uniforms for each profession. The members of his society would elect their professions at the age of ten, marry at the age of fifteen or eighteen, and retire at the age of forty, with the assurance of a livelihood to every individual. Celibacy for those under the age of forty would not be allowed; marriage would be voluntary, but indissoluble for ten years, after which a divorce could be obtained if there were sufficient grounds. The community would care for and educate all children who had reached the age of five. Morelly was convinced that the wants of man can be satisfied by a relatively small amount of labor, and that there is sufficient in the world to supply everyone.[9]

GABRIEL MABLY (1709–1785)

L'Abbé Gabriel Mably was educated for the church, but he abandoned this career for literature and social criticism. In 1741, he became secretary to Cardinal Tencin and remained at his post for seven years when, after a quarrel, he resigned. He then completely withdrew from the world and devoted himself to the study of antiquity and philosophy, and to writing. His literary output was his sole means of support, and from 1748 to his death in 1785 he published fourteen works.

VIEWS

Like many of his contemporaries, Mably believed that politics should be based upon ethics and that ethics should be derived from the nature of man. Once the nature of man is discovered, the policies and measures to be pursued will be evident. Mably was convinced that man is formed by his environment and that in turn man fashions his environment.

Man is selfish, and his conduct is often motivated by self-interest. Man merges into society in response to natural needs, and nature has provided him with sufficient goods for all, if they are shared equally. In his plea for equality, Mably asserted that nature has established no differences among her children since she has given the same senses, feelings, and

9 Martin, *op. cit.*, pp. 243–246; Lichtenberger, *op. cit.*, pp. 114–123.

needs to rich and poor, princes and slaves, masters and servants. Inequality is due to the political laws which violate natural law.[10] "That nature intends all men to enjoy equality is one of Mably's chief contentions." [11] This view is continually repeated—equality is held higher than liberty, for it is the primary gift of nature to man; equality is a source of well-being, for it unites man, lifts him above his self-interest, and promotes good will and friendship, while inequality degrades and humiliates.

Property   The root of inequality is in property, especially property in land. The emergence of property destroyed the inner harmony which had governed man. "Citizens, proud of their riches, have disdained to regard as their equal those who are forced to work for a living."[12] Riches create an overmastering egoism which drives man to increasing accumulation. As man wanders from primitive equality he becomes more and more avaricious and develops false needs and useless desires. Inequality leads to moral decay and the perversion of man's true sentiments. Riches undermine man's true personality, so that the wealthy become slothful; the poor, humble.

Communism   The remedy for the evils of society is a return to the social and moral state indicated by nature. Mably was pessimistic, however, over the possibility of reform. If a favorable occasion for a revolution should arise, it is proper for all to act, since it is a choice between revolution and slavery; less violent change, however, is to be preferred. Mably held that the good legislator is essentially a moralist who will seek to repress antisocial impulses or redirect them into constructive channels. He argued that, being a moralist, the legislator should always hold before him the blessed state of communism existing in the primitive societies that preceded the corrupt age of gold. He held communism as the most perfect social order, but he did not urge men to renounce private property and organize a communistic system.[13]

10 Henri Sée, *L'Évolution de la pensée politique en France au XVIII siècle* (Paris: Marcel Girard, 1925), pp. 253–254.

11 C. H. Driver, "Morelly and Mably" in F. J. C. Hearnshaw, *The Social and Political Ideas of Some Great French Thinkers of the Age of Reason* (New York: Appleton-Century-Crofts, Inc., 1930), p. 236.

12 Quoted by Sée, *op. cit.*, p. 255.

13 Lichtenberger, *op. cit.*, pp. 234–237. There are a number of other socialist writers, the most important being Jean Meslier (1678–1733), Nicholas Henri Linguet (1736–1794), and Charles Robert Gosselin (1740–1820). All of them emphasized, to some degree, the corrupting influence of civilization, and Linguet was not only an economic determinist, but justified revolt against injustice. His views are discussed in André Lichtenberger, *Le Socialisme utopique* (Paris: Ancienne Librairie Germer Bailliere et Cie., 1898), pp. 78–131.

THE FRENCH REVOLUTION

Despite previous criticism of social and economic institutions from a socialist point of view, and the elaboration of several socialistic systems, socialism was not a significant movement during the period of the French Revolution. Some denunciations of unequal distribution of property and some pleas for communism had appeared.[14] The *cahiers* issued before the Revolution demanded the suppression of privilege and the establishment of equality before the law. However, "the Revolution inherited from the *philosophes* [the critics and philosophers of the eighteenth century] a rigorous criticism of property as an absolute right, an ethical defense of communism, and a profound sense that, because the privileges of aristocracy are indefensible, the state might be made to serve the people creatively. The notions had to be applied in a time of crisis, without time to think either of their philosophic significance or their administrative possibility."[15]

THE CONSPIRACY OF THE EQUALS

The French Revolution abolished feudal rights and royal absolutism. Some of the Montagnards were not content with the reforms of the Convention.

Thus Billaud-Varenne, in a tract published in 1793, spoke openly against great wealth. He protested against Voltaire's idea that the worker should be spurred to work by hunger, and he demanded that it be declared that no citizen should henceforth be permitted to possess more than a fixed amount of land, and that no one be allowed to inherit more than 20,000 to 25,000 livres.[16]

In addition to Billaud-Varenne, there were other exponents of communism and partial communism during the French Revolution. Jacques Roux, a former priest, preached an explicit communism and achieved considerable popularity among the laboring poor. The best known of the socialists of the French Revolution was, however, François-Noel Babeuf, who led an unsuccessful attempt to overthrow the property system.

---

[14] Lichtenberger, *Le Socialisme au XVIII siècle*, pp. 425–426.

[15] Harold J. Laski, *The Socialist Tradition in the French Revolution* (London: The Fabian Society, 1930), p. 14.

[16] P. A. Kropotkin, *The Great French Revolution*. Translated from the French by N. F. Dryhurst (New York: G. P. Putnam's Sons, 1909), p. 486.

FRANÇOIS-NOEL BABEUF (1760–1797)

At the age of fifteen, Babeuf became a clerk in a land-surveying office and later served as a land commissioner. He joined a literary society and began to contribute papers on social and philosophical topics.[17] But the French Revolution changed his life and outlook. In the district of Roye he proposed the abolition of feudal tenures and the substitution of a general tax. His proposals were rejected but his popularity increased, and in 1790, he abandoned his work as a land agent and took up a career of political journalism. Two years later he was appointed an administrator and archivist of the Department of the Somme, but after a quarrel with a superior he left. He fled from a similar position at Montidier to escape a charge of forgery in connection with some land titles. He secured a post with the *Bureau des Subsistances* under the Paris Commune. His attempt to prevent dishonesty made him a number of enemies and he was arrested for the old offense at Montidier but was acquitted. Upon his acquittal he returned to Paris in 1795 and launched his *Journal de la liberté de la presse,* which attacked Robespierre and the Commune.[18] He also denounced Robespierre's successful opponents, the Thermidorans. The paper was suppressed but was reissued as *Tribun du peuple.* He was arrested in February, 1795, and was released after seven months by an amnesty issued during the closing days of the National Convention. During this time his views had taken definite shape.

Babeuf was no mere pamphleteer. In October, 1795, having gained an appreciable following, he organized a political society whose aim was the achievement of political and economic equality. It attracted many Jacobins dissatisfied with the turn of the Revolution. In a short time the Society of the Pantheon, which the extreme revolutionaries had founded, had a membership of over 2,000. Babeuf's journal became its official organ. Babeuf proclaimed the doctrine of equality and denounced the holding of private property as the cause of all evil. His agitation was answered by an order for his arrest. He eluded capture, but was soon unable to continue publication of his journal. The Society of the Pantheon was suppressed. Babeuf responded by forming the Secret Directory of Public

---

17 Gerard Walter, *Babeuf* (Paris: Payot et Cie., 1937), contains the facts of Babeuf's life and career.

18 David Thompson, *The Babeuf Plot* (London: Routledge and Kegan Paul, Ltd., 1947), pp. 12–16.

Safety "instituted to restore the people to its rights."[19] It was one of the first underground, conspiratorial organizations and has served as a model for many subsequent groups. Headed by Sylvain Maréchal and Babeuf, the organization was devoted to "equality without restriction, the greatest possible happiness of all, and the certainty of never losing it by force or fraud—such are the benefits the secret directors of public safety sought to ensure to the French people."

In April, 1796, the "Manifesto of the Equals," drawn up by Sylvain Maréchal, was issued as a sort of campaign document. It appealed to the people of France who "during fifteen ages . . . have lived [as] slaves, and [were] consequently unhappy." The manifesto declared equality as "the first vow of nature, first want of man, and chief bond of all legitimate association . . . . From time immemorial, we have been hypocritically told—*men are equal;* and from time immemorial the most degrading and monstrous inequality insolently oppresses the human race." Real, not nominal, equality was demanded, and a prediction was made that the "French Revolution is but a forerunner of another revolution far more grand, far more solemn, and which will be the last." The manifesto denied that the revolutionaries favor the partition of lands: "We aim at something more sublime, and more equitable; we look to *common property,* or the *community of goods!* No more individual property in lands. *The earth belongs to no one.* We claim—we demand—we will the communal enjoyment of the fruits of the earth; *the fruits belong to all.* Let there be no longer any other differences in mankind except age and sex. Upon this 'real revolution' depends the happiness of all mankind."

A statement of principles, *Analyse de la doctrine de Babeuf,* was issued later. According to the "analysis," nature has given to every man an equal right to the enjoyment of all goods, and the "end of society is to defend this equality, often assailed by the strong and wicked in the state of nature; and to augment, by the cooperation of all, the common enjoyment of all." Everyone is obligated to work and none can escape without the commission of a crime. Common work and common and equal enjoyment are the basis of a just society. Only through crime can people appropriate to themselves exclusively the products of the land and industry. Neither rich nor poor should exist in a just society. The object of revolution is to abolish inequality and to re-establish the well-being of all.

[19] Filippo Michele Buonarroti, *History of Babeuf's Conspiracy for Equality.* Translated by James Bronterre O'Brien (London: H. Hetherington, 1836), p. 89. The following quotations from Buonarroti are from pp. 90, 308–309, 314–317, 320, 89, 139.

The document calls also for the restoration of the Constitution of 1793. Usurpation of the powers granted by that constitution is held illegal and counterrevolutionary. An active propaganda was instituted, and many rallied to the cause as the leaders began to discuss the form of insurrectionary government. The setting up of a dictatorship was rejected in favor of a democratic assembly.

The Directory responded by denouncing Babeuf and his followers, charging them with seeking to divide existing property. A law was promulgated in April, 1796, which imposed severe penalties for advocacy of the division of property. Nevertheless, preparations for an armed uprising were begun under the recognized leadership of Babeuf. Tentative decrees, to be issued after the uprising had succeeded, were drafted.

Babeuf's Secret Directory planned to establish a great national community of goods, made up of national property, buildings used for public services, such as hospitals, the property of those who had enriched themselves at public expense, and lands uncultivated by the proprietors; it also planned to abolish inheritance—all property of the deceased was to revert to the state.

Members of the community, except those over sixty years of age, were to labor either in industry or in agriculture. Those between the ages of forty and sixty who surrendered their possessions to the community would not have to perform manual labor, if they had not done that type of work in the past. The length of work day would be regulated by law and all efforts made to substitute machines for hand labor. Income from community property would be distributed among the members of the community so as to furnish each with at least a frugal living. As can be seen, the program was a thoroughgoing reconstruction based upon a lower middle-class view of life—a society of artisans living and working as equals—a form of Jeffersonian democracy.

While the views of Babeuf and his followers are not of great significance as revolutionary doctrines, the techniques of conspiracy they evolved have influenced subsequent radical movements. Power was concentrated in the hands of the Secret Directory, which "conceived the generous resolution of binding to a single point the scattered threads of democracy for the purpose of directing them towards the re-establishment of the popular sovereignty." The plan of organization required the sending of twelve revolutionary agents into various districts and military agents into the army and other branches of the government. At the same time a vigorous and extensive propaganda effort was initiated among the people. A notable amount of success was gained, and plans for seizure of power were made. The government was, however, kept fully informed of developments by one of the leading plotters. According to Buonarroti, seventeen thousand Parisians were ready to take part in the revolt. However, the government was able to step in, and on May 10, 1796, arrested the leaders of the conspiracy, including Babeuf. Two unsuccessful attempts were made to deliver the conspirators.

Forty-seven prisoners were brought to trial on February 20, 1797. The trial continued for more than three months. Troops surrounded the courthouse, and the prisoners were closely guarded. The accused justified their conspiracy on the ground that the government was illegal: consequently the attempt to overthrow it was not a crime but a justifiable act against usurpers. The public prosecutors refused to enter into the question of the legality of the government, and instead confined themselves to demonstrating the facts of the conspiracy. In the end, Babeuf and his leading associate, Augustin Alexandre Darthé, were sentenced to death and seven others to deportation.

Gracchus Babeuf can be regarded as the forerunner of Auguste Blanqui and of the Bolsheviks. His belief in the ability of an armed and well-organized minority to seize power and reorganize society has exercised an influence over the thinking of the extreme left up to our own time. As the first centrally directed secret conspiracy of socialism, the Babouvists devised a model for other revolutionaries to follow. Their methods of infiltration and militancy were copied and further developed by later radicals.

4. SOCIALISM IN THE NINETEENTH CENTURY

The first decades of the nineteenth century produced a proliferation of socialistic ideas, and several theoretical socialistic systems were developed independently and simultaneously as if in response to a collective need. Fourier, Saint-Simon, Cabet, and Robert Owen devised their schemes for social reorganization at about the same time. As Durkheim points out, the authors of nineteenth-century programs of social reconstruction do not aspire to artistic success, nor do they seek to elevate the soul. On the contrary, their purposes are eminently practical.[1] In contrast to the eighteenth-century writers who looked back at a golden past, those of the nineteenth century looked forward to a happier future. The latter wished to go forward to higher and more efficient economic organization and not backward to the time of the innocent and unspoiled savage.

Despite these differences, there are significant similarities between the socialist views of the eighteenth and the first part of the nineteenth centuries. The belief in equality and in the beneficence of God or nature is common to both periods, as is the view that human felicity will be assured by a return to a more natural state. Fourier's conviction that a law of universal harmony could be discovered and Owen's view that man was corrupted by environment echo the eighteenth-century idea of the goodness of nature. Most of the socialist writers of the early nineteenth century were imbued with a belief in equality and leaned upon natural law to reinforce their ideas. They can, however, be divided into two groups. One believes that the state should absorb the economic functions exercised by individuals; Saint-Simon, Cabet, Louis Blanc, and, later,

[1] Emile Durkheim, *Le Socialisme; sa définition, ses débuts, la doctrine Saint-Simonienne* (Paris: Librairie Félix Alcan, 1928), pp. 41–42.

Marx fit into this category. Another group, which contains Fourier and Proudhon within its ranks, stresses the building of the free, autonomous, and decentralized association as the future form of economic activity.

The late eighteenth and early nineteenth centuries witnessed a wide expansion of industrial capitalism, characterized by the socialization of production—organizing large numbers of workers in a factory under central direction. It made possible the accumulation of large fortunes by those able to seize the main chance. Not social rank but ability to exploit the opportunities was the open-sesame for success. Industrial capitalism raised standards of living, but it also separated the worker from his tools and the independent farmer from his land, making both dependent upon an employer for a job. Uncertainty and periodic unemployment became common experiences, and these conditions aroused the attention of reformers. The expansion of factory employment led to the growth of urbanization with its slums, the increase in the employment of women and children, and great disparities in income and wealth.

As new evils are likely to make a more profound impression upon our minds than those to which we have become accustomed, the hardships and sufferings introduced by the new industrialism aroused much fear and attention. Thus social thinkers turned their attention to discovering means by which the misery and insecurity could be overcome. Socialism finally became, at least on the European continent, Marxian socialism. Karl Marx was able to absorb the diverse doctrines and to hammer them into a unified system. No doubt his ability to fuse so many unrelated and contradictory views into a fighting faith represents an achievement of genius; yet many of the views that became part of the Marxian system were either suggested or stated by earlier writers. Saint-Simon, for example, was an outstanding forerunner of Marxian socialism.

SAINT-SIMON (1760–1825) AND THE SAINT-SIMONIANS

Claude Henri de Saint-Simon, a native Parisian, claimed he could trace his origin to Charlemagne. His father was the son of the famous Count Saint-Simon, who played an important role at the brilliant court of Louis XIV and whose lengthy memoirs form an important source of the history of his time. Claude Henri inherited a great name and a sizable fortune. One of the most learned men of the time, D'Alembert, was among his teachers, and from him the boy acquired a deep love of science. He showed his independence at the age of thirteen when he refused to attend Communion and was sent to prison for his recalcitrance. At the age of seventeen he entered military service and was among those Frenchmen who helped the American colonials in the American Revolution, being present at the surrender of Cornwallis. Despite rapid advancement, he was not interested in being a professional soldier and resigned from the army in 1779. He returned to France four years later and tried to organize a project to connect the Atlantic and Pacific oceans by a canal in Mexico; similarly, he proposed to the Spanish government a plan for uniting Madrid and the coast. His plans did not arouse much enthusiasm, and he turned to other tasks.

In common with other titled aristocrats during the French Revolution, Saint-Simon lost his fortune, his social position, and almost his life. He attempted to remain apart from the revolutionary cataclysm engulfing his native land, for while he opposed the *ancien régime,* he did not approve the violence he found around him. In partnership with Count Redern, he began to speculate in church lands, and the depreciation of the assignat was in part responsible for his success. His activity was soon interrupted by the terror which seized France; he was thrown into prison, and there he found time to reflect on the course of events. Upon his release, he turned from the pursuit of wealth to the pursuit of wisdom. He carried out his intention to the full: he studied, discussed, and taught; he took rooms near the Polytechnic School so that he could more easily promote his scientific knowledge. Then thirty-eight years old, he turned toward learning with the eagerness and avidity of a much younger man. He studied physics and physiology with equal enthusiasm, but he did not neglect more mundane activities; the sublime and the disreputable were both examined so that nothing human would be alien to his spirit.

For twelve months after his short-lived marriage in 1801, Saint-Simon entertained lavishly; his small fortune disappeared and he was forced to accept employment as a clerk. During this time, his views were being published and distributed among a limited circle of friends and disciples.[2]

EARLY WORK

Saint-Simon's first work, *Lettres d'un habitant de Genève à ses contemporaires,* was an attempt to discover the laws governing the operation of society. He maintained that in the Middle Ages the clergy constituted

---

[2] *Oeuvres de Saint-Simon.* Edited by Olinde Rodrigues (Paris: Capelle, 1841), pp. xvi–xxix.

the intellectual elite, but since that time it has failed to incorporate the advances of science into its scheme of thought. Consequently, science and theology are no longer a harmonious whole but are at war with each other.

His *Introduction aux travaux scientifics du XIX siècle* was conceived on a grand scale but turned out to be a more modest performance than the author had planned. In it he emphasized the importance of the intellectual classes and illustrated his point by a famous parable.

PARABLE

The "Parable," published as a pamphlet in 1819, raised the question of the possible effect upon French society if it were to lose fifty each of its leading philosophers, scientists, poets, painters, musicians, sculptors, and writers. If France, said Saint-Simon, should lose three thousand of its most eminent intellects, it would require at least a generation for recovery; for these men of great intellect are indispensable to French industry and glory; their loss would be a fatal blow to French culture and French well-being, for they are the true flower of French society and make possible its strength and prosperity.

If, on the other hand, France should lose its leading noblemen, the high officers of the crown, the ministers of state, all the marshals, all the cardinals, archbishops, bishops, grand vicars, canons, judges, and great proprietors:

> Such a misfortune would certainly distress the French because they are kind-hearted, because they could not witness with indifference the sudden disappearance of so great a number of their countrymen. But this loss of thirty thousand individuals, reputed to be the most important to the State, would cause grief merely as a matter of sentiment, for no damage would be caused to the State.[3]

Saint-Simon argued that it would be very easy to fill the vacant places of the aristocracy and royalty for there are many courtiers ready to occupy these ranks.

The prosperity of France, he concluded, rests on the progress of science, the arts, and industry; royalty, titled aristocrats, and high churchmen do little to advance social progress. Moreover, the fact that the latter group absorbs a large part of the social dividend demonstrates that our social organization is imperfect and that men are exploited by ruse and violence. The satire, directed against leading aristocrats who were men-

3 "Parable de Saint-Simon," *ibid.*, pp. 71–75.

tioned by name, led to the trial of Saint-Simon, but he was acquitted.

Saint-Simon followed with a number of other pamphlets dealing with politics, economics, and history. His works had a meager sale. His difficulties became unbearable and he tried to commit suicide; he failed, but his self-inflicted wound caused the loss of an eye. Before his death in 1825, he published his *New Christianity,* which contains his principal views. He left a band of devoted disciples determined to spread his views and philosophy.[4] The views found in his writings are summarized below.

RELIGION

Saint-Simon argued that Christianity has lost its primitive simplicity, and that the church has become corrupt. A distinction ought to be made between divine revelation and the commentaries made upon it by the clergy. What God has said cannot be improved, but the words of the clergy in the name of God are subject to improvement. Christianity should be open to the influences of each period, and it ought to be adaptable to current needs. Only one lesson of Christianity is eternally true, and that is the injunction to love one another. Men ought so to organize their society that it will yield the greatest good to the greatest number. In every word and action we are obligated to seek the prompt and complete physical and moral amelioration of the most numerous class.[5] Religion ought to direct society toward the great end of rapidly improving the condition of the poor. The church has failed, and he accused the pope and the church of heresy on three counts: the improper education of the laity; the false direction given to seminaries, leading to ignorance and incapacity among the servants of the church; and the sponsoring and support given to the Inquisition and the Jesuits, two institutions out of keeping with the spirit of true Christianity.

Although Saint-Simon regarded the pope as guilty of heresy, he did not look with favor upon Luther. He charged that Luther failed to organize the world on a proper moral basis when he had the opportunity; moreover, he failed to carry out the dicta of Christ to organize the world in the interest of the largest and poorest classes. Luther was also charged with introducing an inferior form of worship, for he did not utilize the arts and the ceremonies which appeal to the senses. Saint-Simon held that

---

[4] Maxime Leroy, *La Vie véritable du Comte Henri de Saint-Simon* (Paris: Bernard Grasset, 1925).

[5] St. Simon "Nouveau Christianisme," *Oeuvres,* pp. 94–97.

Luther's emphasis upon the reading of the Bible was demoralizing, inasmuch as the Bible records human error and its contents are too metaphysical.[6]

HISTORY

Saint-Simon divided history into critical and organic periods. Critical periods are defined as those in which social discontent and dissolution are widespread, when a central unifying principle does not exist and men seek innovations; they are characterized by disunion and the development of new social forms. Organic periods are those in which society has a unifying principle, a single philosophy, and existing institutions receive general approval.

A NEW SOCIETY

Saint-Simon, according to his disciples, accomplished the design of Jesus—the establishment of a universal fraternity. In the new society the highest posts would be occupied by the talented men in industry and in the arts. Given such leadership, society would be rid of strife, disorder, and anarchy. Modern society, founded on division and competition, places a premium on the exploitation of man by man—the exploitation of the largest and poorest class by the rich and powerful, who have the power and the means to achieve their immoral designs. In the new society, men would seek justice instead of fortune and power.[7] The society envisaged by Saint-Simon was a universal association accepting the principle, "To each according to his capacity; to each capacity according to its works." In other words, those who contribute the most would receive the highest award.

To carry out the principle, "to each according to his capacity," inheritance would be abolished. The men of talent in each generation would have the opportunity to rise to the top, unhampered by the incompetents who inherit great wealth. Saint-Simon saw the possibility of scientific or intellectual capacity exercising an authority similar to that of the medieval priesthood. The authority would not be imposed but would be universally accepted. Saint-Simon was critical of the subordination of society to the military. He held that this condition is no longer desirable. Progress of civilization has led to a state wherein the industrial classes predominate, and they should be given the major place in society. Leadership

6 *Ibid.*, pp. 106–169.
7 Sebastian Charlety, *Histoire du Saint-Simonisme* (Paul Hartman, 1931), pp. 25–30.

should be placed in their hands, and they should be charged with giving to each class the measure of importance that its service to industry warrants. Saint-Simon based these conclusions on the ground "that work is the source of virtue, and the most useful workers earn the most consideration. Therefore, by both human and divine justice the industrial classes deserve the pre-eminent role in society."[8]

He envisaged the establishment of a great federation of free people, with a central government serving the general interest of each and all. The central government would concern itself with promoting great public works, establishing communications, building canals, and developing colonies in backward nations in order to spread civilization and extend commerce.

FOLLOWERS

After Saint-Simon's death, a school of devoted followers—including a number of gifted men of science and the arts—arose to perpetuate the memory of its founder. At the suggestion of Olinde Rodrigues, a society was formed and a journal, *Le Producteur,* was established, announcing in its first issue that the "age of gold which blind tradition has placed in the past is before us."[9] *Le Producteur* was published for only a year, for its small circulation did not bring in enough money to meet expenses. It was succeeded by *L'Organisateur.*

Leaders Under the leadership of Enfantin and Bazard, lectures explaining the new doctrine were begun in 1827. These lectures emphasized the prevailing anarchy in the arts, sciences, and industry, all of which lack a common unifying idea. The new doctrine called upon men to assume "a bond of affection, of doctrine, and of activity which may unite them: and lead them to advance in peace, with order and love, to a destiny in common; and which may confer on society, on the globe itself, and on the whole universe, a character of union, wisdom and beauty."[10]

The two men who became leaders of the movement complemented each other. Barthélemy Prosper Enfantin (1796–1864), the son of a Parisian banker, was self-confident; endowed with great vigor and eloquence, he aroused affection and confidence. Saint-Amand Bazard (1791–1832) lacked the gifts of the born orator, but he was a keen logician, an able popularizer, and a practical organizer who had come to Saint-

---

[8] Saint-Simon, "Catéchisme politique des industriels," *Oeuvres,* pp. 43–48.
[9] Charlety, *op. cit.,* p. 31.
[10] Sargent, *Social Innovators* (London: Smith, Elder & Co., 1858), p. 52.

Simonism after a career as a revolutionary. Despite differences in temperament, both men cooperated at first to advance the gospel of Saint-Simon.

At first Saint-Simonism was regarded as a literary fad. In 1830, a manifesto was issued, signed by Bazard and Enfantin, in which it was argued that only a change in property relations merits the name of revolution. The Saint-Simonians were attacked in the Chamber of Deputies, and the leaders replied in a letter abjuring the charges of belief in community of goods and wives. The net result was that their views became better known, and to spread the doctrine the *Globe* was purchased in January, 1831, and converted into a *Journal of the Doctrines of St. Simon.*

Universal Association New converts were made, and activity was extended. The aim was a universal association whose purpose would be "the amelioration—moral, intellectual, and physical—of the greatest and poorest class." All privileges of birth were to be abolished, and each would enjoy in accordance with his contribution. Instruction was to be given daily and was to be adapted to the needs of the assembly. Simple exhortations were to be delivered to workers, poetical talks to artists, and more exact lectures to scientists. The official organ, the *Globe,* in addition to discourses on Saint-Simonism, discussed problems of the day. In the proposed abolition of all privileges of birth, Enfantin urged heavy inheritance taxes which were to become heavier as the heirs were "further of kin." His defense of inheritance taxes was that they were levied at the time property changed hands and so would prevent the idleness likely to result from inheritance of large fortunes. Enfantin showed in this, as in other respects, that he was in advance of his time. He defended the creation of banks as necessary to mobilize the resources of the community, holding that banks were not mere lenders of funds but distributed the resources of the community for those uses that were most in demand.

Menilmontant A break between the two chief disciples led Enfantin and his followers to withdraw to Menilmontant, where a communal household was maintained. In the summer of 1832, Enfantin and his leading disciples were prosecuted for illegal assembly and were sentenced to a short term in prison. This resulted in the dispersal of the Saint-Simonians.

INFLUENCE

Many of the Saint-Simonians achieved prominence in art, commerce, and industry. Enfantin himself became a fairly successful engineer. Saint-

Simon and his disciples stressed the importance and merit of talent and industry as against position inherited or achieved by force and violence. Their opposition to great inheritance and their emphasis upon welfare would find wide acceptance in our own time. Opposition to war and violence went side by side with advocacy of a government by an elite, whose dogmas would be accepted by the masses. The belief in authoritarianism and in an elite could be accepted by contemporary fascists, but the emphasis upon industry and world peace would exclude the disciples from the ranks of precursors of fascist ideology. Like other radicals of the mid-nineteenth century, Saint-Simon did not express his views as clearly or as coherently as did later writers, although he anticipated many of their ideas. His differentiation of classes contains the germ of the theory of class struggle, but finer and clearer differentiations are possible. His cyclical theory of history and his emphasis upon industry anticipate later views, and his melioristic philosophy has become an article of faith for later socialists and others.

CHARLES FOURIER (1772–1837)

Charles Fourier was one of the most unusual of the men who planned to reorganize society on a more perfect basis. Fourier loved music and learned to play several instruments. He also attached great importance to the study of the sciences, then on the eve of their greatest influence. He had ambitions to be an engineer, but was induced by his family to engage in business. "Early in his career, Fourier imbibed a strong antipathy for commerce, even an abhorrence of it. He saw the competition and waste, the falsehood and knavery, the monopoly, and adulteration and forms of fraud which are essential characteristics of our competitive and anarchical system of trade."[11] Fourier inherited a substantial fortune when his father died, but lost it in the Lyons uprising against the Convention in 1793. He was imprisoned but escaped death by hiding from the revolutionary army sent to exact reprisals.

Fourier neither led nor instigated popular revolutionary movements, and his later private life was without important incident or significant drama. A poorly paid clerk, he spent his spare moments in extensive reading. He never married; instead, his devotion was given to cats and flowers. He was kind, enjoyed good living and such simple pleasures as

11 Introduction to Charles Fourier, *Theory of Social Organization*, by Albert Brisbane (New York: C. P. Somerby, 1876), p. 3.

following the marching battalions through streets and watching them drill in their gay uniforms. He was precise in temperament and loved order, as shown in his arrangement of society into series, groups, and phalanxes. Daily he arrived at his home exactly at noon in the hope of meeting the philanthropic capitalist who he hoped would finance his plan for reorganizing society.

WORKS

Fourier's regularity was carried into his literary activity. He wrote a definite number of pages each day, and his passion for maintaining a set schedule enabled him to produce a large amount of written work despite his need to earn a living.

In 1808, he published the *Theory of the Four Movements;* in 1822, his major work, *Domestic Association in Agriculture;* in 1829, the *New Industrial World;* and, in 1835, the *False Industry.* His work is a mixture of shrewd insight and fantastic nonsense.

GOD'S PLAN

Fourier assumed that there is a social order which conforms to the will of God, and that it guarantees complete happiness to all mankind. He assumed, too, that the physical and moral universe are both governed by the principle of attraction. Just as Newton had discovered the law of physical attraction, so Fourier ascribed to himself the discovery of the same principle in the moral world. Attraction manifests itself through the passions, which propel man toward an object of desire. According to Fourier, "the mainspring of action is passional attraction." He criticized the conventional view which teaches that man should resist and repress his passions. To him, such a view implied that "God was incapable of organizing our souls, our passions wisely. . . . Imbued with these prejudices regarding the impotence of God, the learned world was not qualified to estimate the natural impulses or passional attractions, which morality proscribes and relegates to the rank of vices."[12]

Fourier admitted that yielding to individual impulse leads to evil, but a different result follows as soon as a number of persons associate together. Then the impulses, which he called attractions, are combined

[12] *Selections from the Works of Fourier.* Translated by Julia Franklin (London: George Allen & Unwin, Ltd., 1901), p. 58. The following quotations from Fourier are from this source, pp. 56, 60, 163, 123, 128, 139, 191, 192. Reprinted by permission of the publishers.

into a series of contrasting groups which stimulate virtue and industry. "The passions, believed to be the enemies of concord, in reality conduce to that unity from which we deem them so far removed." Repressing the passions leads to violence and distortion. On the contrary, we must find a combination that gives the passions free play, which—if allowed a normal outlet—produces universal harmony. Fourier enumerated a long list of passions, and how they affect man's actions.

LABOR IN THE MODERN WORLD

Fourier recognized that labor is regarded under modern conditions as objectionable, but only because it is established on a false principle and is not based on the principle of attraction. Labor should be so organized that it will be attractive, so that man will seek it as a result of passion. He saw in prolonged labor a violation of the will of God. "Instead of working twelve hours with a scant intermission for a poor, dull dinner, the associative state will never extend its sessions of labour beyond an hour and a half or two."

In the modern world labor has become a curse.

[Labor is] says the Scripture very justly, a punishment of man: Adam and his issue are condemned to earn their bread by the sweat of their brow. That, already is an affliction, but this labor . . . we cannot even get it! A laborer lacks the labor upon which his maintenance depends. . . . He suffers from obtaining work at times whose fruit is his master's and not his, of being employed in duties to which he is entirely unaccustomed. . . . The civilized laborer suffers . . . through the maladies with which he is generally stricken by the excess labor demanded by his master. . . . He suffers by being despised and treated as a beggar because he lacks those necessaries which he consents to purchase by the anguish of repugnant labor. He suffers . . . finally in that he will obtain neither advancement nor sufficient wages, and to the vexation of present suffering is added the perspective of future suffering, and of being sent to the gallows should he demand that labor which he may lack tomorrow.

ASSOCIATION

Fourier criticized individual industrial activity, since it leads to dependence and neglect and is opposed to the attainment of perfection. Under individual enterprise the ties of blood are more important than affinity in taste. Individual enterprise fails to utilize the most modern mechanical methods. Under conditions where all participants are not equally interested, fraud and theft are common. Competing enterprises are malevolent; rivals seek to crush competitors, and a conflict between the individual and the collective is inevitable. Finally, wage labor is designated as "indirect servitude, guarantee of misfortune, . . . of despair for the workman in civilisation or barbarism."

Fourier's answer was associated labor, a grouping of individuals on a sufficiently large scale so that all may enjoy the variety of work necessary for the exercise of passional attraction. Fourier did not approve of communism, for he held that the dogma of "community of goods is so pitiful that it is not worthy of refutation." Genuine association, according to Fourier, would be religious. As opposed to the spirit of communism, the spirit of ownership would be stimulated.

Phalanstery   Fourier proposed that work be organized in communities made up of about 400 families, or between 1,500 to 1,600 people "of graduated degrees of fortune, age, character, of theoretical and practical knowledge; care will be taken to secure the greatest amount of variety possible, for the greater the number of variations either in the passions or the faculties of the members, the easier will it be to make them harmonise in a short space of time." An association would be formed among the inhabitants, and capital raised to finance the undertaking. Annually the net return would be divided into three parts: one to be used to pay the interest on the capital; one to be divided among the workers, in accordance with the difficulty of their work; and one to be paid to talent— those who are distinguished in labor either for activity or for intelligence. It is assumed that each man, woman, and child would receive a portion of each fund, in accordance with their contribution to the three sources of production—labor, capital and talent.

In this community of 1,500 to 1,600 people, each would be able to pursue the work most attractive and desirable to him. Moreover, in such a community there would be people of every type of skill. Because of division of labor and large-scale production, output could rise. Gains would also accrue to the community from large centralized storehouses which eliminate the need for the individual granary, and the central kitchen would replace private food preparation. Individuals would be able to work at a number of tasks, so that the evil of monotony would be overcome. Work would be carried on in groups, isolated labor being unknown.

Guaranty of the Minimum   "The first right," said Fourier, "is the right to sustain life, to eat when one is hungry." Society has the duty of securing for the people a minimum of food, clothing, and shelter. As long as man's right to minimum subsistence is not recognized, the social compact accepted by man living in society is nought but a charter of oppression. In nature, man could hunt and fish, pick wild fruit, and pasture his cattle in the meadow. These rights are abolished by civilization; therefore "the poor man can say to his fellow-countrymen, to his native phalanx: 'I was born upon this land; I demand admission to all classes of work practiced here, a guarantee that I shall enjoy the fruit of my labor; I demand that the instruments requisite to prosecute this labor be advanced to me, as a compensation for the right of stealing which Nature has given me.'" It is true that under an individualist regime man works only to support himself and his family. In an associative order, a regime of industrial attraction, men would find work "attractive enough for the multitude to wish to devote to it even the days and hours reserved for idleness."

EFFICIENCY

Fourier believed that under existing conditions man fails to produce up to his full capacity because of the inefficiency of current methods, and that the social problem can be solved only by an increase in output. He therefore urged large-scale production based upon an intensive division of labor. Monotony of work would be overcome by variety and alternative jobs. In his opinion, large-scale production could be carried out only with the aid of vastly increased consumption, and communal feeding would eliminate the waste of individual housekeeping. Phalansteries would produce a variety of goods, and exchange between associations would furnish each with the goods produced by the others.

Fourier's system of associated living stressed efficiency, increased output, and a high level of consumption. In these respects his views coincided with modern opinion. His emphasis upon making work more attractive and allowing each individual to perform the tasks which harmonize with his passions and his capacities has since been recognized as desirable by psychologists and personnel managers. His guaranty of a healthy minimum to all, before the division of the surplus, is another idea which the modern world has partially if not wholly accepted. Fourier's attacks upon competition and his plea for its displacement by associated labor influenced the work of later socialists.

ROBERT OWEN (1771–1858)

Among the early nineteenth-century reformers, none was more dogged and self-sacrificing than Robert Owen, one of the most remarkable Englishmen of his time. His father was a saddler by trade, and his mother came from a family of farmers. He was the youngest of seven children. At the age of ten, he left for London, loaded down with forty shillings and with confidence in his future. Upon his arrival in London he found employment and utilized every spare minute reading the books he found in the well-stocked library of his employer. At the end of his term, he found work with a Manchester firm and remained at that job until he was eighteen, when he accepted an offer—borrowing the necessary money —to go into the business of manufacturing textile machinery.[13]

NEW LANARK

In 1800, Owen took over the management of a cotton mill at New Lanark and began the first of his series of experiments in social and economic reform. From the beginning he was impressed with the importance of environment in shaping human character. In New Lanark, he observed, "the people were surrounded by bad conditions, and these bad conditions had powerfully acted upon them to misform their character and conduct."[14] He decided that the first step toward social and individual improvement was to better the environment in which men lived. Overseers out of sympathy with his views were discharged.

He began a campaign among his workers, against drunkenness and theft, which he attributed to the long hours of work, "the inferior qualities and high prices of everything which they had to purchase for their own use; the bad arrangements in their houses for rearing and training their children . . . ."[15] He established a store where food and clothing, purchased at wholesale prices, were sold to his employees at a cost about 25 per cent lower than in the retail stores. He used the profits from the store to establish schools at New Lanark, which were also open to the children of the surrounding areas. Owen insisted upon cleanliness and

[13] Lloyd Jones, *The Life, Times and Labours of Robert Owen* (London: Swan Sonnenschein, 1895); Frank Podmore, *Robert Owen* (London: George Allen & Unwin, Ltd., 1923); *The Life of Robert Owen, by himself* (New York: Alfred A. Knopf, Inc., 1920).

[14] *The Life of Robert Owen*, p. 78. Reprinted by permission of Alfred A. Knopf, Inc., publishers.

[15] *Ibid.*, p. 86.

good behavior, and he drew up a set of rules providing for the regular cleaning of homes and streets. He urged the villagers to adopt those religious principles they approved, but "at the same time all shall think charitably of their neighbors, respecting their religious opinions, and not presumptiously suppose that theirs alone are right."[16]

Factory Reforms Owen took steps to improve the environment and make possible the education of his employees. Hours were shortened, but total output was not adversely affected. The hiring age was raised to ten years, which at the time was a progressive step, and parents were urged to keep their children at school until the age of seventeen. An attempt was made to limit drunkenness by restriction and punishment, and drinking was reduced. Medical benefits were provided and a sick fund was set up with contributions from the working people. Dwellings were improved and sanitary standards raised. "It was not only the cleanliness, sobriety, and order of the village which impressed the frequent visitors; but the spirit of happiness and goodwill which prevailed everywhere."

Owen was far ahead of his time in kindness and consideration toward his workers. He was, however, an ingrained paternalist, as is perhaps best illustrated by the system of silent monitors he instituted at his plant. Suspended before the individual employee was a four-sided piece of wood about two inches long, each side specially colored, the color in front indicating the individual's behavior the preceding day. Each department had a book of character in which each individual's conduct was recorded. Owen was, however, hampered by his partners, who did not look kindly upon many of his reforms.

Convinced more than ever of the importance of training and environment upon habits and character, Owen felt there was much an enlightened government could do. He advocated the establishment of a labor bureau which could discover the demand for labor throughout the United Kingdom. He was of the opinion that "it ought to be a primary duty of any Government that sincerely interests itself in the well-being of its subjects, to provide perpetual employment of real national utility in which all who may apply may be immediately occupied."

FACTORY ACT

Owen was not satisfied with introducing change into his own establishment, and at a meeting of members of the trade to discuss the removal of

---

[16] Podmore, *op. cit.*, p. 88. The following brief quotations are from this source, pp. 176, 171.

the tariff on wool, he urged them not to overlook the workers who made profits possible. He suggested legislation to prohibit the employment of children under twelve years of age in cotton mills; to limit the working time to ten and a half hours in a twelve-hour interval; and to set educational standards for factory children. Failure to gain approval did not deter him from taking up the fight in behalf of the children. A manufacturer and an employer, he could not be charged with being ill-informed, and his campaign forced upon the state a recognition of its new duties and responsibilities.[17]

RELIEF OF THE UNEMPLOYED

The ending of the Napoleonic Wars brought widespread and acute distress to many sections of the British Isles. Demonstrations, riots, rick-burnings, and the smashing of machinery, the normal accompaniments of severe destitution, made their appearance. Demands for relief and reform by Parliament followed. Repression was not deemed enough, and a special committee from both houses of Parliament was appointed to investigate. Owen was asked to testify, and he presented his "Report to the Committee for the Relief of the Manufacturing Poor."

Owen pictured the great gains in productivity following the invention of machinery, pointing out that while it enabled England to prosper during the war, "new circumstances have arisen. The war demand for the production of labour having ceased, markets could no longer be found for them; and the revenues of the world were inadequate to purchase that which a power so enormous in its effects did produce: a diminished demand consequently followed."[18]

Owen argued that there were three possibilities for the increase of employment: the reduction in the use of machinery, starvation for millions, or useful occupations for the poor and unemployed. Rejecting the first two, Owen presented a program for furnishing useful employment for the poor and out-of-work in colonies with populations of 500 to 1,500. Each colony was to live alone upon a tract of land, comprising 1,000 to 1,500 acres. The big central building was to contain a public kitchen and mess rooms. Other buildings would be designed for schools, a church, and a library. Stables, laundries, factories, and farm buildings would surround the living quarters. The communities were to be as self-sufficient as possi-

17 *Ibid.*, p. 209.

18 Robert Owen, "Report to the Committee for the Relief of the Manufacturing Poor," *A New View of Society.* Everyman's Edition (New York: E. P. Dutton & Co., 1927), p. 158.

ble, and work in manufacturing as well as in farming was to be considered. Children were to attend school for the first few years, then gradually begin manual work.

Owen denied that adequate employment is possible as long as industry is operated without social controls. As productivity increases through the use of machinery, unemployment and distress increase for want "of proper arrangements," and oversupply is the result. Lack of employment does not arise from want of capital or of labor but from "the want of a market." Owen also criticized the standard of value and maintained that "the natural standard of value is, in principle, human labour." Owen believed that shifting from the precious metals to the natural standard would lead to a great increase in demand, as—for a reason which he does not make clear—fluctuations in value would be avoided. The greatest advantage would be that it would enable society to exchange commodities at their prime or labor costs.

Village communities combine the advantages of the country and the city. Common dining rooms lead to many economies, and under wise direction the village communities would become highly productive. Little need for money or private property would exist, for these associations would produce a large surplus which would be used to maintain the young, the aged, and the infirm, to pay taxes and interest on capital, and to barter with other communities.

NEW HARMONY

Proceeding from theory to practice, Owen went to the United States, where he purchased a community founded by George Rapp, at New Harmony, Indiana. It was opened for settlement in 1825, but many of the colonists were frauds and drones. Nevertheless, some progress was made in the first year, and in 1827, a committee to draw up a constitution was elected at a meeting of the community. Social and religious differences led to division and separation, with two new communities being formed. Dissension could not be held in check, and by 1828, the experiment had ended.

COOPERATION

New Harmony ended in failure, but Owen's program inspired the founding in 1821 of the London Co-Operative and Economical Society, which sought "to establish a village of unity and mutual cooperation, combining agriculture, manufactures and trades upon the plan projected by Robert Owen."[19] The Society issued the *Economist* as its official organ. By 1823, the London Cooperative and Economical Society had collapsed; it was succeeded in 1824 by the London Cooperative Society, whose object was to make Owen's views known to the public. Throughout this period cooperative societies spread, and Podmore estimates that by 1830 there were between four and five hundred such societies functioning in England.

Labour Exchanges Undeterred by earlier failures, Owen proposed, in 1832, the setting up of labor exchanges to relieve the artisan from dependence upon the merchant. The value of goods would be measured by labor time, and notes representing this measure would be expanded or contracted in accordance with the increase or diminution of wealth. The labor of an average ten-hour day was to be calculated at the rate of sixpence an hour. It was assumed that this rate was a proper average between the rates of the best and the worst laborer. To the value of the direct labor would be added the value of the indirect labor embodied in raw materials, and the entire amount would be divided by sixpence. The quotient would be the number of labor hours that would be "entered on the labor note." A slight charge was made for the upkeep of the exchanges.

The National Equitable Labour Exchange opened in September, 1832, and at first large deposits of goods in exchange for labor notes were made. The exchange was soon swamped with too many goods, valuation was deficient and management poor; but the idea spread and a number of other exchanges and bazaars were opened. All failed, for the reasons already given.

TRADE-UNION LEADER

Although Owen was essentially a socialist and a cooperator, it became his lot to be the leader of the first national trade-union movement in the world. The growth of trade unions after the repeal of the anticombination laws led Owen to look upon these organizations as future cooperative groups. Early in 1834, the Grand National Consolidated Trades Union of Great Britain and Ireland was organized. More than half a million workers joined. The government, frightened by the growing distress, inaugurated a policy of repression, and in March, 1834, six laborers in Dorsetshire were convicted of administering illegal oaths and were

[19] Podmore, *op. cit.*, II, 350.

sentenced to long terms in prison. A protest parade was organized by the Grand National, but the head of the Home Office, Lord Melbourne, refused to entertain the petition. The Grand National lasted for less than a year, but during its brief life it frightened many people of wealth and power. Thereafter, Owen showed little interest in trade unions, nor was he much interested in the popular agitations for Chartism and the repeal of the corn laws. After the collapse of the Grand National, he tried several other cooperative colonies but they also failed.

While Owen's activities appear as a succession of failures, a deeper examination will reveal the fallacy of this view. He was the inspirer of the great cooperative movement, and a pioneer in factory reform. His insistence on the importance of labor, and his practical steps to ameliorate the conditions of his employees stamp him as a pioneer benevolent paternalist. His emphasis upon training and education and upon the need for a decent environment and healthful conditions of work show him to be a precursor of modern socialistic, liberal, and progressive views. Later-day socialism shares with him the belief in the importance of environment, the evil of competition, and the inevitability of a world of plenty once the true form of economic organization is accepted. Marx and his followers acknowledged their debt to him, and their doctrines show the impact of his ideas. Tirelessly he continued to preach and teach, to all who would listen and follow, his gospel of the influence of environment and education upon human character, and of the need to establish a cooperative way of life. He lacked the winged phrases and the eloquence to stir men's hearts, but his faith and his deeds made up in great measure for what his words did not express. He was a great and good man, who, by self-denying deeds, sought to make the world a better place in which to live.

ÉTIENNE CABET (1788–1856)

Less important than Saint-Simon, Fourier, or Owen, and lacking their breadth and insight, Cabet nevertheless had an influence upon the development of European radicalism. Born at Dijon in a family of coopers, he was destined for the family trade, but delicate health necessitated other plans. At school, Fenelon's *Adventures de Telemaque* exercised some influence over him. At the age of fifteen he became a teacher at a new lycée in his native city, and at twenty-four a full-fledged attorney.

He applied himself to his profession and became known as an adroit lawyer.

At the restoration of the Bourbons to the throne of France, Cabet began his career of opposition. He heartily welcomed the appearance of Napoleon after Elba, and for supporting the usurper, he was barred from the practice of law for three months. Upon his return to the bar, he busied himself defending opponents of the government and thus gained a reputation as a champion of the oppressed. As punishment, the courts of France were again closed to him, this time for a year. He settled in Paris, where he found employment in a law office. Paris, then as now the center of French intellectual life, gave him an opportunity for learning more advanced ideas. Cabet became a member of the antiroyalist society, the Carbonari. He was active in the revolution of 1830 and was elected to the Chamber of Deputies the following year. For an attack upon Louis Philippe in 1832, he was indicted, tried *in absentia,* and sentenced to five years in prison. He was, however, able to have the verdict set aside.[20]

During the Orleanist reaction, he was exiled, in 1834, for five years as an alternative to spending two years in prison. He went to London, which at this time housed many foreign refugees, and turned his attention to literature, philosophy, and history. His criticisms of society were in line with those of eighteenth-century socialists. Seeking to utilize the study of history in order to determine the best system of social and political organization, he came to the conclusion that society everywhere had always been badly organized and that the basic cause of all the disorders was inequality and autocracy and the remedy equality and democracy. Cabet also resembled the social critics of the eighteenth century in his belief that his proposed program could be put into practice anywhere or at any time, and that its success did not depend upon historical evolution or upon a particular stage of human development. Moreover, he also attributed the evils of mankind to violations of the code of nature.

His views were developed in *Voyage en Icarie,* a book purporting to be the diary of one Lord Carisdall, who discovers an isolated community governed on principles differing from those of European nations. According to Cabet, the book is a treatise on morals, philosophy, and social and political economy, and is the fruit of long work, tireless research, and constant meditation, and contains the true principles of social organization.

[20] Jules Prudhommeaux, *Icarie et son fondateur, Étienne Cabet* (Paris: F. Frieder et Cie., 1926), pp. 1–58. The following brief quotations are from this source, pp. 126, 144.

HISTORY OF ICARIE

Under the leadership of Icara, a philosopher and communist, a revolution had taken place in a distant island, Icarie: A program of social reorganization was accepted and a democratic republic which would eventually evolve into a communistic commonwealth established. The nation was divided into provinces and the provinces into communes which were to be self-governing, representatives of the latter making up the national legislature. The government was administered by an executive council. *Transition Program* During the transition period the government of Icarie was to institute national workshops, public housing, and a graduated income tax, with taxes removed from all necessities. Land was to become common property, and agriculture was to be conducted on a large scale by peasant communes. Through taxes and wage regulation, the government was to absorb gradually all private property and all social and economic activities. At the end of the transition period, Icarie was to become a great partnership in which each worked in accordance with his ability and consumed according to his need. Violence and crime as well as luxury and idleness were expected to vanish, and peace, plenty, liberty, and equality to reign. Trade, barter, and money would become obsolete.

In outlining a system of production, Cabet urged that the useful should always precede the agreeable. He believed that work and other aspects of life should be regulated, and that the individual's occupation should have no influence in determining his social worth. As an exponent of equality, Cabet believed that genius and ability are accidental and should not be decisive in determining social worth.[21] Superior merit earns its reward in the satisfaction obtained by the exercise of talent. All are equally esteemed. Among the Icarians, equality of duty would be as important as equality of opportunity. Differences based upon wealth, rank, or position would not exist. Hours of labor would be gradually shortened, to seven hours in winter and six in summer, and work would be made as easy and agreeable as possible.

After the transition period, the land would be transformed into one domain, and the products of the earth and of industry would become social capital to be used for the benefit of all.

In Icarie, education would be controlled by the state and open to

21 Rev. Sylvester A. Piotrowski, *Étienne Cabet and the Voyage en Icarie* (Washington, D.C.: The Catholic University of America, 1935), pp. 94–95.

everyone. Both theory and practice would be used, with emphasis placed upon education as a means of improving human life.

COLONIES

Following the publication of *Voyage en Icarie,* Cabet founded the journal, *Le Populaire,* in which he set forth his views. He published a number of other books and pamphlets, and in 1847, he issued a proclamation, "Allons en Icarie" ("Let us go to Icarie"), in which he called for the establishment of a cooperative colony. Subsequently Cabet secured an extensive grant of land in Texas, and in *Le Populaire* of January 17, 1848, he announced, "C'est au Texas." On February 3, 1849, selected colonists set sail from Le Havre to the new colony in Texas and arrived at New Orleans on March 27. Three weeks after their departure, the government of Louis Philippe was overthrown.

When the colonists reached Texas, they found that they could take possession of the land only on condition that each person build a house on each plot of land by July 1. Also, the grant of land given to the colony was not all in one piece, and each section was to be divided between a land company and the colonists. The experience of the settlers was discouraging, and they and a second contingent were forced by suffering and disease to abandon their Texas project and move to New Orleans.

Upon hearing of the colonists' misadventures, Cabet, who had remained in Paris, decided to join them. Reaching New Orleans, he found only 280 left of the almost 500 colonists. Under his leadership, the colonists settled in Nauvoo, Missouri, in March, 1849, and five years later the colony was "well established and measurably prosperous."[22] Membership had doubled, and a number of industries were set up. Good schools were maintained, and an active printing of books and pamphlets was carried on. Despite increasing prosperity, dissension over the government of the colony arose, and in October, 1856, a minority of 180, including Cabet, withdrew. The struggle was too much for Cabet and he died suddenly on November 8, 1856.

This minority purchased an estate called Cheltenham, a few miles from St. Louis, in May, 1858, but the settlement expired in March, 1864. The majority, who had remained at Nauvoo, found itself in financial difficulties, and in 1860 settled in Corning, Iowa. A number of dissidents rejoined the community and for eighteen years a measure of modest prosperity was enjoyed. During this time a new generation had been rising,

22 Albert Shaw, *Icarie* (New York: G. P. Putnam's Sons, 1884), p. 46.

and a conflict arose between the young progressives, who wanted to asso-ciate with the expanding socialist movement outside the colony, and the old conservatives, who were desirous of following the traditional pro-gram of isolation. The division ended in the courts, which nullified the charter and ordered an equitable distribution of property.

The young or progressive faction kept the name of Icarian Community, and the conservatives became The New Icarian Community. The pro-gressive faction remained in Iowa for eight years, and in 1883 founded a colony, Icaria Speranza, near San Francisco. As the land became valuable, the colonists decided upon a division of property. The conservatives also prospered, and continued for almost twenty years, but communistic living had no attraction for young people in an expanding United States and it was decided unanimously to dissolve on October 22, 1898.

LOUIS BLANC (1811–1882)

Louis Blanc was born into a royalist family. His grandfather was be-headed during the Terror because of his extreme monarchical views. His father accepted the empire and was rewarded with a position at Madrid. Here Louis was born in 1811. With Napoleon's downfall, the family re-turned to France, where Louis was educated at the Royal College et Rodez. He took up tutoring but later turned to journalism. In 1839, he launched the *Revue du progres, politique et littéraire*, which published serially "L'Organisation du travail." So widespread was the approval that the articles appeared in book form and ran through a number of editions.

PRINCIPAL IDEAS

According to Blanc, three great principles have governed history in the past—authority, individualism, and fraternity. The principle of author-ity typified in the long domination of Catholicism is accepted in blind faith and imposes beliefs which must rest upon inequality and autocratic government. This regime ended with Luther and was followed by in-dividualism, which separates man from society, gives him an exalted notion of his rights, but fails to emphasize his duties. Individualism aban-dons him to his own resources and demands that government let him alone. While individualism is an improvement over the preceding sys-tem, it is only a transitional stage to the final goal of history, the rule of fraternity. The latter is founded on solidarity, a recognition that the in-dividual is a member of a great family and that a reorganization of society based upon common consent is necessary. Fraternity and socialism are one.[23]

Blanc had a profound belief in the inevitability of progress, and with it a belief that the desired goal will be reached by educating society, and not by violent revolution, for Blanc agrees with Rousseau that man is by nature a reasonable being. Man is under the tyranny of things; he must be taught how to be free. True freedom is the power to develop one's faculties, something impossible under existing economic organization.

CRITICISM OF COMPETITION

Blanc threfore insisted that competition is the greatest evil of modern society. It fulfills no social purpose, and its operation is a constant source of injustice. Its worst effects strike the workers, whose wages are beaten down to the subsistence level. Competition has impoverished the workman so that he is forced to sell the labor of his children. It does lead to cheaper products for the consumer, but low prices are a device by which the strong subdue the weaker competitor. Once a monopoly is obtained, prices will again rise. He also sees competition leading to a war to the death between countries.[24] As Blanc saw it, the sources of economic power are capital and credit. Emancipation of labor can be achieved only if labor controls these basic resources. As, under present conditions, loans are available only to the rich, Blanc suggested that the government raise a loan and use the proceeds to establish social workshops in the more important branches of industry. These workshops would be equipped with tools and machinery. Workers of good character would be admitted to the workshop on equal terms. After the first year, the workers would have observed each other and learned to recognize each other's ability; thus the workers themselves would be able to select individuals for the several tasks.

The profits of the workshop would be divided as follows: one part to be shared equally by members of the association; a second portion to be allocated for the care of the aged and sick; a third to be used to meet deficits in other concerns and to expand the business of the workshop and increase membership; and a fourth part to be set aside for reserves. Members would have the right to dispose of their wages as they chose, but Blanc thought that a community of labor would lead to a community of

23 J. Tchernoff, *Louis Blanc* (Paris: G. Bellais, 1904), pp. 16–17.

24 Louis Blanc, *The Organization of Work*. Translated by Marie Paula Dickoré (Cincinnati, O. University Press, 1911).

enjoyment. After the Revolution of 1848, the government set up a "commission for laborers," known as the Luxembourg Commission, to examine working conditions. Louis Blanc was its leading member. The national workshops that were set up did not meet with his approval. Contrary to his views, the workers were not employed in their particular trades but all in the shop performed the same tasks. Instead of associated labor, the workshops were directed by government supervisors and the employees received wages.[25] Finally, in June, the government sought to reduce the number employed in a workshop. The Parisian workers rose on the barricades and the Provisional Government gave dictatorial powers to General Cavaignac, who, after a stubborn battle, put down the revolt. Soon the national workshops were closed.

The republic's victory was short-lived. In December, 1848, Prince Louis Napoleon Bonaparte was elected president; in December, 1851, his powers were extended, and shortly thereafter he made himself emperor.

EXILE

Louis Blanc was forced to leave his native land, and with Victor Hugo and Edgar Quinet he refused the amnesty of Louis Napoleon. His exile was a living protest against the usurper, and he returned to his native land only after the collapse of the Second Empire. He served in Parliament and published a journal, the *Free Man,* in which he advocated progress by education and cooperative effort.

Blanc's doctrines prepared the road for later system builders. With Saint-Simon, he recognized the importance of the industrial classes, but he rejected the principle of unequal rewards for people of differing talents. He had more confidence in the state than had Fourier and Proudhon, and in this respect he was in agreement with the later political socialists. He also anticipated Marx in his view that competition leads to monopoly and the struggle for markets. Despite the relative simplicity of many of his views, Blanc influenced the later socialist systems.

[25] Herman Pechan, *Louis Blanc als Wegbereiter des modernen Sozialismus* (Jena: Gustav Fischer, 1929), pp. 124–125.

5. MARXISM

Beginning with the late 1840's, Marxism gained an increasing intellectual dominance over socialist thought and action. For a time the libertarian socialists—anarchists—were its foremost challengers, but gradually the Marxist doctrine spread its intellectual influence over the parties of militant reform in most parts of the world. Its influence was not uniform in all areas where it won a following. Some countries found its dogmas too rigid, modifying them in theory or moderating them in practice. Yet of its appeal to revolutionary groups there can be no doubt. Like the older socialism, Marxism forecast a world of plenty once mankind reformed its economic and social structure. It resembles the eighteenth-century systems in its confidence that human happiness could be attained once the correct social organization was evolved. Marxism emphasizes, however, the historical stages that must be traversed before humanity reaches "the promised land." The marked influence attained by these ideas was due in part to their great logical power and to their passionate exposition by the founder, Karl Marx, and in part to his insistence that his views were founded on a scientific approach devoid of the moralizing of his predecessors.

KARL HEINRICH MARX (1818–1883)

Karl Marx towers over all of his revolutionary contemporaries. Although some of his ideas are a refinement of older views, and many are only the rewording of the doctrines of others, Marx was undoubtedly the most influential revolutionary thinker of the nineteenth century. A great government accepts and disseminates his views with religious reverence. Great political parties in every corner of the world base their policies and programs upon his analyses and predictions, and every branch of social investigation must take cognizance of his criticisms.

Karl Heinrich Marx was born at Trier, Germany. His father, Hirschel, a descendant of a long line of Jewish rabbis, was baptized a Christian when Karl was six years old. Little is known of Karl Marx's mother except that she was descended from a family of Dutch Jews who had settled in Germany in the sixteenth century. Marx came into early contact with the family of Ludwig von Westphalen, whose daughter Jenny became his wife. Through his father he became acquainted with the eighteenth-century philosophies of enlightenment and from the elder Westphalen he learned of Homer and Shakespeare.

Marx made a good record in the schools of his native city, and at the age of seventeen, in October, 1835, he registered at the University of Bonn. From there he then went on to the University of Berlin, where he studied law, literature, philosophy, and history.[1]

In Berlin, Marx had become associated with the group of Young Hegelians—the doctor's club—whose leader, Bruno Bauer, was a member of the faculty of the university. A member of the group, David Strauss, published a *Life of Jesus* in 1835 in which he interpreted Christianity as a nonsupernatural phenomenon and as the product of human thought. Bruno Bauer subjected the Bible to historical criticism and later announced that Christianity was not compatible with rationalism. The *Annals of Halle,* founded by the Young Hegelian Arnold Ruge in 1838, sought to submit to critical examination not only religion but social relations. Ludwig Feuerbach, another member of the group, submitted Christianity to a critical analysis in his *Essence of Religion.* Feuerbach held that the Hegelian idea is only another manifestation of the idea of God. In this volume, Feuerbach argued that reality determines ideas rather than the reverse and that religion has been created by man. Individualism and human selfishness have grown on the religious terrain and man can realize himself only in the collective life of society. Therefore man must substitute the love of humanity for the love of God, and philosophy should turn from the supernatural to science. Marx greeted this volume as marking a return of thought from the heavens down to earth, but he felt that it stopped short of serious criticism of social relations.

The bold hopes of the advanced thinkers were given a severe blow by the German emperor, William I, who instituted a wave of suppression of all liberal views. In the meantime, Marx presented his thesis to the University of Jena and received his doctorate in April, 1841. Deciding to

[1] Karl Vorländer, *Karl Marx* (Leipzig: F. Meiner, 1929), p. 36.

leave Germany, he married Jenny von Westphalen and settled in Paris in November, 1843.

CONVERSION TO SOCIALISM

In his first year in Paris, Marx became acquainted with Heinrich Heine and with many French socialists. Marx and Arnold Ruge began to edit the *German-French Yearbook*, but only one issue was published. The two articles which Marx published in this journal set forth the outlines of his future views. In the "Introduction to a Criticism of Hegel's Philosophy of Law," Marx argued that it was necessary to go beyond a criticism of religion to an examination of political conditions. Here appears his statement that "religion is the opium of the people." In the other article, Marx took issue with his friend Bruno Bauer on the Jewish question. Bauer had sharply attacked what he called the egoistic and particularistic tendencies in Judaism, and had argued that Jewish emancipation could come only through Jews joining the Christian community. Marx reduced the issue to an economic level and argued that when society emancipates itself from the dominance of material goods, characteristic of Jewish life, the Jewish religion will cease to exist.[2]

After the collapse of his literary venture, Marx devoted himself to a study of the historical works of Guizot, Augustin Thierry, and other French historians who had dealt with the history of class conflict. He became acquainted with Proudhon and Wilhelm Weitling, and was highly impressed with their work. He declared that "the German proletariat is the theoretician amongst the European proletariats, as the English proletariat is their political economist and the French proletariat their politician." The tone of the Paris *Vorwärts*, to which Marx contributed, displeased the Prussian authorities and as a result Marx and several other contributors were expelled from France.

FRIENDSHIP WITH ENGELS

During his stay in Paris, Marx began his lifelong friendship with Friedrich Engels (1820–1895). Engels came from a devout and conservative Saxon family, but under the influence of David Strauss he had become a Young Hegelian and had left the church. He served in the artillery guards for a year and acquired a lasting taste for the study of military

[2] Franz Mehring, *Karl Marx*. Translated by Edward Fitzgerald (New York: Covici-Friede, 1935), pp. 93–101. The brief quotations that follow are from this source, pp. 113, 127, 137–138.

subjects. At the completion of his service, Engels went to England and there took a position with his father's spinning firm.

THE HOLY FAMILY

The first joint work of Marx and Engels was *The Holy Family, or a Criticism of Critical Criticism*. It was an answer to an attack upon mass movements by Marx's former intellectual companion Bruno Bauer, who contended that there was a contradiction between the intellect and the masses, and between the idea and the interest. Marx and Engels objected to this dichotomy. On the contrary, they said, "the idea always comes to grief in so far as it is distinct from interest." They declared that every mass interest enters the world as an idea but is invariably carried beyond its real limit and identifies itself with humanity instead of with a class. They rejected Bauer's notion that the state gives cohesion to bourgeois life and affirmed the opposite, that bourgeois life holds the state together.

A CRITICISM OF ENGLISH INDUSTRIALISM

Engels had observed the conditions of labor in England during the early stages of the Industrial Revolution, and in *The Condition of the British Working Class* (1844), he gave a graphic description of the misery and degradation brought on by the new industrialism. Engels visited Marx in Brussels and, after a journey to England, they embarked upon a joint work, *The German Ideology*.

The German Ideology was a long criticism of a number of Marx's former associates of the Hegelian left. Marx's most authoritative biographer detects in it "a tendency to ride a turn of speech to death, to give the statements of their opponents as foolish a meaning as possible by literal interpretation or misrepresentation, a tendency to exaggeration and recklessness of expression."

The German Ideology also dealt with German socialism by criticizing the ideas of Moses Hess, Karl Grün, and others who had developed what Grün called "true socialism." Marx and Engels maintained that "the real state of affairs escapes these 'true socialists,' steeped as they are in their German ideology." The exponents of true socialism, they said, were guilty of separating events from the communistic ideas developed outside Germany and then forcing them into an "arbitrary connection with German philosophy." [3]

3 Karl Marx and Friedrich Engels, *The German Ideology* (New York: International Publishers, 1939), p. 80.

CONFLICT WITH PROUDHON

Marx next turned his intellectual guns upon Proudhon, who for a time challenged Marx and Engels for the position of chief inspirer of the European revolutionary movement. Marx recognized Proudhon's popularity among Latin labor, gained, in part, by his *Système des contradictions économiques ou philosophie de la misère,* in which he "demanded that the value of commodities should be 'constituted' so that the product of one producer should exchange with the product of another containing the same amount of labor. Society was to be reformed by turning all its members into workers exchanging similar amounts of labor." [4]   Marx sought to destroy Proudhon's intellectual influence in his pamphlet, *The Poverty of Philosophy,* a caustic rebuttal of the possibilities of class harmony in modern society. Its polemic violence reveals Marx as an unkind, intolerant duelist who, despite his erudition, is ready to resort to petty name calling.

THE COMMUNIST MANIFESTO

The League of the Just commissioned one of its members, Julius Moll, to request Marx and Engels to affiliate with it. In the summer of 1847, a congress held at London changed the name of the organization to the Communist League, and another meeting was scheduled for later in the year. Marx and Engels, after some persuasion, joined the group. At the second meeting held in November, 1847, Marx and Engels were commissioned to draw up a set of fundamental principles. In February, 1848, the manuscript of what has become one of the more significant documents in history was presented.

Principal Views   The Communist Manifesto makes several ringing statements:

1. The history of all societies is a history of class struggles.

2. All previous class conflicts have in our time become concentrated in the clash between bourgeoisie and proletariat.

3. The modern state is only an executive committee for managing the common interests of the bourgeoisie.

4. The bourgeoisie has abolished all feudal and patriarchial relations and has reduced artists, scientists, and other professions to the status of hired workers.

[4] Mehring, *op. cit.,* p. 149.

5. Through the exploitation of world markets, all countries have been drawn into the bourgeois orbit.

6. In its rule of scarcely one hundred years, capitalism has increased productivity to a greater degree than all past generations. Thus capitalism has been able to throw off its feudal fetters and set up its own rule.

7. At the same time that capital and industry developed, there has arisen a class of modern workers, the proletariat, which feels its growing power and unites against the bourgeoisie.

8. All former social movements were movements of minorities in the interest of minorities; the proletarian movement alone is the movement of the majority in the interests of the majority.

9. The laws, morals, and religion of the old society are, for the proletariat, only bourgeois prejudices, designed to serve the interest of the bourgeoisie.

10. The communists seek to unite the proletariat for the overthrow of bourgeois power to abolish wage labor and private property.

11. Bourgeois society, with its classes and class struggle, shall then be replaced by an association allowing each to develop his capacity to the full.

12. The *Manifesto* closes with a cry that the ruling class may tremble at the approaching revolution, and that the proletariat has nothing to lose but its chains and has a world to gain: "Workers of the world, unite."

The Communist Manifesto is the quintessence of early Marxism.[5] In the hundred years that have passed since its publication, many of the views of the *Manifesto* have been shown to be untenable. Capitalism has proved itself to be much more flexible and tenacious than the authors had assumed. Nor has the proletariat carried out the historic destiny envisaged for it by the authors. Yet the tremendous influence exercised by this document cannot be denied.

Marx and Engels analyzed critically in the *Manifesto* the various political forces then striving for control over the workers' movement and rejected all of them, though they did praise the views of the great utopians, Fourier, Saint-Simon, and Owen. They suggested that the tactics used by the workers' movement in any particular country should be in harmony with the specific historical conditions in that country. Wherever the bourgeoisie was dominant, there labor was urged to fight against it, but in countries where the bourgeoisie was not yet in power, there the com-

5 Vorländer, *op. cit.*, p. 135.

munist parties were urged to cooperate with the bourgeois leftist parties against the ruling classes.

MARX'S RETURN TO GERMANY

The revolution of March, 1848, spread over Europe and engulfed Germany. Marx returned to his native land in April of that year and became the editor of the *Neue Rheinische Zeitung*, a democratic journal published in Cologne. By the autumn of 1848, reaction had gained ground and at the end of September the paper was suspended for fourteen days. The last issue was published on May 19, 1849. The authorities then ordered Marx expelled from Cologne as a "foreigner." Marx left for Paris and then for London, where he lived for the remainder of his life.

LONDON

In London, at that time one of the leading centers for political exiles, Marx re-established his contact with revolutionary circles, and, with Engels, launched a political-economic journal, the *New Rheinland Journal*. Six issues were published. Soon both Marx and Engels found their co-exiles too trying and unrewarding, and Marx began his daily visits to the British Museum, where he gathered much of the data for his monumental work, *Das Kapital*. Immersed in his scientific labor, Marx frequently found his immediate economic problems exceedingly difficult. His family was frequently in real want and were able to survive only by the help of Engels. Yet he never slackened in his work nor in his interest in contemporary events.

After Louis Napoleon's *coup d'état*, Marx published *The Eighteenth Brumaire of Louis Napoleon*, in which he used his great polemic gifts to harass the usurper. Beginning in 1851, for a time he contributed two articles a week to *The New York Tribune;* but even though Engels wrote the articles, Marx found weekly journalism dull and trying as well as a hindrance to his scientific labors.

In 1859, Marx published his first extensive work on economics, *A Critique of Political Economy*. Much of this material was subsequently incorporated in the first volume of *Das Kapital*. In the early 1860's Marx participated actively in the founding of the First International.[6] His attempt to dominate the organization resulted in a break with the anarchist groups led by Mikhail Bakunin and ended the existence of that organization. In his *Civil War in France*, he defended the Paris Com-

6 See Chap. 28.

mune, but his main energies were concentrated upon his work in economics.

MARXISM

The theories of Marx and Engels, or Marxism, must be regarded as a complete social philosophy, or *Weltanschauung,* which seeks to explain the past, examine the social relations of the present, and predict the type of society of the future. It regards all history as a struggle between classes, and historical change as due to changes in productive relations.

THE MATERIALIST CONCEPTION OF HISTORY

The materialistic conception of history starts from the proposition that production, and next to production, the exchange of its products, is the basis of all social organization; that is, in every society appearing in history, the distribution of the products and with it the social stratification into classes and orders, conform to what is produced, how it is produced, and how that which is produced is exchanged.[7]

The views expressed in the above statement were first formulated by Karl Marx in his introduction to *A Critique of Political Economy.*[8] Marx presented a number of propositions which form the basis of his materialistic interpretation of history. They are as follows:

1. In the course of production, men enter into specific relations which give rise, independently of their will, to definite social and economic relations. These correspond to the level of development of the "material forces of production."

2. The sum total of these relations of production constitutes the economic structure of society, the real foundation, on which rises legal and political superstructures and to which correspond definite forms of social consciousness.

3. The form of political institutions and intellectual life of a society is determined by the mode of production.

4. The social institutions determine consciousness, instead of consciousness determining institutions.

5. Once the "material forces" have reached a given level of develop-

---

[7] Friedrich Engels, *Herr Eugen Dühring's Revolution in Science* (Chicago: Charles H. Kerr & Company, 1935), p. 277.

[8] Translated by N. I. Stone (Chicago: Charles H. Kerr & Company, 1904), p. 11–13.

ment, they come into conflict with the existing institutions of production, or the legal system of property relations.

6. The latter now limit the progress of the material forces. This leads
to social tension which results in a revolutionary upheaval ending in
changing the economic base and the superstructure of society. A successful revolution in the structure of production can take place only after the
potentialities of progress of the forces of production have been exhausted.

7. The productive forces developing under capitalism are laying the
basis for the removal of class antagonism which has characterized all
societies.

In other words, the nature of man's economic life has been determined
by the methods of production in use. Economic conditions which result
from methods of production give rise to class divisions, to the evolution of rank and law, to those beliefs which make social and moral customs, and to the sentiments and reflections expressed in art, science, and
religion.[9]

Historical materialism may be summarized thus: Conditions of production, taken as a whole, constitute the economic structure of society; this is
the material basis on which a superstructure of laws and political institutions is raised, and to which certain forms of social ethics, religious and
artistic consciousness correspond. Marx believed that the conditions of
production compel men to make decisions which may not harmonize
with their desires, but are accepted because of conditions of production.
Conditions of production are in turn determined by material forces.

The ultimate causes of social change, according to this view, cannot be
sought in greater human consciousness, "not in better insight into eternal
truth and justice," but in changes in the productive processes. Economic
rather than philosophical causes underlie social change. Man's increasing
recognition of the injustice of certain economic relations demonstrates
that changes in methods of production have taken place, and that these
changes have destroyed the harmonious social relations hitherto existing.

PRODUCTIVE FORCES

The control of productive forces has aroused considerable speculation and debate.[10] "The sum of productive forces, forms of capital and

---

[9] Benedetto Croce, *Historical Materialism and the Economics of Karl Marx*. Translated by C. M. Merdith (New York: The Macmillan Company, 1914), p. 14.

[10] Karl Marx and Friedrich Engels, *The German Ideology* (New York: International
Publishers, 1939), p. 29. See Karl Federn, *The Materialist Conception of History* (London: Macmillan & Co., 1939), Chap. II. In M. M. Bober, *Karl Marx's Interpretation of*

social forms of intercourse, which every individual and generation finds in existence as something given, is the real basis of the conditions of life." [11] Productive forces are made up of physical or natural, and human or social, forces. Among the physical are the fruitfulness of the earth, solar heat, water, wind, and all forms of man-created power. However, these must be combined with human labor force before they become a source of riches.[12] "The mode of production is not synonymous . . . with technique. The concept is much wider. It assumes the ensemble of three agencies, man, nature and technique." [13]

The most important component of the productive forces is a human labor power, embodying both intellectual and bodily elements. Man combines with nature to form the production process. Each of these primary factors conditions the others. The attempt to explain historical causation by a single proposition is not always successful. The utilization of discoveries by industry is an act of will, judgment, and risk. While classically the role of the entrepreneur is to seize any innovations and to exploit them to the full, the degree and the rapidity with which a discovery is utilized depend upon individual temperament, although the objective conditions—materials, markets, and labor force—must be present. Nor can national tradition or psychology be overlooked.

Marxists have answered criticisms of their beliefs with the observation that "intellectual phenomena are more or less important intermediate links in the different historical processes, but being of an ideological nature, they are rooted in the economic system and are ultimately created and determined by the conditions of production." [14] This has reference to the relations between thought and economic processes. Manifesting itself in science, art, and philosophy as a reflection of the structure of production, thought cannot be, according to Marx, independent of historical conditions. "The ideas of the ruling class are in every epoch the ruling ideas: i.e., the class, which is the ruling material force in society, is at the same time its intellectual force." The class which controls the material means also controls intellectual production, so that groups without property become subject to the ruling ideas. The ruling ideas are

History (Cambridge: Harvard University Press, 2nd ed., 1948). Chap. 1 gives an excellent discussion of the meaning of "productive forces."

11 Marx and Engels, *The German Ideology*, p. 29.

12 Heinrich Cunow, *Die Marxische Geschichts Gesellschafts und Staatstheorie* (Berlin: J. H. W. Dietz, 1923), I, 158.

13 Bober, *op. cit.* (1st ed., 1927), p. 17.

14 *Federn*, pp. 26–27.

nothing more than the ideal expression of the dominant material relationship grasped as ideas.

In this instance, we are not dealing with the question whether economic relationships influence the thinking of man, but whether the relations between science, art, philosophy, and religion on the one hand, and the economic structure on the other are such as to make the former dependent upon the latter. Some Marxists contend that Marxism does not hold that the ideology of man flows directly and specifically from economic relations alone. The different legal, scientific, philosophic, artistic, and religious elements also react upon and influence each other. However, the final or total elements of intellectual and spiritual life in every period are determined by the economic system of that society. It is not clear why ideas and ideals cannot be autonomous, and exercise an independent influence upon events.

In discussing the Marxist view of historical causation, it is necessary to recognize that the term "materialist" is not used in the sense that men are guided by material or economic interests alone. Marxists do not deny that ideas and ideals exist in the world and even have some influence. They contend that these are conditioned by productive relations or the economic structure of society. A given type of economic society produces, according to the Marxists, a specific type of ideas and ideals. However, history seems too varied and complex a panorama to be explained by a single principle. While productive forces may play a significant role in history, the Marxists have by no means demonstrated the exclusive or even predominant character of their influence.

DIALECTICS

Marx and Engles assumed that history is largely the record of man's progress from lower to higher social states. Nothing in the universe is permanent; all phenomena are undergoing continual change, which takes place on the basis of contradiction and the union of opposites, called the dialectic.

The dialectic was a method developed by the German philosopher George Wilhelm Friedrich Hegel. According to Hegel, the world was in a constant state of change or development without end or repetition which expressed the universal spirit or idea. This change proceeds by contradiction—thesis and antithesis—and leads to a higher synthesis. The idea, according to Hegel, was anterior to material facts, for reality was, in his opinion, only a manifestation of thought. Marx agreed that the dialectic reveals the real nature of the universe. However, he regarded Hegel's statement as enshrouded in mysticism, for actually ideas are only the reflection of the real world. While Hegel had understood the process of change, his dialectic was actually standing on its head, for instead of the real world reflecting the idea, it is ideas which reflect the real world.[15]

Thus existing economic institutions generate their opposites—contradictions—and out of those conflicts arise higher forms of social organization. Historically these contradictions are the class conflicts. Under feudalism the social contradictions showed themselves in the struggle between feudal lord and serf, which led to the development of a higher socioeconomic form, capitalism. Under capitalism, the capitalist class and the proletariat are the thesis and the antithesis, and out of this conflict Marxists expect a higher form of society—socialism—to evolve.

CLASSES

In society the differences between the developing productive forces and social relations express themselves through class conflict. A class is a group of individuals which occupies a given place in the productive system of society with respect to ownership or nonownership of property and the degree of personal freedom enjoyed or lacking. "Each system of production implies a unique class structure. With a change in the mode of production, the relations of production change and with them the type of classes." [16] A class, according to Marx, arises out of economic or property relations. Capital has thereby created a working class with a common interest. A class is different from an occupational group in that the economic interests of two occupational groups can be in harmony with each other and at the same time be in conflict with other classes. The factor which determines membership in a class is the character of the economic activity performed by the individual, and not the amount of his wealth or the size of his income. Three classes are distinguished in modern society—landlords, capitalists, and laborers or proletarians.[17]

Class Division   The modern division of society into classes has had many forerunners, as emphasized in *The Communist Manifesto*. In fact, Marx defined all history as a series of class conflicts.

[15] Friedrich Engels, *Feuerbach, the Roots of the Socialist Philosophy* (Chicago: Charles H. Kerr & Company), Chap. 4; Karl Marx, *Capital* (Chicago: Charles H. Kerr & Company, 1908), I, 25.

[16] Bober, *op. cit.*, 2d ed., p. 100.

[17] Max Adler, *Die Staats Aufassung des Marxismus* (Vienna: Marx-Studien, 1922), pp. 89–96.

THE STATE

According to Marx's theory of history and classes, the state has no independent existence. It is part of the "superstructure" of society, and its character is determined by the development of the productive forces. The form of the state and the legal relations that arise are rooted in the material conditions of life. According to Engels, "There have been societies without it [the state], that had no idea of any state or public power. At a certain stage of economic development, which was of necessity accompanied by a division of society into classes, the state became the inevitable result of this division." [18]

The state is not power arising outside society, nor is its origin due to the achievement of certain ethical principles. On the contrary, the state arises as soon as society has become involved in irreconcilable economic conflicts; it functions so as to prevent this conflict from coming to the surface and expressing itself in open warfare. Consequently, an illusion is created of a power above society acting to preserve order and preventing an open clash by conflicting groups. The existence of the state is an admission that classes have arisen, and class conflict has developed.

[Since] the state has arisen as a result of these very conflicts, it acts as the instrument of suppression of the ruling economic class. In the several historical epochs, the state has been the representative of the ruling class. In ancient Greece, the state represented the interests of the slave owners; in the feudal system, the state spoke for the feudal nobility; and under capitalism the state expresses the desire and will of the capitalist class.[19]

If the state reflects the irreconcilable conflict in society, and if it is the instrument of the ruling class, it logically follows that it is the organ of a dominating class in order to check the subordinate class. It is, in the words of Lenin, "the organ of class domination, the organ of *oppression* of one class by another."[20] The state regularizes and moderates oppression, and makes it more bearable.

A second feature of the state is its power of coercion.

[18] Friedrich Engels, *Origin of the Family, Private Property and the State.* Translated by Ernest Unterman (Chicago: Charles H. Kerr & Company, 1902), p. 211. The quotations from this source are reprinted by permission of the publishers.

[19] *Ibid.*, p. 201.

[20] *The State and Revolution* (New York: International Publishers, 1932), p. 9. Italics are Lenin's.

This special power of coercion is necessary because a self-organized army of the people has become impossible since the division of society into classes took place . . . . This public power of coercion exists in every state. It is not composed of armed men alone, but has also such objects as prisons and correction houses attached to it . . . . It may be very small . . . in societies with feebly developed class antagonisms . . . . But it increases in the same ratio in which the class antagonisms become more pronounced, and in which neighboring states become larger and more populous.[21]

The state begins as a minor instrument of repression, and expands its power and importance as class cleavages become sharper. The state thus becomes an organized force used by one class to keep another in subjection. It acts to prevent interference with established production and exchange, which are the bases of class exploitation.

Engels contended that in most historical epochs the wealthy had special rights and privileges, and in a democracy this power is exercised indirectly. Either direct corruption or an alliance between the rich and the government is the means of giving power to the wealthy. As for the welfare and noncoercive actions of the state, these are dismissed as unimportant or as a means of deceiving the oppressed.

As the state is an instrument of class domination, it ceases to be necessary once class differences are removed. According to Marx, the proletariat "will substitute, in the course of its development, for the older order of civil society an association which will exclude classes and their antagonisms and there will no longer be political power, properly speaking, since political power is simply the official form of antagonism in civil society." [22]

When workers seize power and transform private property into social property, class differences are abolished, and the state ceases to have any function. In taking over the means of production, the state becomes "superfluous, and then dies out of itself. In the place of the government over persons steps the administration of things and the management of the processes of production. The state is not abolished, it withers away." [23] The termination of the state is the historical goal of the proletariat.

21 Engels, *Origin of the Family, Private Property and the State*, p. 207.
22 Karl Marx, *The Poverty of Philosophy* (Chicago: Charles H. Kerr & Company, 1907), p. 190.
23 Italics in original. Engels, *Herr Eugen Dühring's Revolution in Science*, p. 292.

6. MARXIST ECONOMIC DOCTRINES

ECONOMIC DOCTRINES

Marx's economic views are not reached independently of his views on history and the state. Economics is not a form of pure analysis, but a means of discovering the laws of development of capitalistic society in order to be better armed intellectually to replace it. It must be borne in mind that Marx was not concerned with the same type of problem usually discussed in equilibrium economics, such as the formation of market prices or income, or the incidence of a tax. Whenever such issues are discussed, they are incidental to the major objective, which is to demonstrate how and why labor is exploited, how this class conflict becomes increasingly serious, and why it cannot be lessened by palliatives.[1]

COMMODITY PRODUCTION

Marx's economic analysis is concerned with capitalistic production and with revealing the laws of movement of capitalistic society. The wealth of capitalistic societies presents itself as an accumulation of commodities, and the unit of production as the single commodity. First of all, a commodity is a useful good, a want-satisfying object possessing utility, and consequently having use value. In addition to having use value, commodities also have exchange value. In fact, according to Marx, exchange value is not an accidental relation dependent upon time and place, but is inseparably linked with a substance inherent in a commodity. This common property of commodities is that they are all the product of labor. It is not the specific type or kind of labor we have in view, but "human labor in the abstract."

In the exchange of commodities, exchange value shows itself to be in-

[1] Paul Sweezy, *The Theory of Economic Development* (New York: Oxford University Press, 1942), interprets Marx from the Leninist point of view.

dependent of use value. The value of a commodity is determined by the quantity of labor power contained in the product. In order to eliminate an ambiguity so that value would not be created by idleness and wasteful methods, Marx explains that value of a commodity is the average labor time socially necessary to produce the article under normal conditions of production and with the average degree of skill and intensity customary at the time. If a laborsaving invention reduces the labor time needed to produce a commodity, the value of that commodity will fall by the same percentage as the reduction in labor time. Consequently, commodities in which equal quantities of labor are embodied, or those which can be produced in the same labor time, have the same value, and "as values, all commodities are only definite masses of congealed labor." [2] While human labor creates value, it is itself not value. Human labor becomes value only when it is embodied in some object.

THE FETISHISM OF COMMODITIES

Marx sought to unravel the mysteries of value. The basic difficulty in the problem of value, according to Marx, is that the existence of things qua commodities and the value relation between the products of labor which stamps them as commodities have absolutely no connection with their physical properties and with the material relations arising therefrom. Actually, the exchange of commodities is a relation between men, although it assumes a relation between things. This is what Marx called the fetishism of commodities. He explained the dual character of a commodity in that it possesses use value and exchange value. Marx contended that the material character of things hides their value relations. It is true that the exchange of products of labor is motivated by a desire to exchange products of different uses, but at the same time we exchange homogeneous human labor. In a society of commodity producers, specific private labor is equal to every other kind of labor by virtue of its being human labor. This fact is hidden from view, but it is revealed by going behind the superficial relations of commodities and seeing their true character as values.

EXCHANGE

For exchange of commodities to take place, the products exchanged must possess use values for the person seeking them, and nonuse values

---

2 Karl Marx, *Capital* (Chicago: Charles H. Kerr & Company, 1908), I, 46. Quotations from this source are reprinted by permission of the publishers.

for their owners. At first only superfluous goods were exchanged, but with the development of society the products of labor were produced for exchange. A distinction is gradually developed between the production of a good for purposes of consumption and the production of a good for purposes of exchange. As exchange of commodities expands, the commodity equipped by its nature to perform the function of a universal equivalent becomes established as money.

MONEY OR THE CIRCULATION OF COMMODITIES

Money becomes the material or phenomenal form of the value inherent in commodities—inherent because all of them are embodiments of labor.

Price expresses the value of a commodity in money form. It is only the money name for the labor embodied in a commodity. However, Marx recognized that the price can deviate from value, as the exchange ratio at any particular time and place may not coincide with the ratios of labor time needed to produce the commodity money and the good being exchanged. In the development of money as the universal equivalent of value, Marx made reference to the development of the changing forms. At first the formula Commodity–Money–Commodity appears. The commodity is first converted into money, but the money soon completes the circuit and returns to the commodity form. The circulation of commodities is begun so that the owner may purchase other commodities. Owners of commodities sell in order to buy other commodities.

Formula for Capital   In the course of time, owners of commodities buy in order to sell. Instead of the old formula Commodity–Money–Commodity, a new one appears: Money–Commodity–Money. In the old formula *C–M–C*, the aim is to get a new and different consumption good. Producers of Commodity X exchange it for money and purchase Commodity Y. While X and Y are commodities of equal value, they differ in quality or use value. At this stage the transfer of commodities is determined by the difference in their quality.

A different situation obtains in the circulation of Money–Commodity–Money. Money appears both at the beginning and at the end of the formula. However, upon examination, a quantitative difference is evident. The circuit begins with a specific sum, and it is greater at the end than at the beginning. The added amount or the surplus which appears at the end of the circuit results because the original sum has been transformed into capital. The first form of capital is merchant's capital. However, industrial capital is also money, converted into commodities, which in the course of sale produce a surplus.

THE ORIGIN OF SURPLUS VALUE

It is to be noted that Marx contended that a surplus, or an additional value, results from the circulation of money. However, this surplus does not arise in the process of circulation, for exchange is made on the basis of equal values. The change of values, that is, the addition of a surplus to the original value, arises in the consumption of what Marx called "a peculiar property of being a source of value." This special commodity is "labor power."

LABOR POWER

Labor power is the mental and physical capacity possessed by human beings for working and creating use values. To be able to dispose of his labor power without hindrance, the worker must be a free man, and economic conditions must be such as to separate the worker from his tools so as to make him dependent upon others for employment. The worker is therefore not in a position to sell commodities produced by his labor, but is forced by necessity to sell his labor power on the market. This labor power is purchased by the owners of money which appears as capital. The appearance of labor power as a commodity is dependent upon definite historical conditions, and arises only when the owner of capital meets in the market the free laborer ready to sell his labor power.[3]

Labor power is a peculiar commodity and, like that of all other commodities, its value is determined by the labor time needed to produce it. This means that the value of labor power is determined by the cost of maintaining the individual who supplies it, in accordance with the historic and cultural circumstances of the time.

Creation of Surplus Value   Labor power is bought by the capitalist in order to set it to work producing use values. With the help of tools and machinery, the worker under the direction of the capitalist converts the materials of nature into a new form. The product created in the labor process belongs to the capitalist. It is at this point that Marx argues that exploitation of labor takes place.

Marx reasoned as follows: The value of labor power, i.e., wages, is determined by the amount the worker needs to maintain himself, or

[3] *Ibid.*, p. 189.

differently expressed, the cost of labor is equivalent to the socially necessary labor time needed to produce the labor supply. However, the value of labor or wages and the value of the commodities produced by that labor are of different magnitudes. For the payment of wages, the capitalist is able to appropriate all the output produced during the working day. However, as a worker receives only the value of his labor power and as he continues on the job beyond this time, he creates in the second period an additional amount, surplus value.

Exploitation   Capital is used in the labor process. It appears in two forms—constant capital and variable capital. The constant capital (c) refers to the value of raw or semifinished materials, and the tools and equipment which are used in the productive process. They appear again as part of the value of the product. Nothing additional is added by these factors, since they only transmit values they formerly possessed to a new product. Thus if a machine, whatever the worth, depreciates at the rate of $200 a week and it produces 200 units a week, the machine would transmit $1 of value to each unit of product. Similarly, if the value of the materials used on each unit is $1, the value acquired by every unit of output from this material will equal $1. It is for these reasons that both of these forms of capital are called constant.

Variable capital (v) is the capital used to pay labor. It is called variable capital because in a capitalistic society the worker is required to remain at work and produce values not only up to the amount of his wages—the value of his labor power—but to continue to produce values over and above that amount. This process results in the creation of surplus value, which is the difference between the value of the final product and the value of the raw material, tools, and labor used to produce it.

To illustrate the exploitation of labor we can assume that a firm uses $10,000 in capital ($C$) made up of constant ($c$) expended upon raw material and equipment, and variable (v) used to hire labor. Assuming $9,000 constant and $1,000 variable at the beginning of the productive process we have at the conclusion of the process commodities whose total value equals (c plus v) plus s, where s is the surplus value. The original capital C equaling $10,000 has changed to C' or $11,000. The difference between C and C' is the surplus of $1,000.

The source of this surplus must, according to Marx, be sought in the variable capital, for the constant capital does not expand in value during the production process; it merely reappears at its old value. In the above example, the $9,000 of constant capital would have no part in value creation, and it is only the $1,000 advanced as wages which is important. Accordingly, the working time is divided into two segments: the part of the day in which the employee produces the value of his labor power of (v), and the part used to produce surplus (s). The necessary labor time is the period the worker spends in producing a value equal to wages. The fraction of the working day which extends beyond the necessary working time is designated as surplus labor time, and the labor expended in this period is called surplus labor.

Working Time Under given historical conditions the necessary labor time, or the period in which a value equal to wages is produced, is a given magnitude. In a capitalistic society the working day must be longer than the necessary working time, for it is from the latter portion of the working day that the capitalist derives his surplus value. Therefore Marx argues that the capitalist desires to extend the working day as much as possible, so as to increase the unpaid labor time and surplus value.

Mass of Surplus Value The mass of surplus value derived by the capitalist is the average value received from the employment of one worker multiplied by the total number of workers. It is possible to keep the mass of surplus value constant even if the number of workers employed is reduced. This can be achieved by an increase in the rate of surplus value. Assuming employment of one hundred workers who expend four hours out of an eight-hour day in necessary labor and the mass of surplus value of $400, the employer could increase the rate of surplus value to 150 per cent if he could increase the working day to ten hours.

6 hours surplus labor / 4 hours necessary labor

In the first instance, $400 was advanced in wages of variable capital. It is now possible to dismiss twenty workers, for eighty employees each working ten hours, assuming no change in productivity, will produce an output approximately equal to the output of one hundred in eight hours. Instead of advancing $400 in wages, the employer will need to advance but $320. An opposite result will follow if the working day is shortened. If, for example, the working day is reduced to six hours, then the rate of surplus value would be 50 per cent.

2 hours surplus labor / 4 hours necessary labor

The consequence would be that, everything being equal, the employer would require 25 per cent more labor to do the same quantity of work. The illustrations given indicate that the rate of surplus value, which is the relation of unpaid time to paid labor time, depends only upon the variable capital, and varies directly with the variable capital. Marx recognized that an employer using a large amount of equipment is not likely to earn less surplus value than an employer using a small amount of fixed capital. He therefore promised to solve this difficulty later.[4] Moreover, an implicit assumption is made that changes in the hours worked per day have no effect on output.

Relative Surplus Value   Surplus value may also be increased by raising the productiveness of labor, for the value of the worker's wages is thus lowered. Surplus value produced by increasing the length of the working day is designated as absolute surplus value; the surplus value which arises from a shortening of the necessary labor time to produce the value of wages and which causes a change in the ratios of the surplus and necessary working time is called relative surplus value. To increase the relative surplus value the capitalist is constantly forced to adopt improvements, for in this fashion he lowers the value of labor power, or wages. Competition is another factor stimulating increases in relative surplus value. However, the temporary advantage one employer has over his rivals acts as a stimulant upon others. The consequence is a constant pressure for lowering the value of labor power and increasing the relative surplus value.

PURPOSE OF CAPITALIST PRODUCTION

Capitalistic production is, according to Marx, primarily designed to produce surplus value. The test of a worker's productiveness is the surplus value he produces. Productive work has a specific meaning, one determined by the social relation of production, a relation conditioned historically.

Assuming that labor power sells at its value, it is possible for the capitalist to alter the relations between necessary and surplus labor in the following ways: (1) change in the length of the working day; (2) change in the intensity of work; (3) change in the productivity of labor. If the working day is prolonged, and productivity per hour remains the same, the absolute value will increase. The value of labor power falls and surplus value rises with an increase in the productivity of labor. The reason is that the worker can now produce his wages in a shorter period, and that means that surplus value, or his unpaid working time, increases.

---

[4] Marx did not live to complete his work, and Volumes II and III were finished by his lifelong friend and collaborator, Engels.

WAGES

Superficially, the wage of labor appears as the price of labor, a given quantity of money for a given amount of time. The laborer sells labor power, and the value of this commodity is, like all others, determined by the socially necessary labor time required for its production. Marx contended that while the price paid for labor is the price for the entire working day, the worker in a capitalistic society produces the value of his wage in a shorter period. The wage-form therefore blurs the division of the working day into necessary labor and surplus labor. The wage relation, according to Marx, conceals the fact that part of the working day is, in a capitalistic economy, unpaid. In this fact lies the importance of the transformation of value and price of labor power into the wage form.

Wage differences between countries can be explained by the customary cost of production of the laborer, i.e., by the standard of life as historically developed, the cost of training, and the number of members of the family employed.

ACCUMULATION OF CAPITAL

Money is transformed in the first instance into a means of production and labor power. The commodities produced contain the value advanced plus a portion of surplus value. The commodities then appear on the market, where they are sold and their value is realized in money. This movement forms the circulation of capital. While the capitalist who directly employs labor is the one who extracts the surplus value, he is by no means able to keep control of all of it. He shares it with other capitalists, merchants, and landowners, who claim to perform a function in the totality of social production. Surplus value is therefore divided into a number of parts, and it appears among its several recipients as interest, merchants' profit, rent, and producers' profit. Part of this surplus value is then spent on consumption and part is saved. The latter is added to the capital fund and constitutes capital formation or accumulation.

SIMPLE REPRODUCTION

Production in any society is a continuous process. Consequently, production is at the same time reproduction, for a society must reconvert a part of its products into means of production and semifinished material. Hence a portion of the annual social product is destined for productive consumption. If the capitalistic process is regarded as production, wages can be regarded as an advance out of the owner's capital. However, if the capitalistic process is also one of reproduction, the worker is paid out of the product of his own labor. In this respect it may be proper to assume that the worker receives a part of the product of his labor as wages. It is true that the worker is paid in money, but this is only the "transmuted form of the product of his labor." While the worker is creating new products, a portion of his earlier work is being converted into money which is used to pay the wage earner; Marx contended that this process is hidden by the commodity-form of the product and the money-form of the commodity. Variable capital is only the historical form of the fund out of which labor is supplied with the necessities of life, but which is in fact supplied by the worker himself through his own labor.

Assuming that a capitalist began his business life with a capital of $10,000 and obtained an annual surplus value of $2,000 which he spent on consumption, there would be at the end of five years no change in the quantity of capital. Marx argued that $10,000 in a capitalist's possession at the end of the period was derived from surplus value, for during the period he spent $10,000 on personal consumption. No payment for risk or for organizing the factors is allowed. Therefore, regardless of the initial origin of capital, it is after some time changed through the means of simple reproduction into capitalized surplus value.

Conversion of Surplus Value into Capital   More typically, however, part of the surplus value is consumed by the capitalist, and part is saved. The latter represents the conversion of surplus value into capital, *and is designated as capital accumulation.* This may be illustrated as follows: If a capitalist starts with an initial capital of $100,000 and the annual rate of surplus value is $10,000, he will, if he saves the surplus value and re-converts it, have a capital of $110,000 at the end of the first year. Assuming the same rate of surplus value, he will derive $11,000 in the second year; in the third year his capital will have jumped to above $122,000. In a relatively short time his capital will have doubled. This surplus value that has been appropriated by the capitalist is now converted into capital goods and is used to expand production and for the appropriation of more surplus value. Marx ridiculed the idea that a return to capital is warranted by the capitalist's foregoing consumption, or by abstinence, as it was called in his time. He argued that it is the abstinence of the worker and not that of the capitalist which leads to capital accumulation. The lower the wage, the greater the rate of surplus value and the larger the part diverted to capital accumulation.

COMPOSITION OF CAPITAL

Marx divided the composition of capital into two categories: (1) value composition of capital or the proportion in which total capital is divided into constant capital and variable capital; (2) technical composition of capital or the relation between the means of production and the labor needed for its employment. The relation between the two in terms of value is called the organic composition of capital, or $C/(C+V)$.

Growth of total capital assumes that part of the additional capital will be used for the payment of wages or for variable capital. If the composition of capital remains constant, a definite amount of investment will require a given number of workers. However, if additional workers will be required, wages will rise. This cannot go on indefinitely, for a limit exists to the rise of wages in a capitalistic regime, which limit is set by surplus value, since a wage cannot rise so as to jeopardize the total of surplus value.

However, capital accumulation does not, as initially assumed, proceed without changes in the composition of capital: it is affected by every improvement which leads to changes in productivity. For example, an increase in the productivity of labor usually leads to a change in the technical composition of capital since there is now an increase in the use of raw materials and of machinery. This change is soon reflected in the value or organic composition, for relatively more constant capital and relatively less variable capital are now used.

An increase in the productivity of labor, requiring as it does larger outlays of capital, leads to greater concentration in ownership. This concentration proceeds by constant expansion of capital through accumulation, or increase in capital, as a result of investment of surplus value, centralization, the growth in the size of capital enterprise, and absorption.

Accumulation has less part in this process than centralization. The former depends upon gradual increases resulting from reproduction, while the latter simply alters the quantitative grouping of capital and is thereby much more rapid. Thus the capitalistic means of producing commodities is in a constant state of flux, the result of which is a continual increase of constant capital—machinery, equipment, and raw materials—and a relative diminution of the variable capital—the "wage fund."

OUSTING OF LABOR

Decline of relative variable capital is more rapid than accumulation, for the newly accumulated capital uses a continually smaller proportion of workers. In addition, obsolete machinery is replaced by more productive equipment, resulting in the employment of fewer workers. Consequently, the proportion of constant to variable capital changes, a continually increasing part of the total capital becoming constant capital and a declining part becoming variable capital. Since the demand for labor depends upon variable capital and not upon total capital, the demand for labor falls in relation to total capital. It is true that the variable constituent of capital increases absolutely with the growth of total capital, but only at a constantly diminishing percentage. The rate of capital accumulation must be sharply accelerated to avoid unemployment of labor, for the relative decline in the variable capital appears as an absolute increase in the wage-earning population. This is due to the accumulation of capital, which always brings about a surplus of workers, i.e., greater than the number needed to utilize the accumulated capital. Marx argues that this reserve of workers is the "human material ready for exploitation." They are the partially and totally unemployed. The machine displaces the laborer.

This industrial reserve army stands ready to accept employment when additional workers are needed during seasonal or cyclical upswings. However, as constant capital accumulates, labor is more and more driven from employment. "Taking them as a whole, the general movements of wages are exclusively regulated by the expansion and contraction of the industrial reserve army, and these correspond to the periodic changes of the industrial cycle. . . . The industrial reserve army, during the periods of stagnation and average prosperity, weighs down the active labor army during periods of overproduction and paroxysm; it holds its pretensions in check."[5] The reserve army acts as a continuous threat to the jobs of the employed. "The greater the social wealth, the functioning capital, the extent and energy of its growth, and therefore also the absolute mass of the proletariat and the productiveness of its labor, the greater is the industrial reserve army."

[5] These quotations from Marx are from *Capital*, I, 899, 707, 709, in the edition cited.

Marx is determined to prove that growth of mechanization, increase in capital plant and equipment, and rise in productivity only mean increasing degradation of labor. "It follows, therefore, that in proportion as capital accumulates, the lot of the laborer, be his payment high or low, must grow worse."

The transformation of commodities into money and money into commodities leads, however, to the creation of no value, since buying and selling are in themselves unproductive, although a necessary link in the productive process. It is an unproductive function in the sense that it creates no value. These are dead expenses, and from the point of view of the capitalistic class these expenses are a deduction from surplus value or from surplus products. Circulation of values is distinct from transportation of commodities to consumers, in that transportation adds value to the commodity because of the means of production and the labor used in its process.

In addition to the purely Marxian categories of constant and variable, Marx distinguishes between fixed and circulating capitals. His distinction between fixed and circulating is based upon their different rates of turnover. A single turnover of fixed capital will equal several turnovers of circulating capital. The quantity of value invested in fixed capital must be advanced at once, and portions of this value are successively embodied in commodities. In contrast, the circulating capital has to be continually reproduced. However, individual components of fixed capital have a longer duration and consequently different periods of turnover.

Turnover of capital is important in the Marxist analysis because it influences the annual rate of surplus value. Assuming, for example, a given capital has an annual rate of turnover of ten and a variable capital of $5,000, surplus value of $5,000, the total surplus value produced annually will be $50,000. The annual rate of surplus value is the ratio of the total surplus value annually produced to the variable capital. In this instance it is $50,000 to $5,000 or 1,000 per cent.[6] Difference in the turnover period of capital will therefore lead to differences in the annual rate of surplus value.

6 *Ibid.*, II, 338.

REPRODUCTION AND CIRCULATION OF SOCIAL CAPITAL

The motive for carrying on production is the gaining of surplus value. This process consists in a continual cycle of production and circulation. The individual capitals engaged in these processes form a part of the total social capital, and the entire process is made up of production, a series of exchanges, and individual consumption. The worker sells his labor power and in turn buys commodities for his own consumption as does the capitalist out of surplus value. Out of the annual social product, the capital consumed in production is replaced, and both worker and capitalist draw from the annual social output for their daily needs.

COST PRICE AND PROFIT

According to Marx, the value of a commodity (C) is equal to the sum of constant capital (c), variable capital (v), and surplus value (s). If a firm begins with a total capital of $10,000 divided into $5,000 constant and $5,000 variable, and if the rate of surplus value is 100 per cent, the firm will obtain at the end of the production cycle $15,000. If we subtract the $5,000 of surplus value, we have left $10,000, which is the value of the capitalist's investment in consumed means of production and in labor power. As the surplus value of $5,000 represents the unpaid labor power of the worker, there is a difference between the cost of the commodity to the capitalist, or $10,000, and the "actual" cost of the commodity, or $15,000. Cost price is less than the value of a commodity, for the value is equal to cost price plus surplus value. Surplus value is regarded as "an offspring of the advanced total capital, the surplus value assumes the change of form known as profit."[7] If surplus value is translated into profit, then the value of a commodity is equal to the cost price plus profit. In selling a commodity at its value, the capitalist will realize a profit which will equal the difference between cost price and value. However, the capitalist can realize a profit even if he sells his finished commodity below its value, so long as he sells above cost price.

PROFIT AND SURPLUS VALUE

In the process of capitalistic production, money is both the beginning and the terminal point of the production cycle. The aim is to increase the

[7] *Ibid.*, III, 49.

sum in the process of circulation. As both constant and variable capital must be joined in order to carry on production, the *rate* of gain or profit is calculated on the *total* capital employed. Surplus value or profit is the amount of value yielded in the process of production above cost price. The rate of profit is found by dividing surplus value (s) by total capital (C), or s/C. The rate of surplus value (s) is found by dividing surplus value (s) by variable capital or wages (v), or s/v. Surplus value, or profit, arises within the process of production, and is realized in circulation. As the rate of surplus value is based on the ratio of surplus value to variable capital, and the rate of profit on the ratio of surplus value to *total* capital, the rate of surplus value on two capitals of equal magnitude may be the same, while the rates of profit may differ. For example:

1. Capital A has a total capital of $100,000 divided into $80,000 constant and $20,000 variable. If the yield of surplus value is $20,000 the rate of *surplus value* will be 20,000/20,000 or 100 per cent, the rate of *profit* 20,000/100,000, or 20 per cent.

2. Capital B has a capital of $100,000 divided into $90,000 constant and $10,000 variable. If $10,000 is yielded in surplus value the rate of *surplus value* will be 10,000/10,000 or 100 per cent, the rate of profit 10,000/100,000 or 10 per cent.

In addition the rate of profit is affected by the period of turnover of capital. Two capitals of similar composition, equal rates of surplus value, and the same number of working days will have rates of profit proportionate to their periods of turnover.

CONVERSION OF PROFIT INTO AVERAGE PROFIT

Capitals of the same magnitude, employed for similar periods and exploiting labor at the same rate, may yet yield different amounts of surplus value and profit because of their different organic composition. This follows because surplus value and profit are derived from the variable capital. For example, Capital A of $10,000, divided in $1,000 constant capital and $9,000 variable capital with a rate of exploitation of 100 per cent, will at the end of the cycle consist of $1,000 constant, $9,000 variable, and $9,000 surplus. Capital B of the same magnitude divided into $9,000 constant and $1,000 variable capital with the same rate of surplus value, will yield $1,000 surplus. The rate of profit on A is therefore 90 per cent, 9,000/10,000 and on B only 10 per cent, 1,000/10,000. However, in a competitive economy this cannot be. As Marx put it, "aside from unessential, accidental, and mutually compensating distinctions, a *difference* in the average rate of profit of the various lines of industry does not exist in reality, and could not exist without abolishing the entire system of capitalist production."[8] Marx tried to solve this dilemma by combining all individual capitals into social capital. The rate of return to this total capital would then be the same regardless of its composition. Some commodities will sell below and some above their value. The prices which emerge by calculating the *average* rates of profit for all the branches of industry and their cost prices are called the "prices of production." While different industries, because of the difference in their capital composition, will earn different rates of profit, the latter is equalized by competition. "The price of any commodity which is equal to its cost-price, plus that share of average profit on total capital invested . . . in its production which is allotted to it in proportion to its conditions of turnover, is called its price of production."

Each individual capitalist, therefore, would recover from his sales the value of capital consumed plus this social average rate of surplus value or profit. When the composition of capital in some forms is approximately average, prices of production will usually equal value, and surplus value coincides with profit. All other capitals tend toward the average. Capital tends to move out of those branches with low rates of profit and to flow into those activities which yield a high rate. This in-and-out flow of capital serves to distribute it in such a manner that average profit on capital would be equalized in different branches of industry. This was the long-awaited and somewhat disappointing solution of the relationship between rising surplus value and falling profits and the problem to which attention was called above.

Tendency of Profit to Fall   In the process of accumulation, constant capital has a tendency to increase in relation to variable and to total capital. This tendency operates with respect both to individual capitals in different industries and to social capital as a whole. A relative diminution in the variable capital leads to a relative decrease in the profit, once the rate of exploitation is established. The reason is that a given rate of surplus value will express itself in considerably different rates of profit, according to the different volumes of constant capitals and consequently of total capitals. For example, assuming that of two firms, the first has $9,000 of constant capital and $1,000 of variable, and rate of surplus value of

8 *Ibid.*, p. 183. Italics are mine. The succeeding quotations from *Capital* are also from Vol. III in the edition cited, pp. 186, 247, 256, 423, 743, 759.

100 per cent, profit would equal $1,000 or 10 per cent. The second firm, with $19,000 constant and $1,000 variable, and the same rate of surplus value, would have a profit of $1,000, or 5 per cent. As Marx has argued that the constant capital tends to increase in relation to the variable capital, a falling rate of profit logically follows. However, the mass of total profit may, and actually does, increase, but since total capital increases faster, the *rate* of profit must fall. On a given amount of capital, say $1,000, the rate of surplus value and profit may go down, but if the number of units of $1,000 increases, the *absolute* or total mass of surplus will rise.

The progress of the process of production and accumulation *must*, therefore, be accompanied by a growth of the mass of available and appropriated surplus—labor—and consequently by a growth of the absolute mass of profit appropriated by the social capital. But the same laws of production and accumulation increase the volume and value of the constant capital in a more rapid progression than those of the variable capital invested in living labor. The same laws, then, produce for the social capital an increase in the absolute mass of profit and a falling rate of profit.

This was called by Marx, the "law of the falling tendency of the rate of profit."

CONCENTRATION OF PRODUCTION

The capitalist does not stand idly by in the face of a falling rate of profit. He seeks to improve his position by introducing new devices and undermining his competitor. New machinery and techniques are injected which lead to the elimination of the small producer. However, such steps can be only temporary palliatives, for the trend, inherent in the nature of capitalism, cannot be permanently halted.

CAUSES COUNTERACTING THE FALL IN THE RATE OF PROFIT

While the dominant tendency in a capitalist economy is for the rate of profit to fall, the capitalist is able to utilize a number of devices to counteract the operation of this tendency. He may reduce wages, lengthen hours, speed up production, utilize cheaper foreign raw materials, and exploit the surplus population set loose by the acceleration of the mechanization of industry.

DIVISION OF PROFIT INTO INTEREST AND PURE PROFIT

Profit is divided among several groups of capitalists. The owner of a sum of money transfers its use to another—the industrialist capitalist. In return, the money capitalist—the lender—expects a return which constitutes interest. It is part of the surplus value that is paid in interest. The rate of interest is determined by competition between lenders and borrowers. As interest is derived from profit, and as the rate of profit is inversely proportioned to the development of capitalistic production, "it follows that the high or low rate of interest in a certain country is to the same extent inversely proportional to the degree of industrial development, at least so far as differences in the rate of interest actually expresses differences in the rate of profit."

Ground rent, as distinct from returns on improvements, is a payment for the use of the soil. The landlord receives annually a sum for the lease of his property. Ground rent is therefore based upon the existence of private property in land. "All ground rent is surplus value, the product of surplus labor."

Ground rent takes the form of differential rent, which arises when certain individual capitals can enjoy a greater fertility in a sphere of production than capitals excluded from these advantages. This natural monopoly permits an increase in the productive power of labor. Thus the landowner is able to absorb in rent the difference between "the individual and average profit." It is the outcome of equal investments upon equal areas of land of different fertilities. A second case of differential rent arises when equal quantities of capital successively applied to the same landed area yield unequal returns. In addition, because of his monopoly position, the landlord is able to appropriate absolute ground rent, surplus value. Absolute rent forms a portion of surplus value of commodities. "It is captured by the landlords, who extract it from the capitalists."

CRISES

Periodic breakdowns inherent in capitalism are inevitable and become a threat to the existence of capitalist society. Marx appears to have three theories of crises developed: (1) Underconsumption, (2) falling rate of profit, and (3) disproportionality.[9]

9 Bober, *op. cit.* (2nd ed.), Chap. XII.

Underconsumption refers to the tendency of production to outrun the consuming power of society, for while surplus value arises in production by exploiting labor, it can be realized only by the sale of commodities. Marx maintained that the "last cause of all real crises always remains the poverty and restricted consumption of the masses as compared to the tendency of capitalist production to develop the productive forces in such a way, that only the absolute power of consumption of the entire society would be their limit."[10] Elsewhere Marx argued that income distribution is such that the consuming power of the masses is reduced "to a variable minimum within more or less narrow limits." In other places underconsumption is repudiated, and Marx maintained that crises cannot be solved by wage increases. An underconsumption theory of crises seems out of harmony with the Marxist system, as such a theory implies the crises can be solved by rearranging the distribution of income and that thereby revolution would not be inevitable.

The need to overcome the tendency for the rate of profit to fall is, according to Marx, the basic cause of economic crises. The falling rate of profit takes place at the same time the mass of profits increases with the "growing mass of the employed capital." Profit in this connection refers to all forms of surplus value, and includes rent, interest, and pure profit. A fall in the rate of profit creates a competitive struggle among capitalists for markets, for the "compensation of the fall in the rate of profit by a rise in the mass of profit applies only to the social capital and to the great capitalists who are firmly installed." The owners of small or new capitals must carve out markets for themselves. The struggle leads to overproduction of commodities and inability to sell. Marx maintained that for this reason there is periodical overproduction. Capital becomes more concentrated, but the small, less well-situated capitals are forced into speculative and semilegal channels, for they cannot find adequate returns. As a result there arises a "plethora of that class of capital which finds no compensation in its mass for the fall in the rate of profit—a plethora of capitals [which are] incapable of self-dependent action and placed at the disposal of the managers of large lines of industry in the form of credit." The result is "unemployed capital on one hand, and an unemployed laboring population on the other."

At some point additional capital can find no employment and must remain partially or completely idle. A crisis ensues, and the capital stock

10 *Capital*, III, 568. The following quotations from *Capital* are also from Vol. III, pp. 301, 294, 298.

depreciates because it now earns less than formerly. "The principal work of destruction would show its most dire effects in a slaughtering of the *values* of capitals." Claims on future surplus value *would* suffer from a reduction in receipts. Commodities would be sold only at reduced prices, which means that the value of the capital embodied in them would shrink. Moreover, the entire process of reproduction is based on certain assumptions as to prices, so that a lowering of prices interferes with reproduction. "The chain of payments due at certain times is broken at a hundred places, and the disaster is intensified by the collapse of the credit-system. Thus violent and acute crises are brought about, sudden and forcible depreciations, an actual stagnation and collapse of the process of reproduction, and finally a real falling off in reproduction." However, the decline in prices and values intensifies the competitive struggle, which in turn stimulates innovations and the wider use of laborsaving machinery. Coupled to the depreciation in values, a basis eventually develops for a new expansion of capital. Yet Marx argued that the desire to overcome the falling rate of profit—which inevitably brings about a surplus of workers—must also lead to a surplus or overproduction of capital. This does not signify that too much wealth is being produced, but only reflects the contradictions in the system.

Marx, according to some writers, also developed a disproportionality theory of crises. This has reference to the maladjustments which arise in a competitive economy where decisions are made by a large number of individual capitalists. In other words, it is unplanned, anarchical production that leads to the difficulty. For example, partial overproduction or crop failures, by affecting the income of certain producers, leads to decisions that react upon other entrepreneurs, with the consequence that they modify their income-output policies and further spread economic difficulties. Shortages react on price, which means smaller amounts allocated for wages, and the rate of profit $s/(c+v)$ will tend to decline.

Marx's primary concern was to show that the origin of rent, interest, and profit comes from the exploitation of labor. Exploitation is possible because the worker has to sell his labor power to a capitalist who purchases it for the surplus value he is able to extract from labor. Creation of surplus value leads to growth in capital formation, displacement of labor, periodic crises, and the virtual expulsion of some members of the working force from the labor market. Growth of this labor reserve army leads to steadily worsening conditions of labor, which becomes more revolutionary and anticapitalistic. In addition, the periodic crisis with its uncertainty and unemployment, intensifies the misery of labor. In the face of these difficulties and contradictions, the displacement of capitalism by a socialist society becomes inevitable.

It is not difficult to demonstrate contradictions and shortcomings in Marx's economic analysis. His underemphasis of the importance of demand, and his inability to reduce labor of all kinds to "homogeneous human 'labor' " is never mastered. "We must reduce heterogeneous labours to terms of homogeneous simple labour before prices are settled. But in fact the equation and reduction are made through the prices of the commodities into which the different labour enters."[11] It is also true that Marx, as a former Hegelian, pursued the chimera of absolute value, rather than accepting the prosaic fact that economic value is relative and merely expresses market price.

Marx's theory of history is founded upon the same simple assumptions. There need be no doubt that economic events play an important role in history, but it is certainly an obvious overstatement that economic events are the basis of all human institutions and that government, religion, art, and science have no independent existence. Not only does Marx fail to demonstrate that economics is the base and that all institutions are superstructures, but history shows the fallacy of such a view. The notion of freedom, individual liberty, and rights of man goes back far beyond the fifteenth and sixteenth centuries, and we can find them not only expressed but sought for at all stages of Western history. To dismiss, as mere reflections of economic processes, ideals which have fired the mind and imagination of man and for which they have willingly died seems unwarranted and without adequate cause. Moreover, there is no proof that government is not itself an independent power. Certainly, in a democracy it reflects interests of groups, but there need not be any direct relation between government and economic power. Modern governments, including our own in the United States, have repeatedly acted against the vital interests of certain powerful financial and industrial interests, and while the latter will use their efforts to frustrate what they regard as harmful to themselves, they cannot succeed if the government has public support. Marx's insistence upon his historical law seems to have been designed to demonstrate that unless the capitalistic class is dispossessed, improvement through government is not possible because government is merely the superstructure. History is the best proof of the inadequacy of this

[11] H. W. B. Joseph, *The Labour Theory of Value in Karl Marx* (London: Oxford University Press, 1923), p. 67.

theory. Not only is government important, but man's notion of justice, morality, and ethics is important, for in molding the outlook and action of man, they can change the course of events and reshape human institutions.

Marx mistook for a historic law the irrepressible drive for capital accumulation and increasing exploitation typical of pioneer capitalism. A newly created industrial society faces the need for rapid capital accumulation. Forced savings and low wages and standards are the means by which capital is now accumulated in the Soviet Union, as they were in capitalistic England. Marx confounded a phase of capitalism with its essence. Because of the awful exploitation under early capitalism, Marx projected the growing and irresistible power of capitalism and the growing misery of labor. The domination of politics by economics in early capitalism led Marx to assume that this was an inexorable law. But only in early laissez-faire capitalism is it possible for economic power to dominate the politics of society. In the fascist and soviet type of society, in the welfare state politics is the master of economic groups. Here again a special and transitory situation was converted into a universal principle. Consequently, Marxists were led by their theoretical fatalism to deny the possibility of improvement by the state, and thus the whole modern system of social and welfare legislation is held to be unimportant.

Marx had in mind a pure capitalism, an intellectual construction which perhaps never existed. If social systems could be made pure constructions by abstracting all elements, it is possible to demonstrate the superiority of the particular one a writer favors. Thus we can demonstrate the invisible hand operating in capitalism to maximize social welfare, or the Marxian capitalist dominating society and utilizing all of his power to squeeze out the last ounce of surplus value from the exploited worker. Actually capitalism does not conform to either view.

The significance of Marx's work should not, however, be underestimated even if his economics may not meet the test of rigorous criticism. As Croce points out:

No honest student can deny that his work has been of great historic importance, and it is hard to believe that a book like *Das Kapital* which has been the inspiration of a great movement can be nothing but a tissue of false reasoning as some of its critics have affirmed. The doctrine of the economic interpretation of history has revivified and influenced almost all modern historical research. In a great part of his analysis of the nature and natural development of a capitalist society, Marx has shown himself a prophet of extraordinary insight. Only a great book could become the "Bible of the working classes." [12]

Marx gave to his immediate disciples, then a small, persecuted group, a vision and a certainty of victory. He assured his followers that they were the heirs of the capitalist. Such conclusions have an air of almost divine prophecy, and there is no denying that they are able to inspire confidence in the persecuted that they will inherit the future.

Marx's major importance may be as the inspirer and guide of the Continental socialist movement of the last seventy-five years. The movement itself has divided into a Western and an Eastern branch. While a small segment of the movement was revolutionary, the socialist movement concerned with the real progress of labor took on a more reformist tinge.

The labor and trade-union movements of Continental Europe sprang in part from Marxism, though essentially they have been evolutionary in outlook and policy. However, the amoralism, the intolerance, and the wickedness that are compatible with Marxist philosophy have also blossomed. In the period of 1890–1914, the less attractive features of Marxism were subordinated to more tolerant tendencies perhaps because of the stability and progress of the period; and while doctrinal debates were frequently acrimonious, seldom were dissidents suppressed or exterminated. Up to World War I, the extreme left was inconsequential. With the victory of Bolshevism, the left of Marxism has gained both moral and material support.

Marxism swept aside its rivals and became the chief intellectual armory of the socialist movements of the world. Yet the power it exercised varied from country to country, depending upon the history and traditions as well as upon the competing doctrines.

[12] Benedetio Croce, *Historical Materialism and the Economics of Karl Marx*. Translated by C. M. Merdith (New York: The Macmillan Company, 1914), p. x.

7. *ANARCHISM*

Although scarcely an important group in the contemporary movements for economic reform, anarchism was for a time a rival to Marxism on the Continent. The anarchists rejected capitalism, and accepted the eighteenth-century view of the inherent goodness of man. From the latter hypothesis they drew the conclusion that the evil and wickedness are due to man-made institutions. More clearly than any of their contemporaries, they perceived the dangers inherent in the leviathan state, and their criticisms of government have a vitality and freshness which age has not been able to destroy. However, in common with all types of socialists, they reject competition as an evil, and private ownership of the factors of production as a source of injustice.

Modern anarchism is "the confluence of the two great currents which during and since the French Revolution have found such characteristic expression in the intellectual life of Europe: socialism and liberalism." [1] In common with liberalism, anarchism regards social problems from the point of view of the individual and also seeks to limit the functions of government. With the socialists, anarchists demand the abolition of private ownership of the means of production. However, anarchism is not a single view. It can be divided into two types: the individualist anarchism of Godwin, Stirner, and Benjamin Tucker; and the anarchist communism of Kropotkin, Reclus, and Malatesta.

"Anarchy means, in its ideal sense, the perfect, unfettered self-government of the individual, and consequently the absence of any kind of external government." [2] Anarchism demands both political and economic freedom in the absolute sense. Instead of our present social organization, anarchists would substitute cooperative labor directed solely to the satisfying of wants and not the making of profit. Instead of the present coer-

[1] Rudolf Rocker, *Anarcho-Syndicalism* (London: Secker and Warburg, 1938), p. 21.
[2] E. V. Zenker, *Anarchism* (London: Methuen & Co., 1898), p. 3.

98

cive state, the anarchists advocate a federation of free communities joined by a common economic and social interest and bound by free contract and agreement. The doctrines of anarchism were first promulgated in England by William Godwin, who published the first "great book" on anarchism or liberalism.[3]

WILLIAM GODWIN (1756–1836)

William Godwin presented his views in his book, *Concerning Political Justice and Its Influence upon General Virtue and Happiness,* which was published in 1793. Instead of a universe ruled by God, it would be, according to him, governed by universal reason. Ethical communism was the kingdom of heaven. He believed that there is within us a voice of reason and justice, but no single individual is an infallible judge of what these are. Reason is favorable to virtue, and is capable of leading man to continual progress and ultimate perfection. Men can discover the inherent laws of reason, which stimulate understanding, enlarge virtue, and arouse independence. The essence of virtue and true happiness is the promotion of the general welfare.

INEQUALITY OF PROPERTY

Godwin ascribed the conflicts in society to inequality of property and the laws designed to enhance the power of the rich.[4] Under the existing distribution of property, one man may inherit great wealth, while another has scarcely enough to live on. Unequal distribution of wealth is a check upon progress as it forces many to immerse "themselves in the most sordid cares." It produces idleness, vanity, and ostentation in the rich, and servility, envy, and fraud in the poor. Goods should be distributed so as to promote the general welfare. Disputes over property should be settled on the basis of justice, which demands that none should remain without the necessities while others possess more than enough for their needs.

GOVERNMENT

Godwin depended upon reason to keep men from war and from unsocial conduct. Therefore, government "does not arise out of the nature

[3] Max Nettlau, *La Anarquia a través de los tiempos* (Barcelona: Guilda de Amigos del Libro, 1935), p. 24.

[4] William Godwin, *An Enquiry Concerning Political Justice and Its Influence upon Virtue and Happiness* (New York: Alfred A. Knopf, Inc., 1926), I, 16–24. The following extracts from Godwin's work are from Vol. II and are reprinted by permission of the publishers: pp. 70, 71, 109, 67, 133, 126.

of man but out of the institutions by which he has already been corrupted." Simplifying the social system so that justice is recognizable would then lead the whole of mankind to become honorable and virtuous. Offenders would forsake their errors; otherwise they would face public disapproval and find it more congenial to move to another society. A gradual withdrawal of force and the substitution of reason would finally lead to "the dissolution of political government, of that brute engine which has been the only perennial engine for the vices of mankind."

The object of government . . . is the exertion of force. Now force can never be regarded as an appeal to understanding; and therefore obedience, which is an act of the understanding or will, can have no legitimate connection with it. I am bound to submit to justice and truth because they approve themselves to my judgment. I am bound to cooperate with government as far as it appears to me to coincide with these principles. But I submit to government when I think it erroneous merely because I have no remedy.

Godwin believed that the very nature of political institutions is "to suspend the elasticity and put an end to the advancement of mind." All government has within it an element of tyranny. In absolute governments the tyranny is more open, and in a republic, tyranny adjusts itself to changing opinion. Men have no need for government in order to promote their common welfare, as they will abide by the dictates of reason. Governments continually seek to enlarge their areas and jurisdiction and consequently division and dissension are more likely. "Security and peace are more to be desired than a name at which the nations tremble. Mankind are brethren."

CONSCIENCE

Freedom of conscience and private judgment are articles of faith. "Conscience and the press ought to be unrestrained, not that men have a right to deviate from the exact line that duty prescribes, but because society, the aggregate of individuals, has no right to undertake authoritatively to prescribe to its members in matters of pure speculation." Truth is not a question of mere numbers.

One obvious reason against this assumption on the part of society is the impossibility by any compulsory method of bringing men to uniformity of opinion. Man "is not . . . a perfect being, but perfectible."

The true instruments for changing the opinions of men are argument and persuasion. The best security for an advantageous issue is free and unrestricted discussion. In that field truth must always prove the successful champion.

Man can consult his private judgment and "resist any unjust proceeding on the part of the community." Government "is nothing more than a scheme for enforcing by brute violence the sense of one man or set of men upon another, necessary to be employed in certain cases of peculiar emergency."

METHODS OF CHANGE

Godwin would introduce change by persuasion. "Our judgment will always suspect these weapons with equal prospect of success on both sides. Therefore we should regard all force with aversion." He was convinced that reason was the means and that men would submit to its dictates. Man, he argued, will inevitably discover truth, and "not a sword will need to be drawn, not a finger to be lifted up in purposes of violence. The adversaries will be too few and too feeble to be able to entertain a serious thought of resistance against the universal sense of mankind."

The distinguishing characteristic of Godwin's views is his faith in truth and justice. He was a child of the French Enlightenment for whom reason, justice, and progress were articles of belief. His conviction that the disappearance of government would make mankind more just and reasonable, since it would then be free to exercise its own unspoiled volitions, is derived from the same source. Regardless of the scientific merit of Malthus's *Essay on Population,* it tended to dampen some of the limitless optimism engendered by Godwin. Like others, Godwin failed to take cognizance of the irrational and perverse in man. His bland and unspoiled optimism has a naïve sound for those who are aware of the history of the last fifty years; indeed, of history through the centuries. Godwin's anarchism is an extreme type of middle-class liberalism. It differs from the activist philosophy of Bakunin and other modern anarchists, but his views exercised an influence upon those who followed.

MAX STIRNER (1806–1856)

Another writer whose work was of some importance in the development of later opinion was Johann Casper Schmidt, who wrote under the name of Max Stirner. He attended the University of Berlin, where he came under the influence of Hegel. His views are extremely individualistic and are a form of solipsism. His book, *The Ego and Its Own,* brought sharp criticism from the socialists, and, despite its originality, Stirner did not fare too well. He tried his hand at business, but this attempt was a failure, and his renewed attempt at literary work was far from successful.[5]

VIEWS

Stirner started with the importance and completeness of the individual, whose only object is to express his own individuality. Only individual wants and interests and not religious dogmas or social institutions define the validity of conduct. He rejected the idea of humanity or mankind, for he held that such a concept could lead only to a new domination of the individual. Instead he argued in the *Ego and Its Own* that each individual represents for himself the highest value. The single individual must be the center and starting point of all social thinking. The individual— "das Ich"—is all, the beginning and the end of thought and action.

The past was a period of slavery in which man was subordinated to authority and his impulses were held in check. Neither the ancient world nor Christianity released man from the thralldom which customs and institutions have imposed upon him. The former glorified the state and law, the latter God. Stirner regards the performance of any act motivated by a force outside personal egoism as a form of bondage. Conformance or nonconformance to the wishes of others, to man or God-created morality is of no consequence so long as it satisfies the ego.[6] Individualist anarchism recognizes only the wants of the individual, who is not only unique but the beginning and the end of all existence and experience. In contrast to the anarchist communists, who repudiated all moral imperatives but recognized the validity of ethical standards and instinctive acts which promote the survival and happiness of man, Stirner and the individual anarchists denied the existence of any ethical principles. Stirner repudiated the ideas of race, society, country, humanity. For him they were only intellectual chimeras which the true individualist rejects. The individualist knows only himself, and his actions are for his own pleasure. He has no wish to please any but himself, and he is, therefore, unconcerned with the effect of his actions upon humanity. To him, as for the ancient Sophists, man is the measure of all things, and therefore of all value.[7]

[5] John Henry Mackay, *Max Stirner, Sein Leben und Sein Werk* (Berlin: Bernard Zack, 1910).

[6] Victor Basch, *L'Individualisme anarchiste Max Stirner* (Paris: Ancienne Librairie Germer Bailliere et cie., 1904), p. 237.

[7] *Ibid.*, pp. 259–261.

PIERRE JOSEPH PROUDHON (1809–1865)

In the arena of radicalism, Pierre Joseph Proudhon was a powerful contender for leadership, and his influence, especially in France, has persisted until our own time. He was anti-authoritarian, an opponent of the great state, and a believer in the importance of the dignity of man.

In contrast to the leaders of other brands of early nineteenth-century radicalism, Proudhon did not stem from the wealthy or middle classes; his parents were humble peasants who were never able to overcome their poverty. Early in life he worked in the fields and tended cattle. He was nineteen years old when he left school and took a job as proofreader in a publishing house. His interest in theological questions was aroused, and he acquired a knowledge of ancient languages. Later he traveled through France working at his trade, but frequently he found himself without work and in need. After unsuccessfully trying his hand at business, he resumed his studies, won a fellowship, and published his first work, *What Is Property?*, in which he concluded that property was achieved through theft and was therefore immoral. A year later he issued the second volume of the same title, in which he defended and elaborated his first opinions. His work was confiscated and he was charged with holding subversive views. He was, however, acquitted.

To escape the attention of the government he turned to less controversial topics, and published the *Creation of Order in Humanity*, a work on social evolution. In 1843 he held a job with a shipping company at Lyons which gave him a chance to study banking and industry. The result was the publication, three years later, of *Systems of Economic Contradictions*. He started a paper, *Representative of the People*, in which he could publish his views.

With the revolt of 1848, Proudhon became known as a leader of the "left." He was elected to the National Assembly, but his violent attacks upon the regime led to his imprisonment. In 1851 he wrote *L'Idée générale de la révolution au XIX siècle*, which summarized his views. He devoted the next few years to literary and philosophic work, but the appearance of *De la Justice dans la révolution et dans l'église* forced him to flee to Brussels to avoid imprisonment. He was pardoned in 1859, and returned to Paris, there to continue his literary work until his death.

PROPERTY

Proudhon was not a systematic thinker, yet he presented many penetrating opinions on economics, government, and society.[8] Property is a social product, but it also leads to social dissolution because it excludes as well as includes. This contradiction is universal. Although the right of possession is based upon absolute justice, and without property society could not survive, in a state of private interest, property is a mechanism of fraud and a means of wresting from the producer the results of his labor without the need of a fair, and occasionally any, equivalent. Therefore he does not attack the principle of property in itself. He wishes to universalize it. The problem of property is to prevent an institution, in itself socially useful, from becoming harmful by its excesses. To Proudhon, the control rather than the abolition of property is important. He is irreconcilably opposed to property being used for exploitation. However, he has only the greatest sympathy for those who till their fields to create goods for themselves. Therefore his opposition to property is not unconditional.

COLLECTIVE FORCE

Man has been turned from equality by unreason. Pauperism, crime, war, and revolution are the results of inequality. In turn inequality is directly due to property. Yet Proudhon was an opponent of communism, which he considered an embodiment of oppression and slavery and opposed to freedom and liberty. "I find in it always a character of a governmental autocracy, which is disagreeable to me. I see in it a barrier to liberty of transactions and of inheritances; the free disposition of the soil taken away from him who cultivates it; and this precious sovereignty . . . . forbidden to the citizen, and reserved for that fictitious being, without intelligence, without passion, without morality, that we call the state."[9] With great energy he defended the individual personality. He insisted that all production is collective, intellectual as well as physical, production. For that reason he opposed those who demanded greater returns for men of talent and capacity. "The greatest genius is, by the laws of his existence and by the laws of his development, dependent upon the

8 P. J. Proudhon, *What Is Property?* Translated by Benjamin R. Tucker (Princeton, Mass.: Benjamin R. Tucker, 1876), p. 11–15.

9 P. J. Proudhon, *General Idea of the Revolution in the Nineteenth Century* (London: Freedom Press, 1923), p. 208.

society which created him." [10] The interdependence of all is recognized, and the collective is nothing more than a sum of individuals. As soon as the group acts together, a sum of energy is created which is, properly speaking, not due to any single one of them but can be attributed to their association.[11] This is obvious when one observes the results of the division of labor and compares it with the output of one working alone. This leads Proudhon to one of his basic arguments against property. By showing that cooperative labor augments output, Proudhon was led to conclude that property is theft, for the individual has appropriated the benefits of common labor. To the argument that the employer pays each worker his daily wage, Proudhon replied that the output of a group is greater than the summation of individual production. As all production is necessarily collective, all capital should be social property, and consequently exclusive ownership of property is scorned. In the series of historical variations it undergoes, the antagonism which arises out of property ownership is always resolved by convention.

EQUALITY

Proudhon believed that social functions were equivalent. Intelligence is less unequal than is indicated by our experience in an abnormal world. Intellectual differences are purely accidental and transitory. The tendency in society is toward the equalization of intelligence as in the leveling of conditions.

ECONOMICS

Proudhon observed that the division of labor and competition have both been distorted, so that instead of serving as instruments of progress they have become means of oppression. The division of labor has led to great increases in production, but it has been followed by a declining demand for workers and a subsequent reduction of wages. Similarly, competition has been perverted; for the ten million wage workers, competition does not exist, for them "there is nothing but to struggle among themselves for their meagre stipend." [12] Competition fails as a democratizing agent in industry; it neither aids the worker nor guarantees the honesty of trade, but creates a ruthless mercantile aristocracy.

Value Value has a double character—use and exchange value. "The

10 *Ibid.*
11 Proudhon, *What Is Property?*, pp. 132–137.
12 Proudhon, *General Idea of the Revolution in the Nineteenth Century*, p. 50.

economists have clearly shown the double character of value, but they have not made equally plain its contradictive nature." [13] Proudhon found that an increase in the quantity of goods or use values lowers their exchange values. This represents "antinomy" or contradiction, and means in effect that value in use and value in exchange are in perpetual struggle. "The effects of this struggle are well-known; wars of commerce and of the market; obstructions to business; stagnation; prohibition; the massacres of competition; monopoly; reductions of wages; laws fixing maximum prices, the crushing inequality of fortunes; misery—all these result from the antinomy of value."

Proudhon believed that contradiction can be resolved by a synthesis which he calls "constituted values," or the amount of labor needed to produce a commodity. "Utility is the basis of value; labor fixes the relation between commodities."

Land, Labor, and Capital   He accepted the view that rent arises as a result of differences in the quality of the soil, but in contrast to the traditional opinion, he held that the rightful claimants to the excess production on superior land are those workers employed on less fertile areas.

In common with the early classical economists, Proudhon believed that labor alone was productive, for the worker would without capital supply his wants by labor, while capital would remain inert without labor to give it vitality. He therefore denied that capital is productive. Whatever increases in output are due to the use of capital must be attributed to labor, for capital is simply the product of past labor. Essentially, therefore, capital is unproductive, and rent and interest are due to exploitation and violate the law of fraternity. A natural increase in wealth inevitably leads to a reduction in rent and interest. In fact, these payments may be eliminated by the organization of mutual credit.

CREDIT AND THE BANK OF EXCHANGE

Circulation constitutes the major characteristic of an economy based upon a division of labor. Credit is the most effective manner of facilitating social exchange. To gain the maximum benefits, free and universal credit must be facilitated. "Each has a right to credit," for its perversion is the most active cause of mass poverty. Credit develops as a stage in the

[13] P. J. Proudhon, *System of Economic Contradictions.* Translated by Benjamin R. Tucker (Boston, Mass.: Benjamin R. Tucker, 1888), p. 77. The next two quotations are from this source, pp. 85 and 102.

process of exchanging products, and it arises because those who possess a surplus can only exchange those commodities for a promise to pay a future equivalent. All credit is based upon labor and could not exist without it. Consequently, credit should be controlled by the laboring classes. However, credit, instead of being governed by the producers, is in the hands of intermediaries—bankers. Instead of being used as an aid to workers it has become an engine for the making of money, a means of obtaining the greatest amount of the products of labor for as little exchange as possible. If labor could only control the credit instruments rightfully theirs, it could escape from the thralldom of working for others. Then labor could emancipate itself, set up its own productive units, and enjoy the product of its labor. Consequently, Proudhon advises the socialization of credit.

Proudhon, as we have seen, insisted upon the equality of functions of different employments. Credit would be furnished at cost. To realize the latter, Proudhon proposed the creation of a bank of exchange to establish "mutual credit." All producers and consumers who wished to exchange their goods and services and avoid speculative risks could become members of the bank of exchange. The bank would discount commercial paper and make loans. It would charge 1 per cent to defray the cost of administration. Interest would, in fact, be abolished. Moreover, rents could not, under these circumstances, rise above the amount needed to keep the property in repair. People would not save in order to lend to others at interest and thereby enjoy the fruits of someone else's toil. Accumulation of the products of labor of the many by the few would cease, and the goods produced would be exchanged and enjoyed by all producers. New wants would arise, productive industry would be stimulated, and universal abundance would follow. Proudhon visualized the establishment of an equality of trades and of equal remuneration. The result would not be due to arbitrary laws but to a natural tendency.

CAUSES OF REVOLUTION

Revolution, he held, is necessary and inevitable, a force which should be slowed down but not permanently repressed. Revolutions need not be violent, but there exist two "causes against the peaceful accomplishment of revolutions: established interest and the pride of government." [14]

14 Proudhon, *General Idea of the Revolution in the Nineteenth Century*, p. 17. The following quotations from Proudhon are from this source, pp. 40, 44, 108, 133, 144, 245.

There is a fatality in human history which causes the rich and powerful to refuse concessions at a time when the poor and downtrodden are no longer able to endure the oppression and servitude pressed upon them. A conflict is sooner or later inevitable, and revolution arises out of this conflict. It is "an act of sovereign justice, in the order of moral facts, springing out of the necessity of things, and in consequence carrying with it its own justification."

There was a distinction in Proudhon's mind between political and economic revolutions, and he ascribed the failure of the revolutions of 1789 and 1848 to the concentration of its promoters upon political forms. The revolutionaries failed because of their "total lack of economic ideas, their prejudice in favor of government, and the distrust of the lower classes which they harbored."

GOVERNMENT

Proudhon held that all of us have through habit and custom acquired a prejudice in favor of government, and even unconventional thinkers regard government as a necessary evil. He denied the need or the beneficence of government, for experience shows "that everywhere and always the Government, however much it may have been for the people at its origin, has placed itself on the side of the richest and most educated class against the more numerous and poorest class; it has little by little become narrow and exclusive; and, instead of maintaining liberty and equality among all, it works persistently to destroy them, by virtue of its natural inclination towards privilege."

Proudhon denied that government exists with the consent of the poor or for their benefit. He therefore found no reason for submitting to the laws of the state. "Who guarantees to me its justice, its sincerity? Whence comes it? Who made it?" He denied Rousseau's contention that in obeying the law, the citizen obeys his own will. "But the law has been made without my participation, despite my absolute disapproval, despite the injury it inflicts upon me. The State does not bargain with me; it gives me nothing in exchange; it simply practices extortion upon me." An examination of different forms of government led Proudhon to the same conclusion: government constitutes fraud and violence. He was as mistrustful of representative democracy as of any other form, for "universal suffrage, the imperative mandate, the responsibility of representatives, in fact, the whole elective systems, is but child's play."

There is an incompatibility between justice and government which can be resolved only by the abolition of the latter. Proudhon maintained that the citizen can "live without government . . . abolish all authority, absolutely and unreservedly." He favored the producer's replacing the citizen as "ruler" in society, for economic rights ought to be superior to political rights. The ending of the authoritarian state would lead to the establishment of a republic founded upon local producers' cooperatives based on local administration. Thus local life would revive, coercive authority would disappear, war would cease, and disarmament would follow. Public activity would be guided by justice, assuring local and national freedom. In fact, government would end and administration would begin.

FOLLOWERS

Proudhon failed to create a school or even a movement, although the anarchists claim him as one of their intellectual forebears. Yet he has not been without influence. His antistatism and his distrust of politicians have been inherited by a large segment of the French labor movement, while his belief in low interest rates as a means of inducing prosperity has now become an article of economic faith even among conservative economists. Proudhon lacked the logical power of Marx, as well as his drive and venom. The modesty of his remedies, his emphasis upon localism and federalism, and his opposition to centralized power made it difficult for his followers to build a great political party. Although he was intellectually inferior to his great rival Marx, Proudhon's bias against bigness and central authority is a gospel the modern world needs.

Recently an attempt has been made to picture Proudhon as a forerunner of fascism.[15] Actually, Proudhon was opposed to large states, and believed that it was in the interest of European equilibrium to diminish their size and multiply small states. The latter could be united into federations for defensive purposes. He was convinced that where the state is largest there the danger to liberty is greatest. While Proudhon as an intellectual representative of the peasantry and petty bourgeoisie had many views that might be accepted by contemporary fascists, his emphasis upon the autonomy and freedom of the individual, his belief in liberty, and his antistatism and opposition to centralism would scarcely qualify him for a place in a fascist gallery.

15 J. Salwyn Schapiro, "Proudhon," The American Historical Review, July, 1945.

MIKHAIL BAKUNIN (1814–1876)

In the galaxy of revolutionaries, Bakunin was the one who challenged the dominance of Marx directly. Although he was defeated by his great rival, Bakunin's tactics have been adopted and expanded by the communist parties which blindly follow Karl Marx.

Bakunin's father was a liberal in his youth, and was affiliated with one of the Decembrist societies, but after the accession of Nicholas I to the throne he became a disillusioned skeptic, seeking only to cultivate his lands and raise his children, of whom Mikhail was the oldest. At the age of fifteen, Mikhail was sent to artillery school and three years later he passed his examinations with honor. He was assigned to a peasant village as an officer of the line; but life in the army did not appeal to him and he resigned his commission. He spent part of his time on his father's estate and made frequent journeys to Moscow. There he made the acquaintance of N. Stankevitsch, became a member of his circle, and began to study German philosophy whose conservative influence he at first sought to spread. He met Ogarov and Herzen, both of whom exercised an influence in the shaping of his opinions. In 1841, Bakunin left Russia and settled in Berlin, where he continued his study of philosophy. According to the novelist Ivan Turgenev, Bakunin had become an "enthusiastic follower of the Hegelian philosophy, which appeared as the key to the world's knowledge." [16] Gradually his views became more radical, and at that time he was inclined to the views of the Hegelian left. His interests were, however, largely with philosophic rather than social problems.

In 1842, Bakunin left for Dresden, where he became associated for a time with Arnold Ruge, publisher of the *German Yearbook*. Writing under a pseudonym, he published his first work in October, 1842, "The Reaction in Germany." In this article Bakunin reveals the views which are to characterize his more mature thinking: "Let us confine ourselves to the eternal spirit which only destroys because it is the unfathomable source of life. The desire for destruction is at the same time a creative desire." Bakunin aroused the suspicion of the Saxon government and had to leave for Zurich in 1843, where he met the group centered around Weitling. He spent the winter of 1843–1844 in Berne, but the pressure

---

[16] Mikhail Bakunin, *Sozial-Politscher Briefwechsel mit Alexander Iw. Herzen und Ogarjow*. Ubersetzt aus dem Russischen von Dr. Boris Mimzes (Stuttgart: Verlag der I. G. Gottaschen Buchhandlung, 1895), p. xxi.

of the police forced him to transfer his residence to Paris and he remained there until December, 1847.

In Paris, Bakunin came into contact with Marx and Engels and Proudhon. These years in Paris were the most fruitful in his intellectual development. He recognized Marx's talent and genius, but he was suspicious of his dictatorial temper and his authoritarian views. In contrast, he felt that Proudhon had a much greater feeling for liberty. Bakunin believed that Proudhon, when not engaged in metaphysical speculation, was a true revolutionary, an anarchist. As a result of a speech commenting on the Polish insurrection of 1830, Bakunin was expelled from Paris at the behest of the Russian ambassador. To prevent sympathy for Bakunin, a Russian agent circulated the fiction that he was a czarist spy. Bakunin settled in Brussels, where Marx also lived, but he was repelled by the verbalism of Marx and his friends. To him, Marx was a petty bourgeois.[17] At the time he showed sympathy for the declassed, the *lumpen* or slum proletariat, rather than to the steady and regular worker, and his love of destruction and attraction for the declassed Bohemian is reminiscent of the Nazi mentality. He hoped that the "lumpen proletariat" would become the revolutionary element. Bakunin was inclined to believe in the dictatorship of small groups and a leader who would lead the inert masses on the road to progress.

At the outbreak of the February Revolution in Paris, Bakunin immediately returned to France, throwing himself wholeheartedly into the revolutionary current. The spread of the revolution through Europe found Bakunin trying to keep up with its growth. He visited Leipzig, Cologne, and Breslau in order to take part in events there, and at the beginning of June, 1848, he attended a congress of Slavs at Prague. Under Bakunin's influence, the congress demanded the freedom of all people and called for the convening of an all-European peoples' congress. There was a reference in the resolution to the fact that the Slavs, in contrast to the French and the Germans, had never oppressed other people.[18] Before the close of the congress, the revolts sweeping Europe reached Prague, and bloody street fighting followed. The bombardment of Prague forced Bakunin to flee to Berlin, where he went into hiding. He tried to bring the democratic Slavs into an alliance with the Hungarian revolu-

[17] Mikhail Bakunin, *Oeuvres* (Paris: Ancienne Librairie Tresse et Stock, 1907), II, ix–x.

[18] *Sozial-Politscher Briefwechsel mit Alexander Iw. Herzen*, pp. ii–v.

tionaries, but his efforts met with little success. He arrived in Dresden during the revolt and became one of the leaders of the revolution. In the end, the revolutionary legions were scattered by Saxon and Prussian troops, and Bakunin had to flee for his life. He was seized in Chemnitz, tried, and sentenced to death. His sentence was commuted to life imprisonment. He remained in prison from August, 1849, to October, 1851, when the Austrian government turned him over to the Russian police.

From 1851 to 1854 he was imprisoned in St. Petersburg, later at the fortress of Schlusselberg, and then exiled to Siberia, where he married. He made his escape in 1861, and reached Aleksander Herzen in London by way of Japan and the United States. Bakunin had, despite his imprisonment, a strong predilection for Russia and the Slavs. The idea that Russia was destined to lead the Slavs and all of Europe to a higher order of civilization was always with him, notwithstanding his superficial internationalism. Behind the professional revolutionary there lurked the nationalist and patriot.

Propaganda was renewed with customary vigor. He insisted that propaganda leads to deeds. Committees must be organized and organizations founded. During his stay in London, Bakunin expressed his dissatisfaction with the propaganda of Herzen. The Polish revolt of 1863 sent him from London, and in 1864 he settled in Florence. He lived there and in Naples for the next two years. In the latter city he formed the first section of the First International on the following program: abolition of the state and all of its judicial, political, and social manifestations and reorganization by individual initiative of free commerce. In September, 1857, Bakunin was a delegate to the Geneva meeting of the League of Peace and Freedom. His eloquence and passion impressed the delegates but did not convert them to his radical program.[19] Bakunin's failure to win over this group led to his withdrawal from the organization. He and a minority of seceders then set up the International Alliance of Social Democracy. This was a secret, international, conspiratorial organization directed by a central committee dominated by Bakunin. The International refused admittance to the Alliance, and only after it was presumably dissolved were its sections allowed to affiliate.

[19] About this time Bakunin came into contact with the Russian nihilist, Serge Netchaiev (1846–1882), who despite his youth made a deep impression upon him. Netchaiev organized a secret society, and his murder of the student Ivanov was used by Dostoyevsky as a basis for his prophetic novel *The Possessed.*—H. E. Kaminski, *Bakounine* (Paris: Aubier, 1938), p. 232.

THE ALLIANCE

The Alliance was to be an international organization made up of national sections. The single dominant aim of the organization was revolution. All palliatives or reform measures were held as reactionary. Members were to accept the entire program in its theoretical and practical consequences, and no duty was to rise above the revolution. No member could accept public office without permission of the organization; neither could a member publicly express an opinion contrary to the policy of the Alliance. It was to be a centrally directed and secret organization.

The Alliance aimed at the destruction of all institutions, and at the creation of a society based on free associated labor. As a national organization cannot succeed under modern conditions, Bakunin believed that only a universal revolution could free mankind. The revolution must be universal, socialistic, destructive of the state, and creative of liberty, equality, and justice. The Alliance was to work on two levels: (1) to educate the masses of all countries in the correct political, economic, and philosophic views; and (2) to organize the advanced, the energetic, and the intelligent men of good will in an international revolutionary network for the overthrowing of existing governments.[20]

Bakunin's organizational program of secret conspiratorial infiltration with a closely knit organization of intelligent and energetic men acting under central discipline resembled a modern communist party. While Bakunin's pandestruction appealed to or was independently reached by the fascists of our day, his organizational form was adopted by both communists and fascists.

Bakunin's program brought him in headlong collision with Marx. At the Basle congress in 1869, two currents were apparent in the International: the state socialism of the German, Swiss German, and English delegates; and the antistatist views of the Belgian, Spanish, and French delegates, who were communists, federalists, or anarchists. Bakunin sided with the latter group. A division took place, with Marx and Bakunin as leaders of the respective factions. The differences came to a head at The Hague congress in 1872, when Marx captured the moribund International and had its offices transferred to New York City. Marx let loose his verbal guns and Bakunin was charged with treason and espionage by this unjust master of vituperation and abuse.

Bakunin was opposed to any alliance with bourgeois radicalism. Bour-

20 *Oeuvres*, III, 1–280.

geois radical socialism wished to use the parliamentary state to effect reform, while Bakunin advocated the total abolition of the state and of the politics it personified.[21] The enslavement of labor by those who monopolize the raw materials and instruments of toil is the source of all forms of moral and physical tyranny. Consequently, the economic emancipation of labor is the great end which must be sought. It is not a local or national problem but a universal one for all civilized nations. Justice, truth, and morality must be the basis of conduct of man toward man. We must announce as our aim "No duties without rights, no rights without duties."[22]

VIEWS IN GENERAL

Bakunin, in common with the men of his century, was a believer in continual progress. Man is constantly moving from lower to higher forms of organization. In the progress of mankind, a phase will be reached in which statutory law will disappear. Bakunin was convinced that enacted, or statutory, law belongs to a low stage of social evolution. Legislation by a monarch or a legislative assembly is always a denial of nature, hostile to liberty of the people, and forces upon them a despotic system of laws. Legislation has only one objective, imposing and regularizing a despotic system of laws for the benefit of the rulers. Therefore, all legislation has only one aim, the enslavement of mankind.

The State   As Bakunin saw it, the state rested on force. The state is a negation of liberty, and even the good it sometimes seeks is destroyed because the state commands rather than persuades. It corrupts, for man should do good not because he is ordered, but because he wills it. In addition, the state depraves those who govern; it poisons their hearts and minds. This conclusion is described as a law of social life, permitting no exceptions. Powerful states maintain themselves by crime, and small ones are virtuous from weakness. It is true that at some levels of civilization the state is a necessary evil, but that stage is passing. This does not mean that social living will cease, for only in society does man achieve his fullest development. But men will not be held together by a supreme authority; as free men, they will recognize the common humanity of all. Bakunin argued that he does not reject all authority.

In the matter of boots, I refer to the authority of the bootmaker; concerning houses, canals or railroads, I consult that of the architect or engineer. For such

21 *Ibid.*, VI, 39.
22 *Ibid.*, p. 93.

or such special knowledge, I apply to such or such a *savant*. But I allow neither the bootmaker nor the architect, nor the *savant* to impose his authority upon me. I listen to them freely and with all the respect merited by their intelligence, their character, their knowledge, reserving always my incontestable right of criticism and censure . . . . But I recognize no infallible authority; even in special questions; consequently, whatever respect I may have for the honesty and the sincerity of such or such an individual, I have no absolute faith in any person. Such a faith would be fatal to my reason, to my liberty, and even to the success of my undertakings; it would immediately transform me into a stupid slave, an instrument of the will and interests of others.[23]

FUTURE SOCIETY

In his search for freedom, man will not reject society, for Bakunin felt man's potentialities could be fully realized only under social conditions. But in place of the old social organization built upon force and authority, a society founded upon the natural needs, inclinations, and endeavors of man will be organized. Thus a free union of individuals will rise, the communes will combine into provinces, these in turn into nations, and ultimately the free nations into a world league. Every commune, province, or nation has the right to complete independence, provided such independence does not threaten the freedom of others.

Property In the future, private property will disappear, for it is the consequence and the basis of the state. The future will see private property in consumption goods, but not in the instruments of production and land. Justice demands that each be given the full product of his labor; this can be achieved only by socializing the land and the instruments of production, and turning their management over to agricultural and industrial associations. Bakunin was a collectivist, a believer in producers' cooperation, but opposed to governmentalism. In the name of liberty, Bakunin protested against communism and state socialism. Society should organize itself upon the basis of free union, and should not be managed by authority from above.

Social Transformation The change in property relations and the abolition of the state, law, and religion would be brought about by a violent overthrow of the existing order. Such a social revolution would destroy inequality, the state, and all state institutions. Bakunin believed that revolution was inevitable, and that it would arise from within the people. But it is the job of the enlightened elite to lead, to become the general

23 Mikhail Bakunin, *God and the State* (London: Freedom Press, 1910), p. 20.

staff of the revolution. These leaders must be people of energy and talent, without egoism or selfishness.

IMPORTANCE

Bakunin was not a systematic thinker. He lacked the genius and profound insight of Marx. A superb agitator, a professional revolutionary, he was a vigorous and inspiring leader. Though dictatorial in his relation to his followers, he perceived, albeit vaguely, the dangers of the state socialism envisioned by the Marxists. Long before Professor von Hayek, the followers of Bakunin clearly saw the danger of political socialism to the liberty of man. While they also rebelled at the stultification of the individual by the private ownership of the means of production, they feared that political socialism might lead to the substitution of one tyranny for another. One of the great merits of Bakunin and his followers was their recognition of this danger.

In addition to formulating a criticism of political socialism from an anticapitalistic point of view, Bakunin was also the first modern discoverer of the "ennobling character of organized violence," and of the effectiveness of disciplined conspiratorial groups. He was thus a precursor of Sorel. His tactics of infiltration, or boring from within, and control of a larger group through disciplined minorities have all been adopted and effectively used by the Communists, who claim Marx, Bakunin's opponent, as their founding father. Although Bakunin left many printed works and uncompleted manuscripts, his philosophy is not always discernible. Creative writing was not the strongest of Bakunin's assets. He was, above all, a speaker and an agitator, and he represented the eternal rebel, the man always destined to find tradition, law, order, and organized government unendurable.

PETR KROPOTKIN (1842–1921)

It is to Petr Kropotkin, an eminent Russian thinker, writer, and philosopher, that the modern anarchist or libertarian movement is indebted for many of its ideas. He was a versatile student who wrote authoritatively on natural science, literature, philosophy, law, and government. His family traced its origin to a "Grand Prince of Kieff" and his father "was a typical officer of the time of Nicholas I." He was a member of the corps of pages and an officer of the Cossacks. His travels took him over a large part of Siberia and Manchuria. In 1872 he visited Switzerland, where he came in contact with the Jura Federation, an anarchist group. He returned to St. Petersburg the same year and joined the Tchaykovsky circle. He was arrested in 1874 and two years later succeeded in escaping and going abroad. Most of the remainder of his life was spent in England and in France; in 1883 he was imprisoned in the latter country, being pardoned three years later. He supported Russia in World War I; returned after the Revolution to Russia and opposed the Bolsheviks.[24] Kropotkin was a versatile student who wrote authoritatively on natural science, literature, philosophy, law and government.

Criticism of Society   Kropotkin foresaw a time when private ownership would disappear, and the productive machinery would become the property of society. His "ideal of the political organization of society is a condition of things where the functions of government are reduced to a minimum, and the individual recovers his full liberty of initiative and action for satisfying, by means of free groups and federations—freely constituted —all the infinitely varied needs of human beings." [25]

Kropotkin regards the land, factories, mines, and mills as social products. Discoveries, inventions and the increase of wealth are due to the physical and mental effort of both past and present generations. He argues that the wealth of the world and the machinery of production have been taken by the few. Consequently the worker has no option other than to sell his labor. Necessity forces him to accept the hardest toil, as he is unable to afford the training and education that would enable him to rise above his station. Society is divided into hostile camps which make freedom impossible of attainment. Existence of a privileged class makes necessary a vast army of officers of all kinds sworn to uphold privilege. Were exploitation of the weak majority by a privileged minority abolished, enough goods and services for the well-being of all would be available.

Expropriation   The problem which history has placed before the modern world is the expropriation of private property. However, the problem cannot be solved by legislation for neither existing governments nor any that might arise out of conceivable political changes would be capable of finding a solution for our problems.

Government   Government is due to division of society into a privileged and unprivileged group. Anarchists sympathize with the struggle for political and economic freedom and recognize in the two groups the

---

[24] Most of the facts are taken from P. Kropotkin, *Memoirs of a Revolutionist* (Boston: Houghton Mifflin Co., 1899).

[25] P. Kropotkin, *Anarchist Communism* (London: Freedom Press, 1920), p. 3.

movement for equality. They conclude that "no substantial reform in the sense of political equality, and no limitation of the powers of government, can be made as long as society is divided into two hostile camps, and the laborer remains economically dependent upon the employer." In addition, anarchists are convinced that the political structure must also be modified. Every form of society and economy has its form of government.

Absolute monarchy—that is, court-rule—corresponds to the system of serfdom. Representative government corresponds to capital-rule. Both, however, are class-rule. But in a society where the distinction between capitalist and labourer has disappeared, there is no need of such a government; it would be an anachronism and a nuisance. Free workers would require a free organization, and this cannot have another basis than free agreement and free cooperation without sacrificing the autonomy of the individual to the all-pervading interference of the State. The no-capitalist system implies the no-government system.[26]

The dangers of centralized government are increased when government is given power to administer economic relations. Kropotkin insisted that the popular or mass state is as great a danger to liberty as is any type of autocracy, and he opposed entrusting it with the management of production and distribution. He maintained that the "history of the last fifty years furnishes a living proof that representative government is impotent to discharge the functions we have sought to assign to it. . . . We are beginning to see that government by majorities means abandoning all the affairs of the country to the tide-waters who make up the majorities in the House and in election committees." [27]

FREE AGREEMENT

The breakup of the state is inevitable and is in accordance with the principles of evolution. In place of government, men will combine into free associations. As an example of free agreement Kropotkin pointed to the railway net of Europe operated by a group of independent companies. The Lifeboat Association and the Red Cross were cited as other examples of groups freely combining for a specific purpose without the intervention of government. In the anarchist commune, everyone would perform the necessary tasks without waiting for a government order. He saw multiple associations arising and as each could exercise some power over the others, he believed that each would be inclined to avoid using force.

[26] Kropotkin, *Anarchist Communism,* p. 8.
[27] Kropotkin, *The Conquest of Bread,* p. 41.

Kropotkin visualized the voluntary formation of communes which would join together in free federations, and the federations into larger groupings so that the greatest division of labor would be achieved. The future society is to be based on "free communism," which puts the joint products at the disposal of all.[28]

Common possession of the necessities of production implies the common enjoyment of the fruits of common production; and we consider that an equitable organization of society can only arise when every wage system is abandoned, and when everybody, contributing to the full extent of his capacities, shall enjoy from the common stock of society to the fullest possible extent of his needs.

Anarchists believed that private property should become common property, which means the establishment of communism. However, not communism of the authoritarian school, but a communism without government, a free communism. Under such conditions, the production of necessities would have priority, but because of great increases in productivity that are assumed to follow, man would have time to devote himself to artistic, literary, and other pleasurable endeavors. Moreover, the separation of industry from agriculture would cease, and the dichotomy between physical and mental labor would end.

Distribution Although everyone would contribute to production, the distribution of income would be based upon need rather than upon effort. Kropotkin holds "to each according to his deeds" a false principle, one that would restore all the evils against which he directs his criticism. Moreover, it is not possible to measure adequately an individual's contribution to the social products. Each of us contributes not merely in accordance with our work, because our work is influenced by "past and present labour of society as a whole."

Revolution The new society envisaged by Kropotkin will not come into effect without serious disturbance. He anticipates frightful storms that will sweep aside the old and decayed institutions, so that the people can take possession of the stock of goods and then abolish government. A social revolution is an affair of years and not of days. It demands firmness but not cruelty. Kropotkin is confident that government will crumble when confronted by the wrath of an insurgent people. When government begins to crumble, free association will begin automatically, for, once the

[28] Kropotkin, *Anarchist Communism,* p. 19. The following quotations from Kropotkin come from this source, pp. 21, 22.

compulsive power of the state is removed, natural wants force cooperation.

Kropotkin's criticism of capitalism is similar to that of the socialists and communists. At this point he and they diverge. More concerned with individual freedom, he opposes the control of economic resources by the state as leading to tyranny. He is suspicious of government, and his attacks on governmental collectivism anticipate virtually all that modern criticism has presented. Despite their suspicion, the anarchists have what is almost a naïve faith in man, once he is uncorrupted by the state. While government is evil and a stimulator of oppression, man, freed from the restriction of law, is good and just. Thus, there is joined in the anarchist outlook remnants of the sentimental faith of the Enlightenment with a cold analytic understanding of government. Certainly the anarchists' fears have not been unfounded, but they never recognized the submerged evil that exists in man.

Propaganda by the Deed   As a means of propaganda, the anarchists evolved the technique of "propaganda by the deed," an act of terrorism against a leading individual, an institution, or a community. Its purpose was to stimulate the revolutionary fervor of the masses, to bring to the surface their repressed discontent, and to force an awareness of oppression and injustice.

Anarchosyndicalism   The anarchists inspired the development of anarchosyndicalism. In tactics, anarchosyndicalism accepts the forms evolved by the revolutuionary syndicalists in France in the years 1906–1910. It rejects political activity, and it holds that participation "in parliamentary politics has affected the socialist labor movement like an insidious poison. It destroyed the belief in the necessity of constructive socialist activity, and worst of all, the impulse to self-help by innoculating people with the harmful delusion that salvation always comes from above." [29] The anarchosyndicalists have had a significant influence in the labor movements of France and Spain and a smaller influence in other countries.

[29] Rocker, *op. cit.*, p. 83.

8. GERMAN SOCIAL DEMOCRACY

Marxism became in time the official doctrine of most Continental socialist movements. For over fifty years, German social democracy was the leading socialist party of the world. It had within its ranks the leading theorists, its membership was more numerous, and its activities were more varied than those of any other socialist party. The policies of the party were shaped not only by the doctrines but by the social, economic, and political conditions of the time. In addition, other socialist writers and leaders were active on the German political stage, and their theories and policies helped to shape the character of the movement which developed. The most influential of the early German socialists was Wilhelm Weitling.[1]

WILHELM WEITLING (1808–1871)

The son of a soldier and born out of wedlock, he was able, through the efforts of his mother, to attend school and learn the tailor's trade. As a journeyman tailor, he visited many German cities and finally landed in Paris in 1835. There he joined the League of the Outlawed, a society of German political exiles. Soon thereafter the League split into two factions. One group formed the League of the Just, and Weitling was commissioned to draw up a program. The document was subsequently incorporated into the *Guaranty of Harmony and Freedom,* published at Switzerland, where Weitling settled so that he could more effectively carry on his political work. He also issued a monthly journal, but he was continually harassed by the police. The issuance of the *Gospel of a Poor Sinner* led to his imprisonment and expulsion from Switzerland. Marx

[1] Richard Lipinski, *Die Sozialdemokratie* (Berlin: J. H. W. Dietz, 1927), I, 28–35; Franz Mehring, *Geschichte der Deutschen Sozialdemokratie* (Stuttgart: J. Dietz, 1897), I, 72.

regarded Weitling as a rival, and in a personal meeting he severely criticized his sentimentality and the scientific weakness of his propaganda. The latter pointed to his record, which he held was of greater significance than the cogitations of ivory tower philosophers. Marx angrily answered that "ignorance has never aided anyone." Weitling made his way to the United States, but returned to his native land during the revolution of 1848. He had, however, lost contact with the movement, which was now led by others. He therefore went back to the United States, and remained here until his death.

Weitling's views were strongly influenced by the Christian Socialism of Lamennais and by Fourier. He regarded the unequal division of labor and wealth as the prime cause of human misery. Money is the great evil which leads to oppression and slavery.

He was not altogether clear on the methods to be used in transforming capitalism to communism. Sometimes he foresaw increasing misery driving workers to revolt, and the most reliable revolutionists, he believed, were the dispossessed and the criminals who were to be enrolled in the revolutionary legions. In his more mystical moods, he looked toward a new Messiah to emancipate mankind. Then he would, in the language of a Biblical prophet, denounce the iniquitous money changers, and declare that Christianity was a pure form of communism that had been corrupted by the church.

Weitling's criticism of a capitalistic society was based upon his belief in equality. He believed that history is a record of spoilation and robbery, and that progress is a law of nature, operating in all society. With Fourier, he argued that passions and desires are the basis of social action. Social disorder is the result of a disturbance of equilibrium between desires and the means of satisfying them. Freedom and the harmony of desire and satisfactions lead to social good, as a disequilibrium leads to harm.

In contrast to many of his contemporaries, Weitling recognized the need for a conscious, revolutionary working-class movement, and was critical of the passivity of labor in the face of oppression.

How would the new society be brought about? Through a great leader —a new Messiah—who would transform this evil world into an earthly paradise in which state, church, and class distinctions would be abolished. All would work and share equally in the products of labor and be assured a comfortable existence. None would have power over others, complete harmony would exist, and laws would be needless. "A perfect society needs no government but an administration, no laws but duties, no punishments but remedies."

Although some of Weitling's ideas later became part of the intellectual arsenal of German socialism, it was only in the 1860's that the modern movement arose. In the first half of the nineteenth century, German industry took a sharp turn upward. The *Zollverein* opened a large area to free trade and stimulated German industrial expansion. Steel and coal production, the basis of all great industrial empires, greaty increased. Changes were also taking place in the political sphere. The demand for freedom accompanied the demand for national unity. Leadership in the movement was largely in the hands of middle-class professional people. Some of the reformers recognized the importance of the labor question. One of the more active of them, Schulze-Delitzsch, believed that producers' cooperation was an important means of combating socialism and advocated consumers' loans, raw materials, and producers' cooperatives. His appeal found some response among German workers. Schulze-Delitzsch was not a socialist and he advised labor to avoid politics. His movement attracted the artisans and tradesmen under the motto "Self-Help," and stood in the way of the development of a native socialist movement.

FERDINAND LASSALLE (1825–1864)

The self-help movement was challenged and undermined by Ferdinand Lassalle. Although lacking the theoretical ability of Marx, he brought into existence the first political party of labor, and his views continued to influence the practice if not the theory of the movement. Lassalle, the son of a well-to-do Jewish silk merchant, showed no aptitude for commerce and determined on a career as a writer. He studied at Berlin and Breslau, became a follower of Hegel, and made a notable record as a student. In Berlin he became acquainted with Alexander von Humboldt, the famous naturalist; and in Paris he met Heinrich Heine. Both became his admirers.

Lassalle had planned to continue his studies but became involved in the trials of Countess Sophie von Hatzfeld, then engaged in a divorce suit against her husband. Lassalle became the lady's champion and followed the case for eight years through thirty-six courts. Finally he forced a compromise settlement favorable to the countess. In the meantime serious political changes were taking place. Bitter opposition was provoked by the dissolution of the Prussian Landtag by royal decree in 1848. Lassalle called the citizens of Düsseldorf to armed resistance. He was arrested and charged with inciting to rebellion but was acquitted. He was, however, kept in prison for six months for opposing the government. The trials made him a public figure and he was for a time barred from residing in Berlin.

He was a prolific writer of articles dealing with literary criticism, drama, history, philosophy, and political economy. He divided modern history into epochs dominated by the feudal nobility, the bourgeoisie, and the laboring masses. He held that revolutions are not forced but are brought into being by necessity. Political parties are aids to, but not creators of, revolutions. Therefore, labor ought to organize and bring forth the revolution that is ready to be born. The working class was distinguished from the bourgeoisie and feudal groups in that labor would not become a privileged minority. Therefore a government of labor would abolish self-seeking and the struggle for narrow interests. No need for the "night watchman" state would exist, and the state would become a means for promoting moral and cultural improvement.

ECONOMIC VIEWS

Lassalle argued that under modern conditions the worker must depend upon the capitalist for employment. While production in modern society is conducted on the basis of cooperation, distribution continues on an individual arrangement. Seeking its own expansion as well as division of labor and profit in sale,[2] capital insists upon individual distribution. Communal production and individualized distribution were to Lassalle the basic contradictions of modern society.

Value is determined by the labor time necessary to produce a commodity. Market prices tend to oscillate around value and are influenced by supply and demand. Like that of all other commodities, the market price of labor or wages is determined in the short run by supply and demand, but in the long run by the cost of maintaining the worker and his family. Labor must in the long run earn its cost of production. Relations between capitalist and worker have become cold and impersonal, based as they are upon supply, demand, and price.

Exploitation As labor receives in wages only the average amount needed to maintain itself, the value of the remaining product is absorbed by the capitalist and subsequently divided between the receivers of in-

[2] Ferdinand Lassalle, *Gesammelte Reden und Schriften* (Berlin: Paul Cassirer, 1919), V, 79–80.

terest and rent. He concluded that such a system deprives the worker of part of his product and is therefore a form of disguised robbery.

POLITICS

Lassalle's most important work was to inspire the first independent party of labor in modern times. A new liberal party, the Progressive party, announced its program in 1861. Its main principles were loyalty to the Prussian king and a strong centralized state under Prussian hegemony. Not a single line was devoted to the universal franchise or to democratic rights. While refusing to recognize the special interests of labor, the Progressives supported and sponsored workers' educational and mutual-aid societies. Made up of teachers and members of other liberal professions, the Progressive party sought to direct the energies of labor into innocuous channels. However, a number of leaders tried to induce the German labor movement to strike out on an independent course, and a labor congress was called for February, 1863. Asked for advice, Lassalle answered with his "Open Letter to the Central Committee in Regard to the Convocation of a General German Labor Congress." It marked the beginning of the German labor and socialist movement.[3]

Lassalle here advised the workers to dissociate themselves from all bourgeois parties, including the Progressive party. "The working class must constitute itself an independent political party based on universal equal suffrage."[4] The working class can only serve its interests by the attainment of political freedom, for every labor question is a political question. He announced that the Progressive party, which sought the support of labor, had failed. He then drew the conclusion that the workers must form an independent political party whose principal slogan shall be general, direct, and equal suffrage. On economic issues, Lassalle expounded the so-called iron law of wages, the theory that the worker's wages are limited by the requirements of subsistence as established by custom and habit. Should wages rise above this level, an increase in the numbers of available workers would ensue, and their competition for jobs would succeed in lowering the wage to the previous level. Consequently, the worker cannot improve his lot in a capitalistic society nor can he find relief through the consumers' cooperatives promoted by

[3] Herman Oncken, *Lassalle* (Stuttgart: Deutsche Verlags-Anstalt, 1920), p. 277. *Lassalle's Open Letter to the National Labor Association of Germany.* Translated by John Ehmann and Fred Bader (New York: International Publishers, 1901).

[4] *Lassalle's Open Letter,* p. 8.

Schulze-Delitzsch, for a reduction in prices of goods would soon be followed by a reduction in money wages. There is, according to Lassalle, only one remedy: the worker himself must take over industry through the establishment of producers' cooperatives. The "working class must become itself a monster employer; the whole series of gigantic enterprises. By this means and by this alone can amelioration come, and the iron and cruel law governing wages be abolished." [5] Thus the conflict between wages and profit will disappear and the worker will receive the full product of his toil.

PRODUCER ASSOCIATIONS

However, the workers can establish free producers' associations only by the aid of state credit. The producers' associations would combine to care for the general economic problems and to decide on allocation of resources. As a result of the tying together of the state and the producer, projects would be undertaken which are today neglected.[6] Lassalle's views met with opposition from those who distrusted the state, and he was also severely criticized in the liberal press for urging state credit. However, he was able to establish the Working Men's Association at a meeting of delegates from workers' organizations in ten cities. The Universal German Working Men's Association was strongly centralized, with Lassalle as president exercising dictatorial powers. He was destined to lead the German labor movement for only a year, for he lost his life on August 31, 1864, in a duel. The movement then came under the leadership of Johann Baptiste von Schweitzer (1833–1875).

Side by side with the socialist movement initiated by Lassalle, there arose in Germany another movement influenced by Marx and Engels, who did not approve of Lassalle's views and tactics. Marx disliked Lassalle's attempts to unite the embryonic movement of labor with reaction against the liberals. Marx and Engels also found Lassalle's notions on the state unacceptable, for Lassalle believed he would use the bourgeois state for establishing a socialist society, a view opposed to Marx's theory of the class nature of the state. The leaders of the Marxist wing were Wilhelm Liebknecht (1826–1900), a journalist, and August Bebel (1840–1913), a turner by trade. The latter began his public career as a member of a workers' educational society, formed to promote self-help.

---

5 *Ibid.*, p. 26.
6 Lassalle, *op. cit.*, V, 319–324.

Gradually he became more radical, and, in 1869, he and Liebknecht sponsored a labor congress which organized the Social Democratic Labor party.

PROGRAM

The program of this party called for the establishment of a free democratic republic—a people's state. Existing political and social conditions were denounced as unjust. The struggle for the freeing of the working class was held to be not a class privilege but a means for establishing equal rights and duties for all. The economic dependence of labor upon the capitalist is the source of social and economic evil. The aim of the Social Democratic Labor party was to institute cooperative labor whereby the worker would receive the full product of his toil. Political freedom is the prerequisite for economic freedom since social and political problems are indivisible, and their solution is possible only in a democratic state. Freeing of the working class can be achieved only under the leadership of a unified social democratic party. Emancipation of labor from capitalistic exploitation is a social task in all countries where a modern society exists. The Social Democratic Labor party was therefore a part of the international working-class movement. Its program was clearly inspired by Marx.

Immediately, the Social Democratic Labor party demanded freedom of press, association, and organization; the establishment of a normal workday; limitation of the hours of labor of women; prohibition of child labor; state credit for producers' cooperatives; and democratic guarantees.

FRANCO-PRUSSIAN WAR

The newly organized socialist parties faced a serious problem during the Franco-Prussian War. Bismarck was able by falsification to create the illusion that the German state was in danger from attack by France. For all socialists, but especially for those who were members of the Reichstag, the vital questions were whether Germany was engaged in a defensive or an offensive war, and what were the obligations of socialists in either event. Liebknecht and Bebel, both members of the North German Reichstag, abstained from voting war credits on the ground that both nations were guilty of aggression. Three other members who belonged to Lassalle's group approved the credits. Later Liebknecht and Bebel were arrested and imprisoned for criticism of the war.

GOTHA PROGRAM

Both Marxists and Lassalleans were socialists, divided more on organizational forms than on social philosophy. Common problems in parliament, pressure of the party membership, and rising opposition made the problem of unity urgent. The unity congress met at Gotha in 1875 and organized the Socialist Workers' party.

The program declared that labor was the source of all wealth and culture and that social labor can be performed only within society. In contemporary society the means of labor are monopolized by capitalists, upon whom the working class depends. This dependence is the cause of misery and oppression. Freeing of labor is possible only by transferring the means of production to society. The emancipation of the working class must be the work of the working class itself. Consequently the Socialist Workers' party will use all legal means to undermine the system of wage labor, to end exploitation in every form, and to eliminate all political and social inequality. The Socialist Workers' party recognized the international character of the labor movement. It demanded the setting up of producers' cooperatives with state aid under the democratic control of the workers. It also demanded an equal and secret ballot, and a direct vote on peace and war. Substitution of a people's militia for a standing army, elimination of exceptional laws on the freedom of the press, speech, and assembly, labor's unlimited right to organize, abolition of children's and women's labor, and a progressive income tax were a few of the immediate demands.

Marx was sorely disappointed with the compromises made with the followers of Lassalle. Some of his criticisms appear picayune and academic. For example, he argued: "Labour is not the source of all wealth. Nature is just as much the source of use values." Marx argued against many other paragraphs—loose notions "which Lassalle has put in the place of definite economic conceptions." [7]   Marx also objected to the views on the transformation of the state. According to Marx:

Between capitalist and communist society lies the period of the revolutionary transformation of the one into the other. There corresponds to this also a political

---

[7] Karl Marx, *The Critique of the Gotha Programme* (New York: International Publishers, 1938), pp. 3–6. Mehring, *op. cit.*, II, 355–356.

transition period in which the state can be nothing but the *revolutionary dictatorship of the proletariat.* Now the program does not deal with this, nor with the future state in communist society. Its political demands contain nothing beyond the old familiar democratic litany: universal suffrage, direct legislation, people's justice, a people's militia, etc. They are a mere echo of the bourgeois People's Party, of the League of Peace and Freedom.[8]

ANTI-SOCIALIST LAWS

Unification of the two groups into one party led to a large increase in socialist influence. In the election of 1877, the socialists polled almost a half million votes and elected twelve members to the Reichstag. Their increased influence was noticeable, especially in the large and industrial communities. The electoral success was accompanied by more literary and social activity. However, terrorist attempts upon the life of the emperor furnished Bismarck with a pretext for outlawing open meetings of socialists and forbidding socialist publications.

As a result of its suppression, an anarchist current developed within the Socialist party. Its proponents advocated physical force, violence, and terror as instruments of social reform. These views were rejected, and the leader, Johann Most, and a number of his followers were expelled from the party. At the party convention in 1880, the tactics pursued were approved but the words "by all legal means," which had been inserted into the platform at the unity congress at Gotha, were eliminated from the party program.

For twelve years socialist activity was forbidden, but an underground movement carried on active work. Its effectiveness is shown by the increase in the socialist vote to almost one million. Following the legalization of socialist activity, the convention in Halle, in 1890, took the name of the German Social Democratic party. It was generally recognized that the party's program required basic revision.

ERFURT PROGRAM

The new program, adopted at the Erfurt congress in 1891, remained the platform of the German Social Democratic party for many years. The program declared that the economic development of capitalistic society was leading to concentration of wealth, monopoly, and the destruction

8 Marx, *The Gotha Program,* p. 18.

of small business, resulting in the continued growth of the proletariat, the growth of unemployment, and the sharpening of class conflict. Differences between the propertied and the propertyless classes were being forever widened by industrial crises which were growing ever more serious. Private ownership of the means of production had ceased to be a means of assuring the producer ownership of his own product, and had become, instead, a means by which the capitalist and the landlord deprived the laboring population of its product. Only with the transformation of capitalistic private property into social property and commodity production into socialistic production could the continually increasing productivity of socially organized labor become a source of human wealth and harmony.

This social transformation would lead to freedom for labor and all oppressed groups, but this emancipation could be achieved only by the working class. The struggle of the working class against capitalistic exploitation was necessarily a political struggle, for labor could not conduct its economic struggles or develop its economic organizations without political rights. Labor could not socialize the means of production without gaining political power. It was, then, the task of the Social Democratic party to unify the workers for a conscious struggle. Labor unions could not permanently improve the position of labor, but they were a recruiting ground for political socialism. The common interests of the workers in all countries were recognized, and the development of a world market made the workers of all countries interdependent. The Social Democratic party declared itself united with the workers of all lands.

In addition to this declaration, a set of immediate demands was made for such innovations as the universal and secret ballot, replacement of the standing army by a militia, equal treatment of the sexes, and other meliorative measures.[9]

As can be seen, the Erfurt program was mainly a Marxist document. It speaks of the concentration of wealth, the proletarianization of labor, and the class struggle, but it does not make any special reference to Marx's views on historical development and sources of exploitation. This omission was due, perhaps, to a desire to placate both the revolutionary and the opportunist sections.

The German Social Democratic party saw almost continual progress and, despite checks and rebuffs, became, in 1912, the largest single party

<hr/>

[9] Karl Kautsky, *The Class Struggle* (Erfurt Program). Translated by W. E. Bohn (Chicago: Charles H. Kerr & Company, 1910).

in the Reichstag. While externally it was united, the German party, like socialist parties elsewhere contained conflicting groups. The socialist parties were in fact divided into three groups: The revisionists, or conservatives; the centrists, who were in actual command of most parties; and a small leftist group of real revolutionaries.

Differences arose out of the failure of actual conditions to meet the Marxian blueprint. Instead of increasing misery, labor enjoyed an era of unparalleled progress and continual improvement in standards. Labor unions, cooperatives, and welfare legislation all showed that the workers had a stake in society, and that they were able to improve their circumstances through capitalistic governments. Moreover, equal opposition of labor to all nonsocialist political groups was held by some to be an unsound policy. Experience showed that political factions not socialist in outlook supported welfare legislation and believed in strong economic organizations of labor. The Marxist intellectual scheme did not fit the facts of life. As a result, revisionism appeared with the aim of bringing the theory of social democracy into closer harmony with actual facts. Its intellectual leader was Eduard Bernstein (1850–1932), who, having lived for many years in England, was strongly influenced by the English Fabians and had noted the importance of trade unions and cooperatives in raising the standards of labor.

REVISIONISM

After a short career as a bank clerk, Eduard Bernstein became active in the radical movement. During the period of the antisocialist laws, he edited the *Sozialdemocrat* at Zurich and, after his expulsion, at London. His vigorous campaigns against the German government during his editorship made it inadvisable for him to return after the revocation of the antisocialist laws, and he remained in London as correspondent for the *Neue Zeit*. His observation of Swiss and English social and political conditions and his acquaintance with leaders of the Fabian Society convinced him that the revolutionary views were defective. In a series of articles on the problems of socialism, published in 1896–1898 in the *Neue Zeit*, he criticized the theory of increasing misery and showed that labor had improved its position by legal enactment, trade-union action, and cooperatives.[10] Bernstein also denied that depressions were as widespread

---

[10] The articles were published as the *Voraussetzungen des Sozialismus und die Aufgaben der Sozialdemokratie*. Translated as *Evolutionary Socialism* by Edith C. Harvey (London: Independent Labour Party, 1909).

in their effects as Marxism indicated. To a large extent the views of Bernstein reflected the spirit of the times. The catastrophic predictions of Marx had not been realized. Instead of increasing misery and growing revolutionary tension, the European working class was everywhere improving its economic position and gaining greater political freedom. Growing awareness of the labor movement and increasing social consciousness among large segments of the population were leading to favorable changes in the condition of labor. The task attempted by Bernstein was to bring the theories of socialism into harmony with the facts of political life. The views of Bernstein were denounced by Karl Kautsky (1854–1938) as an abandonment of the socialism of Marx.

THE MATERIALISTIC CONCEPTION OF HISTORY

Bernstein criticized the materialist conception of history by rejecting the view that the movement of matter "determines the form of ideas," and he characterized the historical materialist as a "Calvinist without God." While rejecting predestination as ordained by a divinity, the materialist nevertheless assumed that starting from a certain point in time, all subsequent events are predetermined. Bernstein rejected the notion that the consciousness and will of man are dependent upon material forces. He admitted that Marx and Engels acknowledge the importance of noneconomic factors in history, but he regarded the weight given to the latter as inadequate.

Bernstein also criticized Marx's theory of the class struggle as unsatisfactory. Marx's theory of value was not an adequate "norm for the justice or injustice of the partition of the product of labour." [11] Bernstein did not believe, therefore, that the worker's failure to receive the full value of his work furnished an adequate basis for socialism or communism.

Marx's notion of a tendency toward a polarization of classes was questioned. The evidence that the middle group was being ground into a propertyless proletariat, or raised to the ranks of the capitalists was held inconclusive. The Marxian theory of crises was regarded as unproven—Bernstein believed that general depressions were avoidable, although partial ones were not.

---

11 Bernstein, *Evolutionary Socialism*, p. 39. The following quotations from Bernstein are from this source, pp. 141, 149.

TASKS OF SOCIAL DEMOCRACY

Bernstein did not consider the working class as a homogeneous and undifferentiated mass. Differences in income breed differences in outlook and in living. Through the trade unions some of the differences may be eliminated, and workers may support each other politically and even financially in times of stress, but Bernstein claimed that such sympathy and action is a far cry from economic solidarity.

In contrast to some socialist writers, Bernstein was strongly in favor of consumers' cooperatives, which he regarded as organizations promoting the welfare of the workers. He placed great stress upon the trade union as a democratizing force in industry, but only if it "can further simultaneously the interests of its members and the general good." Similarly, Bernstein believed that to socialists "the security of civil freedom has always seemed to stand higher than the fulfillment of some economic progress." Socialism strives for the development of a free personality; therefore socialism must be a liberating force. Bernstein warned against immoderate attacks upon bourgeois liberalism, which, he felt, also fought for freedom. At the same time, Bernstein emphasized municipal reform and small advances. In sum, Bernstein proposed a gradualistic reform program suited to the needs of his time. It is true that it aroused great anger and stormy polemics among orthodox Marxists. Nevertheless, the socialist movements of Europe accepted his advice even when they denied his views. Of the socialist writers of his time, he was most correct in assessing the temper of the world around him.

Bernstein's views aroused a storm of opposition in the ranks of social democracy, and the struggle reverberated to other parts of the socialist movement. Karl Kautsky rushed to the defence of Marxian orthodoxy, and sought to demonstrate, in a series of articles in *Vorwärts* and in the *Neue Zeit*, that Bernstein was in error.[12] Largely by a mere repetition of Marxian formulas he tried to answer Bernstein's criticisms of the inadequacy of Marxist views on history, the dialectic, and value. Kautsky argued that Bernstein had drawn a false picture of the party's position. He denied that the party was Blanquist and that it favored the use of armed force. In defense of the theory of growing misery, Kautsky made a distinction between physiological and social misery; he admitted that the facts indicate a lessening of physiological misery brought about by in-

---

[12] The articles were later issued in Karl Kautsky, *Bernstein und das Sozialdemokratische Programm* (Stuttgart: J. Dietz, 1899).

creases in real wages and improvements in social services. However, Kautsky argued that labor is excluded from sharing in most cultural progress, and that its improved status is achieved at a slower rate than that of the bourgeoisie. Kautsky pointed to the increase in the employent of women and children as proof of increasing misery.[13]   But it is to be noted that an increase in employment of children in factories is not necessarily common in all phases of capitalism, for with the growth of welfare legislation, a decline in the number and proportion of employed minors has set in. Nor is it certain that an increase in the employment of women is proof of growing misery. An argument might be made that at certain levels of economic development, the entrance of women into industry is due to their diminishing family and home responsibilities and to their rise in social status, and actually is proof of increasing economc welfare. Kautsky also pointed to the growth of large-scale industry, the elimination of the small entrepreneur, and the growing power of capital in the productive process. These presumably cause increasing misery, but it need not follow, as a consequence of such changes, for the standard of living may be raised.

In the main, Kautsky presented no facts to prove the Marxian doctrine of increasing misery of labor as a result of the progress of capitalism. His view was based mainly upon deductions from premises set forth by Marx.

Bernstein's view on the rise of a new middle class is also challenged, for Kautsky argued that technicians, managers, and engineers are merely performing functions from which the capitalist has willingly freed himself. They are subordinates of the capitalist, performing some of his functions, and the growth of the corporate form of business increases the numbers of this group. Kautsky denied that this group constituted a special class and maintained that it embodied, on a microcosmic scale, all the contradictions of capitalistic society.[14]

Kautsky's theoretical criticism was also leveled at Bernstein's practical proposals. The latter had argued that the revolutionary elements in social democracy were traditional and theoretical, but its deeds and policies were reformist. At that time the question of cooperation with nonsocialist parties had, to Kautsky, been settled by *The Communist Manifesto* and Lassalle's "Open Letter." Kautsky recognized no possibility of a social democratic party acting as a party of the proletariat and cooperating with nonproletarian political groups, and he denied the desirability

13 *Ibid.*, pp. 119–124.
14 *Ibid.*, p. 132–135.

of an alliance with these liberals. Social democracy must seek to conquer power as an independent proletarian party unencumbered by alliances with other social strata. All resources must be used to attain independent power.

The issues raised by Bernstein were debated at several party congresses, and the orthodox views overwhelmingly carried the day.[15]

The leadership of the German social democracy, while accepting the words of Marx with almost religious devotion, was in practice and spirit not revolutionary. The real revolutionaries in the German socialist movement were a small faction centered around Rosa Luxemburg, 1870–1919). The differences between the party leadership and the left wing were evident in the latter's advocacy of the general strike.

THE MASS STRIKE

The idea of the general strike was introduced by Rosa Luxemburg in 1904. At first the idea was rejected, but during the Russian Revolution of 1905 the plan gained more adherents. The defeat of the Russian Revolution eliminated the emotional overtones surrounding this issue, and made it one of practical policy. The trade-union leaders were especially opposed to the endorsement of a mass political strike, for they and their unions would be forced to bear the brunt of such an enterprise. The party accepted the view that no general strike would be called without the consent of the trade-union leadership. This did not quiet the agitation of the left wing, which continued to press for a strike.

As shown by Russian experience in 1904 and 1905, the mass strike is "a changeable phenomenon that . . . reflects all phases of the political and economic struggle, all stages and factors of the revolution. . . . It suddenly opens new and wide perspectives of the revolution when it appears to have already arrived in a narrow pass and where it is impossible for anyone to reckon on it with any degree of certainty." [16] The general strike is not an isolated action, but can last for years. There is a reciprocal action between the political and the economic struggle, one influencing the other and becoming merged with it. Such a union is possible only in time of revolution. "The revolution thus first creates the social conditions

[15] *Vorlagen an den Parteitag*, 1903, pp. 298–420.
[16] Rosa Luxemburg, *The Mass Strike*. Translated by P. Lavin (Detroit, Mich.: The Marxian Educational Society, no date), p. 41. The following quotations from Luxemburg are from this source, pp. 48, 71, 79, 88.

in which this sudden change of the economic struggle into the political, and of the political struggle into the economic, is possible, a change which finds its expression in the mass strike."

The mass strike is a "universal form of the proletarian class struggle resulting from the present stage of capitalist development and revolution." The trade unions and the party must act together, for, "in a revolutionary mass action the political and the economic struggle are one, and the artificial boundary between the trade union and Social Democracy as two separate, wholly independent forms of the labor movement, is simply swept away. . . . There are not two different class struggles of the working class, an economic and a political one, but only ONE class struggle which aims at one and the same time at the limitation of capitalist exploitation within bourgeois society and the abolition of exploitations." While these views showed intellectual ingenuity, Luxemburg and her followers had virtually no influence upon the rank-and-file worker. In common with many Marxists, Luxemburg underrated the importance of trade unions, and was critical of their attempt to gain equal authority with the Social Democratic party over German labor. She criticized the conservatism of trade-union leaders, their restricted horizon, and their overestimate of the economic value of organizations of labor.

The trade-union leaders, constantly absorbed in the economic guerrilla war, whose plausible task it is to make the workers place the highest value on the smallest economic achievement, every increase in wages and shortening of the working day, gradually lose the power of seeing the larger connection and of taking a survey of the whole position.

To Luxemburg, trade-union activity could not permanently improve the conditions of the workers, for they could not overcome the permanent contradictions of capitalism. Such a view failed to impress either the trade-union leaders or the rank and file.

9. SOCIAL DEMOCRACY AFTER WORLD WAR I

FACTIONS WITHIN THE GERMAN SOCIAL DEMOCRACY

While it maintained the appearance of unity, on the eve of World War I the German Social Democratic party was split into three hostile factions. On the right were the revisionists, comprising most of the trade-union leadership. They believed, as Bernstein had maintained, in continual and uninterrupted progress and peaceful social evolution. The center was made up of the party leadership who were orthodox Marxists in theory, but reformist in practice. The third group was a small left wing which wanted to combine revolutionary theory with militant behavior.

WORLD WAR I

The Social Democratic party had always been opposed to militarism and war. International conflict was denounced at party congresses, in the press, and in its theoretical literature. The workers of all countries were urged to resist the machinations of capitalists and financiers who, to serve their selfish ends, tried to involve nations in bloody wars. Antimilitarist and antiwar resolutions were a regular feature of socialist gatherings. In the prewar crises the socialists of all countries watched carefully the conduct of the German social democracy as the leading party of international socialism. On the eve of World War I, the Social Democratic party had more than one million members.[1]

[1] Edwin Bevan, *German Social Democracy during the War* (London: George Allen & Unwin, Ltd., 1918), pp. 1–3.

The party denounced the Austrian ultimatum to Serbia in July, 1914, as "so shameless in its manner as well as in its demands that any government which backed down submissively before such a note would have to reckon with the possibility of being flung out by a popular mass movement between dinner and dessert." [2]

On the same day, the directorate of the party issued an appeal in which it demanded that "no drop of German soldier's blood must be sacrificed to the Austrian's lust for power, to imperialist commercial interests." [3]

German socialism was faced with a dilemma. Would it continue its firm stand against war, or would it rally to the Fatherland? At a caucus of Socialist members of the Reichstag, three tendencies appeared. A majority argued that a declaration of war ended political differences and that social democracy must support the nation. Another faction was of the opinion that war was an inevitable outgrowth of capitalism, and that Socialists should not separate themselves from the masses during the conflict. A third faction was explicitly antiwar. The supporters of war were victorious in the caucus, and the motion that the Socialists should support war credits in the Reichstag was approved by 78 to 14. The statement of the caucus declared "We are faced now with the iron fact of war," and "much if not everything is at stake for our people and their freedom, in view of the possibility of a victory of Russian despotism." [4] Fear of Russia was the reason for supporting war credits. For a time the voices of opponents of the prowar policy were stilled by the power of party discipline, but in time they made themselves heard.

Karl Kautsky did not look with favor upon the voting of war credits. Franz Mehring, biographer of Marx and a leading socialist writer and historian, and Rosa Luxemburg organized *Die Internationale,* an antiwar publication suppressed by the government after one issue. Later Rosa Luxemburg, writing under the pseudonym of Junius, charged that the German party was to be condemned more severely than the socialist parties in other lands:

The German Social Democracy has been generally acknowledged to be the purest incarnation of Marxian socialism. It has held and wielded a peculiar prestige as teacher and leader of the Second International . . . Particularly in

2 Quotation, *ibid.,* p. 5.
3 Quotation, *ibid.,* p. 6.
4 Quoted in Evelyn Anderson, *Hammer or Anvil* (London: Victor Gollancz, Ltd., 1945), p. 17.

the fight against militarism and war the position taken by the German Social Democracy has always been decisive. . . . The German Social Democracy was not only the strongest body, it was the thinking brain of the International as well.[5]

Around Luxemburg, a group called the Internationalists, and known later as the Spartacus League, was organized. Karl Liebknecht (1871-1919) a leader of this group, issued the first antiwar appeal to the masses. Even more important was "the Need of the Hour," signed by Kautsky, Haase (1863–1919), and Bernstein, in which it was charged that the war had ceased to be a defensive war and had become an imperialistic war of conquest. These were symptoms of the bitter differences that were rending the party.

OPEN SPLIT

Increasing numbers of socialists in the Reichstag disregarded party discipline and voted against war credits. For such a breach of discipline Liebknecht was expelled from the party. This expulsion did not diminish the antiwar activities of his group, which were much less important than the opposition within the Reichstag. In the spring of 1916 seventeen members who refused to approve the emergency budget were expelled. The opposition then organized the Social Democratic Fellowship as an independent socialist group, and the break was complete.

A conference at Gotha in March, 1917, organized the Independent Social Democratic party. The new party was made up of several groups, for the opposition to the war contained revisionists as well as Marxists. At the foundation of the party, Rosa Luxemburg's Spartacus League became affiliated with it. At the other extreme were Bernstein and his group who, on pacifist and humanitarian grounds, opposed the continuance of the war. Opposition to the war was the common bond uniting these diverse groups.[6]

LAST PHASE OF EMPIRE

In July, 1918, Germany's offensive power was gone, and in August she was unable to fight on any longer. In October, 1918, Prince Max of Baden organized a coalition cabinet which included two Socialists, Gus-

[5] The Junius Pamphlet, *The Crisis in the German Social Democracy* (New York: The Socialist Publication Society, 1918), pp. 10–11.

[6] Eduard Bernstein, *Die deutsche Revolution* (Berlin: Verlag für Gesellschaft und Erziehung, 1921), pp. 20–22.

tav Bauer and Philipp Scheidemann. A request for an armistice was made, and the emperor was forced to abdicate and to flee to Holland.[7]

REVOLUTION

On November 10, 1918, a republican government for Germany was proclaimed in Berlin at the meeting of the soldiers' and workers' councils. A coalition socialist government for Prussia was organized after the Independent Socialists laid down a number of terms accepted by the majority Socialists. A government of six, with three representatives from each party, was chosen. The Spartacus group refused to go along. Other German states followed Prussia's example, and Socialist-dominated state governments appeared throughout the country. Soldiers' and workers' councils had also arisen nearly everywhere, but the majority of socialists were suspicious of these new groups and their proposals. The revolutionary movement was split into several groups, and each group was split into factions.[8]

SPLIT IN THE SOCIALIST GOVERNMENT

The People's Representatives chosen on November 10, 1918, governed Germany through January, 1919, and introduced a number of reforms. An eight-hour day was established, for example, and workers were protected from arbitrary dismissals. However, democratization of Germany and long-run measures against the revival of militarism were not achieved. The government's reforms were of essentially trade-union character. No basic changes were introduced, no important industry was nationalized, no attempt was made to centralize the states, direction of the army was not transferred to hands sympathetic to democracy, and the bureaucracy was not disturbed.

Division over the form of the government appeared. The left favored a soviet, and the conservative socialists a national assembly. A general congress of soldiers' and workers' deputies in December, 1918, decided for a national assembly, thus endorsing the view of the majority Socialists.[9] A clash between a detachment of revolutionary sailors and government

---

[7] Heinrich Strobel, *The German Revolution*. Translated by H. J. Stenning (London: no date), pp. 27–30.

[8] Arthur Rosenberg, *A History of the German Republic*. Translated by Ian D. Marrow and L. Marie Sieveking (London: Methuen & Co., 1936), pp. 24–31.

[9] Bernstein, *op. cit.*, pp. 122–127.

troops led to the resignation of the Independent Socialists from the government.

THE COMMUNIST PARTY OF GERMANY

In the closing days of 1918 the Spartacus League held a conference at Berlin at which the Communist party of Germany was established. A program drafted by Rosa Luxemburg declared that the "Spartacus Union will never assume governmental power except in response to the plain and unmistakable wish of the great majority of the proletarian masses in Germany; and only as a result of the definite agreement of these masses with the views, aims and methods of the Spartacus Union."[10] Although the delegates approved Luxemburg's theoretical formulations, they rejected her advice on a practical political program when they voted against participating in the election for delegates to the National Assembly.

CLASH BETWEEN LEFT AND RIGHT SOCIALISTS

The withdrawal of the Independents from the government led to the appointment of three majority socialists to replace them. In the meantime, demonstrations were suppressed by the government, and this "proved to be the turn of the tide of the German Revolution. It was then that the offensive force of the revolutionary working class was broken." [11]

Government troops were ruthless in their treatment of prisoners. Many were shot, among them Luxemburg and Liebknecht; some were tortured. In despair thousands of workers left the majority Socialists for the Independents. Only in Bavaria was repression absent. There the head of the government, Kurt Eisner (1867–1919), an Independent Socialist, was able to pursue a constructive policy. He was supported by large groups of majority Socialists and peasants. While on his way to the Bavarian Parliament on February 7, 1919, he was assassinated by a counterrevolutionary student, Count Arco. Thus German Socialism lost one of its true statesmen. Following Eisner's death, there was a drift toward extremism, and on April 7, 1919, a Bavarian soviet government was proclaimed. It brought about an attack by monarchists and reactionaries aided by the central government. Munich was captured on May

10 Quoted by Rosenberg, *op. cit,* p. 69.
11 *Ibid.,* pp. 83–84.

2 and a wave of bloody terror was unleashed. Hundreds of innocent victims perished.

THE WEIMAR ASSEMBLY

In the first election to a democratic parliament in the history of Germany, in January, 1919, the two socialist parties polled almost fourteen million votes, or about 44 per cent of the total. The Independents refused to join the government. The majority Socialists thereupon formed a coalition with the middle-class parties on the following basis: unconditional support of the Republic, fiscal reform based on taxation of property and capital, and socialization of basic industries. A Socialist, Philipp Scheidemann, was chosen prime minister, and Friedrich Ebert, also a Socialist, became the first president of the German Republic. The government had to sign the peace treaty, and the performance of this unavoidable act became the basis of the reactionary and Nazi charges that the Socialists had betrayed the nation.

INDUSTRIAL DEMOCRACY

The Socialists dominating the government tried to strengthen the trade unions, and in November, 1918, the trade unions and the associations of employers signed an agreement in which the former were recognized as the representatives of the workers, and collective bargaining was acknowledged as the means for establishing conditions of employment. In addition, the eight-hour day was approved and a committee with equal membership from labor and management was set up to help solve economic and social questions.[12] The government implemented this agreement by enacting an eight-hour workday law, and made written wage agreements legally binding; in some instances the terms were extended to an entire industry. These gains for German labor gave the trade unions an important place in the German economy. Of course they did not—nor did they intend to—revolutionize the economy, for the Socialists who promoted these reforms were reformers and not revolutionaries. The latter were bitterly opposed to the labor-employer agreement, since they feared these agreements would deaden the revolutionary *élan* of the masses.

[12] Anderson, *op. cit.,* pp. 66–70.

THE KAPP PUTSCH

Opposition to the moderate Socialists also came from the reactionaries and monarchists. On March 13, 1920, the Ehrhardt Brigade entered Berlin to establish a military dictatorship. The government fled, and Wolfgang Kapp, an obscure officer, was proclaimed chancellor. However, the workers were not ready to surrender the government to a band of reactionary adventurers. A general strike called by the Socialists and the trade unions ended the Kapp regime. The general strike was largely a trade-union affair. After the strike, the trade unions, through their old leader, Karl Legien, suggested reorganizing the government along the following lines: the two Socialist parties and the Christian and free trade unions were to join in giving the unions an important voice in the government, the leaders and participants in the Putsch were to be punished, the civil service and the army were to be purged, and certain industries were to be socialized.[13] Under left-wing pressure, the Independent Socialists rejected these terms. The majority Socialists thereupon formed another coalition government with the middle-class parties. At the Reichstag elections in June, 1920, the majority Socialists suffered severe losses. Their votes were reduced to slightly above five and one half million; the Independents gained sharply, their total vote being nearly five million. The Communists polled about four hundred thousand votes. The total Socialist vote fell by about two million as compared with the vote in the preceding election, but there was a decided shift to the left. The Socialists left the government and a member of the Center party became prime minister.

SPLIT AMONG THE INDEPENDENTS

As was noted, the Independent Socialist party arose as a result of differences over the war. It was, however, far from united on other issues. Some agreed with the majority Socialists on most issues, while others were actually Communists in outlook. The latter advocated affiliation with the newly formed Communist International. A special congress met at Halle, in October, 1920, to decide the issue. The terms laid down by the Communist International were accepted, and a majority joined the Com-

[13] Ibid., p. 76.

munist party of Germany. A minority maintained their independence, and united in 1922 with the majority Socialists.

MASS RISING FAILS

The Communist party, its membership increased by the adhesion of the Independent Socialists, decided to test its theories of revolution, and directed a rising in the mining area of Mansfield under the leadership of Max Holz. A general strike to support it was called, but both the strike and the revolt failed. Arthur Rosenberg, an experienced observer and a participant in the events, has argued that the Russian Communist leaders were guilty of bad faith, for they realized in 1921 and 1922 that a proletarian revolution was not likely in Western Europe in the immediate future. The proper course, in his opinion, would have been to follow the lead of the Social Democrats, with whom unity should have been effected. Instead, the Communist International, dominated by the heads of the Soviet government, transformed the Western Communist parties into Russian puppets.[14] However, the Socialists had no program to meet the situation. When out of office they were critical of the government's domestic policy, but when holding power they failed to take any steps toward major reform.

The ineffectiveness of the majority Socialists is revealed by the failure of the socialization program. In March, 1919, the government was empowered to nationalize industry, and a Socialization Commission made up of representatives from employer and worker organizations was set up to devise a program. Its work ended in failure. A second commission was set up in 1920, and the employer members concluded a report in which socialization was held impracticable and inadvisable. This represented a substantial victory for the anti-Socialist forces.[15]

INFLATION

In the meantime, Germany experienced an inflation that devoured the savings of the middle classes and enriched speculators. Labor suffered almost as much as the middle group, and there was a constant struggle to maintain real wages. Social tension was intensified but the reactionaries succeeded in ousting the liberal chancellor, Joseph Wirth, replacing

14 Rosenberg, op. cit., pp. 173–175.
15 Anderson, op. cit., pp. 83–84.

him with a conservative shipowner, Wilhelm Cuno. There was danger of
an explosion. It was, however, averted by the French occupation of the
Ruhr.

The occupation of the Ruhr early in 1923 was met by patriotic demonstrations, and the government called for a campaign of passive resistance. The Communists sought to place themselves at the head of the resistance movement, but the influence of the Socialists and trade unions
prevented the complete consummation of this aim. Nevertheless, the fall
of real wages was pushing thousands of workers in the Communist direction, and the refusal of the government to provide even a modicum of relief was adding fuel to the burning discontent. A series of strikes forced
the resignation of the government in the summer of 1923. It was succeeded by a coalition headed by Gustav Stresemann, a leader in the party
of big business, the People's party.

As soon as inflation had passed its crest, the wave of discontent began
to recede. Communist opinion lagged slightly behind events, and an insurrection that had been planned was called off. However, the Hamburg
section of the Communist party had not been informed of the change in
plans and attempted an insurrection in October, 1923. It failed. At the
same time, the central government began to show a more decided reactionary stamp. Labor governments in Saxony and Thuringia were deposed by Stresemann, and the Social Democrats left the cabinet. The
government's program was unaffected, and the end of 1923 the German
economy had weathered the storm. Stabilization had begun and the left
was thoroughly demoralized.

Discussing the reasons for the lack of revolutionary inclination in German labor movement, Rudolf Hilferding, the leading theorist of German
socialism in the 1920's, ascribed it to the substantial prosperity of the
German economy which enabled German labor to gain higher and
higher real wages. Consequently, German labor sought improvement in
its status and pushed the revolutionary and socialist objectives into the
background. European and German labor, soothed by prosperity, lost
its revolutionary fervor and was psychologically unprepared to seize
power. Hilferding claimed that blame for this state of affairs could not
be placed on any particular leader.[16] This interpretation may be correct,
but it is necessary to recognize that neither the Socialists nor the trade
unions were equipped for leadership of a revolutionary mass movement.

16 Rudolf Hilferding, *Die Sozialisierung und die Machtverhältnisse der Klassen*
(Berlin: Verlags-Genossenschaft, 1920), pp. 3–4.

STABILIZATION

The Dawes plan initiated a period of economic stabilization for Germany. After its acceptance in 1924, Germany increased its foreign borrowing, reorganized its currency, and enlarged its trade. The Social Democratic party turned its attention toward domestic reforms—increasing the standard of living for the masses and increasing property and death duties. In fact, the Social Democrats had become more and more the representatives of the trade unions. An explanation of the new conditions was evolved by Rudolf Hilferding. Concentration of capital in the form of trusts and cartels under the domination of banks he declared, represented a change from a competitive to an organized capitalism based increasingly on conscious and organized state direction designed to overcome the competitive anarchy inherent in capitalism. Hilferding maintained that organized capitalism was in fact substituting the socialist principle of planning for capitalistic competition. It was the duty of socialists to aid in the transformation of capitalistic society into a democratic planned society or socialism.[17] These changes tend to moderate the fluctuations of business, with greater stability in the economy ensuing.

During the stabilization period the Socialists prospered, and the party vote rose from six million in 1924 to eight million in 1928. Germany was throughout this time controlled by a middle-class bloc. It lasted up to 1928, when it split apart. In the elections of that year the Socialist vote rose to nine million and the Communist vote to three and one quarter million. The two together polled over 42.0 per cent of the vote, about the same proportion as the Nazis did in March, 1933, when the state machinery was already in their hands. As a result of the large vote, a socialist became chancellor of a coalition government, but only after the party agreed to a number of conditions laid down by President von Hindenburg.

THE CRISIS

By the fall of 1929, economic stabilization had come to an end and Germany succumbed to the depression engulfing the western world. The Socialists were confused, hesitant, and without a policy. The trade unions were largely concerned with day-to-day problems, and the Communists were bewitched by the Russians. As unemployment rose the unions found

17 Rudolf Hilferding, "Probleme de Zeit," *Die Geselschaft,* April, 1924, pp. 1–3.

that the maintenance of wages and hours could not solve or even mitigate the difficulties and sufferings of the permanently or partially unemployed. At the Frankfort congress of 1930, the free trade unions favored a program of public works financed by international credits, and two years later they favored, in a special congress at Berlin, a nationally financed public works program. The same congress came out for an extensive program of socialized industry and for a planned economy. From other parties came demands for curtailment of the budget and for reduction in taxation. An obvious source of tax reduction rested on the cutting of the social services. In March, 1930, the Great Coalition, as the government of the several democratic parties was called, broke up on this issue. Heinrich Brüning became chancellor and instituted a series of emergency decrees cutting salaries, insurance benefits, and social services. Brüning's deflationary remedies failed to bring relief to Germany's sick economy. On the theory that Brüning was the "lesser evil," the Socialists supported him, even though the support was given without enthusiasm. The Communists, in turn, made no distinction between parties, and referred to all of them as fascist, although "social fascist" was reserved for the Socialists.

While the Marxist parties were fighting for dominance, the Nazis were able by their appeal, threats, and falsehoods to raise their votes from 800,000 in 1928 to 6,400,000 in 1930. This increase should have been a sharp warning, but nothing was done to prevent the further expansion of this sinister movement.

The Socialists had no program, and their direct and indirect participation in the government stamped them in the minds of many of the bitter and disillusioned Germans as part of the hated regime. The Communists, on the other hand, were unable to emancipate themselves from their Soviet mentors and to develop a policy based on German realities. The Communists in Germany failed to recognize the difference between a capitalist democracy and a fascist dictatorship.[18] The governments that followed one another in 1932 were incapable of solving the problems. Finally, on January 30, 1933, Hitler came into power.

THE END OF THE GERMAN LABOR MOVEMENT

The Nazis began by outlawing Communist propaganda and followed with other decrees presumably directed toward the protection of the state.

18 Leon Trotsky, *What Next?* Translated by Joseph Vanzler (New York: Pioneer Publishers, 1932), pp. 37–39.

At first the major drive was against the Communists, the Reichstag fire being the visible excuse. Despite the terror, the Socialists and Communists together elected two hundred members to the Reichstag in the election of March 5, a truly remarkable performance. Some trade-union leaders tried to compromise; although they disaffiliated themselves from the Socialist party, their doom was sealed. On May 2, 1933, all buildings occupied by trade-union organizations were seized and the leaders arrested. Six weeks later, the Social Democratic party was outlawed, and in July the process was completed by making the National Socialist Labor party the only legal political party in Germany. Thus ended the German labor, socialist, and communist movements in inglorious defeat. All of them had huge organizations, dozens of magazines and newspapers, hundreds of thousands of enrolled members, and millions of followers, yet none lifted a hand against the Nazi seizure of power. Perhaps the outcome would have been the same had they done so, but the Nazi would have been weakened and their mystical belief in their unfaltering destiny shaken. In contrast to the socialists of Austria and the anarchosyndicalists of Spain, the German labor, socialist, and communist movements surrendered without an open struggle. The ease of victory undoubtedly magnified the confidence and arrogance of the Nazis, and made them more ready to embark upon foreign adventures. Having at best a dispirited and disorganized opponent, they could without fear plan their next step toward world conquest.

10. *AUSTRO-MARXISM*

Marxism was curiously enough the instrument by which the Austrian socialists overcame the elements within the movement that favored a violent policy. Austrian socialism, or Austro-Marxism, as it became known, was able to combine fundamentalism in theory with an opportunist line in practice. Before the party could emerge, it had subdued opponents of gradualist policies within its ranks.[1]

The early Austrian socialist and labor movement is closely tied to the struggle for democratic rights. During the Revolution of 1848 two workers' organizations arose in Vienna. They did not survive for long, and not until 1867 did the workers of Austria establish a permanent educational association.[2] At the beginning, a controversy developed between those who favored the self-help principles of Schulze-Delitzsch and those who advocated political action for labor. The majority concluded that self-help was possibly only for a few workers, and that labor should seek the franchise so that it might win an improvement in conditions through the use of political power.

SOCIAL DEMOCRATIC PARTY

The Social Democratic party was founded in 1868. It demanded freedom of association, press, and assembly; universal franchise; complete religious freedom; abolition of the standing army and its replacement by a people's militia. The government, however, virtually forbade Socialist meetings, dissolved the party, and arrested a number of leaders.

[1] The monumental work of Charles A. Gulick, *Austria from Hapsburg to Hitler* (Berkeley: University of California Press, 1948), should be consulted by the reader.

[2] Ludwig Brugel, *Geschichte der Osterreichischen Sozialdemokratie Wiener Volksbuchhandlung* (Vienna: 1922), I, 84–88. See also pp. 126–127, 141–154, and 228–234 in Vol. I.

149

The suppression of labor activity was for a time only partly successful. A number of labor unions arose in Vienna, and a radical sheet, the *People's Voice* was started. Socialists were active not only in organizing various types of workers' groups, but in agitating for universal suffrage. The government thereupon decided on firmer methods, and all labor organization was sternly suppressed.

THE ANARCHISTS

The Austrian radical movement, at the end of the 1870's, contained an anarchist wing which regarded open political action as an obstruction to labor's efforts to gain its freedom. Johann Most, the German anarchist then in exile in London, was the inspirer of this brand of radicalism. Most advised secret conspiratorial organization of the Blanqui type; his followers regarded the right of franchise as worthless.[3]

This extreme propaganda found some favor among sections of Austrian labor. The moderates recognized that deplorable living conditions and blind reaction were responsible for the success the radicals had gained, but they were convinced that extreme policies could lead only to disaster. At the Brünn congress in 1882, the program of the moderates won a majority. Resolutions were adopted calling for social ownership of the means of production; direct suffrage; freedom of speech, press, and organization; separation of church and state; compulsory education in public schools; displacement of the standing army by a people's militia; and introduction of an eight-hour day.[4]

Although the moderates held a majority, they were not able to control the activity of the extremists. The workers were warned that violent tactics would serve as a pretext for a campaign of repression by the government. The warnings were of no avail. In 1883 and 1884, a number of officials were assaulted and several were murdered by anarchists in pursuance of "propaganda by the deed." With the full support of the community, the government suppressed all socialist activity in Vienna and the surrounding area.

The socialist movement was in confusion. On the side it found itself in a fight with the anarchists, and on the other it faced suppression by the government. The movement seemed destined to waste away in internecine

[3] Max Emers, *Victor Adler* (Vienna: Hans Epstein, 1932), pp. 22–41.
[4] Brugel, *op. cit.*, III, 282.

strife but, largely through the efforts of Viktor Adler, a party professing a common and moderate program was formed.

VIKTOR ADLER (1852–1918)

Adler, born in Prague, came to Vienna at the age of three. He studied medicine, became a physician, and affiliated with the German nationalists. While still a young man, he turned to socialism, to which he devoted the rest of his life. Under his wise leadership, the Social Democratic party became one of the main parties in Austria and one of the most influential on the international scene.

Although Adler was not an outstanding theoretician, he was an adroit realist who knew how to guide his party to influence and power. Under his guidance, Austro-Marxism, while strict in matters of doctrine, became supple and compromising in practice, and some of the leading theoreticians of world socialism were nurtured within its fold. On the practical side, the Austrian socialists succeeded in organizing virtually every aspect, economic and cultural, of the worker's activity.[5] Adler founded the *Equality*, a weekly publication, which he subsidized. He succeeded in bringing the two warring factions together, and thus made possible the later achievements of Austrian socialism.

HAINFELD

At the Hainfeld congress in 1888, the new Austrian Social Democratic party was launched. In its "Declaration of Principles" the party dedicated itself to the freeing of all from economic bondage. The declaration traced the cause of the misery of the masses to individual control of enterprise. Socialization of the means of production not only would lead to the freeing of labor, but would be the fulfillment of a historical necessity.[6] The party declared itself as internationalist, it demanded freedom of speech, press, and assembly, and it asked for the abolition of the standing army and its replacement by a people's militia. On all political and economic issues the party announced it would represent the views of the proletariat.

The newly united party set itself the task of winning Austrian labor. It had to contend with the remaining opposition in its own ranks and the

[5] Emers, *op. cit.*, pp. 51–75.

[6] *Verhandlungen des Parteitages der Österreichischen Sozialdemokratie in Hainfeld* (Vienna: Gleicheit, 1889), pp. 3–21.

repression of the government from without. Nevertheless the party remained active and with all its strength entered into the agitation for the shorter-hour movement. The party also embarked on a campaign for the establishment of universal suffrage, and in 1891 it participated in its first electoral campaign.[7] The development of large factories and businesses with their numerous employees furnished the growing membership of socialism.[8]

At the second party congress in 1891, Adler, the party leader, was able to report substantial gains in activity and in membership. The following year the old differences between moderates and radicals reappeared. Issues such as centralism, federalism, and the role of leadership were basic causes of division. Viktor Adler argued for a united party, defended the support of reforms to improve the condition of labor, and pleaded for the use of political means to attain socialistic objectives. The opposition advocated the building of the party on an economic rather than on a political basis, and deplored the introduction of an overcentralized party organization. Nevertheless, the Hainfeld program was reaffirmed and the party tactics were upheld. The Austrian Social Democratic party steadily increased its influence and, by 1897, virtually all industrial areas voted Social Democratic.[9]

THE NATIONAL QUESTION

As the Austrian Social Democratic party was made up of a number of national groups, some occupying a less advantageous position than others with respect to language, cultural rights, and economic development, the issue of nationalism inevitably intruded itself into party discussions. Moreover, as the national issue became more serious within a particular country, the tension inevitably reflected itself within the party. Austrian socialism was predominantly a German product dominated by men who were culturally Germans and who ruled the party from Vienna. Such a state of affairs was not likely to be permanently suitable to the other nationalities of the Austro-Hungarian Empire. At its Hainfeld congress, the party came out for equal rights for all nationalities living in Austria. However, in 1891, a Czech delegate to the party congress protested against the neglect of Czech national interests by the Austrian party.[10]

7 Brugel, op. cit., IV, 140–156.
8 C. A. Macartney, The Social Revolution in Austria (Cambridge: Cambridge University Press, 1926), pp. 45–46.
9 Brugel, op. cit., IV, 311.
10 Arthur Kogan, Socialism in the Multi-National State. An unpublished doctor's dissertation deposited at the Widener Library of Harvard University, 1946, pp. 98–100.

Viktor Adler was aware of the divisive character of this issue and, while he recognized the cultural value of nationalism, he pleaded for solidarity on the basis of internationalism. The other national parties would not agree and, at the Brünn congress in 1897, separate Socialist parties were set up for each national group living in Austria. The separate national parties of Germans, Czechs, Poles, Italians, Southern Slavs, and Ruthenians sent delegates to an All-Austrian Socialist Congress that met every two years.[11]

At the congress in Brünn in 1899, the national question was dealt with in some detail by the report of the united executive committee of the party. It declared that national disputes were a hindrance to political and cultural development, and that equality of nationalities and language must be recognized. Such recognition was held possible only with the abolition of feudal rights and privileges. Austria was to recognize cultural and language autonomy of all national groups whose governments were to be based on democracy.[12] In contrast to the declaration of the executive committee of the Austrian party the "Czech Socialists shared with the Czech bourgeoisie the desire not only for some vague equality in matters of language but for institutions with economic and political attributes within the framework of the Austrian commonwealth." [13] The demands of the Czechs were at least partially met by the adoption of a resolution calling for a democratic federation of nationalities chosen by direct and universal suffrage, establishment of self-governing autonomous national regions for self-government, and recognition of minority rights. The Austrian Socialist solution of its multinational problem did not meet with the approval of Joseph Stalin, then regarded as an expert on the national question by the Bolshevik faction of Russian socialism. Stalin characterized the separatism as "the destruction of the unity of the working class movement." [14]

Nor were the Czechs satisfied with the solution. Reflecting the rising nationalism of the entire Czech community, the Czech Socialists became more and more separatists. They argued that the leadership of the Austrian party was in fact German or Jewish and that Vienna, the home of

11 *Ibid.,* pp. 128–130.
12 *Verhandlungen des Gesamtparteitages der Sozialdemokratie in Osterreich* (Brünn: 1899), p. 74.
13 Kogan, *op. cit.,* p. 189.
14 Joseph Stalin, *Marxism and the National Question* (New York: International Publishers, 1935), p. 45.

the party center, was in fact a German city. The Czechs felt duty-bound to release themselves from foreign domination.

Because of the close connection between socialism and trade unionism in Austria, the issue of Czech autonomy became a source of division within the Austrian party, for the Czech Socialists insisted that their independence be recognized. The conflict affected every part of the labor, socialist, and cooperative movements. The last All-Austrian Congress attended by the Czechs was held in 1905. In 1911, the Czech separatists organized the Czech Social Democratic Labor party in Austria. While it recognized internationalism and the class struggle, its spirit and action were nationalistic. The split had become serious.

CHARACTERISTICS OF AUSTRO-MARXISM

One of the unique characteristics of Austrian socialism was its domination of all phases of labor. While completely democratic in its relations to government and society, the political branch of Austro-Marxism dominated all aspects of the labor movement—political, economic, cooperative, sport, and leisure-time activity. In many industrial nations trade unions developed prior to, and independent of, labor parties. In Austria, however, the Social Democratic party was firmly established when the trade unions were just taking hold. "Both movements, equally distrusted by the authorities, drew on the same limited supply of activists among the working class." The result was that "leading officials of the union usually held important positions in the Social Democratic Party."[15]

Until the arrival of the suffrage the party organization and the trade unions were almost identical. The utmost care was devoted to developing and training them, to increasing their numbers and bringing them under Socialist influence. . . . Even under the aegis of Adler, whose sense of justice and statesmanship far exceeded most of his successors, the party made every effort, while organizing, centralizing the trade unions movement and leveling up hours and conditions, to get rid of all elements which were not purely Social Democratic.[16]

Austro-Marxism also developed intellectual activities of a very high order. Using the Marxist approach, its theorists sought to illuminate cultural and economic issues. Under the leadership of Adler and his co-

---

[15] Kogan, *op. cit.*, p. 50.
[16] Macartney, *op. cit.*, p. 46.

workers, a division between reformist and revolutionaries was always avoided. "It aimed at never falling too far out of step with the masses without ever surrendering to their revolutionary impatience. Further it attempted to divert these revolutionary energies into channels of reform, while being always ready to use them as bargaining points with the ruling powers." [17]

WORLD WAR I

A majority of the Austrian party supported the war. The antiwar group did not, as it did in Germany, split away from the main branch of Austrian social democracy. The German and Polish socialist groups in Austria based their support of the war on the need to overthrow czarism. So long as Austrian arms were successful criticism was silenced, but with defeats on the battle field the picture changed.

ASSASSINATION OF PRIME MINISTER STURGKH

Friedrich Adler, the son of the founder of Austro-Marxism, led the antiwar socialist movement. He organized a small group in The Karl Marx Association. This, for a time, became the left wing of the Austrian socialist movement.[18] Facing the obstacles of censorship and repression, Adler decided to dramatize his fight against war and autocracy. On October 21, 1916, he shot Prime Minister Sturgkh. Adler's defense awoke a sympathetic response among the masses. He was sentenced to death but his sentence was commuted. The growing left wing was reinforced in the fall of 1917 by the return from captivity in Russia of Otto Bauer, one of Austria's leading theorists of socialism.

In January, 1918, the rations of the workers in Wiener Neustadt were cut, and a strike followed. It soon spread out until it tied up the whole of Vienna and assumed a political character. Demands for ending the war with the Allies were made, and the government promised to initiate negotiations. On the nationalities question—a perennial difficulty—the left wing advocated constituent assemblies for every area and settlement of boundary disputes by plebiscite. These views were accepted by the party majority.

[17] Kogan, op. cit., p. 76.
[18] Otto Bauer, The Austrian Revolution. Translated by H. J. Stenning (London: Leonard Parsons, 1925), p. 28.

REVOLUTION

In October, 1918, the old Austro-Hungarian Empire was in an advanced state of dissolution. On October 29, the workers of Vienna urged the establishment of a republic, and by early fall the Hapsburg monarchy had ceased to exist. This was but a first step and was followed by national and social revolutions.

A political council took over the reins of government. It was a coalition, with the Social Democrat Karl Renner acting as chancellor and Viktor Adler as secretary for foreign affairs. Socialist undersecretaries were appointed in other departments. As a result of the dissolution of the army, a people's militia, organized by Julius Deutsch, was set up to maintain order. On November 11, 1918, at the demand of the Socialists, the emperor abdicated. The prerogatives of the House of Hapsburg were abolished, political privileges were ended, and equal suffrage without regard to sex or class was put into effect. On November 12, the Austrian Republic was proclaimed.

Although a republic had been established without street fighting, barricades, or bloodshed, Austria faced grave economic problems. Suffering from the lack of raw materials and the removal of her agricultural areas, Austria was broken both militarily and economically and was dependent upon outside aid for survival. Moreover, with demobilization, Austria faced serious unemployment. In the face of these conditions, social and political radicalism rose to new heights.

And among the wildly excited homecomers, among the despairing workless, among the militiamen filled with revolutionary romanticism, were disabled soldiers who wanted to avenge their personal injuries upon the guilty social order, were neurotic women whose husbands had languished in war captivity for years, were intellectuals and literary men of all kinds who, suddenly converted to Socialism, were filled with the Utopian radicalism of neophytes.[19]

WORKERS' COUNCILS

As in other countries, workers' councils arose in the cities, and peasants' councils in rural areas. As the cities were dependent upon the countryside for food and were not able to compensate the farmers in manufactured goods, the peasants withheld their produce. The peasants formed

19 *Ibid.*, p. 85.

armed guards—*Heimwehr*—to prevent food requisition. According to Bauer, the moderate policy of Austrian socialism was justified, for the agrarian areas were in a position to starve Vienna, where the major strength of Austrian socialism was concentrated. In the election to the Constituent Assembly, the Social Democrats polled the most votes and had the largest representation, but the party remained a minority in the Provisional National Assembly.

During this period unemployment was acute. In May, 1919, the Department of Social Welfare ordered every firm employing fifteen or more workers to increase its employment by 20 per cent. An eight-hour day and an annual vacation of one or two weeks, depending upon length of employment with a firm, were introduced. A Socialization Commission was established with Otto Bauer as president, and the works' committees were given legal status. Works' committees were set up in every type of enterprise, and these looked after the economic, cultural, and social interests of labor. They also enabled trade unions to establish themselves in many plants where they formerly were weak or nonexistent. Discipline was another function of these committees.

The government also sought to create jointly controlled enterprises to be managed by representatives of the state, consumers, trade unions, and workers' committees. The state provided the plant; the consumers' cooperatives, the trained manager; and trade unions had representatives on the board of management. More extensive socialization was not feasible because of the ownership of Austrian industry by foreign shareholders, or because of the dependence of industries upon foreign supplies or financing.

GROWTH OF SOCIALISM AND TRADE UNIONS

After World War I, Austrian Social Democracy experienced a great upsurge in influence. However, instead of urging the workers to militant action, the leaders had to pacify and hold their followers in check. While Austrian socialism had made a revolution, it was unable, because of the reduced size of the country, to carry the economic revolution very far. Political union with Germany, which would have furnished Austria with sources of foodstuffs and raw materials and the ultimate protection of a large government, was prevented by the Allied governments. The result was that Austria "could accomplish a social transformation only within very narrow limits. Obliged to moderate its pretensions, it remained everywhere poor in heroic actions, dramatic episodes, dramatic struggles. But it was just the privations and impotence of this revolution which constituted its peculiar greatness." [20]

REACTION

The reaction which followed the first revolutionary wave also affected Austria. The Vienna Christian Socialists, made up of reactionary clerical elements, gained the leadership of the more liberal Christian Socialists from the provinces who represented peasant constituencies. In contrast to the first coalition government, which was an alliance of industrial workers and peasants, the second, instituted in October, 1919, was dominated by the Vienna Christian Socialists, who were conservative in politics. The second coalition was barren of accomplishment, and as a result of division over a new defense law, the liberal or Marxist Socialists withdrew and the coalition ceased in June, 1920. After a series of efforts to re-establish it, a government controlled by the Christian Socialists took office in November, 1920.

The new government allowed reactionary irregulars to arm, and the workers' councils followed suit. In the rural areas, the Heimwehr was organized to combat the city workers. While the Socialists, from 1920 on, refused to participate in the national government, they cooperated in six of nine provincial assemblies. Moreover, they controlled the governments in cities, which contained 47 per cent of the Austrian population. Even in the national parliament the Socialists exercised great influence, and important legislation could be enacted only with their approval. A Republican Defense Corps was set up for protecting the working-class movement from armed reaction.

BAUER'S POSITION

The Austrian Revolution dethroned the monarchy and abolished special voting privileges exercised by the nobility. All citizens acquired equality. Otto Bauer (1881–1936), the intellectual and political leader of Austrian socialism, maintained that a political revolution was only half of a revolution, for while it removed political oppression, it failed to change economic relations. He called attention to the uneasiness of the

[20] *Ibid.*, p. 178.

laboring masses who were raising the question of the failure to carry the revolution into the economic as well as the political sphere.

Bauer, however, found a bloody revolution undesirable in the face of Austria's depleted resources and her dependence upon foreign raw materials and credit. He believed that the technical and enginering groups would refuse to work in factories operated by the city workers. A revolution under these circumstances would lead to the production of fewer goods.

THE ROAD TO SOCIALISM

Socialism, according to him, can be reached only by another road. Only through planned and organized activity moving step by step can a socialistic society be built. Bauer maintained that a socialistic society must be one in which more goods are produced than in a capitalistic order. Although a political revolution can be brought about by the use of force, a social revolution is possible only by constructive labor. A political revolution can be consummated in a matter of hours, but a social revolution requires careful and bold action over a period of years.[21]

SOCIALIZATION OF INDUSTRY

Socialization of industry must begin with heavy industry—coal, metal, and steel. They are the easiest to socialize, and are the most highly concentrated. Bauer advocated payment to the owners of heavy industry by a progressive tax upon the capitalists and landlords so that the owners of heavy industry would be compensated out of the proceeds raised by taxes upon all owners.

Directors of industry would appoint managers, set prices, make collective agreements with trade unions, distribute profits and determine new investments. Care would be necessary to prevent the appointment of inferior personnel to leading positions because of personal and political considerations. To avoid such a possibility, committees made up of teachers in technical schools and directors of socialized industries would propose competent members for leading positions.

Purpose of Socialization Socialization of industry would lead to an improvement in the living standards of the employees in the socialized industries; and the income in the form of interest, rent, and profit formerly

21 Otto Bauer, *Der Weg zum Sozialismus* (Vienna: Wiener Volksbuchhandlung, 1921), pp. 6–9.

yielded to the capitalist would then accrue to society. Part of the profit—exclusive of interest and rent—of socialized industry would be used for capital expansion and the remainder divided between the state and workers and officers of the industry. In this fashion all groups would gain by socialization. Some industries would be socialized and leased to cooperatives; others would be controlled and operated by subordinate government units.

Organization of Industry   Industrial organizations would be set up for each industry not socialized and every firm would be required to belong to the proper one. Each organization would be headed by a committee, a fourth of whom would be appointed by the government and would include a representative of trade and industry. These representatives would be charged with protecting the interests of the state and the community. Another fourth of the representatives would be chosen by consumers' groups and would protect those interests; a third group of delegates would be selected by organizations of labor; and a fourth of industry. As a result of the many-sided representation, the central organizations of industry would tend to serve the community rather than a special group.

The tasks of these central industrial groups would be to develop industry technically so as to lower costs. Research directed to improving methods and products would be emphasized. The purchase of raw material and the sale of finished products would be centralized. Prices would be so regulated that the enterpriser would receive a return equal to the wages he might have earned for his contribution to industry. Contracts between labor unions and industry would be made through these central organizations.

Position of Labor   Bauer argued that the development of trade unions destroys employer absolutism in the plant as surely as the establishment of parliament undermines the absolutism of monarchical government. Participation of the workers' representatives in the regulation of conditions in the shop would be on an *ad hoc* basis, and would depend upon the power relations between the two groups. The aim would be to regularize and legalize these relations, so that workers' committees, elected by all employees, would participate in the making of collective contracts. To the extent that wages were not set by collective agreements between the union and the central employers' group, the workers' committee would be charged with this task. It would be the function of the workers' committee to maintain order and discipline and punish violations.

Land ownership The size of agricultural operation that would yield the greatest efficiency would be used for the different crops. Thus a crop that required large operations for most effective results would be raised on large holdings. Whenever better results could be obtained by the use of smaller holdings, such a system would be followed. Large landownings were to be subsidized and landlords compensated in the same manner as owners of socialized industries.

In addition to the socialization of large estates owned by the church, big landlords, and capitalists, there are many small holdings owned by self-employed peasants. Such holdings would remain under private ownership, and operators would be required to engage in a program of planned production. A national plan would be elaborated, which the independent farmer would follow. As the regulator of the prices of the goods which the peasant buys and sells, the state would exercise a predominant influence upon the farmer's real income.[22]

Banking Bauer distinguished between socialization of industry and large estates, and banking, for the banks merely exercise the right to lend other people's money and to create money. No expropriation would take place, but certain powers would be transferred from the banks to the community. Socialization of banking could be achieved by combining all private banks into one national bank, and thus credit would be centralized. The interest rate would be lowered and the power of finance capital broken.

Expropriation Although socialism was the end sought, Bauer opposed brutal confiscation of the wealth of capitalists and landlords. Such a program would lead only to a bloody struggle culminating in the destruction of large amounts of social capital and the pauperization of society. Instead, he advocated a peaceful transition to socialism. His road was one of gradual, orderly change, but he admitted that it might be possible to attain socialism by other means.

Austria was not destined to achieve socialism by peaceful means "for the history of the Austrian Republic is contained in an unusual amount of unusually bitter fights about unusually small matters of social policy." [23] Stripped of a great part of her territory, her economy undermined and dependent on the outside for materials and finance, little Austria struggled to survive. The country was divided into two hostile camps,

22 *Ibid.*, pp. 23–36.
23 Franz Borkenau, *Austria and After* (London: Faber and Faber, 1938), p. 213.

Socialists and Catholics. The Socialists dominated the urban areas and the Catholics the countryside, where the Socialists were feared and hated.

The Socialists exercised a predominant influence upon the municipal governments of the cities and made use of their power in order to establish an advanced form of municipal socialism. Vienna was the chief exhibit of Austria's municipal socialism. Under the leadership of Mayor Karl Seitz, Vienna extended the municipal socialism that had been inaugurated by the clerical politician Karl Lueger. Municipal finances were entrusted to Hugo Breitner, who utilized an extensive variety of luxury taxes to finance the socialist program. The administration in Vienna improved the lot of municipal workers and increased the extent of health and welfare work for all workers. Rent control was introduced and a housing program launched. Land was acquired on which healthful and convenient apartment houses were built. In addition, loans were made to an association known as the "Geisba," which built garden suburbs for those who supplied one fourth of the building costs and paid the remainder in five years at 5 per cent interest.[24] Large apartment houses were constructed which were the envy of housing reformers.

THE LINZ CONGRESS

At the Linz congress in 1926 the party revised its program.[25] Austrian social democracy dedicated itself to a defense of the Austrian Republic and to the democratization of economic and political life. It declared for the right to organize, for improvement in the conditions of labor, and for greater social benefits. It regarded the development of capitalism as having set the stage for its replacement. It pointed out that the functions formerly performed by the individual entrepreneur are now performed by banks, trusts, and cartels. Moreover, capitalism brings into being an organized working class capable of eliminating the social system which created it. Socialization of large estates and large industries was declared necessary, their operation to be turned over to social corporations and cooperatives. Intellectual and artistic activity, the press, the publication of books, the theater, and art was not to be socialized.[26] The Linz program became the basis of the party and the spiritual guide to its activity.

---

24 Robert Danneberg, *Vienna under Socialist Rule.* Translated by H. J. Stenning (London: The Labour Party, 1925).

25 Wilhelm Ellenbogen, "Der Linzer Parteitag," *Der Kampf,* December, 1926, p. 37.

26 *Protokoll des Sozialdemokratischen Parteitages,* 1926, pp. 168–195.

CLASH OF 1927

While it followed a reformist line in practice, the only one possible under Austrian conditions, the Austrian party was revolutionary in theory. It had in its ranks some of the ablest exponents of Marxism. However, it was not possible to introduce fundamental social changes, for the Socialists lacked a majority and were committed to peaceful means.

They had consolidated their position in the cities, but gradually there began emerging secret, armed bands dedicated to the breaking of this influence. In 1927, an armed clash between anti-Socialist terrorists and Socialists led to the killing of two people. When a jury acquitted those accused of the murders, a spontaneous demonstration swept the city. In a series of clashes over a period of two days, ninety were killed and more than a thousand were wounded. This had a serious reaction in the rural areas, where the moribund Heimwehr revived. Socialists now found implacable hostility in the provinces. The conflict between the Socialists and the Heimwehr was the beginning of a struggle that was to have drastic consequences for the country.[27]

The Heimwehr was a rural military organization officered by the rural middle class and made up largely of peasants who had an undying hatred for the Socialists. Two men came to the top as leaders, Major Fey and Prince von Starhemberg. Political conditions steadily deteriorated, and the balance between Catholics and Socialists was upset. With the collapse of the Credit-Anstalt in 1931 the Austrian economy was badly shaken. Monsignor Ignaz Seipel, the leader of the Christian Socialist party, offered to form a government with the Socialists and to introduce a number of fiscal reforms designed to lead the country out of its economic morass. The Socialists, recognizing that these reforms would involve reductions in the social services, refused the invitation. "Here was the law in 'Austro-Marxism.' Hitherto the socialists had cleverly compromised on the one hand and kept their ideological purity intact on the other." [28] They faced a serious problem, however, for their followers as doctrinal Marxists would not agree to compromises. At the same time, a new threat, the Nazis, appeared, and the Socialists faced a decision.

27 Borkenau, *op. cit.,* pp. 229–231.
28 *Ibid.,* p. 246.

DEFEAT OF THE AUSTRIAN REPUBLIC

The local elections of 1932 showed a sharp rise in the Nazi tide, but not at the expense of the Socialists. Urban labor was too well schooled and disciplined to fall a victim to Nazi propaganda. The Nazi gains were at the expense of the clerical faction and, seeking in this split an opportunity to gain power, the Socialists demanded a dissolution of parliament. But instead, Engelbert Dollfuss became chancellor and formed an anti-Socialist coalition which held a majority of one. The government lacked a policy, and its hatred of the Socialists so obscured its vision that it was unable to recognize that the real menace came from the Nazis.

A change in the method of paying railroad men provoked a strike. Dismissal of a number of union leaders followed, and led to a parliamentary crisis.[29] The government was defeated, but it refused to accept defeat on the ground that absentee ballots could be cast. In protest, Karl Renner, the Socialist speaker of parliament and the man who has had the melancholy duty of twice acting as chancellor of Austria after a lost war, resigned in protest as did two other candidates. Instead of dissolving parliament and calling for new elections, Dollfuss insisted that parliament had ceased to exist and that he would govern by decree. A dictatorship based on a modified form of the corporate state and anti-Semitic in policy then arose, but the humiliations and cruelties typical of the Nazi regime were avoided.

The Dollfuss regime launched a campaign against socialist and workers' institutions. More than one third of Vienna's finances were cut off by the central government, and its social and welfare activities were seriously impaired.[30] While the Socialists were aware of the greater threat of the Nazis and were anxious to avoid making a Nazi victory possible, they were not blind to this Dollfuss danger facing them.

In the fall of 1933, an extraordinary party conference decided that a general strike could be called (1) if the government introduced a fascist constitution; (2) if the government illegally deposed the municipal and provincial authorities of Vienna; and (3) if the government dissolved the party or the trade unions.

The Socialists sought to find a way out. An armed rising could not suc-

---

[29] G. E. R. Gedye, *Betrayal in Central Europe* (New York: Harper & Brothers, 1939), p. 73.

[30] Otto Bauer, *Austrian Democracy under Fire* (London: National Joint Council of the Labour Movement, no date), pp. 16, 23.

ceed, but, on the contrary, might open the road for the Nazis. Yet could a great Socialist party of 600,000 members representing 90 per cent of the workers, two thirds of the population of Vienna, the overwhelming majority of the town-dwelling and industrial population of Austria as a whole, and 41 per cent of the Austrian population "supinely surrender"? [31] It did not, but the Socialists realized the difficult decision facing them. Supported by Mussolini, Dollfuss pursued his objective slowly but relentlessly. Although the Socialists had an effective movement and a defense organization (the *Schutzbund*), the government controlled the army and the police. Gradually pressure against socialist groups was increased, for the government had in view the dissolution of the Social Democratic party and the trade unions. In January, 1934, Heimwehr detachments and auxiliary police were stationed in the industrial areas governed by Socialists. The communities were forced to bear the cost of maintenance. Daily the demands of the Heimwehr became greater.

Finally, on February 12, 1934, the government forced a clash. Two days before that, the Heimwehr had been mobilized in Upper Austria and had demanded the dissolution of a number of local municipal councils. A detachment of police and soldiers raided the headquarters of the Social Democratic party at Linz. Resistance, a bloody clash, and fighting spread throughout the city. The information reached Vienna and a general strike began. Arrests followed, and a brutal assault on the residents of a municipal apartment, the Reumannhof, led to open warfare between the government and members of the Schutzbund. The fight spread and the poorly armed nonprofessional Schutzbund fought bravely and vainly. Their cause and their valor deserved a better fate. A number of the captured were executed, among them the secretary of the Gratz Chamber of Labor, Joseph Stanek, and Koloman Wallisch, the Socialist leader of Styria.[32]

Victory went with the government, which flung thousands of Socialists into prison. The party was suppressed, the unions were dissolved, and the property of the labor and socialist organizations was confiscated. Many of the leaders were forced into exile. "To the eternal credit of the Social-Democratic administration of Vienna, be it recorded that after its suppression, all the efforts of its enemies failed to establish a single case of

[31] *Ibid.*, p. 18.
[32] Julius Deutsch, *The Civil War in Austria*. Translated by D. P. Berenberg (Chicago: The Socialist Party, National Headquarters, 1934; Paula Wallisch, *Ein Held Stirbt* (Karlsbad: Deutsch Sozialdemokratische Arbeitepartei in der Tschechoslowakischen Republik, 1935).

corruption during a period when the records of the Heimwehr and Clerical governments stank, as they continued to do after the suppression of the Socialists, with evidence of venal sin." [33]   The Socialists believed that between 1,500 and 2,000 of their number had been killed and about 5,000 wounded.

Thus ended one of the best and most civilized of socialist movements. For the clerical reaction it was a Pyrrhic victory, for it was soon succeeded by the Nazis. While the German Socialists and Communists allowed themselves to be ignominiously suppressed, the Austrian Socialists fought heroically on the streets in what must have seemed a hopeless but glorious fight. Underground activity continued and Austrian socialism never lost its hold upon Austrian labor. Courageous and determined in defeat, the workers were again to turn to the Austrian social democracy as soon as the Nazi yoke was destroyed. Today Austrian socialism is again a small democratic oasis in a totalitarian desert.

[33] Gedye, *op. cit.*, p. 113.

11. *FRENCH SOCIALISM AND SYNDICALISM*

French social movements, operating in the land of numerous socialist theories, also fell under the spell of Marxist doctrines, although Marxism never gained complete intellectual pre-eminence over them. Not only was there resistance from humanitarian and reform socialists, but under the influence of anarchist ideas, the growing labor movement rejected the domination of political socialism.

UNDER THE EMPIRE

As noted in a previous chapter, France had been the home of several varieties of socialism and quasi socialism in the earlier part of the nineteenth century. Socialist activity, concentrated largely around Paris, was virtually destroyed by Cavaignac in the "June Days" of 1848. Louis Napoleon followed a dual policy: on one hand he sought to repress all revolutionary agitation by stern measures, but at the same time he encouraged a system of paternalism with which he tried to win the rank-and-file workers.[1]

The dictatorship of Louis Napoleon rested on the army, big industry, the banks, and large commercial enterprises. Since the French Revolution, combinations of workers were forbidden and only mutual societies could function. A number of the latter were organized in the 1850's, but they were timid and hesitant and required the approval of the authorities. Slowly the growth of industry, the increase in the number of wage earners, and the dissatisfaction characteristic of an expanding industrial so-

[1] Georges Weill, *Histoire du mouvement social en France* (Paris: Félix Alcan, 1924), pp. 1–17.

ciety began to affect the masses. The government sought to direct this dissatisfaction into harmless channels.

In the 1860's, several doctrines were struggling for acceptance by French labor. Militant trade unionism had its supporters, political socialism had a few, but cooperation was the principal philosophy accepted by labor. An important milestone in the growing consciousness of labor was the "Manifesto of the Sixty," which demanded economic as well as political freedom. The most interesting and perhaps the most important revolutionary of that period was Auguste Blanqui.

LOUIS-AUGUSTE BLANQUI (1805–1881)

The son of a professor of philosophy, Blanqui studied both law and medicine, but these were only steps on the road to a revolutionary career. As a young man he became active in the revolutionary currents of his time. He participated in the July uprising which toppled the Bourbons from power. He then became active in the republican organization, the Society of the Friends of the People, which directed its efforts against the monarchy of Louis Philippe. Blanqui was among fifteen members arrested, and at the trial gave his profession as "proletariat." He announced that all the political struggles could be summarized in a war of the poor against the rich, and denounced the regime for exploiting twenty-five million peasants and five million industrial workers. He demanded universal suffrage and a tax on the rich.[2] He and his companions were acquitted. In 1834 he launched a weekly journal, *The Liberator* in which he propounded the gospel of equality.

Blanqui became a leader among the conspiratorial groups of republicans and socialists who haunted Paris in the 1830's. Chief of the *Société-des-Familles,* he was arrested for his activity and sentenced to a prison term of two years. Pardoned after seven months, he reorganized his followers as the Society of the Seasons, a secret conspiratorial group subdivided into "weeks" and "months." Three "months" constituted a "season" led by a chief called "Spring." The "month" was made up of four "weeks" officered by a "July," and a "week" was made up of six members led by a "Sunday." Supreme direction was under the leadership of a secret committee whose chief was Blanqui. On May 12, 1839, Paris witnessed an attempt at a *coup d'état* made by about a thousand republicans. Barricades appeared, but the attempt failed. Blanqui and Armand Barbes

2 Gustave Geffroy, *L'Enfermé* (Paris: Les Éditions G. Cres et Cie., 1926), I, 57–59.

were sentenced to death, but their sentence was commuted to life imprisonment. Released by the Revolution of 1848, Blanqui was again convicted for rebellion, and served in prison until 1859. He was again arrested in 1861, and sentenced to four years' imprisonment. During the Franco-Prussian War, he launched a journal, *The Country in Danger,* as a means of rallying the people to the defense of Paris. He charged the Germans had provoked the war and had prepared for the destruction of France. On the day before the revolt he was again arrested and sentenced to death, but his sentence was commuted to life imprisonment. Elected as a deputy in 1879, he was released from prison. He resumed his revolutionary activity and established a journal, *Neither God nor Master.* Two years later he died.

IDEAS

Blanqui is important as an active revolutionary leader, not as a theoretical thinker. He was a perennial conspirator and believed that a militant and determined minority could seize power. Social conflict was, as he saw it, a struggle between privilege and equality. Privilege he regarded as the cause of violence, competition, and war. In contrast, equality is the promoter of order and social justice. Either equality must triumph or humanity will perish. Blanqui also anticipated the later socialist theorists in his argument that man is not free if he is at the mercy of those who control the conditions of work. His socialist views were simple and ethical. The source of private wealth is immorality. Riches are obtained from conquest, confiscation, pillage, royal favor, war, and speculation; private fortunes can increase only in proportion to the oppression of the proletariat. Wealth is created by man's ability to combine land and labor, and their control should not be vested in any individual. Therefore he concluded that an indispensable source of activity should not be controlled by anyone but the public.

During the Revolution of 1848, Blanqui proclaimed himself a socialist and a Jacobin, and opposed the Provisional Government as too timid and conservative. After the failure of the uprising in June, 1848, he formed his theory that a successful revolution must be based upon the militant revolutionary minority. This view was subsequently developed by Lenin into the theory that the Communists are the advance guard of the proletariat and were therefore entitled to exercise dictatorial power.[3]

Blanqui never commanded a large following, but his was the most rest-

3 *Ibid.,* pp. 69–70, 255; II, 5.

less and active section among the revolutionaries of his time. He has been criticized by socialist writers for failure to distinguish between insurrection and revolution and for underestimatng the importance of the masses. Yet, while his theoretical views are formally denied, the tactics of the Communists, with their emphasis upon conspiracy and the role of leadership, are largely derived from him.

THE COMMUNE

The Paris Commune is important for its part in the mythology of subsequent socialist and communist movements. Its course was closely studied by revolutionaries from Marx to Lenin in order to learn its methods and profit from its errors.

On the eve of the Franco-Prussian War, the tensions in French society were coming to the surface. The declaration of war against Prussia on July 15, 1870, temporarily eased the difficulties.[4] The French army was unequal to its military tasks, and the first defeats led to a reorganization of the government. With the defeat and surrender of Sedan, the Second Napoleonic Empire came to an end. A provisional authority, called a Government of National Defense, made up largely of moderates, was set up in Paris on September 4, 1871. On September 7, the first issue of Blanqui's *La Patrie en Danger* appeared. It demanded the introduction of universal military service and an offensive to relieve Paris.[5]   Instead, the government accepted terms which gave the Germans the right to enter the city. The Parisian workers felt they had been betrayed. Noticing the rise in popular discontent, the Provisional Government left for Versailles. On March 18 the Central Committee was master of Paris and took over the responsibility of government, but the heads of the new regime were uncertain of the course to follow.

The first act of the Central Committee called for communal elections by the people of Paris and an attempt was made to restore the life of the city. Blanqui had been arrested before March 18, and his firmness and leadership were sorely missed. His followers favored an active war against the National Assembly at Versailles, but the Central Committee shied away from taking this drastic step. Instead, the Central Committee tried to establish its legality by holding a communal election on March 26.

4 Frank Jellinek, *The Paris Commune of 1871* (London: Victor Gollancz, Ltd., 1937), p. 49.
5 Prosper O. Lissagaray, *History of the French Commune of 1871*. Translated by Eleanor Marx Aveling (London: Reeves and Turner, 1886), p. 14.

The Commune, as the Parisian government was called, contained twenty-one workers, thirty professional people, and thirteen clerks and small tradesmen. "Thus while the Commune cannot, owing to the undeveloped state of industry at the time, be called truly proletarian, it contained enough workers and representatives of workers to make it something entirely new in the way of governments."[6] The Commune was formally installed on March 28, 1871.

Its difficulties were enormous. Taking power during the unsuccessful war, it sought to rally the people for a defense of the capital. It also had to contend with the implacable opposition of the Provisional Government at Versailles. As the military situation of the Commune became more desperate, a sterner policy was adopted. Opposition papers were suppressed, suspects arrested. But neither sternness nor heroism could hold off the inevitable: on May 28 the battle ended with the troops of Versailles victorious.

Vengeance was untempered by mercy. Paris was divided into four districts and placed under martial law. Denunciation of suspects was conducted on a huge scale. Men and women were picked out for shooting only because their face, figure, or carriage attracted attention. No effort was made to base punishment upon degree of guilt. The carnival of vengeance was presumably a reprisal for the hostages—chief of whom was the Archbishop of Paris—shot by the Communards. No attempt was made to bind the wounds of civil war. Torture and vengeance were the order of the day. Under the direction of General Galliffet, almost twenty thousand Communards were executed.[7] Many others were imprisoned or exiled, and others fled to Belgium, Switzerland, or London. The agitation for a full amnesty lasted a number of years and was finally achieved in 1880.

The character of the Commune has been a source of debate. Professor Mason[8] has denied its socialistic character. Its energies came from the Blanquists, who were not completely socialists. The socialistic measures introduced were few and of a mild variety. The documents issued show no clear-cut socialist orientation. There are some vague phrases on social credit and exchange, on the need for socializing property and the necessity for ending a government dominated by priests, militarists, and monopolists. In practice, the Commune was hesitant and indecisive and only

6 Jellinek, op. cit., pp. 124–125, 173.
7 Lissagaray, op. cit., pp. 383–444.
8 Edward Mason, The Paris Commune (New York: The Macmillan Company, 1930), pp. 296–324.

a few accepted the views of Marx. Nevertheless, the First International claimed the Commune, and sought to rally support for it. The repression that followed and the hostility to radical ideas engendered by the Commune were, for a time, a severe blow to all forms of French socialism. Socialists have regarded the Commune as "the first example of a workers' seizure of power. Thus the Commune became a valuable touchstone upon which the validity of every kind of revolutionary theory could be tested."[9]

REVIVAL OF RADICALISM

The French revolutionary movement was suppressed after the collapse of the Commune. The mutual-aid association was the dominant form of worker society in the 1870's and it was largely through these groups that the philosophy of socialism reappeared. A congress of workers' delegates met in Paris in 1876 to discuss problems of common interest. It steered clear of political issues and instead demanded moderate reforms such as homes for the aged, suppression of night work in manufacturing and free vocational education. This program did not meet the approval of the socialist refugees in London.

However, the moderates' victory was short-lived. Largely because of the influence of the Communard Jules Guesde,[10] the collectivists won control of the new movement. At the congress of 1879, delegates from workers' groups, socialist organizations, and anarchist circles attended. The strong personality of Jules Guesde dominated the scene, and collective ownership of the means of production and political action were endorsed at the labor congress of 1880.[11] The *Parti Ouvrier Français* was formed and a Marxist program adopted.

The social emancipation of the proletariat was held inseparable from its political emancipation, and labor was urged to strike out on an independent political course without alliances with bourgeois groups, for the social revolution could, it was urged, be attained only if the working class avoided alliances with other classes. A few who refused to accept the political program withdrew the following year, but they lacked the energy to build a new movement.

9 Jellinek, *op. cit.*, p. 418.
10 Léon de Seilhac, *Les congrès ouvriers en France* (Paris: Armand Colin et Cie., 1899), pp. 5–49.
11 Alexandre Zévaès, *Les Guesdists* (Paris: Marcel Rivière, 1911).

French socialism underwent a series of splits. Marxist extremism was challenged by Paul Brousse, a former anarchist who organized a socialist party devoted not only to achieving socialism but to promoting day-to-day reforms. The "possibilists," as they were called, were less doctrinaire than the Marxists. Some possibilists came to regard their program as too narrow, and left the group. In addition, the followers of Auguste Blanqui maintained an organization of their own. Outside all socialist groups were the independents, whose appeal was largely to the intellectuals and members of the middle class. Their outstanding leader was Jean Jaurès, who later became the guide and tribune of French socialism.

JEAN JAURÈS (1859–1914)

Jaurès was trained in philosophy and held a lectureship at the University of Toulouse. First elected to Parliament as a left republican in 1885, he rejoined the faculty and completed his doctor's dissertation after his defeat in 1889. His subject was German socialism, and he traced its origin to the writings of Luther, Kant, Fichte, and Hegel. He rejected the view that modern socialism is the result of purely economic forces. Again elected to the Chamber of Deputies in 1891, this time as a Socialist, he soon became recognized as the Socialist spokesman in Parliament. He favored immediate reforms and rejected the harsh conclusions of Marx. In 1897, Jaurès appealed to socialists of all factions to agree upon a common program, and he argued that the route to socialism could not be traced in advance. He believed that progress could best be achieved by supporting the advanced non-Socialist groups in the Chamber of Deputies, a proposal opposed by the Marxists.[12]

The Dreyfus case aroused in Jaurès the greatest moral indignation. Convinced that Dreyfus was innocent, he threw all his energy into his cause. Jaurès felt that it was the duty of socialists to protect those rights "which sum up the meagre progress of humanity, modest guarantees that it has little by little acquired by the long effort of centuries, and the long series of revolutions." [13]

A strong advocate of international peace, he warned, in 1905: "From a European war the revolution might spring forth; and the governing classes would do well to ponder on that—but there might result also for a long period, cries of counter-revolution, of furious nationalism, of stifling

12 Margaret Pease, *Jean Jaurès* (New York: The Viking Press, 1917), p. 43.
13 *Ibid.*, p. 77.

dictatorships, of monstrous militarism, a long chain of retrogade violence, of base hatreds, of reprisals, of slavery."[14]

At international socialist congresses, Jaurès was active in discussions on peace. As the war clouds became heavier over Europe, he used his energies and eloquence to warn against the approaching catastrophe. His efforts were met with vile denunciations in the reactionary and royalist press, but he refused to reply to his detractors. On July 28, 1914, he attended an international mass meeting at Brussels in an attempt to save the peace. Three days later, on July 31, as he was having dinner with friends, he was assassinated by a nationalist aroused by the bitter accusations in the reactionary press.

ATTEMPTS AT UNITY

Jaurès helped to promote cooperation between the several Socialist parties in the Chamber of Deputies. In 1898 the Socialist parties demanded a review of the sentence of Dreyfus. A committee of vigilance was set up, with each of the groups represented by seven delegates.[15] Close cooperation between the several parties appeared realizable, but the propriety of a Socialist entering a cabinet headed by a non-Socialist prime minister was a fresh source of difference.

MINISTERIALISM

In June, 1899, Pierre Marie Waldeck-Rousseau was asked to form a government, and among his ministerial appointments was a leading Socialist, Alexandre Millerand. Marxists and Blanquists charged that participation in a non-Socialist cabinet was a rejection of the class struggle. In contrast, the reformists, led by Jaurès, argued that the class struggle called only for the formation of a Socialist party and that many gains could be won by cooperating with the republican left. The issue was sharply debated at a general congress held in December, 1899. Jaurès defended participation and argued that it was easy to repeat socialist formulas and avoid responsibility. The revolutionaries—antiministerialists— invoked fundamental principles and the class struggle and warned that cooperation with bourgeois governments would lead to the disorientating of Socialism. Finally a majority decided that the class struggle did not

---

[14] Quotation in Pease, op. cit., pp. 125–126.
[15] A-Orry, Les Socialistes indépendants (Paris: Marcel Rivière, 1911).

permit socialists to participate in bourgeois governments, although the congress members agreed that, under exceptional circumstances, the issue of participation would have to be reconsidered.

UNITY

Differences betwen reformists and revolutionists prevented even loose cooperation. Marxists formed the *Parti Socialiste de France,* and rejected all alliances with bourgeois parties; the reformists organized the *Parti Socialiste Français.* The latter cooperated with bourgeois radicals and its leader, Jean Jaurès, was elected vice-president of the Chamber of Deputies in 1902.[16] Reformists favored an evolutionary policy, and stressed the importance of social reform and republican institutions. As a matter of fact, the two socialist groups did not differ on policy as profoundly as their declarations would indicate. Both groups supported the same type of policies within Parliament, but the revolutionaries were more violent in speech. Finally, in 1905, with the help of the International Socialist Congress, the major socialist groups united and formed the *Section Française de l'Internationale Ouvrier.* Its program called for international understanding between labor groups, political and economic organization of the proletariat for the conquest of power, and socialization of the means of production and exchange.[17]

A united party had been established, but differences in doctrine and tactics inevitably reappeared. These were especially in evidence on the questions of war and patriotism. The extreme left favored a campaign against militarism and war, and advocated a general strike to prevent international strife. Many of these views found support from Jaurès. On the other hand, the orthodox Marxists found these opinions unsound. Only Socialism could suppress the possibility of war, and it was a waste of energy to carry out isolated campaigns against militarism.

Differences also developed over the relations of the unions to the party. The Marxists maintained that the party, being fundamentally revolutionary, should lead the trade unions, which were engaged in day-to-day and limited struggles. In contrast, Jaurès argued that the political and economic organizations of labor were of equal value, that neither should

16 Harold R. Weinstein, Jean Jaurès (New York: Columbia University Press, 1936), p. 82.

17 Alexander Zévaès, *Le Socialisme en France* (Paris: Bibliothèque-Charpentier, 1934), pp. 7–8.

seek to dominate the other, and that each had a proper sphere of activity valuable to the working class.

Outside the ranks of the political socialist movement, and even hostile to it, there developed another revolutionary doctrine and movement— French syndicalism. The essential doctrines of syndicalism were developed within the trade unions. The influence of the anarchists, who were opposed to the political involvement and domination of a labor union by a political party, contributed significantly in the evolution of these ideas.

RIGHT TO ORGANIZE

The repeal of the anticombination laws in 1884 opened a new era for French labor. Trade unions obtained legal status and were only required to deposit with the authorities their constitutions, bylaws, and the names of their officers. As the number of unions increased, a meeting to work out a common set of principles was called in 1886. Differences between the moderates and Socialists were in evidence from the beginning. Nevertheless the *Fédération Nationale des Syndicats et Groupes Corporatifs de France* was set up. Under radical domination, the organization approved, in 1889, the use of the general strike.[18] Failure of the moderates to win control finally led to their withdrawal and to the collapse of the organization.

BOURSES DU TRAVAIL

The *bourse* or a delegate body representing a number of local unions also came into existence during the 1880's. First established by the municipality of Paris in 1886, it began as an employment office and soon added a library dealing with technical and economic subjects. Similar institutions were established in other communities and the *bourse du travail* became a central organization for the local *syndicats* (unions). In February, 1892, delegates from a number of cities organized the *Fédération des Bourses du Travail*.[19]

FERNAND PELLOUTIER (1867-1901)

Fernand Pelloutier was the intellectual architect of French syndicalism. A member of a conservative monarchist family, he became a journalist and associated with Aristide Briand. At first a Marxist Socialist, he gradu-

18 Sylvain Humbert, *Le Mouvement Syndical* (Paris: Marcel Rivière, 1912), p. 4.
19 Paul Delesalle, *Les Bourses du travail* (Paris: Marcel Rivière, no date) p. 35.

ally drifted away from political socialism. Instead, he emphasized purely economic forms of struggle and the general strike. His contact with anarchist writers after 1894 led to the strengthening of his antipolitical predilections.

As secretary of the bourses, Pelloutier sought to free the economic movement from all political influences. As an anarchist he opposed central control and direction of workers' activities. He visualized the development of two powerful separate organizations, the *Bourses du Travail* and the *Confédération du Travail*, each with its own functions, but cooperating on mutual problems. These bourses, which were to be local organizations, were to manage the economy after capitalism had been replaced. They were to study the economic character of the areas in which they were organized, the distribution of industry, and the density of population so as to be prepared to administer their local industries. Pelloutier had a mystical faith in the ability of the workers to manage the economy. Therefore his program allowed autonomy to the localities and avoided the dangers of excessive centralization, which he opposed on grounds of principle.[20] His idea was to have the bourses act as centers for mutual aid, teaching, propaganda, and resistance to the employer.

In addition, Pelloutier believed that the bourses should serve as organizations for mutual aid for placement of workers, relieve unemployment, pay accident insurance, and aid migratory journeymen with traveling funds. They should, moreover, organize schools for teaching both trade and social subjects, collect and disseminate economic and statistical information, help set up unions in agriculture and industry, and act as spearheads in the struggle with the employer.

CONFEDERATION GENERALE DU TRAVAIL

The bourses were local groups, and in 1895 the *Confédération Générale du Travail* (C.G.T.) was formed. Later it became the representative of the economic movement of French labor. Soon after its organization, the C.G.T. was captured by militants who advocated the use of sabotage and direct action as tactics in the class war. As a result, the two economic organizations of labor drew closer together and on January 11, 1903, organic unity was achieved.[21]

[20] Édouard Dolléans, *Histoire du mouvement ouvrier* (Paris: Librairie Armand Colin, 1939), II, 37–53.

[21] Léon Jouhaux, *La Confédération générale du travail* (Paris: Gallimard, 1937), pp. 65–67.

The C.G.T. was predominantly revolutionary in outlook. It advocated direct or economic action, the general strike, sabotage, and antimilitarism, although exponents of more moderate views were by no means lacking. The syndicats were required to affiliate with a federation of their crafts or industry and also with a bourse. The C.G.T. was antipolitical in fact, and in 1906 the "Charter of Amiens," a basic syndicalist document, was adopted. The charter accepted the existence of the class struggle and gave as its aim the abolition of classes. The dual struggle of the syndicats was emphasized. The syndicats sought immediate improvements in wages and conditions of labor for the worker; ultimately, however, they aimed to bring about the abolition of capitalism. However, even when the ultimate aim was rejected, workers were urged to support the syndicats as the basis of all struggle for improvement. Labor would be strengthened if the syndicats avoided all political entanglements, but workers in smaller groups or as individuals could participate in political activity if they chose to do so. This section of the charter struck a blow at the efforts of socialists to tie together the economic and political movements of labor.[22] Ultimately the movement was designed for the conquest of control of the means of production. Direct action and the strike were the most effective means of carrying on the struggle against capitalism. Sabotage, a passive form of strike, was another form of direct action. The highest mode of action was the general strike.[23]

The "Charter of Amiens" represented a victory for the direct-action, antipolitical revolutionaries. However, Socialists and moderates remained in the syndicats and continued to press for their point of view. Opponents of revolutionary doctrines held them to be dangerous, as they tended to inflame the workers and arouse the government. Actually the success of the revolutionists was at least in part due to the voting system used at the syndicalist congresses. Voting was based upon syndical units and not upon membership.[24] As organizations, regardless of size, had equal votes and as small groups could more easily be dominated by a revolutionary minority than could larger ones, the adoption of a militant program lost some of its significance. In common with the left-wing political parties, French syndicalism, despite its opposition to militarism, rallied to the defense of France in World War I.

22 *Ibid.*, pp. 77–81.
23 Victor Griffuelhes and Louis Niel, *Les Objectifs de nos luttes de classes* (Paris: Marcel Rivière, 1909), pp. 5–36.
24 David J. Saposs, *The Labor Movement in Post-War France* (New York: Columbia University Press, 1931), p. 23.

GEORGES SOREL (1847–1922)

Syndicalism before World War I derived its inspiration largely from anarchist sources which were opposed to the dominance of the workers' movement by political socialists. Syndicalism then attracted the attention of a number of intellectuals disillusioned with the growing conservatism of political socialism; the most original among them was Georges Sorel. He was a romantic to whom the labor movement represented a means of moral regeneration rather than of physical improvement in the conditions of work. Hating the dullness and pedestrian life of the urban middle class, he hoped that out of the struggle between labor and the bourgeoisie would arise a new and sublime chivalry.

Georges Sorel was an engineer, and for twenty-five years he worked at his profession. In 1892, at the age of forty-five, he retired to devote himself to literary and scientific work. For the next thirty years he published a large number of articles and books. He died in August, 1922, at the age of seventy-six.

Early in life Sorel abandoned Catholicism, but he retained an interest in the origin of religion. Although he rejected its doctrines, he was an admirer of the power and glory of the church. His continual search for truth, the severity of his judgments, and his pessimism place Sorel among the tormented moralists engaged in an everlasting search for the answers to the riddle of life. It was a search which led Sorel to wander from one political camp to another, always dissatisfied with the answers given. Beginning as a conservative, he successively became a democratic socialist, a revolutionary syndicalist, a nationalist and monarchist, and finally he almost returned to one of his early loves when he greeted Lenin as "the giant destined to save the cause of labor." [25]

One of his collaborators observed that he was an indefatigable worker, and that he was always responsive to new ideas. Sorel's most original work was done in the *Mouvement Socialiste* edited by Hubert Lagardelle, who later became a friend of Mussolini and a collaborator during the Nazi occupation. Sorel later associated himself with an antidemocratic review, *L'Indépendence,* to which Paul Bourget and Maurice Barrès contributed.[26]

Sorel was not a systematic thinker in the sense that he developed a

[25] Victor Sartre, *Georges Sorel* (Paris: Éditions Spes, 1937), pp. 12–13.
[26] Edouard Berth, *Du 'Capital' aux Reflexsions sur la violence* (Paris: Marcel Rivière, 1932), pp. 169–174.

logically coherent doctrine. He himself has claimed that he wrote "from day to day according to the need of the moment." [27] This fact may account for the diverse groups which honor his memory.

Sorel's first volume, *A Contribution to a Profane Study of the Bible,* published in 1889, dealt with the causes of the decline of a people. This was followed by *The Process of Socrates,* in which the underlying pessimism of Sorel reveals itself. Sorel saw in pain a unifying force, an element which set up man's guard against the evil always ready to overwhelm him. In contrast, satisfaction is a soporific, "for in the melodic strains of joy one hears the caressing tones of death." [28] Sorel's pessimism arose not from resignation but from the belief that man must fight against decadence, for decline is always more natural and easy than the movement toward grandeur.

Sorel believed that pessimism was "a doctrine without which nothing very great has been accomplished in this world." [29] He believed that pessimism is generally conceived incorrectly. A pessimist is not a man who rails at the blindness of fate or the inconstancy of friends or relations. "A pessimist regards social conditions as forming a system bound together by an iron law which cannot be evaded, so that the system is given, as it were, in one block, and cannot disappear except in a catastrophe which involves the whole." The pessimist does not hold individuals responsible for existing evils, and "he does not dream of bringing about the happiness of future generations by slaughtering existing egoists." [30]

Nor did Sorel concede that progress is a universal law. On the contrary, he regarded this notion as illusory, and blamed the parliamentary democrats for perpetrating this obvious absurdity. Man should be told of the hard road that lies ahead, of the sacrifices that stand before him. It is necessary to graft a "pessimistic conception" of the future of mankind. Man must learn the necessity of struggle, of sadness, and that humanity, like the Wandering Jew, must ever be condemned to march down the dusty plain without repose. It is this spirit of rebellion, rooted in true

27 Quotation in Sartre, *op. cit.,* p. 17.

28 Michael Freund, *Georges Sorel, de Revolutionäre Konservatismus* (Frankfort on the Main: V. Klostermann, 1932), pp. 30–31.

29 Georges Sorel, *Reflections on Violence.* Translated by T. E. Hulme (New York: The Viking Press, 1919), p. 7.

30 *Ibid.,* p. 11.

pessimism, which will arouse the most fervent struggle for the overthrow of capitalism by those consecrated to the moral rejuvenation of man.

HISTORY

Sorel agreed with the essential postulates of historic materialism. Never a slavish follower, he accepted those elements congenial to him, and changed and modified others. Economic conflict and the class struggle are recognized as the locomotives of history. Sorel explained the popularity of Cartesianism in the eighteenth century by the optimism of the bourgeoisie; and Rousseau's ideal of a free citizen by the existence of a prosperous artisan class at Geneva where Rousseau was reared.[31] While recognizing the importance of productive relations, he saw no inevitable connection between means of production and human conduct. Social movements respond to noneconomic influences which are not compatible with absolute determinism. Chance is continually operating in human affairs. This idea he took from the French philosopher Henri Bergson.

The role of great men in history was also recognized. How, he asks, could one deny the influence of Christ, Mahomet, Luther, Caesar, and Napoleon on historical evolution?

VIOLENCE

Sorel was critical of parliamentary socialism. To him it was unclear, unrevolutionary, compromising. Socialists ought to cease appealing to justice and enlightenment of the middle classes; they ought to stop searching for better legislation. The sole function of Socialists is "explaining to the proletariat the greatness of the revolutionary part they are called upon to play. By ceaseless criticism the proletariat must be brought to perfect their organizations; they must be shown how the embryonic forms which appear in their unions may be developed, so that, finally, they may build up institutions without any parallel in the history of the middle class; that they may form ideas which depend solely on their position as producers in large industries, and which owe nothing to middle-class thought; and that they may acquire *habits of liberty* with which the middle class nowadays are no longer acquainted."

An implacable conflict is necessary if the workers are to learn the road that leads to their destiny. By constant criticism the workers would learn to perfect their organizations, so that they form ideas which arise only as a result of their position as producers, ideas which are independent of

31 Sartre, *op. cit.*, p. 85.

middle-class thought. For the compromises of social peace, Sorel urged "proletarian violence" which "tends to restore the separation of classes, just when they seemed on the point of intermingling in the democratic march." [32] He feared the debilitating effects of humanitarianism and social peace, not only upon labor, but upon the nation. He therefore concluded: "Proletarian violence not only makes the future revolution certain, but it seems also to be the only means by which the European nations—at present stupefied by humanitarianism—can recover their former energy." Proletarian violence is in the service "of the immemorial interests of civilization; it is not perhaps the most appropriate method of obtaining immediate material advantages, but it may save the world from barbarism."

The General Strike   The essence of proletarian violence is the general strike. Its practical impossibility did not concern him, for it is not a practical question. Sorel asked only if the idea has power to move the workers and their leaders. To him, the general strike is "the *myth* in which socialism is wholly comprised, i.e. a body of images capable of evoking instinctively all the sentiments which correspond to the different manifestations of the war undertaken by socialism against modern society." In explaining the meaning of "myth" he tells us it "cannot be refuted, since it is, at bottom, identical with the convictions of a group, being the expression of these convictions in the language of movement, and it is in consequence not divided into parts which could be placed on the plane of historical description." According to Sorel, myth was of much importance in history and was capable of mobilizing the strength of the groups believing in it.

Sorel stressed intuition as a method of reaching the truth; the proletarian general strike was a concept which is grasped by intuition rather than by intellectual analysis. The political general strike was regarded by Sorel as a method of noble warfare. The proletariat finds in this instrument a consciousness "of the glory which will be attached to its historical role and of the heroism of its militant attitude."

The Ethics of Violence   Violence is defined as acts of revolt which lead to the destruction of the social order. It is a high and sublime force, clean, honest, and uplifting. There is something heroic in violence which shames the bourgeois virtues of the middle class. There is a mystic purity about it which gives it a heroic form. Strangely enough, Sorel's concep-

---

[32] Sorel, *op. cit.*, p. 90. The following quotations are also from this source, pp. 90, 99, 137, 33, 189, 195.

tion of violence as a purifying and ennobling force did not strike much response among Marxists. Nor were the socialists and syndicalists who opposed Marxism attracted by its heroic mysticism. Instead, the doctrine made a considerable impression upon the young conservative intellectuals, especially those who congregated around the *Action Française,* the royalist publication of Charles Maurras. The glorification of violence cast a spell over writers and politicians, some of whom later became fascists. Sorel's views were nihilistic and destructive. He hated the complacency and smugness of middle-class life, with its search for leisure and comfort. Himself a bookish man who had, during his lifetime, achieved a notable amount of erudition, he hated the man of intellect while glorifying impulse and passion. Instead of intellectual analysis, he emphasized intuition as a means of reaching truth, a doctrine popularized by the philosopher Henri Bergson.

Sorel exercised great influence, not so much upon the French labor movement, as upon intellectuals. The views of the French labor movement—direct action and antiparliamentarianism—were reached independently, as we have seen, and before Sorel had published his principal views. The emphasis upon economic or direct action and the hostility to the political involvement of labor were due to the influence of antiparliamentary revolutionaries. Sorel's views represented something new and, in fact, something alien to the tradition of the Western European revolutionary movement. His contempt for intellect, his criticism of science, and his belief in the primacy of impulse and intuition as means for reaching truth, were all hostile to the "scientific" spirit of Marxism and other revolutionary doctrines. Despite his temporary membership in the Marxist camp, Sorel's spirit was fundamentally hostile to European socialism.

French syndicalism lost its revolutionary fervor and supported the government in World War I.[33] As the war continued, there was some revival of the old militancy, but the majority remained prowar.

---

[33] Roger Picard, *Le Mouvement syndical durant la guerre* (New Haven: Yale University Press, no date), pp. 49–50.

12. FRENCH RADICALISM AFTER
WORLD WAR I

POSTWAR UNREST

In common with most other countries, France suffered from serious strikes in the period following World War I. Inspired by the Russian Revolution, a minority within the trade unions syndicats demanded a more revolutionary policy. It maintained that labor's first duty was to support and to extend the Russian Revolution. The heads of the trade-union movement were attacked for having substituted the national interest for the class struggle. [1] The opposition was made up of militant syndicalists, Communists, and anarchists. Instead of surrendering to the majority, the militants continued their activity, and in 1921, they organized the *Confédération Générale du Travail Unitaire*.

A division within the minority immediately appeared. Militant syndicalists and anarchists, while opposed to reform and compromise, were not favorable to allowing the Communists to control the economic movement. The Communists would not give ground, for, in accordance with their theory, the trade union was to be subordinate to the political party. Therefore a few syndicalist groups split away, hoping to return to the nonpolitical policies of the Charter of Amiens. In contrast, the C.G.T. became increasingly a purely reformist trade union in theory as well as in practice. French syndicalism now became increasingly concerned with security of the job and improvements through legislation and not with the transformation of society.

[1] Édouard Dolléans, *Histoire du mouvement ouvrier* (Paris: Librairie Armand Colin, 1929), II, 298–320.

THE CRISIS AND UNITY

The unification of the economic aspect of the French labor movement was due to the political crisis facing the country in 1934. Using the Stavisky scandal as a pretext, an open assault upon parliamentary institutions was made by reactionary and fascist groups. The C.G.T. stepped into the breach, and appealed for a twenty-four-hour general strike on Februaury 12, 1934.

Fearful that a reactionary victory might unleash a concerted attack upon the Soviet Union, the unions under Communist influence began a campaign for a united front. Begun on the local level, it ended in September, 1935, in organic unity on the basis of the Charter of Amiens.[2]

Unity meant that large numbers of Communists entered the C.G.T. Differences appeared. The Communists then followed a patriotic line under the slogan of "a free, strong and happy France," a line which was opposed by a number of antiwar syndicalists. Each group founded a journal to propound its point of view. Between the pacifists on the one side and the Communists on the other, a third group led by the long-time head of the C.G.T., Léon Jouhaux, attempted to retain its independent outlook.[3]

The pacifist and syndicalist wings did not regard foreign policy as the most significant problem facing French labor. On the other hand, for the Communists there were few other problems, and those of only minor importance.

French labor gained in prestige, in membership, and in standards. The Popular Front government, in office in 1936, won the forty-hour week and other reforms. With the replacement of Blum by Edouard Daladier as prime minister, an attack against labor standards was instituted, inspired by a member of the cabinet, Paul Reynaud. The decrees curtailing labor standards were introduced during the "Munich period" and it

was evident . . . that the communists' opposition to the government's foreign policy was at least as great as their wrath about Reynaud's rehabilitation program. In numerous telegrams of protest which communist-influenced trade unions sent to the Congress (of the C.G.T.) presidium, as well as in some of the speeches, it was suggested that the decrees be regarded as "not existing"; [the demand] for

2 *Ibid.,* pp. 382–386.
3 Henry W. Ehrmann, *French Labor: From Popular Front to Liberation* (New York: Oxford University Press, 1947), pp. 111–114. The quotations in this section are from this source, pp. 95, 148–150, 264.

a resort to the ultimate weapon was distinctly raised. And since it was not within the power even of a successful general strike to nullify legislation, the communist idea could have had no other aim than to overthrow, with the aid of a popular movement, the cabinet which had conducted the Munich accord.

Genuine discontent with the government's policies led to the calling of a general strike in the fall of 1938. The government was well prepared, while confusion and uncertainty existed in the ranks of labor. French labor suffered a serious defeat.

WORLD WAR II

[After the signing of a] non-aggression pact between Nazi Germany and Soviet Russia the communist line was again changed. While the event was unexpected, French communists, similar to those elsewhere, adapted themselves to the new conditions. The appeasement of Hitler by Soviet Russia was defended [by the Communists] and this led to the ousting of communist officials from the unions. Thereupon the communists went underground, dusted off their anti-war slogans and sought to undermine the labor movement and the government.

Like the Communists, the pacifist and appeasement factions were far from enthusiastic about the war. Lacking the discipline and will of the Communists, they manifested their opposition mainly in lukewarm approval of the war effort. With French capitulation in 1940, the appeasers had their day. René Belin, a leading official of the C.G.T., was appointed Minister of Production and Labor by Pétain. The National Council of the C.G.T. refused to approve the appointment, and Pétain's efforts to harness French labor to appeasement was not successful. In revenge, the government formally dissolved the C.G.T. in November, 1940. A labor charter to regulate the position of labor in the community was promulgated in October, 1941; it marked the end of free trade unionism in France. A number of pacifists and some former syndicalists cooperated with Vichy and the Germans, but the majority of French labor followed the old leaders, who created an underground apparatus which became the vital force. With the break between Germany and Soviet Russia, the Communists joined the fight on Hitler. Soon they sought readmission to the underground anti-Vichy trade-union movement. At a meeting of several underground leaders in May, 1943, the Communists were readmitted and actually allowed greater representation at the central office than they had at the time of the Molotov-Ribbentrop pact in 1939. "It appears that during their period of ostracism they had won a stronger position than they held at the time, which was considered by many observers the apogee of their influence within the C.G.T."

Their important position in the underground French trade-union movement coupled with the growth of communist sentiment among French labor gave the Communists an opportunity to entrench themselves. At the first convention of the C.G.T., the Communists were in full control. They have since controlled a majority of the administrative posts in that organization and dominant positions in the leading unions. The antipolitical syndicalist C.G.T. has become the economic arm of international communism in France.

DIVISIONS IN SOCIALIST RANKS

French socialism, like the syndicalist movement, faced a crisis during and after World War I. French Socialists were pacifists and antimilitarists, but once war became a reality, the majority of French Socialists overwhelmingly supported their government. Two Socialists, Marcel Sembat and the old Marxist, Jules Guesde, joined the cabinet as representatives of the Socialist party and not as individuals.[4]

As the conflict continued, antiwar sentiment increased among French Socialists, and the end of World War I found the party split into three factions—right, center, and left. The right wanted to cooperate with the bourgeois left parties for the winning of economic reform. The center advocated a more socialistic policy and sought, in fact, to return to the traditional policies of socialism, of no cooperation with nonsocialist groups. The left was made up of admirers of the Russian Revolution who demanded a militant policy on the economic and political fronts.

THE SPLIT

The left turned out to be the majority and later established the French Communist party, which accepted the theses and conditions promulgated by the Third International. The minority withdrew and re-established the French Socialist party. Soon the Socialists, under the leadership of Léon Blum, regained and even exceeded the strength they had before World War I.

During the 1920's, the French Socialists fought for economic and political reforms, but refrained from joining governments in which other

[4] Alexandre Zévaès, *Le Socialisme en France* (Paris: Bibliothèque-Charpentier, 1934), pp. 92–94.

parties were represented. The threat to the French Republic which followed a financial and political scandal in 1934 forced the Socialists to change their policy. A number of influential politicians were involved in a scandal, and royalist and reactionary groups used this as a pretext for staging violent demonstrations against the republic.

The rioters were a mixed crowd of people, many of them belonging to no particular organization; oddly enough there were even some communists among them. For among the organizations that demonstrated in the Champs Élysées and the Concorde that night was the A.R.A.C., the Federation of Communist Ex-Servicemen. The communists were that night on the side of the anti-parliamentary rioters and when in his recent book on *France Today and the People's Front*, M. Thorez, the communist leader, asserts that the communists organized "anti-Fascist demonstrations on February 6" one cannot help wondering on what evidence the assertion is made.[5]

THE POPULAR FRONT

The C.G.T., with the support of the Socialists, sensed the danger and called a general strike as a protest and a warning against an attempt at a *coup d'état*. The Communists, who had participated in the antigovernment demonstrations, finally recognized the danger of a Fascist victory to Soviet Russia began to cry for a "United Front." All Communist-dominated groups, including satellite organizations, joined the campaign. In the light of their past experience, Socialists were naturally suspicious of Communists bearing gifts, but pressure from the rank and file forced closer cooperation. On August 27, 1934, the United Action Pact was signed by the Communist and Socialist parties. It provided for (1) mobilization of the working class against fascist organizations; (2) defense of democratic liberties; (3) prevention of preparation for a new war; (4) a campaign against fascist terror in Germany and Austria; and (5) the freeing of Thaelmann from prison in Nazi Germany.

Each party was to maintain its separate activities and each had the right to seek new recruits. However, each agreed to refrain from attacking the doctrines and tactics of the other. A number of Socialists were doubtful of the good intentions of the Communists and of the alliance with a group actually under the influence of a foreign power.

A program of political and economic reform was worked out by the

---

[5] Alexander Werth, *Which Way France?* (New York: Harper & Brothers, 1937), p. 56.

"Popular Front." Collective security within the League of Nations was demanded. As to economic reforms, the Popular Front sought the establishment of a national unemployment fund, reduction in the hours of labor, old-age pensions, and a system of public works financed by local and national authorities. For agriculture, the program called for revaluation of agricultural prices, elimination of speculation, reduction of the cost of living, and encouragement of agricultural cooperatives. Finally, a demand was made for a reorganization of the system of money and credit in order to eliminate the power of the "200 families" over the financial life of France. The electoral campaign was successful, and Léon Blum became the first French Socialist prime minister.

The Government of the Popular Front   Blum took office in June, 1936, at a time when France was beset by serious crises on both the domestic and the foreign fronts. Serious strikes, many of which were spontaneous, had paralyzed the economy. Blum himself presided over the negotiations carried on between the C.G.T. and the employers' group, the *Confédération Générale de Production Française*. The outcome was the "Matignon Agreement."

It provided for the acceptance of collective agreements, recognition of the right of the workers to join a regular union, and an increase of real wages from 7 to 15 per cent. Léon Jouhaux, the secretary of the C.G.T., proclaimed the pact as the greatest victory in the history of French labor.[6] The Popular Front government lasted a year and was responsible for the introduction of a large number of reforms. It failed, however, to solve the economic difficulties confronting the country, nor was it able to master the opposition of large industry and finance to domestic reform. Faced by a flight of capital, the government asked for power to meet the threat to the nation's financial stability. The Senate rejected the request, and the government resigned. Four governments succeeded one another in rapid order. Blum tried again, but resigned after three weeks. His successor, Edouard Daladier, approved of the settlement at Munich which turned the Sudeten over to Hitler. His move aroused the left; but at the same time that he pursued a policy of appeasement in foreign affairs, Daladier embarked upon a militant attack on labor at home. His action against the standards of labor led to a general strike, but Daladier remained master of the situation. Labor was defeated.

Crisis   Daladier virtually destroyed the Popular Front. Throughout 1939, international tension was increasing. When war finally came, there

6 *Ibid.*, pp. 320–322.

was grim acceptance of the harsh fact, but no enthusiasm. After the Soviet-German pact, the Communists became lukewarm and then openly hostile toward the defense of their country. They became pacifists. The majority of Socialists in parliament supported Pétain. Nevertheless their party was outlawed.

With the fall of France, Blum was arrested and when brought to trial he demonstrated courage, heroism, and tenacity of the highest order. He defended his political conduct and his part in the Popular Front governments, answering every charge with irony and eloquence. In fact, he placed his accusers in the dock, at least before the bar of history. He refused to retract a single word or excuse a single political act. He charged the reactionaries and deflationists with forcing the masses to unite in a popular front and ended his defense with a charge that loyalty to France had now become treason, and with a prophecy of the future revival and glory of the republic.[7]

AFTERMATH OF WORLD WAR II

The Socialist party participated in the underground exploits during the occupation and reorganized as soon as possible. The first general secretary of the revived party urged it to become the rallying point for revolutionaries and republicans who desired to transform society without sacrificing liberty.

One of the results of the occupation was greater amity between Christians and Socialists. One of the leaders of French socialism, André Philip, took the position that socialism is in effect an institutional technique and not a philosophic system or a faith." Socialism means the socialization of key industries, national direction of the economy, and the accession of workers to the management of affairs. This ideal also embodies respect for the human personality, equality before the law, and the protection of the fundamental liberties as defined by the Declaration of the Rights of Man. Accordingly, Léon Blum pleaded for a Socialist party both democratic and effective. He proclaimed the death of economic liberalism, and urged collectivism, which respects and promotes the human personality. Everyone wishes a society founded on social justice. The object of socialism is to transform the regime of property so that it ceases to weigh heavily upon man. Blum opposed an organic unity with the Communists,

7 Léon Blum, *L'Histoire jugera* (Montral: Éditions de l'Arbre, 1943), pp. 269–348.

for he believed that the Communists were too much under the thumb of Moscow. According to Blum, French Socialists valued liberty won by the French Revolution and, Communists, he said, had no such loyalty, despite their heroic record during the resistance. Discussing Communist patriotism, Blum declared that "all would be simple so long as the position of France coincided with that of the Soviet." Even admitting that the Communists were not financially dependent upon Moscow, he maintained that they were spiritually dependent, and he argued that while Communist discipline was rigid, its propaganda was sinister, and while its organization was homogeneous in form, it was multiple in its ramifications.

Another faction favored close cooperation with the Communists, and the loss of Socialist votes strengthened this trend. In 1946, the opposition to Blum elected a majority to the executive committee. It, however, failed to halt the loss of votes in the following election. The renewed struggle between left and right in the French Socialist party is symptomatic of the dilemma of all socialist parties. If they cooperate with radical parties that are nonrevolutionary in philosophy, they are likely to stimulate opposition from groups within their own ranks that accept the Marxist interpretation of events and who feel sympathy toward the Communists.

Loss of Socialist electoral votes has been severe. It was due in part to the loss of labor, support and in part to the weakness of the socialist administrative and propaganda apparatus. For a time, the party's greatest problem, however, was the left or *Communisant* wing, which believed that it could find common ground with the Communists. Actually the party did not fare any better with the left wing in control of the organization machinery than it had before.

The Socialists in France face a dilemma typical of all "Third Force" groups at present seeking to combine social reform with political liberty. The more positive and less responsible appeals of the Communists have succeeded in weaning large masses of workers from the Socialist ranks, for on the one hand, as good republicans the Socialists cannot initiate or carry out policies that may compromise or jeopardize democratic institutions; on the other hand, without running the danger of losing labor support, the Socialists cannot separate themselves from their historic position of a proletarian party. It is a terrible dilemma that perhaps can be solved only by the return of political and economic stability. Until that time the position of the Socialist party is likely to be uncertain, with a precarious balance between the divergent groups within the party.

On the economic front, the C.G.T. is now completely controlled by the Communists. As a result, under the cover of economic demands, the unions have been used for political purposes. The Communist intention is to undermine the Marshall plan, and by maintaining uncertainty and economic instability they may achieve that aim. A strike movement based upon economic demands, but having political purposes, was launched in the fall of 1947. As soon as its goals became visible, there were large defections, and a National Conference of Minority Groups, known as the Workers' Force (*Force Ouvrière*) was launched in November, 1947, to seek a return of the C.G.T. to first principles. In the following month, the minority movement decided to withdraw from the C.G.T. and set up an independent group, whose membership has about one million members. This secession was based on a desire to restore the independence of the trade-union movement and to free it from the domination of political revolutionaries. The fears of Pelloutier and Griffuelhes that the movement would be dominated by outsiders have come to pass. In the view of the opposition, the trade-union movement has been diverted from its true purpose and made to serve the imperialistic interest of the Soviet Union to the detriment and sacrifice of the trade unions and the French community. The justification of this policy is simply an elaboration of the Marxist philosophy that the trade union is incapable of initiating basic reforms, and that only by becoming an auxiliary of the revolutionary political party does it achieve its highest function. Such a view transforms the union from a democratic body seeking the improvement of its own members to an instrument in the service of a revolutionary general staff.

13. *EARLY SOCIALISM IN ENGLAND*

Marxism was never able to make much headway in England. The rigid and harsh doctrines and the emphasis upon impersonal, amoral historical forces inherent in Marxist formulations never held much attraction for English writers, social critics, and workers. Nor did Marxists play the same role in initiating and extending the labor movements in England as they did in many Continental countries. English socialism grew slowly and almost unobtrusively. While critical of competitive capitalism, it has regarded collectivism as a superior form of economic organization rather than as a historically ordained necessity. Not only the assimilation of ideas from other countries, but also social, political, and economic changes at home as well as the social theories evolved by native writers, shaped the peculiar features of English laboristic socialism.

English "laborism" is a reform type of socialism strongly influenced by humanitarian and Christian traditions on the one hand and the pragmatism of the trade unions on the other. It differs from Continental socialism in that it lacks an organized body of doctrine. It is practical and compromising and regards socialism as a desirable system of economic organization rather than a body of "revealed" dogma.

RICARDIAN SOCIALISTS

The close of the Napoleonic Wars found England's trade depressed, employment low, and social conditions explosive. The misery and destitution were in part responsible for the rise of Chartism as a political movement, for the growth of the first labor organizations, and for the development of socialist ideas based upon the doctrines of classical economics.[1] The Ricardian socialists, as they were called, attacked laissez faire and advocated cooperative rather than competitive production.

[1] Anton Menger, *The Right to the Whole Produce of Labor* (London: Macmillan & Co., 1899).

WILLIAM THOMPSON *(1783–1833)*

William Thompson, a prosperous landowner in Cork County, Ireland, was an admirer of Jeremy Bentham and Robert Owen. From Bentham, Thompson acquired the concept of utility, or the principle that the greatest happiness for the greatest number was the most desirable social end. Its attainment is possible only by a plentiful production and equitable distribution.

Thompson attempted to answer the argument that equal payment would equally reward the indolent and the industrious, and thus remove the stimulus to labor. He rejected the views of his conservative contemporaries, who regarded the capitalist as the creative force in the production of wealth, and profit as the force which sets the creative power in motion. In contrast, Thompson considered labor as the real producer, and argued that the insecurity of labor was the real check on output.[2]

Unequal distribution of wealth is the most salient feature of modern economic society. Abundant production is possible only under a system where the worker is reasonably certain that he will enjoy the use of the goods he has produced. Therefore, abundant production must await equal and just distribution.[3]

Insecurity   Insecurity is due, in Thompson's opinion, to faultiness in the methods of distributing wealth. Following Ricardo, he argued that wealth is the product of labor and that value is equal to labor cost of production using "ordinary skill and judgment." In general, people are capable of producing equal quantities of wealth and the few rich must "abstract" it from the many. This is close to Marx's theory of surplus value. From this premise, Thompson reached the conclusion that under conditions of private property, the producer is denied security, for a large share of his output is taken in the form of rent and profit by owners and landlords. The result is excessive property, luxury, and idleness on the one hand and poverty and need on the other. The existing system is inefficient. It deprives the worker of the incentive to produce to his full capacity because the worker must transfer a part of his product to capitalist and landlord. The competitive system was indicted on two counts. It fails to produce the greatest happiness, for a transfer of goods from the

2 Esther Lowenthal, *The Ricardian Socialists* (New York: Columbia University Press, 1911), p. 21.

3 Max Beer, *A History of British Socialism* (London: George Bell & Sons, 1919), I, 219.

worker to the capitalist results in a greater loss of happiness to the worker than gain to the capitalist, because increases in the increments of wealth by a single person become "successively less capable of producing happiness." [4] Nor is the system efficient, as labor's incentive for all-out production is reduced by the capitalist's "abstraction" of part of the product. In addition, the capitalistic system concentrates economic and political power in a few hands, and allows the capitalist to determine wages and employment.[5]

The System of Security   Thompson then turned his attention to an ideal society, one which assures security. It must be based on "natural laws of distribution" so that the jobs could be freely chosen, exchange would be free and voluntary, and labor would receive the full value it produced. Adoption of these principles would lead to a great increase in wealth and happiness. Natural resources should be equally shared by all, for they cannot be regarded as the product of labor. The young and the old would be entitled to support. Thompson was sure that equality would lead to security and greater happiness; producers' cooperatives financed by the savings of trade unions were the means by which these goals could be attained.

JOHN GRAY *(1799–1850)*

Another of the Ricardian socialists, John Gray, left school at the age of fifteen and accepted employment in a London wholesale house. He became interested in social problems and, in 1815, he assisted Robert Owen in the management of the colony at Orbiston.

Economic Views   "Every necessary, convenience and comfort of life is obtained by human labor." [6] Proceeding from this concept, Gray divided society into productive and unproductive classes. Unproductive groups are those who give "no equivalent whatever for that which they consume." The productive classes produce material wealth.

Gray argued that the unproductive classes live upon the "industry of their fellow-creatures." He denied that they draw their living from their property. On the contrary, they live on the property of others, for the foundation of all property is nothing but accumulated labor. Gray denied

---

4 Lowenthal, *op. cit.*, p. 24.

5 Quotation, *ibid.*, p. 24, from *Distribution of Wealth*. Chap 1, Sec. 8.

6 John Gray, *A Lecture on Human Happiness* (London: Sherwood Jones and Company, 1825), p. 15. No. 2 in Series of Reprints of Scarce Tracts in Economic and Political Science. The following quotations from Gray are from this source, pp. 22, 33, 35, 37, 63.

the right of landowning, for it is "the natural inheritance of all mankind. . . . a habitation belonging to no man in particular, but to every man." No one is entitled to the produce except he whose labor has made the produce possible. The landlord performs no labor, and gives no equivalent for the produce he exacts. Rent should be paid to the nation.

Like rent, interest is held to be "another mode of obtaining labour without giving any equivalent for it; or in other words, of legally and unjustly imposing on other men the task of keeping us in idleness."

Competition is severely criticized. Under existing conditions production is determined by demand and not by need; by profit and not by satisfaction of wants. Demand is determined by the income of the productive and unproductive classes. However, "the quantity of wealth which the labour, the services or the property of individuals enable them to command, is limited by competition between man and man." Competition determines the amount received by the productive classes, and the amount is just enough to support bodily strength and offspring.

Gray advocated the setting up of banks to issue paper currency to encourage industry. Factories would be directed by salaried managers. Goods produced would be deposited in public warehouses, and the producer would receive the full value calculated in labor time. Workers would receive minimum wages and bonuses for superior work. Gray believed that this system would expand and would eventually include all production.

JOHN FRANCIS BRAY *(1809–1895)*

John Francis Bray lived most of his life in the United States, but his book, *Labour's Wrongs and Labour's Remedy,* exercised its influence mainly among the English Chartists. Like those of the other Ricardian socialists, his views influenced the writings of Marx and other radicals. *Views* Bray did not attribute the hardships and misery of labor to the wickedness of governments. On the contrary, he regarded government as the effect and not the cause of social maladjustment. In words reminiscent of Marx, he maintained that "going to the origin of the thing, we shall find that every form of government, and every social and governmental wrong, owes its rise to the existing social system—*the institution of property as it at present exists."* [7] Equality of political power is differentiated from equal political rights. Differences in rights are due to class divi-

---

[7] John F. Bray, *Labour's Wrongs and Labour's Remedy,* p. 17. Italics in original. The following quotations from Bray are from this source, pp. 33, 44, 61.

sion, and changes in the form of government do not, therefore, abolish class differences. Bray examined the conditions under which equality is possible. He argued that all men ought to engage in labor, and that raw materials and the surface of the earth should be made common property. It is difficult "to maintain this natural equality of right to subsistence unless the earth be Common Property." Common property must be predicated upon common ownership of land and man has no "exclusive right to one single inch of land."

Bray had in mind an equal wage for all. He regarded all labor as deserving of equal rewards, for even though all forms of labor "do not appear of equal value to society at large. . . . Such inequality of value . . . is no argument for inequality of rewards." No pecuniary stimulus is needed for man to perform his best work.

In a system of equal exchange, the value of goods is based upon their labor cost of production. Under those conditions, neither interest nor profit is possible, for they arise out of "unequal exchanges." Bray denied that capital and labor have a community of interest. They are hostile to each other, "for the gain of the capitalist is always the loss of the working man." He was not unaware of the importance of capital in increasing productivity, but he felt that capital is the fruit of labor.

THOMAS HODGSKIN (1787–1869)

While perhaps less important than the other three Ricardian socialists, Thomas Hodgskin defined capital in such a way that he may be regarded as a forerunner of Marx. Self-interest was, to Hodgskin, the dominating principle of human conduct. Order and harmony govern the natural world, and man is part of the cosmic scheme. Moreover, the laws which determine the wealth of nations are part of the natural order, discoverable by man. Government interference with economic processes is self-defeating, as it interferes with the natural order. The economists were criticized because they regarded ownership of property as necesaary or natural. Actually it is, according to Hodgskin, based upon artificial rights.

His criticism of capital was based upon the labor theory of value. Neither landlord nor capital is productive, for capital is the product of labor. Labor produces all wealth and is therefore entitled to the total product. Interest is unjustified, and he rejected the theory that interest payments promote abstinence and stimulate savings. Capital could be accumulated by a nation that possessed knowledge and a skilled labor force able to apply it.

As the sole creator of value, labor is entitled to the whole produce of industry. Managers and employers, who, he held, are in fact workers, should be remunerated in accordance with their high ability. Owners of industry should be paid a wage based on their managerial competence, but Hodgskin denied that they are entitled to payments based on ownership.

The Ricardian socialists exercised an influence upon later socialist writers. Their stress upon the labor theory of value and their arguments that payments to the factors other than labor constituted a surplus "abstracted" or extracted from labor were subsequently embodied, perhaps in more refined form in the economic theories of socialism.

CHARTISM

The agitation of Owen swelled the criticism of the anticapitalist writers; they merged and reached their crest in the Chartist movement. Roughly the incubating period of the movement extended from 1825 to 1834. It assumed a nation-wide character and attained its greatest vigor from 1837 to 1842. The views and traditions of Chartism were absorbed by Continental socialists and by English cooperators.

Chartism lacked the unified philosophy and the well-rounded theories of modern radical parties. It is, however, generally accepted that a branch of the Chartists had in view a communistic society. The term "Chartism" is derived from the People's Charter presented by the London Workingmen's Association in 1837, and was largely the work of the Owenite William Lovett (1800–1877). The People's Charter demanded (1) universal suffrage, (2) equal electoral districts, (3) abolition of property qualifications for parliamentary party candidates, (4) an annual ballot and a secret ballot, and (5) payment to members of Parliament. Along with the desire for greater political rights was the resentment against the harshness of the new industrialism. In contrast to the aristocrats who were in the forefront of the movement for political liberty in the eighteenth century, the early Chartist leaders were humble men—writers and workmen. Their claims were not based upon abstract ideas, but upon the need for political equality in order to assure men justice.

LONDON WORKINGMEN'S ASSOCIATION

The London Workingmen's Association was organized in June, 1836, and aspired to unite "the intelligent and influential portion of the working classes in town and country." [8] Equal rights and the removal of restriction upon a "cheap" and honest press were demanded. Only workers were eligible for membership. Propagandists were sent out who succeeded in forming similar associations elsewhere. These proponents of political reform became known as Chartists.

FACTIONS

The Chartists were divided into the moral-force and the physical-force factions. The leader of the former was William Lovett, the author of the Charter and a ropemaker by trade. The moral-force protagonists favored persuasion and education as methods for achieving reform.

The leader of the physical-force group, Feargus O'Connor, was a lawyer, a politician, and an editor of a leading radical paper, the *Northern Star*. His bitter denunciation of the factory system and the poor law reflected the feelings of the masses. If reform could be attained only by violence, O'Connor was not averse to its use.

THE AGITATION

The pent-up resentment of the masses expressed itself through the Chartist agitation. Large meetings at which violence was openly advocated were held through 1838, until a frightened government refused to allow further demonstrations.

A manifesto having a distinct class bias charged the government with despotism and the enslavement of labor. It denounced the degradation of the worker by the machine, and complained that poverty was being regarded as a crime. It urged the masses to fight for justice, peacefully if possible, forcefully if need be.[9] Other measures were also advocated, including the withdrawal of funds from savings banks and their conversion to gold and silver in order to put a strain on the banks. A sacred month or a general strike was also urged. Despite these militant tactics, the Charter was rejected by the House of Commons and the government replied by instituting a campaign of repression. Hundreds were arrested and sentenced to prison for sedition.

The Newport Rising   The defeat of the Charter and the repressive policies of the government evoked countermeasures by the "physical-force"

8 "Address and Rules of the Working Men's Association for Benefiting Socially and Morally the Useful Classes." Quoted by Frank B. Rosenblatt, *The Chartist Movement* (New York: Columbia University Press, 1916), p. 84.

9 *Ibid.*, pp. 167–169.

leaders. An armed rising was planned that provoked the government to sterner action.

The movement, after a short period of decline, revived again in the early 1840's. The revival was due largely to the bitter distress that spread over industrial England in "The Hungry Forties." Spontaneous strikes were converted by the Chartists into political demonstrations. Again the government responded with arrests and sentences to long imprisonment. An attempt to form a combination of Chartists and radical reformers failed. Feargus O'Connor turned his attention to land reform. A plot was purchased and shares were sold to subscribers. The enterprise, however, met with the opposition of many Chartists and its failure hurt the movement's prestige.

Another Chartist convention met in April, 1848, where a demonstration in London and a march on Parliament to present a new petition were planned. Alarmed, the government swore in 170,000 special constables to resist the threat. The meeting was held, but the march on Parliament was abandoned. This was the last gasp of the movement, which disintegrated during the next few years.

CAUSES OF DECLINE

The Chartists failed to attract an important section of the middle class by their agitation. Another handicap was their lack of a unified program. All types of reformers rallied around Chartism, and their differences weakened the movement. This absence of focus was especially evident in the economic views of the leaders. Lovett was a believer in improvement by voluntary means, a cooperator; O'Connor saw Chartism as a means of rebuilding a new peasantry and abolishing slums; J. R. Stephens and John Frost were most anxious to repeal the poor law; James Bronterre O'Brien had a scheme for currency reform and nationalization of land rents; and Ernest Jones stood for modern proletarian socialism.

Important personal differences played a role. Lovett, the believer in moral force, could not placate the followers of O'Connor. The latter was, however, too quarrelsome and erratic to win over the bulk of the leaders. This led to internal bickering and to the weakening of the movement. Perhaps the most important reason was the change in economic conditions. Factory legislation and repeal of the corn laws tended to remove many grievances, so that those seeking practical relief left the party, and only the followers of abstract principles remained.

CHRISTIAN SOCIALISM

Christian Socialism in England was the result of a reaction of a number of talented English churchmen to the evils of industrialism. Its founder, John Malcolm Forbes Ludlow (1821–1911), who had studied in France, had met there many socialists and acquired a knowledge of their principal views. He was able to rally to his side John Frederick Denison Maurice (1805–1872), an Anglican clergyman who had been deeply stirred by the sufferings of the poor. Appointed chaplain at Lincoln's Inn, he became acquainted with Ludlow, who was conversant with current social and political philosophies.[10] They were joined by Charles Kingsley, the novelist, and by Charles Blackford Mansfield. Influenced by the events of 1848, the four launched the Christian Socialist movement. In May, 1848, a weekly, *Politics for the People,* was issued. Its tone was moderate and reserved, and it "aimed rather at the ventilation of grievances, the discussion of problems, the expression of individual views, and the exposition of general principles than at detailed statements or a clearcut policy of reform." [11] It dealt with the general franchise, the possibility of social reform through legislation, the significance of the Bible, and the meaning of freedom, equality, and brotherly love. The discussions assumed that politics for the people must be either atheistic or Christian. "Quite deliberately Maurice and his followers adopted the name 'Christian Socialists,' thereby consciously opposing themselves to . . . 'unsocial Christians and un-Christian Socialists.' " [12]

The first publication did not gain many subscribers and was discontinued. Now they turned to other methods. Meetings with workingmen and others interested in the social problem were held beginning in April, 1849. From personal acquaintance, the Christian Socialists learned that workers looked upon Christian worship with "bitter hostility and repugnance. Scoldings had only driven them away and at the easy platitudes of many of the clergy they had simply laughed." [13] The Christian Socialists were naturally disturbed over the antireligious attitude of the workers, but they were also opposed to the laissez-faire doctrines of the Manchester school.

10 Lujo Brentano, *Die Christlich Soziale Bewegung in England* (Leipzig: Verlag von Duncker und Humboldt, 1883), p. 25.
11 Charles E. Raven, *Christian Socialism* (London: Macmillan & Co., 1920), p. 112.
12 Quoted from the *Christian Socialist,* January 25, 1851, in Cyril K. Gloyn, *The Church in the Social Order* (Forest Grove, Ore.: Pacific University, 1942), p. 134.
13 *The Life of Frederick Denison Maurice.* Edited by Frederick Maurice (New York: Charles Scribner's Sons, 1884), II, 67.

PRODUCERS' COOPERATION

Unwilling to limit themselves to propaganda, the Christian Socialists established in February, 1850, a cooperative workshop for making clothes. "The watchword of the Socialist is Co-operation; the watchword of the Anti-Socialist is Competition. Anyone who recognizes the principle of co-operation as a stronger and truer principle than that of competition has a right to the honor or the disgrace of being called a Socialist." [14]

Several producers' associations were started, but the missionary activities of leading Christian Socialists were perhaps more important than their actual projects. The producers' cooperatives were to demonstrate the existence of an alternative to competition. Eliminating the relation of employer and employee not only would lead to the economic improvement in the conditions of labor, but would remove the basis of the class war. Christian Socialists believed their activity was part of their religious duties, and that "it is the special vocation of the Church in this age to carry out this work . . . to help men to *work* together for the supply of their own necessities and those of others as well as pray together." [15]

The experiments of the English Christian Socialists met with failure. They were unable to overcome the difficulties inherent in producers' cooperatives. Lack of capital, absence of discipline, and stubbornness put an end to their efforts, but they demonstrated that it is possible not only to harmonize cooperation and Christianity, but to show their spiritual similarity and interdependence. As in our own time, they demonstrated that a collectivist view can be based upon a religious as well as a materialist philosophy. Christian Socialism was a doctrine of nonviolent social change based upon religious feeling; it showed that religion is not hostile to fundamental social change. Christian Socialism helped to modify

all future forms of socialism in accordance with the English temperament, by insuring in the ranks of future socialist bodies the infusion of a number of earnest men who regarded socialism as a fundamental part of their religion. Among a people such as the English essentially inclined to compromise and unwilling definitely to break with any belief or custom this service to the cause was an invaluable one, and smoothed the way for the spread of socialism among people who would probably never have listened to it.[16]

14 *Tracts on Christian Socialism*, No. 1.
15 *The Christian Socialist*, April 5, 1851. Quoted in Gloyn, *op. cit.*, p. 137.
16 Brougham Villiers, *The Socialist Movement in England* (London: T. Fisher Unwin, 1908), p. 60.

LIMITED OBJECTIVE

The 1850's and 1860's witnessed a basic change in the attitude of English labor and radicalism. There emerged a strong disinclination to listen to utopian discourses and a strong desire to concentrate upon trade-union work. The leaders of the trade-union movement accepted the orthodox economic views held by the majority of businessmen and by the learned professions.

Victorian trade unionism rejected the utopian idealism of the earlier period, and, in the main, accepted the existing order. The growing trade unions sought to improve the bargaining position of their own members, and not to make the world a better place for all. The first sign of the new spirit was the organization of the Amalgamated Society of Engineers in 1851, accomplished largely through the efforts of William Newton and Robert Allan. "The generous but impracticable 'universalism' of the Owenite and Chartist organizations was replaced by the principle of the protection of the vested interests of the craftsman in his occupation." [17]

The "new model" trade unions were exclusive organizations, and their financial and administrative systems enabled the unions to combine the function of protecting the trade with a system of friendly benefits or insurance. Thus the unions acquired a level of financial stability hitherto not attained. The new movement was a "grass roots affair." It was initiated by workers and not by wealthy philanthropists or religious-minded humanitarians. The watchword of the trade unionist was "no politics within the union." The leaders accepted the capitalistic system, and cooperated with the liberals to gain concessions. This policy of "Lib-Lab" reduced the influence of the socialists in England to a minimum at the time they were gaining ground on the Continent. A few socialist clubs usually existed among the Continental exiles, whose discussions and disagreements sometimes overflowed into native radical channels. The Rose Club, the best known of these groups, was the scene of a dispute between Marxists and anarchists.[18]

While the "new model" unionists dominated the movement in the 1860's, English workers participated in the fight for a reform of the franchise. The London Workingmen's Association, founded in 1866, had as its object "the political enfranchisement of the workers and the pro-

[17] Sidney and Beatrice Webb, *The History of Trade Unionism* (Workers' Educational Association, 1919), p. 217.

[18] G. D. H. Cole, *British Working Class Politics* (London: Routledge and Kegan Paul, Ltd., 1941), p. 81.

motion of the social and general interests of the industrial classes." [19] It was in the Chartist tradition, well to the left of the Junta and the "new model" unionists. After the enactment of the Reform Act in 1867, the London Workingmen's Association urged the support of labor candidates for Parliament, but the organization disappeared after two years of activity.

The next step in the political development of labor was the formation of the Labour Representation League. Both the followers of George Potter and the Junta were represented. The League sought to mobilize the votes of labor so as

to secure the return to Parliament of qualified workingmen-persons who, by character and ability, command the confidence of their class, and who are competent to deal satisfactorily with questions of general interest as well as those in which they are specially interested. Beyond this, it will, where deemed necessary, recommend support as candidates from among the other classes such persons as have studied the great Labour problem, and have proved themselves friendly to the equitable settlement of the many difficult points which it involves.[20]

For a time, it appeared as if the League would eventually emerge as a labor party, but increasingly the League concentrated upon gaining representation of labor in Parliament, and by 1875 it had ceased to exist. Labor leaders showed their lack of interest in a socialistic program, in state intervention in industry, and in legal legislation of conditions of work, but they cooperated whenever possible with the Liberal party in what became known as "Lib-Lab." In the 1880's, a change occurred.

[19] Quotation, *ibid.*, p. 39.
[20] Quotation, *ibid.*, p. 50.

14. *THE ENGLISH LABOR PARTIES*

With the formation of the Democratic Federation in 1881—converted into the Social-Democratic Federation two years later—the modern socialist movement was launched in England. However, it was not the socialism of Maurice or Owen, but of Marx, that was offered the English people.

THE DEMOCRATIC FEDERATION

Dissatisfaction with the Gladstone government, elected after the Midlothian campaign, led to a conference of a number of radical spirits which in turn resulted in the organization of the Social-Democratic Federation on June 8, 1881. Its leader was Henry Mayers Hyndman (1842–1921), the author of *England for All*. The program was radical but reminiscent of Chartism rather than of Marxism. Nationalization of the land and industry, state aid for workers' housing, universal and free education, a legal eight-hour day for employees, public works for the unemployed, graduated income taxes, and redemption of the national debt were part of its program. *Justice,* the first Marxist socialist journal in England, was founded at this time. The organization attracted to its ranks a number of gifted men and women, the foremost being William Morris, the poet. The Social-Democratic Federation became a purely Marxist group. Its agitation did not attract a mass following, but it marked the beginning of an active Marxist propaganda movement.

THE SOCIALIST LEAGUE

The Social-Democratic Federation was dominated by Hyndman, a man of strong and dictatorial temper. Differences had arisen over politics and the means used to spread the doctrine of the organization. Morris strongly opposed centralization and feared state socialism as a new form of tyranny. Instead of political activity, Morris wished to emphasize education.[1] Unable to bridge their differences, Morris and his followers seceded and established the Socialist League on Decmber 30, 1884. A journal, the *Commonweal*, was founded. Morris wrote, spoke, and gave freely of his means. When the group was captured by the anarchists in 1890, Morris withdrew, and the organization ended its existence two years later. Morris then founded the Hammersmith Socialist Society. The manifesto written by him declared that the aim of socialists must be "not the dissolution of society, but its reintegration. The idea put forward by some who attack present society, of the complete independence of every individual, that is, of freedom without society, is not merely impossible of realization, but, when looked into, turns out to be inconceivable." [2]

Morris now came closer to Hyndman's Social-Democratic Federation, and he began to contribute to its publication, *Justice,* and to lecture before its forums. He also tried to unify warring groups of socialists.[3]

Although the Social-Democratic Federation withstood the secession in 1884, it was almost wrecked by accepting financial support from the Tories for two of its candidates. The Tories hoped to split the labor vote and thus defeat the Liberal candidate. The Federation was bitterly assailed, although it was saved from collapse by the severe depression of 1886. Parades and agitation against unemployment were organized, but the Federation's influence declined with the revival of business.

THE FABIAN SOCIETY

The Fabian Society was organized in 1883 by a small group of English intellectuals whose common bond was their belief in collectivism. This group played an important role in the history of British socialism, and though never numerous the members were often able to exercise a significant influence upon British political life. The following resolution, enacted at one of the early meetings, expressed their views:

The members of the Society assert that the Competitive system assures the happiness and comfort of the few at the expense of the suffering of the many and

1 See Max Beer, *A History of British Socialism* (London: George Bell & Sons, Ltd., 1919), Vol. II, Chap. 13. This two-volume work is very useful for the intellectual currents in English socialist movements.

2 Quoted in May Morris, *William Morris, Artist, Writer, and Socialist* (Oxford: Basil Blackwell, 1936), I, 327.

3 H. W. Lee and E. Archbold, *Social-Democracy in Britain* (London: Social-Democratic Federation, 1935).

that Society must be reconstituted in such a manner as to secure the general welfare and happiness.[4]

The Fabian Society advocated collectivism but it was not a doctrinaire socialist group. It differed from other socialist organizations in that it rejected Marx's doctrines of the class war, surplus value, and the materialist conception of history. The Fabians refused to combine with socialist groups promulgating these doctrines.

FABIAN ESSAYS

Chief credit for the establishment and the progress of the Fabian Society belongs to the Fabian essayists, who were experts on many social and economic questions and were ready to present a reasoned examination of every contemporary problem, supporting their conclusions with facts and figures. The results were embodied in a low-priced pamphlet which was widely distributed among workers and middle-class citizens. The Fabians, some of whom were well versed in economics and statistics, were able to use the work of academic writers for their own purposes. In 1912, the Fabian Research Department was set up to investigate numerous economic and political problems. Under the direction of the Webbs and such men as G. D. H. Cole, many phases of English economic and social life were examined. The Fabians avoided the specialized jargon of the Marxists and the dreary discourse on the class war, and dealt with day-to-day problems in easily understood terms.

Socialism as first preached to the English people by the Social Democrats, was narrow, as bigoted, as exclusive as the strictest of Scotch religious sects. *Das Kapital,* Volume I was its bible; and the thoughts and schemes of English socialists were to be approved or condemned according as they could or could not be justified by a quoted text. The Fabian Society freed English socialism from this intellectual bondage, and freed it sooner and more completely than the "Revisionists" have succeeded in doing elsewhere.[5]

The Fabian Society favored municipal ownership of public utilities, factory and welfare legislation, and the strengthening of trade unions as methods of improving the position of the masses. The Fabians also demanded the socialization of rents. In the Fabian view, rents "include all differential unearned incomes, from land, from ability, from opportunity

4 Edward R. Pease, *The History of the Fabian Society* (New York: E. P. Dutton & Co., 1916), p. 32. The quotations from this source are reprinted by permission of the publishers.
5 *Ibid.,* p. 236.

[i.e., special profits], interest includes all non-differential unearned incomes, and thus the State is to be endowed, not with rents alone, but with all unearned incomes." [6]

While the Fabians concentrated their main attack upon unearned incomes, which they regarded as the least defensible aspect of capitalism, they also advocated the "municipalization and nationalization" of enterprise. By taking over enterprises, the state could receive the profits of management. The capitalist is to be compensated by interest-bearing securities. He thus becomes a receiver of unearned income, and fair game for taxation.

Largely intellectuals, the Fabians sought to "permeate all classes, from top to bottom, with a common opinion in favor of socially-created values." [7] The Fabians aimed at making England more democratic by socializing industry, and the members of the society joined other organizations in order to permeate them with Fabian views. The slow advances of the trade unions were in harmony with Fabian aspirations. From the outset, the Fabians were reformist and avoided revolutionary slogans. They stood for democratic control, but at the same time they favored the expert. The Fabian Society has sought to persuade the English people to make their constitution more democratic, and they favored socialized industry so as to free it from dependence upon private capitalism.

The Fabian Society leaned on the theories of Jevons rather than on those of Marx. According to Jevons, value of a good is determined by the utility of the last unit consumed. Therefore, it is possible by transferring units from the rich to the poor to increase the value derived from consumption. In other words, the Fabians argued that a dollar of income has more value to the poor than a similar amount to the rich, and that total utility would be raised by transfers from the rich to the poor. On this basis, high income and inheritance taxes, redistribution of wealth, and government enterprise could be justified by the increase in total utility that would ensue.

THE NEW UNIONISM

The trade unions that had been organized in the 1850's and 1860's—the "new model"—were content with modest gains. Their membership largely limited to the highly skilled workers, the unions sought to win

[6] *Ibid.*, pp. 245–246.
[7] Ernest Barker, *Political Thought in England* (New York: Henry Holt and Company, 1916), p. 219.

concessions on the job, but they also furnished insurance benefits to their members. Politics was avoided, for the leaders did not believe in the possibility or even the desirability of social reorganization. Trade unionists generally approved this policy and "for over twenty years no Trade Unionists questioned its excellence." [8]

An influx of new members and the expansion of some of the semi-skilled unions brought a more militant and socialistic group into the trade-union movement. Socialist leaders also gained prestige from their leadership of the unemployed demonstrations in 1886. Socialism was thereby made known to thousands of workers, many of whom began accepting it as a fighting faith. Another significant event which aided the growth of socialist sentiment among the workers was the dockers' strike at London.

The London dockers were unorganized and bitterly exploited. Under socialist leadership they managed, over the opposition of their employers, to establish a union and win concessions. Success on the London docks had repercussions in other industries and in other sections of the country. The new unions differed in policy and organization from the older societies. As a rule the unions concentrated upon the improvement of economic conditions and avoided fraternal activities. Even more, the "new unionists" brought a changed attitude into the movement. Unlike the older leaders, they were not opposed to government intervention in economic affairs and, in fact, many of the leaders of the "new unionism" were active socialists.[9]

INDEPENDENT LABOUR PARTY

The growing socialistic influence affected the attitude of the trade unions on many social and economic questions. Union members who were socialists were likely to regard economic activity as only one aspect of the struggle for a better world. Political action based upon an independent party was another. Marxism, with its elaborate doctrine and specialized jargon, had little appeal for English labor. There were, however, a group of socialists who, while opposing the policy of labor cooperation with the Liberals, wanted also to avoid the revolutionary slogans of the Marxist Social-Democratic Federation. While favoring socialism as

[8] Sidney and Beatrice Webb, *The History of Trade Unionism* (Workers' Educational Association, 1919), p. 217.
[9] G. D. H. Cole, *A Short History of the British Working Class Movement* (London: George Allen & Unwin, Ltd., 1926), III, 152–164.

an ultimate aim, the group, led by James Keir Hardie (1856–1915), wanted to win over the trade unions by concentrating upon immediate reforms. A first step toward forming an independent labor political party was taken in 1888, when Hardie, the secretary of the Scottish Miners' Federation, stood as an independent candidate for Mid-Lanark. Hardie was defeated, but his candidacy led to the forming of the Scottish Labour party. It was not a thorough socialistic organization. Nationalization of the banks and railways, land reform, and an eight-hour workday were advocated. In the general election of 1892, the Scottish Labour party presented eight candidates. None was successful. A number of journals helped the cause, the most influential being *The Clarion,* edited by Robert Blatchford.[10]

At a conference of delegates in Bradford in 1893, the Independent Labour party was formed. It advocated collective ownership of the means of production, distribution, and exchange. The eight-hour day; abolition of child labor; public provision for the sick, the aged, and widows and orphans; free, nonsectarian education; and public employment of the unemployed were demanded. The Independent Labour party, while adopting a socialist program, made its appeal on an ethical and democratic basis, and not upon the doctrines of class war. The members "used few phrases that were not drawn from the common stock of British thought. They were trade unionists, inspired indeed by socialism, but just as much interested, generally more so, in current questions of wages and hours as any member of the unions to which they belonged." [11]

The socialists who belonged to the I.L.P. did not set themselves up as a race apart from other workers. As a rule, the socialist shared the vices and the virtues of his fellow workers, and frequently he was a local preacher in the Methodist church. Nor did the views of the I.L.P. on questions such as the family, marriage, or religion differ from those held by other members of the community. The party thereby avoided arousing the opposition of those who might favor economic reform, but would oppose attacks upon other social institutions. In fact, on noneconomic issues the member of the Independent Labour party was likely to hold the same views as those of other members of the community. The fact that the socialism was reformist, moderate, and undoctrinaire made it acceptable

10 G. D. H. Cole, *British Working Class Politics* (London: Routledge and Kegan Paul, Ltd., 1941), pp. 128–130.

11 Brougham Villiers, *The Socialist Movement in England* (London: T. Fisher Unwin, 1908), p. 132.

to the British worker. It was a typical British product and its appeal was to conscience rather than to logic.

Branches were organized and propaganda was spread throughout the north of England. The party attracted a group of competent propagandists whose main emphasis in the early years was the need for an independent political party of labor. Although few parliamentary constituencies were gained in the early years, members of the Independent Labour party were elected to local offices, where they gained experience in the art of government and became better known to the public. Nevertheless, the leaders of the Independent Labour party realized that another organization was needed to cement an alliance between the trade unions and political socialism.

LABOUR REPRESENTATION COMMITTEE

Following the formation of the Independent Labour party, the socialists made renewed efforts to win the trade unions to socialism. The older leaders wanted to continue their alliance with the Liberals. To weaken the influence of the socialists, those who did not work at their trade or were not employed by a trade union were excluded as delegates to local trades councils, where the socialistic influences had been strongest; the "card vote," under which delegates' votes were based upon the number of constituents, was also introduced.

Finally, at the Trades-Union Congress[12] of 1899, a resolution to establish the Labour Representation Committee was introduced by the Amalgamated Society of Railway Servants. It instructed "the Parliamentary Committee to invite the cooperation of all working-class organizations to jointly co-operate on lines mutually agreed upon in convening a special Congress of representatives from such of the above named organizations as may be willing to take part to devise ways and means for the securing of an increased number of Labour members in the next Parliament." [13] It was adopted by a vote of 546,000 to 434,000. The committee was made up of twelve members from trade unions, ten from co-operative societies, and two from each of the following: The Fabian

[12] The Trades-Union Congress meets annually to review the progress of the English labor movement, express its hopes and decry its losses. Issues that affect the general interest of labor are discussed and a program and policy are adopted. The Parliamentary Committee, annually chosen, presents its views to cabinet officers and Parliament.

[13] *The Book of the Labour Party.* Edited by Herbert Tracey (London: Caxton Publishing Co., 1925), Vol. I, Chap. 4.

Society, the Independent Labour party, and the Social-Democratic Federation.

To the conference, which met in London on February 27, 1900, the three socialist political groups—the Independent Labour party, the Fabian Society, and the Social-Democratic Federation—sent delegates, as did trade unions with a membership of 500,000 members. Some delegates wanted a pure socialist party based upon a recognition of the class war. Approval of such a proposal would have wrecked the conference. Also rejected was the suggestion that a few proposals be drawn up and candidates for Parliament asked to endorse them. This proposal would have made the formation of a separate party of labor impossible. Instead, the conference approved "a distinct labour group in Parliament who shall have their own Whip and agree upon their policy, which must embrace a readiness to cooperate with any party which, for the time being, may be engaged in promoting legislation in the direct interest of Labour, and be equally ready to associate themselves with any party opposing measures having an opposite tendency." [14] The compromise was the work of Keir Hardie, who, in his anxiety to gain the support of the trade unions, avoided a breach on the issue of an independent political party. The Labour Representation Committee was a compromise, as the trade unions would at the time have refused to accept a socialist party. On the other hand, the socialists had taken the first step toward detaching the trade unions from their alliance with the Liberals. An executive committee of twelve was set up. James Ramsay MacDonald, who was later to become the first Labour prime minister, was chosen secretary.

TAFF-VALE DECISION

Independent political action by labor was immensely stimulated by the Taff-Vale decision. It frightened the trade unions and aroused them to more active political participation. In 1900 an "outlaw" strike was called on the Taff-Vale Railway, a small Welsh line. Subsequently the strike was endorsed by the Amalgamated Society of Railway Servants, and the railroad brought suit for damages against the union and its members. It was generally believed that trade-union funds were amply protected by the law of 1871, but to the surprise and consternation of the trade-union movement, the company received a verdict of 23,000 pounds, plus costs.

14 *Ibid.*, pp. 121–123.

THE LABOUR PARTY

In the general election of 1906, the Labour Representation Committee became the Labour party, an effective political force with which the other parties had to reckon. The Labour party was not at the time a socialist party. Social and economic reforms, especially the overriding of the Taff-Vale decision, were uppermost in the minds of the trade unionists. The importance of the Labour victory was apparent when it forced the government to accept Labour's version of the Trade Disputes Act. The new act exempted trade-unions from damage suits for losses arising out of the actions of members of officers. A new assault against the Labour party developed in 1909, when a member of the Amalgamated Society of Railway Servants—Osborne by name—secured an injunction restraining the union from spending its funds for political purposes. Other unions were also restrained from financing political activities, and these decisions destroyed the Labour party's chief sources of income. The effects of these judgments were mainly reversed in 1913, when Parliament allowed the unions to carry on political activity.[15]

EARLY LEADERS

At the beginning, Keir Hardie, Ramsay MacDonald (1866–1937), Arthur Henderson (1863–1935), and Philip Snowden (1864–1937) were the dominant figures of Parliamentary Labour. MacDonald was a great asset during the party's formative years, but he seriously harmed it when he agreed to head a national ministry in 1931.

Arthur Henderson lacked great oratorical gifts, but he was an earnest, patient organizer. Companionable and kindly, he understood the trade unions and had their confidence. Henderson was not much concerned with the niceties of doctrine and "he had no craving for the social pleasures which attract other men. His only luxury seemed to be work." [16]

Philip Snowden differed from both MacDonald and Henderson in that he was hard and doctrinaire. His attitude may have arisen from a physical disability he suffered in early manhood. Acrid and forthright in speech, he left no doubt of his position. A brilliant and forceful debater, he was a great asset to the Labour party in Parliament. His conservatism in fiscal matters and the fear of national bankruptcy led him to side with Ramsay MacDonald in the crisis of 1931.

15 Cole, *British Working Class Politics*, pp. 200–204.
16 J. R. Clynes, *Memoirs* (London: Hutchinson and Co., 1937), II, 201, 210.

The Labour party perhaps owes more to James Keir Hardie than to the other three. A coal miner's son, he began work at the age of six. Self-educated, he took the first steps for an independent political party of labor in 1888, when he stood as an independent Labour candidate for Mid-Lanark. He was not doctrinaire, and he sought socialism so as to give the average citizen a better chance for a life of decency and dignity.

WORLD WAR I

British labor has always been pacifist in philosophy. Once war was declared, however, the majority of British workers and their organizations rallied to the government's aid. The leader of the Parliamentary Labour party, Ramsay MacDonald, resigned his leadership following the declaration of war and was succeeded by Arthur Henderson. On August 29 the Executive Committee of the Labour party agreed to an electoral truce with the Liberals and the unionists.[17]

Labour Joins the Coalition   Members of the Labour party accepted places in Lloyd George's coalition. The step was generally approved, although the opposition of large sections of the Independent Labour party and the British Socialist party, a Marxian group, was aroused. At the Labour party conference in January, 1916, the adherents of coalition won decisively.[18]

In May, 1917, Henderson was sent by the government on a mission to Russia. He was convinced that an international conference of labor and socialist leaders might help to end the war, and he approved of plans for the calling of such a meeting at Stockholm. Lloyd George strenuously objected to the fact that Henderson, a cabinet member, was working to revive the European socialist and labor movements. Henderson resigned, but the other labor cabinet members remained in the government until the Armistice. At a special conference in November, 1918, it was overwhelmingly decided that the Labour party renew its independence and leave the coalition.[19]

[17] Philip Viscount Snowden, *An Autobiography* (London: Ivor Nicholson and Watson, Ltd., 1934), I, 358.

[18] George M. Barnes, *From Workshop to War Cabinet* (New York: Appleton-Century-Crofts, Inc., 1924), pp. 138–141.

[19] Carl F. Brand, *British Labour's Rise to Power* (Stanford University, Calif.: Stanford University Press, 1941), pp. 50–54.

THE SHOP STEWARDS

Although the Labour party cooperated in the prosecution of World War I, opposition appeared among other socialist groups. The Socialist Labour party denounced the conflict as an imperialist war, and urged its members not to serve in the armed forces. The British Socialist party expelled its prowar faction. Led by Hyndman, this group set up the Nationalist Socialist party, while the British Socialist party carried on its opposition in terms of pacifist or class-war slogans. Although the antiwar agitation had no decisive effect, dissatisfaction with wages and working conditions led to the formation of the shop stewards' group, which later furnished a base for the English Communist party. Shop stewards are union representatives elected from among those employed in a shop to represent the union in the negotiation resulting from a grievance. Usually they are subordinate officers who carry out the official policy of the union. Shop stewards first appeared among the engineers—called machinists in the United States—and they emerged at the head of a faction opposed to the official leadership of the union.

In the meantime, unauthorized strikes forced concessions from the government. New leaders came to the front who were anxious to challenge the established labor institutions and their spokesmen. The shop stewards' movement furnished a favorable opportunity for the antiwar socialists and syndicalists to direct into revolutionary channels the dissatisfaction of the workers with wages and working conditions.[20] A committee was set up to unify the activities of the movement.

The shop stewards' movement soon spent its force and came under complete Communist domination. Transformed into the National Minority Movement in 1924,[21] as an economic arm of the Communist party, it succeeded in penetrating into a few unions.

More widespread among English labor was the opposition to armed intervention in Russia. In the summer of 1920 the London dock workers refused to load a ship carrying arms for the White Armies. Fear of more aggressive support of the White Armies led to a special conference of the Parliamentary Labour party, the Executive of the Labour party, and the Trades-Union Congress. The meeting charged that a war between the Allied Powers and Russia "is being engineered on the issue of Poland,"

[20] J. T. Murphy, *Preparing for Power* (London: Jonathan Cape, Ltd., 1934), p. 147.
[21] Allen Hutt, *British Trade Unionism: A Short History* (London: Lawrence and Wishart, 1941), p. 99.

and declared that "such a war would be an intolerable crime against humanity and therefore warns the government that the whole industrial power of the organized workers will be used to defeat this war." [22] A Council of Action was established to put the decisions into effect. The unsatisfactory replies of Lloyd George to a deputation led to a special conference. On three days' notice, one thousand delegates from affiliated societies assembled. The conference endorsed unanimously the calling of a general strike in case of war.[23] The government retreated. War was not declared and the Council of Action, its tasks accomplished, ceased to exist.

BASIC CHANGES IN THE LABOUR PARTY

At the outset, the Labour party was a federated body. It was difficult, except in a few instances, to join the Labour party as an individual member. Membership could be obtained by affiliating with one of the constituent socialist groups, the Independent Labour party, or the Fabian Society, or through an affiliated trade union. This situation gave the Independent Labour party great influence, although the Labour party was not socialist in either policy or aim. The leaders of the I.L.P. opposed World War I and thereby lost some of their influence with the rank and file supporting the government. Moreover, the collapse of the Liberal party made it mandatory for the Labour party to become a national political party seeking to gain a parliamentary majority. After World War I, the Labour party changed its organizational structure and became an explicitly socialist organization. The Labour party set up an individual member section, and those not belonging to the Labour party through membership in a trade union, cooperative society, or socialist group could join.[24] New local labor parties arose which became very important in local governments.

More important was the elaboration of an explicit socialist program. Up to 1918, the Labour party was mainly concerned with specific and limited reforms. No attempt was made to evolve a complete program or to indicate general objectives. *Labour and the New Social Order,* issued in 1918, was a socialist document. It is

22 Quoted by Snowden, *op. cit.,* II, 560.
23 *Ibid.,* p. 563.
24 C. R. Attlee, *The Labour Party in Perspective* (London: Victor Gollancz, Ltd., 1937), pp. 86–88.

a . . . systematic, and comprehensive plan for that immediate rebuilding which
any Ministry . . . will be driven to undertake. The Four Pillars of the House
we propose to erect, resting upon the common foundation of the Democratic
Control of society in all its activities, may be termed respectively:

    (a) The Universal Enforcement of the National Minimum,

    (b) The Democratic Control of Industry,

    (c) The Revolution in National Finance, and

    (d) The Surplus of Wealth for the Common Good.[25]

The first part deals with the assurance for every citizen of at least a
minimum standard of living by the community. In addition, the program
advocated a policy of public works to balance the cycle. The second demand—democratic control of industry—had reference to public ownership of industry under parliamentary control. The third point called for
a revision of the system of taxation and for a capital levy as a method of
paying for the war. Surplus wealth for the common good means the use
of the country's resources for public ends, including improved education.

As expressed in the Labour party's constitution, its object is "to secure
for the workers by hand or by brain the full fruits of their industry and
the most equitable distribution thereof that may be possible, upon the
basis of common ownership of the means of production, distribution and
exchange, and the best obtainable system of popular administration and
control of each industry and service." [26] The objectives are to be gained
by constitutional action, and violence and revolution as political instruments are rejected. The aims are to be achieved without violating the
rule of law, a priceless treasure of the Anglo-Saxon world. Social reform,
at a slow pace, is preferable to violence for it is unaccompanied by concentration camps, secret police, and arbitrary arrests. The Labour party
has not sought to gain economic security through the creation of civic
insecurity.

THE FIRST LABOUR GOVERNMENT

In 1924 a Labour government took office for the first time. In the
elections of 1922, the Labour party had almost doubled the number of
seats it held in Parliament, and when the Conservatives appealed to the
country on the issue of tariff reform, the Labour party increased its
parliamentary representation by forty-eight. The Conservatives lost

[25] *Labour and the New Social Order* (London: The Labour Party, 1918), pp. 4–5.
[26] Quoted in Attlee, *op. cit.*, p. 137.

ground, and although they remained the strongest party, their numbers in Parliament were fewer than the combined Liberal and Labour votes.

The Liberals agreed to support the Labour party, which accepted the opportunity to form a new government.[27] Ramsay MacDonald was chosen prime minister, Philip Snowden, chancellor of the exchequer, and J. R. Clynes, lord privy seal. Of the twenty cabinet officers, only seven were trade unionists, and a number had little or no record of activity in the Labour party.[28]

The first Labour government was dependent upon the sufferance of the Liberal party for its tenure of office. The fact that no steps could be taken or policy developed without the tacit approval of the latter tied the hands of the government, but the first Labour government showed that it was not lacking in capacity. It re-established relations with Soviet Russia. On the domestic front, it raised old-age pensions, restored the minimum wage in agriculture, and increased expenditure for education and the social services. It also put through an act to finance low-cost housing. The Labour government fell on a rather trivial issue, the prosecution of a Communist writer.

The high light of the following election campaign was a letter, presumably signed by Zinoviev as president of the Executive Committee of the Communist International, which urged the use of pressure upon Parliament so that the pending treaty between Great Britain and Russia would be ratified. The letter, full of the usual Communist slogans, helped to throw many votes to the Conservatives.[29] The Labour party increased its popular vote, but it suffered a net loss of forty-one seats. After the election, Stanley Baldwin became prime minister at the head of a huge Conservative majority.

THE GENERAL STRIKE

No summary of important events of the political movement of English labor can ignore the general strike of 1926. It was an event of momentous importance with a united English labor movement arrayed against industry and the government. Fought over a purely economic issue, the general strike was a dangerous threat to the British labor movement, although the danger remained potential rather than actual. The origin of

27 Clynes, op. cit., I, 341.
28 Snowden, op. cit., II, 605.
29 This letter is republished as Appendix I, ibid., II, 1043–1045.

the strike goes back to the difficulties facing the British coal-mining industry. Soon after the end of World War I, the British coal miners, acting through the Miners' Federation, demanded improved wages and hours as well as state ownership and democratic control of the mines. A Royal Commission under the chairmanship of Justice Sankey recommended nationalization and a measure of workers' control. The recommendations were rejected by the government.

Several other commissions were appointed, but none recommended a solution acceptable to both parties. Early in 1926, the Samuel Commission, the last one appointed before the general strike, recommended downward revision of all but the lowest wages, continuance of national agreements, and an end to government subsidy. The union refused to agree, and negotiations to end the deadlock were futile. Thereupon the miners appealed to the Trades' Union Congress for support.

A majority of the General Council of the British Trades Union Congress was anxious to avoid a general strike, but the refusal of the government to seek a way out forced a reluctant decision upon the leaders. A general strike was called for midnight, May 3, and the reaction was very favorable. Virtually all who were called out responded and remained on strike until the end. It was a remarkable demonstration of labor solidarity unaccompanied by violence. Winston Churchill, then chancellor of the exchequer, raised the cry of civil war and charged that the strike endangered parliamentary government.[30] Actually the trade unions were not prepared for such a venture. British labor is nonrevolutionary and never dreamed of taking power except by constitutional means. The strikers tried to frighten the government and, having failed, they had, in fact, lost the battle.

Termination of the general strike was announced by Arthur Pugh, chairman of the General Council. Only Ernest Bevin stood out for a pledge against reprisals, and for a promise that neogtiations in the mining industry would be resumed.[31] Although the government urged employers to avoid reprisals, many workers lost their jobs. The government introduced the Trade Disputes and Trade Union Act of 1927, which made a strike illegal except in furtherance of a trade dispute in the trade or industry in which the strikers are engaged, and outlawed stoppages seeking to place pressure on the government. Unions of civil service em-

[30] Wilfred H. Crook, *The General Strike* (Chapel Hill: The University of North Carolina Press, 1931), p. 403.
[31] *Ibid.*, pp. 432–433.

ployees were denied the right to affiliate with outside labor groups. The conditions under which trade unions were allowed to make political contributions were changed. Under the law of 1913, unions could contribute to political parties, but members could refuse by "contracting out"—signing a statement of unwillingness to donate for this purpose. The law was changed so that no labor union could collect money for political purposes, except from those members who had agreed in writing to contribute. The miners, for whom the general strike was called, were left to continue their uneven struggle alone. A prolonged strike ate up their meager resources, and in November, 1926, the government enacted an eight-hour law for the mines. Peace was made on a district basis, with the miners in fact starved back to the pits. The penalties against the unions were not repealed until 1946, when the Labour government, commanding an ample majority, pushed the repeals through the House of Commons.

THE SECOND LABOUR GOVERNMENT

The general election of 1929 resulted in the Labour party's becoming the largest party in Parliament, but short of a majority. Labour again took office with Liberal consent and Ramsay MacDonald became prime minister. The Independent Labour party, dissatisfied with the program, refused to abide by the standing orders to support the party in Parliament, and at a special conference of the I.L.P. withdrew from the Labour party in 1932.

CRISIS IN THE LABOUR GOVERNMENT

The most serious issue facing the Labour government was the high level of unemployment. The rise in the number of unemployed, and the reduction in state contributions to the insurance fund, imposed a burden upon the Treasury. In accordance with its promise, the Labour government proposed an increase in benefits to certain groups.[32] However, Chancellor of the Exchequer Philip Snowden was a believer in financial orthodoxy and a balanced budget. In a speech to the House of Commons in February, 1931, Snowden warned that "schemes" involving heavy expenditure "however desirable they may be, will have to wait until prosperity returns . . . and no class will ultimately benefit more by present

[32] Snowden, op. cit., II, 843–848.

economy than wage earners." [33] A committee was appointed to examine the problem and to suggest remedies.

Betrayal by MacDonald The May Committee, with two members dissenting, recommended a drastic reduction of expenditures, the burden falling on the unemployed and teachers. The Labour party leaders and members rejected these recommendations, but the socialist chancellor was convinced that the drastic remedies prescribed by the May Committee were in the interests of labor.

The General Council of the Trades-Union Congress refused to agree to cut in unemployment benefits, and Snowden was advised by Ernest Bevin and Walter Citrine, spokesmen for the congress, that they "oppose any interference with the existing terms and conditions on the Unemployment Insurance scheme, including the limitation of statutory benefits to twenty-six weeks. We were told that the trade unions oppose the suggested economies on teachers' salaries and pay of the men in the fighting services, and any suggestion for reducing expenditures on works in relief of unemployment." [34] MacDonald asked for the resignation of the cabinet officers not approving the cuts. He then became the head of a national government made up of all parties but Labour. In the general election that followed, the Labour party suffered a serious reversal. It was a catastrophic defeat, and it taught Labour the "outstanding lesson . . . that nationalization of banks and big business is necessary to the nation's safety." [35]

RESURGENCE AND THE END OF PACIFISM

With increasing international tension, the Labour party reversed its traditional policy of pacifism in 1934 and demanded the imposition of sanctions against Italy for its invasion of Abyssinia, even if it led to war. Moreover, the reversal was brought about by the trade unionists, dominated by Bevin, rather than by the intellectual socialists.

In a series of conferences from 1934 to 1939 the movement worked out almost unanimously a policy in terms of the interests of the British workers. The attempts, led by Lansbury and Cripps, to retain the traditional pacifist and abstentionist policies of the movement were squarely met and defeated.[36]

33 Quotation, *ibid.,* p. 894.
34 *Ibid.,* p. 942.
35 Clynes, *op. cit.,* II, 209.
36 *Labour's Next Step.* Tract Series No. 252 (London: The Fabian Society, 1940), p. 7.

In the general election that followed, Labour won 154 seats and polled a total of 8,500,000 votes, 2,000,000 fewer than the Conservatives. Clement Attlee was chosen leader of the Opposition.

ATTEMPT AT A UNITED FRONT

With the rise of the danger from the fascist forces, the doctrine of the "united front" was promulgated by a group of English intellectuals, members of the Socialist League, the Independent Labour party, and the Communist party. The Labour party, however, refused to go along. The Labour party regarded the Independent Labour party as incorrigible, for after years of membership in the Labour party, it had broken away in 1932. Communists who followed a foreign line were not sufficiently reliable. In March, 1937, the Executive Committee of the Labour party announced that membership in the Socialist League was incompatible with membership in the Labour party.[37] The Executive Committee of the Labour party based its view on the decision taken at the annual conference in 1934. At that conference, the Communist party was declared ineligible for affiliation with the Labour party. In addition, it was decided to reject "organizations auxiliary or subsidiary to the Communist party." [38] Thereupon the Socialist League was disbanded.

In the Labour party there developed, especially after the debacle of 1931, a deep distrust of intellectuals. The trade unions felt that MacDonald, Snowden, and finally Oswald Mosley, all nonworkers, had betrayed the movement. Increasingly the trade unions sought to exercise a dominant influence in the affairs of the party and to wield the power that their numbers gave them. This was presumably achieved by holding the meeting of the Trades-Union Congress several weeks ahead of the Labour party conference, and marshaling the trade-union vote behind a given point of view. A friendly critic admits that had "the trade unions been in command in 1931, the Labour Party could not have been forced into the equivocal position which it came to occupy over the treatment of the unemployed: for on 'straight' working-class issues of domestic social reform the trade unions can be relied on to take the right views when a crisis arises." [39]

[37] Patricia Strauss, *Cripps* (New York: Duell, Sloan and Pearce, Inc., 1942), pp. 158–161.
[38] An Appeal to the Movement by the Labour Party Executive Committee in G. D. H. Cole, *The People's Front* (London: Victor Gollancz, Ltd., 1937), pp. 353–356.
[39] *Ibid.*, p. 294.

GENERAL OBJECTIVES

Clement Attlee, elected leader of the Parliamentary Labour party in 1935, declared the "aim of the Labour Party is the establishment of the Cooperative Commonwealth." [40] Socialism as it is envisaged by the British Labour party aims to give greater freedom to the individual. State intervention is held to be a means of freeing the individual from oppression, and not a means of placing power in the hands of a small group. Socialism aims at security, the elimination of idleness, and the assurance that all capable of employment will receive jobs.[41]

40 Attlee, *op. cit.*, p. 137.
41 Quotation, *ibid.*, p. 137.

15. *ENGLISH LABOR IN POWER*

BRITISH LABOR AND WORLD WAR II

With the exception of a few extreme pacifists, the entire British working class, exclusive of the Communists, rallied to the defense of England at the declaration of war. In a "Manifesto," the "British Labour Movement . . . declared that there are no international disputes incapable of settlement by peaceful negotiations.

Equally, however, it has always insisted that aggression on the part of any Power must be resisted. It has declared that the use of Force in international disputes must be made forever impossible. The decision of the British Government to resist the latest efforts of conquest by aggression on the part of Hitler therefore receives the full support of the Labour Movement in this country. It has long criticized the policy of the National Government. It stands by that criticism. Had it been followed it believes that a different world would now be in being. But as it stood by Czecho-Slovakia on this principle, so British Labour stands also by Poland.[1]

Similarly, the "Trades Union Congress believes that the Nazi Government, having chosen for its people the way of war, must be resisted to the utmost." [2] The British Labour party refused to join the Chamberlain government, whose weak policies it held, had brought England and the world to the brink of disaster. It recognized, however, the indispensability of an Allied victory to future freedom and progress. At no time were the leaders of the Labour party fooled by Hitler. Hugh Dalton, chancellor of the exchequer in the Labour government, expressed the views of the party: "We knew too much about the Nazis. They had murdered per-

[1] C. R. Attlee and Others, *Labour's Aims in War and Peace* (London: Lincolns-Prager, Ltd., no date), p. 9. The quotations from this work are reprinted by permission of the publishers.
[2] *Ibid.*, p. 11.

sonal friends of ours in Germany—men whom we used to meet at international conferences in the old days. They had suppressed the trade unions, the cooperative societies and the Socialist Party of Germany." [3]

At its annual conference in Bournemouth in 1940, the Labour party declared itself a socialist party, and it conceived of reconstruction in socialistic terms. It rejected "all demands for Dictatorship, whether from the Left or from the Right. We take our stand upon that faith in reason which looks to the declared will of the people as the only valid source of power. So long as that will is nationally respected, we are confident that the historic forms of Parliamentary Democracy provide a highroad along which the nation can pass peacefully from an acquisitive to a Socialist society." [4]

The declaration advocated the transference of the key industries, services, and banks to public authority. Investment is to be directed in accordance with public interest and not with private profit. Public ownership and control of coal and power, of basic transportation, and, gradually, of land must be introduced. Nationalized industries will have to be reorganized to raise their efficiency. "Individual initiative and ability must not be restricted, but must be directed to the service of the community." [5] Control of the location of industry was urged so as to promote public health and preserve the beauties of the countryside.

LABOUR ENTERS THE GOVERNMENT

Labour's attitude toward World War II passed through several stages. From the first the labor movement supported the war wholeheartedly. However, Labour refused to join the government under Neville Chamberlain. Clement R. Attlee summarized this attitude in a speech: "We are supporting this country against aggression, but I must remind you that we are still deeply critical of the government's past, critical of its present, and distrustful of its future." [6] On May 11, 1940, Labour helped to defeat the Chamberlain government, and it entered the Churchill cabinet. Clement Attlee became lord privy seal and deputy prime minister; Herbert Morrison, minister of supply and subsequently minister of home security; Ernest Bevin, minister of labour and national defense; Hugh Dalton,

---

[3] Hugh Dalton, "Peace Must Be Won for Humanity," *ibid.*, p. 139.

[4] "Declaration of Policy by the Conference of the British Labour Party," 1940, *ibid.*, pp. 142–143.

[5] *Ibid.*, p. 145.

[6] Quoted in *Labour's Next Step*. Tract Series No. 252, (London: The Fabian Society, 1940), p. 7.

minister of economic warfare and later president of the Board of Trade. A number of other offices were given to Labour party members.

PLANNED ECONOMIC DEMOCRACY

At the Forty-first Annual Conference in Westminster in 1942, the Labour party declared that

there must be no return after the war to an unplanned competitive society, which inevitably produces economic insecurity, industrial inefficiency and social inequality . . . . It regards the socialization of the basic industries and services of the country, and the planning of production for community consumption as the only lasting foundation for a just and prosperous economic order in which political democracy and personal liberty can be combined with a reasonable standard of living for all citizens.[7]

The conference endorsed nationalization of all forms of transport, a comprehensive scheme of social insurance, an increase in the school age, and more extensive support of the schools.

In its report to the Annual Conference in 1944, the National Executive Committee endorsed the use of fiscal policy to obtain full employment. "The central point in our financial policy for the maintenance of full employment is the maintenance of the total purchasing power of the community. The total money income of the inhabitants of Britain might be, and should be, better distributed, but the total expenditure must not be allowed to fall." [8] Finance was to be made the servant and not the master of industry. New capital issues and capital exports were to be controlled.

ELECTION PLATFORM

Following the defeat of Germany, Labour left the government and forced an election. In a statement of policy, "Let's Face the Future" endorsed by the Blackpool conference, the Labour party called for nationalization of the fuel, power, iron, and steel industries and of the Bank of England. Maintenance of purchasing power to assure high and steady employment, planned investment, and a housing and public works program were advocated.

[7] *Report of the 41st Annual Conference of the Labour Party, 1942,* p. 110.
[8] *Full Employment and Financial Policy.* Report by the National Executive Committee of the Labour Party to be presented to the Annual Conference, 1944, p. 3.

Under peace-time private ownership, not only has unemployment become part of the pattern of the economy, but many of the basic industries have become crippled by inefficient organization. This is the unhappy legacy of their unplanned growth and the unrestrained competitive struggle for profit. Such inefficient organization prevents the workers from gaining a decent standard of living and condemns them in some cases to work in what are little more than slum factories.

The Labour party's answer "is nationalization of those basic industries which can no longer be left to the unplanned anarchy of monopoly capitalism." [9]

In addition, the party advocated the promotion of agriculture; the retention of the new food services such as factory canteens and free milk for mothers and children; an extensive housing program; nationalization of the land with the initial right of local authorities to acquire the land for public use; compulsory schooling to sixteen years of age; and free adult and secondary education for all. It promised to put into immediate effect an extensive program of social insurance so as to guarantee all a minimum standard of living.

ELECTION VICTORY

In a campaign of unusual violence, the Labour party won a decisive majority. A Labour government was organized with Clement Attlee as prime minister; Herbert Morrison as lord president of the Council and leader of the House of Commons; Ernest Bevin as foreign secretary; and Hugh Dalton as chancellor of the exchequer.[10]

For the first time in history, a political party dedicated to democratic socialism has gained power in a great nation. Consequently, upon the shoulders of the Labour party rests more than the destiny of a socialistic government. Even though power was won at a time when England faced the gravest economic problems in several decades, success or failure may well determine whether basic changes are possible without dictatorship. The Labour party aims for a democratic, planned socialistic economy which will guarantee to each person certain minimum protection. The Labour party, however, came to power at an inopportune moment, in a period in which Britain finds her economy beset with some of the greatest difficulties in her history.

[9] *Labour Party Bulletin,* June, 1945, p. 65.
[10] *Ibid.,* January, 1946, p. 145.

Soon after taking office, the government indicated that nationalization is "an essential part of a planned economy that we are introducing into this country . . . designed to help in promoting full employment, economic prosperity and justice for all." [11] In his speech the prime minister argued that the programs of nationalization are "not the result of some *a priori* theorizing. They come out of hard and practical experience and close study of the problem involved." [12]

In October, 1946, the government pushed through a bill for the nationalization of the Bank of England. Nationalization of the coal mines, communications, electric power supply, inland transport, and civil aviation followed. A bill to nationalize the steel industry was introduced in 1948. Fair prices determined by impartial boards are paid to former owners. Nationalized industries are managed by boards appointed by the appropriate minister. For example, the nationalized coal industry is managed by the National Coal Board appointed by the minister of fuel and power. Like the Tennessee Valley Corporation, the board is independent with respect to its day-to-day operations, but is subject to parliamentary supervision to which it submits periodic reports. Nationalization will, of course, not instantaneously solve all the problems. In the coal industry the National Coal Board was faced not only with the immediate problems of increasing the output of coal and the need to increase the labor force, but also with the necessity of making concessions to the miners. The concessions were a sign of good faith, and the government was able to convince the miners to forgo the five-day week. A non-labor government might have faced considerably more economic pressure from the workers.[13] Of course, there is danger that nationalization may be carried too far. The dispute over the desirability of nationalizing the iron and steel industry is an example of the type of problem that confronts a government seeking to carry out a long-advocated policy, the economic wisdom of which may only eventually be clear.

The British economy is in a real sense a mixed economy, and may remain so for many years. British socialism is pragmatic and not doctrinaire, and it would not adopt a policy of socialization for socialization's sake. The speed of nationalization is governed by expediency, by available administrative ability, and even by the strength of the opposition.

[11] Clement Attlee, "What Labor Has Done." Speech delivered at the 45th Annual Conference of the Labour Party, June 11, 1946, p. 2.

[12] *Ibid.*, p. 2.

[13] See the discussion in Trades-Union Congress, *79th Annual Report*, 1947, pp. 332–341.

In a socialism that does not rely on concentration camps, respect for minorities and for public opinion does not, however, leave the government powerless to influence and direct the economy. Although only a small proportion of industry has been nationalized, steps have been taken to influence the direction and extent of private investment by the Borrowing Control and Guarantees Act.

This Borrowing Bill is going to regulate permanently access to the capital market. In the future raising of new capital, the decision is going to be determined, not by the relative profit expected to be obtained from this or that new issue, nor by the plausibility of company promoters; it is going to be determined by priority in the national interest; by that and nothing else.[14]

Under the terms of the Borrowing Bill, investment is regulated, and loans must be approved by the Capital Issues Committee, acting with the advice of the National Investment Council. Should private demand for capital fail to reach a level held necessary, the Treasury can make loans to investors up to fifty million pounds annually, and more if necessary. In addition, the first two budgets of the Labour party made sweeping reductions upon the poorer income taxpayers and upon the taxes of the housewife.[15] On the other hand, surtaxes and estate taxes—death duties —were raised.

The Labour government is regulating industrial location under the Distribution of Industries Act passed during the war. Before a factory is built, a license must be procured, and the government has used this power to distribute factories in the onetime depressed areas. The government has also embarked upon a short-term and long-term housing program. The former is designed to take care of immediate needs through the erection of prefabricated houses, and the remodeling and seizure of unoccupied houses. By 1948, the government had rehoused more than four hundred thousand families. In addition, it hopes to rehouse the working class in four million well-arranged modern homes by 1956. The results have only been fair. A program has been evolved for planned rebuilding of slum areas in the hope of shifting population from cities to towns. Labour believes in land nationalization and will work toward it. But, as a first step, the state and the local authorities were given power to acquire land for public purposes. County councils are to be allowed to acquire land and to plan land use.

14 Hugh Dalton, "Financing Labour's Plan." Speech to the 45th Annual Conference of the Labour Party, June 14, 1946, p. 2.
15 *Ibid.*, p. 1.

In the field of social insurance, the Labour party has gone beyond any of the earlier schemes. Under the National Insurance Act, adopted in August, 1946, employer, employee, and the state make contributions, and every person has insurance "from the cradle to the grave." Standard benefits are paid to single persons in the event of unemployment, sickness, and old age, and since July, 1948, contributors have paid a single weekly contribution. Maternity grants and widows' pensions, guardians' allowances (for orphans), retirement pensions, and death grants will also be paid. The government has improved the industrial accident compensation law and has sponsored the Families' Allowance Act under which five shillings are paid weekly for all children under school-leaving age except the first. Plans for supplementing these payments by free milk and by school lunches have been devised. The scheme provides for all benefits for those employed irrespective of position. The self-employed are insured for sickness only. Under the National Assistance Act, the Labour government swept aside the remnants of the Poor Relief Law enacted in the reign of Queen Elizabeth. Under the new law, relief of the needy poor is transferred from the local authorities to the national government. A National Assistance Board administers the system. A single weekly contribution paid under the National Insurance Act entitles contributors and their dependents to free and comprehensive medical service. The National Health Act provides complete medical, specialist, and hospital services, available without charge and without limitation to every man, woman, and child irrespective of station or income, except that patients can choose their doctors and physicians their practice. Doctors are free to come into the system or remain outside it. Patients can avail themselves of private service if they wish to do so.

The government has taken over all hospitals and has grouped them together. According to the Labour party,

The confidential relation between doctor and patient is an indispensable part of a satisfactory health service. It is becoming apparent, however, that the present system of organizing and paying for the doctor's services has become increasingly unsatisfactory from the standpoint of the nation, of the patient, and of the doctor himself. The patient is not getting a service that is preventative, comprehensive, open to all and fully efficient. In the Labour Party's opinion, therefore, it is necessary that the medical profession should be organized as a national, full-time, salaried, pensionable service.[16]

[16] *National Service for Health,* The Labour Party.

The National Health Service aims to provide every form of treatment needed by the patient. Family physicians, specialists, clinics, hospitals, nurses, medicines at a small charge, and appliances are provided for all. There was widespread and vigorous opposition to the health scheme from the medical profession. Physicians objected to the basic salary set by the government and to the losses involved in the abolition of the sale of medical practice. Compromises were finally made, and although they were not completely satisfactory to the majority of doctors, they were accepted and the plan was put into operation on July 5, 1948.

The school-leaving age was raised to fifteen immediately and to sixteen as soon as more schools are available. Secondary education has been made compulsory, and children leaving school at the age of sixteen will attend special county colleges several times a week at their employers' expense. Scholarships for free university and technical schooling have been increased.

The trade unions were perhaps most pleased by the repeal of the Trade Unions Act, framed after the general strike of 1926. Although the government has been vigorous in action, the opposition of more conservative groups has by no means been allayed. In the foreign field, the Labour government has had to grapple with the problems resulting from two decades of appeasement and from a devastating war. Bevin's policy with respect to Russia has not displeased believers in a democratic world and opponents of the new Soviet imperialism.

However, the government has no illusions with respect to the magnitude of the problem it faces. In the *Economic Survey for 1947* presented to Parliament by the prime minister, the seriousness of the difficulties was clearly outlined. The government recognized that there

is an essential difference between totalitarian and democratic planning. The former subordinates all individual desires and preferences to the demands of the State. For this purpose, it uses various methods of compulsion upon the individual which deprive him of the freedom of choice . . . . But, in normal times, the people of a democratic country will not give up their freedom of choice to their government. A democratic government must, therefore, conduct its economic planning in a manner which preserves the maximum possible freedom of choice to the individual citizen.[17]

Actual economic planning in England must remain cognizant of the fact that economic decisions are made by thousands of organizations and in-

[17] *Loc. cit.* (London: His Majesty's Stationery Office, 1947), p. 5.

dividuals, and that the public is accustomed to the exercise of choice. Moreover, as England must depend upon the import of food and raw materials, it must export, and that means competing with foreign countries in price, quality, and other terms of sale.

Aside from long-run programs of developing a number of basic industries, the government is seeking to evolve a system of economic planning based upon

an organization with enough knowledge and reliable information to assess our national resources and to formulate the national needs. A set of economic "budgets" which relate to our resources, and which enable the Government to say what is the best use of resources in the national interest. A number of methods, the effect of which will enable the Government to influence the use of resources in the desired direction, without interfering with democratic freedoms.[18]

England also faced the task of directing labor into peacetime industries. It was to be expected that, under existing conditions, labor would not necessarily move into industries where the need was greatest: the difficulty is that England, with its over-all shortages and the need to build up its exports, cannot offer pecuniary attractions that would normally distribute labor through the branches of industry. As a result, the Labour government was forced to introduce in August, 1948, schemes for the direction of labor. Workers leaving their jobs will be able to get new ones only through the government employment offices. In addition, the government seeks to channel labor into essential industries. The difference between the English system and the one prevailing in totalitarian countries is that an independent labor movement exists in England. The unions can check any tendency of the government to extend controls beyond the point that appears necessary. Perhaps the experience under the Control of Engagement Order best illustrates the difference between democratic and totalitarian socialism. At the end of a year of operation, the Labour exchanges filled 4,519,000 vacancies, and the total number directed totaled 29, or 1 in 156,000. Even if the 338 coal miners and 129 agricultural workers ordered to remain in their trades are included, the figure for deliberate direction is still 1 in 9,000.[19]

At the end of World War II, England faced very serious problems. England is a large importer of food and raw materials which, before World War II, were paid for by the export of commodities, the sale of

18 *Ibid.*, pp. 5–6.
19 *Labour Party Bulletin,* December, 1948, p. 183.

shipping, insurance, and other services, and the income from foreign investments. During World War II, England was forced to liquidate much of her foreign holdings, and she lost a large part of her shipping. In addition, she acquired added liabilities of almost twelve billion dollars. Consequently, she is unable to pay for the large purchases abroad, which are indispensable to her industries. The loans from the United States and Canada were not enough to prevent the development of the "dollar crisis" in the middle of 1947.

Basically the 'dollar crisis' that came to Britain in the middle of 1947 was the delayed result of the great loss of wealth that Britain suffered at home and abroad during the war. At home, war damage was estimated at $6 billion; depreciation and obsolescence amounted to $3½ billion; shipping losses to $3 billion. Overseas, Britain sold capital assets valued at $4½ billion and incurred further liabilities amounting to $11½ billion. The total of nearly thirty billion was equal to about one-third of Britain's pre-war national wealth.[20]

Faced with an immediate need for sharp increases in exports to pay for imports, Britain found herself in serious financial difficulty, especially after July 15, 1947, when sterling became fully convertible for current account. The "dollar crisis" was not due nearly so much to the incompetence of the Labour government, as to the insatiable need for dollars induced in part by the extensive economic destruction of the war and the need for American goods in England and other countries.

The dollar crisis of 1949, while caused by the same basic conditions, is due to long-run changes in the British economy and in the trading relations of the countries of the world. Prior to World War II, Britain purchased more from the United States and Canada than she paid to them. However, these deficits could be offset by Britain's earning surpluses in other countries. The pattern of multilateral trade operated so that no single country had a surplus with the rest of the world. Otherwise the country having the deficit could find no means for paying the deficit out of its current resources. For all countries the demand for each other's goods and currencies would balance, and as trading deficits would be small and not too frequent they could be met by short-term financing or gold movements. This pattern of world trade was somewhat distorted by World War I and virtually shattered by World War II. In contrast to the experience of the major countries of the world, the economy of the

20 *Labour and Industry in Britain*, September–October, 1947, p. 175.

United States expanded and became more productive during World War II. The solidity of the United States economy has aided in the reconstruction and revival of the economics of other countries, but it has also created very difficult problems of payments between countries. In 1947 the net payments by foreigners to Americans were twenty times as great as they were prior to World War II, and, in 1949, they were about twelve times as large. Other dollar areas in North and South America have also amassed large balances with nondollar nations. Consequently, it is not possible for the nondollar nations to balance their accounts with the dollar countries as the former have large overall deficits with the latter. The nondollar areas cannot earn a sufficient amount of dollars from each other to keep multilateral trade going automatically.

The British position can best be appreciated by recognizing that prior to World War II, England paid for only 27 per cent of her exports from the dollar area, and made up the difference by dollars earned from investments in dollar countries, earnings from other sterling area countries[21] which had a surplus with dollar nations, and the sale of gold mined in the sterling area. These methods are no longer available. British dollar income from investments has been sharply reduced, the other countries in the sterling area have deficits because of their greater dependence upon the dollar area for raw material. The dollar price of gold has remained stable while American prices have risen sharply.

To meet deficits in the balance of payments, Britain and other sterling countries have drawn on their gold and dollar reserves. However, this process cannot be continued, for adequate reserves are needed to finance the short-term trade and services of all the sterling countries. The British deficit to the dollar area was substantially reduced in 1947 and 1948, but rose sharply in the first quarter of 1949, because of the large increase in British payments for imports from dollar countries, a decline in prices and sales of sterling area raw materials and British exports in the United States, a decline in income from the sale of oil by English companies.

The British did not see the possibility of further reduction in imports, for they have been strictly regulated. Consequently, devaluation was tried, in the hope of stimulating exports from the sterling area to the dollar area. Devaluation will lead to rises in cost-of-living items, and perhaps to demands for wage increases. Some of the effects of devaluation may

---

21 Countries having close financial ties with Great Britain and whose trade was largely carried on by agencies located in Britain and much of whose capital came from British investors.

thereby be lost. At least this drastic step has demonstrated the willingness of the government to accept unpleasant remedies.

We must not lose sight of the fact that the Labour government took office when England suffered from economic difficulties of unparalleled severity. The tremendous losses of war, the loss of foreign investment, and the deterioration of key industries—the most important being coal mining—created problems of great magnitude. English socialism was introduced under the most adverse circumstances, at a time when its economy has lost many of its traditional advantages.

The Labour government has, however, been criticized for lack of prudence, for following an unwise policy of capital expansion which imposed unnecessary burdens upon the people because "big government-sponsored programmes give rise to pressure that makes it impossible for industry in general to add to its working capital or even, in some cases, secure adequate maintenance of its existing capital." [22] Capital outlay exceeded current savings plus gifts from abroad. The value of democratic discussion was never shown to better advantage, for the government was forced by critics and events to revise downward its plan for capital expansion.

In addition, the Labour government's program for expanding the social services has been under attack. It "is important that working people should be provided with amenities in all various industries and factories. But, where it involves capital outlay, postponement is necessary . . . . This principle is not beyond the comprehension of the ordinary man; it was well understood during the war." [23]

The author of the above lines, an eminent economist, then criticizes the government's housing program on the ground that it means diverting resources from more urgent uses.

It is, of course, true that a nation may establish a level of social services it cannot afford, especially a nation which has to import a large amount of its food and raw materials. Such a program can lead to deficits in the balance of payments. One must, however, not overlook the political importance of demonstrating to labor that the government will make reasonable provisions for social improvement. A Labour government which followed the advice of economic theorists, with an exclusive eye on the pure economics of a situation, would not remain in office. Moreover,

22 Roy Harrod, *Are These Hardships Necessary?* (London: Rupert Hart-Davis, 1947), p. 29.
23 *Ibid.*, pp. 88–89.

workers disillusioned with a Labour government that failed to improve the lot of the lower-income group might turn to more radical remedies. One needs only to compare the labor strife that followed World War I with the disciplined calm of the present period to recognize the difference in the reaction of labor. It is sheer snobbery to examine the reactions and expectations of entrepreneurs to given events, and not regard the reaction of the laboring millions as worthy of attention. A glance toward postwar France, with its unsettled industrial conditions, underlines the great achievement of the Labour government in winning the workers' consent to a program of austerity and greater effort.

Criticisms of the extensive re-equipping of industry have also been made. Here it is necessary to guard against overambitious schemes which consciously or unconsciously seek to emulate the Five-Year Plans of the Soviet Union. Yet British industry obviously needs drastic overhauling if it is to be able to meet the obligations that rest upon it. "American man-hour output ranges from 131 percent to 597 percent of the British." [24] The wide gap in output between the United States and England is due largely to differences in the level of mechanization. A low rate of mechanization adversely effects equipment producers, who as a consequence limit their research and development. "The condition of factory buildings in the industries surveyed [by Working Parties] is even worse than the condition of equipment. In some cases, the majority of buildings are more than 50 years old." [25] Many of the industrial buildings are unfit for housing modern machinery; they interfere with the efficient arrangement of machines and the smooth flow of materials.

The Reid Report of March, 1945, emphasized the same problem. The British coal-mining industry had failed to increase its efficiency as compared with American mines as well as with German and Dutch mines. "One of the reasons for the failure of the British mining industry to increase its productivity undoubtedly lay in the inadequate rate at which it had improved its capital equipment of all kinds." [26] The need for improved efficiency is generally recognized, and the setting up of the Anglo-American Joint Production Council is evidence of such awareness.

One of the more serious problems was the adverse balance of payments. Britain's unfavorable position in this respect was already apparent be-

---

24 *Technological Stagnation in Great Britain* (Chicago: Machinery and Allied Products Institute, 1948), p. 10.

25 *Ibid.*, p. 27.

26 Ian Bowen, *Britain's Industrial Survival* (London: Faber & Faber, 1947), p. 110.

fore World War II; in 1938, Britain's adverse balance of payments was £70 million. It has risen sharply, and in 1947 the deficit on the balance of payments reached £630 million. Britain's unfavorable position is due preponderantly to causes outside the control of the Labour government. As Britain's receipts from interest and from profits and dividends from shipping are much lower than before the war, she faces the problem of selling a sufficiently large volume of exports so as to begin moving toward earning enough to meet her needs.[27] As a consequence, an export drive was organized and a strong effort made to avoid buying from the dollar area.

Exports in 1947 reached 120 per cent of 1938, and by December, 1948, they reached 148 per cent of that base.

In 1948, the deficit in the balance of payments declined from £630 million in 1947 to £150 million. The deficit, in 1948, on visible trade is about the same as in 1938, but the income from services is about one eighth that of 1938. Since World War II, the terms of trade have shifted against England so that a much larger volume of exports is needed to purchase the same amount of imports as in the 1930's. On invisible items, a deficit of £192 million in 1947 was converted into a surplus in 1948. This change was brought about by a reduction in military expenditures in Germany, but there was also some improvement in income from shipping. Returns from investment were, however, slightly lower. Actually England's surplus with the nondollar world cannot clear her dollar deficits, as the nondollar countries are also short of dollars. She must increase her exports to the United States.

It is worth while to quote the severe but fair critic of the government, *The Economist*:

It is not often realized, either in this country or particularly in the United States, how well the British record in the last three years shows up in comparison with that of other countries that found themselves in a roughly similar predicament. Is there another country in the world that has been willing to impose such crushing taxes on itself for the sake of financial rectitude, or that has been willing to carry on its own reserves the burden of other countries' trade deficits? . . . Judged by any absolute test of what is necessary or desirable, there are many defects in British economic policy which have not been passed over wholly in silence in these columns. By the relative test of what others have done, the record is magnificent.[28]

27 Economic Survey for 1948, p. 17; *Parliamentary Debates (Hansard) House of Commons Report,* April 6, 1948, p. 41.
28 *The Economist,* September 25, 1948, p. 483.

This achievement has been carried out by a Labour government which has had to overcome the suspicion of many segments of the movement. Workers who are suspicious of increasing production and who regard the administrators of the nationalized industries as another employer create difficult problems which manifest themselves in wildcat strikes.[29] Yet it would not square with the facts to deny that there is increasing recognition of the community point of view. A leading trade unionist has argued:

It is a good thing that we as Trade Unionists recognize that we have a responsibility, not only to our members, but to the community and the nation at large. All the efforts of Trade Union leaders and the speeches of the rank and file from this rostrum this afternoon indicate to me at least a growing desire amongst this great Trade Union movement to accept its responsibility even to the extent of saying unpopular things and undertaking unpopular tasks . . . . . We should not hide our heads in the sand. We should not seek to deceive ourselves. We need more coal, we need more steel, we need more cotton, we need more ship-building, we need more production of every kind. I say to you and also the rank and file of the Trade Union movement that the time has come from the point of view of our dignity and with a sense of obligation to the nation, we ought to outlaw restrictive practices, condemn unofficial stoppages and get rid of every retarding agreement which stops production from reaching the highest possible maximum.[30]

In line with this view the Trade-Union Congress published a report, in November, 1948, on productivity which outlined methods to be used in increasing per capita output. Considerable, but not enough, has been achieved in this respect. It is no easy task to reverse the suspicion and fear of laborsaving methods built up over generations. Yet the report shows that the leaders of unions are aware of the problem and are trying to meet it.

Socialists face the problem of overcoming long-held views with respect to output and efficiency. Socialists have assumed that problems of production will be solved by capitalism, and that a socialist society would not be bedeviled by difficulties arising out of low output. Events show, however, that while changes in the social structure may eliminate disparities in income, they do not automatically and immediately raise productivity. There is still need to increase efficiency if the people are to be assured reasonable minima.

[29] National Coal Board, *Annual Report and Statement of Accounts* (London: His Majesty's Stationery Office, 1948), pp. 17–20.
[30] *Report of the 47th Annual Conference of the Labour Party,* 1948, p. 205.

Minimum guarantees—another problem that faces a socialist government—are desirable and necessary, but cognizance must also be taken of reality. Unfortunately, scarcity has not yet been overcome, and socialist communities, if they commit too large a portion of their incomes to social guarantees, may find their cost structure overburdened and incapable of meeting competition on foreign markets. On the other hand, democratic socialist governments are subjected to continual pressure by their constituents for improvements. Education is needed, and much has been done.

Under the leadership of Sir Stafford Cripps, the government has followed a policy of austerity, has kept down domestic consumption, and has used its resources to promote exports. The interference with the market mechanism has aroused widespread criticism among professional economists, who are convinced that prices are the best device for distributing resources. Although there is merit in this view, it is doubtful if an economy where decisions were made exclusively on the basis of highest profits would have gained labor's cooperation. Professional economists who believe maximum profits are the best guides for investment decisions usually preach restraint and hard work to labor. They also assume competitive conditions and not the monopolistic realities. It is doubtful if their preachments would have prevented the widespread demands for higher wages. The fact is that output has risen in many industries and the possibility of further improvement is favorable, perhaps because of the government's ability to gain labor's support.

The English experience has shown that so far the workers can learn the hard lessons of patience and restraint. It is doubtful whether any other kind of government could have exacted the cooperation and sacrifice that the Labour party has secured. Despite the criticism that has rightfully been made, the Labour government has introduced its program without the slightest attack on the basic civil liberties. The doctrinaire pronouncements of Lenin and even the preachings of the uncompromising laissez-faire protagonists are being given the lie by English experience. However, it may be too soon to judge. The union of democracy to socialism in England is the most significant social experience in the history of our time and perhaps of all time. Even opponents of socialism have a stake in its success, for it will show whether fundamental economic change and the destruction of vested interests can be made peacefully without civil war, concentration camps, or slave labor. Democratic socialism may have very serious weaknesses in developing the highest level of income. It may be that unrestrained or limited capitalism is more efficient in allocating resources and in stimulating innovations and technical progress. Even though a socialist system does not destroy freedom of speech, press, religion, and assembly, it may nevertheless be open to objection on economic and personal grounds. Yet, in this world of change, much of it violent and undesirable, we must seek to salvage what we can of our heritage of freedom. Social experiments need not be approved, but we must tolerate them, and improve and change them if realities fail to meet our expectations.

16. *THE SWEDISH MIDDLE WAY*

Sweden's socialist movement was influenced largely by the German social democracy. Although the movement faced the ideological conflicts common to the socialist parties of other countries, it developed policies that were peculiarly its own. These policies showed a daring and ingenuity which the other Continental socialist parties frequently lacked. Directed toward meeting a crisis situation, they demonstrated that socialist policies need be neither extreme nor doctrinaire.

Utopian socialistic ideas popular in France were introduced into Sweden in the 1830's by Per Götrek. He presented the views of Saint-Simon and Cabet to the public and later translated *The Communist Manifesto* into Swedish. Socialist ideas did not, however, gain a large audience. The liberals' demand for constitutional reform and free trade attracted a wider following.[1]

In the 1870's the intelligentsia became increasingly concerned with social problems. This concern showed itself in the founding in Stockholm of a labor institute and in the establishment of social-reform societies in the universities. Moreover, the social criticism embodied in the dramas of Strindberg and in the work of the Norwegian Ibsen made an impression during this period.[2] Labor was, however, largely excluded from political life by the laws governing the franchise.

The first labor movement in Sweden was promoted by liberals who formed a number of study groups in the 1860's. A congress of these groups, held in Stockholm in 1870, issued a set of modest suggestions. The fear of God and the practice of thrift were the remedies for labor's ills. Trade unions grew in the 1860's, although the printers had formed

1 John Lindgren, *Från Per Götrek Till Per Albin* (Stockholm: Albert Bonniers Förlag, 1936), pp. 8–9.
2 Rudolf Heberle, *Zur Geschichte der Arbeiter Berwegung in Schweden* (Jena: Fischer, 1925), pp. 15–17.

such organizations earlier. With the spread of a more militant spirit, socialist groups were organized.[3]

Under the leadership of August Palm, the first modern socialist program was presented in 1882 by the Swedish Social Democratic Labor Association. It was based essentially on the Gotha program of the German social democracy. Palm was also instrumental in establishing in Stockholm in 1884 a Social Democratic Club made up largely of intellectuals. The club blamed the misery of the masses on the existing social organization, which allowed private ownership of land and the means of production. This was said to lead to the appropriation of the products of labor by a few and to result in the misery and uncertainty of the many. Socialists, it declared, had no desire to pervert the historical course of social evolution, for they recognized that the growth of larger and larger enterprises was inevitable. Overproduction, coupled to increasing unemployment and misery of labor, was also held inevitable, and workers were urged to organize into unions for the improvement of their lot and for the setting up of producers' cooperatives.[4] In addition, the program demanded the ending of indirect taxation and its replacement by progressive income and inheritance taxes, limitation of the hours of labor of women to ten a day, prohibition of the labor of minors under the age of fourteen, and protection of the aged, sick, and infirm.[5]

SOCIAL DEMOCRATIC PARTY

By 1889, social democratic views had spread sufficiently to make the launching of a political party possible. No program was elaborated, the delegates being content to base themselves upon the Gotha program of the German social democracy. Although violent revolution was rejected, the party declared itself ready to direct the masses if, driven by misery and suffering, they rebelled against their oppressors. The demand for universal suffrage was placed in the forefront,[6] and the tactics to be pursued for its achievement became a leading problem for Swedish socialism.

Lack of success in the elections of 1890 led to the development of an anarchist current which, for a time, diverted some energies into utopian

---

3 H. J. Branting, "Le Mouvement ouvrier suedois," *Revue Socialiste*, May, 1894, pp. 596–609.

4 Heberle, *op. cit.*, pp. 21–23.

5 Herbert Tingsten, *Den Svenska Socialdemokratiens Ideutvekling* (Stockholm: Tidens Förlag, 1941), I, 139–140.

6 Heberle, *op. cit.*, pp. 26–27.

channels. However, under the leadership of Hjalmar Branting (1860–1925), violence and "propaganda by the deed" were rejected. For many years Branting edited the *Social Democrat;* and while he was philosophically an orthodox Marxist, in practice he was a reformist.[7]

From the beginning, Branting sought to mediate between the revolutionary and reformist wings. He was convinced that both socialism and democracy could be won by peaceful means. Opposed to the gradual reformism of Branting were the more militant and revolutionary elements for whom democracy was a historic lie and parliamentary government a form of the modern class state. This view was rejected by the Swedish party, which generally accepted the Marxian categories, although never wholeheartedly. For example, the party recognized noneconomic factors as important in history. Nor did the party accept completely the Marxist prognosis with respect to industrial development. The theory of increasing misery was somewhat modified, for Hjalmar Branting believed that socialism could be ushered in gradually by an intelligent and socialistically schooled working class. Although the German socialist movement exercised a great influence upon Swedish socialism, the Swedes were not theoretically minded, and the doctrinal wars that rent the other socialist movements were never important.[8]

Swedish socialists revised their program at their fourth congress in 1897. The program contained a list of general propositions embodying the party's ideology and a set of immediate or practical demands. In contrast to other political parties, the Social Democratic party declared its aim to be the safeguarding and promotion of the spiritual and material culture of the masses. It described the main cause of current evils as due to the private ownership of the means of production, which, desirable at one stage of history, had led to the concentration of wealth on the one side and to the creation of a propertyless wage-earning class on the other. These conditions have forced labor to organize as a class in order to raise its wages and improve working conditions. In addition, the program declared that the Social Democratic party was also organizing to acquire political power for the working class and to transfer the means of production, transportation, forests, mines, factories, manufacturing, machinery, and land from individual to social ownership.

---

[7] G. Henriksson-Holmberg "Die Entwicklungsgeschichte der Arbeiter-bewegung in Schweden," *Archiv für die Geschichte des Sozialismus und der Arbeiterbewegung,* 1916, VI, 58–59.

[8] Tingsten, *op. cit.,* pp. 26–27.

A political program capable of realization under capitalism was also presented. It included a demand for progressive income and inheritance taxes; state-supported credit; protection of labor by an eight-hour day; prohibition of the employment of minors under fourteen years of age; the prohibition of all nightwork not required by technical conditions; abolition of the truck system of wage payment; supervision of all branches of industry by government inspectors; aid by the government to the sick, aged, and infirm; and the guaranty of freedom of speech, press, and assembly.[9] In most respects, the Swedish socialist program now followed the Erfurt program of German social democracy.

GROWTH

At its organization in 1889, the Social Democratic party counted a little more than 3,000 members. Progress during the early years was slow, the party's membership reaching but 10,000 by 1895. Two years later, the first socialist, Hjalmar Branting, was elected to Parliament. By the turn of the century the Social Democratic party had transformed itself from a representative of a scattered number of workers into a rapidly growing and important political movement. The party in its early years was led by several journalists.[10] The only leader of worker origin during the early years was August Palm, the founder of modern Swedish socialism.

Swedish social democracy increased in numbers from 10,000 members in 1895 to 86,000 in 1915. Similarly, the party's representation in Parliament increased sharply, especially after the reform of the franchise in 1907–1909.[11]

WORLD WAR I

Swedish social democracy faced a critical period during 1914–1920. Growing differences developed between the moderate majority and a left wing strongly influenced by the Russian Revolution. The left charged the party leadership with overconcentration on day-to-day reforms, and were, in turn, accused of lack of clarity and of infatuation with radical phraseology. The moderates opposed the revolutionary road to power; to them the problem was not to divide existing wealth but to increase production. A revolution, they argued, would reduce output for a long time because of the lack of experienced administrators and technicians. On the

9 *Ibid.*, I, pp. 143–144.
10 *Ibid.*, pp. 144–145.
11 *Ibid.*, p. 197.

other hand, gradual collectivization would lead to nationalized production and the substitution of the waste of competition by organized planning.[12] They advocated gradual socialization of some basic industries and support of consumers' and producers' cooperatives. These differences led to a break, and the setting up of a left-wing group.

The discussions after World War I led to the appointment of a commission to revise the party's program. The new program declared the Swedish social democracy as differing from other political parties in its desire to reorganize bourgeois society so as to free the worker and assure the spiritual and material progress of society. The modern system of capitalistic production was held to be the chief weakness of modern civilization, for it allowed the few to control the means of work of the propertyless majority, and created an unbridgeable gulf between worker and employer. The program declared that ownership of capital had become a means by which the worker was deprived of a part of the product of his toil. To oppose the power of the capitalist, the worker was forced to organize in trade unions and consumers' cooperatives. Conscious of his historic mission, the worker will bring into being a new productive organization free from rent, interest, and profit. The growth in the power of capital is obvious, as is its dominance over industrial production and natural resources, its undermining of the independence of the middle and artisan classes, and the growth of banking and share capital. Social democracy will organize for the winning of political power and the establishment of a socialist society.[13]

In addition to the expression of general principles, the program contained a number of demands that could be introduced immediately. They included direct taxation, a progressive income tax with minimum exemption and a steeper rate for unearned income, and a tax on wealth, especially that which is inherited. Social capital was to be secured through taxation. Free trade was advocated, and foreign commerce was to be placed under social control. Accident, sickness, maternity, and unemployment insurance was advocated, as were pensions for the aged and the invalided and for orphans and widows. A demand was also made for the establishment of eight hours as the normal working day, prohibition of nightwork unless necessitated by technical conditions or by general welfare, at least thirty-six hours' continual rest for every worker per week, prohibition of employment of children under fifteen years of age,

12 *Ibid.*, pp. 242–243.
13 *Ibid.*, pp. 251–252.

protection against industrial risks and establishment of industrial inspection, free industrial training at public expense, maintenance of satisfactory minimum-wage standards by government regulation, extension of safety regulation to home industries, freedom of immigration and emigration, the right of all foreign workers to enjoy the advantages of industrial safety and insurance, and international agreement to secure the rights of labor.[14]

The program also demanded planned management and social ownership of natural resources, industrial establishments, credit institutions, and the means of transportation and communication. The program of socialization was to be introduced gradually, beginning with the large monopoly industries. Gradualism and slow improvement rather than revolution were emphasized, and the owners of nationalized property were to be compensated. In the same spirit, the promotion of cooperative enterprises was held to be not only a defense against capitalistic exploitation, but a future form of social organization with great potentialities for development.[15]

On the agricultural question, the program recommended the forced purchase of large landed estates by the government, the taking over by the government of neglected estates, the protection of the interests of the poor and working farmer, the social control of agricultural land transfer, and the protection of the small holders and renters against foreclosure.

As can be seen, Swedish socialism has been, from the beginning, revisionist in temper. Swedish Socialists gradually increased their parliamentary representation. In 1917 Socialists entered a coalition government, and three years later a purely Socialistic government was formed. Socialists were in office a number of times in the 1920's, and in 1932, Per Albin Hansson formed a government. He served as prime minister from 1932 until his death in 1946, and was succeeded by another Socialist. Party membership between 1920 and 1936 increased from 143,000 to 368,000.[16]

Swedish Socialism has developed no special doctrine, and perhaps even its practical accomplishments have been exaggerated by enthusiasts outside the country. Yet there can be no doubt that some of the methods used have been unique, and Sweden has attempted by fiscal policy and the use of its natural resources to overcome serious economic crises. Be-

14 *Ibid.,* pp. 236–265.
15 *Ibid.,* pp. 271–272.
16 *Ibid.,* pp. 286–287.

fore compensatory spending was popularized by Lord Keynes and his followers, the Swedish Socialists were applying such a policy.

CRISIS

Sweden faced a serious economic crisis in the early 1930's, and in March, 1933, its unemployed reached 186,561, the highest in the history of the country.[17]

CRISIS POLICY

With the arrival of the world crisis, the Socialist party appointed in the fall of 1931 a committee to work out a policy for the emergency. The result was a number of proposals in Parliament for relieving the unemployed. Heretofore work relief was carried on by reserve projects supervised by the state and the local community. Subsidies were appropriated for the payment of wages which equaled between 30 and 90 per cent. Reserve projects required the approval of the State Unemployment Commission, which determined the number of unemployed to be hired on the project and the amount of subsidy to be paid. Communities could operate their own project if no subsidy was asked of the central government. This system of work relief sought to discourage workers from remaining on reserve projects unless absolutely necessary. In addition, the reserve projects aimed to avoid competing for labor with private industry. The Socialists regarded this system as unjust, heartless, and inflexible. They argued that reserve projects compelled all to perform unskilled labor and left no room for salespeople and mechanics. A worker might, as a consequence, lose his skill. Moreover, workers were sometimes sent away from home—when reserve projects were at some distance—and lost contact with the labor market. Consequently the Socialists wanted to engage the unemployed on projects of general use and pay them market wages. They argued it was more economical to put the unemployed to work at market wages, for their subsequent expenditures would increase consumption and purchasing power and thereby exercise a favorable influence on the economy.[18] It was hoped that the policy would lead to an increase in prices and thus aid agriculture and other producers of raw materials.

[17] Bjarne Braatoy, *The New Sweden* (Edinburgh: Thomas Nelson & Sons, Limited, 1939), p. 8.
[18] Tingsten, *op. cit.*, I, 331–333. Gustav Möller, *Swedish Unemployment Policy* (New York: The Royal Swedish Commission, 1939), pp. 7–10.

At the party congress in the early months of 1932, the party leadership wanted approval for a policy of handling the economic crisis by fiscal means and increased economic planning. A leftish group, led by George Branting and Fabian Mansson, advocated a plan for socialization beginning with the banking system, and charged the party leadership with being too hesitant and conservative. The radical group was defeated, and a moderate policy launched.

The socialist government which came into power in 1932 held the view "that it would be possible along new lines to achieve far more than had been attempted . . . and indeed experience has afterwards confirmed the correctness of this view." [19]

PUBLIC WORKS

The government inaugurated a policy of public works that aimed to relieve unemployment and to stimulate recovery. Emergency public works projects instead of work relief were instituted under open labor market conditions. An inventory was undertaken to discover which projects were desirable from a social point of view, and no distinction was made between those which yielded direct employment on the site and those which stimulated employment in material-producing industries.

Above all, attention was paid to the creation of possibilities for an expansion of the building industry, which is, together with iron and steel, the most important industry from an employment point of view and which furthermore indirectly provides employment within a series of other industries.[20]

Facilities were increased for loans for constructing city apartments and rural homes. The construction of government buildings was accelerated so that a six-year program was completed in two years. A wide variety of nonliquidating communal projects was started. In 1933, the Riksdag appropriated 215,000,000 kronor for combating unemployment, as compared to an appropriation of 28,000,000 kronor in 1932.

It is, therefore, impossible to describe the expansion of the state's activity as insignificant in comparison with a vacancy left by the reduction of private investments. As a matter of fact, considerably over one hundred thousand persons were employed directly or indirectly on reserve and emergency projects during the second half of 1934—a rather impressive achievement when it is recalled

19 Arthur Montgomery, *How Sweden Overcame the Depression* (Stockholm: Albert Bonniers Boktyckeri, 1938), p. 75.

20 Möller, *op. cit.*, p. 15.

that the registered and reported unemployment never exceeded 190,000 and during 1934 amounted, on the average, to 115,000, seasonal unemployment included.[21]

The Social Democrats rejected any monetary policy which suggested the financing of nonliquidating projects by taxation. As the projects approved for 1933 were about 80 per cent nonincome producing, the carrying out of such a financial policy would have made necessary a virtual doubling of taxes. Such a policy was rejected, and a borrowing program inaugurated. At the time, funds were plentiful, the interest rate was low, and money could be obtained on favorable terms. To avoid the shifting of an excessive financial burden to the future, higher inheritance and income taxes were introduced, the proceeds from which were used for amortizing the loans. Thus the principle of balancing the budget over the business cycle rather than annually was introduced.[22]

THE BUDGET

Swedish budgetary policy developed during the depression of the 1930's when unemployment rose sharply. The budget is balanced not annually but cyclically. It is divided into a current account and a capital account. The Socialist government decided to increase its expenditures on public works despite unbalancing the budget. In the depression years of 1933–1934 between 27 and 29 per cent of the budget was financed by loans.[23] Two types of budgetary expansion have been tried. One has for its aim the increase of the aggregate purchasing power during a depression; the other aims at transferring income from the high-earning to low-income groups. In addition to tax income, the government derives income from operating the railroads, the postal and telephone service, hydroelectric power stations, and forests, and from capital investments in loan funds and stocks, and fees and charges.[24]

GOVERNMENT CONTROL

The Swedish government indirectly controls most public utilities, the post office, the telephone and telegraph system, the leading railways, most

---

21 *Ibid.*, p. 23.

22 *Ibid.*, p. 44.

23 Geoffrey Wilson, "Budgetary Policy" in Margaret Cole and Charles Smith, *Democratic Sweden* (London: Routledge and Kegan Paul, 1938), p. 69.

24 Ernest Wigfors, "The Financial Policy during Boom and Depression," *The Annals of the American Academy of Political and Social Science,* May, 1938.

of the electric power production and a significant part of the forests; also, directly and indirectly, the Riksbank, radio, air transport, manufacture of tobacco, and liquor wholesaling. Public ownership was introduced by non-Socialist political groups and was accelerated by the Socialists. Sweden follows two plans of public operation; directly by a government department, or through a state-owned company, which operates as a state monopoly. The state company is similar to a private company except that the government owns the majority of shares.

AGRICULTURE

In agriculture, Sweden is already a managed economy. The import of sugar is monopolized and the production of beet sugar in Southern Sweden is secured under cover of monopoly price. The imports of cereal are regulated by the obligation of the mills to use home produce. Import restrictions and import duties, administered so as to regulate the price of imported animal fodder, assist in the control of livestock and animal produce.[25]

Sweden has sought to make farm life attractive. A system of price regulation has gradually grown up which assures the farmer approximately the same standard of living as he enjoyed in 1925–1929. The interrelations of prices were taken into account; it was recognized that guarantees of the price of one agricultural crop might have a harmful effect upon the production of other crops, as farmers might find it profitable to shift from the unguaranteed to the guaranteed crop.

A central fund has been set up to secure equality of benefit among dairy farmers. A charge is levied on all milk sold, and added revenue is collected from import duties on fodder and from an excise duty on margarine. The monies thus collected are used to help exporters of butter. In the distribution of subsidies, local conditions are taken into account. The fund is administered by the State Agricultural Board, which cooperates with the producers' associations. Although self-government is encouraged, the national rather than sectional interests are emphasized in the "final evolution of a managed Swedish agriculture."[26]

Prices have been raised deliberately, and in this program the producer has been favored. Yet Swedish agriculture did not suffer as a result of an unfavorable export position. Nor were the people in general opposed to a managed and subsidized agriculture. "It has made for that equality of liv-

25 Braatoy, *op. cit.*, pp. 68–69.
26 *Ibid.*, p. 70.

ing conditions which is the dominating ideal of Swedish society. It provided a material basis for that equality in control of public affairs between various sections of the Swedish people which is now being realized." [27]

The program of the socialist government was based on the theory that the course of business development could be controlled.

The idea of the Government was by means of its financial policy to effect an adjustment between good and bad years, to repay in a forthcoming period of revival loans taken up during the depression with a view to enabling the expansion of public works. This program was in fact realized . . . . . and indeed the entire plan of 1933 was developed and carried out with great success from the financial point of view.[28]

Steady improvement in industries that produce for the home market led government officials to the opinion

that even a small country like Sweden, with the economic structure on which it is based, is not reduced to the necessity of passively surrendering to every international economic fluctuation; on the contrary, our liberty of action is relatively wide and we are by no means incapable of influencing our cyclical position through the medium of our own economic policy.[29]

CONTROL OF NATIONAL RESOURCES AND RAILWAYS

Forest land covers a large part of Sweden, and the expansion of the forests has been increasingly subjected to government control. Not only does lumbering provide a needed supplement to many farmers' incomes, but the forests are the basis for Sweden's paper and pulp industry. Exploitation of forests is regulated, as are the quarters of lumber workers. The government has, for many years, owned a large share in the most important iron-ore mining company in Sweden. In addition, a royalty upon one half of the ore produced has been required. In 1938, the government transferred to state ownership all ores yet to be discovered on private lands.

The main Swedish railway lines have been under government control, but local feeder lines have operated under private ownership, and

27 *Ibid.*, p. 71.
28 Montgomery, *op. cit.*, p. 76.
29 Quotation, *ibid.*, p. 83.

their rates were subjected to government rule. A comprehensive program of nationalization has been undertaken.

Power is produced by both government and private agencies, but they supplement each other. Private power companies supply mainly individual industries, whereas government power serves local, district, and national transport needs. In addition, the government controls the sale of alcoholic liquor and has in view a reasonable return on invested capital, but no increased revenue as a result of greater sales. The state also has a monopoly on the import and wholesaling of tobacco.[30]

Although private enterprise can operate freely within a socialized and monopolized area, the government stands ready whenever it is found necessary, to initiate a detailed control of a particular industry. The government may compel an industry to unite into an export association, such as the quarry industry, or, by imposition of standards, may control an industry which seeks a subsidy.[31]

CONSUMER COOPERATIVES

First attempts to establish consumer cooperatives were made as early as the middle nineteenth century, but the "modern period of consumer cooperative development in Sweden may be said to have started in 1899: in that year *Kooperative Förbundet,* a central federation for the local consumer cooperative societies was founded."[32]

Progress was steady, but unspectacular. In 1936 the affiliated societies numbered more than 700, and their total sales reached almost 450,000,000 kronor. Since World War I, the cooperatives have been themselves financing a rapid expansion and they have been setting up larger business units. By 1937, the cooperatives handled about 12 per cent of the total retail business and approximately 20 per cent of the retail food trade. By 1941 the enrolled membership of 740,000 covered about one third of the families in Sweden.[33] Swedish consumers' cooperative enterprises are as a rule larger than private distributors and employ a lower ratio of workers to value of trade than these latter distributors. Conse-

---

30 Braatoy, *op. cit.,* pp. 76–85.
31 *Ibid.,* pp. 89–90.
32 Mauritz Bonow, "The Consumer Cooperative Movement in Sweden," *The Annals of the American Academy of Political and Social Science,* May, 1938, p. 175.
33 *Ibid.,* p. 176.

quently, a Swedish consumer cooperative can be said to be efficiently managed. In 1941, Kooperative Förbundet produced about 137 million kronor of goods, about half of its wholesale turnover.[34]

Profits are divided as follows: Subscribers of shares receive a limited rate of interest. At least 15 per cent of the remainder is allocated to reserves, and the rest is divided among customer-members in proportion to their purchases. Swedish cooperatives have followed a price policy which benefits buyers at noncooperative stores as well as their own members. "The consumer cooperatives have utilized their economic superiority to regulate retail prices downward in relation to wholesale prices..[35] Customers of cooperatives have thus benefited from lower retail prices and from dividends on purchases.

ACTION AGAINST MONOPOLISTS

Swedish consumer cooperatives have taken other steps to fight against monopoly. In certain industries, the cooperatives have directly intervened against monopolistic enterprises. The first venture of this kind was the establishment of a margarine factory by Kooperative Förbundet in 1921. As a result, prices of margarine were forced down. Intervention in other industries followed. Action was taken by the cooperatives against the milling cartel and the galosh cartel, and monopoly pricing has been destroyed in the distribution of superphosphate, oatmeal, macaroni, and other products. Perhaps the best-known move was against the international electric-bulb cartel, in which case the establishment of a cooperative factory at Stockholm forced a 40 per cent reduction in prices. Consequent upon this lowering of prices, imports of bulbs were reduced and exports increased. Thus employment rose and the electric-bulb industry was aided by technical improvements.[36]

Readiness by the cooperative movement to take active steps to curb monopoly has led to price reduction, and products with an elastic demand have been sold in greater volume. Productive capacity was thereby more fully utilized. On balance, the real income of the community is increased because of more effective utilization of the nation's productive capacity, and the increase in real income is expressed for the consumer in lower prices. By controlling between 20 and 30 per cent of an industry's

[34] Thorsten Ode, "The Consumer Cooperatives," in *Sweden: A National Survey* (New York: Swedish News Exchange, no date), pp. 113–115.
[35] *Ibid.*, p. 177.
[36] Bonow, *op. cit.*, pp. 180–181.

output, the cooperative movement has been able to prevent monopolistic pricing and monopoly profits.

Sweden managed to stay out of the war, but it had to suspend its social welfare program. A number of economic controls were imposed. Domestic shortages of raw materials, the diversion of resources to armaments, and the curtailment of exports made restrictions inevitable. A twenty-seven point postwar program was presented by labor and the Socialists in 1944. The program was divided into three sections: (1) full employment; (2) fair distribution of income and higher living standards; and (3) greater efficiency and output. The following program[37] was declared for the prevention of a postwar slump: the coordination of the level of employment under state control, a general scheme to coordinate investments under a system of regional planning, utilization of export markets with state-aided export credits, a long-run housing plan, cheaper consumer goods, state support of agriculture in the form of loans and subsidies, stand-by public works ready for use if a decline in employment should take place, a rise in the standard of living for the masses, leveling of wages, and improved social security.

The economic forces which promote a more effective utilisation of the productive resources of the nation must be husbanded and strengthened . . . . Sweden's national economy must be controlled more and more by the democratic forces of the community—a) because production and distribution must be better adapted to the needs of the masses, and b) because we must utilise an important but hitherto unexploited asset, e.g. the active interest of all those engaged in productive work in common economic problems.

The report criticized private monopolies which increase prices, and the existence of "too many firms manufacturing consumer goods." To this end the Social Democratic program demanded planning

to enable full use of all national productive resources, so as to give every able-bodied citizen security in employment and all citizens a livelihood compatible with the general production output.

All forms of economic activity should be coordinated under State control, and natural resources as well as industrial undertakings, credit institutions, transport and communications, etc. should be transferred to national ownership, where necessary to the realisation of this aim.

[37] *The Post-War Programme of Swedish Labor* (Stockholm: Landsorganisationen, no date), p. 5. The following quotations are from this source, pp. 132, 136, 138.

It is clear that the degree of nationalization and state control is to be determined by realistic considerations rather than by any theory. However, private interests will not be able to block government action deemed necessary for the common welfare. The government has begun to carry out parts of its social welfare program. Old-age pensions were raised, compulsory vacation for workers was increased, and a health insurance system, to be fully effective in 1950, was established. A children's allowance scheme was also introduced.[38]

After World War II, Sweden experienced an appreciable expansion in income. However, the country faced a serious problem because of the increased demand for imports occasioned by the reduction of stocks during the latter stages of the war, by the need for replacing obsolescence, and by higher consumer income. The large increases in exports, which began after the Armistice, leveled off as soon as stocks were used up, and deliveries could be made only from current output. As a result, heavy deficits were experienced in Sweden's foreign trade. The consequence of the unfavorable balance of trade was a diminution in gold and foreign exchange reserves. The government had to restrict imports and to try to encourage purchases from nondollar countries. Some restriction on the improvement of domestic industry also had to be imposed.[39] Sweden was too generous in granting credits to foreign countries, but the disintegration of the European economy, especially the German, has undoubtedly severely affected Sweden.[40]

Despite the many problems facing the country, and despite criticism, the Social Democrats lost only three seats in the second chamber of the Riksdag in the election of September, 1948. It demonstrates the desire of the people to continue the steady and unspectacular development of the last fifteen years.

[38] Tage Lindbom, *Sweden's Labor Program* (New York: League for Industrial Democracy, 1948), pp. 52–53.

[39] Bengt Senneby, "Sweden's Foreign Trade Crisis," *Skandinaviska Banken*, January, 1948, p. 16.

[40] Arthur Montgomery, "Post-war Economic Problems in Sweden," *Lloyds Bank Bulletin*, April, 1948, p. 32.

17. AMERICAN RADICALISM

The failure of Marxism to gain a large following in the United States is perhaps due to the fact that here social, political, and economic adjustments have always been made before they could develop into a state of crisis.[1]

American workers have not regarded and do not regard themselves as an oppressed class. Having won the right to vote early in the history of the nation and therefore having had the right to choose the people who govern them, American workers have never felt that they labored under special disabilities. Moreover, the greater opportunities available in the expanding economy, the greater fluidity of classes, and the real social democracy that have existed in the United States tend to minimize class feelings. Generally, American workers do not regard themselves as members of a lower class, but as citizens of a free, democratic commonwealth. Consequently European forms of social radicalism have not prospered in the American environment. Yet foreign radicalism has exercised an indirect influence upon American labor. In addition, what has been called native radicalism, whose roots are primarily in agrarian areas, has also gained prominence.

The first modern socialist ideas were brought to the United States by European immigrants in the 1850's. Owen's and Fourier's views had attracted some, but their adherents were largely middle-class writers and intellectuals. In contrast to the native, largely agrarian radicalism of Jackson and the frontier, the radicalism of the immigrant worker was urban in origin and directed its appeal mainly to the city worker.

---

[1] Selig Perlman, in his highly suggestive *A Theory of the Labor Movement* (New York: The Macmillan Company, 1928), Chaps. 5–8, discusses the particular characteristics of the American environment.

WILHELM WEITLING

Under the leadership of Wilhelm Weitling, who settled in the United States in 1849, the scattered organizations of German immigrants formed in New York, in 1850, a Central Committee of United Trades. Similar bodies were established in other cities. *Die Republic der Arbeiter* was launched as an official organ of the organization.

A national convention was called in Philadelphia and delegates representing members of forty-two organizations in ten cities assembled and endorsed Weitling's proposal for an "Exchange Bank." The bank was to allow producers of useful commodities to deposit their products in exchange for a certificate of equivalent value. The certificates could be used to purchase any article deposited at the bank at cost. The General Workingmen's League, as the organization became known, never started its bank of exchange. Weitling, the driving force of the movement, withdrew as a result of personal differences. A monthly magazine, *The Revolution*, edited by Marx's friend Joseph Weydemeyer (1818–1860), was launched to present Marxian ideas. The General Workingmen's League lasted until 1860.[2]

THE COMMUNIST CLUB

The Communist Club was organized in 1857. During the Civil War the club was inactive, but it was reorganized in 1867 and participated in the forming of the "Social party of New York and Surrounding Area." A moderate program was formulated in the hope of attracting native-born workers. It contained a demand for a graduated income tax; an eight-hour law; the issue of paper money to be limited to the United States government; abolition of all laws discriminating against people on the basis of race, sex, or religion; and stricter laws against election frauds. Among the officers chosen was Marx's friend F. A. Sorge.[3]

THE FIRST INTERNATIONAL

The General German Labor Union then became Section 1 of the International Workingmen's Association (the First International), and

2 Morris Hillquit, *History of Socialism in the United States* (New York: Funk and Wagnalls Co., 1903), pp. 160–168.
3 *Ibid.*, pp. 169–170.

other sections were soon established among native and German workers.[4] As the affiliates of the International in the United States grew in number, the Central Committee of the International Workingmen's Association of the United States was set up in 1870. A controversy between the pure socialists and the reformers began almost immediately, and lasted until the end of the organization in 1876.[5]

NATIONAL LABOR UNION

A rise in the number of workers organized into unions led to demands during the 1860's for closer cooperation. Among those in the forefront of this movement was William Sylvis (1828–1869) of the molders' union. It was the "defeat of the Iron Molders' International Union that caused Sylvis to shift his emphasis from trade unionism to social reform."[6] The disastrous strikes of 1867–1868 shattered his hopes for progress through trade unionism and he turned to other methods. Cooperation, he believed, would eliminate class conflict by removing the cause for class differences. However, cooperation was also a defense against hostile employers. Sylvis's view was favored by the machinists' and blacksmiths' unions and by many local trades assemblies. Unity was attained by the organization of the National Labor Union in 1866, which favored a labor party, cooperatives, land for all from the public domain, and an eight-hour day. At its second convention in 1867, the National Labor Union issued its program called the "Second Declaration of Independence." The National Labor Union combined within itself many diverse groups: "Trade unionists, eight-hour champions, cooperators, women's rights advocates, immigrants, Negroes, and farmers were brought together."[7]

Differences over pressure politics and independent political action appeared. In addition, the socialist unionists of New York were opposed to concentrating upon antimonopoly and monetary reform. The Central Committee of the International Workingmen's Association, the Marxist group, refused to send a delegate to the congress of the National Labor Union of 1871 because the latter had increasingly become a bourgeois and farmer reform group. The Central Committee sought to develop close

---

[4] Herman Schlüter, *Die Internationale in Amerika* (Chicago: Deutsche Sprachgruppe der Sozialist Partei de Ver. Staaten, 1918), pp. 78, 90, 107–115.

[5] Hillquit, *op. cit.*, pp. 203–204.

[6] Jonathan Grossman, *William Sylvis, Pioneer of American Labor* (New York: Columbia University Press, 1945), p. 189.

[7] *Ibid.*, p. 232.

relations with the native labor movement, and the literature of the Central Committee was reprinted in A. C. Cameron's *Workingmen's Advocate* of Chicago, the leading paper of the period.[8]

SOCIALIST LABOR PARTY

One of the many efforts to organize the socialists of the United States led to the formation of the Social Democratic Working Men's party in New York in 1874. It sponsored the convention in Philadelphia in 1876 which formed the Working Men's party of the United States. A year later it became the Socialist Labor party of North America.[9]

Soon thereafter the Socialist Labor party became embroiled in a dispute with the anarchists, some of whom had joined the party. The dispute centered around the Educational and Defense (*Lehr und Wehr*) societies formed to defend socialists against attack and to act as a counterforce to the police and militia. The Executive Committee of the Socialist Labor party disapproved of the societies and a sharp debate on the issue, ensued.

Differences over the armed clubs mirrored the increasing division over the use of violence as a revolutionary weapon. At the time, "propaganda by the deed" became popular with some sections in the revolutionary movement. Those who opposed the use of the ballot box and favored physical force were anarchists who were then called "social revolutionaries."

The anarchists had met in London in 1881 and set up the International Working People's Association as a loose federation. "Propaganda by the deed" was recognized as a proper form of revolutionary activity. Individual and collective violence were approved.[10] Delegates from the United States participated in the congress and approved the decisions. Following the congress, the New York Social Revolutionary Club joined the new International and invited other groups to follow. A conference in Chicago in 1881 was not an impressive gathering. The congress voted to organize workers on a local, national, and international basis for the abolition of the evils affecting society. Promotion of trade unions, organi-

---

8 Schlüter, *op. cit.*, pp. 127–128.

9 Hillquit, *op. cit.*, pp. 207–210.

10 Henry David, *The History of the Haymarket Affair* (New York: Rinehart & Company, 1936), pp. 65–66; Rudolf Röcker, *Johann Most: Das Leben Eines Rebellen* (Berlin: Fritz Kater, 1924), pp. 123–135.

zation of revolutionary action, and participation in politics in order to demonstrate its fraudulent character, were advocated.[11]

JOHANN MOST (1846–1906)

The early life in Germany of the leader of anarchism in the United States, Johann Most, the son of a noncommissioned army officer, was beset by cruelty and harshness. Long sickness had left his face permanently scarred, and a too severe stepmother and an exacting employer, to whom Most had been apprenticed, left an indelible imprint upon him. Although he lacked a formal education, Most traveled widely as a young man and learned to know the world and the revolutionary movement of his time. He became active in the International, and in 1869 was sentence to a month's imprisonment for an inflammatory speech at Vienna. The following year he was arrested for treason and after a few months in prison he was expelled from the country.

He later returned to Germany, where he became active in the socialist movement and was elected to Parliament in 1874. He served until the enactment of the antisocialist laws, when he was expelled from Berlin. Most now went to London, where he published the *Freedom,* but for glorifying the assassination of Alexander II of Russia by the Nihilists he was sentenced to prison for sixteen months. After his release in December, 1882, he came to New York, where he was greeted as a martyr to oppression.

Most toured the United States, receiving enthusiastic receptions from his followers and extensive publicity from the daily press. He inspired the setting up of anarchist groups in many communities, which led to a congress of anarchists and social revolutionaries at Pittsburgh in October, 1883. A national organization, the International Working People's Association, was established and the "Pittsburgh Declaration" issued. The purpose of the movement was "the destruction of the existing class government by all means, i.e. by energetic, implacable, revolutionary and international action. The free exchange of equivalent products between the producing organizations themselves and without the intervention of middlemen and profit making." [12]

11 David, *op. cit.,* pp. 67–74.
12 Quoted by Hillquit, *op. cit.,* p. 238.

THE EIGHT-HOUR MOVEMENT
AND THE HAYMARKET AFFAIR

The progress of American radicalism was interrupted by the Haymarket affair. At its convention in 1884 the Federation of Trades and Labor Unions of the United States and Canada had voted for the establishment of an eight-hour day by May 1, 1886. The anarchists threw themselves into this agitation with great energy. Not that they were convinced of the desirability of this step, but it served as a convenient means of agitation.

Chicago was a stronghold of the revolutionaries, who became leading speakers at shorter-hour meetings. A demonstration near the McCormick Reaper Works on May 3, 1886, was attacked by the police. Six were killed and many wounded. August Spies, who had been addressing the strikers during the attack, was outraged by the brutality and hurried to the office of the *Arbeiter-Zeitung*, where he wrote a circular headed "Revenge," which called for vengance. About two thousand attended a protest meeting held at Haymarket Square on the following day. The mayor found it peaceful and advised against police interference. Nevertheless, when the gathering was about to break up, a large platoon of policemen marched up and ordered the meeting to disperse. At this point a bomb was thrown at the police; it exploded, killing one and wounding others. Firing from both sides now began, and when the battle ended seven policemen had been killed and almost sixty wounded. In addition four workers were killed and about fifty wounded.

A wave of indignation, fanned into fever heat by the press, followed. Those who addressed the Haymarket meeting and the board and staff of the *Arbeiter-Zeitung* were arrested and subsequently indicted for murder. One of the defendents escaped, another turned state's evidence, and Albert Parsons, who could not be found, later voluntarily surrendered. Eight were brought to trial on June 21, 1886. The accused were not charged with personally participating in the murder, but with by word and speech inciting to murder which eventually led to the killing of policeman M. J. Degan. Not only was this theory open to serious objection, but the drawing of the jury and the conduct of the judge made the trial a farce. After forty-nine days of trial, six of the defendants were convicted and sentenced to be hanged, and one to fifteen years in prison. Appeals to the appelate court were in vain. Two of the seven asked the governor for executive clemency, which was granted. Louis Ling committed suicide in prison, and August Spies, Albert Parsons, Adolph Fischer, and George Engel were hanged on November 11, 1887.

Six years later, Governor John P. Altgeld pardoned the three defendants then in prison. He "had not granted the pardons because the men had been sufficiently punished for their acts, or for reasons of expediency: he was freeing [them] because he believed that they were not legally convicted of the crime for which they had been tried." [13]

The Haymarket affair, a tragic episode in the history of American radicalism, focused attention on the movement and aroused fear and hatred against it. Assessment of the effect of this tragedy upon the subsequent progress of American radicalism is not easy. However, Professor David, in his definitive study, believes it did little to slacken the progress of the radical and labor movements.[14]

GROWTH OF SOCIALIST INFLUENCE

By 1879 the Socialist Labor party had spread to twenty-five states and counted ten thousand members. However, the return of prosperity reduced the membership, and the party found the going more difficult.

A combination of reformers, Socialists, and single taxers participated in a municipal campaign in New York in 1886. After the election, an inevitable dispute took place between the Socialists and the single-tax followers of Henry George. At the United Labor Party Convention in Syracuse in August, 1887, the Socialists were beaten.

After the expulsion of the Socialists, a platform endorsing the single tax was adopted. To salve their wounds, the Socialists organized the Progressive Labor party. The single taxers also faced a division. Friction developed between Henry George and Father McGlynn over independent political action. George wanted to cooperate with the Democrats in the campaign of 1888, but McGlynn insisted on an independent policy. George and his followers split away. A national convention was called in Cincinnati in May, 1888, and the United Labor party was launched on a platform of free trade and the single tax. A presidential ticket was nominated, but it polled few votes in the election of 1888.

At its convention in 1889, the Socialist Labor party drew up a new platform which denounced plutocratic exploitation and urged "'honest

---

[13] David, op. cit., p. 493.
[14] Ibid., pp. 535–536.

citizens to organize under the banner of the Socialist Labor Party into a class-conscious body . . . so that held together by an indomitable spirit of solidarity under the most trying conditions of the present class struggle we may put a summary end to that barbarous struggle by the abolition of all classes." [15] Steady gains were made until 1899, when the S.L.P. reached the zenith of its power. In 1892 the first Socialist presidential ticket was launched; it received 21,152 votes in six states.

SOCIALIST TRADE AND LABOR ALLIANCE

Although polling a small popular vote, the Socialists exercised a much greater influence within the labor movement, and sought the adoption of socialist resolutions at union conventions.[16]

The Socialists were rebuffed by the American Federation of Labor when, after an acrimonious debate, the latter refused to seat a delegate representing a Socialist political group. Again in 1894 the A.F. of L. refused to endorse a socialist resolution. Thereupon the Socialist Labor party tried to capture the Knights of Labor. When it failed, the party set up, in 1896, the Socialist Trade and Labor Alliance as its industrial arm. From the beginning, this group was of slight importance, but its failure did not diminish the venomous attacks of Daniel De Leon, the leader of the Socialist Labor party, upon the American Federation of Labor.

Daniel De Leon (1852–1914) Daniel De Leon was born in Venezuela, studied in Germany, and came to the United States in the 1870's. He taught at Columbia University, joined the Socialist Labor party in 1890, and became the editor of its official English journal, *The People,* two years later. An orthodox Marxist, he was cocksure, intolerant, and narrow. He became the intellectual and moral autocrat of the Socialist Labor party and retained an absolute hold upon its dwindling membership. Uncompromising and dogmatic, he had, despite his extensive erudition, no understanding of American labor or of the realities of American life. His venom and unfairness created a wide gulf between the trade unions and the socialist movement. Locked in his Marxist ivory tower, he never sympathized with nor understood the real contributions of American unionists. Having failed to dominate the trade-union movement, he inspired the Socialist Trade and Labor Alliance, which he hoped would be the economic arm of his party.

15 Appendix II in Hillquit, *op. cit.*
16 John R. Commons and Associates, *History of Labor in the United States* (New York: The Macmillan Company, 1935), II, 510–532.

The vituperative fanaticism of De Leon finally met with resistance. His bitter attacks upon the honest labor-union officials aroused a number of socialist groups against him and led to a schism in the ranks.[17]

THE SOCIALIST PARTY

The Socialist party, which for many years had carried the banner of socialism, arose as a result of the collapse of the American Railway Union. The latter was launched as an industrial union of railway workers in 1893, and in a short period it enrolled about 150,000 members. A victory over the Great Northern Railway in April, 1894, increased its prestige. It decided to throw its strength behind the workers on strike against the Pullman Company. Over the protests of Governor Altgeld, federal troops were sent to Chicago, and the injunctions against the strikers and their leaders were used for purposes of ending the walkout. The strike was lost, and several strike leaders, including Eugene Victor Debs, were sentenced to jail for violating the injunction.

Convinced that his effort to build an industrial union of railwaymen had failed, Debs favored the colonizing of some western state in order to set up a limited or partial form of socialism. In June, 1897, the Social Democracy was established. Colonization was subsequently rejected, and a program of political action formulated. The name "Social Democracy" was adopted.

The faction opposed to De Leon within the Socialist Labor party set up an organization of its own, held a convention in February, 1900, nominated candidates for president and vice-president of the United States, and took steps to unite with the Social Democracy. A joint ticket was eventually chosen, despite some opposition in the Social Democracy party. Formal union took place in 1901, when the Socialist party was launched.

Although its gains were not spectacular, the Socialist party made solid and steady progress. The party polled the highest percentage of votes in 1912, when it mustered 5.9 per cent of the total votes cast. In 1910, the Socialist party elected its first congressman, Victor L. Berger from a Milwaukee district, and Meyer London from a New York City district four years later. In addition to electoral gains, the Socialists exercised widespread influence in many trade unions, and while the leaders of the

---

[17] Nathan Fine, *Labor and Farmer Parties in the United States, 1828–1928* (New York: The Rand School of Social Science, 1928), pp. 147–183.

American Federation of Labor were antisocialist in philosophy, the So-cialists were always a vigorous and respected minority group inside the labor movement.

Within the party two divergent tendencies existed from the beginning. On the one side were the revolutionaries, who believed that the function of a Socialist party was to emphasize the need for socializing productive property, install socialism, and disregard immediate reforms as useless palliatives. In addition it was hostile to trade unionism and emphasized rank-and-file rule. They were called "impossibilists." On the other side were the reform or evolutionary socialists, who favored winning office through the ballot, advocated reforms, and regarded socialism as an ideal of the future rather than an issue of the present. This faction was known as the "possibilists." From the beginning the possibilists and impossibilists were at war. Differences were especially sharp on the trade-union ques-tion, with the possibilists in general favoring working within the conservative trade-union movement. On the other hand, the revolution-ary socialists frequently favored supporting insurgent or dual unionism.

THE INDUSTRIAL WORKERS OF THE WORLD

Among the dual unions that came to the fore the Industrial Workers of the World was the best known. Organized in 1905 by militant socialists, it opposed the conservative policies of the American Federation of Labor. After two years of internal bickering, the Industrial Workers of the World directed its appeal to the most exploited sections in the American economy, the unskilled migratory worker then employed in agriculture, horticulture, lumbering, and road construction, and to the unorganized, foreign semiskilled workers neglected by the craft unions. Essentially it was a doctrineless movement resembling the Spanish anarchosyndicalist National Labor Federation. The Industrial Workers of the World adopted the syndicalist dogmas of the general strike, direct action, and sabotage. Many Socialists did not favor this movement, and opposed especially the advocacy of violence. The issues came before the conven-tion of the Socialist party in 1912, and the constitution was amended so as to bar from membership anyone who advocated sabotage or direct ac-tion. The amendment led to the withdrawal of some members from the party ranks.

WORLD WAR I

At the beginning of World War I, American Socialists took an antiwar position. However, differences made their appearance as soon as the possibility of American involvement became apparent. A special convention called in St. Louis to decide the issues divided into three groups: an antiwar majority, which was pacifist as well as Socialist; an antiwar minority that emphasized a revolutionary antiwar policy; and a very small prowar group. The majority report urged "active and public opposition to the war," unyielding opposition to conscription, and consistent propaganda against military training. It also called for socialization and democratic management of great industries. The adoption of this report led to the withdrawal of some of the prowar minority.

SPLIT

As in other countries, the Socialist party in the United States faced a split between the right and left wings following World War I. Differences between possibilists and impossibilists had existed from the beginning of the party's history, but the differences never came to an open break. However, the Bolshevik Revolution convinced the left-wingers that a revolution was imminent in the United States and that the Socialist party was obligated to lead it. Following what has since become known as standard Communist tactics, an attempt was made to capture the Socialist party. The heads of the Socialist party refused to allow the capture of their organization, and as a result two Communist parties were established, the Communist party and the Communist Labor party. Later the two merged to form the United Communist party. The merger followed a period of raids and persecution instigated by A. Mitchell Palmer, the attorney general of the United States, which drove the Communists "underground." A more balanced government attitude finally made it possible for the Communists to begin functioning as a political group without being subject to police interference.

During the Communist party's underground existence, the American Labor Alliance and, later, the Workers' party, were the legal arms of the Communist party. Subsequently, the Workers' party changed its name to the "Communist Party of the United States." Representing the Communist movement in the United States, it was affiliated with the Communist International until the latter's dissolution in 1943, and has to this day mirrored faithfully the ever- changing party line as laid down by the International leadership. In energy and drive, the membership of the Communist party excels that of other left-wing organizations. Communists in the United States show the same type of discipline and the same monolithic views as the Communists of other countries. Close knit and infiltrating, they operate directly through unwary "innocents" and disguised members who bore their way into labor and other types of political and cultural organizations. Communists have been fairly successful in winning important positions in several newly organized labor unions.

AGRARIAN RADICALISM

Socialism is in the main a philosophy strongly influenced by European writers, and at the beginning its chief recruiting ground was among foreign workers. In addition, an indigenous movement centering largely in the agrarian areas became a frequent component of the American political scene. As a rule, the farmer movements lacked an elaborate philosophy. They usually yearned for a simpler state of affairs and opposed monopoly, railroad discrimination, or "sound" money. Lower transportation rates, higher prices, or lower interest charges were customary demands.

GRANGERS

The Granger movement represented the protest of the farming community against discrimination, exorbitant charges, and high-handedness of the railroads. To remedy these evils, the farmers turned to the Grange, or the Patrons of Husbandry, which had been founded in December, 1867. The organization sponsored the advancement of agriculture through the education of the farmer. At first the movement spread slowly, but by the early 1870's, the Grange had established itself as an important farmers' society.[18]

In 1873, the founders were retired from power and were replaced by more aggressive organizers. Granges spread rapidly, and by 1873 only four states out of the then thirty-two did not have them.[19] The following year, at a national convention of Granges held in St. Louis, the general purpose was declared to be the advancement of the interests of the order, the nation, and humanity.

[18] Solon J. Buck, *The Agrarian Crusade* (New Haven: Yale University Press, 1921), pp. 3–5.
[19] *Ibid.*, p. 27.

The expanding organizations became in the 1870's political instruments for the farmers. In some instances the old parties were used; and where the Grangers, as they were called, were rebuffed by the older politicians, they established new parties. "Known variously as Independent, Reform, Anti-Monopoly, or Farmers' Parties, these organizations were all parts of the same general movement, and their platforms were quite similar." [20] The reformers demanded regulation of corporations, especially those engaged in railroad transportation, and economy in government. The Granger agitation led to the regulation of railroad rates, both directly by the legislature and by railroad commissions appointed by the state legislatures. These laws were challenged in the courts, and in *Munn* v. *Illinois*,[21] the United States Supreme Court upheld the right of the state to regulate a business clothed with a public interest. The Grangers scored some notable political successes, but by 1874 the movement was on the decline. Many of the state laws were repealed before they received a trial, and the movement expired.

GREENBACKISM

With the fading out of the movement for regulation of the railroads, the greenback agitation made its appearance. Demands for inflation are the hardy perennials of American politics. Beginning with the colonial period, demands for a cheaper dollar have been advanced by the farming sections, and these demands have at times been too loud and too potent to be ignored. In the 1870's and 1880's the issue revolved around the retirement of greenback currency.

During the Civil War more than $400,000,000 in inconvertible paper notes were issued by the government.[22] The greenbacks declined in value in relation to gold, and after the Civil War an attempt was made to retire them and resume specie payments. Congress forbade further retirement in 1868, but a bill permanently increasing the currency by $400,000,000 was vetoed by President Grant in 1874. This became the basis of the greenback agitation.

Greenback Party   Greenback clubs arose in many parts of the country, and the convention of the National Independent party at Indianapolis in 1876 invited independent men to join ranks in the movement for finan-

20 *Ibid.*, p. 31.
21 94 U.S., 113 (1876).
22 Wesley C. Mitchell, *A History of Greenbacks* (Chicago: University of Chicago Press, 1903).

cial reform and industrial emancipation.[23] Peter Cooper was nominated for president and polled about 80,000 votes.

In the 1870's there were indications of the cooperation of the Greenback and Labor Reform Parties in several states. In all the states labor reformers and greenbackers were two branches of the same party being formed in the country to deal with economic problems that the old parties were not taking up.

Union was finally achieved at a conference in Toledo in 1878.[24] The National party was the name chosen by the labor reformers and advocates of cheap money, but it was usually known as the Greenback-Labor party. Monetization of silver, an adequate money supply, and a graduated income tax were planks in the platform presented to the country.[25]

EDWARD KELLOGG (1790-1858)

Greenbackism was inspired by Edward Kellogg, whose *A New Monetary System* first appeared in 1849 under the title of *Labor and Other Capital*. The work made a deep impression upon farmer leaders. Kellogg believed that "some cause is operating with continual and growing effect to separate production from the producer. The wrong is evident, but neither statesmen nor philanthropists have traced it to its true source; and hence they have not been able to project any plan sufficient for its removal." [26]

According to Kellogg, "money governs the distribution of property, and thus affects in a thousand ways the relations of man to man."

He attacked the distribution and centralization of wealth. "In addition to these evils all civilized nations are every few years visited with great revulsions in trade. Outstanding debts become unsafe, and many debtors bankrupt." However, Kellogg denied that depressed trade is caused by overproduction. Instead, he insisted that it lies "in the power that governs the distribution of the products."

Kellogg emphasized that the power of general acceptance of money is due to its being a legal agent. In other words, the power of money is derived from its property as legal tender. "It is clear that gold possesses no

23 Commons, *op. cit.*, II, 169.
24 *Ibid.*, pp. 240–242.
25 *Ibid.*, pp. 245.
26 Edward Kellogg, *A New Monetary System* (New York: Kiggins, Tooker and Co., 1868), p. xv. The following quotations from Kellogg are from this source, pp. 17, 27, 72, 184, 266, 274.

peculiar or inherent excellence to endow it with power to determine the value and control the use of all other things. But when it is made the agent of . . . these legal powers, it becomes necessary to acquire the gold in order to discharge debts; and the quantity of the metal being limited, its owners are enabled from the necessitous a very high price for its use."

He saw in the high interest rates a serious evil, and urged that it be sharply reduced. "In the United States if interest were reduced to one or to one and one-tenth percent, useful production would probably increase from twenty-five to fifty percent." Interest is the means whereby the producer is robbed of his labor, enabling the capitalist to accumulate large profits. A monetary system must be perfected which will break the power of the capitalist.

Fluctuations in price levels was another evil, for "a currency constantly fluctuating in value, by varying rates of interest, is no more suitable as a medium of exchange than an elastic yardstick is fit for a measure of cloth; that justice requires uniformity of value, and that our present currency is devoid of that quality."

REMEDIES

Kellogg regarded gold and silver as an inadequate basis for a proper monetary system. Limited in quantity, they are incapable of providing an adequate supply of money. Moreover, its scarcity makes for fluctuation in value, and thus money loses its stability. Consequently, Kellogg advocated the issuance of paper money adequate in amount to fulfill all needs. The banks would cease to issue notes; instead, a national currency would be provided by the central government. Money would be supplied to borrowers on proper security, and a rate of interest set that would "secure to labor and capital their respective rights and . . . fix the interest at that rate." The plan required the central government to set up what he called a Safety Fund, the money of which was to be secured by mortgages and would constitute legal tender. People could always loan to the Safety Fund at an annual rate of interest of 1 per cent. Money would be legal tender and could always be converted for income.

Kellogg would guard against overissue by allowing the conversion of money into government bonds at a rate of interest below that paid on mortgages. Convertibility of money into bonds and bonds into money give a flexible currency and destroy the power of banks and monopolists to rule production. The theory that social injustice could be remedied only by legislation and political action on the part of farmers and laborers contained a powerful appeal to the interests and democratic traditions of those classes which were confronted by the rising capitalism of the post-war period. Equally attractive was the statement that these ends could be achieved without any infringement of liberty of contract, private enterprise, and private property in production and business. Thus in spite of its similarity to the conceptions of Marx and Proudhon, and to the financial proposals of Louis Blanc, Marx and Lassalle, Kelloggism remained essentially American in method and appeal.[27]

In common with other movements inspired by agrarian discontent, the Greenbackers found the farmer unresponsive to their message as soon as the "sun of prosperity was beginning . . . to disrupt the clouds of depression." [28] Moreover, the crops of corn, wheat, and oats raised in 1880 were large and prices good. "When the farmer had large crops to dispose of at renumerative prices, he lost interest in the inflation of the currency." [29] Thus the vote of 1880 represented the high-water mark of Greenbackism, although a presidential ticket with General Benjamin F. Butler at the head was nominated in cooperation with the Anti-Monopoly Organization of the United States. The latter had met in Chicago in May, 1884, demanded regulation of corporations, and nominated General Butler for president. The combined ticket polled 175,370 votes.[30] Noticeable was the diminished vote in the agricultural areas.

FARMERS' ALLIANCE

Farmers who had been active in the Grange were induced to join other organizations as soon as it declined. The new movement centered around farmers' clubs or alliances, and were formed initially to protect them from horse thieves and land sharks, and to promote cooperative purchasing.

Soon the movement turned to politics, and the constitution was amended to make participation easier. Organizers were sent out and alliances formed in many southern states. Similar organizations were arising in the northern areas, and by 1880 enough local groups had been established to support a national organization. Its object was "to unite the

27 Chester McArthur Destler, *American Radicalism 1865–1901* (New London: Connecticut College, 1946), p. 55.
28 Buck, *op. cit.*, p. 95.
29 *Ibid.*
30 *Ibid.*, p. 97.

farmers of the United States for their protection against class legislation, and the encroachments of concentrated capital and the tyranny of monopoly." [31] The Farmers' Alliance demanded just taxation of property, an income tax, and regulation of interstate commerce.

SUBTREASURY SCHEME

A subtreasury scheme was evolved that required the abolition of banks as federal depositories. In their place, warehouses would be established in every county which would offer for sale annually $500,000 worth of farm products. Farmers could deposit their crops at these warehouses and receive a loan in legal tender up to 80 per cent of current value. Interest of 1 per cent would be charged. Unless redeemed within one year, the crops would be sold at public auction.

COOPERATIVES

Cooperative creameries and grain elevators were also promoted, but politics became increasingly the objective of the Alliance. The culmination of the political tendencies came in 1889, when the Farmers and Laborers Union and the Northwestern Alliance and the southern group met in St. Louis to effect a merger. No basis of agreement could be reached.

The proliferation of farmers' organizations was visible testimony of underlying dissatisfaction. Infiltration into the Republican and Democratic parties was tried, but the policy was not fully successful. Despite the reluctance of some leaders, the Alliance entered the political campaign of 1890 and forced adoption of some of its principles by the Republican and Democratic organizations.

PEOPLE'S PARTY

In addition, independent tickets were entered in some states. The fair amount of success these had stimulated demands for a national convention to prepare for the presidential elections of 1892. As a result, the Knights of Labor, the Colored Farmers' Alliance, the National Farmers' Alliance, the Farmers' Alliance, the Farmers' Union, and the Citizens' Alliance set up a national committee to coordinate the activities of these liberal organizations. In the meantime, a conference of delegates from labor, farmer, and reform groups met in Cincinnati in May, 1882, and

[31] Quotations, *ibid.*, p. 118.

launched the People's party of the United States of America. Resolutions were adopted calling for a coalition of progressives; if the coalition was not effected, a convention for nominating presidential candidates was to be called.

Having failed to come to an agreement with the other parties, the first national convention of the People's party opened at Omaha on July 2, 1892, with more than 1300 delegates. General James Weaver was nominated for president and General James B. Field for vice-president. The ticket received 1,041,577 popular and 22 electoral votes.[32]

THE SILVER ISSUE

From the beginning, the demand for cheap money was high on the Populist list. "Free silver, on the other hand, although not ignored in the earlier period, did not attain foremost rank among the demands of the dissatisfied classes until the last decade of the century and more particularly after the panic of 1893." [33] To placate the resentment of the silver-producing areas the Silver Purchase Act of 1890 was passed, but it failed to halt the downward slide in the value of silver. The Populists agreed to support the champion of silver, William Jennings Bryan, the Democratic candidate for president in 1896. Placing Thomas Watson of Georgia as candidate for vice-president was a concession made to the "middle-of-the-road" group which opposed the nomination of Bryan. It was hoped that the identity of the Populist party would thus be preserved. The maneuver failed, and marked the end of the People's party, although independent presidential candidates were presented to the voters in the elections of 1900, 1904, and 1908, when they polled relatively few votes. Agrarian discontent was to manifest itself for a time through the two regular political parties. In 1915, the Nonpartisan League made its appearance in North Dakota.

The Populists feared big business and felt that older parties were the servants of wealth; by their agitation they helped to break down party loyalty and create greater political fluidity. The demands for a more elastic currency, paper money, easy credit for the farmer, and protection of agricultural income were later adopted by subsequent administrations.[34] Maximum fulfillment was not to be attained, however, until the New Deal administration of Franklin Roosevelt.

[32] Haynes, *op. cit.*, pp. 261–268.
[33] Buck, *op. cit.*, p. 155.
[34] John D. Hicks, *The Populist Revolt* (Minneapolis: University of Minnesota Press, 1931), pp. 404–423.

NONPARTISAN LEAGUE

Discontent with conditions also led to the formation of the Nonpartisan League, which aimed to devise a program to protect the economic position of agriculture. As a result of the contemptuous rejection of the demands of the farmers by the North Dakota legislature in 1915, A. C. Townley began the organization of the Nonpartisan League. A five-point program demanded state ownership of terminal elevators, flour mills, packing houses, and cold-storage plants; state inspection of grain and grain dockage; exemption of farm improvements from taxation; state hail insurance on the acreage-tax basis; and rural credit banks operated at cost.

The movement spread rapidly, elected a governor in North Dakota, established strong organizations in other states, and formed a National Nonpartisan League. Instead of setting up as an independent political party, the League entered the primaries and tried to capture the nominations for the old party candidates it endorsed. The high point of its success was reached about 1920. From then on it steadily lost strength, and it has since become a faction within the Republican party of North Dakota. As a reform party it was, like its agrarian predecessors, highly unstable. By 1920, organized urban radicalism, which was represented by the Socialist party, had likewise lost much of its influence. Agrarian radicalism, which seemed on the point of active revival with the success of the Nonpartisan League, soon ran its course.

FARMER-LABOR PARTY

Dissatisfaction following the close of World War I led a number of Socialist and ex-Socialist labor officers to promote a Labor party. A second group, the Committee of Forty-Eight, was made up of liberal intellectuals full of ideas but with a small following. Nevertheless, the presidential candidate nominated in 1920, Parley Parker Christensen, polled over a quarter of a million votes.

CONFERENCE FOR PROGRESSIVE POLITICAL ACTION

The hostile attitude of government, the increase in injunctions, and judicial restrictions upon labor in the early 1920's led to the calling of a conference by the heads of a number of large labor organizations. In contrast to the activity for a labor party, which was supported mainly by local groups, this movement was sponsored by powerful internationals. Virtually every type of progressive group was represented at the conference in February, 1922, and a policy of allowing each state to adopt a policy of independent political action or of working within the old parties was adopted. The nominations of conservative candidates on both the Republican and Democratic presidential tickets in 1924 forced the Conference for Progressive Political Action to call a convention and nominate Robert M. La Follette for president. He ran on what was largely an antimonopoly platform, interlarded with criticisms of judicial usurpation and Wilson's foreign policy. Although he carried only his own state, Wisconsin, he made—considering the lack of financial backing, organization, and time—a truly remarkable showing. He polled almost 5,000,000 votes. Nevertheless the railroad unions, which were the chief supporters of this venture, felt uneasy. An independent political movement, they feared, would lessen their influence with Congress, where laws regulating railway labor conditions on interstate carriers were made. It might thereby seriously weaken the position of their unions. Consequently they withdrew from further participation, their withdrawal marking the end of another independent political movement.

After the collapse of the Conference for Progressive Political Action, the Socialist party was back on its own. It ran Norman Thomas for president in 1928, but he polled a small vote.

A DECADE OF OPTIMISM

Throughout the 1920's, the general feeling was that the United States had solved the problem of the business cycle and periodic depressions. Optimism was widespread, and only critical and sophisticated observers were able to perceive the chinks in the armor of the American economy, but they were regarded as Cassandras who found pleasure in predicting disaster for their fellow countrymen. For the great majority, it was a new era of good wages and high employment, and a living testimony to the fairness and efficiency of a free-enterprise economy.

The causes of the depth and duration of the depression of the 1930's have been a topic for prolonged learned, and unlearned discussion. Whatever may have been the reason for the decline, its disastrous consequences cannot be denied. Beginning with the collapse of stock prices in the fall of 1929, the decline continued until the production of goods was down by more than one third. Pay rolls moved even lower. They were less than 40.0 on the basis of 1926 = 100.0. Not only were suffering and destitution rampant in the cities and in industrial areas, but agricultural income, which had never recovered from the price collapse of 1921, now tobogganed even lower.

18. *THE NEW DEAL*

THE NEW ADMINISTRATION

President Franklin Delano Roosevelt took office when hunger demonstrations were spreading through the cities and foreclosure riots were commonplace throughout the countryside. He therefore had to proceed upon two fronts. Moreover, the absence of any significant organized radicalism either in the city or in the country meant that he had to improvise a program and use his political talent to push it through Congress. Absence of a *strong* progressive or socialistic movement made it impossible for him to embark upon any program that involved fundamental change in economic relations, even had he so desired. While the country demanded change, it did not, by electing Franklin D. Roosevelt, ask for revolution, for Norman Thomas, the Socialist candidate, polled less than 900,000 votes and William Z. Foster, the Communist nominee, slightly above 100,000. Roosevelt had been elected as a protest against the unbearable economic conditions, and as he was forced to relieve both agriculture and industry, the policies evolved were sometimes contradictory. He was not and never pretended to be a revolutionary, and the absence of any numerically large radical groups hampered the development of a program that would break with the past.

Social and political radicalism, both urban and rural, were moribund, and there existed only inchoate and desperate dissatisfaction ready to be churned into a sinister and dangerous force by a silver-tongued demagogue. The eternal greatness of Roosevelt rests in part on his recognition that a dispirited and disillusioned populace was a danger to the survival of democratic freedom, on his deep sympathy for the common man, and on his ability to push his improvised program through a Congress basically hostile to his objectives.

277

Indeed, his great political virtuosity saved the United States from the danger of having foisted upon it a quasi-fascist dictatorship. The need to act on several fronts—succor the unemployed, aid the farmer and rescue the businessman, while improvising policies that might lead to permanent recovery—largely accounts for the seeming contradictions of the Roosevelt program. Although the ideas and policies of the New Deal were far from new, the New Deal is unique in that its leader actually created a political group to help him rather than being himself the product and chosen leader of an antecedent political faction.

"The notion that the New Deal had a preconceived theoretical position is ridiculous. The pattern it was to assume was not clear or specific in Roosevelt's mind, in the mind of the Democratic Party, or in the mind of anyone else taking part in the 1932 campaign." [1] He and the majority in the party were convinced that a humanitarian program was needed and desirable. Making life better for the ordinary man was accepted by Roosevelt, his supporters, and his party as a prime objective.[2] There was, however, no precise or even general program. At the beginning, the Roosevelt administration faced the need for embarking upon an emergency or "rescue" program. The farmers, urban workers, and small businessmen needed help, and so programs of relief were launched. "But there was no central unified plan. There wasn't time or organization for that. The New Deal grew out of these emergency and necessary rescue actions. The intellectual and spiritual climate was Roosevelt's general attitude that *the people mattered.*" [3]

RELIEF

Swift action was needed. The Federal Emergency Relief Administration was the first step in a relief program inaugurated two and one-half months after Roosevelt took office. It was by no means a complete answer, but "it kept people alive and instilled courage." [4] It was not a theory of relief that Roosevelt had in mind, but people; and although well-fed people told hundreds of jokes about the shovel-leaners, Roosevelt was always impressed by the real contributions made by these programs. And they were many.[5]

1 Frances Perkins, *The Roosevelt I Knew* (New York: The Viking Press, 1946), pp. 166–167. The quotations from this source are reprinted by permission of the publishers.
2 *Ibid.*, p. 167.
3 173. Italics in original.
4 *Ibid.*, p. 185.
5 Miss Perkins describes Roosevelt's reactions to the relief projects on pages 186–188, *ibid.*

Virtually no serious thought had been given by the federal government to unemployment. The Hoover administration had been adamant against federal aid to the needy, for it regarded care of the destitute as a local responsibility. Persistent pressure forced a minor concession. The Reconstruction Finance Corporation was authorized to lend to states and local governments up to $300,000,000 for the relief of the needy. Under the leadership of President Roosevelt, Congress enacted the Federal Emergency Relief Act on May 12, 1933. With an appropriation of $500,000,000, and one almost twice as large in February, 1934, the federal government sought to aid in relieving destitution. It marked a milestone in American political history, for the federal government explicitly accepted obligations to aid the destitute. Relief standards were raised, work relief was at first slowly introduced, and a Work Division of the Federal Emergency Relief Administration was set up to direct this phase of the relief program.

During 1935 the federal government tried a new approach. In order to differentiate between the unemployed and the chronically poor and disabled, the Works Progress Administration was created. It had the responsibility of providing work for several million idle and destitute workers who were able and willing to work. The chronically unemployed were turned back to the states for aid. This program has been described "as a halfway house between 'pure made work' and a public works program as usually understood." [6] Wage rates were far below prevailing rates, and varied among sections and among urban and rural communities. As 90 per cent of the workers employed on a project had to be drawn from the relief rolls, and as the expenditures per worker employed were kept low, the program fell short of being a public works program. Moreover, the type of project was usually, although not always, one which would "return dividends in social benefits and aesthetic pleasure rather than in cash or even in taxable capacity." [7] Yet the Works Progress Administration was the staff and hope of millions. Artists, actors, and students were given a chance to participate.

In addition, thousands of miles of roads were built, bridges, tunnels, and airports constructed, and school buildings and recreation centers provided for many communities. The work-relief program aroused an avalanche of criticism among conservative people and those fearful of the

[6] The Editors of *The Economist* (London), *The New Deal: Analysis and Appraisal* (New York: Alfred A. Knopf, Inc., 1937), p. 10.

[7] *Ibid.*, pp. 10–11.

effect of budgetary deficits upon financial solvency. Other charges were also made. Waste, favoritism, and political use of funds were charged. Nevertheless, as the editors of *The Economist* noted, "Against them must be set admiration for the amazing rapidity with which the vast organization was improvised and for the imaginative humanity with which it has been administered." [8]

SOCIAL SECURITY

For the first time the United States government embarked on a program of social security involving unemployment insurance, old-age benefits, and aid to the blind and to the destitute aged. Although it was by no means adequate, it marked a significant step in the evolution of a program of aid against loss of income. Actually there was little organized support for social security, and the American Federation of Labor opposed it until 1932. Only a few social workers, radical labor people, and students of the problem favored it. Mass support was certainly lacking.

LABOR

On the labor front, the Roosevelt administration, by a series of laws beginning with Section 7 (A) of the National Industrial Recovery Act, tried to protect labor's right to organize and to bargain collectively. Section 7 (A), the (Wagner) National Labor Relations Act, and the Railway Labor Act of 1934 gave to organized labor the protection needed to expand its organizations and to penetrate into the hitherto unorganized mass-production industries. On the wage level, the administration pushed through the Public Contracts and the Wages and Hours laws to bolster wages. The marshaling of millions of workers into unions and the recognition by the leaders of labor of their dependence upon government made the heads of American unions more hospitable to government intervention in economic affairs and more aware of the benefits to be derived from political action. It has meant the appearance of a new force in American politics, one whose voice is likely to become increasingly powerful with time.

AGRICULTURE

In the 1920's the farmer progressively faced a danger of insolvency. During World War I he had benefited from the world's need for his products, and prices rose sharply. With increasing farm prices and in-

8 *Ibid.,* p. 15.

comes, land values skyrocketed and the margin of cultivation was pushed out. Marginal land that should have lain fallow was drawn into use.

Unfortunately the high prosperity did not last. An era of agricultural deflation began in the fall of 1920 and lasted for more than a decade. Prices slid downward until they were, in some instances, lower than they had been for fifty years. Farm income slumped from $15,000,000,000 in 1919 and about $12,000,000,000 in 1929 to slightly above $5,000,000,000 in 1932. At the same time, while agricultural prices and income were declining, the prices of manufactured goods either remained stable or declined at a slower rate. A number of remedies were tried. The Packers and Stockyards Act of 1921 forbade control of prices and other monopolistic practices by the packers. Amendments to the Federal Reserve and Federal Farm Loan Acts authorized the Federal Farm Loan Board to set up twelve federal intermediate banks each with capital subscribed by the government. The Agricultural Marketing Act of 1929 was another device. The law created a Federal Farm Board to encourage the development of agricultural marketing cooperatives. Trying to prevent the piling up of surpluses of farm commodities, the board set up the Grain Stabilization Corporation, which purchased large amounts of grain and succeeded in holding the domestic price of wheat above the world price. Similar operations were tried in cotton, and the attempt by the Cotton Stabilization Corporation to stabilize cotton prices led to serious monetary losses. Farmers were then urged to restrict acreage, but this plea fell on deaf ears, since no inducements for carrying out the program were provided.

With the onset of the depression of the 1930's, the farmer suffered another blow. Gross farm income, which had been between $11,000,000,-000 and $12,000,000,000 between 1922 and 1929, fell to about $9,500,000,-000 in 1930 and $6,968,000,000 in 1931 and $5,531,000,000 in 1932. Although other prices also fell, they did not decline as rapidly as did farmers' income.

The New Deal's Agricultural Adjustment Act was the major instrument for curing the ills of agriculture. Farmers were given benefit payments to supplement the amounts they derived from their crops. A small part of the funds was withdrawn from the public treasury, but the larger part was raised by taxes on the processors of agricultural commodities. It was assumed that these payments would be made out of profit margins or shifted to the consumer in the form of higher prices. Payments were conditioned upon the farmer's restricting his acreage so that total supply would be such as to restore agricultural prices to parity, defined as the relationship between agricultural prices to nonagricultural prices in 1909–1914.[9]

The agricultural scheme has been criticized on the ground that the most prosperous peacetime years were used as a basis for parity; and that the forward shifting of part or all of the processors' taxes to the consumer was inequitable. Many people objected most strenuously to the restrictive part of the program, believing that such a policy was immoral in a world of want. It was also subjected to the ridicule of political wits. Yet a group of expert foreign observers concluded "there is no room for doubt that the position of the American farmer has improved greatly, and much more rapidly than the position of the country as a whole, since 1932." [10]

Ever-Normal Granary The ever-normal granary system was proposed after the invalidation of the AAA in the Hoosac Mills case by the United States Supreme Court. The Court held that regulation of agriculture was not a proper exercise of Congressional power, as such powers were reserved to the states, and that the processing taxes were used to purchase "submission to federal regulation." Under the ever-normal granary system, federal loans were to accumulate surpluses in good years, and the stocks liquidated in poor crop years. Crop production was to be adjusted to the evolving supply and demand situation. A shift from acreage control to soil conservation was made in the Soil Conservation and Domestic Allotment Act of February, 1936, so as to meet the Court's objection.

The apparent object of the law was to preserve soil fertility, promote the economic use of the land, and re-establish and restore agricultural income. Funds were appropriated and payments were made to induce farmers to shift their crops and to restrict acreage in soil-depleting crops and increase it in soil-conserving crops. Under the Agricultural Adjustment Act of 1938, the soil-conservation program was continued. Benefit payments were made to producers of certain crops, and the effort to restore parity of agricultural to other income based on the 1909 to 1914 ratio was continued. Upon the recommendation of the secretary of agriculture, loans by the Commodity Credit Corporation were authorized whenever certain enumerated crops appeared to be in excess of domestic and export needs, or if farm prices were below a given percentage of

9 Leverett S. Lyon and Victor Abramson and Others, *Government and Economic Life* (Washington, D.C.: The Brookings Institution, 1940), II, 913–914.
10 *The New Deal: Analysis and Appraisal*, p. 62.

parity. Farmers participating in the conservation program were allowed to borrow a larger percentage of the parity price than nonparticipants. If payments made in connection with acreage allotment under the conservation plan failed to control output, "marketing quotas" were to be imposed after a referendum of the producers of the crop in question. Only when approved by at least a two-thirds majority were quotas imposed.

Crop insurance was another aid to the farmer. Surpluses were diverted into relief channels or to processors of agricultural commodities who could convert particular surplus commodities into low-price uses while maintaining price differentials in the principal markets. Export subsidies to enable the farmer to sell on the world market were also tried. Indirect aid to the farmer was given by the Rural Electrification Administration, which helped in the development of generating and transmission facilities for rural users. A program of aid to low-income families was for a time in effect. In sum, the aid given to agriculture was varied and substantial, and was proportionately greater than that received by any other economic or vocational group. Moreover, it continued much longer than aid to labor. Yet the farmer was the first to desert the Roosevelt standard despite the substantial help received. Although he himself was a beneficiary of government aid, the farmer looked askance at other aspects of the Roosevelt program, especially its prolabor policies. While not averse to receiving a benefit check, the farmer remained an unrepentant individualist benefiting by government price supports. There is something humorously contradictory about the Farm Bureau Federation's demanding that the government get out of business, while asking higher price guarantees for the farmer. As a rule, the farmer is not a reformer nor material for a reform party, for he is quite content with the *status quo* as long as his market is protected. Concessions to labor or efforts to introduce reforms of no immediate significance in the solution of their own problems found no sympathetic response in these quarters. The farmers soured on the New Deal and became its open enemy, and their return to the New Deal standard in 1948 was motivated by the fear of losing price supports rather than by any hankering for a reform program. Yet the farmer is not an opponent of public power, regulation of business, or managed money. A basis for cooperation on a reform program by labor and agriculture can be discovered, but certainly never on a Marxist foundation. Roosevelt did gain labor support, and while he could always depend for large majorities in the urban and industrial areas, he did not enjoy the unqualified endorsement of the labor leaders. The split in the labor movement made even more difficult the building of a solid political labor base for a program, faction, or party. The A.F. of L., long accustomed to think of itself as *the* labor movement, was likely to regard equal treatment of its opponent, the C.I.O., as favoritism. Moreover, with the increase in competition between the rival unions, political cooperation became virtually impossible.

A complicating factor was the significant role then played by followers of the Communist party line in political activities of C.I.O. unions, especially on the local level. The influence of the Communists made the building of a political group to operate in the primaries or elections much more difficult. Roosevelt could temporarily organize those conflicting elements, for the urban workers and most of the leaders almost instinctively recognized their debt to him. Without his power to weld them together, the New Deal forces began to disintegrate, and the much-vaunted Political Action Committee showed that its strength was derived from Roosevelt. The effect of Roosevelt's policies was perhaps best observed in the presidential elections of 1948. Frightened by the action of the Eightieth Congress, labor poured out more money and energy than ever before in an effort to defeat legislators hostile to its program. Its unity undoubtedly contributed to the outcome of the presidential election. The results again demonstrated the weak appeal of Marxist views to the American worker. Not only was Henry Wallace's vote very low for one who had attained his political position and whose campaign was not hampered by financial problems, but his vote in the industrial areas was as low as in the middle-class sections.

Roosevelt has, if anything, reinforced the American belief in the possibilities of gradualism and the American distaste for Marxist policies. Roosevelt's confidence, firmness, and good humor reflected themselves in the mood of the people. The bleak gloom which had settled over the country in the early 1930's began to dissipate. He did not give final answers, and in many cases his remedies failed to get at the root of the trouble. Yet his bold and confident actions restored the faith of many in the efficiency and generosity of democratic government. He in fact made possible the working out of solutions by democratic means in an environment of free and representative government.

19. *THE FIRST RUSSIAN REVOLU-TIONARY MOVEMENT*

The Russian revolutionary movement arose within the framework of an absolutist state. Although feudalism lasted longer, and orthodoxy and absolutism exercised a greater effect on thought and feeling, European ideas found a hospitable reception among some members of the intelligentsia but were bitterly rejected by others. European ideas and ideals that reached Russia could, because of differences in history and institutions, be transmuted into something else. Absence of the franchise and of freedom of the press, speech, and assembly, coupled with Draconian measures against reformers, gave a singular stamp to the Russian revolutionary movement. This should not be overstressed, for ideas and movements devoted to Western ideals of freedom and parliamentarianism were by no means absent. Even among the Marxists, the Menshevik faction aspired for democracy and individual freedom. The liberals and large segments of the Social Revolutionaries valued freedom as a priceless possession worth risking personal liberty and even life to attain. Although it cannot be denied that the movements devoted to individual freedom were swept aside, we should recognize that the totalitarianism of the present regime, while a development of the belief of the leaders of the victorious October Revolution in dictatorship, did not come into its dominating position at once. It was a steady growth and perhaps a natural outcome of the initial Bolshevik policies.

THE DECEMBRISTS

The movement for democracy and freedom that spread through Europe in the late eighteenth and early nineteenth centuries did not leave Russia untouched. The pioneer democrat, Aleksandr Radishchev, attended the University of Leipzig, where he acquired a knowledge of Western liberal ideas. His *Voyage from Petersburg to Moscow,* published in 1790, was a merciless if veiled criticism of serfdom and the wretchedness and oppression that filled his native land. On philosophic grounds he believed that every great movement of reform inevitably degenerates. The early Christian church and Protestanism showed this tendency, and he believed that the French Revolution—in the midst of which he lived—would undergo the same evolution. Even though his ideas did not gain a wide audience, he was arrested and sentenced to death. His sentence was, however, commuted to exile and he spent six years in Siberia.[1]

The Napoleonic Wars brought Russian soldiers and officers into direct contact with the thought and institutions of Western Europe. Many were impressed by the greater freedom in the West, and a movement to bring Russia into line with the more progressive countries of Europe was begun. The Union of Salvation or Society of Time and Faithful Sons of the Fatherland, a secret society, was established by a group of army officers.[2] Among the first recruits was the future leader of the revolt against the autocracy, Pavel Pestel. He was the outstanding personality of the movement and gave force and direction to its work.[3] On many points the revolutionists were not able to agree on a program or tactics, and they split into two groups. The more militant group led by Pestel demanded an end to feudalism and the creation of a society based on the welfare of the majority. It advocated a unified central state in which with Russian nationality and culture would be dominant. Class and caste distinctions were to be abolished, and landed property was to remain the property of the state, each cultivator being allowed to use enough land to support five persons.[4]

REVOLT

After the death of Alexander I, the revolutionaries launched a revolt in December, 1825. The Decembrists, as they have been called, were defeated and their leaders arrested. A committee headed by the new czar,

---

[1] Thomas G. Masaryk, *The Spirit of Russia.* Translated by Eden and Cedar Paul (London: George Allen & Unwin, Ltd.), I, 146–148.

[2] Anatole G. Mazour, *The First Russian Revolution* (Berkeley: University of California Press, 1937), p. 66.

[3] Ludwig Kulczycki, *Geschichte der Russischen Revolution.* Translated from Polish to German by Anna Schapise-Nenrath (Goth: Friedrich Andreas Pertles, 1910), I, 84.

[4] Mazour, *op. cit.,* pp. 110–116.

Nicholas, investigated the revolt and some of the accused were personally interviewed by him. In June, 1826, a court was appointed to try the Decembrists. The trial was a farce, for the accused were allowed no defense and no counsel. Five leaders, including Pestel, were hanged, and others were sentenced to prison and exile.[5]

The Decembrists were, in fact, the first revolutionaries of modern Russia. Their defeat has been ascribed to lack of decisiveness, fear of setting in motion the undisciplined feudal masses, and absence of a precise program or plan of procedure. Despite their defeat, the Decembrists exercised a great influence upon the Russian revolutionary movement. They gave inspiration and courage to many of the younger generation and, according to Aleksandr Herzen, "the cannons of St. Petersburg had awakened an entire generation."

While the revolt of the Decembrists inspired many of the Russian youth, it frightened the emperor and the autocracy. Nicholas I developed an almost pathological hatred of change, and regarded the maintenance of his autocratic power as part of a divine mission. Every progressive idea was repressed, and he insisted that Russia must be founded on the principles of autocracy, nationalism, and orthodoxy. He established the dreaded secret service. The censorship became severe, and all the great Russian writers felt the lash of his cruelty.[6]

Nevertheless, progressive and revolutionary ideas were not entirely repressed. In the 1840's, socialistic ideas gained some popularity among university students.

ALEKSANDR HERZEN (1812–1870)

Aleksandr Ivanovich Herzen, the son of a high nobleman, is the outstanding revolutionary of this period. Herzen's father was a freethinker and a Voltairian who regarded Russian orthodoxy as a necessary tradition useful in keeping the people in check.[7]

Herzen, at the University of Moscow, studied literature, science, and philosophy. His interests were, however, not limited to abstract study. He examined contemporary events and the influence of Peter the Great upon Russia. He concluded that Russia was part of Europe, and that

[5] *Ibid.*, pp. 209–220.

[6] J. W. Bienstock, *Histoire du Mouvement revolutionaire en Russia* (Paris: Payot et Cie., 1920), I, p. 37.

[7] Alexander Herzen, *My Past and Thoughts.* Translated by Constance Garnett (London: Chatto and Windus, 1924), Vol. I.

they were both tied together by their common Christian faith. Europe is a common whole, moving toward freedom and liberty and extending the classic civilization inherited from Greece and Rome. Peter, by stimulating Western forms, hastened Russia along the inevitable line of progress.[8]

PRISON

In 1834, Herzen and a number of others were arrested on charges of chanting political verses, and Herzen was exiled to the provinces. He was allowed to return to Moscow in the fall of 1839, but a chance remark in a letter to his father came under the eye of a member of the secret police and he was again exiled to Novgorod, where he remained two years.

At the time of Herzen's return from his second exile in 1842, Russian intellectual society was immersed in the study of the views of Hegel, from whose ideas all ideological groups seemed to gain comfort. For the reactionaries, "the real is the rational" gave moral sanction to the autocracy; the liberals, in turn were more attracted by Hegel's emphasis upon constant change. Herzen believed that the Hegelian conflict of opposites was a formula for progress, a process whereby the present is transformed by struggle, and a proof that society is in constant search of a new equilibrium. After a time Herzen became less concerned with the theoretical issues and abandoned metaphysics for the study of history and social conditions.[9]

PROPERTY

Herzen held property to be necessary for man, a means of freeing him from the tyranny of chance and of securing his dignity and independence. Yet the ownership of property also has a baser side. It inspires waste and greed. There is a danger that in accumulating riches, man will become a slave to material things. Accumulation of property should, therefore, be limited so that the human spirit may never be subjugated by the pursuit of gain.

As can be seen, Herzen's criticism of property was moral rather than economic. To him property was the basis of inequality, and he believed that injustice arises from the division of property rather than from its nature. In his opinion a group adds something to individual output. The employer, in paying his employees separately, ignores the fact that a

---

[8] Roul Labry, *Herzen* (Paris: Bossard, 1926), pp. 122–126.
[9] *Ibid.*, p. 263.

group produces more than the arithmetical sum of the output of its individual members.[10] Property is thus an appropriation, by a few, of the results of collective labor, a monopoly on some of the goods that belong to the group. Herzen, while never clearly formulating a plan for the socialist future, was attracted by the views of Fourier.

Herzen's socialism was based upon his desire to improve man rather than to increase wealth. He justified change by moral rather than by economic considerations, and he believed that basic change could be achieved only by a social revolution. Political equality is an illusion if it is not supported by an equality of fact; liberty is not privilege written into a constitution, but the right of man to develop his faculties freely. Those who possess only power to labor are at the mercy of the rich. Private property has allowed the rise of a moneyed class as tyrannical as the feudal lords of the Middle Ages.

DEPARTURE FOR WESTERN EUROPE

Herzen left Russia in 1847 with his mother and family. He reached France on the eve of the events of 1848, but his hope, as was that of many others, was doomed to disappointment. He denounced the counterrevolution, opposed Louis Napoleon, and was forced to flee to Switzerland, where he acquired Swiss citizenship.

After the defeat of the Continental revolutions, Herzen settled in London in 1852, where he lived for twelve years. He established a Russian press and issued the *Polar Star* in 1855, and the immensely successful *Bell*, which was read by all sections of Russian society, and eagerly examined by Alexander II. In the *Bell*, Herzen came out for freedom against tyranny, for reason, as opposed to superstition, and for the free growth of the people, as opposed to government reaction. For Russia he demanded an end to serfdom, land for the peasantry, abolition of censorship, independence for Poland, and freedom for Russia.[11]

Disillusion The experience in Paris, and the rise of reaction everywhere, convinced Herzen that Europe was incapable of establishing socialism. He then became more sympathetic to the views of the Slavophiles, although he refused to admit it. Since Europe is no longer capable of progress, it has bequeathed to the world its highest thought, socialism. The Slavic people have, among other qualities, the germ of socialism,

10 Herzen, *op. cit.*, VI, 296–297.

11 A. I. Herzen, *"Kolokol" Izbranniya Stat'i* (Geneva: Volnaya Russkaya Tipografiya, 1887), pp. 1–3.

and it is possible for Russia to vitalize and increase its growths. Herzen emphasized that the germ of socialism is to be found in the *mir,* the peasant commune, which, if not complete socialism, is an element that can be strengthened. He urged the throwing off of the past so as to allow the socialist elements to thrive. He believed that Europe was decadent, having nothing to teach Russia, which alone carries within itself the destinies of humanity because she has remained outside the dying European tradition. It is Russia, rich in hope, full of the fervor of youth, upon whom the hope of humanity rests.[12]

"*The truth and justice* of old Europe are falsehood and injustice to Europe which is being born." In contrast, "Russia is quite a new State— an unfinished building in which everything smells of fresh plaster, in which everything is at work and being worked out, in which nothing has yet attained its object, in which everything is changing, often for the worse, but anyway changing. In brief, this is the people whose fundamental principle, to quote your opinion, is communism, and whose strength lies in redivision of the land." [13] Herzen saw as the great hope the peasant commune "which has saved the Russian people from Imperial civilization, from the Europeanized landlords and from German Bureaucracy . . . . This circumstance is of infinite consequence for Russia." [14]

In Herzen the revolutionary is ultimately combined with the Russian patriot, and his idea of Russia as a land destined to lead humanity to a better world is a dogma accepted by the Soviet leaders in our own day. Russia, in contrast to the West, Herzen held, subordinated the individual to the collective; and the peasant commune was Russia's defense against the pauperism and proletarianization of the West. In the 1860's Herzen's influence was almost spent. He lost his following among the liberals because of his defense of the Polish insurrection of 1863. The radical youth turned to other leaders, and toward the end of Herzen's life his following among revolutionaries in Russia was small. He himself recognized this fact.[15] Yet he is important as a Russian revolutionary thinker, for he was among the first to affirm that Russia could evade capitalism. Although this view was rejected by the Russian Marxists, they did feel a similar dislike for Western institutions. The belief in the special mission of Rus-

---

[12] Labry, *op. cit.,* p. 348.
[13] Herzen, *My Past and Thoughts,* VI, 222–223. Italics are Herzen's.
[14] *Ibid.,* pp. 228–229.
[15] Herzen, "*Kolokol*" *Izbranniya Stat'i,* pp. 726–729.

sia with a hatred of non-Russian nations is not uncommon in the Soviet Union today.

REVOLUTIONARY CIRCLES

Most of Herzen's reputation as a publicist and writer was achieved during his editorship of revolutionary journals in other lands. During the 1840's the first revolutionary study circles appeared in Russia. Most of the members were free thinkers and utopian socialists, principally followers of Fourier. Politically, they were republicans, constitutional monarchists, or federalists. The inclinations of the several groups differed. Some concerned themselves with social problems, others with literary and philosophic issues. The best-known group was the Petrachevsky circle, to which Dostoyevsky belonged. It discussed the conditions of the peasantry as well as constitutional questions. Most members of the circle favored the abolition of feudalism and wanted public trials, political freedom, and relaxation of the censorship.[16] Their discussions came to the attention of the authorities, who arrested the members, twenty-one of whom, including Dostoyevsky, were sentenced to death. The sentence was commuted to life imprisonment while the accused were lined up in the square for execution, an event that produced a deep and lasting effect on Dostoyevsky.

THE ABOLITION OF SERFDOM

In the ukase abolishing serfdom, the serfs were given their civil rights and were to receive a portion of their land. Ownership of this land was vested in the village commune, the mir, and payment was to be made to the landowners. The peasant community was allowed to regulate its own internal affairs and appoint its own leaders, and was answerable for taxes and order. The manumitted peasants did not receive the lands individually. Payment for the land was made in government bonds bearing 6 per cent interest. The peasants were required to pay one fifth in cash, and then for a period of forty-nine years to pay off the balance of the four fifths, plus 6 per cent interest. Taxes of various kinds were added.

The abolition of serfdom in 1861 failed to solve the land problem, nor did it allay the widespread discontent. The peasant felt he had been

16 Kulczycki, *op. cit.*, I, 268–276.

cheated, for even while he was a serf he believed the land was his, although he himself belonged to the landlord. There appeared at this time —the 1860's—the intellectual, both nobleman and commoner, but especially the former, who felt a sense of guilt over the misery and suffering prevailing in Russia. Influenced by the philosophic currents predominant in Western Europe, these noblemen preached the individual's right to unfettered expression, and they felt that the masses were entitled to the same rights, which could be achieved only through socialism. Not free to present their ideas and harassed by the authorities, the idealists developed a philosophy of materialism and a faith in science which the novelist Ivan Turgenev called nihilism in *Fathers and Sons*. Bazarov, the hero of this novel, personified this type. In the 1860's, the *Narodniks*, or populists, made their appearance.[17]

The Populists were socialists who believed that Russia, because of the absence of an urban proletariat and industrialism, could escape Western capitalism, with its uprooted proletariat, misery, and slums. The peasant's way of life was idealized, and the peasant commune regarded as a mutual form of socialism in harmony with Russian historical development.[18]

NIKOLAI CHERNYSHEVSKY (1828–1889)

The most representative of the early Narodnik point of view was Nikolai Chernyshevsky, who at the University of St. Petersburg absorbed the influence of German philosophy and became a materialist.[19]

LITERARY ACTIVITY

Chernyshevsky joined the staff of *The Contemporary*, edited by the poet Nekrasov. He displayed great energy and wrote articles on literary, critical, and historical subjects, which won him a prominent place among democratic and radical writers of his time. He turned to the study of political economy, for he became convinced that this was Russia's central problem.[20]

[17] Frederick C. Barghoorn, "D. I. Pisarev; A Representative of Russian Nihilism," *The Review of Politics*, April, 1948, pp. 196–197.

[18] Nicholas Berdyaev, *The Origin of Russian Communism* (London: G. Bless, The Centenary Press, 1937), pp. 66–67.

[19] Georg Steklow, *N. Tschernyschewski, Ein Lebensbild* (Stuttgart: J. Dietz, 1913), pp. 5–7; N. G. Tschernyschewski, *La Possession Communale du Sol* (Paris: Marcel Rivière, 1911), pp. 1–2.

[20] Steklow, *op. cit.*, pp. 8–14.

PHILOSOPHY

Chernyshevsky was a materialist, and to him morals and ideas were conditioned by historical circumstances. He was optimistic with regard to the possibilities of progress, although he recognized that it did not continue in an upward line. Nevertheless, progress was an objective historical necessity, independent of the will of man. He recognized the dependence of ideology upon economic relations. Systems of thinking as well as governmental ideals were conditioned by the interests of the ruling class. Therefore he held that reactionaries represent the large landowners, the clergy, the bureaucracy, and the army. Liberalism reflects the interests of big industry and commerce. Communists and socialists, called reformers to avoid censorship, are the representatives of the interests of labor. Constitutional reform offers no final solution, but freedom of speech, press, and assembly is of great importance. To exercise an important influence in society reformers must be supported by a powerful movement. Realization of any important objective requires power, and as long as revolutionaries lack power they must wait. Chernyshevsky was skeptical of the secret societies and the advocacy of armed uprisings by determined minorities. Only by mass support would success be assured. Although the masses may be too tired from the drudgeries of labor to comprehend an involved political program, revolutionaries can win support by defending the former's interests. They will thereby gain sympathy for the cause and embark upon determined steps for the seizure of state power.[21]

Economics and Socialism   Having concluded that economic factors were extremely important in historical development, Chernyshevsky studied the subject closely. In his chief economic work, *Notes on Mill's Principles,* he discussed productive and unproductive labor, and attempted to show that the former is socially useful and the latter harmful. This approach enabled him to criticize capitalism from the standpoint of advantageous and harmful production. Capital is defined as the product of labor serving for the production of goods of high social need. His value theory is Ricardian, and he maintained that the division of the national income between rent, profit, and wages was characteristic of capitalism. This threefold distribution of income is the basis of class conflict. As the size of each share is determined by the proportions paid to the other two, conflict over the division of income must ensue. There was, in his mind, a

21 *Ibid,* pp. 49–50.

distinction between national wealth and the welfare of the people. The former rests upon increased production and the latter upon just distribution.

From his economic analysis, Chernyshevsky concluded that the system of private property in production was outmoded. Capitalism was a historical and not an eternal phenomenon. With further historical development, capitalism, like its predecessors, must give way to another social system. He argued that wage labor is exploited and is a final stage of slavery. Contemporary relations of labor and capital are historically conditioned and must disappear and be replaced by a system in which the worker is also proprietor.[22]

While Chernyshevsky recognized the progressive character of modern industry, he saw its negative aspects in its proletarianizing of the masses; in the debt burden imposed upon the small producer, who is unable to utilize and advantages of modern technical progress; in the exploitation of the wage worker and small proprietor by great capitalists; in unlimited competition, concentration of capital, and progressive decline of wages as a result of competition for jobs.[23]

Capitalism leads to the steady degradation of labor, and must be pushed aside and replaced by socialism, which will make possible continued technical and human progress. The natural consequence of capitalism is socialism; one leads to the other. Socialism is a means of developing the human personality. "We recognize nothing higher on this earth than the human personality." [24] Only when the means of labor are controlled by those who use them will this be possible in the highest degree.

The People   Chernyshevsky placed his hope upon the Russian peasantry. He urged the new generation to bring the people to socialism and the new life. "Go to the people," he urged the younger generation in his novel, *A Vital Question*.[25] The responsibility for the educated classes to furnish leadership and guidance, a theme repeated by later writers, is emphasized by Chernyshevsky. In this novel, Chernyshevsky pictures the younger generation going among the people so that they might learn its mode of living and its thinking.

Realizing Socialism   Chernyshevsky's views on the seizure of power resembled those of Blanqui. In backward countries, such as Russia, it is

22 *Ibid.*, pp. 57–66.
23 *Ibid.*, p. 69.
24 Quotation, *ibid.*, p. 70.
25 Translated by N. H. Dole and S. S. Skidelsky (New York: Thomas Y. Crowell & Company, 1886).

possible for socialists to seize power and lead the masses to a higher social and economic level without passing through capitalism. He believed that the communal administration of landed property in Russia makes it possible to go direct to socialism. He argued that the peasant commune made Russia a natural place for socialism, for the peasant is not, as in Western Europe, a strong individualist. Communal ownership can therefore serve as a favorable starting point for socialist development.

Following an increase of unrest, Chernyshevsky was arrested in 1867, and a campaign against him was opened in the conservative press. After several years in prison, he was exiled to Siberia in 1866, and not until June, 1889, was he allowed to return to his home in Saratov.

DIMITRI PISAREV (1840–1868)

Following Chernyschevsky, the views of Dimitri Pisarev influenced the thinking of the younger members of the educated classes of the 1860's. Pisarev was born in Orel, and received his first education from his mother. In St. Petersburg, he later attended a Gymnasium and in 1856 he entered the university. He was attracted to modern ideas, joined an advanced study circle, and made his debut as a writer on the question of woman's emancipation. He turned to literary and social criticism, and although his first articles were uneven and betrayed awkwardness, they also revealed firmness in tone and expression.[26] He proclaimed his confidence in progress. "We must see in history the development of humanity, its tendency to perfection. This tendency is sometimes deformed; humanity passes through epochs of struggle and moral ill health, but she moves forward despite trials and deviations."

Pisarev had absolute faith in science. He pleaded for the emancipation of woman and opposed serfdom. In discussing education, he argued that its task is to avoid smothering liberty in the name of duty, nor must it extirpate the impulses which surge within us. Rather, education ought to seek to conciliate impulse and liberty so that we will not be carried to irrational heights. He was, however, unable to carry the intellectual and moral burden he had placed upon himself; and in 1859, he suffered a breakdown because of overwork and financial difficulties. The following year he resumed his labors, accepting the view that egoism

26 Armand Coquant, *Dimitri Pisarev et l'ideologie du nihilisme russe* (Paris: Institut D'Etudes Slaves, 1946), pp. 40–46. The following quotations from Pisarev are from this source, pp. 47, 77, 78, 184, 219–220, 244.

should be the basis of morals and a sure guide to the general interest.

In his writings he showed compassion and understanding of the masses. He opposed those who reviled their shortcomings and lacked understanding for the Russian people. "Every cultivated reader will admit that to discover the peculiarities and the needs of our people is the task of our epoch." A concern for the people, which became a characteristic of the intelligentsia of his time, is often expressed by Pisarev. "Society is finally beginning to recognize the responsibility resting upon it, of making the masses conscious of ideas." The masses have an equal right to a humane and cultured existence, and without their advance progress is impossible. The great task of the age is the enlightenment of the masses so that they will become participants in the progress of society. The publicist, savant, and artist have an obligation to educate the masses and to show them the direction of social evolution.

In philosophy Pisarev accepted the simple materialism of Moleschott and Karl Vogt, who sought to explain social phenomena on the basis of material conditions such as the effect of food and climate upon man. He later elaborated a determinist theory that the individual is fashioned by his environment and the views prevailing in his time. History can be influenced by an increase in knowledge or propaganda, but not by single great individuals. He, however, maintained that each person has inalienable rights which even the state must not touch. Pisarev's views became increasingly radical, and in 1862, the police seized one of his manuscripts in which he bitterly assailed the regime whose overthrowal, he was convinced, constituted the only hope of honest people. His ideas led to his arrest, and after a prison term his views underwent some change. He now thought that an outright struggle with the police was premature, and he advised propaganda as a method. Social improvement depends upon the assurance of minimum standards to man. There exists in society those with advanced ideas, who have mastered, in a measure, a knowledge of science and who recognize its possibilities for the improvement of physical and moral life. Such individuals have the obligation to cultivate, enrich, and deepen their personality. However, they must concentrate upon their own improvement only to be better equipped to aid and lead the masses.

Pisarev's ethics were based upon the rational utilitarianism of the Benthamite variety. According to him, morality is not due to goodness of heart or superior virtue, but to a recognition that to steal and to kill are undesirable. Crime would cease if all members of society recognized its disadvantages, but one "cannot inculcate this salutary knowledge in a savage or a proletarian whose thoughts are continually towards a struggle against hunger. A moral man must be a thinking man, and the faculty of thought is strengthened and developed only when the individual succeeds in escaping from the yoke of material necessity." He was concerned with the moral development of the individual, but he recognized that only by achieving a minimum standard of life is moral growth possible. To Pisarev the basic need was the development of the individual, and he saw no conflict between healthy individual egoism and the general interest. Individual and social prosperity are tied together; social solidarity is an advantage to all, and the realist is the thinking worker. In contrast, the manual worker is enslaved by the machine, which is an instrument capable of emancipating labor but is used instead to enslave it. The realist is bound to work for the emancipation of the enslaved without at any time counting upon their support. A Russian realist must base his efforts on Russian conditions. He must aid the people, for only by overcoming their ignorance can he do so. It is necessary to create in Russia a yearning for education and culture. This awakening must be brought about by the educated classes, whose task it is to infiltrate among the masses and to arouse the people. "The destiny of the people will not be decided in the popular schools, but in the universities." The awakening and guiding of society is the task of its best representatives.

PETR LAVROVICH LAVROV (1823–1900)

Lavrov was the link between Russian and Western socialism. Son of a wealthy landowner, he was educated at an artillery school, where he became an instructor in mathematics. His first publication was on military topics, but he also had other interests. An article on Hegel attracted his attention, and after some study he published articles on philosophy, history, and religion. His growing radicalism led to his arrest in 1866 and to exile. During his exile, he published the *Historical Letters,* which made a deep impression upon educated Russian youth. The *Letters* came at a time when many Russian students gave up their careers in order "to go to the people" and preach the gospel of socialism.

With the help of several friends, Lavrov was able to escape from exile. He landed in Paris in 1870, joined the First International, and made the acquaintance of Marx and Engels. He left Paris after the Commune and founded the *Forward* in Zurich in 1873. His fundamental Narodnik views did not change. He resigned three years later and devoted his talents to scientific, literary, and revolutionary work.

PROGRESS

Lavrov defined progress as the development of individuality in its physical, intellectual, and moral relations, and as the embodiment of the principles of truth and justice in social institutions.[27] He defined the minimum conditions needed for progress, the most important being that the advanced minority capable of critical thought should have an opportunity for full development and leadership. The large mass has no part in progress, for it is governed by custom and convention and is incapable of critical thought. The majority is too weighed down by its daily cares and too little trained to play a role in progress. Truth and justice are perceived by the leaders who make up the critical minority. Historically the advanced and intellectual minority has sought to improve the position of the majority and enlarge the number of those capable of critical thought. By improving the conditions in which the majority lives and by stimulating its intelligence the minority raises the level of social solidarity. From this reasoning, Lavrov draws the conclusion that the suppression of the advanced minority will lead to an end of progress. On the other hand, civilization will be undermined if the few exclude the majority from enjoying the fruits of progress.

Lavrov, as can be seen, emphasized the importance of the advanced minority and its obligations, as well as the need for the minority to develop the highest moral ideals. His views encouraged the "going to the people" of the 1870's; and although Lenin's theories were basically different in most respects, he later emphasized the importance of the advanced minority in the revolutionary movement and in the overthrow of czarism and capitalism.

History forms a special province of investigation. In the field of history, the subjective method must be used. The historian cannot deal with all facts. He must select, and his selection is based not upon objective criteria but upon the judgment of the historian. This constituted, for Lavrov, the subjective method. He argued that historians select those facts which will harmonize with their historical views. Moreover, as we observe the flow of history through time, we recognize certain phenomena as normal

27 Peter Lawrow, *Historische Briefe*. Translated from the Russian into German by S. Davidow (Berlin: Akademischer Verlag für sociale Wissenschaft, 1901), p. 69.

and others as abnormal. Such a view is, according to Lavrov, purely subjective. For example, conservatives regard the *status quo* as normal and revolutionary agitation as abnormal. The reverse judgment would be made by revolutionaries.

From the above, the conclusion is inevitable that no acceptable criterion of what is historically normal exists. Consequently, history can use only the subjective method, and must be distinguished from the natural sciences.

CULTURE

Lavrov's subjectivism is related to his ideas on the difference between the history and the culture of a people. Culture is the traditional habits and customs. History begins in the first instance with the rise of an intellectual minority capable of submitting the historical tradition to historical criticism from the point of view of truth and justice. In modern society many groups remain outside the streams of history. Among the most obvious and important of this group are the intellectual representatives of the ruling classes, who refuse to give leadership to the masses and the exploited and overworked, who possess neither the time nor the ability for critical thought.

SOCIALISM

Lavrov charged that the economic relationships of his time were based on inequality and that they limited the freedom of the mass of the people. Competition stimulates hostility among men, interferes with the highest moral development of millions, and prevents the extension of human solidarity, which is one of the marks of progress. The growth of solidarity is possible only on the basis of cooperation and collective labor. A change in economic relationships would put an end to the struggle for existence by the majority and to the profit seeking of the dominant minority. A socialistic society based on cooperative labor would, in Lavrov's opinion, promote favorable conditions for the development of the human personality.[28]

Lavrov's basic ideas did not undergo any fundamental change throughout his long revolutionary activity. His wide contacts with Western European revolutionaries and their ideas enabled him to present these views to the younger generation of Russian revolutionaries. However, he

28 *Ibid.*, pp. 322–324.

never accepted the views of the Marxists that capitalism was inevitable in Russia, nor their belief in a strong centralized state.[29]

PETR TKACHEV (1844–1885)

In contrast to Lavrov and his moderate views, Petr F. N. Tkachev is to be regarded as a leading exponent of revolutionary activism. A student of law at St. Petersburg, he was expelled from school for participating in a student demonstration. In 1862 he was arrested and imprisoned for three months, and in 1869 he was again arrested. This time he was imprisoned for four years. The year following his release he went abroad to escape arrest.

VIEWS

Tkachev was primarily a revolutionary who emphasized the use of force as a means of establishing reform.[30] This is the primary premise of his activities. In his first years abroad, he collaborated with Lavrov's group, but he broke with it when he urged the establishment of a revolutionary dictatorship. He and a number of followers founded the *Tocsin* to propagate views which were close to those held by Blanqui.

Inequality Physical, intellectual, economic, and political inequalities are the result of social injustice. The existence of inequality justifies the use of force. Equality will be achieved only when envy and competition are banished by the conscious minority, the moral and spiritual leaders who constitute the select few in the population. The militant minority must assume the spiritual and moral guidance of the masses. Until the revolution, the leadership is purely moral, for it faces the power of the state. It is the duty of revolutionary parties to transform this moral leadership into material force. As all power in modern society is concentrated in the state, the revolution can be realized only by the seizure of state power.

Seizure of Power Once power is seized, the function of the revolutionary state is of a double character—negative and positive. The negative aspect is the struggle, the repression of opponents by a centralized and disciplined organization. The essence of the creative function is the organi-

---

29 F. I. Dan, *Proiskhozhdenie Bolshevizma* (New York: New Democracy, 1946), pp. 79–85.

30 Berdyaev, *op. cit.*, pp. 80–81; Michael Karpovich, "Forerunner of Lenin: P. N. Tkachev," *Review of Politics*, July, 1944, pp. 336–350.

zation of a new society based upon moral and intellectual activity founded upon constant and systematic effort, and built by the will and the understanding of mankind. The destructive and creative functions of revolution must be sharply differentiated. Only when power has been seized can the revolutionary parties initiate a parliament and introduce the following economic, political and legal reforms:

1. Transformation of the peasant commune into a collective based on cooperative labor and cooperative use of the means of production.
2. Gradual abolition of private ownership of land.
3. Creation of brotherly love and solidarity, the elimination of the cash nexus in the economy.
4. Replacement of inequality by equality.
5. Abolition of the subjection of women and children to the arbitrary rule of the husband and father.
6. Gradual introduction of self-management of the commune, and the steady weakening of the central government and the eventual abolition of its rule.[31]

Tkachev paid much attention to the mechanics of revolution and revolutionary organization. He believed that only a conspiracy could overthrow the state and that only a strictly centralized and hierarchical organization could direct the revolutionary movement. He emphasized the necessity for forcible seizure of state power, and then only when there was a possibility of success.[32]

Although he favored closer relations between the Russian revolutionary movement and European radicalism, he did not believe that Russia offered a favorable soil for a labor movement based upon the urban proletariat. In an *Open Letter* addressed to Friedrich Engels, Tkachev emphasized the absence of a developed industry, an urban proletariat, a literate population, and a middle class which were the prerequisites for a labor movement of the Western European type.

EARLY REVOLUTIONARY ORGANIZATIONS

TCHAYKOVSKY CIRCLE

In the 1870's, a number of groups espousing revolutionary ideas were organized. In contrast to the earlier period, the revolutionaries were more concerned with practical work than with theories and their groups were

[31] Kulczycki, *op. cit.*, II, 183.
[32] Karpovich, *op. cit.*, p. 349.

influenced by the views of Pisarev, Lavrov, Tkachev, and Bakunin. In 1869, the Tchaykovsky circle was formed in St. Petersburg.[33] Made up of university students, it hoped "to bring about a union of the advanced elements among the students first of St. Petersburg, and afterwards all over Russia, and then proceed to make connections among the workers and peasants and gradually prepare a revolutionary upheaval." [34]

"GOING TO THE PEOPLE"

By 1872, revolutionary circles had been organized in the principal Russian cities, and the works of foreign and native radical writers were distributed.[35] Soon a campaign of "going to the people" began. Many young revolutionaries gave up their careers to work and teach the people in the villages and the workers in the towns.[36]

Two views were held by those who were "going to the people." The "propagandists" who followed Lavrov believed that peaceful persuasion would bring about socialism in the future. In contrast, the "insurrectionists," who were followers of Michail Bakunin, believed that revolutionaries ought to learn from the people, who are socialists by instinct. It is the task of the intelligentsia to unite the local dissatisfaction and occasional riots into a mighty revolution that will sweep aside the existing order. It is proper to encourage "banditry, impersonation of pretenders to the throne. No one knows the hour of the people's vengeance, but so much inflammatory material had accumulated among the people that a small spark would easily flare up into a flame, and the latter into a gigantic conflagration." [37]

For the first time the educated revolutionaries made direct contact with the masses, and although the reaction of the peasantry and labor was scarcely what the idealists had expected, the latter for the first time

33 For Bakunin's views see Chapter 5.

34 G. H. Perris, *Russia in Revolution* (London: Chapman and Hall, 1905), p. 200. Nikolay Tchaykovsky, one of the founders of the circle and whose name it carried, is thus quoted.

35 *Ibid.*, pp. 201–203; L. Deich, *Rol'evreev v Russkom Revoliutsionnom Dvizheni* (Berlin: Grane, 1923), pp. 51–53.

36 L. Tikhomirov, *Russia, Political and Social* (London: Swan Sonnenschein, 1892), pp. 161–162. Tikhomirov was a leader of the revolutionary movement who subsequently repudiated his views and edited a conservative journal. However, he never betrayed his former colleagues.

37 Vera Figner, *Memoirs of a Revolutionist*. Translated from the Russian (New York: International Publishers, 1928), pp. 50–51.

met those they were seeking to recruit and inspire. Actually, many peasants were hostile to the revolutionaries, some of whom were turned over to the police. Easily identified, the propagandists found they were vulnerable, for a stranger arriving in a peasant village would soon be recognized. Propagandists then established themselves in groups being careful not to disclose their identities. This was called "building colonies." Despite such precautions, many were seized.

REPRESSION

Aroused by increasing agitation, the government began a campaign of repression. Hundreds were arrested for political crimes, imprisoned, and then released. More than a thousand arrests were made from 1873 to 1877.[38] In many cases the prisoners were harshly treated by the police and the jailers. News of maltreatment aroused the anger of those outside, and individual acts of vengeance were directed against the more brutal guards, informers, and officials. From isolated acts, terrorism became a system.

"LAND AND FREEDOM"

In 1876, a number of revolutionary circles under the leadership of Mark Nathanson established a national organization, Land and Freedom, a name of the society taken from an earlier revolutionary society of the 1860's. Because existing social relations were, according to the group, based on fraud and violence, it advocated their replacement by a system of collective ownership of land by the communes and of factories and mines by workers' guilds. The St. Petersburg group was given the power to select a small executive committee to undertake the task of organization.

Its activity was as follows: active and passive agitation to stimulate revolts and riots; stimulation of strikes, peaceful protests, and petitions; organization of a fighting detachment to start and direct a general uprising; establishment of relations with other radical groups; and maintenance of propaganda campaigns among students and factory workers.[39]

[38] Stepniak, *Underground Russia* (New York: Charles Scribner's Sons, 1883), pp. 24–26; Perris, *op. cit.*, p. 211.
[39] Kulczycki, *op. cit.*, II, 214; A. J. Sack, *The Birth of the Russian Democracy* (New York: Russian Information Bureau, 1918), pp. 49–50.

PROPAGANDA

Land and Freedom conducted an extensive campaign in the villages. In contrast to the "older" agitators, its propagandists emphasized current difficulties and problems rather than distant ideals. In 1876, Land and Freedom held its first public demonstration before the Kazan cathedral in St. Petersburg. Sparsely attended, it was addressed by Georgi V. Plekhanov, the future founder of the Russian Marxist movement. A number of the participants were arrested, but the speaker escaped.

The peasants were frequently unable to comprehend the propagandists, who found themselves against a stone wall. Nor were the revolutionaries more successful in the cities. Like the people in the village, the city worker showed scant sympathy for the new doctrines. A feeling began to permeate the revolutionaries that terrorism against landlords and officials, including the czar, must be introduced. As the avenues of peaceful agitation and education were closed, terrorism, it was thought, was justifiable. Moreover, the czar showed his severity by increasing the sentences of the 193 revolutionists tried by the Senate.[40]

During the visit of the St. Petersburg chief of police, General Trepov, to the Preliminary Detention Prison, a political prisoner who failed to greet him was stripped and flogged. It was decided to punish this indignity, but before any action could be taken, Vera Zasulich, living under police supervision in a village, went to St. Petersburg and during an interview shot the general. She surrendered to the police, and her trial aroused a wave of sympathy in her behalf. She was acquitted and escaped abroad. Aleksandr Solovyev had fired at the czar and was executed. The shooting of General Trepov by Vera Zasulich encouraged the use of terrorism and marked the beginning of its organized employment against spies and leading government officials. A proclamation was issued explaining the need and justification for terrorism under the conditions existing in Russia, and the terrorists signed the leaflet "Executive Committee." [41]

DIVISION

A controversy over the effectiveness of terrorism developed. The more energetic of the revolutionaries believed terrorism justified and that it

---

[40] Figner, *op. cit.*, pp. 62–66.
[41] Kulczycki, *op. cit.*, II, 241–242; David Footman, *Red Prelude* (New Haven: *Yale University Press*, 1945), pp. 80–81; Figner, *op. cit.*, pp. 69–70.

awakened a sleeping nation. Another group felt that terrorism led up a blind alley and exposed the best people to brutal reprisals. The conference called at Voronezh, in June, 1879, to decide the issue was attended by fourteen persons. The proponents of terrorism met separately at Lipetsk, and decided that terrorism was justified so long as the Russian people were without the right to discuss political and social changes and to determine their laws by a freely chosen legislature. The project of assassinating the czar found favor, for it was hoped that the event would be followed by a general revolt. The terrorists formed a centralized organization directed by a Special Executive Committee. After the adjournment of the session in Lipetsk, the general conference convened at Voronezh. Heated discussions took place between the terrorists, who emphasized the importance of political freedom, and the old Narodniks, who did not regard political freedom as of much use to the people. Terror, they argued, was unwise and demoralizing, and many heroic fighters would be needlessly sacrificed because of its use. A compromise was impossible, and Land and Freedom split into two groups. The terrorists organized the People's Will, and the moderates, the Black Distribution.[42]

THE PEOPLE'S WILL

Complete division gave the terrorists a free hand. In a series of statements, the program and tactics of the People's Will were disclosed. The People's Will declared itself socialistic and advocated social ownership of mines and factories. In common with the Narodniks, it believed that the Russian peasantry was inclined to socialism. Its program demanded popular assemblies chosen by universal suffrage exercising supreme authority; large local autonomy for provincial assemblies; independence of the commune as an economic and administrative unit; nationalization of land; complete freedom of speech, press, assemblage, and conscience; universal suffrage without property or other qualifications; substitution of a people's militia for a standing army.[43]

First on the agenda was political freedom, but the leaders of the People's Will also aimed for a socialist revolution. Revolution would be

42 Kulczycki, *op. cit.*, II, 281–289; Footman, *op. cit.*, pp. 99–108. For the philosophy of terrorism, see Karl Nötzel, *Die Grundlagen des Geistigen Russland* (Jena: Eugen Diedericks, 1917), pp. 180–198.

43 Tikhomirov, *op. cit.*, pp. 145, 177–178.

promoted by an unfavorable war, instinctive and spontaneous uprisings among the people, bankruptcy of the state, and other complications. Terrorist action against leaders of the government and society would engender fear and demoralization in the ranks of the ruling class and at the same time encourage the masses to revolt.

CENTRALIZATION

A secret central organization or executive committee was established to direct revolutionary work among workers, peasants, and students. It was to develop connections with people influential in political and army life.

Under the control of the Executive Committee a "fighting organization" was set up to organize a campaign for the assassination of Alexander II. Since the leaders of the People's Will were convinced that it was necessary to reach right to the top, the preparations, the failures, and the final success of this enterprise are a fascinating example of conspiratorial technique.[44] The czar's habits and movements were studied, and revolutionaries even became employees at the place. Several attempts were made, and at last on March 1, 1881, Alexander was killed by a bomb thrown by a member of the People's Will, Grinevitski. Soon thereafter a proclamation to the "Workers of Russia" denounced Alexander II as "a ravening wolf," guilty of exiling and murdering and misusing the Russian people, for which crimes he deserved death.

Within ten days[45] an "Open Letter" was sent to the new emperor, Alexander III. The Executive Committee fully sympathized with his "deep sorrow," and it informed the new emperor that the assassination of his father was neither accidental nor unexpected. On the contrary, events of the last years had made it inevitable. Although the power of the government to imprison and torture was recognized, the document asserted that new fighters would fill the vacant ranks, and the struggle would continue. Russia stood at the crossroad of revolution or peaceful development. Members of the People's Will would turn to peaceful tasks to help in the cultural growth and development of their fellow countrymen.

COUNTERATTACK

The government did not stand by idly. A ruthless hunt for the assassins was begun. Five were arrested, and the leader of the fighting organiza-

---

[44] Footman, *op. cit.*, p. 112.
[45] Stepniak, *op. cit.*, pp. 265–271, gives the full text.

tion, A. I. Zelyabov, who had been in prison during the assassination, asked that he be tried with the other five for he had participated in organizing the deed. They were convicted and all were sentenced to be hanged. Death sentence was suspended in one case and the other five were hanged on April 3, 1881. An energetic campaign to exterminate the other revolutionaries was launched. Many were arrested or forced to flee. By 1887, the People's Will had collapsed.[46]

[46] The reader should also consult David Shub, *Lenin* (New York: Doubleday & Company, 1948), and Bertram D. Wolfe, *Three Who Made a Revolution* (New York: The Dial Press, 1948), two important contributions to our knowledge of the history of the Russian revolutionary movement.

20. *RUSSIAN MARXISM*

BEGINNING OF MARXISM

Not only the failure of terrorism but the social and economic changes that were taking place within Russia were directing the interests of Russian radicals toward Marxism, then on its first upward wave in Western Europe. The increasing number of industrial workers and the inevitable labor disputes convinced some revolutionary groups that Russia was destined to repeat the experience of Western countries, and that agitation among the urban proletariat was likely to yield the most desirable results.[1] Instead of finding city workers degenerate peasants, the revolutionaries discovered them receptive and lively students.[2] Agitation among factory workers increased during the 1880's, and semi-Marxist groups were established in a number of cities and industrial centers.[3] The most significant of these early groups was the League for the Emancipation of Labor organized by Georgi V. Plekhanov (1857–1918), the founder of Russian Marxism, in Geneva in 1883. The group tried to inspire a socialist movement among the urban workers, and it criticized the older Narodnik views. Like other Marxists, Plekhanov emphasized the role of the industrial proletariat as a liberator of society, and denied the possibility of Russia's going directly to socialism.[4]

The leaders—Plekhanov and Paul Axelrod (1850–1928)—had joined the revolutionary movement in the 1870's, and placed high value

[1] Y. Martov, "Razvitie Krupnoi Promyshlennosti i Rabochee Dvizhenie do 1892," *Istorya Rossii* (St. Petersburg: Granat, 1909), VI, 114.

[2] G. V. Plekhanov, "Russian Workingmen in the Revolutionary Movement," *Free Russia*, November, 1891, p. 8; "Personal Recollections," *ibid.*, December, 1891, pp. 14–16.

[3] A. S. Bubnov, *VKP* (Moscow: Izdatelstvo, Gosudarstvennoe Sotsialno-Economichskoe, 1933), pp. 212–213.

[4] J. W. Bienstock, *Histoire du mouvement révolutionaire en Russie* (Paris: Payot et cie., 1920), p. 288.

upon the revolutionary potential of the proletariat. The two came from completely different backgrounds. Axelrod was the son of a poor Jewish family and was educated in the Russian public schools. He joined the revolutionary movement as a young man, having first been attracted to anarchism. Gradually he went over to Marxism and remained active in the revolutionary movement until his death in 1928. He was one of the leaders and theorists of the Menshevik faction.

Plekhanov, the son of a landowner, first came into contact with the revolutionary movement while a student. He became a Narodnik, and was a leading participant in the demonstration before the Kazan cathedral in December, 1876. He escaped arrest, but he was forced to leave the city. After a time he returned to St. Petersburg. His participation in the strikes of 1878 earned him the title of "Our Eagle."

A year later, in 1879, became the editor of *Land and Freedom*. He moved toward a Marxist position and published *Socialism and the Political Struggle* in 1883. The following year he went abroad and did not return until after the revolution of March, 1917.[5]

It is as the creator and intellectual leader of Russian Marxism that Plekhanov ranks high. In *Our Differences*, published in 1884, he analyzed the social and economic development of Russia and attempted to undermine the views of the Narodniks. Under the name of N. Beltov, he published, in 1895, *On the Development of the Monistic View in History*, in which he sharply criticized the subjective philosophy of the leading Narodnik theorists.[6] Works on philosophy, history, social science, and economics flowed from his pen, and he was regarded as an excellent critic and essayist.

In the split between Bolsheviks and Mensheviks, Plekhanov at first sided with the former, but his opposition to dictatorial tactics pushed him to the other side. After some hesitation, he supported the Allies against Germany in World War I. He returned to Russia after the March Revolution, and settled in St. Petersburg. He opposed the Bolshevik seizure of power, but ill-health kept him from political and literary activity.

Marxist ideas were gaining increasing attention in the late 1880's and 1890's. According to Martov, there were, in the early 1890's, about a dozen groups or circles conducting Marxist propaganda. In 1894, Peter

---

5 See Introduction to G. V. Plekhanov, *God'Na Rodinie* (Paris: Povolzky, 1921).

6 J. Martow, *Geschichte der russischen Sozialdemokratie*. Translated from the Russian into German by Alexander Stein (Berlin: J. H. W. Dietz, 1926), p. 14.

Struve published legally his *Critical Notes,* and at the same time the illegal publication of Lenin, *Who Are the Friends of the People and How
Do They Struggle Against the Social Democrats* appeared. One of the
more important publications was Tugan-Baranovski's study on Russian
manufacturing, in 1898, in which he sought to show the growth of
capitalistic industry and exchange relations in Russia. Like all the Marxists, he tried to prove that Russia could not escape the economic development and stages known to the nations of Western Europe, and that the
Narodnik views were reactionary. Lenin was among the Marxists who
joined in the attack upon the older peasant socialism.

LENIN (1870–1924)

Vladimir Ilyich Ulyanov, historically known as Lenin, came from a
professional family, his father having been an inspector of schools, and
his mother, the daughter of a physician. An older brother, Aleksandr,
had been executed in 1887 for participating in a plan to assassinate the
czar. During his study of law, Lenin was expelled from the university for
radical activity. He became a confirmed Marxist, and translated *The
Communist Manifesto* into Russian. He settled in St. Petersburg in
1893, where he joined a Marxist group and entered the fight on the
Narodniks with his pamphlet, "What the 'Friends of the People' Are and
How They Fight the Social Democracy."[7] Lenin became active among the
St. Petersburg factory workers and, in 1895, helped organize the St.
Petersburg League of Struggle for the Emancipation of the Working
Class. He was arrested in 1895, and later was exiled.

MARXISTS AND THE NARODNIKS

Marxists of all persuasions viewed the Narodniks as reactionary and
unhistorical. They were critical of their emphasis upon the subjective
method and the role of the individual in history and their insistence
that Russia differed from the West. The Narodniks or peasant socialists
regarded Russia as a special case, with the peasantry being instinctive
communists, and they treated the inevitability of capitalistic development in Russia as a Marxist mirage. The Narodniks' opposition to the
development of capitalism in Russia was also based on their belief that
the intellectuals would, in a capitalistic society, become its servant rather

7 *Selected Works* (New York: International Publishers, 1935), I, 389–453.

than strive for the freeing of the masses. The Narodniks stressed the freeing of the peasantry and the development of producers' cooperatives (artels). Lenin, in contrast, strongly advocated a revolutionary party along Western European lines, for he refused to recognize a special rule of development for Russia. Like other countries, he argued, Russia was developing toward capitalism, and her emancipation lay in the creation of a proletarian workers' party.

LEGAL MARXISM

Throughout the 1890's, the Marxists, while continuing their war upon the Narodniks, were themselves divided. The legal Marxists were critical of the view that regarded Russia as a special case and that claimed she could escape the development of Western Europe. This group believed that capitalism was a progressive system for Russia, that industry and trade were desirable, and that Russia was developing along capitalistic lines.

A second group not only was desirous of using Marx's ideas to justify capitalistic development, but was composed of active revolutionaries in the sense that they sought to build a socialistic organization along Western European lines. Among the leaders of this group were G. V. Plekhanov, Paul Axelrod, and V. I. Lenin. Largely through articles and pamphlets they sought to present their ideas before Russian society. In March, 1898, a number of independent Social Democratic groups met illegally at Minsk, and organized the Russian Social Democratic Labor party. A central committee was elected and a manifesto issued outlining the tasks ahead. It described the Russian working class as ready to carry the burden in the struggle for political freedom. Soon after the meeting the officers of the new party were arrested and their printing plant was confiscated.

ECONOMISM

In the latter 1890's the entire international socialist movement was divided by the revisionist controversy, aimed at revising the basic views of Marx and Engels. In Russia, this movement took the form of economism, a belief that the labor movement must concentrate upon the struggle for the improvement of the conditions of work. Therefore the energies of the workers' movement must be directed toward the achievement of economic benefits, rather than toward the attainment of distant ideals.

Political activity was to be left to the liberals. In contrast to Lenin, Plekhanov, and other orthodox Marxists, the "economists" did not believe that propaganda for day-to-day improvement in the conditions of labor was an instrument for drawing the workers into a political struggle. The economic movement was an end in itself, and the labor movement had no political aspirations beyond this. The views of the economists were published as "The Credo," in which an independent political party of the working class was rejected. These views were immediately put under sharp attack by a number of Russian Marxists, who scorned the role of political cooperation with the liberals, and advocated exclusive concentration upon trade-union activity.[8]

"WHAT IS TO BE DONE?"

Of outstanding importance in the development of Lenin's views was the publication of his "What Is to Be Done?"[9] This pamphlet was devoted to an attack upon economism and to an examination of the nature of a revolutionary political organization. Lenin maintained that the

history of all countries shows that the working class, exclusively of its own effort, is able to develop only trade-union consciousness, i.e. it may itself realize the necessity for combining in unions, to fight against the employers and to strive to compel the government to pass necessary labor legislation, etc.

The theory of Socialism, however, grew out of the philosophic, historical and economic theories that were elaborated by the educated representatives of the propertied classes, the intellectuals. The founders of modern scientific socialism, Marx and Engels themselves belonged to the bourgeois intelligentsia. Similarly, in Russia, the theoretical doctrine of Social-Democracy arose quite independently of the spontaneous growth of the labor movement; it arose as a natural and inevitable outcome of the development of ideas among the revolutionary Socialist intelligentsia.

As can be seen, it was Lenin's contention that the workers are capable of reaching independently only the level of trade unionism, and that revolutionary ideas are developed by intellectuals and then channeled into the labor movement. Lenin distinguished between organizations of workers and organizations of revolutionaries.

8 "The Credo" and Lenin's answer in behalf of seventeen Social-Democrats can be found in *Selected Works*, I, 516–517.

9 New York: International Publishers, 1929. The immediately following quotations from Lenin are from this source, pp. 33, 105, 131.

The political struggle carried on by Social-Democrats is far more intensive and complex than the economic struggle the workers carry on against employers and the government . . . . The workers' organizations must, in the first place, be trade organizations; secondly, they must be as wide as possible; and thirdly, they must be as public as conditions will allow. On the other hand, the organizations of revolutionists must be comprised first and foremost of people whose profession is that of revolutionists.

A revolutionary political party was a more limited group than a trade union. The political party was made up of professional revolutionaries who were to energize and direct the masses. Lenin demanded the setting up of a strong centralized secret organization. He denied that democratic selection of members was possible under Russian conditions. Therefore he advocated: "Strict secrecy, strict selection of members, and the training of professional revolutionists."

BOLSHEVISM AND MENSHEVISM

The Russian Marxist movement developed slowly, and although its leaders engaged in many theoretical arguments, some of which like revisionism, were common to the socialist movements of other countries, the crucial difference was over the character of the party organization. This issue arose at the Second Congress of the Russian Social Democratic Labor party held at Brussels and at London. It turned on the following question: Who was to be regarded as a member of the party? Lenin proposed that a member of the party be "one who recognizes its program and supports the Party materially as well as by *personal participation in one of the organizations of the Party*." (Italics in original.) Martov opposed this definition, and suggested that a member of the party be regarded as one who worked *"under the control and guidance of the organizations of the Party."* [10]

Lenin sought to give membership in the party a narrow definition, while his opponent Martov—later the leader of the Menshevik faction— urged a broader definition. Lenin wanted the party to be "the vanguard, the leader of the vast masses of the working class, the whole (or nearly the whole) of which works 'under the control and guidance' of the Party, but which does not and should not, as a whole, join the Party." [11]

[10] Lenin, "Account of the Second Congress of the R.S.D.L.P.," *Selected Works*, II, 349; Martow, *op. cit.*, pp. 79–91.

[11] Lenin, "Speeches Delivered at the Second Congress of the R.S.D.L.P.," *Selected Works*, II, 360.

He wanted a party of workers, activists, responsible to the central organs of the party. Instead of a political party of the Western European type, Lenin sought a disciplined, centrally directed organization of professional revolutionists, a unified organization, in which the minority submitted to the will of the majority. In essence, Lenin favored a militarily disciplined, warrior organization with the central committee of the party as the directing general staff. The earlier revolutionary movements were based on a loose type of discipline. Lenin wanted, however, to go beyond that point. He wanted complete subordination of the individual, and while from the viewpoint of political organization his plan was a stroke of genius, it marked the beginning of the emphasis upon discipline, suppression of personal opinion, and subordination of the individual that reached its highest point in the dictatorship of Stalin.

The Bolsheviks elected a majority, including Plekhanov and Lenin, to the editorial board of the official organ, the *Spark*. The Mensheviks requested the enlargement of the editorial committee so as to include three former editors; the rejection led them to withdraw from party committees. The following year the Mensheviks gained control of the party organizations, and some of the Bolsheviks favored a policy of conciliation of the two factions. But instead, Lenin and his followers set up a Bureau of the Majority Committee, which demanded the convening of a general party congress. The Bureau established in Geneva the *Forward* as its official organ. The Third Congress of the Russian Social Democratic Labor party met in London in the spring of 1905, but it was largely a Bolshevik affair. The Bolsheviks elected a central committee made up of members of their own faction. Acting alone, the Mensheviks chose an organization committee to head their group.

With the spread of the revolutionary movement in 1905, the Bolshevik Central Committee and the Menshevik Organization Committee called a united congress. The Fourth Congress met at Stockholm in the spring of 1906, with the Mensheviks holding a majority. Consequently, the resolutions were of Menshevik complexion. At the Fifth Congress held in London in the spring of 1907 the Bolsheviks had a slight majority over their rivals, but the deciding votes were held by the organizations representing several nationalist groups. This was the last party congress until the summer of 1917.[12]

12 Olga Hess Gankin and H. H. Fisher, *The Bolsheviks and the World War* (Stanford University, Calif.: Stanford University Press, 1940), pp. 13–16.

JULIUS MARTOV (1868–1923)

The leader of the Mensheviks and Lenin's opponent to the last was Julius Martov (Zederbaum), who joined the Marxist wing of the revolutionary movement as a young man. At the party congress in 1903 he stepped out as the opponent of Lenin's advocacy of an ultracentralist organization of professional revolutionists. Martov held that the workers had to bring about their own emancipation, and he opposed Lenin's views on dictatorship and centralism. In World War I he took an international position, and opposed war patriotism. After the February Revolution he favored the conclusion of peace and agrarian reform and a socialist coalition government that would introduce reforms and summon a constituent assembly. During the early part of the Bolshevik regime he favored land and other reforms, but on theoretical and moral grounds he vehemently opposed terrorism and the denial of democratic rights.[13]

Martov was a man of outstanding intellectual and moral stature. Despite their animus and frequently unreasoning hate toward political opponents, both Lenin and Trotsky have written admiringly of Martov's intellect and character. He was a revolutionary and an internationalist, but he was also a democrat and a believer in minority rights. He never allowed his vision of a new society to obscure the importance of existing gains, and because of his vehement and uncompromising opposition to the increasing totalitarianism of the Bolsheviks, he was forced to leave Russia.

THE NEO-POPULISTS

Although the People's Will was destroyed as an organized force, its ideas persisted in Russian radicalism. The outstanding writer of the neo-Populists was Nikolai Konstantinovich Mikhailovsky (1842–1904), who accepted the subjective teachings of Lavrov. Mikhailovsky stood for the many-sided development of the human personality. He believed that the full man has the highest value—for all science and art have only one purpose, the service of man. The human personality, its destiny, and its interest must be the cornerstone of our theoretical thought. Truth de-

[13] Raphael Abramowitsch, "Julius Martow und das russischen Proletariat," *Der Kampf*, July 1923, pp. 180–188; Yu Martov, *Zapiski Sotsialdemokrata* (Berlin: 1923).

pends upon the perception of man, and although it may exist independently of our senses, we must be aware of it.

There are, according to Mikhailovsky, two types of truth—one makes us aware of phenomena and the relations between them. A second type of truth has to do with phenomena which satisfy the intellectual needs of the observer. The second group can be apprehended only through the subjective method. The subjective method, in Mikhailovsky's sense, consists in the realization that human experiences do not enter consciousness in pure form, but are judged and evalued. Therefore, sociology cannot deal, as do the physical sciences, with necessity, but with the possible and with justice. One can make moral judgments only if one assumes free will and not necessity.

He recognized that the conflict between necessity and freedom was insoluble. Man has an obligation to strive for justice, and it is this striving which gives an aim to history. The subjective consciousness of freedom is a fact which cannot be demonstrated, but upon it rest personal responsibility and moral values.

Progress has meaning only because of human thought. Man is the bearer of historical development because he sets aims before himself. Not all historical change constitutes progress, but only that which leads to the development of the human personality. Progress is an extensive differentiation, a wide division of labor. To Mikhailovsky it is not individual adjustment to environment that serves progress, but the transformation of environment by human personality so as to achieve a powerful many-sided development of all human qualities. It is the steady approach to social unity.[14]

Personality expresses itself only in labor, and the people are only the laboring people. Work is therefore the tie that binds the individual personality to society, and the true interests of the individual and of society are the same. Like Chernyshevsky, Mikhailovsky differentiated between people and nation. He admitted that the people may not recognize their interests; to make them do so was a task he assigned to the farsighted personalities capable of critical thought.[15] From emphasis upon human personality, he and his followers developed a theory of individual terrorism that would eliminate those individuals who interfered with progress.

In Russia, Mikhailovsky argued, the labor question was different from

[14] N. K. Mikhailovsky, *Sochineniya* (St. Petersburg: Wolf, 1896), pp. 18–29.
[15] Nicholas von Bubnoff, "Der Geist des Volkstümlichen russischen Sozialismus," *Archiv für Sozialwissenschaft und Sozialpolitik,* Vol. LV, 1926.

that in Western Europe. What was needed was not the development of industry and finance, but a strengthening of the peasant commune. This was the first and major recommendation. The neo Narodniks were upposed to the growth of large capitalistic industry and all of the institutions of capitalism.[16]

SOCIAL REVOLUTIONARIES

Socialists of the Populist school continued to exist despite the suppression that followed the assassination of the czar in 1881. Despite the criticism of the Marxists, they refused to accept the view that capitalism and a proletariat were inevitable in Russia. The dissolution of small peasant holdings did not, according to the proponents of Narodnik views, follow the Marxist predictions. Moreover, they believed that the peasants were good material for a Socialist party, in fact even better than the city workers, and they regarded the working class as made up of the peasantry, urban labor, and the intelligentsia and not of the industrial proletariat alone. Finally, the Narodniks differed from the Marxists in that the former regarded socialism as a new moral force in society while the latter regarded it as a reflection of the class struggle.[17]

After the collapse of the People's Will, a number of revolutionary circles, *Narod Voltsy*, appeared in different parts of Russia, and the idea of a national union of revolutionaries was never abandoned. A first attempt made in 1888 failed. The famine of 1891–1892 stimulated a revival of this wing of the Russian revolutionary movement. A Narodnik group in St. Petersburg issued in 1891 a proclamation written by N. K. Mikhailovsky in which the measures taken by the government to alleviate the famine were severely criticized. Other printed material was also issued by this group.[18]

Under the leadership of an old Narodnik, Mark Nathanson, a revolutionary circle in the guise of a literary society was organized in Saratov, and became the center of revolutionary activity. A conference at Satatov in 1893 denounced the policies of the government as leading to moral and economic ruin. A "People's Rights party" was set up. A year later

[16] M. Tugan-Baranovskii, *Russkaya Fabrika V Proshlom I Nastoyashchem* (Moscow: Sotsialno-Economicheskoe Izdatelstvo, 1938), pp. 440–444.

[17] P. P. Maslov, "Narodnicheskiya Partii," in *Obshchest-vennoe v Rossii*. Edited by J. Martow, P. Maslov, and A. Potresov (St. Petersburg: Obshchestvennaya Polza, 1914), pp. 89–95.

[18] General Alexandre Spiridovitch, *Histoire du terrorisme russe*. Translated by Vladimir Lazarevski (Paris: Payot et cie., 1930), pp. 28–30. General Spiridovitch was chief of the Kiev section of the Secret Police. His work is based on official documents.

the party had established groups in a number of cities, including Moscow and St. Petersburg. A journal was issued, edited by N. K. Mikhailovsky, who announced in an editorial that "liberty was the source of progress and the means of developing the political life of a nation." [19] A series of raids in April, 1894, led to the collapse of the movement.

The scattered groups in many parts of Russia were finally unified in national organization, the Social Revolutionary party, in 1900. A central committee was set up, and all the branches of the Social Revolutionary party were placed under it. The party declared that the abolition of the autocracy was its foremost task. Agitation was to be conducted among industrial workers, the intelligentsia, and the peasantry. Terror was a recognized weapon, but legal agitation was also to be conducted.[20]

First Years The Social Revolutionary party attracted to its banner not only many "old Narodniks" and students determined to employ terror, but also small scattered circles of revolutionaries. At its head was the Central Committee directing all activities among the intelligentsia, urban labor, the peasantry, and the army. Its campaign among the peasants brought a circular from the minister of interior urging the use of all means to suppress the agitation in the countryside. Where the peasantry predominated, the Social Revolutionary agitation exceeded in importance that of the Social Democrats.[21]

Terror At the beginning of its existence, the party set up a special group—a fighting detachment or committee to direct the terror. Minister of Interior Sipiaguine and the Procurator-General of the Holy Synod, K. P. Pobiedonostzev, were the first on the list. The minister was assassinated by the terrorist, Stepan Balmachev, who dressed in the uniform of an aide-de-camp and gained easy access to the building in which a meeting of the Council of State was going on. The preparations for the attempt on Pobiedonostzev miscarried,[22] but the terrorists succeeded in assassinating Interior Minister V. C. Plehve.

In a manifesto, the Fighting Section justified the assassination because Plehve had savagely persecuted the members of the People's Will, and was opposing the rising tide of revolution by police terror. The manifesto repudiated terrorism in a free country, "but in Russia, where despotism

19 *Ibid.*, p. 47.
20 Maslov, *op. cit.*, pp. 96–99.
21 *Ibid.*, pp. 101–102.
22 *Free Russia*, October 1, 1904, pp. 72–73.

excludes all possibility of an openly conducted political movement . . . we are compelled to use the force of revolutionary right against tyranny." [23]

First Open Congress After the first Russian Revolution, the First Congress of the Social Revolutionary party was held in Finland, in December, 1905. In his opening statement, the president of the congress defended political terror as a weapon against autocracy. After analyzing the development of class conflict under capitalism, the program declared that the "task of revolutionary Socialism is to free all mankind, to suppress all forms of struggle between individuals, and to eliminate all forms of violence and exploitation of man by man." [24]

The party demanded freedom of speech, conscience, press, and assembly; the establishment of the right to strike; freedom from illegal search and seizure; universal direct and secret suffrage without regard to sex, religion, or nationality; the establishment of a federative democratic republic; and the recognition of freedom of the different national groups. Although the party declared itself opposed to bourgeois property, its agricultural views were founded on the recognition of the traditional forms of life of the Russian peasantry, and on a conviction that the land cannot belong to anyone and the right to its use is conferred by labor. A future form of communal land administration was outlined.

Whoever accepted the party's program was subject to its orders, and anyone belonging to one of its groups was declared a member. The Central Committee, chosen by the party congress, was charged with the ideological and practical direction of the party. Political terror was recognized as an indispensable means of struggle against the Russian government. [25]

Split in the Party Soon after the First Congress, two tendencies developed, the opposition and the Maximilists. The opposition favored the democratizing of party life and had its main strength in Moscow. After a raid on the offices of the Mutual Credit Society of Moscow which netted several million in loot, the opposition organized itself under the name of the Moscow Organization of the Social Revolutionary party. [26] The Maximilists advocated socialization of land, factories, shops, and

23 *Ibid.*
24 Spiridovitch, *op. cit.,* p. 297.
25 *Ibid.,* Chap. XI.
26 *Ibid.,* p. 392.

mines, and of all other forms of private property. Leading terrorists and the most active "expropriators"—those who seized government and private funds for revolutionary purposes—went over to the Maximilist side.

Like all revolutionary groups, the Social Revolutionary party faced severe difficulties after the failure of the revolt of 1905. Its committees were disrupted and wiped out, and its propaganda was reduced to impotence. Leading activists were forced into hiding or to flight abroad. The party regained its equilibrium after a time, and a terrorist campaign was planned. Leading terrorists were, however, discovered and arrested before they could initiate their work. It appeared that an *agent provocateur* was operating in the highest circles of the party. Such a suspicion was in itself a disintegrating force.[27]

The Affair Asev   Terror was the principal means utilized by the party. Its purpose was to avenge indignities and brutalities against revolutionaries and the people. Terror required a centralized military organization. The constant arrests of active terrorists and the frustration of the most carefully laid plans led to a suspicion that a traitor was present in the highest circles of the party. The Central Committee had been warned of this by an employee of the Secret Police. V. L. Bourtzev, a Russian revolutionary publicist living abroad, came to the conclusion that Evino Azev, a leading member of the Fighting Section, was on the pay roll of the Secret Police. At first an inquiry led to Asev exoneration, but Bourtzev persisted and was able to prove Asev a traitor and a spy.[28] The discovery was a serious blow to the party.

Division in World War   The outbreak of World War I created a crisis within the Social Revolutionary party. A majority supported the war, but the internationalist group was in opposition.

Perhaps the most important conclusion which emerges from a brief review of the Social Revolutionaries is that they were aggressive proponents of democratic government and the rights of man. It is incorrect to maintain that Russia was absolutely without a democratic tradition. In fact, from the Decembrists to the Revolution of 1917, the democratic groups were in the forefront of the revolutionary movement. Even among the Social Democrats the democratic current was not absent. The Mensheviks certainly believed in political democracy and freedom.

27 Maslow, *op. cit.*, pp. 132–135.
28 Boris Savinkov, *Memoirs of a Terrorist.* Translated by Joseph Shaplen (New York: Albert and Charles Boni, 1931), pp. 312–350.

POLICE SOCIALISM

To combat the influence of the revolutionaries, the czarist government sponsored a conservative labor movement loyal to the autocracy. The leader, S. Zubatov, a revolutionary who became head of the Moscow Secret Police, was convinced that it was necessary to win the confidence of the masses in order to wean them from revolutionary propaganda. To carry out his program, he organized, in 1901, the Society of Workers in the Moscow Mechanical Trades.[29] These police unions were not able to contain the rising discontent which broke out in 1902 and 1903 and continued to gain momentum during the Russo-Japanese War.

Since the antiwar sentiments adversely affected the position of the government, it stood ready to support schemes for allaying popular discontent. Father George Gapon believed that workers' discussion groups would help to relieve social tension, and he organized the Gapon Society of St. Petersburg Workers, and it developed a wide influence. The dismissal of several members of the association by the Putilov works was a signal for a general walkout and by January 7 virtually all industrial activity ceased. Moderate demands were presented. They included an eight-hour day, minimum wages, improvement of medical aid, and no discrimination against strikers. Convinced of the justice of their cause, the strikers decided to march to the czar's palace and present him with a petition of grievances. As the unarmed, ikon-carrying, prayer-chanting procession approached the czar's palace, it was fired upon by troops, who killed a large number and wounded many others. The revolutionary tide began to swell, and in August, 1905, the czar ordered the convening of an advisory Imperial Duma. This move failed to assuage the discontent, and in October, 1905, a general strike in Moscow was quickly followed by a nation-wide walkout. The czar dismissed the extreme reactionary Pobiedonostzev, appointed the liberal Count Witte as prime minister, and established by proclamation freedom of speech, press, and assembly; and an elected Duma.[30]

[29] S. P. Turin, *From Peter the Great to Lenin* (London: P. S. King and Son, 1935), pp. 56–62.

[30] Father George Gapon, *The Story of My Life* (London: Chapman and Hall, 1905), pp. 138–238.

FIRST SOVIET

During the strike movement, a Soviet of Workers' Deputies was organized with a lawyer, Georgei Khrustalev-Nosar, known as Khrustalev, as president, but with Trotsky in fact the real leader. The soviets which started in St. Petersburg spread to other centers. Trotsky attempted to guide the revolution through the soviets but the movement failed. The defeat of the revolt forced the leaders of all Russian revolutionary parties to flee, and revolutionary activity and publications were sternly suppressed.[31]

FACTIONAL WARFARE

With the defeat of the revolt, a period of reaction set in. Debates among revolutionists on various theoretical and tactical questions led to splits, divisions, and combinations. In all of these arguments, Lenin showed himself determined and single-minded. The divisions between Mensheviks and Bolsheviks were such that each group was in fact a distinct political party, and the breach was never healed. The two factions approached the problem of revolution differently. The Mensheviks considered the Russian Revolution as a liberal bourgeois revolution; consequently they hoped for the establishment of democratic reforms. They themselves would serve as a sort of socialist opposition, abstaining from government responsibility and pushing the government to more positive steps. Lenin, in contrast, championed a joint dictatorship of the proletariat and peasantry which "gives the impulse to every democratic revolution. These lower classes are the proletariat with the addition of millions and millions of poor townspeople and villagers."

Another serious dispute arose over the liquidation of the illegal branch of the party. Lenin, who had settled in Geneva, as well as some of the Mensheviks, fought against the liquidators. Division over the boycotting of the Duma also took place. Lenin opposed this step, although it was supported by a group of Bolsheviks centered around the newspaper *Forward*. In addition, Lenin entered the lists against those who sought to dilute the philosophical foundations of Marxism by harmonizing it with the empirical monism of Mach and Avenarius. In *Materialism and Empiric Criticism,* Lenin attacked his opponents as reactionary and as wordmongers.[32]

31 Leon Trotsky, *My Life* (New York: Charles Scribners' Sons, 1931), pp. 175–201.
32 *Selected Works*, XI, 89–408.

In the meantime, factional warfare and government repression had a very destructive effect upon socialist activity. The attempt by the Central Committee in 1910 to compose the factional differences was unsuccessful. In 1912, the Bolsheviks called a conference in Prague, and set up a central committee. The Mensheviks and the followers of Leon Trotsky (1879–1940) denounced this action and called a conference for August in Vienna. Attempts to unify the warring Russian factions were also made by the German Social Democratic party, and by the International Socialist Bureau, but they failed. As a matter of fact, the withdrawal of the Bolshevik deputies from the Social Democratic group in the Duma widened the breach between the two factions. Further efforts by the International Socialist Bureau in 1913 also failed.[33] In July, 1914, a conference of Russian Socialist groups was held in Brussels under the sponsorship of the International Socialist Congress. A resolution drafted by Karl Kautsky was approved by all groups except the Bolsheviks and the Lettish Central Committee.

REVIVAL

The period of reaction lasted up to about 1911, and then the revolutionary movement began to show new vigor. In the spring of 1912, the killing of almost three hundred workers on strike in the Lena gold fields set off a wave of nation-wide demonstrations. The increase in revolutionary agitation coincided with the approach of World War I. Lenin seemed to recognize the coming changes, for in 1912, he moved to Cracow, Galicia, in order to be closer to Russia. At the outbreak of the war he was arrested, but the efforts of Austrian Socialists secured his release. He arrived in Berne in September, accompanied by Gregory Zinoviev with whom he collaborated in editing the Russian *Social Democrat*. In contrast to the Socialists of other countries, the Socialist deputies in the Duma, both Bolshevik and Menshevik, refused to vote war credits.

WORLD WAR I

Lenin took up a relentless struggle against the prowar Socialists of every country, whom he characterized as "opportunist" and "chauvinist." In a thesis on the war, he charged the support of the war budget as "a direct betrayal of Socialism," and he regarded the conduct of the major-

[33] Gankin and Fisher, *op. cit.*, pp. 89–90.

ity of leaders of the Second International as showing the "ideological collapse of that International." [34] He opposed any conciliation with the right or center of international socialism and instead of peace, he urged the "changing of the national war into a civil war."

ZIMMERWALD AND KIENTHAL

Both the Mensheviks and the Bolsheviks sent representatives to the Zimmerwald conference called to initiate international socialist action for peace. Lenin led a group of eight, advocating a complete break with the prowar Socialists, the launching of a militant revolutionary policy, and an end to the support of war by all Socialists. A second Socialist conference in April, 1916, at Kienthal showed greater sympathy for Lenin's point of view. Early in 1916 Lenin moved from Berne to Zurich, where he continued his theoretical work; in the summer of 1916 he completed his monograph, *Imperialism, the Highest Stage of Capitalism.*

IMPERIALISM

Lenin's views on imperialism were based upon his study of *Imperialism* by the English liberal, John A. Hobson, and *Finance Capitalism* by the German Social Democrat, Rudolf Hilferding.

STAGES OF CAPITALISM

Lenin differentiated between early capitalism, which was characterized by free competition, and monopolistic capitalism, with its trusts, mergers, combines, and cartels. These large organizations eliminated the "old type of free competition between manufacturers, scattered and out of touch with one another and producing for an unknown market." [35] Instead, the monopolists make estimates of potential capacity and demand and divide the market among themselves. "Production becomes social but appropriation remains private." [36]

ROLE OF THE BANKS

In the monopolistic stage, the banks undergo a transformation and become powerful enterprises controlling virtually all resources. The change

34 "Lenin's Thesis on War" in Gankin and Fisher, *op. cit.,* p. 141.

35 V. I. Lenin, *Imperialism: The Highest Stage of Capitalism* (New York: International Publishers, 1939), p. 25.

36 *Ibid.,* p. 25.

of the banks from the position of a "modest intermediary" into a powerful monopoly represents one of the basic factors in the conversion of competitive capitalism into capitalistic imperialism. The concentration and the growing power of the banks give them a supreme position in industry and make the industrialist dependent upon them; the bank officials begin to supervise and to control industrial enterprises by gaining positions on their boards.

The increasingly important role of the banks in the economy and the concentration of production in monopoly units which follows the merging of banking with industry are the chief characteristics of "finance capitalism."

The latter is monopoly capitalism which, instead of seeking markets for the export of goods, seeks outlets for the export of capital. Investment of capital in economically backward areas yields a higher rate of return. However, it speeds up the development of capitalism in the capital-importing regions, and thus it leads eventually to a sharpening of crises. The desire to export capital and to control sources of raw materials has led to the division of the world among capitalistic powers, and has stimulated colonial conquest.[37] The foreign policy of finance capitalism is a means of achieving the economic and political division of the world. On the one side are the powerful imperialistic nations and on the other, the colonial and dependent peoples.

CAPITALISTIC IMPERIALISM

Capitalistic imperialism is a high stage of capitalism, the monopoly stage. This definition includes finance capital, which is bank capital monopolized by a few banks working in combination with monopolistic manufacturers. According to Lenin, the following features are observable:

1. Concentration of capital and production so that monopolies are of paramount importance in economic life; combination of bank and industrial capital which leads to the creation of "finance capital";

2. Export of capital as distinct from commodity exports;

3. Creation of world-wide capitalist monopolies which share the world among themselves;

4. Completion of the territorial division of the world among the great capitalistic powers.[38]

37 *Ibid.*, pp. 79–84.
38 *Ibid.*, pp. 99–109.

Parasitism and Decay of Capitalism   The economic basis of imperialism is monopoly, which in turn leads to decay and degeneration. Monopoly prices reduce the incentive for technical improvement, and thus imperialism introduces a parasitic element into capitalism, developing a *rentier* class of bondholders who do not participate in production, and "whose profession is idleness." [39] Export of capital introduces this parasitism on a national scale, as it allows an entire nation to profit by exploiting a distant country. As a result, there arises a rentier state—a parasite state. A handful of rich nations are able to enjoy high monopoly profits, which give them the opportunity for corrupting the upper stratum of labor, the aristocracy of labor. This upper stratum loses its interest in revolution and is attracted to reformism and to trade unionism. However, the struggle between capitalistic powers for colonial possession must lead to an open conflict between the great powers for the redivision of the world. This epoch of wars will continue until capitalism is overthrown.

[39] *Ibid.*, p. 100.

21. *THE RUSSIAN REVOLUTIONS*

The war revealed the rottenness of the Russian state. Its economic life undermined, state finances disorganized, and the ruling power bankrupt, a crisis was inevitable. Food stocks ran low in the cities, and the railroads were hampered by their inability to replace rolling stock. Discontent was high, and finally came to the surface with a strike at the Putilov works. A week later the city of Petrograd was paralyzed by a general strike. Troops refused to fire on demonstrators. An informal meeting of the State Duma on March 12, 1917, authorized the Council of Elders to appoint a Provisional Committee, which soon became the Provisional Government, with Prince G. E. Lvov the chairman of the Union of Zemstvo as prime minister and A. F. Kerensky, a right-wing Social Revolutionary, as minister of justice. N. S. Chkheidze, a Menshevik, refused to join the government. The Provisional Government took over full power at the abdication of the czar.[1]

SOVIETS

On March 12, the Provisional Executive Committee Soviet of Workers' and Soldiers' Deputies was formed in Petrograd, and it was resolved to refrain from participating in the Provisional Government.[2] Soviets of Workers' and Soldiers' Deputies also arose in many sections of the country. Like the Petrograd organization, these were made up of representatives of soldiers, workers, and socialist parties. A conference held on April 11–16, with more than four hundred representatives present, formed the All-Russian Central Executive Committee.

[1] Leon Trotsky, *The History of the Russian Revolution*. Translated by Max Eastman (New York: Simon and Schuster, 1932, 3 vols.); it is an authoritative exposition.
[2] Frank A. Golder, *Documents of Russian History* (New York: Appleton-Century-Crofts, Inc., 1927), pp. 255–293.

THE BOLSHEVIKS

The All-Russian Central Executive Committee of the Workers' and Soldiers' Deputies was at first dominated by the Mensheviks and the Social Revolutionaries. The Bolsheviks, at first undecided and divided among themselves, became, under the sharp prompting of Lenin,[3] opponents of the Provisional Government. Lenin was for destroying the government, for arming the workers and the poor peasants, and for instituting a workers' and peasants' government.

Allowed to pass through Germany from Switzerland in a sealed train, Lenin arrived in Petrograd on April 16 and received a warm welcome. He soon defined his position in the *April Theses,* in which he characterized the war as an "imperialist war." He opposed the Provisional Government and called for a republic of soviets of workers', peasants', and soldiers' deputies. Lenin raised the slogans for immediate peace and land to the peasants. Both slogans gained wide popularity and reflected the desires of the masses. Increasing opposition to the provisional regime caused its reorganization, but the crisis was not halted.

An armed demonstration in Petrograd in July, 1917, led to a temporary reverse in the fortune of the Bolsheviks. Lenin and others were forced into hiding. But in August the government faced a new crisis. Suspicion that General Kornilov aspired to become a dictator led to his dismissal, but he refused to leave. Instead, he moved a squadron of troops on Petrograd. The left closed ranks, the movement was suppressed, and the general arrested.

This unsuccessful attempt strengthened the hand of the Bolsheviks, and a swing to them was clearly in evidence. To counteract the movement, the government set the elections for a constituent assembly on November 25. It failed to allay the discontent. In September the Petrograd Soviet accepted the Bolshevik view on the organization of authority, and on October 8, Leon Trotsky was chosen chairman of the Petrograd Soviet.[4]

Lenin proposed that the Mensheviks and Social Revolutionaries form a government in which the Bolsheviks would not participate, although they would tolerate it. The Mensheviks and Social Revolutionaries refused, and the Bolsheviks began preparations for an armed uprising. A

[3] See "Letters from Afar" in Lenin, *The Revolution of 1917* (New York: International Publishers, 1929), I, 27–63.

[4] Golder, *op. cit.,* pp. 577–584.

letter of protest against this step was signed by two members of the Central Committee and leading Bolsheviks, Zinoviev and Kamenev. Lenin replied to their protest by a bitter denunciation of the letter and its authors.[5]

On November 7, 1917, the Petrograd Military Revolutionary Committee, under the leadership of Trotsky, declared the Provisional Government ended. Commissars were sent to the front urging soldiers to support the revolution. The Second All-Russian Congress of Workers' and Soldiers' Deputies, which opened on November 17, 1917, under the control of the Bolsheviks, decided to take government power. It planned to end the war through a democratic peace, and divide the land among the peasants, democratize the army, and place industry under workers' control. All local authority was to be transferred to the Soviets of Workers', Soldiers', and Peasants' Deputies, who were to enforce order. Capital punishment at the front, which had been restored by Kerensky, was abolished.[6]

FIRST STEPS OF THE REVOLUTIONARY GOVERNMENT

The first steps taken by the government were directed toward ending the war. The craving for peace was one of the important factors in the rise of the Bolsheviks, and Lenin utilized this desire to the full. Moreover, Lenin considered the war a clash between rival imperialisms, and he saw no reason to continue the struggle.

The Revolutionary Government undertook to solve the land question, being guided by Lenin's slogan, "All land to the peasants." The landlord's right to ownership of the land was abolished. All estates—monastic, church, private, and royal—were transferred to local land committees. The land became the property of the people, and was turned over to those who worked upon it. A Provisional Workers' and Peasants' Government, known as the Soviet of People's Commissars, was formed to govern the country until the meeting of the Constituent Assembly.[7]

[5] James Bunyan and H. H. Fisher, *The Bolshevik Revolution* (Stanford University, Calif.: Stanford University Press, 1934), pp. 59–66; Trotsky, *The History of the Russian Revolution*, III, 88–166; John Reed, *Ten Days That Shook the World* (New York: The Modern Library, 1934).

[6] Runyan and Fisher, *op. cit.*, 109–122.

[7] *Ibid.*, pp. 125–133.

Kerensky immediately sought the aid of officers and troops at the front. Within Petrograd a Committee to Save the Country and the Revolution was organized to fight the Bolsheviks. While the armed conflict was in its early stages, the Bolsheviks proposed an alliance of all socialist parties upon terms which the others would not accept. The Mensheviks and the Social Revolutionaries of the right feared that the domination of the government by the Bolsheviks would lead to a regime of terror. Some opposition came also from a minority of Bolsheviks, who resigned from the Bolshevik Central Committee. For their public opposition to the decision of the Central Committee, they were threatened with deprivation of party posts and with expulsion.[8]

SEEKING PEACE

An armistice was proposed to Germany, and negotiations were begun in December, 1917. The British ambassador pointed out that separate negotiations constituted a violation of the agreement between the two countries signed on September 5, 1914, and warned that the Germans would impose a harsh and imperialistic peace.[9] He was not mistaken.

The Brest-Litovsk Treaty forced upon the Soviet government deprived Russia of 1,267,000 square miles of territory, holding about 62,000,000 people, approximately one fourth of her territory and 44 per cent of her population; one third of her crops and 27 per cent of her state income; 80 per cent of her sugar factories; 73 per cent of her iron; and 75 per cent of her coal. Of the 16,000 industrial establishments in Russia, 9,000 were in this area.[10]

Lenin believed that the Russian military position precluded any successful opposition to the Germans, and he was therefore inclined to accept the peace terms despite their harshness. A number of others favored the waging of a revolutionary war. The *Communist,* opposed to Lenin's views, was issued by a group of opposition Bolsheviks. As usual, Lenin stood by his guns. He recognized the peace as a humiliating one, but he saw no alternative to accepting the German terms. The Seventh Congress of the Bolshevik party approved Lenin's position; and an extraordinary session of the Congress of Soviets approved the treaty by 784 to 261 votes. The Social Revolutionaries of the left repudiated the

8 *Ibid.,* pp. 197–209.
9 *Ibid.,* pp. 268–275.
10 *Ibid.,* pp. 523–524.

treaty, and resigned from the Soviet of People's Commissars. Thus the government, which had at the beginning been a coalition of Bolsheviks and Social Revolutionaries of the left became now a one-party government.[11]

DICTATORSHIP OF THE PROLETARIAT

After the victory of "October" (November 7), the Bolsheviks decided to transfer state power to the soviets and to organize a Provisional Workers' and Peasants' Government.[12]

The soviets were, however, confronted by a meeting of the Constituent Assembly, which had been chosen to establish a new government. It was to open on January 18, 1918, but Lenin coined the slogan, "All power to the soviets." Lenin charged that the Constituent Assembly represented the hidden power of the capitalists and conciliators, and that it must be suppressed. When it refused to accept the "Declaration of the Rights of the Toiling and Exploited Peoples," which would have placed all power in the hands of the soviets, it was forcibly dissolved.[13] Thus many of the old revolutionaries who had suffered in Siberia and were imbued with democratic ideas were removed from the scene by the dictatorial Lenin.

Soon after the suppression of the Constituent Assembly, the Third Congress of the Soviets opened. It instituted "a dictatorship of the toiling masses." A resolution by Stalin declared the Russian Soviet Socialist Republic a federation of soviet republics "founded on the principle of a free union of the peoples of Russia." The highest governmental body was to be the All-Russian Congress of Soviets of Workers', Soldiers', Peasants', and Cossacks' Deputies. In the intervals between its meetings, the All-Russian Central Executive Committee was to be the highest governing body.[14]

THE STATE

In his interpretation of the nature of the state, Lenin leaned, as usual, upon Marx and Engels. He intended to restore the teaching of the

11 *Ibid.*, pp. 525–540.
12 Russia uses the Julian calendar; hence November 7 is in October in Russia, and hence "October" Revolution.
13 Decree in Bunyan and Fisher, *op. cit.*, pp. 384–386.
14 Resolution in Bunyan and Fisher, *op. cit.*, pp. 396–397.

founders to its original purity, and to rescue the theory from the distortions of opportunists. The state arises because of irreconcilable class conflicts, and the existence of the state demonstrates that reconciliation between classes is impossible. It is a means of class domination, an instrument used by the master class to suppress the masses. According to Lenin, it cannot stand above classes, nor can it be used by a suppressed class to fight the ruling group.

Between capitalism and a communist society lies an intermediate period—a transition stage; in which "the state in this period can only be the revolutionary dictatorship of the proletariat." [15] To free itself from the rule of the capitalist, the proletariat must, according to Lenin, "overthrow the bourgeoisie, conquer political power, and establish its own revolutionary dictatorship." [16] Only when class differences are abolished will the dictatorship of the proletariat end. Once exploitation of labor has ceased, men will become accustomed to observing social rules without compulsion. With the end of exploitation, the need for a repressive apparatus will cease to exist.

PROLETARIAN STATE

Lenin differentiated between a capitalist and a proletarian state. The former is organized by a minority in order to keep a majority in subjection. A temporary proletarian state is founded by a majority to keep a minority of exploiters in check. According to Lenin, the proletarian state, with its wide mass basis, is in fact a majority acting against a small minority. Under communism, a distant and millenial hope, the state in any form would become unnecessary, for there would be no need to maintain a struggle against any part of the population.[17] This condition would be attained only in the higher stages of communism. It is at the high stage of communism when the chief sources of social inequality—antagonism between mental and physical labor—disappear. At this stage the principle, "From each according to his ability, to each according to his needs," would be realized. People would then have learned to observe the basic rules of social relations; they would have attained a level of productivity so that they would voluntarily work according to their ability;

---

[15] V. I. Lenin, *State and Revolution* (New York: International Publishers, rev. ed., 1935), p. 71.
[16] *Ibid.*, p. 70.
[17] *Ibid.*, p. 71.

and the narrow selfishness encouraged by capitalism would have disappeared. Before this higher state of communism, the strictest control over the state must be enforced by the armed workers.

Lenin's simplified and somewhat naïve version of the state obviously neglects many aspects of government which are nonrepressive, at least in the class sense. The dictatorship of Stalin is perhaps the best answer to Lenin's belief that the state will gradually diminish its functions with the decline in the ownership of private property. The Stalin regime is the most absolute and dictatorial in the world, not because of the traditional class differences but because men love power, a problem Marx gave scant attention.

Not all Marxists accepted Lenin's views. Karl Kautsky, the leading Marxist of Western Europe, held that the "'dictatorship of the proletariat as a means for the introduction Socialism must . . . be rejected." [18] Assuming that the dictatorship is victorious in the civil war, the inevitable consequence is the paralysis of political and intellectual life in general. Hopeless torpidity seizes the masses, from whose energetic and intelligent activities alone socialism can come and the democratization of autocratic capitalism.[19] Kautsky maintains that "in arbitrariness, in force, in irresponsibility of the State power, the Bolshevist dictatorship goes far beyond tzarism." [20]

Otto Bauer, the leading theorist of Austro-Marxism, believed at first that the Bolsheviks were the executive organ of the entire working class. He indicated, however, that by the middle of 1918, a gradual change had taken place. The Soviet government acquired more power, built its bureaucratic apparatus, and created an army. As the power of the bureaucracy increased, the influence of the masses diminished. Thus the Soviet apparatus was getting stronger, but the masses were getting weaker. Bauer points out that the concept "Dictatorship of the Proletariat" came to have an entirely different meaning from the one it had during the early days of the October Revolution. It is no longer a dictatorship of the proletariat, but a dictatorship of the idea of a proletariat. It is a special type of socialism, despotic socialism.[21]

18 Karl Kautsky, *The Labor Revolution* (London: George Allen & Unwin, Ltd., 1925), p. 85.

19 *Ibid.*, p. 86.

20 *Ibid.*, p. 89.

21 Otto Bauer, *Bolschevismus oder Sozialdemokratie* (Vienna: Wiener Volksbuchhandlung, 1920), pp. 59–63.

A leading militant of pre-World War I socialism, Rosa Luxemburg, concludes that

with the repression of political life in the land as a whole, life in the soviets must also become more and more crippled. Without general elections, without unrestricted freedom of press and assembly, without a free struggle of opinion, life dies out in every public institution, becomes a mere semblance of life, in which only the bureaucracy remains as the active element. Public life gradually falls asleep, a few dozen party leaders of inexhaustible energy and boundless experience direct and rule." [22]

This prophetic statement demonstrates that the most radical Western European socialists capable of independent thought opposed dictatorship and feared its degeneration.

THE USE OF POWER

The Provisional Soviet Government found itself in internal and external difficulties. On December 20, 1917, the Extraordinary Commission to Fight Counterrevolution and Sabotage (Cheka) was set up to exterminate internal enemies. Later its functions were enlarged to include negligence of duty, profiteering, and banditry. The Cheka became a dreaded instrument of revolutionary vengeance. It sought "*to cut off at the roots all counter revolution and sabotage in Russia; to hand over to the revolutionary court all who are guilty of such attempts, to work out measures for dealing with such cases; and to enforce these measures without mercy.*" [23]

CIVIL WAR

The seizure of power by the Bolsheviks in November, 1917, did not give them control over the entire country. An organized revolt led by high officers, and centering in the Territory of the Don Cossacks, broke out in December, 1917. Attempts were made by antigovernment groups to create a broad anti-Bolshevik coalition, and to recruit an armed force capable of conducting a successful struggle. At the same time,

[22] Rosa Luxemburg, *The Russian Revolution*. Translated by Bertram D. Wolfe (New York: Workers Age Publishers, 1940), pp. 37–38.
[23] Bunyan and Fisher, *op. cit.,* p. 296. Italics in source.

separatist movements aiming at the setting up of regional governments arose in many sections.

The armed opposition and passive resistance confronting the Bolsheviks accelerated the movement to the left. Another sign of the new conditions was the change of name from the Social Democratic Labor party (Bolshevik) to Russian Communist party. Lenin was anxious to disassociate the Russian Communist party from the European socialist movement, which, in his opinion, was corrupt and chauvinistic.

THE ARMY

Confronted by armed opposition, the Bolshevik leaders took steps to create a revolutionary fighting force. In March, 1918, Leon Trotsky was appointed commissar of war and chairman of the Supreme War Council. He began to build an army. Old officers were used whenever possible, as they possessed technical military training. To assure the loyalty of these commanders, military commissars were introduced. The commissar, representative of the government in the army, was to educate the soldiers politically and to prevent the old officers from betraying the Revolution. Compulsory military service for all male citizens between the ages of eighteen to forty was reintroduced to raise a fighting force.[24]

THE TERROR

Six weeks after taking power, the Bolsheviks, as was already mentioned, established the Extraordinary Commission to Fight Counterrevolution and Sabotage, the Cheka. Under the leadership of the revolutionary ascetic, Felix Dzerzhinsky, the Cheka became an effective and dreaded instrument of political terror. Dzerzhinsky expressed his belief in organized terror, which he regarded as "an absolute necessity during times of revolution." Capital punishment, which had been abolished in the first days of the Revolution, was restored. The Cheka acted swiftly and without mercy. Those suspected of counterrevolutionary activities were quickly tried and sentenced to prison or execution.

Following the attempt to assassinate Lenin by Fania Kaplan Roid, a Social Revolutionary of the right, and the murder of M. Uritsky, the head of the Petrograd Cheka, the Soviet government formally instituted a Red Terror. The Social Revolutionaries of the right and members of conservative organizations were seized as hostages, and many were executed. Ter-

24 See *ibid.,* pp. 572–574, for the text of the decree.

ror spread throughout the country, and in one day five hundred hostages were shot in Petrograd.[25] The Cheka did not investigate or try to investigate; it struck. Communist leaders regarded it as the fighting arm of the Revolution.[26]

INTERVENTION

As early as December, 1917, the French prime minister, Clemenceau, suggested that the Japanese be asked to send an expeditionary force to Siberia. The Allies were not unanimous on this question. Great Britain expressed no desire to intervene against the Bolsheviks, but was willing to fight against the Germans on Russian soil upon the invitation of the Soviet government. The United States questioned the wisdom of the intervention of Japan. The latter, however, sent an expeditionary force to Siberia in April, 1918, despite the attitude of the United States.[27]

This was not the only intervention of the Allied governments in the affairs of Russia. A Czechoslovak army, which had been organized on Russian soil to fight the Central powers, clashed with the Soviet government. The Czech army was leaving Russia through Siberia, and in the conflict between Czech detachments and the Bolsheviks, the Czechs managed to occupy a number of strategic points. In July, 1918, the Allied Supreme War Council made its decision to intervene,[28] and the British landed a small force at the port of Murmansk. The British were subsequently joined by French and American detachments. England and France also began to encourage anti-Communist movements aiming at the replacement of the Soviet government.

For a time the outlook for the survival of the Soviet government was not promising. Successively the government overcame the forces of Admiral Kolchack, and a volunteer army under General Denikin, whose forces overran a large part of the Ukraine. The Soviet government also repelled an attack upon Petrograd led by General Yudenich. The drive against Denikin succeeded, but his forces were reorganized under Baron Wrangel. At the same time the Soviet government faced a serious threat from the Poles, who occupied Kiev. A successful Russian counteroffensive brought to the Poles the assistance of the French General Weygand, who

---

[25] Bulletins and statement from All-Russian District and Local Chekas, in James Bunyan, *Intervention, Civil War, and Communism in Russia* (Baltimore: The Johns Hopkins Press, 1936), pp. 237–250.
[26] For statements of Latsis, a leading Chekist, and Dzerzhinsky, see *Ibid.*, pp. 261–276.
[27] *Ibid.*, pp. 60–73.
[28] Resolution of Supreme War Council, *ibid.*, pp. 106–107.

inflicted a serious defeat upon the Soviet troops. An armistice was reached on October 12, and the Soviet forces turned their attention to the army of General Wrangel. The latter was completely defeated and forced to flee the country. With the defeat of Wrangel ended the last armed attempt to depose the Soviet government.

THE KRONSTADT UPRISING

Different from the other uprisings was the revolt of the Kronstadt sailors, who had led the revolt against the czar and the Provisional Government. Now they rebelled against the Bolshevist concentration of power, and demanded that anarchists and left-wing socialists be allowed to enter the soviets. A program was drawn up demanding freedom of speech, press, and assemblage for anarchists and left-wing socialists; the abolition of political commissars in the armed services; the cessation of food requisitioning; and the re-establishment of free trade. For a time the uprising seemed a serious threat, but it was suppressed; the ringleaders were shot and others were imprisoned.

22. THE SOVIET ECONOMY

SOVIET ECONOMIC DEVELOPMENT

At the time of their acquisition of power the Bolsheviks were not prepared with a detailed economic plan. Workers' committees, shop committees, and trade unions began seizing factories and directing their operations. Frequently the new directors were unversed in industrial management and operated their enterprises without regard for the welfare of the general whole. To eliminate this particularism and gear the single enterprise into the economy, a system of workers' control of industry was established. The "organs of workers' control" had the authority to supervise production, fix output quotas, determine costs, and oversee business correspondence. The decisions were binding on the owners and could be revoked only by superior "organs of workers' control." [1]

THE SUPREME COUNCIL OF NATIONAL ECONOMY

The next step toward unifying the economic activity of the country was the setting up of the Supreme Council of National Economy for organizing, regulating, and planning economic life. The council had the power to "confiscate, requisition, sequester, and consolidate various branches of industry, commerce, and other enterprises in the field of production, distribution, and state finance.[2] The decrees in December. 1917, and in April, 1918, nationalized the banks and set up a foreign-trade monopoly. They were aimed in the same direction—centralizing control of economic processes. The government was at the same time nationalizing many enterprises. Lenin who was then opposed to rapid nationalization, advocated the nationalization of large industries and the subjection of small enterprises to government regulation. Large basic in-

[1] Decree in James Bunyan and H. H. Fisher, *The Bolshevik Revolution* (Stanford University, Calif.: Stanford University Press, 1934), pp. 308–309.
[2] For the text of the decree, see *ibid.,* pp. 314–315.

338

dustries would be socialized, small enterprises would remain in private
hands, and some units would be state-owned but leased to private operators. Lenin referred to this system as "state capitalism." However, the
political power in society would be in the hands of the institutions of the
working class, the soviets.[3]

These policies were opposed by a leftist group within the Bolshevik
party, and also by the Social Revolutionaries of the left. Both groups
wanted the nationalization speeded up. But Lenin advocated moderation; he also suggested a long-range study to determine the future economic development of the country.

The attempts to work out an effective economy on the basis of workers'
control of industry operated by former managers were not successful.
Clashes between workers and directors, the inefficiency of "workers'
control," and the spreading civil war kept production at low levels. The
crisis caused a change in policy, and ushered in what is known as "war
communism."

WAR COMMUNISM

The period lasted from 1918 to the spring of 1921.[4] The increasing
disorganization and the collapse of the food supply induced the government to nationalize all enterprises with a capital of more than one million rubles. Nationalized industries were placed under the control of the
Supreme Council of National Economy, which sought to eliminate all
market relations and establish a system of barter.[5]

Strikes and stoppages of work were forbidden. "Those instigating a
strike" were declared "enemies of the proletarian revolution, assisting
capital in its fight to regain power, and inevitably [helping] to increase
starvation and disorganization." [6]

War communism was not a carefully developed scheme, but was improvised to meet the emergencies due to revolution and war. In a narrow
sense, war communism must be considered as a war and not as a purely
economic phenomenon. It was not possible under conditions of civil war
to formulate a unified plan. Much of the energy of the leaders had to be

[3] K. Leitas, *Recent Economic Developments in Russia* (Oxford: The Clarendon
Press, 1922), p. 84.
[4] L. Kritsman, *Die Heroische Periode der Grossen Russischen Revolution* (Vienna:
Verlag für Literatur und Politik, 1929), p. 123.
[5] Decree on nationalization in Bunyan and Fisher, *op. cit.*, pp. 397–398.
[6] For the decree see *ibid.*, pp. 401–402.

diverted to war purposes, and the government never knew what areas were controlled by itself or by its enemies.

With the nationalization of industry, it became necessary to overcome localist tendencies, and the appointment of industrial managers was taken away from the shop committee. The authority of factory managements was reduced. *Glavki,* committees made up of five to seven members, were set up to administer branches of industry. These Glavki were subordinate to the Supreme Council of National Economy.[7] They combined the enterprises in a specific industry and subordinated the single enterprise to the general control. In addition, the function of the Glavki was to plan and direct production.

EARLY LAND POLICY

The land decree of November 8, 1917, followed the program of the Social Revolutionaries of the left, who were given control of the Commissariat of Agriculture. Land belonging to estate owners, crown appanage estates, convents, and monasteries were handed over to regional or district soviets. Land belonging to peasants was not confiscated.[8] Old scores were settled with landlords, and burning of property and crude allocation were not uncommon. In February, 1918, the government nationalized all land, and ordered plots given to all citizens, the size depending on the size of the family. Collective farms were to be encouraged.

Soon thereafter the government grain monopoly was established, prices were fixed, and all surplus grain had to be surrendered. A merciless war was declared against the peasants who failed to cooperate, and led to a break between the Social Revolutionaries of the left and the Bolsheviks.[9] Unable to procure sufficient grain, the government set up village committees composed of the lowest-income group to distribute grain and farm implements and to organize communal cultivation and harvesting.

The committees frequently failed to pay the peasant in manufactured goods for his grain. Moreover, they were inclined to distribute the seized grain in the villages rather than ship it to the cities, where the need was very great. Opposition among the well-to-do peasants to requisitioning was also encountered. It soon became necessary to dispatch armed detach-

[7] *Ibid.,* pp. 413–416.

[8] Alexander Baykov, *The Development of the Soviet Economic System* (Cambridge: Cambridge University Press, 1946), pp. 17–18.

[9] Decree and protest of these Social Revolutions in Bunyan and Fisher, *op. cit.,* pp. 461–463.

ments of considerable size to collect the grain by force. At one time between 20,000 and 45,000 armed men were engaged in this work.

Even during the early period, the Soviet government sought to develop communal land tilling and to encourage a consolidation of small peasant farms. Large Soviet farms under the auspices of the People's Commissariat of Agriculture were also organized.

THE END OF WAR COMMUNISM

The attempt to bring all production under the control of the government met with serious difficulties. Production and distribution sharply declined, for the Soviet government was as yet not strong enough to repress all opposition. Conditions in the spring of 1921 were serious. The preceding harvest had yielded about half the average prewar crop. Nevertheless the commandeering of agricultural surpluses was ruthlessly carried out. The situation in industry was scarcely more favorable, for lack of raw materials interfered with operations. An understanding with the peasantry had to be reached in order to provide the cities with minimum of food and industry with raw materials.

The lack of correlation among the Glavki, or boards who managed industries, was another difficulty. As each acted independently, enterprises might not be able to procure special parts or needed materials. The absence of complementary goods would on occasion seriously hamper industrial operations.[10]

A high degree of centralization was another evil. Enterprises were unable to order parts and equipment, regardless of how small the orders were, except through the Glavki. Wasted effort and delay were inevitable. Some Glavki found themselves unable to deal with the great mass of detail which passed through their hands. Proper records, competent accounting, and knowledge of inventories were needed. Lack of system in the procurement, storage, and delivery of goods and ignorance of technical capacity or technical problems were also common.

The growing bureaucratization of economic life aroused opposition among industrial workers.[11] Consequently, industrial output sank sharply,

10 Boris Brutzkus, *Economic Planning in Soviet Russia* (London: Routledge and Kegan Paul, Ltd., 1935), p. 106; Frederick Pollock, *Die Planwistschaftlichen Versuche in der Sowjetunion* (Leipzig: Hirschfield, 1929), pp. 116–119.

11 Maurice Dobb, *Russian Economic Development since the Revolution* (New York: E. P. Dutton & Co., 1928), pp. 129–165.

with the greatest decline in the basic industries. Professor Prokopovicz has estimated that industrial output in 1920–1921 reached 30.1 per cent of the base in 1913; the number of workers were less than half of 1913, and productivity slightly above one third of 1913.[12]

Politically, war communism was leading to division between town and country. Forced requisitioning was imperative during the Civil War, but it aroused strong opposition as soon as the war crisis had passed.

THE NEW ECONOMIC POLICY

Faced by a catastrophic decline in industrial and agricultural output, the Soviet government temporarily retreated from its program of nationalization. It embarked upon the New Economic Policy, the aim of which was to restore industry and agriculture. The market in grain was reestablished, small enterprises operating for profit were allowed, and the large, nation-wide industries were formed into trusts that operated so as to earn a profit. Forced requisitioning of grain was abandoned, and a tax in kind substituted.[31] The government occupied the "economic heights," the strategic sectors of the economy, which included big industry, the banks, transportation, and foreign trade. Hedged in by these state-controlled organizations, the revived capitalistic activity of the peasant and small trader could be held within narrow limits. The general supervision of economic policy was placed in the Commissariat of Labor and Defense.

Lenin had assumed that the revolution in Russia was part of a series which would sweep Europe. However, Russia found that she stood alone as a socialistic nation, and her economic backwardness and the peasantry threatened the existence of the Soviet state. Lenin admitted that the Bolsheviks had been defeated in their "attempt to adopt the principles of production and distribution by the tactics of 'direct assault,' i.e. by the shortest, quickest and most direct route. The political situation in the spring of 1921, revealed to us that retreat to the position of state capitalism, the substitution of 'seige' tactics for 'direct assault' tactics was inevitable on a number of economic questions." [14] In line with the more liberal policy, a new unit of account, the chervonets, was issued in

---

12 S. N. Prokopovich, *Russland's Volkswirtschaft Unter Den Sowjets* (Zurich: Europa Verlag, 1944), pp. 181–182.

13 Lenin, "Speech on the Food Tax," *Selected Works*, 149–163.

14 Lenin, "The New Economic Policy," *ibid.*, p. 286.

October, 1922, backed by a 25 per cent gold and foreign exchange reserve.

There was some revival of industry and agriculture in the early years of the N.E.P. However, the recovery was at different rates, with agricultural output increasing almost twice as fast as industrial production. The result was a more rapid increase in industrial prices as compared to agricultural prices. Part of the rise in prices was due to monetary factors, for despite the issuance of the chervonets, the paper ruble, which was still in circulation, depreciated even more rapidly than before. As a result, the Soviet economy faced the "scissors crisis" in the winter of 1923–1924. This term was used to describe the disparity in the relations of agricultural and manufacturing prices. Like the two blades of an open pair of scissors, prices tended to move farther and farther apart. Moreover, the position of the blades was reversed in this period. Agricultural prices, which in 1922 could be expressed by the upper blade of the scissors, in 1923 occupied the lower position. The favorable harvest in 1922 changed the price situation of agricultural goods. Industrial prices, however, lagged behind because industry had not experienced as great an improvement. The consequence was the developmnt of wide price disparities. The "terms of trade" had moved in favor of the town, and the danger of a restriction of acerage by the peasants again emerged.

The government decided to close the scissors, or force down prices of industrial goods. At the Thirteenth Congress of the party, it was decided to lower prices. Currency reform was introduced, and the issuance of the old ruble ceased. Beginning in October, 1923, prices of industrial goods were reduced through the introduction of economies and lower profits to government enterprises.

By allowing a limited private market in agricultural produce and by encouraging private industry of certain types, the N.E.P. stimulated the growth of a capitalist sector in the economy. However, the belief that, in a competitive struggle between the socialist and the capitalist sectors, the former would inevitably win was not borne out by events. There was fear that the capitalistic elements, especially in agriculture, were gaining in strength. A faction within the Communist party advocated more rapid and extensive nationalization of both industry and agriculture based on planning. Before the change from the N.E.P. to rapid collectivization could be introduced, a violent ideological struggle took place between three factions, each of which espoused a different line of economic development. The right favored continuance of the liberal policy; the left, led by Trotsky, favored rapid industrialization and the building of collectives in agriculture. Stalin took a middle position. After his victory over the opposition, the Soviet economy embarked upon its first Five-Year Plan, with the objective of accelerating the nationalization of industry, the collectivization of agriculture, and the destruction of all capitalistic elements in Soviet society and economic life.

PLANNING

Planned and directed production was from its inception an ideal of the leaders. In February, 1921, the State Planning Commission (Gosplan) was set up under the leadership of the engineer and old revolutionary, G. M. Krzhizhanovsky. The preceding year, the State Commission on Electrification had been appointed, and its program of electrifying the country had received an enthusiastic endorsement from Lenin. The Gosplan, frequently called the "economic general staff," was at first made up of about forty people, the majority of them engineers and specialists, and it was charged with working out a general economic plan and the means for its realization.

Partial plans were submitted to the governing authorities from time to time. In 1925, the Gosplan introduced control figures, which were general guides to production for 1925–1926. They were regarded as indicators or estimates for the government bureaus, and sought to answer questions in regard to productivity, direction, tempo, and other changes in the economy.

THE FIVE-YEAR PLANS

At the end of 1927, the Gosplan presented its first Five-Year Plan for the reconstruction of the economy of the Soviet Union. It covered the period from October, 1928, to January, 1933, and was intended to bring all industry and agriculture under a single unified plan. According to G. T. Grinko, who was then vice-chairman of the Gosplan, among the essential objectives of Soviet planning are nationization of agriculture, credit and industry, and a state monopoly of foreign trade.[15] Under socialism the whole economy of a country becomes a huge single enterprise. With this in view, the planning of the whole national economy is

[15] G. T. Grinko, *The Five-Year Plan of the Soviet Union* (London: Martin Lawrence, 1931), p. 13.

not only possible but absolutely necessary.[16] The "plans have the force of law." [17] The tasks set out by the plans are realizable, but obviously they involve a high expenditure of mental and physical energy. The plans seek to establish an economic program for a relatively long period, one which permits a redistribution of resources to obtain the desired end.[18] The plan not only fixes objectives for five years, but may provide for the completion of some tasks in a shorter period. "The plan solves one of the fundamental problems which determine the rate of increases of production, namely the problem of distributing the whole yearly output between accumulation and consumption." [19] It indicates the amounts and kinds of goods that are to be made, and how they are to be distributed between investment and consumption. It "provides for the distribution of all the elements of personal consumption among the various classes and groups of the population . . . . lays down prices, wages, taxes and all other elements of the financial plan, which . . . . serve to distribute and redistribute the monetary resources . . . ." "The plan determines the sum total of the inter-relations between the economy of the U.S.S.R., as a whole, and world economy as whole, and each separate country in particular." [20]

PLANNING PRODUCTION

The Gosplan received general directives from the Communist party and the Council of Ministers. Such directives indicated the general priority of tasks and the price, wage, and investment policies that were to be followed. On the basis of these directives, plans were drawn up for various industries, combined into a whole, and submitted for approval to the Council of Ministers. An attempt was made to maintain a rate of development of the separate branches of the economy so that adequate raw materials and complementary goods would be available for processing industries.

Upon its approval, the plan was submitted to the different ministries,

16 Obolensky-Ossinsky, "The Premises, Nature, and Forms of Social Economic Planning," in *Socialist Economy in the Soviet Union* (New York: International Publishers, 1932), pp. 11–12.

17 Stanislas Stroumline, *La Plannification en U.R.S.S.* (Paris: Editions Sociales, 1947), p. 14.

18 Ch. Bettelheim, *La Plannification sovietique* (Paris: Librairie des Sciences Politiques et Sociales, 1939), p. 83.

19 Obolensky-Ossinsky, *op. cit.*, p. 27.

20 *Ibid.*, p. 28.

the Glavki, and factories which, after examining the program, suggested modifications to the Gosplan. The Gosplan finally coordinated the suggested changes, and transmitted it in final form to the various ministries and Glavki, whose duty it became to carry out their part of the plan. Each ministry and each Glavk has a planning department to supervise and divide production among single plants.[21] As a result of the experience accumulated over the years, the procedure has been shortened. Plants may now initiate their own plans for the following year, provided they do not violate the general directives of the preceding period. Plans must then be submitted to Glavki or ministries, who coordinate them with those submitted by other plants. Finally, the Gosplan carries out similar supervision and coordination for all Soviet industry.[22]

In addition to the central planning organization, autonomous republics, regions, Glavki, and single plants maintain planning units which may evolve independent plans, subject to approval of the higher planning authorities. On the plant level, planning does not differ in essence from the type carried on by the entrepreneur in a private economy. Questions such as quantity, type, and quality of output, labor force and wage payment, reductions in the various costs, and plant and output expansion are some of the subjects covered in the independent plans of the single enterprise.

The Gosplan has a responsibility not only for the formulation of the general plan, but also for its execution and adjustment. Consequently check ups on fulfillment are continually made so as to institute adjustments indicated by actual experience. The plan of production is a unified system of output programs, of cost, input, and output. At least theoretically, each element fits in with all the others. Basic to Soviet planning are the programs of capital expansion, which have been given a preeminent place.[23]

INDUSTRIAL ORGANIZATION

The organization of industry has undergone a number of changes. Nationalization succeeded workers' control. Regional and local economic councils, subordinate to the respective soviets, were formed to manage

21 Bettelheim, op cit., pp. 89–91.

22 Gregory Bienstock, "The Planning of Industrial Production," in Management in Russian Industry and Agriculture (New York: Oxford University Press, 1944), pp. 49–50.

23 Maurice Dobb, Soviet Planning in Peace and War (New York: International Publishers, 1943), p. 33.

some industries. Medium and large plants were organized on an industry-wide basis under the control of "chief committees" or Glavki. Both the territorial councils and the Glavki were subordinate to the Supreme Economic Councils. However, with the growing centralization of industry, the functions of the territorial councils were limited to local industries producing for the local market. Trusts organized on a regional basis, and serving as intermediaries between the single plant and the Glavki were formed and reorganized.[24] It was found that the industrial structure was too cumbersome. In October, 1932, the combines operated by Glavki and trusts were reduced in size and increased in number. Simultaneously, the Supreme Economic Council was split into the People's Commissariats (ministries) for Heavy, Light, Timber, and Food Industries. Since then, industry has been further divided, and an increasing number of ministries set up to manage them. National industries are either controlled directly by a minister representing the central government or controlled through a minister representing a constituent republic. Industries catering largely to a local market, or using mainly local resources, are controlled locally. Auxiliary industries are controlled by the minister of the industry served. Economic activity has been, since 1937, coordinated by the Economic Council.

Industries are operated by the minister in charge of the industry, who appoints the heads of Glavki and trusts and supervises their functioning. The ministry of an industry is divided into Glavki and the latter may in turn be split into trusts. The division may be due to the need of putting a subindustry or an area under the direct control of a smaller agency. Managers of individual plants are usually appointed by the Glavki or the trusts and are subject to their orders. Industrial commissariats (ministries), Glavki, and trusts are divided into planning, finance, supply, sale, and accounting departments, and the heads of the different organizations are ultimately responsible to the commissar (minister), who holds the power to appoint and dismiss.

BASIC PRODUCTIVE UNIT

The basic productive unit is the enterprise. It has its own finances, fixed and circulating capital, and an account at the State Bank. Although the plant manager is in charge, he can neither buy nor sell without the approval of the higher authorities, the Glavk or the minister. He is sub-

[24] Leonard E. Hubbard, *Soviet Labor and Industry* (London: Macmillan & Co., 1942), p. 117.

ordinate to higher economic organs, and he has to act within the restrictions imposed upon him by the general plan and the higher authorities. The restrictions go beyond those imposed upon a plant manager employed in a capitalistic economy. The latter must, of course, conform to the price, output, and wage policies of his board of directors, but managers of Soviet plants are severely limited as to the reorganization of their labor force, use of their wage fund, and purchases of raw materials and equipment.[25]

Although the manager is subordinate with respect to the Glavk or industrial commissariat, he has virtually full authority in dealing with his subordinates, whom he can hire or dismiss. In absolute charge, he has the responsibility for carrying out the plan in all its details. He has the authority to set rates of wages and provide for the protection of the health and welfare of labor.

THE ROLE OF THE COMMUNIST PARTY IN INDUSTRY

Like the position of other groups, the role of the plant manager has undergone some changes. Up to 1938, the party was dominated by older revolutionaries, and some conflict in attitude existed between party officers and industrial managers, even though both groups aimed to serve the interests of the government. Gradually a change in favor of the industrialist took place, especially after the purges of 1937–1938, when many of the old Bolsheviks were executed. As a result, party members who traced their membership back to the heroic period of revolution and intervention sharply declined in number. In addition, the functions of the trade unions were redefined, and their chief tasks became the promotion of industrialization. Gradually the plant committees lost their power, which was absorbed by the managers. Trade-union committees continue to discuss factory problems, but they are tending to lose their character as defensive organs of labor, and are becoming increasingly instruments of management.[26]

TRADE UNIONS

Labor unions did not make much progress under the czarist regime, and only 24 unions existed on the eve of the Revolution. The release of labor from restraint stimulated widespread organization, and at the

[25] Bienstock, *op. cit.*, pp. 4–13.
[26] *Ibid.*, pp. 23–31; Hubbard, *op. cit.*, pp. 96–97.

trade-union conference in June, 1917, 967 unions with a membership of 1,475,429 were represented. A decision to organize on an industrial basis was approved.[27]

In the struggle between the Bolsheviks and their opponents, the trade unions sided with the former. At the first trade-union congress at Petrograd in January, 1918, 273 out of 416 delegates voted for the Bolshevik motions against 66 for the Menshevik and 21 for the Social Revolutionary. The Bolshevik resolution, in its turn, declared against the neutrality of the trade unions, which were to participate in the work of economic direction.[28] The unions during the first years had considerable power in industry, and were of great importance throughout the period of workers' control. They were forced to shift their activity, at least to some degree, and direct their interests to wider problems. The unions were charged with the enforcement of labor laws and were authorized to carry out a number of educational and cultural activities.

At their second congress in January, 1919, the trade unions acquired a definite organizational setup. The industrial form of organization was retained. Finances were centralized. The government of the union was based on democratic centralism, which means subordination of the minority to decisions taken. The central organization was to have the authority to represent the union. Decisions taken by the higher authorities of the union are obligatory upon those below. The same structural pattern was to be followed by all unions. Local unions were organized in enterprises, and these were combined into local, regional, and finally into an All-Union organization in an industry. The separate unions were combined in an All-Union Central Council of Trade Unions, which is the central organization for the Russian unions.

In the late 1920's, three points of view on the position of the trade unions in a socialist state were presented. A syndicalist view was espoused by Shlyapnikov and Madame Kollontai. In their opinion the trade unions should have an important voice in the appointment of factory heads and in the management of industry. A second group headed by Trotsky proposed to place the unions under government control, for Trotsky could not visualize the trade unions as distinct from the Communist party. He wanted the control of the unions centralized and their directors named by the government. A group of ten—comprising, among

27 Michel Rolnikas, *Les Syndicats professionnels en U.R.S.S.* (Paris: Librairie Technique et Économique, 1936), p. 57.
28 *Ibid.*, pp. 73–76.

others, Lenin, Zinoviev, and Stalin—maintained that the trade unions had a special function to perform as the training ground for millions of nonparty workers. "The trade unions establish a connection between the vanguard [Communist party] and the masses." [29]

During the N.E.P. the trade unions signed collective agreements with enterprises on hiring and conditions of work. A number of wage categories were established, and to begin with a ratio of about five to one was set up between the basic wage and the highest one.[30] The labor code established a minimum hiring age as well as a system of social insurance which covered temporary and permanent disability, unemployment, and illness. Unemployment insurance has since been abolished. The social insurance schemes are still administered by the unions. During this period the Soviet trade unions were regarded as "schools of communism" which, while organizing the workers around their daily interests, took cognizance of the needs of the economy and the country. The unions sought to stimulate the workers' interest in building socialism, but they were also in part concerned with the direct interests of labor.

A number of the old leaders of the Soviet trade unions, including the head, M. Tomsky, were removed in 1929 on the ground that they had not mobilized the trade unions adequately in behalf of the Five-Year Plan. The new chief of the Soviet unions reproached his predecessor for concentrating too much on day-to-day activities of the workers and neglecting the building of socialism. As a result, the functions of the unions changed.

The functions of Trade Unions as organizers of labor as a productive force are exercised through factory wage commissions, which in spite of their name are concerned more with raising the productivity of labor than with obtaining higher wages and better conditions of work. In capitalist enterprises such commissions would be regarded as organs of the employers.[31]

Trade unions participate in wage fixing in that they are consulted about general wage policy, but their efforts are directed toward removing inequities rather than with securing the highest wage rate.

[In] a socialist planned economy it seems hardly conceivable that wages could be left to be settled by free play of bargaining, for the simple reason that the level

---

[29] V. I. Lenin, "Trade Unions and Mistakes of Trotsky," *Selected Works* (New York: International Publishers, 1935), IX, 5, D. Antoshkin, *Professionalnoe Dvizhenie V Rossi* (Moscow: BTSSPC, 1925), pp. 297–300.

[30] Rolnikas, *op. cit.*, p. 98.

[31] Hubbard, *op. cit.*, p. 157.

of wages, determining as it does the level of consumption (and hence the scale of production not only of the consumption-good industries but also of the investment-good industries), is one of the crucial elements in the whole plan, and to leave it as in part an unknowable factor when constructing the plan would be to make complete planning of economic life virtually impossible.[32]

Irrespective of the type of economy, some conflict between managers and workers in the plant is inevitable. A manager's position is partly dependent upon his ability to keep down costs, and he may therefore try to whittle down the workers' standards.

COLLECTIVE AGREEMENTS

Collective agreements between trade unions and management were accepted early in the Revolution as the method of setting rates of wages and working conditions. The system broke down during the Civil War, but it was re-established during the N.E.P. Although many of the relations between the employee and the enterprise were defined by law, the collective agreement defined rates and methods of pay and many other conditions affecting the workers in the shop. The making of collective contracts declined in the 1930's, and a few were written for 1935. From that time to 1946 no collective contracts were written or renewed. As collective contracts died away, trade unions and plant committees gradually ceased to participate in fixing wages in the plant.[33]

Collective agreements were revived in 1947, however, as a means of promoting the fulfillment of the postwar Five-Year-Plan. The collective agreement is regarded as an important means for attaining and exceeding the production goals of the Five-Year-Plan, and of improving the material and cultural conditions of labor and technical staffs.[34] The collective agreement is essentially, although not entirely, a means for seeking to achieve the objective of the plan. Most of the emphasis of the plenum of the All-Union Central Council of Trade Unions, which dealt with collective agreements, was put on the means for bringing about the fulfillment and overfulfillment of the plan. The trade unions were ordered to help strengthen discipline, fight against slackness and inefficiency, instill principles of safety, improve the workers' technical ability, and their cul-

[32] Maurice Dobb, *Soviet Economy and the War* (London: Routledge and Kegan Paul Ltd., 1941), p. 68.
[33] S. M. Schwartz, "Management and Employees," in *Management in Russian Industry and Agriculture,* p. 41; V. M. Dogadov, "Etapy Razvitiya Sovetskogo Kollektivnogo Dogovora," *Izvestiya Akademii Nauk SSSR* (Economics and Law), Mar.–Apr. 1948.
[34] *Professionalyne Soyuyzy,* May 1, 1947, p. 1.

tural and political education. There was also a reference to improving the conditions of labor, but no reference to wages. They remained under the exclusive control of the government, and increases in rates were possible only with increased productivity.

WAGE TRENDS

The leaders of the October Revolution sought to eliminate wage differences. Their equalitarian policies, however, undermined morale and sapped effort, and a change in policy was necessitated. The population was divided into categories, and each group was allowed a different ration, with the highest allocated to those performing important state functions or heavy physical labor. This plan failed to solve the problem of declining labor productivity. The result was the re-establishment of wage payment based upon the productivity of the wage earner. Real wages, according to Professor Prokopovicz, sank to below 50 per cent of 1913 in the first part of 1922, and rose continually to 1928–1929, when they exceeded the prewar levels by more than 15 per cent.[35] Wages then began to sink again but the trend was reversed by 1938. The same author found that in addition to his wages, the Soviet worker receives many services at low or no cost which, in fact, raise his real wage above the level shown in the index. Such additions are low rent or rentless housing, free heat, light, and water, and the free use of bathing and laundry facilities. Moreover, industry bears the costs of social insurance from which the worker benefits.[36] This is, of course, true, but social insurance is no monopoly of the Soviet Union, and these benefits are not included in the calculation of real wages anywhere else.

Another student of the Soviet economy believes that the "standard of living of the Soviet workman is undoubtedly higher than in pre-Soviet years, and lately has been steadily rising. But it is equally true that this standard which he enjoys at the end of the third Five-year Plan is still far below that of workmen in other industrial countries."[37] Steady employment and the opportunity of all working members of the family to hold steady jobs, he argued, have in fact raised the standard of living beyond the level indicated by examining only the changes in real wages.

35 Prokopovicz, op. cit., pp. 283–300, 302.
36 Ibid., p. 302.
37 A. Yugow, Russia's Economic Front for War and Peace. Translated by N. I. and M. Stone (New York: Harper & Brothers, 1942), p. 212.

Granting the accuracy of this analysis, it is still evident that the Soviet government has performed no miracles. During the same period, real wages rose at a much greater rate in the United States than in Soviet Russia, and the United States began with a much higher base. It is true that the great amount annually allocated for investments affects the real income of the Soviet worker, but the fact remains that the rise in the standard of living of the Russian worker has not been unusual for a rapidly developing industrial economy, even if one accepts the most sanguine estimates made by the government. It is, of course, argued that the benefits of rapid industrialization in Soviet Russia will eventually accrue to the worker, while in a capitalistic nation it is of advantage to the captalist. This is scarcely true, for the benefits of industrialization are widely, even if not evenly, spread around in a capitalistic economy.

WAGE SETTING

Both time and incentive rates are used as methods of wage payment. Piecework is extensively used in wage fixing. A study of processes and the average worker's capacity is made by rate fixers, who determine standards or norms. The tasks are revised whenever changes in technical processes or methods of work are introduced. Piecework is designed to stimulate quality and quantity of output, to increase payment to labor, and to raise the worker's interest in his job.[38]

The Central Committee of the Party decided on its own authority that norms must be raised and instructed Trade Unions to help put the change into effect. Officially of course the workers, having realised that their daily tasks were not within their capacity, were only too glad to work harder for the glory of Communism and in defence of the Soviet Union. Those who did not see that way and felt aggrieved, were guilty of *petit bourgeois* tendencies, so their opinions did not count.[39]

Once the task is fixed, the rate for the job is set by wage fixers. The job is rated on the basis of skill required, difficulty, danger, and other conditions. Those exceeding their tasks are paid higher rates. The method is an adaptation of Taylor's differential piece rate. There are wide disparities between the wage of the lowest-paid and the highest-paid workers.

Under the plan a given amount is allocated for the payment of wages, which is a wage fund. In turn this is divided among industries and enter-

38 N. G. Alexandrov and G. K. Moskalenko, *Sovetskoe Trudovoe Pravo* (Moscow: Yuricliheskoe Izdatelstvo, 1947), pp. 178–183.
39 Hubbard, *op. cit.*, p. 106.

prises, and the amount each can pay out is set. It is thus clear that no actual negotiations over the amount of wages can take place. Once the plan determines the total amounts to be paid out, one group can profit only at the expense of another. Real wages can, however, be increased by rising productivity, leading to lowered prices.

Inequality in wages, while never absent, increased after 1931.[40] The theory that a Soviet economy sets equal wages for all grades of labor was attacked in 1931 by Stalin, who charged that high labor turnover was due

to incorrect organization of the system of wages, an incorrect wage scale, [and] a leftist leveling of wages. In a number of enterprises the wage scales have been drawn up so that there is almost a total disappearance of difference between skilled and unskilled labor, between simple and difficult labor. Leveling results in that the unskilled workers take no interest to become skilled . . . .

The wage scales should be drawn so as to take into consideration the difference between skilled and unskilled labor, between easy work and hard work. We cannot tolerate that a roll-mill worker in metallurgy should get the same wages as a sweeper. We cannot tolerate that an engine driver on the railroad should get the same wages as a copying clerk.[41]

There has been, as all admit, an increase in nonwage social benefits. However, against the nonwage benefits must be placed the increase in compulsory labor. The Soviet Union has experienced a high labor turnover which indicates that freedom of choice is not entirely absent in the Soviet labor market. As a matter of fact, labor turnover and absenteeism have been serious problems in the Soviet Union since the first days of the regime. Full employment undoubtedly acts to encourage shifting between jobs and remaining away from work. The chief reason for labor turnover and absenteeism is dissatisfaction with the job. Rather than make the jobs more attractive, the Soviet government directed its efforts to penalizing workers for absenteeism and job shifting. In December, 1938, unjustified absenteeism from the job—lateness of more than twenty minutes was counted as an absence—of three times in one month or four times in two months was ground for dismissal. Work books, which a worker had to deposit with management upon employment, were also issued in 1938. The conduct of the worker on the job was indicated in the book, which was carried with him from job to job. Moreover, a work-

40 Abram Bergson, *The Structure of Soviet Wages* (Cambridge, Mass.: Harvard University Press, 1944), p. 129.
41 Joseph Stalin, *The New Russian Policy* (New York: The John Day Company, 1931).

er's insurance benefit was adjusted in accordance with the time he spent in the same enterprise.

In 1940 measures for the control of labor were extended. Workers were prohibited from leaving their jobs without the permission of management. Violations were punishable by imprisonment. Compulsory enrollment in vocational schools of young people from fourteen to seventeen years old was decreed; upon graduation they could be assigned to work by the government. Subsequently, a decree established the right of the government to transfer workers and technicians from one plant to another. The transfer was not to lead to material losses on the part of the person transferred; failure to agree was punishable by imprisonment. This system was not abolished after the war.[42]

There has been, in addition, a revival of slavery within the Soviet Union. Political prisoners and others have been transported to different parts of Russia, where they have been forced to work under the most severe conditions. Estimates of the number of slave workers vary from five million to fifteen million people.[43] Certainly any discussion of Soviet labor and welfare must take account of the individual and collective tragedy involved in forced work.

MONEY AND BANKING

The leaders of the October Revolution looked with equanimity upon the inflation which spread over the country. During the era of war communism an attempt was made to abolish money and to replace it by rationing. During the N.E.P. it became necessary to introduce monetary and banking reform.

Soon after the October Revolution, the banking system was nationalized. All bank assets, except claims of depositors, were seized. Limitations were put upon the amount that could be withdrawn at one time. A State Bank (*Gosbank*) was established in 1921. During the N.E.P. the need for a stable currency became acute, and at the end of 1922 the chervonets was established. With the increase in commercial activity, a banking system able to finance trade and industry became necessary. A number of banks were established, each of which was to furnish short- and long-term credit to certain types of enterprises and cooperatives. The

42 Alexandrov and Moskalenko, *op. cit.*, pp. 122–132.
43 See British charges in *The New York Times*, July 28, 1949.

Gosbank supervised the operations of the others.[44] Later short-term credit activities became concentrated largely in the Gosbank.

CURRENCY

The chervonets equals 10 rubles and is an obligation of the Gosbank. It is issued in notes of 1, 2, 3, 5, 10, 25, and 50 units. Treasury notes are also issued in rubles. Bank notes are covered by 25 per cent gold, precious metals, or foreign exchange.[45] The legal reserve is not too important, as it can be varied at the will of the authorities, and the volume of currency can be fixed in accordance with the plan and the need for circulating media to carry on the business of the economy. Both the bank notes and the treasury notes are inconvertible and are under the control of the Gosbank.[46]

BANKS

The financial system provides the economy with a unit of account, and makes possible the reduction of all resources to a common denominator, the ruble. All banks are owned and operated by the government. The most important, the State Bank or Gosbank, is the chief source of short-term credit. Its capital is subscribed by the state, and its supervision is in the Ministry of Finance. Fifty per cent of its profits are paid to the Treasury, and a large part of the remainder goes for reserves, which accumulate until they equal the statutory capital. Deposits of private persons are accepted in the savings banks operated under the direction of the Ministry of Finance. Interest is paid on both private and institutional accounts, the savings being invested in government bonds.

The Gosbank furnishes the economy with an adequate money supply and enterprises with short-term credit; it also supervises accounting procedures. By its control over credit and monetary circulation the bank plays an important role in the carrying out of the current plan. In the planned economy the Gosbank functions as a center of credit, economic accounting, and emission of currency.[47] It is vitally important to the planned economy, for its monetary and credit policies influence the dis-

[44] Leonard E. Hubbard, *Soviet Money and Finance* (London: Macmillan & Co., 1937), pp. 11–15.

[45] Arthur Z. Arnold, *Banks, Credit and Money in Russia* (New York: Columbia University Press, 1937), p. 146.

[46] W. B. Reddway, *The Russian Financial System* (London: Macmillan & Co., 1935), p. 16.

[47] R. O. Halfina, "Pravoe Polozhenie Gosudarstvennogo Banka USSR," *Izvestiya Akademii Nauk SSSR* (Economics and Law), Jan.–Feb. 1947, 3–8.

tribution of real resources. The Gosbank cannot, however, embark upon a policy out of line with the economic plan, for it is even more closely tied to the government than is a central bank in an economy of private enterprise. The Gosbank is in fact the principal organ for carrying out the economic plan.

Enterprises and institutions must keep an account with the Gosbank, and these accounts are utilized for making payments between business enterprises. Before a firm can deliver raw materials or machinery to another, the receiving enterprise must order payment at the bank; delivery will not be made unless the bank certifies that the receiving enterprise has sufficient funds to make payment. Enterprises cannot grant credit or be debited without the approval of the bank.[48] This is logical, for the activities of a single enterprise are conducted with the object of achieving the goals of the plan rather than of earning maximum profits.

The Gosbank assumes an important part in the distribution of resources among industries and enterprises. Each enterprise is allowed a given amount of working capital, which must be allocated for fuel, raw materials, and semifinished products. Its manager has some independence in the allocation of resources among these separate funds, but its credit requirements must conform to the "Credit Plan," which is elaborated by the ministers and the State Bank and is in fact a part of the economic plan. The amount of credit each enterprise is permitted is determined by the Credit Plan. The bank will not lend to an enterprise unless the loan will be used in accordance with the plan, and it can recall loans improperly used. It is possible to shift assets from one account to another, but if a bank loan is needed, the banking authorities must receive a description of the state of the different accounts and know how the working capital is being used in order that the bank can ascertain the solvency of the enterprise and its compliance with the economic plan. If conditions are in order, the loan is granted and the firm is given a credit on current account or else payment is made on behalf of the firm for supplies.[49]

In addition, there are four other types of bank. The *Prombank* or industrial bank is charged with distributing the budgeting grants made by the general plan for national economic development. This bank is in fact a department of the Commissariat of Finance, and it administers the investment funds set aside by the economic plan. It also supervises ex-

48 Reddway, *op. cit.,* p. 18.
49 *Ibid.,* pp. 34–36.

penditures in order to determine that funds advanced are used only for purposes properly authorized by the annual Financial Plan.

The *Tsekombank* finances housing and cultural or educational establishments. Like the Prombank, it checks the activities of its clients, which must conform to the general plan. The *Vsekobank* provides investment funds for cooperatives of all types. The funds are secured by the purchase of shares by cooperative societies, and by contributions from the profits of these organizations. These deposits cannot be withdrawn. The agricultural bank (*Selhozbank*) finances long-term agricultural credit in the form of nonreturnable grants, and repayable loans. The bank pays interest on collective farm funds, and a lower rate on other deposits.[50]

DISTRIBUTION

In the fall of 1918, the government abolished private trade. Distribution of goods was carried on by government stores and cooperatives. Rationing was introduced, lasting until 1921. The introduction of the N.E.P. restored private trade, which continued until 1929, when it was again suppressed. The government again undertook the distribution and rationing of essential goods. In 1932, factory administrators were given the power to issue ration cards to industrial workers. Gradually there developed the commercial shops which sold nonrationed goods. By 1936, rationing was ended, and goods were sold at state stores and cooperatives at a controlled price.[51]

Along with other economic activities, distribution of consumers' goods is determined by the plan. Commercial institutions, called "syndicates," were set up to buy raw materials for groups of enterprises organized in a trust, and to sell the output of their enterprises to distributing organizations.[51]

Retail trade in the cities is operated by chains of government stores which form a *Torg* whose board of directors is appointed by the minister of trade of a federated republic, a province, or the All-Union. A Torg operates large shops which have considerable control over their budgets and management, and over smaller units under the direct control of the Torg. In the towns and villages, cooperative stores are the retail outlets.

50 Hubbard, *Soviet Money and Finance,* pp. 84–86.
51 Leonard E. Hubbard, *Soviet Trade and Distribution* (London: Macmillan & Co., 1938), pp. 58–59, 191.

They are bound together in district, regional, and provincial groups, headed by the *Tsentrosoyuz*, which executes the government decisions affecting the cooperatives. It also has final authority over the plans of the lower organizations for distributing consumers' goods and making large capital outlays.

At the beginning of the first Five-Year Plan, syndicates were abolished. In their place commercial divisions were set up by the trusts. Later wholesale distribution depots for different products were organized. These depots were under the direction of an All-Union minister or a local provincial trading organization. The commercial divisions of trusts may sell to large retail shops and to the wholesale depots, which in turn distribute the goods through their areas. The trading organizations must fit their programs into the general plan so that distribution between groups and regions is equitable and the goods distributed are in demand at the point of sale.

Contracts are made between distributing organizations operating at different levels and are of two types—general contracts and local or direct contracts. General contracts are concluded with large producers of consumers' goods. A minister of an industry—All-Union or republic—or the head of an industrial trust may conclude an arrangement with a central trading organization—state or cooperative—for the sale of a given commodity. Local and direct contracts are then made by subordinate trading and industrial organizations for supplementing and extending the contract.[52]

At their organization, Torg and cooperative outlets are given a fund of capital—supplied by the government or by members of cooperatives—in accordance with the turnover and size of their stock of goods. Turnover periods for goods are fixed so that they are not kept off the market, and the holding of excessive stocks is discouraged. Trading organizations are allowed to borrow from banks for financing their operations, but loans must be repaid at the end of the turnover period. Wholesale and retail enterprises keep, at the Gosbank, "a Special Advance Account and a Giro Account—more or less equivalent to a current account." [53] Upon the receipt of a consignment, a trading enterprise signs a note which constitutes authorization to the bank to pay the "amount of the invoice." This is debited to the trade organization's advance account. Receipts deposited by the trading organization are credited to its advance account:

52 *Ibid.*, pp. 116–117.
53 *Ibid.*, p. 132.

at the end of the turnover period the receipts deposited by the trading organization normally are sufficient to repay the bank's original outlay. The surplus or profit is transferred to the current fund, and is used to pay wages and other expenses. An enterprise which fails to conform to its turnover plan will have its credit curtailed by the bank. The latter is also authorized to investigate trading enterprises showing losses and to check on prices paid suppliers.

In addition to the state and cooperative trading, an appreciable amount of goods is sold in the peasant (*kolkhoz*) and producers' co-operative markets. About 25 per cent of the peasants' income, in 1935, came from the sale of produce in the open market.[54]

Collective farms are allowed to sell their surplus in the kolkhoz market, an open space with a few booths. In large cities the market comprises shops, stalls, and some tables from which produce, mostly foodstuffs, is sold. Under the law, buying on these markets is limited to private persons, and state organizations are barred from purchasing. The kolkhoz cannot employ salesmen, and a member of the collective must be appointed to the task of selling. In addition to the produce of the collective farm, the individual peasant sells produce of his own. About three fifths of this latter comes from the dividend in kind earned by the peasant for his work on the collective farm. The remainder comes from the private gardens of the peasant.

PRICES

Prices are fixed and set in accordance with the plan and are an instrument for effecting the government's economic policy. Prices generally equal costs of labor and raw materials, plus an allowance for depreciation and planned profit, if the enterprise is reasonably efficient. The earned, planned profit is divided into three parts: one part is taxed, another is deposited with the industrial bank for purposes of capital expansion, and a third part is used for the enterprise. Should profits be larger than those planned, the added profit is divided into the same three portions, but the enterprise can use a large proportion of its part for bonus payments to labor and the staff. Since the government has a trade monopoly, it is the exclusive middleman, a fact which enables it to fix prices to both producer and consumer. Depreciation charges are included in prices; how-

54 *Ibid.*, pp. 126–130, 144.

ever, they cannot be freely used by an enterprise, but must be utilized in accordance with the plan. Enterprises are thus banned from building up large cash reserves, and as the Gosbank supervises the use of working capital, failure to meet or an effort to evade the plan would be readily detected. Agricultural prices are set as follows: Agricultural units are required to deliver to the state a given percentage of their output at set prices. The remainder of the produce can be sold to consumers at the regular city markets, or to state organizations and factories at conventional prices which exceed by 20 to 40 per cent the prices set for the produce that must be delivered to the state.[55]

The Soviet government has had several types of retail prices in operation. These were normal or town prices at which only a limited amount of goods could be purchased. Country prices were paid by the peasants at village stores for manufactured goods, and were approximately the same as normal prices. Commercial prices several times as high as town prices were charged for unrationed goods. Open-market prices were used in selling agricultural produce bought by state organizations and factories.

The Soviet Union financed World War II in part by the issuance of currency. The increase in the money supply coupled with the reduction in the available consumers' goods led to sharp increases in prices. The currency reform of 1948 was designed to diminish the supply of money and thus reduce demand and prices.

Rationing was abolished in 1948, and the sale of food and industrial goods was placed on an open-trade basis. Commercial and rationed prices were abolished at the same time and unified state retail prices were introduced. The prices of bread were reduced 12 per cent and cereals 10 per cent, a very sharp decrease as compared with the prices in the commercial stores. Prices of other foodstuffs were kept at the then existing rationed prices. Prices for industrial goods were raised above rationed prices, but they were lower than commercial prices.

With these price changes went a reform of the currency. Those who presented cash received 1 new ruble for 10 old ones. On money already on deposit in savings banks, the exchange rate was 1 new ruble for 1 old one up to 3,000 rubles. On larger deposits, it was 1 for 1 on the first 3,000 rubles, 2 new ones for 3 old ones on the next 7,000 rubles, and 1 new ruble for 2 old ones on all amounts above 10,000 rubles. Three price zones were set up, and prices were to vary between the zones. but were to

55 Hubbard, *Soviet Money and Finance*, p. 135.

remain uniform within a zone. Prices of many consumers' goods were reduced from 10 to 12 per cent.

THE FUNCTION OF PRICES

Consumers can exercise choice in the goods they buy and the prices they offer. As in capitalistic countries, consumers have the freedom to buy or not to buy, but the consumer is not able to determine the division of the national product between consumption and investment. Consumers in the Soviet economy exercise choice but not sovereignty. Consumers can buy or refuse to buy, but they cannot determine, except remotely and indirectly, the volume of goods, the types of goods, and the direction of the economy's development.

Demand and Supply Demand cannot affect normal prices, which are set by the government. Price fluctuations are possible in the commercial markets, and prices will be influenced by consumer demand and by the amounts of commodities the government allocates to the commercial outlets. In a capitalistic economy, prices are determined by consumer demand, which in turn influences the distribution of the factors. In the Soviet economy, the decision on distributing the factors is made by the government. The price of a commodity, in the noncontrolled sector, will be influenced by demand, but a high price will not induce the government to divert more resources for its production.

Wholesale prices are not based upon supply and demand in the market, but are used for accounting purposes. They are used to record the prices at which raw materials and finished goods are sold by state enterprises to each other or to cooperative retail distributors. Prices are based on the costs of the preceding year, minus the planned reduction in costs for the current year.

Retail prices are arranged so as to cover planned costs of production, including the planned costs of wholesale and retail distribution organizations, transportation, and normal profit and turnover tax. Prices are adjusted on the basis of the purchasing power of the population. The turnover tax on commodities is adjusted in accordance with the plan of the planning authorities; by increasing or diminishing the turnover tax, it is possible to restrict or enlarge consumption. This regulation is thus one of the means of directing resources.[56]

56 M. I. Bogolepov, *Sovetskaya Finansovaya Sistema* (Moscow: Gosfinizdat, 1945), pp. 9–11.

THE NATIONAL BUDGET

As the government controls all resources, the budget is one of the factors determining their distribution. Based upon its needs, each governmental unit has its own budget. The state budget is divided into three categories: (1) the local budget, (2) the budgets of federal republics, and (3) the All-Union budget. The budgets of these three governmental units are tied together and constitute the state budget. Outlays from the budgets fall into the following categories: (1) about 40 per cent is for the national economy, the remainder going to (2) social and cultural activities, (3) defense, (4) administration of government, (5) repayment of government loans, (6) social insurance, and (7) other expenditures.[57]

The budget is worked up under the general direction of the party and the government. It must dovetail with the general plan and is in fact one of the means for effecting that plan. Estimates of receipts and expenditures are made by the various authorities, and must be approved by the minister of finance. All expenditures by the state, irrespective of the unit of government, are listed, and require final approval by the Council of Ministers.

Government revenue from the socialized economy is raised largely through a turnover tax on business transactions, and between 1933 and 1937, 67.4 per cent of all taxes was raised by this method.[58]

A tax on profits is also a source of revenue. The earnings of collective farms, loans, premiums on insurance, and a progressive income tax are all relatively minor sources of government revenue. The turnover tax is a means of draining from the consumer the income that arises as a result of large capital investment. Another source of revenue consists of subscriptions to state loans and savings deposits invested in state bonds.

The quantity of savings in the Soviet Union is not determined mainly by individual decisions. Moreover, the individual, to repeat, has no voice in determining how much of the national income is to be saved or spent. The government allocates the amount for capital expansion in accordance with its preconceived plan. For the entire community the annual amount available for consumption is fixed. In Soviet Russia, lending to the government by citizens does not enable the government to increase the goods it has produced, for the government already owns all of the

---

[57] K. Plotnikov, "Gosudarstvennyi Byudzhet Sovetskogo Soyuza," *Financy SSSR ZA 30 Let* (Moscow: Finansovoe Izdatelstvo SSSR, 1947), pp. 160, 179.

[58] *Ibid.*, p. 168.

productive resources. Likewise, the turning over of funds by the citizens to the government will not enable it to purchase more goods, for the government already commands all. It is clear that a Soviet citizen's consumption is not restricted, as in capitalistic countries, by the division of his income between savings and consumption. It is the consumption made available by the state which determines the Soviet citizen's standard of life. Total money payments are made to those engaged in production of capital and consumption goods. Prices of consumption goods must, however, be high enough to recover the outlays on both types of goods; otherwise the community would be building up large amounts of surplus cash. However, this cash could not be used for investment, nor would it affect the direction of investment. An individual with large reserves of cash could use them to buy goods on the commercial markets now or in the future, but his decision would have no effect upon the kind and quantity of goods produced.

Similarly, profits have no effect on the direction of industry. Profits, as in capitalistic economies, arise whenever prices of sale are above costs. Profits can be used for plant expansion, are paid to the government in the form of taxes, and can, in part, be used for improving the conditions of labor.

THE FINANCIAL PLAN

All financial activities comes under the Financial Plan. These include the state budget and all the state activities involving monetary expenditures. The Financial Plan includes the Credit and Cash Plans, and is designed to promote efficiency and to control inventories and capital formation. In relation to the Gosplan, the General Financial Plan parallels the Materials Plan of the former, for they are two sides of the same program, as expenditures for new investments and inventories must be provided by the General Financial Plan. Inflation is avoided if planned investments and the funds allocated are in balance.

THE CREDIT PLAN

Long-term capital expansion is planned by the Gosplan, and the funds are provided by the Credit Plan. Banks are allowed to allocate funds to enterprises in accordance with and up to the planned amounts. By maintaining a check upon pay rolls and other expenditures, the banks prevent the misdirection of funds, and thereby are important instruments for carrying out the general plan. Cash is seldom exchanged between enterprises, and payments for goods and services by one enterprise to another is usually made by the bank's transferring funds from the accounts of the buyer to the seller.

Short-term credit may be either planned, unplanned, or given to cover goods in transit. Enterprises can apply for a loan to a bank, and it is granted if the request harmonizes with the Credit Plan. The Gosbank may temporarily grant an unplanned loan, but this must be repaid within thirty days, and can be extended only by the higher authorities. Enterprises can also receive loans to cover the value of goods in transit; such a loan is retired upon receipt of payment from the customer.

THE CASH PLAN

The main problem of the Cash Plan is to match the flow of purchasing power held by consumers with the value of consumers' goods offered on the market. By subtracting from total personal income payments, government revenue and loans, plus increases in savings bank deposits, the government finds the net purchasing power in the hands of individuals. These estimates are then compared with the Materials Plan, and the government knows the amount of currency needed to bring purchasing power and consumer goods into equilibrium. The Cash Plan is then elaborated; it may aim for decreasing or increasing the monetary circulation, which can be diminished by more rapid tax collection or by encouraging subscriptions to government loans.

FOREIGN TRADE

Absolute monopoly of foreign trade is one of the basic instruments of Soviet economic policy. In April, 1918, foreign trade was nationalized; it was exclusively conducted by the Commissariat for Foreign Trade and Industry. The government controlled foreign trade so as to prevent an inflow of consumption goods; otherwise foreign exchange needed to pay for capital imports would be used to pay for consumption goods. In addition, state control enabled the government to fix internal prices regardless of the effect of imports on the price level. Prices of exports and imports were set without consideration for principle of comparative costs; instead, import and export policies were fitted into the economic plan as a whole.

At the head of the foreign-trade activity was the minister (commissar) of foreign trade. Offices were scattered through local and regional communities, and trade delegations were located in various countries. The minister negotiated trade treaties, approved export and import quotas, authorized transactions, and devised the financing of trade.

Foreign trade under the Soviets has never reached the value achieved under the czar. Neither agricultural nor industrial exports attained the yearly average of 1909–1913. The highest level was reached in 1931, when exports were 64.9 per cent and imports 78.0 per cent of 1913 exports and imports. Beginning in 1932, Soviet imports and exports declined, never regaining their former position. The decline has been explained by Soviet economists as due to the establishment of new productive resources which made it possible to produce at home equipment formerly imported. The need to export in order to pay for imports was thereby reduced.[59]

Whatever the reasons, foreign trade, like other economic relations, is subordinate to political objectives. Imports and exports can, within limits, be increased or lessened in accordance with political rather than economic needs. Moreover, government monopoly makes dumping easy, and even products short at home may be offered for sale abroad. The foreign-trade monopoly is supposed to eliminate the middleman's profits and aid in capital accumulation.[60]

EXPORT AND IMPORT PLANNING

First consideration in the Soviet foreign-trade program is given to estimating the kind and volume of imports. Exports are then planned to meet imports so that foreign exchange will be available to pay for them. Moreover, foreign trade is geared into the general plan of economic development so that imports have consisted largely of capital equipment and machine tools. Actually, foreign-trade operations are conducted by a number of government corporations, each specializing in certain types of goods. Each corporation is assigned a level of expenditures in harmony with the general scheme. Imports are made by industrial or merchandizing companies which must transmit the orders to an importing company. If the order is in harmony with the plan, a license is issued and quota-

[59] Alexander Baykov, *Soviet Foreign Trade* (Princeton, N. J.: Princeton University Press, 1946), pp. 46–47, 55.

[60] Mikhail V. Condoide, *Russian-American Trade* (Columbus, Ohio: The Bureau of Business Research, Ohio State University, 1946), pp. 33–34. The following quotations from Condoide are from this source, pp. 36, 45.

tions on prices, credit, and delivery are requested from the trade delegations abroad.

Exports are utilized only to the extent that they are needed to pay for imports.

Decisions as to the nature and structure of Soviet exports at any given time are based on comprehensive estimates as to what promises greater advantage for Socialist economic purposes: to use available material resources, for which a market abroad exists, directly for the needs of the national economy, or to use the industry through exports and with the proceeds of their sale to purchase necessary goods abroad or to pay for technical assistance of foreign experts.

Under the over-all scheme, the Commissariat of Foreign Trade draws up a plan in consultation with its agents. The plan must be approved by the planning authorities. Estimates of exports are based on resources available and on the possibilities of sale. The estimates are prepared by agencies which deal in production and distribution of commodities, guided by the analysis of foreign demand for Soviet products.

FUNCTIONS OF MINISTRY OF FOREIGN TRADE

The Ministry of Foreign Trade plans the export and delivery of goods, fixes selling prices, and checks on quality. Agents of the commissariat are scattered through the different areas. Abroad, the Ministry of Foreign Trade is represented by agents and delegations. Foreign trade is financed through the Valuta plan—"a balance sheet of monetary transactions between the Soviet Union and foreign countries as expected to take place within a definite period of time in the future."

The Valuta plan is made up of noncommercial currency transactions—cost of foreign missions and technical personnel—and currency involving commercial transactions. An attempt is made to include all expected quantitative and qualitative changes of the foreign-trade organizations, and to relate these changes to the general economic plan.[61]

AGRICULTURE

Although the Communists had turned the land over to the peasants, because of shortages of manufactured goods the peasants refused to sell their crops for low-value rubles. The Bolsheviks were forced to requisition crops, and the peasants refused to plant more than was needed by

61 *Ibid.*, pp. 48–49.

the countryside. The government retreated, and the N.E.P. restored the market in grain. The more capable peasants prospered, and there developed class differentiations in the village. The well-to-do peasants called "kulaks," or fists, were farmers who could afford to hire help; middle peasants were those who worked their own land but hired no labor; then came the many poor peasants who, whether or not they owned a small plot of land, worked for wages on the property of others.

At first the Bolsheviks had hoped to unify the middle and poor peasants against the kulaks, and win them for collective farming. The "alliance" of city workers and the peasants, the *smychka* was a failure. A faction within the party, the right wing led by Bukharin, argued for concessions to the peasantry in the hope of encouraging large crops and raising the level of agriculture. At first, Stalin favored a middle course between concessions to the peasantry and drastic repression of private property, as advocated by Trotsky.[62] The Fifteenth Party Congress, in 1927, adopted resolutions for the suppression of the kulaks and for basing socialism upon a collectivized agriculture.

COLLECTIVIZATION

A drastic change in agricultural policy was introduced in 1928, marking a sharp swing to the left. The government introduced a contract system under which the peasants were required to deliver to the state organizations the surplus harvest at prices set by the government. Prices and amounts to be delivered were fixed upon information supplied by the village soviet, generally controlled by the poor peasants. This system, in fact, resembled the grain requisitioning of the period of war communism.

In January, 1930, the Central Committee of the Communist party decided that 25 per cent of the area under cultivation in 1929 would have to be brought into collectives. This program was carried out so quickly that by March, 1930, 60 per cent of the peasant homesteads in the Soviet were collectivized.[63] The objective of collectivization was to increase the productivity of agriculture so that the rapidly expanding industrial population would receive at least a minimum subsistence. In addition, the Soviet leaders were committed to the mechanization of agriculture, in-

---

[62] Leon Trotsky, *The Revolution Betrayed*. Translated by Max Eastman (New York: Doubleday & Company, 1937), pp. 21–44.

[63] Leonard E. Hubbard, *The Economics of Soviet Agriculture* (London: Macmillan & Co., 1939), pp. 100–107, 110.

volving the use of tractors and combines, possible only on large farms. The peasants, temperamental individualists, were, however, unwilling to enter into collectives. A policy of great pressure was accordingly deemed necessary and was ruthlessly applied. The class war was carried to the village.

The peasant population was divided into the three categories mentioned above—the rich, the middle group, and the poor. Steps were taken to eliminate the rich peasants by proportionately heavier taxation; the middle peasants, while treated somewhat more lightly, were also subjected to severe exactions. The movement for collectivization was directed by the poor peasants, who were backed by the Soviet power. In their haste to create collectives, the leaders neglected to take into account the passive resistance of the peasants, who slaughtered half of the total head of livestock in the space of four years. The government accepted the challenge, and instituted a regime of repression and terror. About five million peasants were deported to Siberia or the Far North, one fourth of whom are said to have perished.[64]

Other consequences also ensued. Chaos in the village was one, and the deepening crisis led Stalin to call a halt in a letter, "Dizziness from Success," issued in March, 1929.[65] Stalin sharply attacked the impetuousness and the lack of moderation of the drive for collectivization. Although the more brutal methods were modified, the struggle for collectivization continued. Passive resistance by the peasants brought a sharp reduction in grain output, and, in the winter of 1932–1933, a serious famine faced several sections of the country. Blame for this situation rests very largely upon the government, which sought to drive the peasants into collectives against their will. On the other hand, the Communist leaders were determined to destroy the power of the peasants to blackmail the government by starving the cities. The Soviet government brutally and decisively demonstrated to the peasants that if starvation was to follow their failure to carry out the government's policies, it would be the peasants and not the supporters of the Soviet power—the urban proletariat—who would starve. Despite the harshness of the methods and brutal confiscations, or perhaps because of them, the policy of forced collectivization led, by 1933, to the virtual transformation of the individual agricultural economy into collective farms. Peasants were compulsorily enrolled in cooperative farms or kolkhozy. At the beginning of World War II, the

64 *Ibid.*, p. 117.
65 Joseph Stalin, *Leninism* (London: George Allen & Unwin, Ltd., 1933), II, 280–286.

29,000,000 small individual farms were transformed into 242,000 kolkhozy, containing 93.5 per cent of all peasant farms and 99.3 per cent of all arable land.[66]

KOLKHOZY

The kolkhoz is a union of peasants in a collective farm, all of whom irrevocably surrendered their land, livestock, equipment, and draft animals to the productive unit, the kolkhoz. Each family can retain a cow, poultry, and hogs and sheep for its own use. Any worker or peasant can become a member except those who slaughter their animals and sell their implements before application. An entrance fee is paid by all. A proportion of the property brought into the collective by the individual is credited to the reserve, and the remainder is regarded as the member's share in the collective. The proportion deposited in the reserve increases with the size of the individual's wealth. Working and administrative expenses are paid out of the collective's net income. All work is performed by the members themselves, and workers can be hired only under special circumstances.[67] In some kolkhozy, the members could raise produce on garden plots, but this right was not always granted by the elective officials. The lack of inducement led to a decline in effort by the peasants, and the result was unfavorable to both peasants and townspeople. Consequently, in 1932, the government allowed the collectives and their members to sell part of their products on the uncontrolled markets, and it devised a plan whereby the compulsory collection of agricultural produce by the government would be only a fixed amount per unit of land planted.[68] This gave the peasants some notion in advance of the demands that would be made upon them in the form of government collections, and removed the arbitrary element. It also allowed the kolkhozy to dispose of the balance on the open market and thus gave a stimulus to increased effort.

OPERATION OF A COLLECTIVE FARM

As noted above, work on a collective farm is carried on by the members, with hired labor utilized in emergencies only. All are required to work, except that women are exempt one month before and after childbirth.

66 Yugow, op. cit., pp. 45–46.
67 Hubbard, The Economics of Soviet Agriculture, pp. 125–127.
68 Ibid., pp. 129–130.

Remuneration is on a piecework basis. Work is carried on in groups called brigades. Every member receives an advance up to 50 per cent of the money due him, and 10 to 15 per cent may be paid in kind. The general assembly is the controlling agency. Between meetings affairs are managed by the administration elected by the assembly. The latter accepts new members, expels old ones, approves and confirms annual production plans, makes contracts for expenditures, and draws up the rules. Theoretically a collective farm is a self-governing agricultural cooperative.

In 1934, the Soviet government allowed each farmer to appropriate for his own use between 1 and 2½ acres of land. In 1939 and 1940, the government sought to limit the peasant's right to this acreage and increased the compulsory deliveries required. Again the peasantry reacted unfavorably, and in April, 1940, and January, 1941, decrees establishing the basis of compulsory deliveries of grain, wool, eggs, and so on, were revised. The deliveries are based on the amount of land owned by the kolkhozy. Previously the kolkhozy had to deliver produce on the basis of the quantity of land sown, and meat and milk deliveries were based on the size of the herds. This meant that an increase in acreage cultivated or in the herds raised would automatically increase the government's requisition. The incentive for additional production was diminished. As a consequence, new decrees appeared which set fixed amounts to be delivered to the government based upon the land owned by the collective. Since anything raised above those amounts belongs to the collectives, an incentive for raising productivity has been created. A second decree established supplementary pay for increasing crop yield.

The government has tried every means to strengthen the collective farm. A decree issued in May, 1939, required each collective farmer to spend at least sixty to one hundred days on the collective farm. Failure to comply could be punished by expulsion and loss of all rights to share in the assets of the collective farm. Hours of work during harvests were extended from 9.6 hours to from sunrise to sunset. These decrees and others aimed to tie the peasant to the collective more closely and to discourage the use of his energies to cultivate the small piece of land allowed him for private use.[69]

Machine Tractor Stations Closely connected with the collective farms are the machine tractor stations, machine shops which provide farm machinery to the collective farms: combines, threshers, tractors, and other agricultural implements. They are purely government institutions which

[69] Prokopovicz, *op. cit.*, pp. 170–171.

service the collective farms at fixed fees, and provide advice on technical and agricultural problems. The M.T.S. control all large agricultural machinery and can thus help to determine agricultural policy. The mechanization of agriculture presumably led to sharp increases in agricultural productivity. Nevertheless, horses were used extensively in parts of Soviet agriculture before World War II and even more widely thereafter. *Agricultural Administration*   At the head of the agricultural administration is the minister of agriculture, who draws up the long-term plans. Several kolkhozy are associated together in larger villages or larger units. At all levels, the ubiquitous official representing the Communist party is present. The heads of the kolkhozy are, as a rule, party members and may not even be agricultural workers. Supervisors, labor organizers, accountants, and agronomists make up the technical directors of the kolkhozy, but the actual administration is done by the Presidium or Executive Committee. Kolkhoz land belongs to the government, and cannot be sold. Similarly, work animals are the collective's property; some of the cattle and poultry are owned by the collectives, and some by individuals.

Small plots are now allowed to each family and income from them is privately owned. That from the collective is divided among the government, the collective, and the individuals. After the government charges have been paid, the law requires deductions for seed, cultural needs, equipment, and capital constructions. The remainder is paid out to members.

The workday is the unit of measurement, and seven varieties of work have been devised. The number of workdays credited depends not only upon the duration but upon the type of work performed. Efficiency will also affect the number of workday credits. After all necessary payments have been subtracted, the remainder constitutes the collective's income. The days worked are added and then divided into the total income of the collective and the value of a day worked is thereby obtained.

According to one student, so "far as can be calculated from the figures allowed to be published by the Soviet government, the average grain yield throughout the country is now no greater than on the private estates before the Revolution, but is certainly better than on pre-war peasant land." [70] In fairness to the Soviet effort, the same author points out that the grain-growing areas have been extended into areas where the yield is likely to be small. "Nevertheless, however one regards the grain problem, the enormous amount of capital invested in the means to produce agri-

[70] Hubbard, *The Economics of Soviet Agriculture*, p. 253.

cultural machinery, in land improvement, in the selection and breeding of new and improved seed grain, in supplying chemical fertilisers, etc., has resulted in a disappointingly small improvement in the yield of the soil." [71] Professor Hubbard admits, however, that collectivization has on the whole been a good thing for the country and that it holds the possibility of raising the future level of agricultural output. The collective has become the predominating form of agricultural enterprise in the Soviet economy, and even the Germans were unable to destroy it during their occupation of Soviet agricultural areas.

ECONOMIC TRENDS

Industrial expansion in the Soviet Union has been uneven. The disproportionate development of industries has been a source of difficulty. Nevertheless, during the last thirty years, the growth of heavy industry, power, coal, electrical machinery, and chemicals has been on an extensive scale. Consumer industries, on the other hand, have registered a more modest growth. This is in line with the Soviet policy, which seeks to emphasize expansion of capital goods industries. We can even admit the claims that progress has been on a scale unprecedented in history, although they are open to question. Yet economic progress by no means justifies the loss of the most elementary freedoms, the one-party state, secret police, administrative exile, and the slave-labor camps. The Russian people, called upon to build socialism by their ruthless masters, have no voice in deciding on the distribution of income, the rate of investment, and the level of consumption. These decisions are made for them, and as they move into the fourth decade of dictatorship, they find their hopes of a life of plenty almost as unfulfilled as in the bleak days of the 1920's.

Despite her economic progress, Russia is still behind the principal capitalistic nations on a per capita basis of production of virtually all important commodities. It is likely that a greater willingness to allow foreign capital to enter, under limited and defined conditions, would have lifted some of the burdens from the backs of the population. However, the Soviet leaders were convinced that such a step might have jeopardized their control over the economy, so they followed a system of raising capital by limiting consumption or by forced savings. In its eagerness to industrialize the nation, the government has starved the people of consumption goods. In part, the rapid tempo was due to the needs

[71] *Ibid.*

of national defense, but in part it was caused by the eagerness and speed to build industry. At present, the threat of foreign invasion is gone. Certainly the strongest nation in Europe, against which no effective force could be mustered, can afford to relax after its heroic struggles. But instead, the Five-Year Plan for the Rehabilitation and Development of the National Economy of the U.S.S.R. in 1946–1950 calls for an investment "of 205 billion rubles in 1950 [in 1926–1927 prices] as compared with 138,500,000 rubles in 1940, which represented an increase in industrial output of 48 per cent as compared with the pre-war year of 1940." [72]

72 *The Great Stalin Five-Year Plan for the Restoration and Development of the National Economy of the U.S.S.R. for 1946–1950,* Information Bulletin, Embassy of the Union of Soviet Socialist Republics, 1946, p. 4.

23. GOVERNMENT AND PARTY IN THE SOVIET UNION

THE ROLE OF THE PARTY

All of Soviet life, whether social, political, or economic, is dominated by the Communist party. Although earlier revolutionary organizations in Russia exacted loyal discipline from their members, the Communist party differs in that it has achieved power in a great country and can impose its decisions by force. Formed as the Bolshevik Faction of the Russian Social Democratic Labor party in 1903, it changed its name in 1918 to distinguish itself from right and center socialists.

The Communist party is not a political party in the Western sense: a group of people freely united for the achievement of definite political aims through the winning of office or through the exercise of pressure upon the government. The Communist party of the Soviet Union must be regarded as part, perhaps the most important part, of the governmental apparatus. The process of becoming a powerful governmental organ was already at work in the first years of the October Revolution. It was accelerated in the 1930's, culminating in the purges of the middle 1930's. The influence of the "Old Bolsheviks" was ruthlessly uprooted, and the party membership is now largely made up of leaders of industry, trade, and the army. Instead of reflecting a proletarian movement, the party now consists of the elite of the nation; the thirty years that have passed since the October Revolution have changed its character. Instead of a persecuted band of conspirators, the party is the directing organ of a great and expanding nation. It is not a hunted band of idealists, but a society of ruthless pragmatists skillful in the use of all the arts of power. Not the oppressed and the heavy-laden but the proud and the ambitious make up its membership. During the war, the gates were opened more freely, and a critical student of Soviet affairs estimates that the Communist party in the Soviet Union attained a membership of 5,700,000, the highest in its history.[1]

The Communist party permeates and directs the political, economic, and cultural life of the Soviet Union. Party cells exist in every type of functioning institution—factories, mines, railways, armed services, and educational and government organizations. Beginning with the local cells, the party is arranged in a number of layers stretching from the local area to the region, district, and union republics, and ending in the All-Union organization. All members and party institutions conform to what is called democratic centralism, which means majority rule and the maintenance of strict party discipline. Decisions made by the higher bodies of the party are absolutely binding upon its lower bodies. Meetings of local regional and All-Union party conferences are held periodically. Delegates from lower party bodies are chosen for the higher ones. The different party bodies select executive committees who guide not only the party, but the various institutions in their area. The executive bodies select secretariats, made up of a smaller and more important group of members who are the actual guides and directors of party policy. Closely identified with the party is the Young Communist League (*Komsomol*). It resembles the party in organizational structure, and its chief functions are to indoctrinate the Soviet youth with the theories of Marxism-Leninism and to assist the party in carrying out its tasks. Young people between the ages of fifteen and twenty-six are eligible. Below the Komsomols are the Young Pioneers, from the ages of ten to sixteen, and the Octobrists, from the ages of eight to eleven. Both organizations are designed to spread the official ideology and encourage an interest in scientific and political questions.

The highest organ of the Communist party is the All-Union Congress. At the beginning of the Revolution, the party congresses met annually; now they meet once every three years. Reports and discussions are presented upon a variety of topics affecting domestic and foreign policy, and decisions are then formulated. In the early years, debate and argument over policy were common. But recently the infrequent meetings and the growth of a simple, monolithic view have reduced the party congresses to "policy-propagating organs."[2]

---

1 S. Schwartz, "Kompartya Poslye Voyni," *Sosialisticheski Vestnik,* December 10, 1945.
2 Julian Towster, *Political Power in the U.S.S.R., 1917–1947* (New York: Oxford University Press, 1948), p. 150.

THE CENTRAL COMMITTEE

At the head of the party is the Central Committee, made up of seventy-one members. From these members the Organizational Bureau (Orgburo) and the Political Bureau (Politburo) are appointed. The Central Committee's power has declined over the years with the expansion of the influence of the Politburo and the Orgburo. These two institutions, first set up in the fall of 1917 to supervise the seizure of power, became permanent in 1919.[3] Since then the Politburo has become the foremost directing body in the Soviet Union. It supervises and directs all the important political and economic activities, and all matters of basic policy fall within its scope. The Orgburo supervises the organizational work of the party. As a coordinator of the work of the Politburo and the Orgburo, the Secretariat, whose members are chosen from the Central Committee, was set up to carry out the will of the various organs of the party. The secretary-general of the Secretariat was a member of both the Politburo and the Orgburo, a post obtained by Stalin in 1922. It was in this post that he was able to destroy his opponents and subordinate the party organs to his will.

After the Revolution, Lenin emphasized the need for the strictest selection in accepting new members even workers. At the same time he ascribed great importance to the occasional cleansing of the party.[4] These are the periodical *Tschistkas* or cleansings, when members are called to account for their official and nonofficial acts. Those not measuring up to the party standards are expelled. During Lenin's lifetime, differences of views were allowed on questions upon which the party had not yet taken a position. Thus differences on peace, trade unions, and the industrial tempo arose; they were debated in the press and at party meetings. The party was based on what has been termed "democratic centralism," that is, the authority of the Central Committee was to be based upon the confidence of the rank and file. The party was held to be the "vanguard of the working class," its most conscious and determined segment. That meant, inferentially, that the party was superior to the mass and had a superior understanding of policy and tactics. Party leaders were above the party rank and file, and thus a hierarchy was established. As long as Lenin lived, his power was unquestioned. He was the intellectual and

3 *Ibid.*, pp. 157–158.
4 V. Molotov, *The Communist Party of the Soviet Union* (New York: Workers' Library, no date), p. 9.

tactical superior of his colleagues; none ranked with him, and his authority was unmatched.

Lenin suffered an apoplectic stroke in 1922, and although he recovered sufficiently in 1923 to perform some political work, he died in 1924. With Lenin's illness, the problem of succession became pressing. Lenin's closest associates were the "Old Bolsheviks," men and women who had belonged to his faction and with whom he had strong political as well as personal ties. Moreover, these Old Bolsheviks occupied most of the important political and economic posts. One of the most powerful of these posts, that of secretary-general of the party, was occupied by Joseph Stalin. From this position, Stalin was enabled to gain control over the party machinery and to place his own adherents in important positions. In contrast, Leon Trotsky, who had been second in command in the October Revolution, had joined the Bolshevik faction as late as 1917. Even though Trotsky enjoyed great prestige within the country, the Old Bolsheviks looked upon him as an outsider. It was also known that Trotsky had held views different from those of the Bolsheviks on many questions. Trotsky's characteristics—imperious temper, lack of tact, and pride —are qualities which do not endear a politician to those working closely with him.[5]

TROTSKY

Leon Trotsky (1879–1940) (Lev Davidovich Bronstein), the leading collaborator of Lenin during the Revolution and later Stalin's chief opponent, became interested in the revolutionary movement while a student at the Gymnasium. For a short time he was a Populist, but he soon became converted to Marxism and joined a Marxist circle. In 1898, he was arrested and imprisoned at Odessa and later exiled to Siberia. He escaped and made his way to Zurich, and then to London to see Lenin. This occurred before the break between the Bolsheviks and the Mensheviks, and while Russian Social Democrats were not yet divided into warring factions. In the split of 1903, Trotsky sided with the Mensheviks. Trotsky attributed his attitude to the influence of Martov, Axelrod, and Zasulich.[6] He did not remain with the minority for long, and he finally disassociated himself from both factions. By then Trotsky was recognized

---

[5] Max Eastman, *Since Lenin Died* (London: The Labour Publishing Company, 1925), Chap. I.

[6] Leon Trotsky, *My Life* (New York: Charles Scribner's Sons, 1930), p. 161.

as one of the more outstanding writers in the Russian revolutionary movement. His nickname Pen (Pero) is striking testimony to his capacity.

THE REVOLUTION OF 1905

In the Revolution of 1905, Trotsky occupied a leading place, and after the arrest of the president of the soviet, at St. Petersburg, Trotsky became the directing head of the revolt. With the collapse of the Revolution, Trotsky and other leaders were arrested, and Trotsky was sentenced to enforced exile, but again he escaped. An exile for a second time, he resumed his socialist activity abroad. In 1908, Trotsky founded a Russian socialist paper (*Pravda*) in Vienna. In 1912, Trotsky and the Mensheviks called a conference of Marxian socialist groups in the same city. Lenin and the Bolsheviks refused to attend. During the Balkan War Trotsky acted as war correspondent, and contributed to the Russian liberal and socialist press. At the outbreak of World War I, Trotsky was in Vienna, but the intervention of the Austrian Socialist leader, Viktor Adler, enabled him to escape internment and leave for Zurich.

In November, 1914, Trotsky crossed the French frontier as a correspondent for a Russian liberal journal. After his arrival in Paris, he joined the staff of *Our Word*. He attended the meeting of socialist anti-war internationalists at Zimmerwald, and later he was ordered expelled from France by the Ministry of Interior. He went to Spain, but he was deported on a steamer leaving for New York, where he arrived on January 13, 1917.

In New York, Trotsky joined the staff of a Russian socialist paper, the *New World*. After the March Revolution, Trotsky left for Russia, only to be removed from his ship at Halifax by the British naval authorities. The intervention by the Soviet of Soldiers' and Workers' Deputies, however, forced his release at the end of April. Upon his arrival in Petrograd in May, 1917, Trotsky threw himself into the political maelstrom rising in Russia. Since 1904, Trotsky had remained outside both the Bolshevik and the Menshevik factions, and his "Inter-District" group merged with the Bolsheviks in July, 1917.

After the October Revolution, Trotsky became a close co-worker of Lenin, occupying the posts first of commissar of foreign affairs and then of war. Under the direction and leadership of Trotsky, the Red Army defended the revolutionary government against internal enemies and foreign intervention. In the public mind, at least, Trotsky occupied, in the early years of the Revolution, a post second to that of Lenin. With

Lenin's illness and death, a radical change took place; a group led by Stalin set out to reduce Trotsky's importance.

FIGHT FOR POWER

Opening the struggle for control, Trotsky, in 1923, criticized the domination of the party by the Central Committee. Trotsky appealed to the youth, and sought to make the leadership more responsive to the will of the party membership.[7] He urged greater inner democracy and less bureaucratism. Against Trotsky, who was at the time war commissar, three leaders—Kamenev, Zinoviev, and Stalin—formed a bloc. Of the three, Stalin was the least known to the outside world. Kamenev was the leader of the Moscow party, and Zinoviev headed the Leningrad section. The Leningrad Provincial Committee, dominated by Zinoviev, indorsed the expulsion of Trotsky from the party; and Kamenev urged the exclusion of Trotsky from the Politburo. Stalin opposed both of these steps, "for we know that the policy of lopping-off might entail grave dangers for the Party."[8] The union of Stalin, Kamenev, and Zinoviev was sufficient to defeat Trotsky, who was unable to gain dominance over the party, the government, and policy. However, the union of the three was soon disrupted. The occasion was the formulation by Stalin of the theory of socialism as a possibility in one country alone. Originally the Bolsheviks had believed that the Russian Revolution was the first of a series of socialist revolutions which would sweep Europe and lead to the establishment of universal socialism. However, the failure of European revolutions lead to the elaboration of Stalin's theory of socialism in only one country. The view was conditionally supported by a more conservative group, at the head of which stood Rykov, the chairman of the People's Commissars, Bukharin, the leading theorist, and Tomsky, the head of the trade unions. Stalin argued "that the proletariat, having seized power in Soviet Russia, can use that power for the establishment of a fully socialised society there. For this to be possible the Russian workers need the sympathy and the support of the workers in other lands; but it is not essential that there should have been a victorious proletarian revolution in these other lands."[9] This was a pragmatic view, but Stalin's victory was perhaps due

---

[7] Arthur Rosenberg, *History of Bolshevism from Marx to the First Five Years' Plan.* Translated by Ian F. D. Morrow (New York: Oxford University Press, 1939), pp. 193–195; N. Popov, *Outline History of the Communist Party of the Soviet Union* (New York: International Publishers, 1935), Part II, p. 201.

[8] Joseph Stalin, *Leninism* (London: George Allen & Unwin, Ltd., 1933), I, 447.

[9] *Ibid.,* p. 56.

more to his political astuteness than to the logical cogency of his arguments.

STALIN (1879–   )

Trotsky's great opponent, Joseph Vissarionovich Dzugashvili (Stalin),
a Georgian, entered a theological seminary at Tiflis at the age of fourteen. He became an energetic revolutionary, and under the name of Soso
he was active in the Tiflis and Batum areas.[10] In 1902, Stalin was arrested
and exiled to Siberia.

In January, 1904, Stalin escaped from Siberia. By now a professional
revolutionary, he sided with the Bolsheviks in the split between the factions, taking an active part in the "expropriations" that followed the
abortive Revolution of 1905. Stalin did not show much predilection for
theoretical analysis, and the little he published at the early stage of his
career shows him an orthodox Marxist of the Bolshevist persuasion and
without great originality of mind. Arrested again in 1908, he was exiled to
the province of Vologda, but he escaped in July, 1909. He returned to
Baku and resumed his underground activity until March, 1910, when
he was again arrested and again exiled to Vologda. Exile came to an end
in the spring of 1911, when Stalin fled and reached St. Petersburg. In
September, 1911, he was once more arrested and sentenced to three years'
exile. Soon thereafter he escaped again, and the close of 1911 once more
found him in St. Petersburg. In February, 1912, Stalin's importance as a
revolutionary was recognized by his election to the Central Committee
of the party, and later by his designation to direct the work of the Bolshevik deputies in the Duma. Soon thereafter, in February, 1913, he was
denounced by the *agent provocateur* Malinovsky, who, while in the employ of the Secret Police, was a member of the Central Committee and
leader of the Bolshevik delegates in the Duma.[11]

Stalin was arrested and again exiled, but after the March Revolution
he appeared in Petrograd, where he took his place with the Bolshevik
leaders. A hostile biographer has argued that there "is nothing about
Stalin in the military works, or the historical memoirs and studies on the
Russian Civil War . . . . Stalin's share was not discovered until

---

10 A critical biography is Boris Souvarine's, *Stalin* (New York: Longmans, Green &
Co., 1939).

11 See Bertram D. Wolfe, "Lenin and *Agent Provocateur* Malinovsky," *The Russian
Review*, Autumn, 1945, pp. 46–49.

1929." [12] This seems too severe, for subsequent events have revealed that Stalin is not without great military talent, and that his almost super-human firmness and determination must have been valuable assets to the Revolution.

Stalin was elected by the Central Committee to the Politburo, originally established in 1917, to direct the insurrection. After Lenin and Trotsky, Stalin was regarded as the most important member. The Politburo of seven was established because of the difficulty of calling a meeting of the Central Committee, whose members were likely to be widely scattered, and because, during the Revolution and immediately after, decisions had to be made quickly. Gradually the Politburo achieved almost dictatorial power, and Stalin, as its secretary and directing head, managed to become virtually supreme.

In 1922, Stalin became secretary-general of the Communist party, succeeding Molotov, who became his assistant. While exercising extra-legal functions, the Communist party was in fact the government of Russia. It made decisions on men, policies, and administration. Thus a chief officer of the Communist party might exercise tremendous power in the government without occupying any government post.

Beginning with the Civil War in the 1920's, relations between Trotsky and Stalin became strained. During Lenin's illness, Stalin, Kamenev, and Zinoviev united to become the dominant trio (*Troika*) and succeeded in diminishing Trotsky's influence. After the congress of the Russian Communist party in 1925, Stalin's victory over the opposition was certain. A split between the members of the dominant Troika now developed, with Stalin on one side and Zinoviev and Kamenev on the other. A new turn occurred when Kamenev and Zinoviev joined Trotsky in an "Opposition" to Stalin. Bitter personal recriminations flared up, and attacks and criticisms from past factional controversies were resurrected and published. Lenin's denunciation of Kamenev and Zinoviev as "deserters" [13] was published, while the opposition demanded the publication of Lenin's testament, which had been suppressed and in which Stalin is described as "rude and ambitious."

The differences between Stalin and Trotsky may have been basically due to personal antipathies, but the issues were fought out on a theoretical basis. According to Trotsky,

[12] Souvarine, *op. cit.*, p. 222.
[13] Despite his denunciations, Lenin gave them both important posts.

Marxism proceeds from world economy, not as a sum of national parts, but as a mighty independent reality, which is created by the international division of labor and the world market, and in the present epoch, predominates over the national markets. The productive forces of capitalist society have long ago grown beyond the national frontier. . . . To aim at the construction of a *nationally isolated* socialist society means, in spite of all temporary successes, to pull the productive forces backward even as compared to capitalism. To attempt, regardless of the geographic, cultural and historical conditions of the country's development, which constitutes a part of the world whole, to realize a fenced-in proportionality of all the branches of economy within national limits, means to go to a reactionary utopia.[14]

Trotsky did not believe that socialism was realizable, except on an international plane. This doctrine regarded socialism as possible only after a series of revolutions. In other words, the Revolution must be continued, and its spread awaited and encouraged. Only by the Revolution's extending beyond the borders could socialism in Russia be victorious. On the negative side, the opposition accused Stalin of proposing a Thermidorian reaction.[15] Terms such as "Cavaignac" were applied to Stalin, and charges that he was corrupting the party were hurled against him.[16] Trotsky was especially critical of the growing power of the Central Committee, of the de-emphasizing of independence, and of the increasing importance of repression. "The G.P.U. has become a decisive factor in the life of the Party." [17]

Quoting a close co-worker, Christian Rakovsky, an Old Bolshevik and former Soviet ambassador, Trotsky sums up the changes in the Communist party:

In the mind of Lenin, and in all our minds . . . . the task of the party leadership was to protect both the party and the working class from the corrupting action of privilege, place and patronage on the part of those in power, from *rapprochement* with the relics of the old nobility and burgerdom (sic), from the corrupting influence of the N.E.P., from the temptation of the bourgeois morals and ideologies . . . . We must say frankly, definitely, and loudly that the party

14 Leon Trotsky, *The Permanent Revolution*. Translated by Max Schachtman (New York: Pioneer Publishers, 1934), pp. ix–x.
15 Thermidor was the month in which Robespierre was overthrown by the conservative reaction.
16 Leon Trotsky, "The Soviet Thermidor," in *The Revolution Betrayed*. Translated by Max Eastman (New York: Doubleday & Company, 1937), pp. 86–114.
17 *Ibid.*, p. 100.

apparatus has not fulfilled this task, that it has revealed a complete incapacity for its double role of protector and education. It has failed. It is bankrupt.[18]

SOCIAL BASIS OF THERMIDOR

Trotsky defines the "Soviet Thermidor as a triumph of the bureaucracy over the masses." [19] It was due to the fatigue of the masses, the debilitating and destructive effects of the Civil War, and the growing bureaucratization of the ruling group. At no time does Trotsky face the problem that dictatorship cannot be the road to freedom. Despite the brilliance of his mind, his great talent in description and characterization, and his wide learning, Trotsky's intellectual horizon was limited, for he saw the world from behind Marxist blinders. He could not and would not admit that Stalin's Russia was a logical consequence of Lenin's revolution, and was perhaps even inherent in Marxism. The suppression of bourgeois liberals and dissident Socialists in 1918 was a preparation for the outlawing of opposition Communists. The latter was a logical extension of the former, and not a perversion of the Revolution.

Trotsky presented a formal argument that, according to Lenin and other socialist writers, the state apparatus becomes weaker in direct proportion as the system of class exploitation is diminished. But he found that while the exploiting classes have become weaker, the power of the state apparatus has been increased. This purely formal argument, copied from Friedrich Engels, bears in fact no relation to the living reality, and demonstrates that a man of talent can become a victim of philosophic fictions. Perhaps it might have been more revealing, though less orthodox, if Trotsky had searched history for the nearly nonexistent examples of men with great power ready to sacrifice it upon the altar of the public weal. He would have discovered then that the desire to hold power and the willingness to yield it do not appear psychologically as simple as the founders of "scientific socialism" had believed. The anarchists, whose theoretical poverty the Marxists had always scorned, seem to have understood the mechanics of power better than the self-confident Marxists.

A variation of the Thermidorian theme is Trotsky's view that the "Stalin regime," rising above a politically atomized society, resting upon a police and officers' corps, and allowing no control whatsoever, is an aspect of Bonapartism, a Bonapartism of a new type not before seen in

18 Quoted by Trotsky, *ibid.*, p. 101.
19 *Ibid.*, p. 105.

history. "Stalinism is a variation of Bonapartism in the sense that it rests upon an antagonism between an organized and armed Soviet Aristocracy and unarmed toiling masses." Its rise Trotsky ascribed to the "dilatoriness of the world Proletariat in solving the problems set for it by history." In many of its features Stalinism, according to Trotsky, resembles fascism. At the Fifteenth Congress of the party in 1927, Trotsky and seventy-four of his followers were expelled and the opposition was crushed.

STALIN'S VICTORY

A part of the opposition, led by Kamenev and Zinoviev, submitted statements repudiating their views, and asked readmission to the party. Trotsky continued his opposition, and in 1929 was expelled from the country. He was allowed, by the Turkish government, to live on Prinkipo, an island near Constantinople. He continued a bitter struggle against Stalin for the remainder of his life. In Norway and finally in Mexico, he continued until his assassination his bitter and brilliant denunciations of Stalin's policies. Although they were frequently sharp and justified, they remained unheeded in the Soviet Union. Despite his opposition, Trotsky always considered the Soviet government a workers' state. He did admit that it suffered from what he called bureaucratic distortions, but these he blamed on Stalin.

The assassination of Sergei M. Kirov, the Communist leader of Leningrad, in December, 1934, let loose terrible reprisals against opponents. Ceaseless investigations, mass trials, and deportations followed. In contrast to former years, this campaign was directed primarily against Communists. Symbolic was the suppression in May, 1935, of the Society of Old Bolsheviks. The repression gained impetus, and in 1936, sixteen former leading oppositionists, including Zinoviev and Kamenev, were tried, convicted, and shot. Next on the list were leading military officers, who were tried and executed in the spring of 1937. A spreading wave of terror engulfed thousands, and in March, 1938, the trial of twenty-one leaders of the rightist-Trotskyist bloc opened. Among them were Bukharin, a leading theorist, and Rykov, a former head of the Soviet, both of whom had once supported Stalin against Trotsky and made his victory possible. They and sixteen others were shot and the remaining three were sentenced to long imprisonment. Thousands of well-known and less important figures were exiled or shot. The Revolution was being liquidated.

THE RIGHT DEVIATION

Stalin had beaten the opposition by virtue of two factors. Perhaps the most important was his control over the organizational machinery of the party, his concentration of power, and his readiness to use it for personal aims.[20] Lenin recognized these qualities in Stalin and proposed to take action against him, but he was unable to do so because of illness. Another factor in Stalin's victory was the support of the more conservative group within the party. This group favored a slower growth of industrialization and a lenient policy toward the middle and even wealthy peasants. The leaders of the right wanted in a sense to continue the agricultural policy of the N.E.P., and to encourage increased production by higher prices. But, strangely enough, once he had defeated the opposition, Stalin embraced its program of accelerated industrialization and the carrying of the class struggle to the countryside. The latter policy meant suppression of the kulaks and collectivization. Stalin therefore turned upon his erstwhile supporters, and in the Sixteenth Congress the "right was completely defeated." [21] Stalin now gained complete control of the party, becoming more and more dictatorial in his methods. Intraparty discussion ceased, and decisions were now increasingly handed down from the top.

The Communist party has become the instrument of the powerful will of the Politburo. Through the Tschistka, or cleansing, politically unreliable elements are eliminated. In the first cleansing or purge in 1921, one third of the more than 500,000 members were removed from the party. Smaller purges were conducted in 1924 and 1926, but a momentous purge followed Stalin's victories over the oppositions of the left and the right, when more than 1,160,000 members were expelled from the Communist party. At the same time, large numbers of new members were recruited from among the mass of the population. As the party fell more under the dominance of Stalin and his close co-workers, it lost much of its former character. Under Lenin and until the defeat of the opposition groups, party membership conferred many privileges. The individual member was personally inviolate except for serious political crimes. Party problems were discussed and debated. Under Stalin, meetings are infrequent and debate is rare. In fact, thousands of former Communists have been arrested, exiled, or shot.

20 "Testament of Lenin" in Leon Trotsky, *The Real Situation in Russia* (New York: Harcourt, Brace and Company, 1928), pp. 320–323.
21 Stalin, *Leninism*, II, 197–252.

LEADERSHIP OF STALIN

Under Stalin's leadership and until Allied aid reached it, the Soviet government overcame the fearful attack of Nazi Germany. Certainly World War II demonstrated that the Soviet leaders were not incompetent or corrupt. The Russian soldier has always fought heroically, but never under better and more determined leadership. Some of the lag in improvement of living standards must be attributed to the fear of a foreign attack, which compelled large-scale investment in heavy, at the expense of light, industry. The official doctrine—derived, soundly or not, by Marxian analysis—that an alliance of capitalistic nations would attack the socialist fatherland, was not borne out by events. Yet the fear of an attack was not unjustified, for Russia was invaded by Nazi Europe, while the most advanced capitalistic democracies were her comrades in arms. Stalin's policies have led the Soviet Union to victory and greatness. Today it is one of the powerful nations of the world casting its shadow across Europe and Asia. But there is no relaxation of the harshness and suppression of its early years. Instead of permitting greater freedom, the Soviet government is repressing all traces of difference of opinion within the country and is pursuing an aggressive foreign policy which resembles the worst type of old colonialism.

What we see in Russia is a new development, and though the regime speaks in the name of Marxism, it is doubtful if Marx would acknowledge that the brutal dictatorship is the realization of his theories. Although Marx was ready to lead a revolt in behalf of socialism, he placed great value on freedom and democracy. Stalinism owes more to autocratic Russia, where the notion of a band of "dedicated" leaders and disciplined organization has, as we have seen, a long history. Lenin's view that the mass must be led and directed has been carried forward by Stalin until an entire nation bows before the arbitrary will of a small group of leaders. Such an outcome is scarcely the dream of Marx and his early followers.

Nor have the visions of a free and better life been fulfilled. One might not deny that the population enjoys a higher standard of living than it did under the czarist regime. That seems faint praise, for rising living standards have not been absent in any capitalistic country developing from an agricultural to an industrial economy. One need only examine superficially the economic history of Western Europe and the United States in the nineteenth and twentieth centuries to notice substantial advances in living standards, literacy, and security. Of course, capitalistic nations suffer from periodic unemployment of varying severity. Perhaps that is the chief criticism to be made against them. Yet Soviet society offers much less security of person, and it is a question whether loss of personal rights and freedom is not too high a price to pay for economic security, even if economic security is possible only under a totalitarian regime. Certainly no evidence suggests that the stringent controls over speech and opinion are needed in the U.S.S.R.

There is no reason to hold that a socialist society cannot be one guaranteeing personal freedom and the inviolability of the individual. The Soviet government is both socialist and Russian, and although a democratic tradition was by no means absent in Russia, it was never a virile one. Lenin's organizational forms were derived from the conspiratorial experience of his revolutionary predecessors, but, unlike them, he was not an admirer of democracy. Conspiratorial techniques constructed to wage war against a czarist autocracy were welded onto the Russian government in the fires of civil war. Serving as a means of repressing counterrevolution, they have become instruments of group and personal power. The argument by supporters of Stalin that freedom of speech and opposition will jeopardize one of the strongest governments in the world sounds like weak apologetics. Russian experience again demonstrates that power, once granted, seized, and consolidated, is seldom or ever surrendered.

FORMAL GOVERNMENT

The Soviet government has become a military or police socialism. The formulator and director of policy is the Communist party. All citizens eighteen years of age or older, except the insane or criminal, are allowed to vote for a deputy to the soviet. These institutions—soviets—are organized on a local basis as city and village soviets elected by the citizens. The local soviets elect executive committees to carry on their work while they are not in session. The local soviets are linked to district soviets, which are in turn linked to regions, provinces, autonomous republics, and All-Union soviets. The Union of Soviet Socialist Republics is, as its name implies, made up of a number of autonomous republics, like the Ukraine, White Russia, and so on. The highest state organ is the Supreme Soviet, with two houses. One house, the Council of the Union, is chosen according to electoral areas, a deputy for every three hundred thousand people; the other house, the Council of Nationalities, is chosen by Union and autonomous republics. Twenty-five deputies represent a Union republic, eleven an autonomous republic, five an autonomous region, and one a national area. Election is for a term of four years, and sessions of the Supreme Soviet are held twice a year. At a joint session of the two houses, the Presidium of the Supreme Soviet is chosen. The Presidium is made up of a president, sixteen vice-presidents, a secretary, and twenty-four other members. It issues decrees, calls the Supreme Soviet into session, and, between meetings of the Supreme Soviet, can declare war, sign treaties, proclaim martial law, and so on.

The chief administrative and executive organ is the Council of Ministers, formerly called the Council of People's Commissars, appointed by the Supreme Soviet. The Council of Ministers directs all economic, political, and cultural work. The autonomous republics are similarly organized. The Council of Ministers enacts into law numerous rules affecting industry, labor, education, and any other activity coming before it. It also examines and amends the plans and budgets of various agencies.

The Soviet government has gained many successes. It has industrialized the nation, it has made Russia strong and respected, and it has introduced universal education and a most enlightened racial policy. These are on the credit side. But it has also introduced the police state, it has no respect for personal liberty or security, and it spurns freedom of speech, press, or criticism. France, bled almost white and reduced from her once pre-eminent position, can afford to respect freedom, but one of the greatest powers in the world, the Soviet government, declares that freedom of speech and criticism would endanger public order. Soviet Russia proves that the anarchists' attack upon Marx[22] and his disciples was more than empty rhetoric. One need only read the stories of Soviet refugees, even if one grants exaggeration, to recognize that in many respects the Union of Soviet Socialist Republics represents a step backward, a reversal of Western European history with its emphasis upon the integrity and freedom, the dignity, and the value of the individual.

We must recognize that the Soviet government has inspired vast enthusiasm for its programs and policies outside its own borders. There are sufficient grounds for assuming that this admiration is due to the will to believe that exists in people who need some imaginary Shangri-La, and not a little to the many imperfections of our own way of living, the re-

---

[22] It may be well to note that although Marx was dictatorial in temper, his theories do not necessarily imply dictatorship. Marx wanted democracy for the human race and thought that *only* communism would assure it.

moval of which would be the best guarantee against communism. Unfortunately, beliefs, often more than realities, can inspire people with enthusiasm, self-sacrifice, and heroism. The vision of these enthusiasts is blurred by neither doubt nor realities, and empirical proof of Soviet realities is as powerless to affect the views of a believer in the Soviet heaven as it would the views of believers in other miracles. One can admit the progress made under Stalin's leadership and yet realize that the road of the Soviet would be a road backward for Western nations, a road of disaster to humanity.

24. ITALIAN SOCIALISM AND FASCISM

Italian socialism was influenced by Marxism and anarchism over a period of years. In the end, Italian socialism accepted a Marxist philosophy, but its policies were hesitant and uncertain. Almost from the beginning, the party was rent by differences over theory, and in the hour of the greatest danger to itself and Italy—the eve of fascism—it was in the midst of a crisis that came into being as a result of the emergence of communism.

The modern Italian socialist movement arose during the struggle for national unity, and Carlo Piscane (1818–1857), the first modern Italian socialist, was closely connected with this struggle.[1] During the 1860's, there existed throughout Italy local workers' groups influenced by the republican doctrines of Mazzini and Garibaldi, and Mikhail Bakunin sought to convert these groups to socialism.[2]

Bakunin arrived in Italy in January, 1864, and immediately started his campaign to undermine Mazzini's influence. By 1866, he had won enough followers to launch his *Libertà e Giustizia,* the Italian branch of the International. Its program consisted of seventeen articles, including a demand for universal suffrage; recall of elected representatives; election of executives; freedom of speech; press, association, assembly, and religion; a progressive income tax; abolition of standing armies; a state based on spontaneous federation; and free public education.[3] For the next few years the Italian revolutionary movement was dominated by Bakunin, and it supported him in his break with Marx.

In April, 1873, the second convention of the Italian International was

[1] Nello Rosselli, *Carlo Piscane nel risorgimento italiano* (Turin: Fratelli Bocca, 1932), pp. 1–60.
[2] Max Nettlau, "Bakunin und die Internationale in Italien bis zum Herbst 1872," *Archiv für die Geschichte des Sozialismus und der Arbeiterbewegung,* 1912, II, 277.
[3] Humbert L. Gualtieri, *The Labor Movement in Italy* (New York: S. F. Vanni, 1946), pp. 61–62, 112.

held, despite opposition from the police. The congress declared itself as atheist, materialist, anarchist, and federalist. A revolt was attempted at several points by small groups of revolutionists, and at Castel del Monte the conflict lasted five days. Arrests and imprisonment followed the failure of the revolt. As the anarchist current receded, Marxism began to attract followers. Nevertheless, the followers of Bakunin made another attempt at insurrection. Its failure marked the end of the influence of the Bakuninist International.

REGROUPING

During the 1870's a regrouping of revolutionary forces took place. In July, 1879, socialists complained of the isolation of revolutionaries, their preoccupation with logic, and their avoidance of the masses. The *Revista Internazionale de Sozialismo,* launched in 1880 to propagate more practical views,[4] was the beginning of a reformist socialist movement.

PARTITO OPERAIO

In 1880, the *Partito Operaio* was organized, with its main strength in the northern part of the country. It was a moderate organization which demanded reform rather than socialism. The law of 1882 extended the right of suffrage and gave the city workers the right to vote. A number of Socialist candidates for Parliament were nominated. Andrea Costa was the first Socialist to enter that body. Four years later, the Socialists elected four candidates. Frightened by these successes, the government dissolved the party.

IL PARTITO DEI LAVORATORI

Although political socialism was suppressed, the movement was by no means destroyed. The democrats and republicans had defeated, in 1889, an endorsement of socialism at the Congress of Labor Societies; but two years later, at Milan, the socialists won an endorsement for the formation of a *Partito dei Lavoratori.* The program called for the emancipation of labor and the destruction of the economic and political monopoly of the capitalist class. In contrast to its predecessor, this party was not anti-intellectual and did not seek to limit itself to manual workers.[5] The

4 Roberto, Michels, *Storia critica de movimento socialista italiano.* "La Voce" (Florence: 1921), p. 75.

5 Pietro Nenni, *La Lutte des classes en Italie* (Paris: Bibliothèque de Documentation Sociale, 1930), p. 51.

movement was aided by Antonio Labriola, subsequently a Marxist of international renown, and Filippo Turati, a well-to-do Milanese lawyer, editor of *Critica Sociale*. This magazine gained an important position in the intellectual life of Italy. In time Marxism absorbed the remnants of the more primitive revolutionary groups, such as the followers of Mazzini. There remained, however, an anarchist group which accepted the class struggle and the economic views of Marx but rejected political action.

IL PARTITO SOCIALISTA

The constitution of the *Partito dei Lavoratori*, elaborated in 1891, did not become effective until the Genoa congress a year later. At this congress a decisive break between the anarchist and socialist tendencies in the revolutionary movement took place. Speaking for the socialist view, Turati maintained that while anarchists and socialists were equally critical of the existing order, they did not agree on the direction of social change nor on the tactics to be used in promoting it. A union was impossible. The socialists therefore withdrew and organized a new party.

In its program the class struggle was recognized, and the exploitation of labor by the capitalist was pronounced a social fact. Socialization of the means of production was proclaimed as an objective. Trade-union efforts toward amelioration of the lot of labor were endorsed, and a campaign for the conquest of power to expropriate the expropriators was proclaimed. A program for the immediate improvement of the conditions of labor was approved.[6]

In the following year the party met at Reggio-Emilia, where its name was changed to *Partito Socialista dei Lavoratori Italiani*. A final break with the anarchists was made, and political action and the formation of a parliamentary group in the Chamber of Deputies were endorsed.

FASCI DEI LAVORATORI

In the latter part of 1890, the *Fasci dei Lavoratori* was organized in Catania, Sicily. At first it aimed to be a mutual-aid society, but under the militant leadership of Garibaldi Bosco, it took on a more revolutionary character. A backward agriculture and a harsh form of landlordism were widespread in Sicily. The movement spread rapidly, and at the peak of its influence counted about 300 groups with a total membership of ap-

---

6 *Socialismo e socialisti in Italia*. Compiled by Alfredo Angiolini and Eugenio Ciacchi (Florence: Nerbini, Casa Editrice, 1919), pp. 208–245.

proximately 200,000. In 1893, government buildings were seized and stores pillaged. The Central Committee demanded the abolition of the flour tax, an inquiry into the administration, and the setting up of producers' cooperatives to alleviate the suffering of the people. General Francesco Morra was sent into Sicily with full power to restore order. Martial law was proclaimed and a number of leading Socialists were arrested and sentenced to prison.[7]

The repression forced the Socialists to hold their third convention in secret in 1895. Hitherto, the party had been made up of autonomous workers' groups. There was no way of ascertaining how many individuals in any group adhered to the socialist program. Consequently serious disputes between socialists, anarchists, and republicans were inevitable. The party now substituted individual membership, a move which freed it from dependence upon other labor groups. A year later, in 1896, the *Avanti*, an official daily, was established.

A YEAR OF CRISIS

Increasing social discontent, caused largely by the rise in the cost of bread, which was an important part of the Italian workers' diet, led to demonstrations and clashes with the police. Milan, the leading center of labor and socialist activity, was a rallying point for much of the discontent. Martial law was declared in May, 1898, and an attempt to suppress a demonstration led to the shooting of several hundred and the killing of a number of demonstrators. Arrests of more than eight hundred followed, and a number, including Turati, were given long prison terms.

General Luigi Pelloux was appointed to stem the radical tide. The attempt of the general to wipe out the freedom of the press and assemblage and the right to strike was challenged in Parliament, and the left prevented the enactment of this repressive legislation. Gabriele d'Annunzio, the poet, to whom we shall refer later, was elected as a conservative deputy but allied himself with the extreme left. The repression ended with the assassination of King Humbert by a youthful anarchist who sought to avenge the dead of Milan. With the accession of Victor Emmanuel III to the throne, a change in government policy was introduced. The new king was presumably liberal and democratic, and his appointment of the chief of Italian political compromisers, Giovanni Giolitti, marked a new era in Italian politics.

[7] Michels, *op. cit.*, pp. 160–168.

MAXIMUM AND MINIMUM PROGRAMS

In Parliament, the socialists maintained an alliance with the bourgeois left. Some doctrinal confusion was a normal consequence of this alliance. At its congress in Rome, in 1900, the Socialist party instituted a program made up of two parts, a set of ultimate and a set of immediate demands. The ultimate demands contained the usual Marxist statement of the existence of class conflict and the need of the workers to organize as a class for the conquest of political power. The minimum or immediate program was distinguished from bourgeois reform programs in that the former was a means to an end, and not, as were bourgeois reforms, an end in themselves. Immediate demands were made for universal suffrage; freedom of speech, press, assemblage, and organization; the development of all types of working-class organizations—cooperative, legal, and economic; absolute neutrality of the government in disputes between capital and labor; freedom to organize trade unions and to strike; improvements of conditions of labor; abolition of nightwork for women and children; and nationalization of railways and mines. A committee was appointed to present to future conventions modifications and amendments of the minimum demands.[8]

The elaboration of minimun and maximum programs was an attempt to bridge the gulf between the two groups. The reformists wished to avoid violent and extreme policies, which they believed were due to immaturity and lack of judgment. The more radical group looked upon the reformist policies as a betrayal of the revolution and as destined to lead the workers in the direction of mere bourgeois reform.

The two tendencies first tested their strength at the annual party meeting at Imola in 1902. The party had grown in influence and power, and about eight hundred delegates from every part of Italy attended its sessions. In the first test, the reformists carried the day. They were practical politicians desiring to cooperate with the bourgeois radicals and anxious for gradual and peaceful reform. While professing vague revolutionary aspirations, they were more interested in immediate results. Turati, the political and spiritual head of the Italian socialist movement, was convinced that socialism could be attained only by evolutionary means.

Turati was gifted with a brilliant literary style, and did not speak to the Italian workers with the cold arguments of the economist or with the axiomatic

[8] *Ibid.*, pp. 212–222.

formulae which do not give the opponent the benefit of a doubt. Rather he spoke like a crusader avenging the rights of the people in the name of humanity and of social justice. His power of argumentation was magnetic and fascinating to the masses. His socialist mission was carried on with an almost religious fervor.[9]

Although victorious at the convention of 1902, the reformists did not have their own way. In fact, the left was able to win a large following among the workers, especially with the rising social tension which Italy experienced in the years immediately preceding World War I. At the party convention in Bologna in 1904, the reformists again carried the majority. After a lengthy debate, a resolution was passed declaring that the class struggle does not permit a socialist to participate in a bourgeois government.[10] The reformist faction was again challenged by a revolutionary group at the Congress in Rome in 1906. This time it was the revolutionary syndicalists who took up the battle.

Syndicalism was rejected, but a third current, "integralism," triumphed for a short time. The integralists accepted the socialization of the means of production as the objective and the class struggle as the means. While recognizing the desirability of using legal means, they reserved the right to employ more militant tactics whenever necessary. Alliances with non-socialist parties were disapproved, as was the support of the government in Parliament without approval of the directing committees of the party. Although the integralists believed themselves more revolutionary, their program was in fact not unacceptable to the reformists.

At the outset the Socialists were republicans by conviction. With the change in the attitude of the monarchy toward social reform, the anti-monarchical sentiment became somewhat lessened. At the outbreak of the Italo-Turkish War over Libya, the Socialist Congress at Modena disapproved of supporting it. As a result, the Socialist party faced another crisis. An attempt on the life of the king led two leaders of the extreme right within the Socialist party to affirm their loyalty to the monarchy. This action raised protests, and a special congress was called to decide the issue. Under the leadership of Benito Mussolini, the left won a majority control of the party and of the official daily, *Avanti*. The extreme right was expelled.[11] Mussolini became the spokesman for the party

[9] Gualtieri, *op. cit.*, p. 304. See also Count Carlo Sforza, *Contemporary Italy* (New York: E. P. Dutton & Co., 1944), p. 159.

[10] Michels, *op. cit.*, p. 264.

[11] Nenni, *op. cit.*, pp. 106–108; Ivaone Bonomi, *From Socialism to Fascism* (London: Martin Hopkinson and Co., 1934), pp. 10–11. A defense of the reformist position can be found in Ivanoe Bonomi, *Le Vie nuove del socialismo* (Rome: Sestante, 1944).

view. Fanatical and intolerant, he was destined to deliver violent and destructive blows against Italian and international socialism after his coming to power in the 1920's.

WORLD WAR I

With the outbreak of the war, Italian Socialists faced a dilemma common to the Socialists of other countries. A member of the Triple Alliance, Italy failed to join the Central Powers. Italian Socialists opposed the war, and Mussolini, the editor of the *Forward,* led, in the first months of the war, the campaign of opposition. He soon changed his attitude and was able to launch, with French government funds delivered by the future Communist deputy, Marcel Cachin, a prowar daily, *Il Popolo d'Italià.* He was expelled from the Socialist party. The party neither approved nor sabotaged the war. After the disaster of Caporetto, many on the right in the party rallied to the nation's defense. Turati affirmed that in the face of an invasion, it was the duty of Italian Socialists to rally to the defense of the country. This view aroused a strong reaction on the left, which demanded that the supporters of war be excluded from the party. Nevertheless, the Socialists were, for a time, able to prevent division in their ranks.

AFTER WORLD WAR I

The Russian Revolution stirred Italian socialism to its depths, and, inspired by its glories and achievements, a number of left-wing socialists longed to emulate the Russian example. Not successful in this objective, their activities led to a split in the socialist movement which later served to weaken its resistance to fascism and made the rise of Mussolini easier. At the congress of December, 1919, the party took a radical tack, but the *Confederazione Generale del Lavro,* the central organ of the trade unions, adhered to a more conservative program. The Confederazione had always been socialistic in outlook, but its socialism was reformist rather than revolutionary in temper. At this point differences between the party leadership and the Socialist members in Parliament appeared. The former were inclined to veer toward the left and were admirers of the Russian Revolution, the example of which they hoped to follow. In contrast, the latter feared that radical verbiage would create illusions among the masses and might force the party into risky adventures. The Confederazione Generale del Lavro shied away from a radical program. Instead, it favored universal suffrage for both sexes, disarmament, the suppression of tariff barriers, the right of nations to self-determination, the recall of troops from Russia, the creation of a chamber representing the trade unions with the right to initiate laws, and the establishment of a republic.

Italy faced a grave crisis. Discontent among the workers and the demobilized troops presented serious problems. Strikes spread, and clashes between nationalists and Socialists became frequent. In the meantime, the rising cost of living and the other difficulties not unusual in a postwar period were constant sources of growing dissatisfaction. Under the hammering of the members of the left, who were dissatisfied with domestic conditions, and those of the right, who were angry at the limited international successes, the government was forced to resign and was succeeded by a more liberal regime.

THE NITTI REGIME

The Nitti ministry, which took office, was confronted by a series of crises. Many of the left regarded it as only a stopgap, a sort of Kerensky regime which would soon give way to something more revolutionary. The founder of the Italian Communist party was of that opinion.[12] While tension mounted daily, a new element, an extreme nationalist group, made its appearance. The port of Fiume, denied to Italy, symbolized the injustice done to her. Gabriele d'Annunzio marched on Fiume at the head of a band of armed volunteers, a gesture that showed the right was not without courage or armed resources.

REVISION OF THE SOCIALIST PROGRAM

The Bologna congress of the Socialist party met in a highly charged atmosphere. Proclaiming that the proletariat would meet violence with violence, it voted to adhere to the Third International and to work out a basis for cooperation with the labor unions. The program was overwhelmingly accepted, but the division between left and right had not been bridged. Nevertheless, the Socialist party entered enthusiastically into the election campaign of November, 1919, and managed to poll more than 1,800,000 votes. The Socialists returned 156 delegates to Parliament,

12 Nenni, *op. cit.*, p. 143.

controlled 2,022 communes, and had a membership of more than 300,000.[13]

OCCUPATION OF THE FACTORIES

Despite their victory, the Socialists were divided. A left wing would have liked to follow the bolshevist example, but the right shrank from organized violence: The Old Fox, Giovanni Giolitti, was called back to power, but he proved unequal to the task. While political jockeying was going on, a crisis developed at another point. The metal workers had won important concessions in the summer of 1919, and demanded a further revision in wages the next year. The employers refused, and the workers countered by occupying the factories. The example of the metal workers was followed by others.

In the crisis the government, after attempts at conciliation, stood aside. Employers, finding themselves without government support, peacefully withdrew. The issue was thus transformed beyond a struggle over wages. It was a question now of surrender or of social revolution, for the employers refused discussion of all issues as long as their factories were occupied. A conference of the heads of the Socialist party and the Confederazione Generale del Lavro met in September, 1920, to decide on a policy. Some of the representatives of the Socialist party maintained that since the occupation of the factories was political, it was important to expand the movement into a revolutionary campaign for the seizure of power. The head of the labor federation, d'Aragone, advocated the more limited objective of demanding a greater voice for labor in the management of industry. The demand could, in fact, be made and granted within the framework of capitalism. This view prevailed.

On September 15, 1920, Prime Minister Giolitti called a meeting of representatives of labor and industry. No agreement could be reached, and a law was introduced for the appointment of a commission of twelve, six from each side, to present a program for granting the workers a voice in the management of industry. This proposal, the basis for the withdrawal of the workers from the plants, was approved by the metal workers. Thus ended an episode then regarded as a prologue to revolution.[14] The effect upon the party was very serious, for it demonstrated that its revolutionary proclamations were empty wordmongering. At the same

---

[13] Bonomi, *op. cit.*, p. 36.
[14] Nenni, *op. cit.*, pp. 179–181.

time the government, while weak and vacillating, was able to ride out the storm safely, even though with lost prestige.

DIVISION AMONG SOCIALISTS

After this serious setback of the socialists, there arose a danger even more grave. Aroused by what they regarded as unfair treatment by the Allies in the making of the peace, the Italian people responded with a deep feeling of patriotism. The fascist movement, incoherent, doctrineless, and adventurist, seized the opportunity and became the militant champion of patriotism and the noisy opponent of the left. During this critical hour, the Italian Socialist party faced a communist-engineered split. Heretofore, the Socialist party, with its ally the Confederazione Generale del Lavro, had dominated the radical and labor movement, although syndicalist and anarchist groups also existed. On some major issues, all radical organizations cooperated.

Consequently the congress of the Italian Socialist party in 1921 met in Livorno under a cloud. Demands that the party accept Moscow's twenty-one points were presented, among these being a demand for the ousting of the reformists. A three-day division appeared: the outright communists stood ready to accept the decisions of the Second Congress of the Third International—they received 58,000 votes; the center, which polled 98,000 votes, stood ready to accept the doctrines of the communists, but would not vote to exclude from the party their old comrades of the right; a third group—reformists—polled 14,000 votes. Thereupon the communists withdrew and formed the Communist party.

ATTACKS UPON THE LEFT

At a time when the left faced the most serious challenge in its history, instead of showing a united front, it divided itself into mutually warring factions. Armed *squadristi* made their appearance and Socialist and labor leaders were subjected to assaults so brutal that they were sometimes fatal. In the elections of 1921, the Socialists polled over 1,500,000 votes and the Communists almost 300,000. At the Socialist congress in the following year, another split took place. The Maximalist Socialists, led by Seratti, broke away from the reformist minority. Seratti subsequently joined the Communists. While the Socialists and Communists were warring between themselves, the Fascists were able to gain a victory over all of these factions.

Italian fascism has been influenced by the syndicalist doctrines of Sorel and by the nationalists, Enrico Corradini and Alfred Rocco. Sorel gained widespread attention in Italian radical circles, many of his articles having been first published in Italy in the *Avanguardista Socialista* of Milan, edited by Arturo Labriola, and in *Il Divenire Sociale* of Rome, edited by Enrico Leone. Fascism was influenced by syndicalism, which had a number of adherents among the organized workers. Economic organization by labor goes back to the Torino printers, who fought against a reduction in wages in 1848. Throughout the 1860's and 1870's attempts were made to establish unions in a number of trades. The visit of a delegation of Italian workers to Paris in 1889 stimulated a movement for establishing *bourses du travail* in their native land. The outcome was the founding of chambers of labor, *Camere del Lavro,* in a number of cities.

Following the formation of chambers of labor in a number of cities, a convention was held in Parma in 1893 at which a program was drawn up. These groups were to act as the central organization for the separate unions in their area, improve the legal position of labor, and seek recognition in affairs affecting the workers' legal status. At the beginning, the movement showed a trade-union orientation rather than a revolutionary one.[15]

The spread of organization among industrial and agricultural labor led, in 1902, to the setting up of a national secretariat. It lacked authority, and at the initiative of the metal workers, a national trade-union congress was convened in Milan in 1906. Over 200,000 workers were represented, and a clash between the reformists and the syndicalists followed. Despite the opposition of the latter, the Federation of Labor (*Confederazione del Lavro*) was organized from the national unions and local chambers of labor. Management was placed in the hands of a bureau of nine members under an executive committee of thirty. The bureau was to direct the Italian economic movement of labor, and to develop cooperation between the trade unions, the cooperatives, and the Socialist party. Close cooperation with the latter was worked out, and a moderate policy was adopted. Membership in the Federation increased steadily, and more than 300,000 workers were affiliated with it on the eve of World War I. In 1920, the Federation, at the crest of its power, reached a membership of 2,150,000 members, 760,000 of them peasants and agricultural workers.[16]

15 Margherita Hirschberg-Neumeyer, *Die Italienischen Gewerkschaften* (Jena: Gustav Fischer, 1928), pp. 15–22.

16 L. Rosenstock-Franck, *L'Économie corporative fasciste en doctrine et en fait* (Paris: Librairie Universitaire J. Gamber, 1934), p. 9.

SYNDICALISM

A group of militants who refused to accept the moderate program of the Federation and its alliance with the political socialists held a congress at Parma in 1907. Despite the differences between the syndicalists and the reformists, both continued to belong to the Federation. Among the militants, two views were held: one favored the formation of a separate organization, and the other advocated infiltrating the conservative Federation to change its views. By 1912, the former view carried the day at the congress of Modena and a group of syndicalists formed the militant Italian Syndicalists' Union (*Sindicale del Lavro*).[17] Around this group gathered the Sorelians, the believers in the nobility and purifying power of violence, and the mockers of moderate democratic socialism. One of the future ideologists of fascism, A. O. Olivetti, heaped contempt upon the modest efforts of the Socialists to ameliorate the conditions of labor. Speaking then as a militant syndicalist, Mussolini's future commissioner described the Socialists as the best and most effective defenders of capitalism.[18]

Intellectually, Sorel's doctrines on the virtues of violence exercised a great influence upon Italian fascism. Arturo Labriola, a leading Italian syndicalist, likened revolutionary syndicalism to imperialism, for, according to him, it exhibited the same energy and proclivity for expansion, and the same disregard for sentimental humanism. From the ranks of the syndicalists came some of the leading fascists. Some were ardent patriots; a prominent syndicalist was Edmondo Rossoni, who had edited an Italian syndicalist paper in the United States, and founded in 1918 the Union of Italian Labor, which, beginning with a membership of 130,000, reached 500,000 by 1920. It was a syndicalist organization, emphasizing the usual ideas of direct action and love of force. Contempt for parliamentary government, democracy, and humanistic values, and devotion to violence as an ennobling and elevating element were the syndicalist ingredients of the fascist brew concocted by Mussolini and his *condottieri*. Yet Italian fascism, unlike Nazism, must be regarded as an aborted offspring of socialism, because it was closely linked to syndicalism, which was itself part of the socialist current.

Nationalism was the other source of fascist philosophy. The adherents

17 *Ibid.*, pp. 198–202.
18 Quoted from *Mouvement socialiste*, March, 1910, in Rosenstock-Franck, *op. cit.*, pp. 9–10.

of nationalism proclaimed its incompatibility with liberal individualism. Liberalism was a force that divided society, that led to many of the problems of the modern world. The nationalists urged the rediscovery of national patriotism and class collaboration based upon the national interest.

BENITO MUSSOLINI (1883—1944)

Much of fascism, its rise and decline, was greatly influenced by Benito Mussolini. His father, Alessandro, was a self-educated internationalist who helped to spread radical ideas for which he served time in prison. A believer in cooperation, he was a known radical who spoke out for his ideas. Benito's mother, Rosa Maltoni, was a village schoolteacher. A year after their marriage, Benito Amilcare Andrea was born. He was sent to school at Faenza and later he attended a technical school and a teachers' college, where he procured a teacher's certificate. He was a serious and studious youth, fond of reading, solitude, and physical exercise. For a time he lived in Lausanne, Switzerland, where he edited a socialist paper and attended Pareto's lectures at the university.[19] From there he went to Berne, mingling with the revolutionary refugees living there. He was expelled, returned to Italy, and began writing for the more extreme socialist press. At that time, Mussolini was on the extreme left, and he bitterly denounced the reformist tendencies of Italian socialism. In 1910 he founded *The Class Struggle* and led an active fight against the reformists. Two years later Mussolini became a member of the Central Committee of the party and editor of the *Forward,* the official daily, published in Milan.

Generally the Italian people sought to remain out of World War I. The nationalists were the only group who did not share this view. As the war continued, the Italian government began negotiating with both sides in an effort to gain the most favorable terms. Some politicians believed Italy could gain most by abstaining from hostilities, but Prime Minister Antonio Salandra, Baron Sidney Sonnino, and the king decided that it was desirable to intervene on the side of the Entente, and on April 26, 1915, the Treaty of London, which took Italy into the war, was signed.

Italian Socialists were pacifist in outlook, and at first Mussolini followed the same policy. However, on November 15, 1914, Mussolini and

[19] Giorgi Pini, *The Official Life of Benito Mussolini.* Translated by Luigi Fillari (London: Hutchinson and Co., 1939), pp. 15–17, 37.

Filippe Naldi founded *Il popolo d'Italia,* which, while claiming to be a socialist journal, launched a malignant campaign against Mussolini's former associates. Also favoring intervention were the newly organized *Fasci di Combattimento,* which favored war on revolutionary groups. The term *"Fascio"* (plural, *"Fasci"*) refers to a group or cluster, and organizations bearing such a name appeared under Bakunin's inspiration in the 1870's. The groups that flourished between October, 1914, and May, 1915, were made up of republicans, socialists, syndicalists, and anarchists favoring Italy's participation in World War I. These *Fascisti* did not last long, but many of the members joined the fascist movement after World War I. Following the Caporetto debacle, a group of deputies opposed to a compromise peace formed the *Fascio di Difensa Nazionale,* or Group of National Defense.[20]

Following the war, Italy faced a period of social and economic difficulty. Organized groups, or squads, began to appear. The young nationalists founded a black-shirted military group and which became known as squadristi, famed for their readiness to bludgeon political opponents into submission. At the beginning, the fascist organizations took on the political coloration of the particular group and locality in which they arose. In many cases the Fasci had vague revolutionary aspirations, and the Milan Fasci, dominated by Mussolini, aspired to be revolutionary proletarians fighting for a reborn Italy and not for vested interests.[21]

Upon the initiative of Mussolini, forty-five delegates from fascist organizations met in Milan on March 23, 1919. At this meeting were delegates widely differing in their views. Anarchosyndicalists, *arditi,* free masons, futurists, and ultraconservatives attended. The largest number came from the Fasci of the 1914 and 1915 vintage, and from leftist prowar interventionists; the latter imposed their views on the first program. The delegates voted to fuse and to establish the *Fasci Italiani di Combattimento.* A reform program indorsed votes for women, the calling of a national assembly to draw up a new constitution, the establishment of labor councils endowed with legislative powers, an eight-hour day, participation of workers in industrial management. Munition plants were to be nationalized and a national militia for defensive purposes was to be founded. A capital levy, the seizure of a portion of property owned by religious or-

---

[20] Giuseppe Prezzolini, *Fascism.* Translated by Kathleen Macmillan (New York: E. P. Dutton & Company, no date), pp. 1–2.

[21] Herbert W. Schneider, *Making the Fascist State* (New York: Oxford University Press, 1938), p. 56.

ganizations, and the abolition of clerical privileges were also advocated. In foreign affairs, the delegates favored annexation of Fiume and Dalmatia and opposed imperialism.

As in most European countries, Italian labor tended, after World War I, to move to the left. In March, 1917, the Socialist party and the Confederazione Generale del Lavro jointly set forth a program in which they proposed no forcible annexations, the recognition of national rights, immediate disarmament for all people, and abolition of custom barriers. On the domestic front, the program demanded a republican form of government, abolition of the Senate, social insurance, minimum wages, and collective labor agreements. This was a moderate socialist program of immediate demands. Growing unrest and a movement to the left within the socialist ranks transferred control of the party in 1918 to a more radical faction. The new majority in the Socialist party did not regard the program as adequate. The left wing or Maximalists were in control.[22] Fond of using radical slogans and enamored of Russia, they were without a plan for handling current problems or of ministering to existing needs.

Into this maelstrom stepped Mussolini, temporarily a politician without a party. For a time he fished in leftist waters, perhaps because he knew them better than the others. He supported strikes, and remained on good terms with the syndicalists. In March, 1919, he again flirted with the labor movement, and supported the sit-down strike of metal workers at the Franchi-Gregorini plant at Dalmine. Later he praised the new method of industrial struggle. Thus the first factory occupation took place under the auspices of budding fascism. His party did not, however, make a good showing in the elections of November, 1919.

More militant tactics were now increasingly used. Armed bands, arditi, intensified their attacks against Socialists and Socialist institutions. The occupation of the port of Fiume by d'Annunzio aroused a large amount of patriotic enthusiasm, and provided fascism with a model of action.

Although the fascists made no appreciable gains in the elections of 1919, the Socialists won 156 seats and polled 1,846,000 votes, or 32 per cent of the total. The Popular party (*Popolari*) elected 100 members, so that these two parties held a majority. However, the Socialist party was controlled by its left wing to which slogans and illusions were as meat and drink. At the Bologna congress in 1919, a radical program was evolved, and adherence to the Third International was unanimously

[22] A. Rossi, *The Rise of Italian Fascism* (London: Methuen and Co., 1938), pp. 11–12.

approved. With the Socialists, the largest party, refusing to join a bourgeois government, Italy faced a continual cabinet crisis.

LABOR MILITANCY

The General Confederation of labor, closely tied to the Socialists, had increased its membership from 321,000 on the eve of World War I, to 2,200,000 at the end of 1920. This was a symptom of widespread discontent, which manifested itself in a large increase of strikes. In March, 1920, Italian industrialists met at Milan and formed the General Confederation of Industry designed to rally employers for offensive and defensive action against labor. A further antilabor step was taken in August, 1920, by the organization of the General Confederation of Agriculture. Against these gathering forces, the left pursued haphazard and doctrinaire policy. Schooled in opposition, the Socialists had no problem to meet this crisis, and sought only to avoid responsibility. The statement of the Socialist leader, Claudio Treves, in the Chamber of Deputies on March 30, 1920, illustrates the Socialist dilemma. "This is the crux of the present tragic situation; you can no longer maintain your existing social order, and we are not yet strong enough to impose the one we want." [23] This is a serious admission of impotence born out of political dogmatism. Treves, who belonged to the right wing, had little responsibility for the party policy then being made by the left-wing Maximalists. Actually the left seemed to be living in a fool's paradise, oblivious to political reality. Two years before the "March on Rome" the National Council of the Socialist party was directing the party executive to draw up a program for the establishment of soviets in Italy.

In May, 1920, the Federation of Metallurgical Workers opened its negotiations with the employers. Failure to agree led to nation-wide sitdown strikes which, while resulting in concessions, aroused and frightened employers and conservative middle-class people.[24] Mussolini did not oppose the sit-down strikes; in fact, he informed Buozzi, the secretary of the metal workers' unions, that he favored them.[25] At this time, Mussolini was trying to win the mass following of the Socialists, whom he had deserted at the beginning of the war. His whole campaign of 1919 and 1920 was in competition with the Socialists. "During the occupation

---

23 *Ibid.*, p. 73.
24 See above, page 399.
25 Rossi, *op. cit.*, p. 27, 73.

of the factories he not only showed himself favorable to the step taken by the workers, but glorified it as the sign of a new economic order." [26] Indeed, Mussolini, in his efforts to win mass support, tried to outbid the Socialists.

A change in the political mood became evident after 1920. Failure of the occupation of the factories and the negativism of the left pushed many into the opposite direction. As the radical tide ebbed, Mussolini began to change his political views. "He had been ultrarevolutionary as long as social revolution seemed possible. He became reactionary as soon as the social revolution seemed impossible." [27] As the strength of the Socialists declined, the power of the fascists increased. They gained widespread support in the latter months of 1920 and in the early months of 1921. In part the growing influence of fascism could be traced to the aggressive and sometimes unwise tactics of the agricultural workers' unions.

The Federation of Agricultural Laborers engaged in long strikes in which they forced the farmers and *mezzadre* to take part. The latter were allowed to harvest half their crops, the half of which was their due, but the landlord's share they had to leave in the fields . . . . Such methods were resented by the public, who saw no reason in them, and were only carried out by the strikers under compulsion, and with qualms of conscience.[28]

As a result an opposition made its appearance and was the opening which the fascists skillfully used.

Another serious error made by the Socialists was their suspicion of and contempt for the ex-soldier. It was foolish to hold the men who fought responsible for the declaration of war; such an attitude could only turn millions against their traducers. This was actually the result of a blind and stupid policy based upon empty sloganeering and doctrinaire philosophizing. The fascists began to use organized terror, and armed bands raided Socialist, Communist, trade-union, and cooperative headquarters, burned buildings and property belonging to opponents, and assaulted all who opposed them. Organized punitive expeditions were launched; a trade-union, cooperative or leftist political center would be surrounded, the members assaulted, and the building fired. Socialist city councilors were rounded up, forced to resign their offices, and expelled from the

---

[26] Luigi Sturzo, *Italy and Fascismo*. Translated by Barbara Barclay Carter (London: Faber and Gwyer, 1926), p. 101.

[27] Gaetano Salvemini, *The Fascist Dictatorship in Italy* (New York: Henry Holt and Company, 1927), p. 52.

[28] Rossi, *op. cit.*, pp. 92–93.

areas. These acts of terrorism were carried on with the connivance of the central authorities.[29]

In the years that immediately followed World War I, Italy faced an almost perennial crisis. With the Socialists refusing to participate in any non-Socialist government, a return to political stability was not possible. To extricate himself from his difficulties, Prime Minister Giolitti called an election in 1921, but the outcome was indecisive. The Socialists and Communists lost some ground; the Italian Popular party gained seven seats; but the fascists, who obtained thirty-five seats, made substantial progress. Instead of being a successful maneuver, the elections of 1921 led to the fall of Giolitti and his replacement as prime minister by the old Socialist, Ivanoe Bonomi.

THE FASCIST PARTY

In an attempt to curb violence, a peace treaty between the Socialists, the labor unions, and the fascists was signed, but a militant wing led by Dino Grandi and Italo Balbo resigned from the directorship of the Fascist party. Their resignations refused, the issues were taken up at the party's congress of November, 1921. Mussolini was now convinced of the need to transform the fascist movement into a political party. The proposal for such a change met opposition. Moreover, the Fascisti were made up of diverse elements who at the time could not agree.

Mussolini favored a "conservative" type of fascism, one that was anti-Socialist at home and imperialistic abroad. Emphasis would be placed on discipline and the supremacy of the national interest above that of all classes. Others favored a romantic type of national syndicalism, opposed to both the left and the right, with syndical government substituted for parliamentarianism. A third view somewhat in between the other two was also presented. A program was drafted, and the three views found expression in it. The most important result was the establishment of the National Fascist party. The congress also repudiated its truce with the Socialists.[30]

The preamble declared: "The National Fascist Party is a Voluntary militia placed at the service of the Nation. The prosecution of its activity is based upon these three principles; order, discipline, hierarchy." [31] The

---

[29] Salvemini, op. cit., pp. 62–63.

[30] Schneider, op. cit., pp. 75–78.

[31] Quoted in Herman Finer, Mussolini's Italy (New York: Henry Holt and Company, 1935), p. 310.

Central Committee was elected at the party's congress and was headed by Mussolini, the Duce. The committee had disciplinary powers over members. Within the Central Committee was a small National Directorate whose duty it was to enforce the decisions of the congress. The Directorate resembled the Politburo of the Russian Communist party, and it chose the secretary-general. On a local level, twenty members could organize a group either on a professional basis or as a fighting squad. Local groups were joined in provincial federations, and provincial congresses chose provincial committees and secretaries. These were subordinate to the general-secretary. After Mussolini took office, the squadristi were dissolved, and the militia, a pretorian guard ready to cudgel and murder opponents, was established. Admission to the party came only after an investigation, and those who failed to meet its standards were eliminated.

In the meantime, the Bonomi government faced a crisis, and the prime minister resigned. Luigi Facta, a lieutenant of Giolitti, came to the helm. He failed to take strong measures against fascist violence and the squadristi were again set loose against their opponents. During this time the left was increasingly paralyzed. The Communists had seceded and set up a shop of their own, and the Socialists were irresolute and divided. Division in the ranks of the Socialists was not ended by the defection of the Communists. A left wing endorsed virtually the entire program of the Communists. Some were, however, eager to find a way out of the impasse. On June 1, 1922, Socialist members of Parliament adopted a resolution that they would support a government dedicated to restoring peace and order. A national council of the Socialist party was summoned; it passed the resolution proposed by Seratti, the left-wing editor of the *Avanti*, which condemned support of a non-Socialist government in power even indirectly by abstention from voting.[32] Every move of the reformist Socialists to find a way out of the political morass was blocked by the left or Maximalists. The advice of the moderate leaders that Socialists support the forces aiming to restore peace and order was rejected by the left-wing Socialists and Communists. Thus a mobilization of anti-fascist strength was made impossible.

Indeed, under the fascist hammer blows the working-class movement seemed powerless. The Federation of Labor, one of the chief targets of fascist attack, dissolved its alliance with the Socialist party. In addition, differences between the right and left factions in the Socialist party were aggravated by the sharpening crisis. The right wanted to support the

[32] Rossi, *op. cit.*, pp. 199–200.

government, while the left opposed collaboration. At the congress of the Socialist party in Rome in October, 1922, the Maximalists won by a close vote. Seratti, the leader of the left, showed himself unaware of political realities. His doctrinaire phrases reveal an infatuation for revolutionary formulas unworthy of a practical politician. The defeated reformists broke away and formed a party of their own.[33]

THE MARCH ON ROME

The position of the Facta cabinet had become intolerable. Maneuvers for a successor were going on behind the scenes, but the Fascists decided to force the hand of the government. Discussion of revolution went on openly in the fascist press. The government showed its impotence by allowing fascist violence to go unpunished, and by drifting along with events. Soon after their congress in 1922, the Fascisti assembled at Civitavecchia, north of Rome. They were organized on a military basis under the leadership of a quadrumvirate nominated by Mussolini. A demand was made that the government resign. Faced by these armed bands, the Facta cabinet stood by helpless and hopeless when a firm stand might have saved parliamentary government—and perhaps Italy, and the world—rivers of blood and tears. The moral resolution of the key individual is in such instances of great importance. At a crucial hour in history, when Italy needed a man of heroic proportions, the head of the government was but a third-rate politician.

The Fascists demanded that Facta resign, and a march on Rome was ordered to begin on October 26, 1922, to be completed two days later. Under pressure the government did resign. When its resignation was not accepted, the government decided on martial law, but the king declined to proclaim a state of siege, for "the advice of certain army chiefs decided the King to refuse his signature to the decree proclaiming martial law."[34] Thus no resistance was put up against several thousand armed men who would have easily succumbed to the opposition of an organized military force. A few thousand Fascists seeped into Rome, while the king negotiated with the Fascist Directorate. On October 30, 1922, Mussolini was appointed head of the government. Thus began the Fascist era, which ended in the ruin of his country. His first cabinet included representatives of all parties except Socialists and Communists. Not a hand was

---

[33] Panfilo Gentile, *Cinquanta anni di socialismo in Italia* (Milan: Longanesi & C., 1948), pp. 153–156.
[34] Sturzo, *op. cit.*, p. 119.

raised against the victory of Fascism, and the labor and socialist units stood by helplessly waiting for the ax to fall. It should be noted that during the "March on Rome," Mussolini was away resting at Milan.

In his first address to the Chamber of Deputies, Mussolini employed the method of "brag, bluff, and bullying" for which he later became internationally famous.[35] He was given extensive power, but opposition to his demands was by no means absent in Parliament or in the country. Leading the opposition in Parliament was Giacomo Matteotti, a right-wing Socialist, fearless and unintimidated by the fascist squadristi. Mussolini had ordered a plebiscite in April, 1924, in the hope of destroying his opponents. Matteoti vigorously assailed on the floor of Parliament the frauds practiced in the election. On June 9, Matteoti was abducted in an automobile and murdered the following day. His body was discovered in a wood on August 16. The evidence indicated that Mussolini was not unaware of the plans for the assassination, and to quiet indignation he reshuffled his cabinet.[36] It was an opportune moment for the opposition, and had it possessed resolute and adroit leadership, Fascism might have collapsed. With Matteotti dead, none was there to lead the fight. Mussolini and his movement weathered the storm; in fact, the crisis established the regime on a firmer basis.

After the publication of Cesare Rossi's statement implicating high Fascist officials in the violence against opponents, Mussolini began to curb the press and destroy the opposition. The Socialist party was reduced to inaction, and opposition deputies who had absented themselves from Parliament as a protest against the Fascist tactics were formally deprived of their seats. Arrest, imprisonment, exile of political prisoners, and reorganization of the state were begun. The prime minister was made responsible only to the king, parliamentary control over the cabinet was removed, and control of local government was placed more firmly in the hands of the central authorities.

THE REORGANIZATION OF THE GOVERNMENT

Perhaps the most important action of the Italian Fascists was the attempt to establish a government upon a new basis. A commission for constitutional reform was appointed in August, 1924. In its report in

[35] Schneider, *op. cit.*, p. 86.
[36] Giacomo Matteotti, *The Fascisti Exposed*. Translated by E. W. Dickes (London: Independent Labour Publication Department, 1924).

July, 1925, the commission recommended the creation of a corporative state based on three corporate chambers. Later in the year, representatives of the fascist syndicates and the Confederation of Industry met and decided that the fascist syndicates were the only representatives of the workers, and the Confederation of Industry was recognized as the sole spokesman for industry. Strikes and lockouts were outlawed in the public service and were to be allowed in private industry only after approval by the authorities. This program was known as the Pact of Vidoni. In April, 1926, the law on collective labor relations was enacted, and in July of the same year rules for enforcement were issued.

THE LAW OF APRIL 3, 1926

Employer and worker syndicate organizations were given legal recognition. An employer syndicate had to represent at least one tenth of the employers engaged in the particular trade or industry. Similarly, labor syndicates, to gain recognition, were required to have at least 10 per cent of all workers in the category or industry as members. In addition to economic protection of members, the syndicates were obligated to promote their moral and patriotic education, and to aid them materially. The legally recognized syndicates were to represent all those in the particular occupations for which they functioned. While other syndicates could exist, only those which were legally recognized could appear before the Labor Court set up for the settlement of labor differences. Strikes and lockouts were outlawed, and collective contracts could be imposed upon employers in a particular category, even if they did not participate in negotiations.

At the same time, a decree created the Ministry of Corporations, and in March, 1927, the duties of the corporations were defined. The charter was officially proclaimed in April, 1927, by the Grand Council, and became a law by legislative enactment in December, 1928. The charter declared that the state was supreme and rose above parties. Although it recognized private initiative in economic activity as desirable, it held that economic affairs are a national concern and are properly a subject for state regulation. An extensive system of social insurance, paid vacations, and minimum standards was introduced. Labor organizations were placed under the guidance of local Fascists and control over their affairs was removed from the rank and file. "Thus the associations have declined from being truly representative and militant organs of masters and workers into organizations for better disciplining of labor and capital, run by fascist officials subject to appointment, control and dismissal by the Government." [37]

Individual and collective differences were settled by labor courts. Disputes between a labor union and an employer association were settled by a court of three judges and two technical advisers of unimpeachable reputation. Decisions applied to all employed in the category in which the dispute arose. However, before giving a decision, the chairman of the court had to attempt conciliation.

NATIONAL COUNCIL OF CORPORATIONS

Mussolini was the head of the National Council of Corporations, and had authority to delegate his functions to the minister of corporations. The National Council was made up of seven sections: liberal professions and arts; industry and artisans, with a subsection of each; agriculture; commerce; land transport and inland navigation; sea and air transport; and banking.

When the subject for decision is of interest to the entire syndical and corporative order of the State, and in the cases specifically mentioned in the present law, the section of the Council shall be convoked in General Assembly. The participants therein shall be, in addition to the Minister for Corporations, the Minister for the Interior, the Minister for Agriculture and Forests, the Secretary of the National Fascists, the Undersecretary of State for Corporations and all representatives designated by the syndical confederations of employers and workers for the corresponding sections.[38]

The National Council of Corporations advised on issues affecting national production and sought to promote increases in output, culture, and national art. It dealt with matters affecting the interests of syndical associations and directed expenditures, propaganda, the labor exchanges and relief carried on by the syndical associations.

Whatever may be the theory, the corporations were instruments of the Fascist party and engines of control. According to Mussolini, "Corporativism overcomes Socialism as well as it does Liberalism: it creates a new synthesis." [39]

[37] Finer, *op. cit.*, p. 507.
[38] Benito Mussolini, *Fascism* (Rome: Ardita, 1935), p. 145.
[39] Quoted by Finer, *op. cit.*, p. 502.

ESSENCE OF FASCISM

Behind the elaborate façade, fascism was naked adventurism. Its leader, a socialist turncoat, had imbibed the doctrine of violence from the syndicalist theorists popular at the turn of the century. After World War I he saw an opportunity to mobilize the disillusioned and the violent into an armed and militant phalanx. As an ex-Socialist, Mussolini knew the art of mass agitation, and he used the popular discontent to create a new movement, antisocialist and antidemocratic.

After Socialism, Fascism trains its guns on the whole block of democratic ideologies and rejects both their premises and their practical applications and implements. Fascism denies that numbers, as such, can be the determining factor in human society; it denies the right of numbers to govern by means of periodical consultations; it asserts the irremediable and fertile and beneficent inequality of men who cannot be levelled by any such mechanical and universal device as universal suffrage.

According to Mussolini,

Fascism rejects the absurd conventional lie of political equalitarianism, the habit of collective irresponsibility, the myth of felicity and indefinite progress. But if democracy be understood as meaning a regime in which the masses are not driven back to the margin of the State, then the writer of these pages has already defined Fascism as an organized, centralized, authoritarian democracy.[40]

Mussolini regarded fascism as something new in history. To some extent he was correct, as fascism was absolutism of a party open to all, irrespective of class or caste, and resting upon a wide base. "A party governing a nation! totalitarianism is a new departure in history. There are no points of reference nor of comparison. From beneath the ruins of liberal, socialist and democratic doctrines, Fascism extracts those elements which are still vital." What these elements are, and how they may be identified, we are not told. Mussolini believed that the twentieth century was the century of the collective and the state. "The key-stone of the Fascist doctrine is its conception of the State, of its essence, its functions, and its aims." For Fascism the State is absolute, individuals and groups relative. Individuals and groups are admissible in so far as they come within the State.

Mussolini gave the state a mystic meaning. To him, the state was a

---

[40] *Ibid.*, pp. 21, 23. The following quotations from Mussolini are also from this source, pp. 25–26, 27, 29.

spiritual and political force for securing the economic, judicial, and political organization of the country. The state guards and fosters the spirit of the people as it has been historically developed by its customs, language, and literature. The state is the past, present, and future of a people. He regarded the fascist state as revolutionary

for it anticipates the solution of certain universal problems which have been raised elsewhere, in the political field by the splitting-up of parties, usurpation of power by parliaments, by irresponsibility of assemblies; in the economic field by increasingly numerous and important functions discharged by trade-unions and trade associations with their deputies and ententes, affecting both capital and labor; in the ethical field by the need felt for order, discipline, obedience to the moral dictates of patriotism.

War was the spiritual crucible of fascism, according to one of its more eminent philosophers, Giovanni Gentile. The war reanimated the youth of Italy, who threw off the spiritual yoke of liberalism and socialism. Fascism thus burst forth as a violent cry of youth, which was not illegal, but was the expression of the new idea.[41] Even its serious thinkers saw in fascism only an extreme anti-intellectualist manifestation of violence supposed to reflect youthful ardor and eagerness. The emphasis upon violence led not only to the forcible suppression of internal opponents, but finally to foreign adventures which ended in disaster.

The fusion of aggressive nationalism with state interventionism failed. Despite Mussolini's temporary success in destroying his opposition, he tragically overrated the military capacity of a nation poor in natural resources. During the peaceful era, his bluff and braggadocio were unchallenged. The emptiness of his posturing and the papier-mâché edifice of Italian fascism were tragically revealed after Italy's entrance into World War II.

POSTWAR

With the ending of the war, parliamentary government was restored, and the Communist and Socialist parties began to function. From the outset, the Communists advocated the tactic of a "united front," and Pietro Nenni, the leader of Italian socialism, wholeheartedly embraced this idea. With the exception of those in Eastern Europe, the Socialist party of Italy was the only large Socialist organization which favored

41 Giovanni Gentile, *Che cosa e il Fascismo* (Florence: Vallecchi Editore, 1925), pp. 123–124.

close cooperation with the Communists. This policy encountered increasing opposition from those within the party who opposed the antidemocratic tendencies of the Communists.

Finally, Gustav Sarragat decided, in February, 1947, to break away and form a new party. He carried about one third of the Socialist members of Parliament with him. Since December, 1947, he has cooperated with De Gasperi's government. Sarragat's party, the *Partito Socialista dei Lavoratori Italiani* (the Italian Workers' Socialist party), is made up of the people around the *Critica Sociale,* largely pre-Fascist reformers, and another group organized around *Iniziativa Socialista,* made up of younger and more radical people. Sarragat's forces were strengthened by the defection of Ivan Matteo Lombardo from Nenni's group.

The Sarragat Socialists refused to cooperate with the "Popular Front" of Nenni and the Communists. In the elections of 1948, 26,000,000, or 92 per cent of these eligible citizens voted. About 13,000,000 votes were received by the Christian Democrats. The Popular Front, made up of Communists and Socialists, polled 8,000,000 and the Independent Anti-Communist Socialists polled about 2,000,000. The Christian Democrats received 307 out of 574 seats in the Chamber of Deputies. Out of a total of 182 seats won by the Popular Front coalition, the Communists gained 138; the Socialists elected 36, and the Independents, 6.[42]

The election was thus a major disaster for the Socialists. Meeting in Genoa in July, 1948, the Nenni Socialists took a middle position between Sarragat and Togliatti. Not wishing to join with Sarragat or with the Communists, they followed an intermediate, compromising course, fearing to move toward Sarragat or away from the Communists. The compromise was a victory of the center, but the issue of cooperation with the Communist party remains unsettled.[43] Nenni was for a short time ousted from power, but he has regained control over a weakened Socialist party. Some wanted complete disassociation from the Communists while others wanted to continue this union.

Although the Communists were defeated in the elections, they controlled the main segment of the Italian labor movement, the *Confederazione Generale Italiano di Lavro.* This fact gave the Communists a powerful instrument with which they could restrain the opposition. The

---

42 Mario Einaudi, "The Italian Elections of 1948," *The Review of Politics,* July, 1948, pp. 346–349.

43 Ferrenbach, "Il Congresso della delusione," *La Critica politica,* July–August, 1948, pp. 248–252.

workers could be mustered at will and a government embarrassed. There are always grievances and occasions to stir up strife, ostensibly for the correction of economic injustice, but actually designed to further political ends. The Communists have won a major position within the labor movement, and their dislodgment may be possible only with the improvement and stabilization of economic conditions.

25. *CHRISTIAN SOCIALISM*

The spread of liberal capitalism and the rise of modern socialism directed the attention of a number of Christian writers and leaders to the need for grappling with social problems. Although these Christian Socialists did not advocate a uniform gospel, all of them saw the solution of present problems in the return to the teachings of Christ. Society can be saved from disaster by a return to the Christian order almost completely forgotten by modern man. All Christian Socialists are critical of the competitive and profit-making principle. For them a return to Christian teachings implies going back to a cooperative way of life undermined by the expansion of modern capitalism. As a result, a number of Christian Socialist or quasi-socialist doctrines were developed which urged the substitution of cooperative or associated labor for competition. In some instances the autonomous activity of labor is stressed; in others government aid is advocated. "All are agreed that cooperative labor is only possible in a society which is interpenetrated by the spirit of Christ." [1]

A common element in the work of all Christian Socialist thinkers was their desire to impregnate society with religious principles. The material welfare of individuals is important only in that it enables us to lead a true Christian life. Among the earliest Christian Socialists Hugues Félicité Robert de Lamennais occupied an important place.

HUGUES FÉLICITÉ ROBERT DE LAMENNAIS (1782–1854)

Lamennais was from old bourgeois stock and came under the influence of Rousseau. For a time he was inclined toward nationalism, but later changed his views and turned in the direction of religion, subsequently

[1] Rev. M. Kaufmann, *Christian Socialism* (London: Kegan Paul, Trench, Trubner and Co., 1888), p. 25.

being ordained a priest. His study on religious indifference attracted wide attention. In it he developed the thesis that the church could be regenerated only through liberty, and mankind through the church—a doctrine of liberal Catholicism. For a time he advocated a government founded on a theocratic basis, which was expressed in the proposition "that without the Pope there is no Church, without the Church there is no Christianity, without Christianity there is no religion and hence no society." [2]

CRITICISM

Lamennais's criticism of social conditions was based upon religious grounds. The fecundity of nature is a sign that God has provided for all, and if some are lacking necessities, it is because man has violated the natural order of God, has broken the original unity, and has transformed men into enemies. Evil passions and egoism have armed man against man, rapine has destroyed security, and war has devastated the world. Laws for the profit of some and the misfortune of others have been enacted. While actually slavery exists in only a few parts of the world, exploitation is widespread. Those who labor are frequently in worse predicament than the slave, for they lack security during unemployment, sickness and old age. Excessive self-love destroys in us the love of others. Distinctions based on money abound, and out of them grow an idle rich and a proletariat, poor, propertyless, and resentful.[3]

The revolution of 1830 brought the bourgeoisie to power. It was an age of utopias, of secularism, of anticlericalism. Lamennais and his followers established *L'Avenir* (*The Future*), whose aim was to liberalize the Catholic Church and to Catholicize the liberal state. They demanded an end to the interference of the state in religious matters, and to the suppression of state salaries paid to the clergy. They also advocated freedom of education, the right of association and popular elections, a free press and the right of the individual conscience. The church was, however, not too eager to become embroiled in these activities, and Lamennais's doctrines were pronounced dangerous. Lamennais submitted on religious questions, but he reserved the right to conduct activities on behalf of his country and of humanity.

In 1834 he published his most popular work, *Words of a Believer*, in

[2] Charles Sigfried Pearson, *The Politico-Social Ideal of Hugues-Félicité Robert de Lamennais* (New York: The Graduate School of New York University, 1936), pp. 1–2.
[3] F. Lamennais, *Le Livre du peuple* (Paris: H. Delloye, 1838), pp. 2–19.

which the militant Christian socialist appears. It advocated the organization of labor on the principle of fraternal associations, the substitution of self-sacrifice for self-seeking as the motivation of human activity, and the elimination of the evils of competition by promoting friendly cooperation.

Lamennais defended revolution as part of the divine plan, and held that no obligation existed for obeying a bad prince. Regardless of the objectives of revolutionaries, revolutions are the result of the universal need for a new social order conforming to the law of progress, which he regarded as necessary and providential. It is resistance to progress that breeds revolution, and it is true wisdom to assist those movements which cannot be prevented; otherwise society must face sudden shocks and violent commotions.

CHRISTIAN SOCIALISM

Society is composed of two classes, the rich and the disinherited. The proletarians are the backbone and conservators of society, the creators of wealth. Although they are the most numerous, they have been unjustly reduced to a state of slavery and ignorance. Lamennais, despite his other views, rejected such doctrines as the class struggle and materialism. He maintained that the interests of the workers did not differ from those of other social groups. Nevertheless, he feared the socialism of his day, Saint-Simonism and Fourierism, because they would destroy liberty and bring into being a despotic slavery. He rejected all views which would realize happiness by sacrificing liberty. Concentration of power in the hands of the state was to him no remedy. Yet he would allow limited intervention by the state to prevent the degradation of the working population. It is the duty of the state to create the conditions under which a worker can secure education, capital, and the assurance of the right to work; and to aid those unable to find employment.

Even though he opposed the socialism of his time, Lamennais was truly a precursor of some types of collectivism. He thought more of equality than of liberty, and criticized the notion that men are free if they are economically dependent. The solution of the social problem was dependent upon a change in the distribution of goods. However, improvement in the conditions of the poor lies not in abolishing private property, but in developing a society in which everyone can become a property owner. These ends can be attained by abolishing privileges and monopolies and by making the instruments of production accessible to all. These two measures, combined with a system of association, would, little by little, establish an equitable distribution of wealth.

Lamennais believed that the proletariat can be emancipated by removing the legal fetters which prevent free association, eliminating the intellectual fetters through a vast system of free education, and ending the material fetters by making capital available. Although he recognized that the worker should enjoy given rights, he also emphasized his duties to his family, community, and country. Man has a duty to labor, to observe the rights of others, and to practice equality and justice.

INTERNATIONALISM

Each people owes to the other justice and charity, and all should use their utmost efforts to unite the nations of the world and to destroy the prejudices which keep them apart. Each nation, following its own genius, determined by its own climate and history, performs the particular function that Providence has assigned to it. Nations have common rather than conflicting interests, and the good of one is the benefit of the other.

Lamennais's social views do not constitute a unified system. He recognized the evils of capitalism and the harmful effect it had on man's spiritual life. Like other Christian reformers, he regarded economic reforms as a means of making it possible for man to lead a Christian life.

SCHOLASTIC SOCIALISM

Postwar Europe has seen a significant spread in socialist ideas advocated by religious-minded individuals who invoke Christian teaching in support of their views. The attitude of major scholastic economists parallels in many instances the views of the bitter opponents of Catholicism, the Marxists. The answer of scholastic economists to the problems of our time is "the establishment of an organic or corporate economy in which bargaining between organized vocational and industrial groups is to supplant the market form of organization." [4] Scholastic socialism has found an audience, and there are signs that it is not without influence in the United States. The movement itself goes back to a much earlier period.

BISHOP VON KETTELER (1811–1877)

The entry of the Catholic Church into the social arena in Germany was contemperaneous with the beginning of the first labor movement. Its

[4] Abram L. Harris, "The Scholastic Revival: The Economics of Heinrich Pesch," *Journal of Political Economy*, February, 1946, pp. 39, 56.

leader was Wilhelm Emmanuel von Ketteler, who, after studying and practicing law, turned to theology and the Catholic Church. The turbulent events of 1848 changed von Ketteler from a secluded pastor of a Christian flock into an active politician. He was elected to the National Assembly at Frankfort, where he attracted wide attention by a funeral sermon at the bier of two conservative leaders killed in a street riot.[5] His delivery of this sermon made a deep impression, and two years later he was appointed Bishop of Mainz. He showed a deep realization of contemporary social problems, and appreciated the significance of the socialist creeds then being hammered out by a number of writers and politicians. He encouraged the *Gesellenvereine,* workers' clubs established by Father Adolf Kolping (1813–1865), and supported low-cost housing ventures for workers.

Now Ketteler, who had followed the agitation of Ferdinand Lassalle, stepped into the arena of public discussion with his *Christianity and the Labor Question,* in 1864.[6] Strongly influenced by Larsalle's views on economic problems, it was severely critical of liberalism and competition. He argued that the "labor question touches the material needs of the Christian people; this consideration alone . . . gives me the right to discuss it publicly. Viewed in this light the labor question is also a question of Christian charity." [7] He charged that unlimited liberty and the domination of capital exposed the workers to the fluctuations of the market. For the worker, liberty is an illusion and consists of selling his labor at a low wage. Free international trade means competition with low-paid labor from abroad. Now Ketteler did not look with favor upon the movement for self-help, for this is possible only for the fortunate few, the more skilled and able, who may be in a position to rise to the rank of employer; it is not possible for labor in general, for wages, as Lassalle had shown, are governed by the "iron law." [8]

Although economic liberty has increased production, by exceeding the proper limits, it has degraded labor. Now Ketteler saw the real difficulty in that the worker was dependent upon others and could not help him-

[5] George Metlake, *Christian Social Reform* (Philadelphia: The Dolphin Press, 1912), pp. 7–24.

[6] Wilhelm Emmanuel Freihern von Ketteler, *Die Arbeiterfrage und das Chrisenthum* (Mainz: Franz Kircheim, 1864).

[7] William Edward Hogan, *The Development of Bishop Wilhelm Emmanuel von Ketteler's Interpretation of the Social Problem* (Washington, D. C.: The Catholic University of America Press, 1946), pp. 113–115, 108.

[8] Émile de Laveleye, *The Socialism of Today.* Translated by Goddard H. Oppen (London: Field and Tuer, no date), p. 124.

self. He outlined the remedy. First the spirit of man must be redeemed from atheistic materialism, and true Christianity must be embraced. We must succor the poor, the sick, and the incurable. The truths and precepts of the church, with its cultivation of the mind and heart, are also offered labor. He approved of organization for the

fundamental characteristic of the labor movements of our day, that which gives them their importance and significance and really constitutes their essence, is the tendency, everywhere rife among workingmen, to organize for the purpose of gaining a hearing for their just claims by united action. To this tendency, which is not only justified but necessary under existing economic conditions, the Church cannot but gladly give her sanction and support.

It would be a great folly on our part if we kept aloof from this movement merely because it happens at the present time to be promoted chiefly by men who are hostile to Christianity. The air remains God's air though breathed by an atheist, and the bread we eat is no less the nourishment provided for us by God though kneaded by an unbeliever. It is the same with unionism: it is an idea that rests on the divine order of things and is essentially Christian, though men who favor it most do not recognize the finger of God in it and often even turn it to a wicked use.[9]

Von Ketteler felt that Christianity alone can direct unionism so as to make it of maximum benefit to labor. "The future of unionism belongs to Christianity." In addition, he proposed cooperative producers' associations, arguing that "whoever works for another, and is forced to do so all his life, has a moral right to demand security for a permanent livelihood. All the other classes enjoy such security. Why should the working class alone be deprived of it?" The social question is intertwined with Christianity, for the Gospel commands us to be our brother's keeper. Von Ketteler denied that the problems can be handled by charity and almsgiving; and, as wages are reduced by the competition of the market, he would take steps to abolish the influence of the market on the worker. His remedy was cooperation.

May God in His goodness bring all good Catholics to adopt the idea of the cooperation associations of production, upon the basis of Christianity! Thus alone can salvation be brought to the labouring classes. The freedom promised by Liberalism is like Dead Sea fruit, fair on the outside, but dust and ashes within. Liberalism proclaims freedom of contract; but for the laborer without capital, it is merely freedom to die of hunger; for how can he live if he does not accept whatever conditions may be imposed upon him? Freedom to go where he likes is

9 These quotations from von Ketteler are from Metlake, *op. cit.*, pp. 127, 128, 134.

another meaningless phrase; for is not the workingman who has a wife and children tied to the spot where he is settled? How can he seek employment elsewhere, when he lacks the means of satisfying his first needs? Freedom of labor; what is it except the competition of laborers reducing wages to the lowest point? Free trade, what other result has it except to enable the rich to buy what they want in the cheapest market, and to reduce the working man to the level of those who can subsist upon the least? Christianity, practically applied, can alone bring it about that those liberties of which capitalists now reap the entire profit, may also benefit the laborers. Catholic charity has already established countless institutions of every kind, convents, schools, refuges, hospitals, succour for all needs and infirmities! To-day it is the laborers to whom aid must come. This is the special mission of Catholicism.[10]

Von Ketteler's views made a deep impression, and he gained a fairly large following.

FRANZ CHRISTOPH MOUFANG (1817–1890)

Von Ketteler's position in the hierarchy, his earnestness, and his passionate campaign for social justice created wide interest in his teaching, especially among the clergy. One of his leading disciples, Franz Christoph Moufang, engaged in parliamentary and journalistic activity. Like von Ketteler, he looked upon industrial capital as the great enemy of society, and favored the independent craftsman, the factory worker, and the farmer. Although he recognized that this world could not be a paradise, it was a denial of justice for the 90 per cent to remain in need while the 10 per cent have a surplus.

Moufang recommended three sources of aid for the working population. Foremost was religion, then the family, and finally the association. The weak must join together to oppose the strong. A union of workers is desirable, not to fight the employer, but to organize against exploitation and against the harshness of capital. In other words, Christian Socialism fights against the exploitation of labor, but still more against the oppression of the middle class by large capital.[11]

Moufang did not believe that self-help was adequate to relieve the lot of the worker. Legal protection was needed; it should regulate the length of the working day as well as wage levels, prohibit the labor of women and children, and control working conditions. The worker is not an inert machine, but a human being made in the image of God and with natural

10 Quotation in Laveleye, *op. cit.*, pp. 127–128.
11 August Erdmann, *Die Christliche Arbeiterbewegung in Deutschland* (Stuttgart: Dietz, 1909), p. 51.

rights. Nor can the principle of competition be recognized for labor, although it may be proper for commodities. Moufang had in mind the development of a labor code similar to commercial, maritime, and civil codes. Under the labor code, relations between masters and apprentices, labor and capital would be regulated.

He followed both von Ketteler and Lassalle in advocating state support for workers' societies. He pointed to state subsidies for railroads and other improvements requiring large capital investment. Surely the worker could ask for the same treatment. In addition, Moufang demanded the reduction of direct and indirect taxes and the military burdens borne by the worker. The wealthy, their pockets bursting with wealth, are exempt from taxes, while the burden is placed upon the worker. Reform is necessary on this point, and militarism could be abolished and thus one of Germany's greatest evils eliminated.

Finally, the state should end the tyranny of capital; while Moufang denied that the acquisition of wealth is illegitimate or un-Christian, he deplored the enrichment of a few at the expense of the many. Under Moufang's leadership, the *Christliche-sociale Blätter* was established. It assailed competitive capitalism and urged Christian Socialism.[12]

FRANZ HITZE (1851–1921)

The work of von Ketteler and Moufang was carried a step further by Father Franz Hitze. Like them, Hitze held that the church must concern herself with social questions. The church has never shut her eyes to evils, and he pointed out that the questions of property, interest, labor, charity, and wages have been discussed by St. Thomas and other Catholic thinkers.

The best means for defeating democratic Socialism is to take up its truths, eliminating from them what is erroneous.

We must also render our teaching of social economy conformable with the teachings of our faith, loudly proclaiming our Christian ideal in the midst of errors and confusion of the social question, and showing clearly how the modern economic developments may and must conform to that ideal.[13]

He believed that the great concentration of capital was pushing the artisan and the farmer into the ranks of wage workers. Large capital overwhelms the smaller capital in the field of competition so that it is more

---

12 Laveleye, *op. cit.*, pp. 128–132.

13 Quoted from an address by Hitze in Francesco S. Nitti, *Catholic Socialism*. Translated by Mary MacKintosh (London: George Allen & Unwin, Ltd., 1911), p. 144.

and more concentrated in fewer and fewer hands. At the same time the proletariat faces increasing misery. In examining economic progress, Hitze found that technical discoveries and increasing productivity lead to greater wealth for the capitalist and to misery for the worker. He came to the conclusion that a modern wage earner's lot is inferior to that of a slave in former times.[14] The slave was certain of minimum subsistence, and as he represented an investment to his master, he was assured against extreme suffering. In contrast, a free worker has no assurance that when his strength is used up he will not be cast aside and replaced by a stronger and better worker.

Socialism Hitze accepted the socialist criticism of capitalism. However, so long as man remains what he is, collectivism will fail to bring relief. He regarded the optimism of socialists and communists as due to their failure to understand man, his original sin, and its influence; and to realize that this life is only a transient moment on the road to eternity.[15] He also questioned the desirability of socializing the product of labor, for the exertion of the individual would be reduced when he no longer gained from hard work, and thus the total product might fail.

However, he recognized the important contribution made by socialism in its criticism of our present social order. Both Marx and Lassalle made worthy contributions in their criticisms of capitalism. Socialism has, however, no positive remedy. The church must step into the breach, for she alone can provide the leadership to pull man out of the social morass. A revival of morality and well-being is possible only under her leadership. With the aid of the state, producers' associations and cooperatives can be set up. Hitze's sympathies were largely with the peasants, for he saw in them a healthy element and a barrier against the corruption and irreligion of urban life. He advocated reforms of corporations and the stock exchange, charging that they were dominated by Jews. Like many German reformers who based their views on religion, he was a pronounced anti-Semite.[16] His petty bourgeois views are also manifested in his eagerness to keep the peasant on the land and to protect the artisan against the encroachment of the factory. For the relief of the worker, he urged reduction of the hours of labor and protection against unnecessary hardships.

He was, however, convinced of the necessity for replacing the present

14 Erdmann, *op. cit.*, 55.
15 *Ibid.*, p. 57.
16 *Ibid.*, p. 60.

social organization; and he advocated the replacement of capitalism by a medieval guild society, for he was more concerned with saving the middle class from being ground down into the proletariat than in creating a society in which the proletariat would dominate. In a word, "Herr Hitze is the founder of middle class Socialism." [17]

He also opposed the principle of majority rule, for he saw in it "permanent revolution." We must again become conservative. Instead of an elected parliament subject to every type of social strain, he would introduce a body representative of different interests, corresponding to the medieval guilds. Each class would have equal representation, irrespective of its numbers. Instead of turning economic activity over to the state, Hitze would organize the trades. He was convinced that

the reign of individualism and Liberalism is in reality nothing else than the reign of despotic hypocrisy, which satisfies neither the wants of the community at large nor the interests of production. The future belongs to Socialism, whether it be absolute Democratic Socialism tending to revolutionize the state, or the healthy conservative, relative Socialism of the trade corporations. *A social organization of the nations is the only possible safe solution of the social question.*[18]

Hitze held that the social question is not independent of religion. Reorganization of the economy on a socialist basis offers the only solution. His system of socialism would reorganize the trades so that they would become political as well as economic institutions.[19]

CHRISTIAN SOCIETIES

Following Bishop von Ketteler's injunction of "association on Christian principles," the 1860's witnessed the beginning of the formation of Christian workers' groups. There were savings, credit, and consumer cooperatives, and in some instances labor unions. In 1868, at the suggestion of the Elberfeld Society, the Catholic Social party was established. Freedom to organize and freedom from the overwhelming oppression of capital were the objectives it professed to seek.[20] The movement spread, and at the meeting of 1870, fourteen societies were represented. The principal issues discussed were credit, savings, self-help, and consumers' cooperatives. The Catholic Social party gained a large number of followers by

17 *Ibid.*, p. 64.
18 Quotation in Nitti, *op. cit.*, pp. 150–151.
19 *Ibid.*, 153–154.
20 Erdmann, *op. cit.*, p. 76.

adopting the Catholic journeyman's clubs founded in 1847 by Father Kolping.

Kolping maintained that the worker lacked a strong moral faith and a leadership which he could trust; he lacked a place where he could spend his evenings and where he could concern himself with spiritual and intellectual problems; he lacked an opportunity for technical education. The worker must be won back to religion, and a spirit of love and sacrifice must be revived within him. Organizations under the leadership of the clergy must be initiated which will make possible the achievement of these ends.[21] For Kolping the labor question was essentially a moral one. He wanted to avoid all larger social issues for he was convinced that scant aid would be obtained by any means other than religion and virtue.

To carry out his views, he organized the Catholic labor movement, a general assembly which met at least once every five years. It was managed by a general executive between conferences; at the head of each local group stood a member of the Catholic clergy.[22] In 1891, some Catholics wanted to establish religious labor organizations, but their proposal did not gain wide acceptance. However, the attempt of a socialist union to speak for the miners of the Ruhr brought a reaction. In October, 1894, the first Christian miners' union was established at Essen. The movement spread to other sections.

Actually the first Catholic labor organization which aimed to improve the conditions of labor by economic means was founded in 1879. Its purpose was to introduce Christianity into labor relations.[23] Disavowing any revolutionary designs, the movement was eminently conservative; it declared that the restoration of Catholic principles in industry would bar all threats of revolution. It sought to avoid disputes with employers, to abstain from political activity, to counteract the influence of social democracy among labor, and to protect the economic interests of its members. In 1899, this organization held its first congress at Mainz. In 1901 a federation of Christian labor unions was effected.

The basis of the new grouping was interdenominational; it rested on the principles of Christianity and forbade the discussion of religious differences. The unions sought improvement in conditions of work, but within the existing social and national framework. Sickness insurance and

21 *Ibid.*, p. 18.
22 *Ibid.*, pp. 181–182.
23 *Ibid.*, p. 204.

other forms of insurance were advocated and the common interests of labor and management were recognized.[24]

AUSTRIA

The Catholic social movement spread to Austria. Rudolf Meyer, (1839–1899), convert to Catholicism, fled Germany and settled in Austria, where he became an intellectual leader of Catholic socialism. He criticized liberal economics on the ground that it shows more interest in production than in the producer, more in wealth than in people. He agreed with Marx's criticisms of capitalism, and he maintained that "Christian reform is not possible unless its promoters are convinced that property confers no rights whatever on the person of our fellow-man, but only duties toward him." [25] Capital does not assume any duties toward labor or toward the other agent of production, land. Consequently, modern society is subject to an unstable equilibrium, for capital has the power to ignore justice. Wise and prudent laws were, in his opinion, needed to prevent the excesses of capital. Meyer advocated state intervention to rectify the distribution of wealth. In common with the Marxists, he affirmed that the interests of labor are opposed to those of capital, and with unrestricted freedom of contract the worker has no means of improving his position. He not only urged stricter and more extensive regulation of interest rates, but believed that the state should continually enlarge its activities. The principal activity of government, he believed, should be to develop small holdings and even to aid in their growth. In addition Meyer proposed the setting up of pension systems upon a contributory basis by each trade and the settlement of disputes between employers and employees by arbitration. In common with other Catholic writers, he urged the organization of trades and industries into corporations. As a first step he advocated limitation of the hours of industrial labor, regulation of the employment of women and minors, and improvement in factory laws and their effective enforcement.

Like Rudolf Meyer, Baron Karl von Vogelsgang 1818–1890 was a Prussian and a Catholic convert. A forceful opponent of economic liberalism, he maintained that under the old order private property was allowable only in exchange for benefits rendered to the community. All private

[24] Theodore Böhme, *Die Christliche nationale Gewerkschaft* (Stuttgart: Kohlhammer, 1930), p. 58.

[25] Nitti, *op. cit.*, p. 207.

property had its correlative duties. In an individualist community, property which has been a social patrimony becomes subject to individual use and abuse. He argued that the bourgeoisie which had overthrown the old order had fooled the people, who have unwittingly brought about their own ruin, for capitalism came with the triumph of the bourgeoisie. Under capitalism, wealth is individual property; it has rights but no duties except to obtain for its owners the highest possible return. The principle of the highest gain as the single basis of calculation manifests itself more clearly in money capital, which pushes its tentacles into every aspect of economic and social activity.

Under the growing influence of money, the proud worker is degraded to a propertyless proletarian. Similarly, the present laboring under a load of debt suffers the same fate. These evils require strong measures, and von Vogelsgang held that

Catholics. . . . deceive themselves in believing that the solution of the social question may be effected through the sole intervention of the Church, excluding that of the State. We can never hope to see the establishment of a social organization based on justice towards the weak, unless under the influence of Christian laws. But neither must we allow ourselves to be led away by illusions; we must try and understand that it is impossible to oppose any remedy to the evils of modern society, infested as it is by capitalism, without an energetic intervention on the part of the state.[26]

As a way out, von Vogelsgang urged corporative organization of workers on the basis of trades and industries under the supervision of the state.

Perhaps to a greater degree than elsewhere, the Austrian social Catholic movement exercised a strong attraction for the feudal aristocracy.

In Austria, because capital and industry were there so largely in the hands of Jews, and because Jewish millionaires were rapidly becoming landed magnates, the older, Christian aristocracy of birth was moved to reassert its authority by intervening in the labor question, as the more or less disinterested defender of the industrial proletariat against the industrial capitalist and financier. Feudalism thus found its *revanche* for the attacks of the capitalists and financiers upon the feudal regime.[27]

Austrian Catholic socialism inspired the work of the Viennese mayor and anti-Semite Karl Lueger, who was close to von Vogelsgang. Although

---

[26] Quotation from von Vogelsgang, *ibid.,* p. 222.
[27] Parker T. Moon, *The Labor Problem and the Social Catholic Movement in France* (New York: The Macmillan Company, 1921), p. 131.

Lueger introduced a number of municipal reforms, his narrow outlook and anti-Semitism influenced the Hitler movement and bore much evil fruit for his country and the world.

BELGIUM

Catholic political action in Belgium was tied closely to the conservative interests. In 1868 the Federation of the Catholic Workers' Associations was founded; it published the *L'Économie chrétienne*. The leader of the Catholic labor movement in Belgium, L'Abbé Pottier, advocated the views of St. Thomas Aquinas. He divided law into natural and civil, with property based on the latter. On many contemporary issues—strikes, employment of women and children, collective bargaining—Pottier took an advanced position.[28] Catholic socialism, as it has been called, did not have a large following in Belgium until after World War II.

FRANCE

The growth of socialist influence among industrial labor led the founder of the modern French Catholic social movement, Vicomte Armand de Melun (1807–1877), to seek a reconciliation of the church and the wage earner.

Trained for the foreign service, De Melun gave up his career, after the July Revolution of 1830, to devote himself to the relief of the poor. He established a magazine in which he discussed the social problems of the time, and after the Revolution of 1848, he turned from charitable work to the sponsoring of social legislation.

Melun sought to steer a middle course between communism and laissez faire. Society, in his opinion, was obligated to protect the worker against ignorance, sickness, vice, and poverty. He wanted a positive policy, one that would prevent rather than ameliorate. His program called for maternity hospitals, day nurseries, orphan asylums, popular education, vocational training, and welfare associations, as well as measures to encourage thrift and alleviate distress. He also wanted to develop groups of employers and workers who would convert the wage system into a profit-sharing arrangement.[29] He was followed by René de La Tour du

28 Moon, *op. cit.*, pp. 134–135.
29 *Ibid.*, pp. 48–51.

Pin, who attacked the heartlessness and cruelty of economic liberalism. This reformer advocated a corporate order and charged that the dogmas of the French Revolution had been used to destroy the workers' organizations which Du Pin would revive and empower to regulate many aspects of production.[30] Thus labor would again acquire its former dignity. In addition, Du Pin advocated many reforms which would lighten the worker's burdens and give him more security.

ALBERT DE MUN (1841–1914)

Sharing Du Pin's views, but more active in public affairs, was Count Albert de Mun, who, with several associates, launched the Committee for the Establishment of Catholic Workingmen's Clubs. A manifesto called upon the privileged class to save the people from revolutionary doctrines by a policy of aid to labor and an understanding of its problems. The first club was founded in a poor section of Paris in 1872. With the spread of the movement, branches were established in many places. A historian of French labor and socialism explained the small membership by the urban worker's opposition to religion.[31]

De Mun was a monarchist and so favored a restoration, but he was also critical of individualism and laissez faire. He advocated legislation for the reduction of the hours of labor; the regulation of child labor; the raising of the school age; compulsory sickness, old-age, and accident insurance supported by joint contributions of employers and employees; and boards of arbitration to settle labor disputes. In the sphere of labor organization, he also advocated a guild system whereby both labor and capital would organize, with workers receiving a share in the management of industry. Ultimately the guild organizations would be given extensive regulatory powers.[32] The Catholic social movement in France did not develop a large popular following, but it sought to spread its influence through oral and written propaganda and study courses. It has had more influence since World War II.

RERUM NOVARUM

Catholic social action was greatly encouraged by Pope Leo XIII's encyclical letter, *Rerum Novarum*, issued in May, 1891. In it the pope ex-

---

[30] Georges Hoog, *Histoire du catholicisme social en France* (Paris: Éditions Domat Montchrestien, 1946), pp. 18–19.

[31] Georges Weill, *Histoire du mouvement social en France* (Paris: Félix Alcan, 1911), p. 405.

[32] Moon, *op. cit.*, pp. 101–112.

pressed alarm at the conditions then existing and declared "that some remedy must be found, and quickly found, for the misery and wretchedness which press so heavily at this moment on the large majority of the very poor." [33] While recognizing modern evils, the pope attacked the socialists who appeal to envy and hate and maintain that the remedy lies in transferring ownership from private to public bodies.

Ownership, the pope argued, is frequently the result of thrift and is in fact an embodiment of past wages. A remedy that would deprive an owner of his rightful property, he reasoned, is manifestly against justice. Rulers of the state should act with justice so that the poor are protected against avarice and oppression. "Whatever shall appear to be conducive to the well-being of those who work, should receive favorable consideration." One of the first concerns should be "to save the poor workers from the cruelty of grasping men who use human beings as mere instruments for money making." The pope favored regulation of the hours of labor, protection of women and children against excessive toil or labor under harmful conditions, and a minimum wage that will "be enough to support the wage earner in reasonable and frugal comfort."

True social reform, he urged, was dependent upon the cooperation of the church, the state, and organizations of labor. "Man should not consider his outward possessions as his own, but as common to all, so as to share them without difficulty when others are in need." He advised against violence by labor, and pointed out that no practical solution of the labor problem can be found without dependence upon religion. In alleviating conditions the state can help provide for the welfare and comfort of the workers, and also restrain revolutionary agitation. Catholics were urged to support trade unions, but the pope left it to the national experience of the different countries to decide the scope and type of organization.

QUADRAGESIMO ANNO

The views of Pope Leo were affirmed and elaborated in the encyclical letter, *Quadragesimo Anno,* issued in May, 1931, by Pope Pius XI. He points to the influence of *Rerum Novarum* in promoting a Christian social science. "The Encyclical has become in truth a memorable document." Pius points to and approves the encouragement of Christian

[33] *Encyclical on the Condition of the Workmen* by Pope Leo XIII.

labor unions given by his predecessor and he holds it is our "right and our duty to deal authoritatively with social and economic problems."

In this letter the following ideas are stressed: Property has a two-fold aspect, individual and social. Man has a right to own property, but it must be put to proper use. Men must therefore take into consideration not only their own advantage but the common good. "Each class. . . . must receive its due share, and the distribution of created goods must be brought into conformity with the demands of the common good and social justice, for every sincere observer is conscious that the vast differences between the few who hold excessive wealth and the many who live in destitution constitute a grave evil in modern society." The worker needs a wage that will enable him to support his family, to save for all contingencies, and to provide something for those he leaves behind. The pope urged the "re-establishment of vocational groups," and the substitution of the principle of "social justice and social charity" for free competition.

The pope was hostile to communism, but he admitted that programs of moderate socialism "often strikingly approach the just demands of Christian social reformers." Cooperation is therefore possible between reformist socialism and Catholic Social Action, although the pope criticized the socialist views on property.

GUILD SOCIALISM AND DISTRIBUTISM IN ENGLAND

The interest of English Catholics in social reform was due to their opposition to many of the practices of competitive capitalism. The extensive welfare activities of Cardinal Manning revealed to many English Catholics the social derelictions of a capitalistic society. Others followed his example, and concerned themselves with the problems of the poor. At first this effort was largely directed to charitable activities, but the conviction that charity was not enough steadily gained ground.[34]

The Catholic Social Guild was founded in Manchester in 1909 to combine the scattered activities of Catholics concerned with social problems. The guild devoted itself to the study of social questions. It marked the beginning of the Catholic social movement which "stands for the continous

[34] Georgiana Putnam McEntee, *The Social Catholic Movement in Great Britain* (New York: The Macmillan Company, 1927), p. 173.

action of Catholics, in union with the Church, directed towards the establishment of social relationships on a basis corresponding to Catholic conceptions of well being." [35]

As defined by Pope Pius XI, Catholic Social Action is concerned with "works of evident importance in relation to the needs of modern society and adapted to moral and material interests, especially those of the people and the poor classes." [36]

The guild socialists and "distributists" were closely related to Catholic Social Action. They maintained that instead of ending the evils of industrialism, traditional orthodox socialism would intensify them. They were critical of capitalistic competition with its emphasis upon mass production and low costs. In contrast the program of the guilds urged the setting of just prices and wages and the limiting of competition to quality. Guild socialism "attacks the wage system and directs attention to the danger of the Servile State—evils with which every working man is familiar—while it presents him with a vision of a new society in which he may take pleasure in his work." [37]

The guild socialist movement was formally started in 1912. Before that time a group of antistatist reformers led by Gilbert and Cecil Chesterton and Hilaire Belloc attacked both the corruption of capitalism and the dangers of socialism. Capitalism was charged with materialism, neglect of quality, destruction of the creative spirit, and degradation of the individual; socialism was held to be a danger to freedom and liberty.

THE FOUNDERS OF GUILD SOCIALISM

The leaders of guild socialism were writers and professional people. All were critical of modern society and assailed both capitalism and socialism. The mistakes of contemporary economics were held to rest on a basically false philosophy of life

on the belief that work at the best is a disagreeable necessity that it is desirable to reduce to a minimum. In former times it was the normal thing for men to find pleasure and satisfaction in their work. But this is no longer the case. The vast majority of people today do not look for any such pleasure. They work in order to get money to live. Their hearts are not in their work, their real interests

---

[35] Henry Somerville, *Studies in the Catholic Social Movement* (London: Burns Oates & Washbourne, Ltd., 1933), p. 1.

[36] *Ibid.*

[37] Arthur J. Penty, *A Guildsman's Interpretation of History* (London: George Allen & Unwin, Ltd., 1920), p. 299.

are outside, either in the pursuit of pleasure, or in some hobby or occupation extraneous to their daily work.[38]

Two reasons appear to have caused this unfortunate attitude: work is performed at the direction of profiteers; and, work is monotonous and boring. Self-expression through work is, however, a spiritual necessity. The great evil is the specialization of labor engendered by industrialism. It is not opposition to the division of labor as practiced in simpler economic societies, but the splitting of a trade into separate processes which reduces men to automatons and machine tenders, undermines the moral and spiritual life, disintegrates the personality, and leads to worry and insecurity.

The subdivision of labour attacks the crafts; scientific management attacks the man. Its acknowledged object is further to increase output by the elimination of all the motions of the arms and fingers and body that do not directly contribute to the fashioning of the article under process of manufacture. As such it completes the dehumanization and despiritualization of labour begun by the subdivision of labour.[39]

Guildsmen assume that the essential social values are human values, and that Society is to be regarded as a complex of associations held together by the wills of their members, whose well-being is its purpose.[40]

A realization of democracy is possible only by extending it to the economic sphere.

The omnicompetent State, with its omnicompetent Parliament is thus utterly unsuitable to any really democratic community, and must be destroyed or painlessly extinguished as it has destroyed or extinguished its rivals.

The proponents of guild socialism contended that true democracy is based on functional representation, which is the selection of a representative not for the purpose of representing the constituency "in all aspects of citizenship, but only to choose some one to represent his point of view in relation to some particular purpose or a group of purposes, in other words, some particular function."

Guild socialists criticized the approach to the labor problem through price theory. Labor, according to them, is not a dehumanized commod-

---

38 Arthur J. Penty "The Obstacle of Industrialism," in *The Return of Christendom* (London: George Allen & Unwin, Ltd., 1922), p. 134. Reprinted by permission of the publishers.

39 *Ibid.*, p. 136.

40 G. D. H. Cole, *Guild Socialism* (Philadelphia: J. B. Lippincott Company, 1921), pp. 4, 23, 46.

ity, but a human being. Labor must be free both politically and economically. Guildsmen also maintained that work of the best quality can never be achieved in a society where production is governed by financial considerations. Since the citizen's character is strongly determined by his employment, guildsmen argued that "the wage system is the one great barrier against human emancipation." [41]

GUILDS

A guild would be made up of all hand and brain workers in an industry and would include manual, technical, and managerial workers. Following what is called that functional principle, each guild would receive autonomy in its own area. Guilds would be of two types: the industrial, including manufacture, transportation, and agriculture: and the civic, including professions. Guilds would be national in scope and would handle problems such as markets, the purchase of raw materials, and the relations of the guild to other groups. In actual factory management the local guild would play a principal role. Supervisors and foremen would be selected by the guilds and would be responsible to them. Each local guild would choose a local committee, and each of these would select representatives to the regional and national bodies.

Under the guild arrangement the worker would be paid whether he were employed or idle. This program would be based on the individual's need and would continue whether he were well or ill. Guilds would be brought together through a system of guild councils or congresses, which would handle interguild problems and adjust differences. A commune made up of representatives from the guilds and from cooperative societies would represent the interests of consumers. Communes would deal with allocation of resources, with differences among guilds, and with external relations, and would exercise coercive powers. The commune would, in fact, be a "joint body representative of all the major interests and functions in the guild society." [42]

Tactics Tactics of guild socialism have much in common with those of the syndicalists, since both regard the trade union as the vehicle for achieving their aims. Trade unions would be transformed from bargaining agents into instruments of social reorganization, as a first step in the transition from craft or quasi-industrial unions into industrial organizations. By

41 Quoted from S. R. Hobson, *National Guilds*, p. 58, by Niles Carpenter, *Guild Socialism* (New York: Appleton-Century-Crofts, Inc., 1922), p. 147.
42 Carpenter, *op. cit.*, p. 189.

gradual encroachment upon the employer's domain, a functional guild society would be achieved.

Guild socialism is in fact a variant of syndicalism. The absence of violence in its program is perhaps due to its English origin, but its general criticism of parliamentary socialism and of the collectivist state has much in common with the syndicalists, as does the desire to use the trade unions. What distinguishes the guild socialist from the syndicalist is the former's emphasis upon quality and his opposition to many of the technical as distinct from the economic evils of modern society. Moreover, the guild socialist wishes to return to conditions of a better day—those of the Middle Ages.

DISTRIBUTISTS

Like the guild socialists, the distributists are opposed to modern economic organization. Their cure is wider or universal ownership of property. G. K. Chesterton, a leading distributist, felt that "the present system, whether we call it capitalism or anything else, especially as it exists in industrial countries, has already become a danger; and is rapidly becoming a death-trap." [43] Modern industrialism dominated by plutocracy has made Christianity not only unrealizable, but for the majority, even incomprehensible. This state of affairs is not accidental, but is a result of the breakdown of medieval standards and of the institutions based upon them. "Society—a harmony of interwoven purposes, communally organized—gave place to the State, with its monopoly of power for the glorification of its rulers, till the heresies of individualism came to take their intellectual vengeance for the suppressed truth of the claims of human personality." [44] Industrialism has transformed property from a socially useful institution into an instrument of greed. As "our free modern society in which the means of production are owned by a few . . . [is] necessarily in unstable equilibrium and it is tending to reach a condition of stable equilibrium by the Establishment of Compulsory Labour Legally Enforcible Upon Those Who Do Not Own The Means of Production For The Advantage of Those Who Do." [45] Belloc saw the develop-

---

[43] G. K. Chesterton, *The Outline of Sanity* (London: Methuen and Co., 1926), p. 22.

[44] Maurice B. Reckitt, "The Idea of Christendom in Relation to Modern Society," in *The Return of Christendom*, p. 20. Reprinted by permission of George Allen & Unwin, Ltd., publishers.

[45] Hillaire Belloc, *The Servile State* (London: T. N. Foulis, 1912), p. 3. Reprinted by permission of Henry Holt & Co. The following quotations from Belloc are also from this source, pp. 16, 81, 82, 99, 164.

ment of two classes, the free and the unfree, the latter assured by society of minimum standards. Such a society would avoid the strains and tensions of a capitalistic economy, but it would acquire the characteristics of a "Servile State."

The Servile State The Servile State is defined as "arrangement of society in which so considerable a number of the families and individuals are constrained by positive law to labour for the advantage of other families and individuals as to stamp the whole community with the mark of such labour." Men are free if they labor in response to a desire for creative effort or for monetary reward or because of need.

Capitalism, with its concentration of wealth, lays the groundwork for the Servile State. Belloc looks back upon the sixteenth century as the beginning of the evil. With the dissolution of the monasteries and the acquisition of their property by men of wealth, the concentration of property in a relatively few hands began. Capitalism is fundamentally unstable, for "the means of production [re] confined to a body of free citizens, not large enough to make up properly a general character of that society, while the rest are dispossessed of the means of production, and are, therefore, proletarians." Capitalism is based on private ownership, but ownership is not distributed in many hands. In addition, the great majority is without property, politically free but economically without power. From this condition, "it is a necessary inference that there will be under Capitalism a conscious, direct and planned exploitation of the majority, the free citizens who do not own by the minority of owners." Such a society cannot last because it is subject to increasing strain which arises as a result of the divergencies between the moral basis of society and actual social facts. Strain arises, too, as a result of the insecurity which capitalism imposes upon the majority of its citizens.

Solutions Belloc envisaged three possible substitutes for capitalism: slavery, socialism, and property. Man, in view of the traditions of the Western world, will reject a conscious imposition of slavery. Therefore, Belloc argued no reformer would dare to attack the existence of freedom. (This seems a bit optimistic in the light of more recent developments.) Consequently, it is only by changing the distribution of property that reform can be brought about. Two possibilities are envisaged: property can be put in many hands, can be widely distributed; or it can be abolished by placing it in the hands of political officers. The latter is collectivism or socialism. The other solution, wide distribution of property, leads, in contrast, to the distributive state. The proponents of the distributive state are believers in the traditional way of life as exemplified by Christianity.

The test of the Servile State is the existence of laws which distinguish between citizens on the basis of their economic status. Belloc saw the encroachment of the Servile State in the attempt to mitigate the insecurity of the wage earner by compulsory laws and by laws settling wage minima.

We can note in the distributists' criticism of socialism most of the arguments recently advanced by von Hayek. However, in contrast to von Hayek, they do not regard the opportunity for money-making in a free market as either a cardinal virtue or as the test of freedom. To them, economics is subordinate to the good life and does not determine it. To the distributists, freedom is threatened by capitalism, and only by diffusion of property can serfdom be avoided. In common with the Marxists, they envisage the collectivist state arising as a result of the inherent evils in capitalism. In common with Christian socialists, they see the danger of a powerful state in which the individual is reduced to a minor cog; accordingly they advocated a return to widespread property ownership and the elimination of the dominating role of the machine. Like the modern guildsmen, the distributists want to go back to a simpler society, to one in which man controls the tools of his trade and receives joy not only from consuming goods and services but from creating the goods society needs.

26. *REACTIONARY SOCIALISM*

Criticism of competitive capitalism was not limited to those who sought a world of peace, plenty, or greater creative possibility in another system. There were also the reactionary critics who attacked capitalism as a disintegrating social force and looked askance at the humanitarian internationalism advocated by the socialists. This movement, "reactionary socialism," regarded both liberal capitalism, with its emphasis upon individual freedom and laissez faire, and socialism, with its advocacy of international peace and abundance, as its enemies. Although statements of these views can be found in a number of countries, they found their most extreme and virulent expression in Germany. Carlyle and Ruskin, in England, attacked industrialism from antidemocratic points of view; in Germany, socialist views with a strong nationalist tinge were developed by Fichte, by Rodbertus, and, to some extent, by the court preacher, Christian Adolf Stoecker, as the answer to the problems of the time.

JOHANN FICHTE (1762–1814)

Johann Gottlieb Fichte, who was born in a commoner's family, received his first education from his father. He attracted the attention of a nobleman who sent him to a private school; then he finished his studies at the universities of Jena and Leipzig. Upon graduation he served as a private tutor at Zurich, but he soon became absorbed in historical and philosophical studies. At first he leaned to popular sovereignty, and during the French Revolution he defended the right of the people to change their government.

Despite the opposition of conservative circles, he was appointed, in 1794, to the faculty of the University of Jena. He was then a liberal and a democrat, strongly influenced by Rousseau. His stay at Jena was marred by personal disputes and attacks upon his views. He resigned and settled in Berlin, where he joined the circle of Friedrich von Schlegel and Schleiermacher. At first he sympathized with the romantic school headed by the Schlegels, but later he veered in another direction. In 1805, he was appointed to a professorship at the University of Erlangen, but Napoleon's victories forced him to move to Konigsberg. He returned to Berlin in 1807, where he delivered his "Addresses to the German Nation" in which he urged the unity of Germany under the leadership of Prussia. After the founding of the university at Berlin he served as its rector. His impetuous and domineering disposition made him an unsatisfactory leader, and he resigned. He died in 1814, after a short illness, at the age of fifty-two.[1]

At the beginning, Fichte was an ardent Jacobin, defending the French Revolution and arguing that all have the right to leave one political society and form or join another. In substance this constitutes a revolution. He assailed the monarchical form of government as selfish and harmful, for the monarch is always seeking to perpetuate and to enlarge his own rule. Fichte did not long continue this line of thought, however. From an exponent of democracy and cosmopolitanism he changed to an ardent champion of a strong state and a strong nationalism.

The state, he next held, is the basis of freedom through contract. Although it can obtain its objective through education, it must, when necessary, compel submission, for compulsion is based on the sovereignty of the general will. In addition to its educational mission, the state has economic functions. It must guarantee the right to work, and thereby assure freedom and security.[2]

Fichte rejects the notion that the area of state activity should be restricted. On the contrary, the state has the obligation of arranging economic activity so that all will find their proper place. Man satisfies his wants through work, and work should be organized so as to give the maximum satisfaction and happiness to all. His notion of property is related to work, and not to ownership of tangible goods. Property is the right to engage freely in a particular economic activity, and at the same time exclude others.[3] His notion of property is more in harmony with the views of the medieval guilds than with those of a capitalistic society.

To the state is given the power to determine how property, or the

---

[1] Robert Adamson, *Fichte* (Edinburgh: William Blackwood and Sons, 1881), pp. 8–104.

[2] Johann Gottlieb Fichte, *Die Geschlossene Handelsstadt* (Vienna: 1801), pp. 9–12.

[3] *Ibid.*, pp. 84–96.

right to work, is to be used. Producers are the basis of the nation, and he divides them into three groups: those employed on raw materials, on fabrication, and on distribution.

VALUE

Fichte did not regard the precious metals as a proper medium basis for currency. The use of gold and silver to measure value is both artificial and harmful. He advocated grain as a more adequate standard of value, for it is indispensable to the maintenance of life, and is both necessary to and acceptable by all. Therefore he urged the creation of a unit of account based on a bushel of grain. He suggested the issuance of paper or leather notes that would circulate within the country.

Fichte's state would be a closed one, an autarchy. When it had reached its ultimate development it would not be in contact with other states. Thus any commodity could be converted into a national money; in a closed state the intrinsic value of money is slight, for the entire circulation represents only the value of goods.[4]

FOREIGN RELATIONS

Consistent with his belief in autarchy, Fichte wanted to begin limiting trade with other nations. He recognized the immediate difficulty of such a step, but claimed that eventually it could be achieved. Foreign trade would be allowed in those products which, due to climate or the absence of natural resources, could not be produced domestically. International intercourse would be limited to artists, writers, and scholars. National isolation promises the establishment of the highest possible well-being and would enable each citizen to enjoy his proper share of goods and services.[5] Fichte was convinced that his system would lighten the burden of the individual, aid in the reduction of taxes, and eliminate the need for armaments and wars. As a result the nation would develop a particular national character, and "the people will be attached to their fatherland with a fervent love; a high conception of national honor will be fostered."[6]

Fichte believed that the Germans represented a superior type, and he was anxious that it should not be diluted by foreigners. Germans must

[4] *Ibid.*, pp. 67–74.
[5] *Ibid.*, pp. 195–203.
[6] H. E. Engelbrecht, *Johann Gottlieb Fichte* (New York: Columbia University Press, 1933), p. 80.

protect their common characteristics and "avert the downfall of our nation which is threatened by its fusion with foreign peoples."

A primary problem for any epoch is the growth of self-seeking which affects subjects and then rulers and results in a "weakened handling of the reins of power which describes itself in alien words humanity, liberality and popularity." Such feelings are more truly described as "slackness and unworthy conduct." The sad state of things can be changed by education, but not one which exhorts to morality and the good life. Instead, Fichte favors education which moulds the vital impulses and actions.

Fichte defines all the nations of Europe as German, except the Slavs. However, some nations have lost their pristine Germanic purity; they have been corrupted. In contrast true Germans have an original language which demonstrates the ancient lineage of the Germans, who are an *Urvolk*. The criterion of "the German" is the belief in continued racial progress, a belief in Germanic goodness and in its mission.

Only by creating confidence and knowledge will there arise a new Germany. He believed in the creation of a Germany free from foreign influence—independent of world trade, "a closed commercial state would lead to prosperity and the development of the true German spirit."[7]

Fichte in fact anticipated the main Nazi economic policies—autarchy, quotas, armaments, living space, and fiery nationalism. Thus, he may be regarded as an early national socialist.[8]

THOMAS CARLYLE (1795–1881)

Although scarcely on the same level as a philosopher, Thomas Carlyle resembled Fichte in his glorification of the state and his hatred of industrialism.

Carlyle's early life coincided with a period of great distress and unparalleled misery. His father, a farmer and stonemason, found it difficult to earn a living, and this experience aroused the son's deep sympathy for the poor and oppressed. During his studies at Edinburgh University he gave up hope of becoming a minister and turned to literature. He published *Sartor Resartus,* and through Madame de Staël came into contact with Goethe and other German writers. He translated Goethe's

[7] Johann Gottlieb Fichte, *Addresses to the German Nation.* Trans. by R. F. Jones and G. H. Turnbull (Chicago: The Open Court Publishing Co., 1922), p. 4, 231–233.

[8] Rohan D. C. Butler, *The Roots of National Socialism* (New York: E. P. Dutton & Co., 1942), pp. 43–44.

Wilhelm Meister and wrote a life of Schiller. These marked the beginning of a long literary career. In 1839 he entered into a discussion of political problems with his *Chartism*. It is to be noted that he was a student and admirer of German culture and helped to introduce German writers and ideas to England.

Carlyle witnessed the distress at home and abroad which followed the Industrial Revolution. He saw the rise and decline of Chartism, the expansion of the franchise, and the onsweep of reform. Many of the changes he greeted with angry imprecations. The world was facing a crisis, and Carlyle devoted himself to saving man "from the crushing effects of industrialism by restoring to him faith in his humanity; and thus to create through him and his fellows a new society resting upon humane relations." [9]

He opposed the scientific, mechanical, and naturalistic tendencies and wanted to substitute mystery, wonder, and imagination. He rebelled at the prosaic character of a world debilitated by industrialism. What outraged him perhaps more than any other aspect of capitalism was unemployment. The Calvinist to whom work was nature's priceless gift was appalled at the idea that men were without a living, decaying in senseless idleness because none would supply them with work. To deny work is to deny life, not only in the economic sense, but more profoundly in the sense that in work lies the secret of life. Through purposeful effort, man creates order out of chaos, and builds something new and worthy. From the nobility of work, Carlyle concluded that the ablest should be the governors.

What was the remedy for the prevailing disorders? The selection of proper leaders, who by strength and character could lead weaker men out of their thralldom. He therefore scorned democracy and a people's movement, and placed, instead, his faith in the great man.

Vehement in his criticism of laissez faire and the classical economics, Carlyle complained of the senseless sufferings to which man was subjected by modern industrialism:

And yet I will venture to believe that in no time, since the beginnings of Society, was the lot of those same dumb millions of toilers so entirely unbearable as it is even in the days now passing over us. It is not to die, or even die of

9 Frederick W. Roe, *The Social Philosophy of Carlyle and Ruskin* (New York: Peter Smith, 1936), p. 88.

hunger, that makes a man wretched . . . . . but it is to live miserable, we know not why; to work sore and yet gain nothing; to be heartworn, weary, yet isolated; unrelated, girt-in with a cold universal Laissez-faire.[10]

Democracy cannot give the answer for it is incapable of finding any heroes to govern the people.

Carlyle's contempt for democracy and for Parliament as a body of idle talkers led him to place his faith in the select few men of genius. He was repelled by humanitarianism, which he regarded as a sickly creed unworthy of strong men or virile nations. Reform of society must begin by the organization of labor by the state, and by the discarding of the cash nexus which binds employer and employee under capitalism. In its place he would substitute permanent life tenure with a just wage and just conditions as determined by experience. The doors of opportunity must be opened to all, and talent is to be the only credential for the topmost offices that society can bestow.[11] His attacks upon industrialism were continued throughout his life. Uncurbed laissez faire was under constant attack. He demanded leadership and responsibility from those who govern.

Although Carlyle saw the evils of his own time clearly and attacked them with great force, his belief in the heroic virtues and his strictures against Parliament resemble the antidemocratic opinion of a contemporary fascist. Like the latter, he believed in strong governors and a centralized state. As we have seen in our own time, strength and power are not immune to selfish temptations; and decisions that are not subject to review are likely to be burdensome and unjust. Carlyle saw the evils of his own time clearly, but it is doubtful if he was capable of prescribing a remedy.

JOHN RUSKIN (1819–1900)

Ruskin was first attracted to literature and the arts. Beginning in 1843, he published a series of studies on painting and architecture designed to arouse a better appreciation of beauty among his countrymen.

Gradually he became aware of social problems, and "he decided to give

---

10 Carlyle, *Past and Present*.

11 Benjamin Evans Lippincott, *Victorian Critics of Democracy* (Minneapolis: The University of Minnesota Press, 1938), p. 42.

up his art work and deal with a world that made art all but impossible." [12] He became convinced that great art cannot flourish in a world of ugliness and deformity. "How can the springs of English national life to-day be purified so that a true national art may once more be possible? What are the taints of conduct and character, what are the vices and defects of the social order which must be removed before a true national life blossoming in art is attainable?" [13]

Ruskin, like Carlyle, revolted against the empty utilitarianism, corruption, and pauperism he held to be part of his time. Idleness he denounced as the greatest evil afflicting mankind, and he found scant relief from the dreary social panorama no matter where he looked. He therefore decided to examine political and economic questions from a fresh point of view. He attacked economics for confusing the pursuit of commercial wealth with political economy; he also maintained that many assumptions of economic science were erroneous and would lead to social harm. Man is motivated not only by self-interest but by affection and love of beauty.[14]

Ruskin regarded work not as an evil to be avoided but as "a source of supreme delight." Like his master Carlyle, Ruskin abhorred the materialism of his time, the ugliness of the factory towns, and the lack of beauty in the lives of the factory operatives. Devotion to money-making was a sordid business, and he was convinced that large wealth could be achieved only by exploiting the poor. Once an individual has accumulated capital, he argued, he is in the position of using the labor of others for his own profit. Although he admitted that savings may be due to thrift, he concluded that it is the use of savings to employ others which creates differences among rich and poor. Ruskin also recognized, perhaps to a greater extent than many contemporaries, that wealth is a form of power; and that the capitalist does not seek mere accumulation, but power over the lives of men.

Has not the man who has worked for the money a right to use it as he best can? No; in this respect, money is now exactly what mountain promontories over public roads were in old times. The barons fought for them fairly;—the strongest and cunningest got them; then fortified them, and made everyone who passed below pay toll. Well, capital now is exactly what crags were then.

12 *Ibid.*, p. 61.
13 John A. Hobson, *John Ruskin, Social Reformer* (London: James Nisbet & Co., 1899), p. 39.
14 *Ibid.*, p. 62.

Ruskin maintained that wherever the accumulation of money is the main object "it does harm both in the getting and spending." [15]

Political economy also errs in condoning inequality in wealth and in failing to raise the question of the origin of differences in wealth, or of whether wealth was obtained by moral or immoral means. It emphasizes only acquisitiveness, which often leads to ostentation and vulgarity and the denial of beauty.

Ruskin denied that competition was an equitable means of determining price. "Since profit, not excellence of work, is the admitted motive, the individual producer is purely self-engrossed, his selfishness not being tempered by any sense of social service: in all the processes of buying and selling this selfishness is accentuated by the sharp antagonism between himself and his competitors." [16] Nor would competition necessarily compel the creation of the best possible product. Moreover, work should be a source of joy and should be sought in the same manner as a creative artist seeks and enjoys his activity. Man should not be driven to work by need, but by the desire to express himself.

THE RIGHT SOCIAL ORDER

The basis for all of Ruskin's proposals was the belief that everyone "must do the work which he can do best, and in the best way, for the common good and not for individual profit, receiving in return property consisting of good things which he has honestly got and can skilfully use." Ruskin therefore advocated state supervision of marriage, and to develop both physical and mental faculties, he would supply each child with good food, housing, clothing, and education.

He would allow each person to perform the job for which he was best fitted, and he hoped to limit income. He favored the establishment of a system of guilds which, like their medieval predecessors, would regulate quality, quantity, and price. However, he left room for profits, for master guildsmen could, after paying wages and sick and old-age pensions, retain the remainder.

He opposed monopoly in the ownership of land, and argued that the state should encourage peasant proprietorship. Land should belong to those who use it and not to absentee landlords. He also favored a

15 John Ruskin, *The Crown of Wild Olive* (New York: Merrill and Batzer, no date), p. 21.
16 Hobson, *op. cit.*, p. 131. The following quotations from Ruskin are from this source, pp. 154, 179, 184, 185.

"publicly organized industry for use . . . . the abolition of rent and interest . . . the establishment of a labour-basis of exchange." His views thus seem to be a combination of single tax and socialism. In contrast to Continental socialism, but in harmony with the English variety, Ruskin believed that religion could perform a vital function. There is a place for "spiritual authority, derived from the Fatherhood of God, and administered on earth by divinely appointed bishops and by a hierarchy of 'orders' penetrating all the details of social life."

Ruskin was a believer in authority and a critic of democracy. "It is not merely a disbelief in the efficacy of representative institutions, but a deeper distrust of the ability of the people to safeguard or advance their true interests." He is an exponent of order and he has only scorn for the doctrines of liberty and equality. Liberal democracy was, for him, a disruptive force and a negation of reason.

Ruskin's criticism of modern industrialism was frequently shrewd and penetrating. He saw its ugliness and misery, but he failed to appreciate its more attractive qualities. Modern industry has raised the living standards, even though not sufficiently, and it has made available many comforts to the poor that otherwise would be denied them. A wealthy art critic may decry the cheapening of life and goods, but the ordinary man, wearied and dulled by overwork, could not in ages past enjoy the artistic beauties nor consume the finely fashioned goods chiseled by master craftsmen. Ruskin's criticism fell partly off the mark, his hatred of liberty and democracy foreshadowing the anticapitalist movements of the twentieth century.

JOHANN KARL RODBERTUS (1805–1875)

Johann Karl Rodbertus did not exercise an influence on the mass movements inspired by socialism. Some writers sometimes regarded him as entitled to question the originality of Marx's formulations, and Friedrich Engels regarded the charges that Marx had plagiarized from Rodbertus as deserving of an answer.[17] Although a conservative, Rodbertus reached socialist conclusions.

Rodbertus, a member of a German academic family, lived the life of a landed proprietor. He was a member of the Provincial Diet and of the Constituent Assembly in 1849. For a short time he served in the cabinet.

17 See Preface to Karl Marx, *Capital* (Chicago: Charles H. Kerr and Company, 1913), Vol. II.

With the onset of reaction, he retired to his estates, where he devoted himself to social and economic studies until his death.

Rodbertus looks upon society as a growth, "the instinct which impels man to combine into societies, at first in small groups, then in larger ones, but always with a constant straining towards extension, it is the social principle encountered in history." [18] It is "the growing union of individuals in history, widening its range in successive periods, and always increasing its strength."

Political government gives expression to the common social existence and to the capacity of a particular society to combine its conflicting units. The direction of social life is to some degree determined by economic forces. The essential feature of economic life is labor, and "labor is the cost of wealth"; only upon the recognition of this principle can a correct theory of distribution be evolved. As long as wealth does not become luxury, inequality may be avoided. However, poverty and wealth are relative terms. Poverty is defined as the inability of any person to supply himself with the commodities proper to his place in society. Consequently, Rodbertus argued, as the working class advances, its wants increase, and consequently its feeling of poverty must be greater even if its income is the same. This is akin to Marx's theory of increasing misery, as interpreted by those who believe that Marx implies *psychological misery*.

In contrast to Marx, Rodbertus believed that progress can be obtained most effectively by compromise. Progress in one direction sometimes leads to lack of progress elsewhere. This is a sort of "opportunity cost" of progress. Inequality of wealth makes possible the development of an educated class which fosters and expands our cultural heritage.

THE STATE

Rodbertus assumed that the transition of society into a state or national existence opened up for it greater possibilities. A modern state allows for a wide division of labor which, he held, is the basis of modern civilization, and the foundation upon which modern culture rests. However, the division of labor makes for greater association and for a greater dependence of parts upon the whole. Rodbertus believed that society has taken only a first step and that what we need is a greater association, the

[18] E. C. K. Gonner, *The Social Philosophy of Rodbertus* (London: Macmillan & Co., 1899), p. 60. The following quotations from Rodbertus are from this source, pp. 65, 76, 79, 105.

impediment to which exists in private property of land and capital, an "undue survival of a form of property which at one time was admittedly a necessary part of a necessary system."

Rodbertus saw the modern state as lacking in social principles, for

social functions . . . . which should be performed by society are in the hands of individuals who act in accordance with individual motives, and so in place of social ordering and direction of production, all the direction that there is, lies in the blind and expensive workings of competition; a condition of things due to the existence of private property in land and capital.

Owners of capital and land, the means of production, direct the economic mechanism, and are involving the state in serious danger.

VALUE

Like Marx and the classicists, Rodbertus held value to be dependent upon labor. Although labor is the cause of all value,

in modern competitive society it stands in a different position, since under the pressure of competition, and in the face of ownership in private hands of the land and capital necessary for production, the amount given to labor is prevented from rising above the amount necessary to its maintenance. In this way labor itself is treated as a marketable commodity exchanging against its cost of subsistence as other commodities exchange according to their costs of production, and what is called surplus value is exhibited.

Surplus value is the difference between that which those who work should receive in exchange for their labor by right of its claim as the sole producing force, and that which they do receive when their wages and salaries are measured along the line of subsistence.

DISTRIBUTION

The national income is divided into wages paid to labor and rent paid to owners of property. Rent is used to designate all forms of property income rather than merely the return from land. Acquisition of rent depends upon the worker's producing a surplus in excess of his subsistence, and upon the existence of social institutions permitting appropriation of the product of labor by a class of owners. Rent is divided among several types of property owners. Rent on capital is paid to the capitalist, and land rent is paid to the landlord; both are based on possession.

In the division of the national income, every increase in the productivity of labor must lead to a relatively diminishing share to labor.[19] Thus depression, overproduction, and pauperism arise. Therefore an increase in national income leads to more physical poverty for the majority because the buying power of the majority of society continually diminishes.

To repeat, according to Rodbertus, interest and profit are forms of rent arising out of ownership and lending of capital, and ground rent is derived from ownership of land. No rent is possible unless the worker produces a surplus beyond the amount needed for his maintenance. No surplus could exist if it were not taken from the worker and given to others. The ability of others to appropriate the surplus[20] is based on the system of ownership, and on the worker's ability to produce a surplus in excess of his subsistence. As an increase in productivity of labor enables the worker to produce his maintenence in a shorter period, the portion going to land and capital steadily increases with economic progress. Rodbertus drew the conclusion that, as a consequence, labor would be excluded from the advantages of technical progress, and the position of labor would deteriorate while the nation as a whole improved its standards.[21]

CRISIS

Industrial crises are ever-recurring modern phenomena, the result of an incorrect division of the social product into wages and profit, which inevitably leads to underconsumption. The income going to labor is sufficient to buy back only part of the output, and an eventual cessation of production is inevitable. The division of the social income means that landlords and capitalists are unable to consume the entire amounts received by them. In contrast, labor, capable of greater consumption, is not provided with sufficient purchasing power to secure it. Investing the income not spent for consumption is only a temporary palliative, for investment in capital leads to increasing output of consumers' goods and makes the problem of underconsumption more serious.[22] Nor is the problem solved by investing in plants producing luxury goods, for the receivers of rent are unwilling to consume all of their income, and when the new equipment is available, a surplus of luxury goods will be pro-

[19] Carl Rodbertus-Jagetzow, *Deutscher Staat und Sozialismus* (Potsdam: Alfred Prote, 1935), pp. 78–84.
[20] *Ibid.*, pp. 61–64.
[21] *Ibid.*, pp. 7–11.
[22] *Ibid.*, pp. 42–43.

duced. Rodbertus saw this condition as becoming worse rather than better, for with increasing productivity, the proportional share going to labor tends to diminish.[23]

SOCIALISM

For the future, Rodbertus visualized a socialist system in which private property in the means of production would be absent. The state would control and direct industry. He did not fear that the nature of the demand for goods would be unknown to the central authority. The difficulty involved was recognized, but he believed that it could be overcome by reference to past and present production. As gain would not be a motive for economic activity, Rodbertus believed that the state would produce only what is useful. State control of capital would make possible its increase and replacement whenever required. Labor would benefit, for it would not be forced to wait on demand or be idle. National income would be divided among producers in accordance with their contribution to production. Under these conditions political freedom is not important, since it is only desirable as an instrument for attaining a more equitable economic position.[24]

A number of remedial measures could be immediately taken: restriction of the incomes from land and capital; prevention of absolute and relative reductions in wages; protection of labor against unemployment.

Rodbertus, while not a believer in force and violence, was a collectivist who placed little emphasis upon political freedom, and glorified the state. His intellectual arsenal contained some of the weapons that could be used by the National Socialists. In contrast to Marx, Rodbertus placed Germany above class and party. He was less a socialist than a nationalist.

EVANGELICAL-SOCIAL MOVEMENT

"The Evangelical-Social Movement has, fundamentally, one single aim which is expressed in the name itself." It began in Germany as a result of the dissatisfaction of Christian clergymen and writers with the social evils of the time. In speech and writing, the evils of capitalism were subjected to sharp criticism.

23 Karl Rodbertus, *Overproduction and Crises.* Translated by Julia Franklin (London: Swan Sonnenschein, 1898), p. 49.
24 Karl Rodbertus, *Die Forderungen der Arbeitenden Klassen* (Frankfort on the Main: Vittorio Klosterman, 1946), p. 9.

The movement, largely concerned with the religious aspects of the problem, sought to set in motion the whole moral and religious force of Evangelical Christianity for the help of those masses of mankind who not so much through their fault as of our social conditions, have an uncertain livelihood, unhealthy dwellings, insufficient food, too little employment, too low wages, too long hours, and unsuitable work-places, and thus suffer in their whole intellectual and moral development.[25]

Yet the movement itself ended in this blind alley of anti-Semitism, and helped to prepare the ground for Nazi propaganda.

JOHANN WICHERN (1808–1881)

Johann Wichern, the pioneer and leader of evangelical social thought and the creator of the "Inner Mission" or Home Mission, introduced the idea of social Christianity in Germany in 1848. He demanded the application of the Christian spirit to social and economic relations. Wichern not only advanced an idea, but sought to bring practice into line with theory. In the name of Jesus he established homes for neglected boys and trained workers for home-mission tasks. While aware of the need of basic reforms, Wichern largely concerned himself with personal benevolence. "Wichern is certainly the father of the evangelical-social idea, but not the originator of the Evangelical-Social Movement, which aims at transforming the idea into action by means of social reform." [26] His activity aimed at reform, and was not designed to introduce changes in social and economic conditions.

VICTOR AIMÉ HUBER (1800–1869)

Victor Huber tried to carry further the views of his friend Wichern. The modern social problem was due, he believed, to the existence of a rootless and propertyless proletariat. After his graduation from the University of Göttingen, Huber became interested in cooperation, and tried to interest the conservative public in this movement. Unable to gain the support of the conservatives, but undeterred, he continued to devote himself to the promotion of his objective.

Instead of stressing a proletarian revolution, he believed that society

25 Paul Göhre, *The Evangelical-Social Movement in Germany*. Translated by Janet and E. Kay Shuttleworth (London: Ideal Publishing Union, 1898), p. 9.
26 *Ibid.*, p. 15.

must "by means of voluntary effort re-collect the isolated atoms in cooperation, and by the re-union of employers and employed in the process of production as well as of distribution. But this depends on the re-awakening of the fraternal spirit, and therefore must have religion for its basis." [27] Christian love was the force which unites man with man and produces a spirit of self-sacrifice and devotion to the common good.

Huber proposed "Inner Colonization," the forming of colonies of about one hundred and fifty families. A central power plant would supply energy, and food would be purchased wholesale and prepared jointly. Thus money, fuel, and labor would be saved. Machinery would be purchased from a fund set up by common voluntary savings. All forms of cooperation—producers', consumers', and credit—were approved. However, they were to be promoted through the self-help of workers and the aid of Christian men of culture and property, and not by the state. Well-to-do Christians were obligated to foster cooperatives, which were the embodiment of brotherly love, solidarity, mutual aid, and peace. Huber stressed not mere beneficence and alms but Christian social reform. Mistrusting political action, he hoped the workers would depend upon the leadership of Christian men of wealth and education.

RUDOLF TODT (1839–1887)

Rudolf Todt, another leader of evangelical reform, approved of the criticism voiced by the socialists, but he opposed what he claimed were their atheistic and communistic ideas. He advised Christian leaders to take a position against economic injustice and thus reassert their leadership for social peace. He demanded that the wealthy acknowledge their Christian responsibility and recognize the worth of labor and the fact that the worker is not a commodity. He pleaded against undue concentration on worldly goods to the neglect of spiritual wealth. His practical program called for a revival of the laws against usury; reform of limited-liability laws; establishment of credit banks for landed property and loans for workers and tradesmen; acquisition by the state of banks, dwellings, and insurance companies; setting up of "compulsory corporations in every trade all over the empire"; and the establishment of insurance against sickness, old age, and accidents. He demanded that the

27 Rev. M. Kaufmann, *Christian Socialism* (London: Kegan Paul, Trench, Trubner & Co., 1888), p. 143.

church be fearless on social subjects and that candidates for holy orders be trained in political economy.[28]

He argued that "every Christian *must* be a socialist, but not a social-democrat. To the atheistical social democracy we must oppose a Christian Socialism." Holy Scripture must be the basis of social reform, which could be founded not on individual benevolence but upon organized political action. Despite his belief in political action, Todt was conservative in his outlook and "true Christian-social Christianity was only conceivable to him in a conservative garb."

Todt attempted to carry his ideas into practice and helped to form the Central Union for Social Reform. The organization was to prepare a program of social improvement based on religious and monarchical principles. Adolf Stoecker became one of its leaders and began to advocate a violent anti-Semitism.

CHRISTIAN ADOLF STOECKER (1835–1909)

Christian Adolf Stoecker recognized that the urban workers were becoming hostile or indifferent to the church. Their indifference, if not their hostility, was due to the failure of Christian leaders to concern themselves actively with the social and economic problem of the masses.[29] Under his leadership, the Christian Social party was founded. It espoused Christian principles and rejected social democracy as atheistic. Among the party's objectives were the lessening of the gap between rich and poor and the bringing about of a greater measure of security. It favored "introduction of compulsory associations, separate ones for each trade, but extending throughout the whole empire." [30]

Compulsory arbitration and funds for widows and orphans were to be established. Trade associations were to be allowed to protect their members' interests, and state control was to be exercised over funds. A progressive income tax and one on stock exchange transactions were to be imposed and labor conditions regulated.[31]

At first the members of the Christian Social party were workers, but

28 Göhre, *op. cit.*, pp. 28–29. The following quotations from Todt are from this source, pp. 30, 43.

29 Walter Frank, *Hofprediger Adolf Stoecker* (Hamburg: Hanseatische Verlagsanstalt, 1935), pp. 13–17.

30 Quotation in *Göhre, op. cit.*, p. 59.

31 *Ibid.*, 59–60. The following quotations are from this source, pp. 74, 75.

soon ceasing to gain new members among Berlin workmen, it began to attract largely middle-class people.

Nevertheless many new members joined the Party, but they no longer were factory operatives, but artisans, small shop-keepers and small officials. Also a small number of the so-called higher classes, scholars and students, retired officers, even aristocrats. But the majority were artisans, shop-keepers and officials. Naturally this majority wished and demanded to have their own interests represented and fought for by the new social party when they joined it. The fulfillment of their wish found expression in anti-Semitism which soon became the real program of the Party.

This was a natural outcome "of the almost total withdrawal of the Berlin operatives . . . and the entrance of the Berlin lower middle-class with its interests into the Party."

Stoecker's agitation was an early and perhaps less violent form of Nazism. It combined a superficially radical social program with Jewish hatred. Stoecker attributed the social evils of our time, not to the concentration of industry, but to the concentration of money which debilitates and destroys the middle class. Stoecker boasted in a speech to the Prussian Landtag in 1893 that he had transformed anti-Semitism from a literary topic to a political problem. He was an early "racist" demagogue, who sought to channel the growing social discontent against the Jews rather than against capitalism. His appeal was successful with the middle classes, which faced Jewish competitors in business and the professions. Stoecker showed that illogical racist views could gain a following although conditions were not yet ripe for a racist to win power.

27. *GERMAN REACTIONARY SOCIALISM*

NATIONAL SOCIALISM

The chief ideas of national socialism, nationalism, racism, and social-ism can be traced to a long line of writers and politicians. In this regard German national socialism differs from Italian fascism. The latter was in-fluenced by the doctrine of Sorel and by French syndicalism, itself a variant of Marxism and anarchism. Therefore fascism can be traced to Marxism, although its extreme nationalism and "heroism" would mark it as a degenerate form of the Marxist system. In contrast, the intellectual lineage of national socialism shows no trace of the Marxist influence, for both Marxism and Marxists were always hostile to racism and racists. Moreover, as we have seen, there are direct lines of thought in Germany in which can be found all of the dogmas which subsequently became articles of faith of the Nazi movement. Emphasis upon the peculiar na-ture of Germanic qualities can be found in Fichte, as can the doctrine of autarchy and state socialism. Nazism is unrelated and even intellectually hostile to Marxism. The latter rejects the emphasis upon national traits. Instead of recognizing anything peculiar or unusual about races, Marx-ism asserts that races and people as well as individuals are the malleable materials of environment and history.

The leaders of Nazism were all hostile to Marxist ideas. Not a single one ever showed understanding of or sympathy for the Marxist cause. In the unsettled era between the two world wars, these men could come to the top because Marxism, as embodied in the German social democ-racy and the Communist party, lacked a program. In the eyes of many, these groups were an official opposition whose litany sounded as stale and uninspiring as the claims of those in power. Following the close of World War I, thousands of army officers found themselves without a career.

"And since these intellectuals in uniform found no career and no bread in the breakdown after the peace, their officer days remained for many the high point of their existence; the hope for a return of the golden days remained their secret ambition." [1]

Perhaps if Germany had not faced a series of crises, these ambitions would have remained unrealized, but the period was one of trouble and turbulence in which new ideas and slogans finally carried the day. The defeat of German arms in World War I was denied by these Germans, and the Allied victories were attributed to conspiracy and betrayal on the home front. The volunteer military or free corps that spread throughout the country subsequently furnished the storm troopers and elite formations of the Nazi party.

On March 7, 1918, Anton Drexler organized the Committee for Independent Workmen in Munich. Its purpose was the securing of an honorable peace for Germany. This small group, composed of about forty people, constituted the beginning of the National Socialist German Workers' party,[2] which was later destined to conquer Germany, Europe, and for a time, to subjugate directly a greater surface of the world than any group or conqueror in history had done.

Drexler, a locksmith by trade, while opposed to the socialistic trade unions, did not approve of the *status quo*. He sought a patriotic socialism, one that was nationalistic and German in mood and action. During 1918, Drexler had joined a group that claimed to be promoting peace along working-class lines; as a result of this experience he reached the opinion that a militarily disciplined labor party was needed. With the advent of the German Revolution, Drexler reorganized his group in 1919 as the German Workers' party, which later became the National Socialist German Workers' party.[3] The first chairman was Karl Harrer, whose place was subsequently taken by Anton Drexler.[4]

ADOLF HITLER (1882-1945)

The movement was dominated and molded from the beginning by Adolf Hitler, an Austrian and the son of a minor official. One of the most evil and repellent figures in history, he was nonetheless a politician of

[1] Konrad Heiden, *Der Fuehrer* (New York: Lexington Press, 1944), pp. 20–33.

[2] Konrad Heiden, *A History of National Socialism* (New York: Alfred A. Knopf, Inc., 1935), p. 3.

[3] *Ibid.*, p. 7.

[4] Adolf Hitler, *Mein Kampf* (Boston: Houghton Mifflin Company, 1941), pp. 505–506.

some genius on the domestic and international plane. The enormity of his crimes is matched only by the size of his achievements. There have been many, and there shall be infinitely more, attempts to diagnose this diabolical figure, but his greatness as a political strategist and his ability as a tactician will probably never be denied. A hateful and disgusting individual, he was yet one of the great masters of the art of politics and government.

Adolf Hitler was not an outstanding student. At an early age he left for Vienna, where he began the study of art, but, his money exhausted, he found employment as a bricklayer's assistant. He refused to join a labor union, and was forced from the job. His enmity toward the socialist and labor movements may have stemmed from this hapless experience in Vienna. He now turned to the study of architectural drawing.

During this time, Vienna was governed by the Christian Socialist party, which was anti-Semitic in outlook. Hitler developed a racist anti-Semitism in contrast to the religious anti-Semitism of Karl Lueger, the Viennese bourgomaster. Franz Borkenau has explained Hitler's views on the ground that many successful Austrian Jews were baptized and were thus protected from religious anti-Semitism.

In 1912, Hitler moved to Munich, and with the outbreak of World War I, he joined the German army. His regiment participated in heavy fighting, suffered high losses, and Hitler won the Iron Cross.[5]

Upon his release from military service Hitler was attracted to the postwar agitations which were stirring Germany. The national socialist movement grew slowly, but from the beginning it drew to its ranks an aggressive following of young soldiers and others ready to brawl and fight. Hitler almost immediately assumed leadership, and, after he ousted Anton Drexler, the founder and chief of the party, he was in command as its President. This victory of 1921 was due to strong financial support and to his political astuteness.[6]

From the beginning, Hitler's appeal was made to the middle classes, who were being crushed between the rising working class and expanding capitalism. Clerks, shopkeepers, and minor officials unable to keep up with rising prices while seeing their "inferiors," the workers, gain in prestige and economic position, found in Hitler a fiery spokesman for their voiceless anger.

This mass, neglected by fate and the new German government, was

[5] Hitler has given the facts of his life in *Mein Kampf*.
[6] Heiden, *A History of National Socialism*, pp. 51–53.

especially enraptured by Hitler's anti-Semitism, for had it not suffered at the hands of Jewish competitors? What is even more important, the Nazi leaders, convinced, erroneously, that the German socialist and labor movement had built its power on cunning and deception, worked out techniques of mass agitation unrivaled by any other political party.

On November 9, 1923, a *Putsch* in Munich was attempted under Hitler's leadership, but it was put down. Hitler and a number of followers were tried and condemned to nine months' imprisonment. That the trial was used to good advantage can be seen from the thirty-two seats in the Reichstag captured by the Nazis in the elections of May, 1924. For a time this was the high mark of Nazi success. Internal dissension and stabilization of economic conditions brought about the party's decline. In 1928, it elected only twelve deputies to the national parliament.

However, it had grown to a membership of sixty thousand, and Germany was on the eve of a great economic and political crisis. In 1929, Hitler concluded an arrangement with Dr. Alfred Hugenberg, the leader of the German Nationalist party, to protest against the Young plan, which spread reparation payments over sixty years. The annual payments were to reach a maximum by 1965, and then progressively decline. The operations were to be carried out through an international bank, and Germany could ask for a revision in the event of an unforseen crisis. The economic crisis that spread over Germany in 1928 had swelled the ranks of Hitler's party. Germany's unemployed jumped from three million to six million in the years between 1930 and 1932. These official figures underestimate the actual number of the unemployed and take no account of the partially employed.[7]

From the beginning, the Nazi party had organized "defense sections" to protect its meetings against opponents. In August, 1921, the *Sturm Abteilung* (Storm Detachment) was established, presumably for gynmastics and sports. Hitler defined its aim in the first regulations: "The S.A. is not only intended to be a means of defense for the movement, but above all a training school for the coming struggle for liberty." [8] Recruited mainly from the ranks of the former free corps, and headed by an able freebooter, Captain Ernst Röhm, these were to become the Nazi shock troops. Later the S.S. (*Schutzstaffel*) was organized. They were the elite fighters, the guard detachments who were loyal to Hitler personally.

[7] *Ibid.*, pp. 122–125.
[8] Quotation, *ibid.*, p. 82.

To these troops was entrusted the protection of the leaders; they were the eyes and ears of the party, the bravest corps.

PRINCIPLES OF NATIONAL SOCIALISM

National socialism, as its name implies, was a fusion of socialism and nationalism. Its socialism was petty bourgeois rather than revolutionary. Its economic program was epitomized in the twenty-five points originally formulated by Gottfried Feder in 1920. It demanded abolition of unearned incomes, confiscation of war profits, socialization of trusts, and reform of the agrarian law. In addition it preclaimed the "Good of the state before the Good of the individual." According to Hitler,

Feder's merit was that he outlined, with ruthless brutality, the character of the stock exchange and loan capital that was harmful to economy, and that he exposed the original and eternal presupposition of interest. His arguments were so correct in all its [sic] fundamental questions that those who criticized them from the beginning denied less the theoretical correctness of the idea but rather the practical possibility of its execution.[9]

Actually the Nazi party never developed a coherent economic theory. The leadership was made up of freebooters, declassed intellectuals, and small middle-class people; hence it was likely to be biased against big business, and to advocate an unintegrated socialist policy.

FOLK STATE

The "folk state" was another Nazi dogma. According to Hitler,

the highest purpose of the folkish State is the care for the preservation of those racial primal elements which, supplying culture, create the beauty and dignity of a higher humanity. We as ARYANS, are therefore able to imagine a State only to be the living organism of a nationality which not only safeguards the preservation of that nationality, but which, by a further training of its spiritual and ideal abilities, leads it to the highest freedom.[10]

Like many of his ideas, the notion of "folk" can be traced to earlier writers. The idea of the importance of the German *Volk* was first examined by the German historian Johann Gottfried Herder in the latter part of the eighteenth century. Nations, he maintained, had distinctive qualities, and behind these national qualities stood the national soul or

[9] Hitler, *op. cit.*, p. 283.
[10] *Ibid.*, p. 595.

genius. Following Herder, Karl Friedrich von Schlegel argued that the highest form of state was the one embracing all members of one tribe or folk. According to him

[the] older and purer and more unmixed the racial stock, the more national customs it will have, and the more national customs and steadfastness and attachment to these, the more it will be a nation. . . . . . Every state is an individual existing independently for itself; it is unconditionally its own master; it has its peculiar character and governs itself according to its peculiar laws, customs and usages.[11]

The next and final step in the development of racial mythology was taken by the historian Joseph Görres, who, writing in the first part of the nineteenth century, argued that it was the tie of blood which held the "folk" together.

No human power can hold back a folk which matures within itself to great historical character. . . . What is above all necessary is that in the center of the nation a firm and definite public opinion should form itself which expresses decisively and unmistakably the peculiarities of the racial strain.[12]

Closely related to the idea of the importance of race or "folk" is the notion of the superiority of the German people. Ideas of the superiority of the Germanic races were woven into the inner texture of Nazi doctrine. At first formulated by Count Arthur de Gobineau in his *Essay on the Inequality of the Human Races,* it was accepted by the composer Richard Wagner and further developed by Wagner's son-in-law, the expatriate Englishman, Houston Stewart Chamberlain. These views gained wide acceptance in nationalist circles, and Hitler held that

[if] one were to divide mankind into three groups: culture-founders, culture-bearers and culture-destroyers, then as the representative of the first kind only the Aryan would come in question. It is from him that the foundation and the walls of all human creations originate and only the external form and color depend on the characterisitcs of the various people involved.[13]

Side by side with the glorification of the Aryan went a bitter denunciation of the Jew. The latter attitude was also part of the tradition, for Fichte, Görres, Wagner, and Chamberlain were violent anti-Semites, and

[11] Quoted from Schlegel, *Philosophische Vorlesungen aus den Jahren 1804 bis 1806,* II, 57, in Raymond Murphy and Others, *National Socialism* (Washington, D. C.: U. S. Government Printing Office, 1943), p. 6.
[12] Quotation from Görres, *Gesammelte Schriften,* III, 413, *ibid.,* p. 6.
[13] Hitler, *op. cit.,* p. 398.

Hitler surpassed them all. With Hitler, anti-Semitism was an obsession, but it was used with diabolical cunning and it undoubtedly brought a sympathetic response from the *déracine* petty bourgeois and placeless professionals that abounded in Hitler's Germany. It appealed to the prejudice, hate, and folly that is found in all people, especially a people suffering severe economic and political trials.

FÜHRER

With the racist principle went the doctrine of the "leader." Antidemocratic ideas have always had a following among German intellectuals. In the years following World War I they were presented by Moeller van den Bruck,[14] who urged the avoidance of decadent parliamentarianism. What the German people needed was a leader and not a counting of hands. Once the true leader came to the fore, the masses would follow, and the democratic and socialist parties would be driven to perdition.

Between the leader and the people stood the party, an elite ruling class. Although authority within the nation comes from the people, it is the ruling group organized in the party which expresses the people's will. The party is the select and most conscious part of the German people and

the Party stands above and beside the State as the wielder of an authority derived from the people with its own sovereign power and its own sphere of sovereignty . . . . . The legal position of the party is therefore that of a completely sovereign authority whose legal authority and self-sufficiency rest upon the original independent political authority which the Führer and the movement have attained as a result of their historical achievements.[15]

The Nazi party was an elite, its members ultimately responsible to, and deriving their power from the leader. National Socialist ideology gave the most important place to the "leader." A leader is an absolutist monarch who has been catapulted to the top by a mass movement and is above the law. He is the absolute ruler of the state machine, and it is to him rather than to the nation or the people that fealty is sworn. Franz Neumann has described this doctrine as "charismatic leadership." [16] It is

[14] *Germany's Third Empire.* Translated by E. Lorimer (London: George Allen & Unwin, Ltd., 1934).

[15] Quotation from Gauweiler, *Rechtseinrictungen und Rechtsaufgaben der Bewegung* in Murphy, *op. cit.,* p. 42.

[16] Franz Neumann, *Behemoth* (London: Victor Gollancz, Ltd., 1942), pp. 73–81.

clear that National Socialism had no elaborate theory. Offering only a vague program of reform, it appealed to the frustrations and prejudices of Germans. Events, nevertheless, favored the Nazis. Had not the German economy been engulfed by the world crises, the Nazi party might never have won power, for the temporary stabilization in 1924 had not only halted the progress of the Nazis, but had in fact reduced it to an annoying but far from powerful minority. Germany and the world might have been saved from their most agonizing experience.

Who was to blame for the Nazi rise to power? At this stage in history the answer is not simple. Certainly the failure of the left to solve or even to ameliorate the mounting crisis in the German economy contributed to the rise of the Nazis. The Social Democrats and the trade unions lacked a positive policy. Their claim that they were hampered by the Communists may be true but is nevertheless irrelevant. If the Social Democrats had had anything to offer, the Communists would never have been able to make their substantial gains during the crisis. The fact is that the Social Democrats and the trade unions have never had a policy capable of coping with a severe depression, one likely to put a strain on the social fabric. Attuned to making small and steady gains, they are left bewildered and without a plan by a sharp social crisis.

Nor did the Communists show any greater awareness of the situation. Bewitched by the Marxist analysis, they were unable to visualize any answer to the crisis but the one they derived from perusing the Marxist classics. To them the situation and the answer were simple. Consequently they continued their policy of encouraging a division between labor and the forces of the left, justifying their policy by the specious argument of "unity from below" as if it were possible to unite two movements on a common program except through the leaders, who are, in fact, appointed stewards of their organizations.

The Nazis, whose gains in earlier elections were not alarming, gained 107 seats and polled 6,400,000 votes in the elections of September, 1930. Such staggering gains in so short a time were without parallel in German history. A series of maneuvers now began, with a substantial number of industrialists playing with Hitler. Efforts to find an alternative government to the one the Nazis offered were made, but no combination showed ability to cope with the crisis. For a time it seemed that General Kurt von Schleicher might succeed. He had a program for establishing a wide coalition which he hoped could ride out the storm and prevent the Nazis from taking power. Moreover, there were signs that the Nazis had reached their peak and that the tide was receding. But these signs were false. Hitler and the Nazis showed that they were not to be easily cast aside, and played their hand in masterful fashion.

> The game which the National Socialists played with the Communists in the last months of their fight for power will always be remembered as a masterpiece of political strategy. They systematically shattered the political order of Germany by fighting in the streets with the Communists and collaborating with them in Parliament. In the Reichstag they destroyed the basis of government; on the streets they destroyed the peace.[17]

Von Schleicher's attempt to govern met with failure. The large industrialists hated the Weimar Republic, the trade unions, and the left. Here was a chance to smash the whole body of social legislation and free themselves from the trade-union octopus. Other hopes were not absent. Nationalists looked forward to a rearmed and militant Germany, again on the prowl for loot and conquest. The issue that was to raise Hitler to power was the payment of subsidies to the East Prussian Junkers. Von Hindenburg, himself a member of these families, forced the resignation of von Schleicher, whose government was replaced by a Nazi-Nationalist combination on January 30, 1933. Whatever hope may have existed that the Nationalists could keep a check on the Nazis was soon dispelled. By a series of bold steps the Nazis suppressed the opposition, utilizing the Reichstag fire, set by themselves, to suppress the Communists, then the Socialists, the trade unions, and finally all other groups not part of the Nazi system of organization. A totalitarian state with Hitler as absolute dictator was instituted, and the fearful campaign of suppressing internal opponents and waging foreign war was begun.

The Nazis had no definite program of social reorganization. Aside from power, they were not certain what they wanted. However, the Nazis did not achieve power in order to become the cat's-paw for financiers and industrialists. At many points the Nazis agreed with those groups—but not on the subject of sharing power. The Nazi ranks were not closed to men of property, but the latter derived their strength from membership in the Nazi party rather than the reverse. Although the rich and powerful flocked to the Nazi banner, it was rather an indication that those in power are usually courted; than a sign of subservience of the Nazi to those possessing great wealth.

With the advent of Hitler to power, the German economy was sub-

[17] Heiden, *Der Fuehrer*, p. 526.

jected to many controls. Franz Neumann, in his interesting book on Nazism, argues that the economy remained capitalistic. His view is based upon what he conceived to be the relation between economics and politics.[18]

He is convinced that economics determines politics. However, this is true, now and then, in a democratic, capitalistic society where economic pressures can be exercised by powerful economic groups upon government. In a totalitarian regime, economic decisions are not autonomous; they can be directed by the state up to and including confiscation and imprisonment. Undoubtedly the Nazis had in mind geographic expansion and economic domination over other peoples. However, these ambitions do not demonstrate Nazism as a capitalistic form of imperialism. In their foreign conquest and lootings, the Nazis extended the principles and techniques they had applied to Jewish economic assets within. These were seized as booty for the advantage of insiders, the party, or the government. What is more important is their regulation of economic decisions; the allocation of resources among different uses was made on a principle other than individual profit. The government made these decisions on the basis of the national interest, defined, of course, according to its own views.

ECONOMIC POLICIES OF NATIONAL SOCIALISM

The basic law for regulating business was enacted on February 27, 1934. Later in the year, a national economic chamber and the working community of chambers and industry were set up. As in other fields of activity, the leadership principle was established in economic life. Businessmen were required to join chambers operating in their industry. A number of giant combines, of which the Hermann Göring properties were the largest, were organized. Neumann explains these ventures as follows: "A gangster can survive only if he becomes honorable." However, in a gangster society, the standards of honor are set by gangsters. We are told, "Only an economic basis, providing him with a steady income and giving him social status, will open the way for him in society. The Hermann Göring works constitute the attempt of the party to prove the economic basis for the party's rule." [19]

18 Neumann, *op. cit.*, pp. 181–186.
19 *Ibid.*, p. 247.

This passage indicates how even an able investigator can become so carried away by an idea that it becomes a Procrustean bed for his think ing. In a society where the party absolutely dominates all forms of activit and sets the social standards, it has no need to assure its position b seizing economic enterprises. Neumann then rightly shows that the exist ence of monopolistic restrictions, while they allocate resources differentl from the practice in a completely free market, does not change the rela tionships of the agents of productions in the economy. It is true tha capitalism nowhere exists in pure form; it is controlled to some degree b government monopolies.

Three economic changes in German fascism have been defined: th substitution of organized government intervention for a free market; th destruction of free labor organizations; and the abolition of democracy.[2]

Since one of the main objectives of the Nazis was the creation of a wa machine, the economy was subordinated to that purpose. Private enter prise and private profit were allowed, but decisions of entrepreneur were circumscribed by the needs of creating war machinery. As the Nazi consolidated their power, they placed industry under increasing regimen tation, organizing it into several functional groups that consisted of na tional, economic, and trade groups. National groups were the leadin organizations; below them were economic and functional groups. Mem bership was compulsory, all enterprises being forced to join. In addition territorial organizations, chambers of industry and commerce, were se up and unified into a Federation of the Chambers of Industry and Com merce. Heads of both types of groups were appointed by the Reic Ministry of Economics in accordance with the leadership principle Chairmen were obligated to lead their organizations in accordance wit the principles of National Socialism.

The economic groups and territorial chambers were instruments o the Nazi government whose tasks were to see that the latter's objective were promoted. The government was guiding the economy in a directio chosen by itself rather than allowing the market to decide; hence th economy must be regarded as noncapitalistic. In addition to these agen cies, which exercised considerable power over economic decisions, th Office of the Four-Year Plan was created in October, 1936, for achievin Germany's independence from foreign economic influence. The offic

[20] Otto Nathan, *The Nazi Economic System* (Durham, N. C.: Duke University Pres 1944), p. 3.

handled questions affecting production of raw materials, allocation of all resources, pricing, and foreign exchange.

AGRICULTURE

Direction of agriculture was placed in the hands of the Reich Food Estate set up in September, 1933. Membership was compulsory for all engaged in raising, processing, and distributing food products. The Food Estate could issue binding orders upon all subject to its jurisdiction. At the head of the organization stood the Reich Farm Leader, who appointed an advisory council. Sections were set up for carrying out educational and technical activities and for regulating control of production, processing, and distributing agricultural products.

MONEY AND BANKING

From the beginning, the Nazi government took control over the monetary and banking system. In a capitalistic economy, the function of the investment banking system is to allocate savings among different uses: commercial banks provide short-term credit to business, safety and profitability being the guides. A controlled economy imposes different obligations upon its money and banking system, and upon taking office the Nazis placed credit institutions under the control of the government. Under the Credit Act of 1934, a government commissioner was appointed to administer the law. He "could request balance sheets, profit and loss accounts, and any books or documents" of credit institutions. He was empowered to call and to attend meetings of stockholders.[21]

In addition, control of foreign exchange was introduced. Free international trade was abolished, and individual traders had to secure permission for any transaction involving purchase of foreign exchange. Payments in foreign exchange made to German nationals were deposited in the Reichsbank and were checked for accuracy by requiring exporters to record with the authorities the value of goods shipped out of the country. Failure to declare exports, or misstatement of their value, was a punishable offense. Foreign exchange offices were set up, and permits for imports had to be obtained. In addition, the foreign exchange offices were charged with determining the desirability of specific exports and imports and with regulating their direction and price. The net result of these

---

21 The financing of domestic recovery is discussed in detail in Kenyon E. Poole, *German Financial Policies* (Cambridge, Mass.: Harvard University Press, 1939).

regulations was the imposition of a controlled system of foreign trade directed toward serving the government rather than private traders.

PRODUCTION

The Nazis were determined that the productive system should serve the objectives of the government rather than the profit of producers and the choice of consumers. It happened that the aims of the Nazi government were preparation for war; hence the economic system was geared to this overshadowing purpose. If the Nazis had had other objectives in mind, the economic system would have been compelled to serve them. The economic characteristics of Nazism, while closely tied to war-making, need not necessarily have been directed toward that end. It is true that the system had war as its chief *raison d'être*, but it is by no means certain that this was inevitable. Production quotas were issued to enterprises, which were instructed on the type of material that could be used for making certain commodities. Through these orders the type and variety of national product produced were determined by the government.

Regulation of investment logically followed. Restrictions upon the use of scarce material or those needed for military purposes were instituted. Added to the restrictions were efforts to direct capital into grooves the government deemed desirable.

Labor Relations During its rise to power, the Nazi party had relentlessly attacked the free trade-union movement as Marxist, and the Nazi leaders had threatened to smash the unions as soon as they had seized power. This part of the program was carried out with dispatch. Theodore Leipart, the leader of the free German unions, tried to reach a compromise with the Nazis, and ended their alliance with the Social Democrats. But this move failed to appease the Nazis. The funds of the free and Christian trade unions were seized, and their leaders driven to prison or exile.

On January 20, 1934, the law regulating national labor was promulgated. It applied the leadership principle to the plant. The employer became leader of the plant and his employees were his followers:

[both] shall work together to further the purposes of the undertaking, and for the common good of the people and of the State.

As between the leader of an undertaking and his followers, the leader shall make all decisions concerning the undertaking.

He is to take care of the welfare of the followers. The followers are to keep faith with him in the spirit of solidarity in a joint enterprise.[22]

In theory, differences between worker and owner were abolished, for conflict no longer existed, and the interests of the community were paramount. An enterprise community, *Betriebsgemeinschaft,* was established. The employer, or leader, had a responsibility to his workers, the followers, but both were obligated to serve the community. Leaders had sole responsibility for conditions within the plant, but each plant employing twenty or more workers had to publish a schedule of its wages, hours of labor, and working conditions. To prevent misuse of the leader's authority, special committees to review the rules were appointed. If a majority of the special committee disapproved the regulations, it could recommend changes to the trustees of labor, appointed by the National Department of Labor.

The trustees of labor enjoyed wide powers and could amend or change any rules adopted by the employer. In fact, they had the functions formerly performed by the trade unions and government agencies engaged in conciliation and arbitration. The trustees of labor, who served as a safety valve, could prevent the imposition of onerous conditions. They were subject to the Ministry of Labor and could issue "industry rules" setting up normal conditions in industry. Their principal job was to preserve economic peace, and they had the authority to cancel rules.

Wage Policy Wages were held at depression levels. Subsequently, minima were introduced, and incentive systems to encourage output were utilized. At the beginning, the government's policy of stabilizing wages was effected by using the masses of the idle, but later the policy was enforced by limiting mobility. In June, 1938, the government authorized the trustees of labor to set maximum as well as minimum wages as a means of limiting labor changes, and with the outbreak of war the trustees used their authority to reduce wages.

Courts of Social Honor Courts of Social Honor were set up in each economic district to hear cases against employers and employees charged with violating communal obligations. Offending employers and disloyal workers could be brought before these tribunals, but few cases actually were. However, in a few instances, an employer was dismissed as a plant leader, which in fact meant he ceased to be an employer. These courts

[22] Quoted from the Law for the Organization of Labor in C. W. Guillebaud, *The Social Policy of Nazi Germany* (Cambridge: Cambridge University Press, 1941), p. 20–21.

also heard charges against unjust dismissal, and were able to award damages to those whose separation was held unjustified.

LABOR FRONT

After abolishing the trade unions because they were liberal and Marxist, the Nazi party set up the Labor Front under the headship of Dr. Robert Ley, a dissolute alcoholic and habitué of the Bohemian underworld. All employers and employees, except Jews, were eligible for membership and virtually all joined. The Labor Front kept a watch on industrial relations, carried on party propaganda, and initiated a program of leisure-time activity.

EMPLOYMENT

When the Nazis came to power, Germany was confronted with the most serious unemployment problem in its history. Hitler launched his Four Year Plan, which included a vast public works program financed by credit expansion. Women were forced from the labor market, and subsidies for home improvements and plant replacement were given. Employment was spread by shortening hours. The general attitude of the National Socialist party toward the problem of unemployment was embodied in the principle of the "right to work," and the ability of the government to abolish unemployment gave it great prestige among the masses, even if its success was based on armaments and war.

COMPULSORY LABOR

In May, 1934, the Nazis limited the migration of labor, and as the economy approached full employment, the flow of labor was increasingly regulated. After February, 1935, employment books were required of all German workers to serve as records of training and work experience. Under a law enacted in June, 1935, all Germans of from nineteen to twenty-five years of age could be required to perform compulsory "service of honor." As the Nazi economy was, from the beginning, geared to war, compulsory labor was analogous to military service. The function of the National Labor Service was to inculcate in the German youth a community spirit, and to promote respect for manual work. In addition, the government limited the amount of labor turnover by prohibiting the quitting of jobs in certain industries without the approval of the em ployment office. In the field of social insurance the Nazis continued the earlier institutions.

PRICES

Although the entrepreneur continued to control the firm, a government-sponsored "accounting system was imposed upon him, in connection with price control, enabled the government to supervise and control minute aspects of the enterprise and every single move the entrepreneur made." [23] The Nazi war preparations produced large-scale economic expansion. The government instituted a system of price regulation and attempted to limit the effect of shortages, especially of foreign-produced materials, upon prices. Only increases in costs were held to justify price increases. The Nazis sought to maintain a stable price level, and therefore had to prevent the price and cost changes that would normally follow in a free market. Moreover, the allocation of resources among enterprises kept prices in check.

The Nazi economic changes were a means of preparing the nation for war and conquest. Could the movement have risen and prospered without an aggressive foreign policy? Given Germany's economic position at the time the Nazis came to power, the absorption of the unemployed into industry was an immediate and pressing task. It might have been done by expanding public works and government activities of various kinds. However, the Nazis had been infected by the reactionary, nationalistic collectivism of German writers who hated democracy and freedom because in part they express the people's desire for peace. In addition, the Nazis regarded humanitarianism with contempt, and although they utilized the desperate economic situation to appeal to the needy and unemployed, their philosophy and aims were more concerned with national domination than with economic welfare. The German people, who had given the Nazis a mandate, were to pay a high price for their action. They were to be led inexorably down the road to war and disaster, much of it to be shared by a large part of humanity.

23 Nathan, *op. cit.*, p. 216.

28. *THE FIRST AND SECOND INTERNATIONALS*

International solidarity has been the goal of revolutionary groups throughout the nineteenth century. The rise of Marxism has strengthened this urge, for Marxism insists that class solidarity across international lines is more real than the national solidarity of conflicting classes within the nation-state. Non-Marxist socialists, on the other hand, dream of international solidarity as a means of increasing prosperity and assuring universal peace. The drive for international solidarity has led to the setting up of organizations which hoped to eliminate wars through joint effort, and also one—the Comintern—that aspired to be the directing guide of an international revolutionary party. Concentration upon international problems has also stimulated intellectual activity among radicals who sought to explain the causes of international conflict, and has thus inspired the development of theories of imperialism.

A movement for combining the radical groups of different nationalities into one international body arose in the early part of the nineteenth century, when an attempt was made to bring the German refugees living in Switzerland into contact with the Exiles' League, organized in Paris in 1834. At the request of the German states, the refugees were expelled.

In Paris the League of the Just was formed as a successor to the Exiles' League, and the London refugees were in close contact with this group. Close connection between the foreign refugees and the Chartist movement was established, and William Lovett, the leader of the moral-force faction of Chartists, helped to establish in 1842 the Democratic Friends of All Nations. The following year the Fraternal Democrats was founded. Its aim was to establish democratic republics and organize them into a free federation.

THE COMMUNIST LEAGUE

The refugee circles in this period were highly unstable. Organizations followed each other, and splits and divisions on questions of philosophy were common. In June, 1847, the Communist League was formed, and it commissioned Marx and Engels to draw up *The Communist Manifesto*. After the abortive revolts of 1848, the movement was seriously weakened. Differences between the followers of Marx and a utopian group led by Karl Schapper and August Willich resulted in a division, and by 1851 the Communist League had passed from the scene.

THE FIRST INTERNATIONAL

In the 1850's, the English labor movement revived under what the Webbs called the "Junta," a group of influential leaders of a number of skilled unions who advocated a conservative policy. Attempts at international unity were repeatedly made but without success. The London Trades' Council, founded in 1860, organized a popular demonstration for the Italian revolutionary leader Garibaldi, and two years later a meeting supporting the North in the slavery struggle in the United States was held in London under the same auspices.[1]

In 1862 a delegation of French workers sent to the London exhibition established cordial relations with leaders of English labor. At a demonstration held in St. Martin's Hall on September 28, 1864, it was decided to launch an international labor organization. Headquarters were to be in London; a provisional committee of twenty-one, among them were a number of well-known English trade unionists, was set up; and Karl Marx was appointed to draft the rules and a constitution.

THE INAUGURAL ADDRESS

In *The Address and Provisional Rules of the International Workingmen's Association*, Marx sought to steer a middle course. Although he argued that the conditions of the laboring population had not improved in the period between 1848 and 1864, he pointed to the great victory of the ten-hour law. State interference in the conditions of work constituted a triumph of the philosophy of labor over that of the capitalists. Another evidence of progress was the spread of the practices of consumers' coop-

[1] G. M. Stekloff, *History of the First International* (London: Lawrence, 1928), pp. 34–35.

eratives as developed by the Rochdale Pioneers. The success of cooperation showed that labor was capable of managing industry, and demonstrated the possibility of free associated labor. Large-scale cooperative labor could be organized only on a nation-wide basis with the support of the state. Therefore the workers must first of all conquer political power.

The *Address* urged the international unity of labor not only for mutual assistance, but

"to master . . . the mysteries of international politics, to watch the diplomatic acts of their respective governments, to counteract them if necessary by all means in their power when unable to combine in simultaneous denunciations, and to vindicate the simple laws of morals and justice which ought to govern the relations of private individuals as the rules paramount in the intercourse of nations. The fight for such a foreign policy forms part of the general struggle for the emancipation of the working classes.

The *Address* drafted by Marx was adopted. A general congress was summoned for 1866.

FIRST CONGRESS

On September 3, 1866, the First Congress of the International Workingmen's Association opened at Geneva. It lasted five days and was attended by forty-six delegates representing twenty-two sections of the International.[2] A constitution and a program were adopted. The local branch was defined as the unit; locals in a specific country elected a federal council, but branches were autonomous, and could join together and elect district councils. At the head of the International stood the General Council elected by the General Congress; it was the supreme governing body of the International. The General Council conducted the business of the International between congresses, acted as a connecting link between sections, issued periodical reports, and accumulated statistical information on working conditions in various countries.

The International Workingmen's Association (First International) was intended as an instrument for bringing the workers' organizations of the different countries into closer relationship. All of the intellectual and organizational tendencies seeking a place in the labor movement sought to dominate the International. Followers of the Frenchman Proudhon,

2 Edmond Villetard, *History of the International*. Translated by Susan Day (New Haven: George H. Richmond Company, 1874), pp. 102–125.

putschists influenced by the revolutionary Blanqui, socialists led by Marx, and English trade unionists were among those seeking a place of power. At the beginning, leadership went to the followers of Marx, who were anxious to push the workers' movement in political directions. To Marx, the fundamental need was the establishment of working-class political parties.

THE CONGRESSES OF THE INTERNATIONAL

Seventy-one delegates attended the Second Congress at Lausanne, the largest delegation coming from Switzerland. The Proudhonist idea of a people's bank was endorsed. The function of the state in relation to war among the nations was also discussed, and a resolution demanding political freedom adopted.

The Third Congress met at Brussels in 1868 with ninety-nine delegates attending. War was one of the principal issues. A resolution protesting against war and urging a strike to prevent it was adopted. The congress advised that courses in technical and scientific studies be offered, advocated a reduction in hours of labor, and endorsed mutual credit. For the first time the International also endorsed communism.

The Fourth Congress, at Basle in September, 1869, had Bakunin among its seventy-five delegates. Among its decisions was an endorsement of socialization of the land, after a fight between the collectivists and followers of Proudhon. A dispute arose between followers of Marx and Bakunin over the right of inheritance. Both sides favored its abolition, but differed in that the Marxists looked upon abolition as possible when "the proletariat had attained political power." Bakunin argued that abolition of inheritance was immediately possible and could be used as a base for an attack upon the political system. This was a first clash in what was to become a fierce struggle between the two giants of European revolution.

INNER CONFLICT

Bakunin had been a member of the League of Peace and Freedom but at the Second Congress of this organization in 1868 his views were rejected and he and his associates established the International Alliance of Socialist Democracy. The alliance endorsed atheism and the abolition of religion; political, economic, and social equality; equal opportunities for all children; rejection of political action; and international solidarity of labor.[3] A secret group formed within it was given direction over the movement. A request for affiliation with the International Workingmen's Association was rejected by the latter's General Council. The alliance, as is evident, was a secret conspiratorial organization not unlike the modern communist movement. It was dominated by a secret group and sought to permeate other working-class associations to gain control over them. It was difficult for the Marxists and the Bakuninists to work in the same organization. The latter felt that labor's participation in politics constituted a betrayal of the cause, and that the reform advocated by Marx would lead to political tyranny. Bakunin regarded the measures advocated by the socialists as puny palliatives which in the end would take the edge off labor's revolutionary fervor. He was especially contemptuous of the labor aristocracy and parliamentarianism. Only by destroying the state and all vested interests could labor emancipate itself from exploitation.

The Franco-Prussian War interfered with the Fifth Congress of the International; instead a conference of the General Council was held in London in September, 1871. The opposition to Marx was organized in the Bakunin group, now operating in part openly and in part secretly. Each side sought to win the national sections to its view.

THE HAGUE CONGRESS

The differences came to a head at The Hague congress held in 1872. At the outset, the feeling between Marxist and Bakuninist delegates was bitter. The dispute centered around the powers to be exercised by the General Council, and around political action. The Marxist favored vesting power in the General Council, and emphasized the need of a labor political party. Opposite views were held by the Bakuninists. Although Marx and his followers were able to carry the day on the powers of the General Council, they recognized that the opposition was actually the stronger faction. They accordingly voted to transfer the headquarters of the General Council from London to New York on the theory that the International would thus be saved from the anarchists. An investigation made of the Bakunin group reported that its rules were founded on principles hostile to those of the International and recommended the expulsion of Bakunin and his close followers. This act marked the end of the First International.

The Marxists have maintained that they represented the interests of

[3] Stekloff, *op. cit.*, pp. 154–155.

industrial labor, and that the anarchist followers of Bakunin expressed the interests of the small bourgeoisie, the declassed workers, *(lumpen proletariat)*, and the poor peasantry. Bakunin, who was opposed to all government and to the building of a political party of labor, rejected Marx's dictum "that every class struggle is a political struggle." Other points of difference arose from the policy of infiltration and secret control preached and practiced by Bakunin and his followers. It must be noted that Bakunin's tactics have been adopted by the most orthodox Marxists of our time, the Communists.

ANARCHIST CONGRESSES

Bakunin's influence was especially potent in the Latin countries, and an attack upon the International came from one of Bakunin's strong-holds, the Italian Federation. Upon the adjournment of The Hague congress, in 1872, a special congress convened at Saint-Imier, Switzer-land. This congress endorsed the autonomy of the national federations, and denied the right of any congress to impose its views upon a separate affiliated group. The congress delegates declared themselves as anti-authoritarian collectivists or federalists. Subsequently they acquired the name of anarchists. The Saint-Imier congress declared "that the destruc-tion of every kind of political power is the first task of the proletariat." Even the temporary use of politics in the furtherance of the emancipa-tion of humanity was held to be vain and illusory. A number of other congresses were held by the anarchists in the 1870's; the socialists, in-creasing their strength throughout this period, met at irregular intervals in international gatherings of their own.[4]

FOUNDING OF THE SECOND INTERNATIONAL

When the First International, the International Workingmen's Associa-tion, transferred its seat from London to New York in 1872, a formal international organization of the socialist movement ceased to exist. The following two decades witnessed, however, widespread progress in the local socialist and labor movements of Europe. With the revival of radi-cal activity went a renewal of interest in the re-establishment of socialist

[4] James Guillaume, *L'Internationale* (Paris: Tresse et Stock, 1909), Vol. III, deals with the Anarchist congresses.

internationalism. Two labor congresses opened on July 14, 1889, the hundredth anniversary of the storming of the Bastille. The reformist congress was dominated by the French possibilists and English trade unionists; the congress of the revolutionists—the more important meeting—was opened by Edmound Vaillant, and among its delegates was Wilhelm Liebknecht. An overwhelming majority of the 391 delegates came from France, which sent 221; Germany had 81, the remainder coming from seventeen other countries. A reading of the demands is perhaps an excellent index of the progress since made in Western European countries and in the United States: the eight-hour workday, prohibition of the labor of children under the age of fourteen, and of nightwork of women and minors under eighteen. Over the objection of the anarchists, the need for political action was recognized, and May 1st was declared a labor holiday.[5] The dispute between the socialists and anarchists was resumed. The latter opposed political action, for they were convinced that political power exercised by socialists would be as oppressive as power exercised by any other group. Opposition was expressed to standing armies, and unity with the reformist socialist group was advocated.[6]

THE SECOND AND THIRD CONGRESSES

The Second Congress of the Second International held at Brussels in 1891 was given over largely to a discussion of militarism and the relations of the political parties of socialism to trade unions. A resolution advocating the formation of an international trade-union body was rejected as premature; socialists were urged to support in parliamentary elections only those candidates who approved the abolition of capitalism; and the workers were urged to protest against all preparations for war. An attempt by the Dutch anarchist Nieuwenhuis to get a sharper declaration against war failed.

At the Third Congress in Zurich in 1893 the questions of antimilitarism and the general strike were again in the forefront of discussion. Opposition to the general strike in case of war was strong among the German delegates, who felt that an invasion by Czarist soldiers would impose the obligation of national defense upon socialists. Endorsement of the general strike was defeated; a resolution was adopted urging the

---

5 *Protokol des Internationalen Arbeiter Kongress zu Paris, 1899* (Nuremberg: Worlëin, 1890), pp. 122–124.

6 J. Lenz, *The Rise and Fall of the Second International* (New York: International Publishers, 1932).

workers to keep in view their revolutionary goal and to reject all compromises with bourgeois political parties. The anarchist problem again emerged. At the preliminary conference in Brussels, it had been decided to admit only trade unions and socialist parties which accepted the need for political action by labor, which meant that the workers would use their political franchise and the electoral machinery to promote the interest of labor and to conquer political power. Gustav Landauer, an anarchist, charged that such a resolution interfered with free opinion, but the German leader, Bebel, argued that a line had to be drawn somewhere and those who could not agree were free to form an international of their own.[7]

EXCLUSION OF ANARCHISTS

The London congress held in the summer of 1896 finally and definitely excluded the anarchists. Those who represented trade unions were recognized as delegates, but none holding a mandate from an anarchist group was seated. At this congress the French independent socialists were given a place. The congress resolved that socialism could be attained only by winning political power and urged universal suffrage, the secret ballot, and the initiative, referendum, and recall. The congress also demanded the abolition of standing armies, the institution of a people's militia, and the arbitration of international differences.[8]

MINISTERIALISM

Improvement in the position of labor in the last decades of the nineteenth century led many socialists to doubt the validity of a strict Marxian interpretation of events. In Germany the reformist current manifested itself as revisionism; in France the controversy between reformist and revolutionary socialists was centered in the issue of a socialist's joining a bourgeois cabinet. In 1899, Millerand entered the cabinet headed by the left republican Waldeck-Rousseau. Millerand contended that the Republic was threatened by a reactionary *coup d'état* and that it was the duty of Socialists to prevent this disaster. The Marxists, led by Guesde, and the Blanquists, led by Vaillant, bitterly assailed this step. Jaurès warmly defended Millerand's conduct, and the question of ministerialism was brought before the congress. The resolution by Kautsky recognized

---

[7] *Protokol des Internationalen Sozialistischen Kongress, Zurich, 1893* (Zurich: Grütliverwins, 1894), pp. 5–10.

[8] *International Socialist Workers and Trade Union Congress, London, 1896* (London: Twentieth Century Press, 1896), pp. 9–10.

that the entrance of a Socialist into a bourgeois government can be justified only by an emergency, and the judgment whether or not such an emergency exists is a matter of tactics and not principle. This position was vigorously attacked by the left, but Kautsky's resolution was adopted by a vote of twenty-nine to nine[9]—a clear indication that the socialist parties of Western European countries reflected increasingly the non-aggressive mood of the working classes. Steady improvement in political and economic status made the extreme phrases and ideas of the revolutionaries seem utopian. Had the socialist groups accepted the views of their left-wing factions, they would have been reduced to impotence. Despite the charge of treason and betrayal commonly made by the revolutionary socialists against the reformists, the political insignificance of the left demonstrated more clearly than their finely argued dialectics that they had misjudged the mood of the workers.

At the same congress, Rosa Luxemburg moved the resolution against militarism and cited the growth of colonial imperialism and the danger of war that followed from the increasing national rivalries.[10] Socialist members of parliaments were urged to vote against military appropriations, and Socialist parties were advised to prevent their governments from adventures that lead to war. An International Secretariat set up with headquarters at Brussels was to collect documents and exchange information. Émile Vandervelde, its first president, was succeeded in 1903 by Camille Huysmans, who served for many years.

At the Amsterdam congress of 1904, a group of French Marxists again decried socialist participation in a bourgeois government. Jaurès passionately defended ministerialism, and insisted that it had saved the Republic. Bebel, who acted as chief spokesman for the revolutionary view, took the doctrinaire position that it made little difference whether a government was a monarchy or a republic, for the state is always but an instrument of class rule. The discussion revealed wide differences of opinion among the delegates. Between the revisionist right and the revolutionary left were a large number of delegates who wanted to preserve unity within the International.

THE STUTTGART CONGRESS OF 1907

Militarism and the colonial question were the principal issues discussed at the Stuttgart congress. Three resolutions on militarism and in-

[9] *Cinquième congrès socialiste international* (Paris: Société Nouvelle de Librairie et d'Édition, 1901), pp. 59–90.

[10] Lenz, *op. cit.*, pp. 48–53.

ternational conflict were presented. One called for the repudiation of bourgeois patriotism and asked the socialists to answer a declaration of war by a general strike and insurrection. Another resolution recognized war and militarism as due to capitalistic production, but held that the call for a general strike and insurrection would be harmful; therefore the remedy prescribed was a vigorous campaign for organizing the workers for socialism so that the cause of war would be eliminated. A third view held international solidarity to be superior to national interests and called for action on a national and international scale to prevent war by all means.[11]

Opening the debate, Bebel, the leader of the German Social Democrats, declared that the general strike, desertion of troops, and insurrection were not practical in Germany as antiwar measures. A French leftist, Gustav Hervé, ridiculed Bebel's sentiments and criticized the German party as an admirable machine which lacked a revolutionary conception. Its discipline was one of death, and its internationalism a lie. The French leader, Jaurès, demanded, as he had previously at Amsterdam, the maximum action against war, while criticizing Hervé's antinationalism; Hervé, according to Jaurès, forgot that a nation is a repository of tradition. The essence of capitalism is and was "C'est la loi d'airain de la guerre", and the proletariat ought to check it by all means. An amendment submitted by Rosa Luxemburg, Lenin, and Martov declared that wars are the result of competitive armaments, and that it is the duty of the proletariat and their representatives to prevent them. Should wars arise despite the efforts of labor, the economic and political crises generated should be used as a means for ending capitalism. A subcommittee brought out a compromise which was unanimously adopted. It traced wars to capitalism, and urged the proletariat to use all means to prevent them.[12]

THE COPENHAGEN CONGRESS

The Eighth Congress, meeting in Copenhagen in 1910, had before it a number of resolutions on peace and disarmament. The subcommittee reported a resolution which reaffirmed the socialist opposition to war and militarism, warned of competitive armament races, and declared that the danger of war would not cease until capitalism was ended. The Stuttgart resolution was affirmed, and socialists were urged to use all means to end

[11] *VII Congrès sociliste international 1907* (Brussels: Veuve Désiré, 1908), pp. 111–117.
[12] *Ibid.*, pp. 165–166, 179–182.

the capitalistic system in the event of war. The Bureau of the Socialist International was instructed to convene an emergency congress for devising action if the threat of war appeared. The general strike as a weapon against war was rejected.[13]

EXTRAORDINARY CONGRESS OF 1912

Increasing international tension led to the convening of an extraordinary congress in 1912. Pleas against war and for peace were made. The congress declared that it was the moral duty of the workers to prevent war, and predictions that a proletarian revolt would follow an armed conflict were made.

IMPERIALISM

In connection with war and colonial questions, Marxist writers have developed several theories of imperialism, the most important being those of Rudolf Hilferding, Rosa Luxemburg, and Lenin.[14]

According to the Marxist view, the ultimate basis for modern imperialism is the appropriation of surplus value by the capitalist. Imperialism complements the protective tariff, which establishes a monopoly of the home market for native capitalists. All Marxists, and, in fact, all socialists, agreed to these propositions; however, they differed on details. The first significant Marxist view was developed by Karl Kautsky, who argued that the discovery of the New World and the Industrial Revolution had brought to an end the old imperialistic policy. Instead of exploiting the native races, the policy of free trade favored humane treatment of the native population. Instead of a brutal policy typical of the older imperialism, the new form emphasized philanthropy. The driving force behind this new policy was the desire to build up markets for goods and to educate prospective customers. However, with the development of capitalism, a reversion toward the old forms took place because of the change-over from the export of products to the export of capital.

[He] called attention to the way in which "high finance" was beginning to exert an influence over the state which old-fashioned individual capitalism in the free-trade era had never dreamed of, and [to the fact] that it was particularly successful in pressing for the new acquisition of colonies, or stricter control of

---

13 *Huitème Congrès socialiste International, Copenhagen, 1910,* pp. 191–193, 211–213.
14 For Lenin's views, see Chapter 20.

existing ones, as new and more profitable fields of investment for surplus capital.[15]

HILFERDING

Kautsky's view contained little that was novel. Rudolf Hilferding carried the discussion to another plane and strongly influenced subsequent Marxian views on the question. Starting from the Marxist assumption of a tendency of the rate of profit to fall, Hilferding examines the means of overcoming this tendency by capitalists' setting aside competition. Both vertical and horizontal combinations arise as a result of the desire to eliminate competition. Mergers are another means of attaining this objective, as are cartels and trusts.[16]

The Role of the Banks   The development of capitalistic industry leads to the growth and concentration of banking, which becomes a vital force in the promotion of the highest level of capitalistic concentration in cartels and trusts. Each—bank and cartel and trust—reacts upon and stimulates the growth of the other. With the development of capitalism and its credit institutions, the dependence of industry upon the banks increases. Hilferding maintains that an ever-larger part of industrial capital does not belong to the entrepreneur, but is borrowed from the credit and banking systems. On the other hand, banks find it necessary to invest an ever-growing part of their funds in industry. The capital of banks that is used as industrial capital is called "finance capital." [17] Finance capital arises with the joint-stock company or the corporation and reaches its highest point with the spread of monopoly in industry. The power of the banks over industry is thereby continually increased. As capital reaches the highest level, finance capital becomes its most important form. Finance capital is the apogee of capitalism. The mobilization of capital and the greater role of credit transform the role of the money and banking system. Banks increase in power and become the founders of enterprise and then, as finance capital, dominate industry.

Policies of Finance Capital   Finance capital represents the unification of all forms of capital—industrial, commercial, and bank. Now all are under the direction and leadership of high finance. This unity leads to the abolition of competition and to a change in the relations of the

---

15 E. M. Winslow, *The Pattern of Imperialism* (New York: Columbia University Press, 1948), p. 154.

16 Rudolf Hilferding, *Das Finanzkapital* (Vienna: Volksbuchhandlung, 1927), pp. 234, 236–249.

17 *Ibid.*, p. 283.

capitalistic class toward the state. The national, bourgeois state arose in the struggle between the early capitalistic entrepreneur and the state privileges and monopolies of the great merchant companies. Consequently, the struggle against mercantilism was a struggle for economic, and later for industrial, freedom. Monopoly industry, according to Hilferding, strives for a tariff in order to exploit native consumers by charging at home higher than world prices.[18] Through the tariff the home market is assured to home industry, and the world economy becomes split into a group of single state economies.

Export of Capital   The introduction of tariffs reacts unfavorably upon costs for, reducing the international division of labor, it raises the costs of production, and depresses profits. As free trade does not appear a desirable alternative, the capitalist, to prevent the shrinking of his profit, is forced to enlarge, by exporting capital, the size of the economic area in which he operates. An export of capital is defined by Hilferding as an export of value, which creates surplus value in the importing nation. A distinction is made between a capital export and a transfer of capital by a person who moves himself and his capital from one country to another. The former takes place, according to Hilferding, when the exported capital is owned by an investor who lives elsewhere and disposes of the surplus value it yields.

Capital export is made possible by differences in the profit rates of several countries, for the less-developed countries have a much higher rate of return than the older and more developed capitalistic nations. A higher return is due to lower wages and lower rents. Existence of higher returns is a powerful magnet for capital exports. Moreover, privileges and monopolies can be obtained, and all of these factors make for higher profits. Export of capital raises the productivity of labor in the colonies and at the same time increases production in the exporting country. Sharp increases in production raise the demand for labor, wages are raised, and industry prospers. This cycle, according to Hilferding, creates the appearance that the tendency for conditions of labor to deteriorate, inherent in capitalism, has been overcome.[19]

Finance Capital and Export of Capital   The development of finance capital creates strong pressure for capital export, and the struggle for markets to dispose of surplus commodities is replaced by a struggle among national banking monopolies for sources for capital exports, each

18 *Ibid.*, p. 386.
19 *Ibid.*, pp. 394–397, 400.

seeking to stake out a colonial empire. The policies of finance capital follow three specific directions: (1) the establishment or winning of the largest possible economic area; (2) the exclusion through tariff walls of foreign competition; and (3) the exploitation by monopolies of the protected areas.

Economic rivalries between nations are sharply increased by the development of finance capital, for backward nations serve as outlets for the surplus capital of advanced nations. The struggle for colonies leads to increasing tension between economic areas. Consequently, finance capital advocates a powerfully armed state.

Hilferding maintains that finance capital has shed the economic liberalism of early capitalism, with its emphasis upon individualism, competition, and free trade. Finance capital seeks power and not freedom. It must be able to protect its interests in the foreign markets and be powerful enough to follow a policy of colonial expansion. The need to expand introduces a change in the outlook of the capitalist class, which ceases to be more or less peace-loving and humanitarian. Instead of peaceful ideas, finance capital develops doctrines of power and domination of foreign peoples based on racial supremacy.

Finance capital is thus characterized by great concentration of power, by demand for monopoly of the home market, and by an aggressive expansionist policy abroad. By eliminating and absorbing the medium and small-scale producer, finance capital accelerates the movement for the socialization of production. It thus creates a broad basis for socialism. By forcing state intervention into economic affairs, finance capitalism destroys the fiction that the state is a neutral mediator between classes, and the state stands revealed as an instrument of the dominating class. Finance capital is the highest state of capitalism, the completion of its role and destiny. Beyond it is socialism.[20]

ROSA LUXEMBURG (1870—1919)

Rosa Luxemburg was another Marxist who sought to develop a theory of imperialism to explain the tendencies in capitalism. Beginning with the assumption that the driving force behind the economic activity of the capitalist is the creation of surplus value, she draws the conclusion that this is achieved through the process of reproduction of capital. The capitalist does not cease operating when his production cycle is completed. He is not satisfied to pocket the surplus value he has appropriated

20 *Ibid.*, pp. 412, 426, 474–477.

and withdraw from productive activity. Appropriation of surplus value at a progressive rate is the aim of the capitalist. Such progressive increase is possible only by the expansion of production or, as it is phrased by Luxemburg, of reproduction.[21]

Capital expansion is the result of transforming some of the accumulated surplus value into additional active capital. Luxemburg traces this process through several stages: (1) production must lead to the creation of surplus value; (2) surplus value must be realized in money form; (3) a portion of the realized surplus value is converted into capital; (4) the increased capital leads to an increase in the output of goods, part of which constitutes additional surplus value. When the new surplus value is converted into money, the cycle of capital expansion is completed. In order to dispose of his increased mass of goods, the capitalist needs an enlarged market.

The essential difference between simple and expanded reproduction consists in the fact that under simple reproduction, constant capital and variable capital are transformed at the end of a production period into goods. These goods are sold and the money thus obtained is used to purchase new plant, equipment, raw material, and labor of the *same* magnitude. The whole of surplus value filched by the capitalist is consumed by him, and production is conducted on the same scale and with the same amount of capital as in the previous cycle.

Expanded reproduction means that the capitalist does not consume all of his surplus value, but uses part of it to enlarge his plant and equipment, so that the total surplus value will increase. Expanded reproduction is characteristic of all progressive capitalistic societies. It constitutes, in fact, capital formation. The idea of Luxemburg seems to imply that savings come exclusively from profits.

Expanded reproduction leads to an increase in the goods produced. Consequently, new purchasers or additional demand must be discovered; otherwise the capitalist will fail to sell his total stock. At first the problem is simple. Goods produced under conditions of expanded reproduction replace those formerly sold by the now displaced competitor. Such a change simply means the replacement of one capitalist by another. Luxemburg concluded that an increase in the total capital of society is possible only if society contains, in addition to workers and capitalists, persons who receive their means of support from either the laboring or the cap-

---

21 Rosa Luxemburg, *Die Akkumulation des Kapitals* (Berlin: Vereinigung Internationaler Verlags-Anstalten, G.M.B.H., 1923), p. 9.

italistic class. In other words, the accumulation of capital is based upon the existence of noncapitalistic elements in society who can consume the surplus produced by expanded reproduction. For its existence and progress, capitalism requires noncapitalistic forms of production. Noncapitalistic social groups are needed as an outlet for the accumulated surplus value, as a market for means of production, and as a reservoir for wage labor. The peasantry, to the extent that agriculture has not become capitalistic, the colonial people, and others living in economically backward areas are among the principal noncapitalistic elements in the modern world. Capitalism, while utilizing the noncapitalistic areas for its own expansion, also helps to change the backward areas from noncapitalistic to capitalistic. Under the influence of capitalistic expansion, the backward areas increase their commercial activities and become capitalistic. Thus capitalism itself undermines the noncapitalistic areas which are vital to its continued progress, for it transforms and destroys all the more primitive productive forms.

Imperialism thus arises, according to Rosa Luxemburg, from the constant and insatiable need of capitalists for new spheres of exploitation. Existence of noncapitalistic areas is the *sine qua non* of capitalism, for capital expansion depends upon their existence. Such expansion has not been effected altogether by peaceful means, for capitalism has, from the beginning, utilized force and violence to penetrate economically backward areas. In these violent penetrations, the capitalist has had the effective aid of the state. It is through its invasion of colonial and backward areas that capitalism helps to maintain itself.

Imperialism is therefore the political expression of capital accumulation in its struggle for control of noncapitalistic areas. As a consequence of the higher development and the continuing sharpening of competition of capitalistic countries for the profitable exploitation of noncapitalistic areas, imperialism becomes more potent and aggressive and stimulates the clash of interest between capitalistic nations. Consequently, militarism performs a useful function in capital expansion and is an accompaniment of accumulation.[22] In the first phases of capitalism, militarism conquered the New World and India; later militarism conquered colonial areas and, undermining their primitive economies, made possible the proletarianization of their working population and the introduction of capitalism. The ever-present need to find noncapitalistic areas will bring on the convulsions and clashes which will eventually destroy the system.

[22] *Ibid.*, pp. 13–14, 289, 361–368.

Luxemburg's main thesis was that to monetize surplus value the goods have to be sold. But there is no purchasing power for the masses to buy goods; therefore *export* the goods. But she fails to see that the exported goods are not given away, but are paid for with imported goods. The lack of purchasing power brings the problem, chased through the window of exports, back through the door of imports. Her theory is weak. If the export is capital equipment, the picture remains unchanged: we are *paid,* and with *imports.* Who buys the imports?

29. *INTERNATIONALISM AFTER 1914*

FACTIONS

Like its constituent parties, the Second International, although unified on the surface, developed discordant tendencies. In a real sense the International was a loose agglomeration of socialist parties of various countries. Centralized authority and organized discipline were absent, and every national party could follow its own program. While the International and many of its constituent groups were proclaiming their revolutionary faith, most countries experienced a large expansion in trade-union membership and in protective legislation. These developments were responsible for the rise of a reformist current. Aiming to revise the Marxist doctrines so that they would conform to political realities, revisionism began in Germany and had its counterpart in other countries.

The disputes in the German and French parties reflected the divisions everywhere. International socialism, before 1914, was divided into three groups. On the right were the reformers made up of German revisionists, the English Fabians, and the French possibilists. Kautsky was the official spokesman of orthodox Marxism, and his views were shared by men like Jules Guesde in France. While accepting the major tenets of Marxism, this second group sought to utilize political action. Using Marxist phrases, they cooperated with the revisionists in advocating day-to-day reforms. The smallest section, the third group, contained the leftist revolutionaries who wanted to return to pure Marxism in both theory and practice. This group was led by Antonie Pannekoek and Rosa Luxemburg and was supported by Lenin. They regarded the state as an organ of class domination and advocated revolutionary action.

WORLD WAR I

    International socialism faced its most serious challenge with the out-
break of World War I. The assassination of the Austrian Archduke
Franz Ferdinand at Sarajevo by a Serbian nationalist led to a series of
maneuvers which plunged the world into a terrible war. Socialist internationalism had been founded upon a belief that the solidarity of labor
transcended national boundaries and that international class solidarity
was superior to national interest. These lofty views did not stand the test
of events. Socialists in every warring country joined governments of national unity. There were, of course, exceptions, mainly on the left, but
the majority stood by their governments. The threat of war was responsible for demonstrations led by socialists in Germany. The International
Socialist Bureau met at Brussels on July 29, and the socialist congress
scheduled for Vienna on August 23, 1914, was advanced to August 11.
A large mass meeting held at Brussels on the day the Bureau assembled
was addressed by Hugo Haase, the chairman of the German social democracy, who charged Austria with responsibility for the impending war.
    Jaurès, the tribune of French socialism, cried out for peace. Two days
later he was dead, assassinated on the last day of July by a demented
"patriot." On August 1, 1914, Hermann Müller arrived in Paris. He conferred with the leaders of French socialism and assured them that the
socialists in the Reichstag would not vote for credits. Nevertheless, as
war became a reality, the socialist members of the Reichstag gave way to
the patriotic fervor which seized all other citizens. The parliamentary
members of the German Social Democratic party agreed in caucus,
seventy-eight to fourteen, to vote war credits; and at first the fourteen
opponents voted with the majority in accordance with party discipline.
Leading Marxists, such as Heinrich Cunow, supported the war, while the
revisionist leader, Eduard Bernstein, opposed it on pacifist humanitarian
grounds. In Austria, the majority voted to support the war. French socialists, while at first reluctant, changed their views as soon as they
learned of the German invasion. The Belgian socialists took a similar
position. In England, only a few members of the Independent Labour
party, including Snowden and MacDonald, refused to support the war.
On the whole, Russian socialists opposed the war, but a number of
prominent exiles, including Plekhanov and Deutsch, pleaded for the support of the fatherland.
    The prospect of war and the capitulation of the great majority of

socialists to war enthusiasm destroyed the entire internationalist structure that had been erected during a quarter of a century. Leading socialists in every country believed that international socialism could best be promoted by serving the national interest. Two groups stood out against this view. One group was the centrists, who opposed the war but were not ready to break with their old comrades. Their opposition was largely based on pacifist principles. Some of the reformist socialists, notably Bernstein, were in this group. Kautsky, the pre-eminent theorist of the Second International, also defended an antiwar position, but his views lacked the revolutionary vigor of the more leftist opponents of war. The other group stood on the extreme left. It was small in number at the outset, but it made up for its size by vigor and enthusiasm. It urged a complete break with the socialist supporters of war, who were denounced as chauvinists and social patriots.

As the war continued, efforts to revive the international socialist movement began. The first international conference of socialists was held at Lugan, Switzerland, and was attended by representatives of the Italian and Swiss parties. The conference called for a speedy termination of the slaughter. Meanwhile, opposition to the war increased. In Germany, Karl Liebknecht, Franz Mehring, and Rosa Luxemburg organized an opposition to the dominant views. In her "Junius" pamphlet, Luxemburg demanded a fight for peace based on the class struggle. In France, opposition to the war arose in the ranks of the syndicalists; in Great Britain, as noted above, the Independent Labour party stood against it from the outset.

In the forefront of the opposition to the war was Lenin, then the leader of the majority faction of the Russian Social Democratic Labor party. Lenin's views were presented to the International Woman's Conference, held at Berne, Switzerland, during March, 1915. He and his group favored a complete break with the prowar socialists and called for a revolutionary struggle. These views were rejected and more moderate antiwar views adopted.[1]

ZIMMERWALD

At a conference of antiwar socialists initiated by the Italian and Swiss socialists at the little Swiss village of Zimmerwald in September, 1915, differences arose between the extreme left and the more conservative

[1] Olga Hess Gankin and H. H. Fisher, *The Bolsheviks and the World War* (Stanford University, Calif.: Stanford University Press, 1940), pp. 286–308.

majority. About twenty of the delegates were anxious to declare for peace between nations, and avoid an open break with the majority socialists supporting the war. The former group might be regarded as the right wing of the conference. In addition there were a center group and the extreme left, led by Lenin. The majority called for a revival of international socialism and an end of the war. A more radical statement was submitted and independently issued by the left. It was signed by five delegates, among them Lenin, G. Zinoviev, and K. Radek. An International Socialist Commission was appointed to maintain the organization.

The conference did not receive much attention, and its decisions were not closely examined then. In the meantime, the differences between prowar and antiwar socialists were becoming more acute. In Germany an open schism developed when a majority of opponents of war refused to bow to party discipline and approve war credits. When, as a result, they were forced out of the parliamentary Social Democratic group, they took the first step in the direction of forming an independent political division. In Germany, three tendencies were now apparent: the extreme right, or majority; the center group, with a substantial following; and a small leftist minority.

In other countries, the same division was appearing. The efforts to break with the majority socialists supporting the government were accelerated by the Zimmerwald movement and gained many adherents as the war continued. The rank and file of socialism and labor showed increasingly its dissatisfaction with the prowar policies.

KIENTHAL

In the meantime, the International Socialist Commission decided to call a conference, which convened at Kienthal, Switzerland, on April 24–30, 1916. Forty-four delegates were present, a number being prevented from attending by the police or by inability to get passports. Two views were in evidence, the left and the center. The left, while much stronger than at the first conference, was still a minority. Dominated by the views of Lenin, the left wanted a more decisive break, not only with the right-wing supporters of war, but also with the pacifist groups who, while opposing war, did not advocate the conversion of the national war into a proletarian revolution.

Differences between the two Zimmerwald groups grew increasingly sharper, with Lenin favoring a break with the less revolutionary elements. Believing that a new revolutionary international was needed, he not only attacked the prowar socialists but showed little patience with the group disposed to what he called "social pacifism." This was dominated by men such as Kautsky in Germany, Turati in Italy, and Longuet in France, who, while opposed to the war, were not ready for revolutionary *coup d'etats*. Efforts to revive the International were also made by members of the right.

THE SECOND INTERNATIONAL DURING WORLD WAR I

Leaders of the Second International sought to preserve their organization. Soon after the invasion of Belgium, Camille Huysmans, the head of the International Socialist Bureau, removed the Bureau headquarters from Brussels to The Hague. He tried to maintain relations with all socialist groups, but he was under continual pressure to call a general meeting. After several unsuccessful attempts to call such a conference, a meeting of delegates from Allied countries only took place. The socialist parties of Belgium, France, Russia, and Great Britain sent representatives to a meeting held in London in February, 1915, and presided over by Keir Hardie. The conference denounced the invasion of Belgium and France and brought forth a set of "War Aims" which foreshadowed Wilson's subsequent proposals. The responsibility of trying to maintain international relations between socialist parties fell to the International Socialist Bureau, which finally arranged a conference of minority and majority socialist parties for Stockholm in 1917. But the Stockholm conference failed to meet, the failure being largely due to the fear and suspicion that Allied prowar socialists entertained toward their German colleagues, and the opposition of the Russian Bolsheviks to all socialists not belonging to their faction.

With the end of World War I the efforts to revive the International were renewed. However, the task of rebuilding the shattered international edifice was not easy. The cleavage that had taken place could not be bridged, and bitterness, hate, and suspicion now divided the socialists of the world. On the extreme left were those who looked to the Bolsheviks for leadership, but even the non-Bolsheviks were divided between those who had favored the war and those who had been opposed to it but recognized that the prowar group, while mistaken, was neither chauvinistic nor composed of traitors to the working class. In an attempt to revive the Second International, delegates from a number of socialist parties met at Berne, Switzerland, under the chairmanship of Hjalmar Branting.

A bitter debate over war guilt almost wrecked the conference, but cooler counsel prevailed. Resolutions were endorsed favoring a democratic peace, an international labor charter, the use of parliamentary institutions, freedom of speech, and personal liberty to obtain socialism. Violence and dictatorship were debated, with a minority led by Friedrich Adler and Jean Longuet clamoring for a more militant policy. No agreement was reached, and both resolutions were placed in the minutes. A permanent committee headed by Branting and Huysmans was appointed to put the conclusions of the Berne meeting before the Peace Conference and to take steps for a revival of the Second International.

Uniting the shattered socialist forces was an insuperable task. The left had split away and formed the Communist International, but the controversy between the right wing and the former center continued. Nevertheless, plans for the reconstitution of the Second International went on. Delegates from a number of socialist parties met at Geneva in August, 1920. In contrast to the size and enthusiasm of former meetings, the Geneva conference was a small and spiritless gathering. It followed the line of the English Fabians, and came out for a policy of gradual socialization, with compensation to be paid to the displaced capitalist. London was selected as the temporary headquarters and an executive committee was chosen. Irreconcilable differences between the Second International and the Third, then in process of formation, were evident.

THE COMMUNIST (THIRD) INTERNATIONAL

With the victory of the Bolsheviks in October, 1917, unity of the socialist forces became impossible. Lenin had bitterly attacked the chief socialist parties of Europe for having "become disloyal to all their convictions and tasks." [2] He and his co-workers regarded the social democrats as betrayers and reactionaries with whom unity could not and should not be obtained. Therefore he and his associates initiated steps to form a new, more revolutionary, disciplined, and centralized International. On January 24, 1919, the Russian Communist party joined with several minor European communist groups in calling for the organization of a new revolutionary International. The need was held to be due to the bank-

---

[2] V. I. Lenin, *The War and the Second International* (New York: International Publishers, 1932), p. 8.

ruptcy of the Second International and the inability of centrist elements in the old socialist parties to adhere to a revolutionary program.[3]

The congress was opened by Lenin, with representatives from thirty-seven nations present. In the "theses" he presented, Lenin defined the difference between dictatorship in general and dictatorship of an oppressed class over its oppressors. Bourgeois parliamentary democracy was but a means of suppressing the toiling masses and keeping them in subjection. He denied the claim of the bourgeoisie to any rights. To him the demand for "freedom of assembly for the exploiters" was only a hypocritical pose.

The congress declared itself the heir of the revolutionary groups that had gathered at Zimmerwald and Kienthal, proposed steps to enlarge the membership, and elected an executive committee of the Communist (Third) International. Gregory Zinoviev, subsequently shot during one of the purges, was chosen president, and Angelica Balabanova, secretary. In contrast to its predecessors, the Communist International was to be an active and directing center of world revolution, marshaling its subordinate national parties behind a common revolutionary policy. Its purpose was the overthrowal of capitalism, the establishment of the dictatorship of the proletariat, and an international Soviet republic to abolish class oppression. The International Congress was the supreme body, and its Executive Committee exercised direction between congresses. Only communist parties were eligible for admission.[4]

Dictatorial tactics were new and unknown to the socialist movement, and it was assumed by some that despite the theoretical pronouncements, a wide variety of views and opinions would be tolerated. Consequently a number of socialist parties applied for affiliation with the Third International. Many were rejected, for the communist leaders held that the International "was threatened by the invasion of indecisive and hesitant groups who had not yet broken with the ideology of the Second International." [5] To avoid the lessening of revolutionary fervor, the Second Congress held in Petrograd from July 17 to August 7 laid down twenty-one points which had to be met by all political groups seeking admission to the Communist International.

3 *Thèses, manifestoes et résolutions adoptès par les I, II, III et IV congrès d'Internationale communiste* (Paris: Bibliothèque Communiste, 1934), p. viii.

4 *Ibid.*, pp. 7, 37–38.

5 *Ibid.*, p. 39.

THE TWENTY-ONE POINTS

The twenty-one conditions or points required were as follows: (1) all organs of the press to be controlled by the party; (2) all followers of reformists and centrists must be removed from responsible posts in the labor movement (even if it meant replacing experienced leaders with simple workers); (3) an illegal apparatus must be created by all communist parties; (4) persistent communist propaganda in the armed services must be conducted; (5) systematic and steady propaganda must be conducted in the countryside; (6) social patriotism, pacifism, and the League of Nations must be attacked; (7) open rupture with socialists of other persuasion must be brought about, and leading socialists, mentioned by name, were to be excluded; (8) colonial imperialism must be denounced and fought; (9) persistent infiltration and work in trade unions and cooperatives must be carried out; (10) conservative socialist and noncommunist trade unions must be fought; (11) communists who belong to parliament must be subject to control of the party's central committee; (12) "parties belonging to the Communist International must be built up on the principle of democratic *centralism*. At the present time of acute civil war, the Communist Party will only be able fully to do its duty when it is organized in the most centralized manner, if it has iron discipline, bordering on military discipline, and if the Party center is a powerful, authoritative organ with wide powers, possessing the general trust of the Party membership." [6]

Condition (13) required that communist parties were to make periodic "cleansings" of membership so as to eliminate petty-bourgeois elements; (14) parties belonging to the Communist International "must give every possible support to the Soviet Republic"; (15) an overhauling of old party programs must be undertaken as soon as possible, and the program must be approved by the Communist International or its Executive Committee; (16) "all decisions of the congresses of the Communist International, as well as decisions of its executive committee, are binding on all parties affiliated with the Communist International"; (17) every party that seeks to join the Communist International must "bear the name: Communist Party of such and such country (Section of the Third, Communist, International)"; (18) party organs must publish the important documents of the Third International; (19) a convention must

[6] O. Piatnitsky, *The Twenty-One Conditions of Admission into the Communist International* (no date or place; italics in the original), pp. 27–30.

be called by parties seeking admission to discuss their obligations; (20) parties which seek to join the Third International must organize themselves so that their leading committees are made up of members two thirds of whom adhered to the Communist International before the Second Congress; (21) members who reject the conditions or the principles of the Third International must be expelled.[7]

In addition to the issuance of the twenty-one points, the Second Congress defined the immediate tasks of the communist parties as the overthrowal of the bourgeoisie and the organization of all exploited classes by the advance guard of the proletariat, the Communist party, so as to reduce to impotence the small traders, farmers, and others inclined to rally around the capitalistic groups. Normal stimulus, but not artificial hastening, of the revolution was held possible and imperative. Actual preparation for the conquest of power under a proletarian dictatorship was urged upon all communist groups.[8] On the trade-union question, the congress urged infiltration of the reformist organizations so as to convert them to a revolutionary policy.

The expectation that proletarian revolutions in Western Europe would follow World War I was not realized, and the Third Congress recognized "that the war did not have as its immediate consequence a proletarian revolution, and the bourgeoisie has some grounds to register this fact as a great victory for itself." [9] Recognition that the revolutionary tide was no longer rising induced the abortive movement for a united front.

"THE TWO-AND-A-HALF INTERNATIONAL" OR THE VIENNA UNION

A center group had hoped that all the forces of international socialism could be gathered under one tent. While unwilling to accept the disciplined authoritarianism of Moscow, it was inhospitable to the reformism of the Second International. The center group sought the reconciliation of all the forces of socialism, and, as that was impossible, it set off on an independent course. Upon the invitation of the British Independent Labour party, delegates from several countries assembled at

[7] *Ibid.,* pp. 30–32, 39–41.
[8] *Ibid.,* pp. 42–43.
[9] *Theses and Resolutions of the Third World Congress of the Communist International* (New York: The Contemporary Publishing Association, 1921), p. 29.

Vienna in February, 1921. After criticizing both the Second and the Third Internationals, the International Working Union of Socialist Parties, called the Vienna Union, was set up. This group was popularly known as the "Two-and-a-half International." Its main objective was the unification of international socialism, and as a result of its efforts the executives of the three Internationals met in the Reichstag building in April, 1922, to explore the possibility of joint action.

AN ATTEMPT AT A UNITED FRONT

On April 2, 1922, representatives of the Second International, the International Working Union of Socialist Parties, and the Third International met to devise a program of unity under the chairmanship of Friedrich Adler of the Austrian Social Democratic party and leader of the Vienna Union. In opening the meeting Adler declared that we "of the International Working Union of Socialist Parties have undertaken this experiment with the knowledge that the position of the world proletariat is such that it is imperative, in spite of all differences which may exist, to make an attempt to unite its strength for certain concrete purposes and actions." [10] Clara Zetkin, speaking for the Third International, took a few shots at the reformists and proposed that all groups oppose a new imperialist war and the Treaty of Versailles and defend the Soviet Union.[11]

Vandervelde, the spokesman for the Second International, demanded "guarantees of reciprocal good faith . . . against attempts to break up the unity of the workers in such countries as Belgium and England where this unity is still maintained." [12] Moreover, he asked the freeing of political prisoners held in Russia, the removal of Red Army troops from Georgia, and the establishment of freedom of speech, press, and assembly in Russia.[13]

A subcommittee tried to find a basis for agreement, and proposed that an Organization Committee of nine, three from each group, be set up. The Russian delegates agreed to allow a socialist deputation to attend the trials of the social revolutionaries charged with sabotage, and to re-

---

[10] *Official Report of the Conference between the Executives of the Second and Third Internationals and the Vienna Union* (London: The Labour Publishing Company, 1922), p. 7.

[11] *Ibid.*, pp. 12–19.

[12] *Ibid.*, p. 24.

[13] *Ibid.*, p. 60.

examine the issue of Georgia, but it would not yield on the question of "boring-from-within" other organizations of labor outside Russia.

The committee of nine elected by the conference of the three Internationals met in Berlin in May, 1922. Representatives of the Second International charged that the agreement had not been fulfilled, and that attacks upon their leaders by the Communist International had continued. In turn, Karl Radek, speaking for the Communist International, charged that the Second was disrupting the "united front." No agreement was reached on any of the important issues, and the conference broke up in failure.

MERGING OF SECOND INTERNATIONAL AND VIENNA UNION

Although the Vienna Union resented the attitude of the Second International, which was held as partly to blame for the collapse of the negotiations on unity, events were pushing the Vienna Union and the Second International together: the Moscow trials of social revolutionaries made a bad impression; in addition, the growing reaction at home had brought about a unification of the independent and majority socialists in Germany. The victory of fascism in Italy and the growing conservatism of the masses as a result of the stabilization of economic conditions emphasized the need for unity among the various socialist parties.

Convinced that unity with the communists was impossible, the Vienna Union and the Second International took steps to merge their forces. Preliminary meetings were held at The Hague in December, 1922, and in January, 1923, a call for a meeting was issued to all socialist and labor parties that accepted these principles: (1) the economic emancipation of labor from capitalistic domination could be achieved by the independent political and economic action of labor; (2) unity of the Amsterdam trade-union movement was essential; (3) in case of war, the policy adopted should be based on The Hague Peace Congress of 1922; (4) the Labor and Socialist International should be recognized as essential to war and peace; (5) the organization would not affiliate with any other political International.[14]

On May 21, 1923, more than four hundred delegates representing forty-three parties in thirty countries, met at London. The meeting, which lasted for three days, discussed imperialist peace, international

[14] *Report of 23rd Annual Conference of the Labour Party* (London: 1923), pp. 5–6, 14–15.

reaction, and the eight-hour day. On the first issue the congress declared that the "peace treaties violate all economic principles; they have thus prolonged and intensified the depression and postponed economic reconstruction." The resolution charged the ruling class with preparing a new world war.

The resolution on international reaction urged vigilance upon the labor movements of the world lest the capitalists in their own countries promote reaction abroad. It urged that workers "combat with all their strength all endeavors by the imperialist powers to intervene in the home affairs of Russia or cause a fresh civil war in that country." [14]

Both the Vienna Union and the Second International were dissolved, and the Labor and Socialist International was set up. Congresses were to be held at least every three years, but provisions for convening special congresses were made. An Executive Committee was chosen which was to elect a bureau made up of nine members who could meet quickly on urgent matters and summon the Executive Committee when necessary. The latter appointed Friedrich Adler of Austria and Tom Shaw of England as the joint secretaries. The Labor and Socialist International recognized the existence of the class struggle and the need for political and trade-union action to bring about the emancipation of labor. Close relations with the International Federation of Trade Unions were established.

Although operating under a new name, the Labor and Socialist International was in fact a continuation of the Second International that antedated World War I. It sought to unify the labor and socialist movements of the different countries, but it was not a centralized, disciplined organization whose constituent units were obligated to accept a common policy. From time to time, manifestos and resolutions were issued, but differences in attitude rendered agreement on basic issues impossible. Nevertheless, studies were made on disarmament, colonial problems, fascism, and other questions. No party was bound by the resolutions passed at the congresses, since each might be facing special problems which it was permitted to solve in accordance with its own views.

THE COMINTERN IN THE RUHR

During this period the Communists suffered a severe blow in Bulgaria, where the party was suppressed after an unsuccessful coup. Within Germany the occupation of the Ruhr by the French initiated a series of events which led to another defeat of the Communists. In August, 1923, a number of widespread strikes forced the resignation of the government headed by Chancellor Cuno. The Socialists, who had abstained from the coalition, joined the new government of Stresemann. Faced by a deepening political crisis, the German Communists decided on a *Putsch*. It was to start as a defense of the left-wing Saxon government, then threatened by the *Reichswehr,* and to spread through the entire *Reich*. The attempted revolt fizzled, with a few hundred Communists defending themselves heroically in Hamburg. The Hamburg rising, it seems, was due to a mistake in orders. Although the Hamburg Communists fought bravely, "'the big masses of the Hamburg proletariat remained completely indifferent." [15]

TURN TO THE LEFT

Following the German debacle, the Comintern executed a turn to the left. Now instead of "a united front," a slogan of "united front from below" was promulgated by Zinoviev, who described it as a tactical maneuver.[16] This move meant an unceasing attack upon the leadership of the trade unions and the socialist and labor parties. Carrying out this tactic of infiltration, the Soviet labor unions sought to gain admission to the International Federation of Trade Unions. They failed, but they found the English trade unions more hospitable.

Beginning in 1924, the communist parties had to adhere more closely to the line promulgated by the Communist International, the Comintern. Application of pressure led to splits in the Norwegian and Polish parties. The future conduct and policy of the Comintern were already obvious: it aimed to direct and control all affiliated parties.

CHINA

Although a detailed description of the Comintern in China is not possible, communist ideas began to play a role in that country in the early 1920's. Lenin had defended the view that the "revolution" would come as a result of an alliance of the Western proletariat with the colo-

[15] Franz Borkenau, *World Communism* (New York: W. W. Norton & Company, 1939), p. 252.
[16] *Le Congrès de l'Internationale communiste* (Paris: Librairie de l'Humanité, 1924), p. 38.

nial peoples and that China represented a testing ground. Sun Yat-sen, the leader of the Chinese Revolution, sought and procured the aid of Russian revolutionary leaders. Borodin, a former resident of the United States, was sent to Canton as political adviser in 1921; and General Galin-Bluecher, who also perished in the purges, became the military adviser to Chiang Kai-shek, a brother-in-law of Sun Yat-sen. The Kuomintang, or People's party, directed the program in which the communists cooperated. Substantial success was gained at first, despite the defection of some conservative groups from Canton. In 1925, Sun Yat-sen died, and he was succeeded by the leader of the left wing, Wang Ching-wei.

A sudden change in the fortunes of Chinese communism took place in March, 1926, when Chiang Kai-shek overthrew the government and arrested hundreds of communists and their sympathizers. Communist detachments fought heroically, but events were against them. The legions of Chiang Kai-shek swept aside with an iron broom all opposition. In July, 1927, the Russian embassy at Peking was raided, and the group of Chinese communist leaders found there were executed. A desperate attempt to stage a revolt in Canton in December, 1927, was mercilessly crushed.

THE THREE PERIODS

At the Sixth Congress of the Communist International in 1928, the years following World War I were divided by the Executive Committee into three periods. The first period witnessed a tremendous revolutionary upsurge throughout the world. It saw the February and October Revolutions in Russia, a revolt in Finland and Hungary, the establishment of a short-lived Soviet Republic in Bavaria, the occupation of the factories in Italy. Although the high tide was reached in 1919, the period lasted until 1923, and ended with defeats for the Bulgarian and German communists. The second period is characterized by the strengthening and consolidation of capitalism. Stability and expansion of capitalism beyond the levels attained before World War I are the attributes of the second period. This stabilization created a base for social democratic activity, and some believed that the terrain was favorable to the growth of the influence of the communists.[17] Therefore a more vigorous campaign against reformism, by which was meant social democracy and the

17 *La Correspondance internationale,* August 1, 1928, pp. 1–17, 160.

trade unions, was begun. This program led to the characterization of social democrats and trade unionists as "social fascists." The "third period" was presumably the opening of a new revolutionary epoch.

SOCIAL FASCISM

The noncommunist labor movement was subjected to attack for being allied with fascism or for at least unconsciously aiding it. In Germany this line of reasoning induced the communists to cooperate with the Nazis and reactionary nationalists against the socialists. In 1931 the communists aided the Nazis in the referendum campaign to overthrow the provincial government of Prussia in which the socialists had occupied an important place. This policy followed from the theory that the differences between the labor movement and the fascists were slight.[18] The proposed "united front from below" meant that the communists would seek to distinguish between the leaders of the reformist labor movement and their followers. How such a feat could be achieved was never explained.[19]

A united front from below was never realized. With the rise of Hitler and the sharp upsurge in his influence, the German Social Democratic party, through its official organ, the *Vörwarts,* appealed for a common front with the Communists. Hitler was then on the threshold of power. In addition, the Bureau of the Labor and Socialist International issued a manifesto on January 19, 1933, announcing its willingness to reach a common understanding with the Communists on the pressing issues of the day. Nothing came of this effort except an exchange of correspondence. In October, 1934, when the international situation had become more menacing, representatives from the Communist International met with leaders of the Labor and Socialist International but no agreement could be reached.[20]

The Communist International was in a real sense dominated by the Russian party, with the communist parties of outside countries morally and financially dependent upon it.

[18] Borkenau, *op. cit.*, pp. 341–344.
[19] O. Pjatnizki, *Die Bolschewisierung der kommunistischen Parteen der kapitalistischen Lande* (Moscow: Auslandischen Arbeiter, 1932).
[20] John Price, *The International Labour Movement* (New York: Oxford University Press, New York, 1945), pp. 87–88.

THE UNITED FRONT AND THE HITLER-STALIN PACT

The complete victory of Hitler and the rising fascist tide in France finally awakened the directors of international communism to political reality. The change of tactics was stimulated by the dangers to the Soviet government rather than by solicitude for world labor. Cooperation between communist and socialist parties began in France and was followed by extending the cooperation to nonlabor groups. In July, 1934, the Communist and Socialist parties of France signed an agreement, the pact for Unity of Action, against fascism. The policy of the Popular Front was initiated, under which alliances were promoted between all opponents of fascism, including bourgeois liberals. From the extreme radicalism of the third period, international communism had swung to the most thorough reformism. The policy of promoting alliance with socialists and liberals was continued until the Hitler-Stalin Pact of 1939.

THE MOLOTOV-RIBBENTROP PACT

With the signing of this pact, a swing to the left was swiftly executed, and the international communist movement dusted off its revolutionary slogans to be hurled by its orators at the governments and nations fighting for their lives against Hitler's tyranny. Communists everywhere found little difference between Hitler's Germany and the democracies of the West. Antiwar and anti-imperialism (meaning England) became popular catchwords for the followers of the Comintern. But a new reversal became necessary when Hitler unloosed his war machine at the Soviet Union in June, 1941. Communism became reformist, patriotic, and conciliatory. As a gesture toward Western public opinion, the Presidium of the Communist International announced its demise on May 22, 1943.

For many years the Communist International had been nothing but a mouthpiece for the Soviet Foreign Office. Supported by Soviet funds and prestige, it used the communist parties of other countries as pliable instruments for carrying out the needs of Soviet foreign policies. Although the Second International demonstrated that international cooperation against the national interest was not likely, the Third International showed that no group had sufficient insight, training, or experience to act as a general staff for the revolution. The Third International, in its aim to serve the Soviet government, neglected the interests of the workers of other countries, who were but pawns on Moscow's chessboard. No recognition was ever given of dissimilarities in training and experience or to the conditions of different countries. Nor was the political maturity or backwardness of different countries taken into account. A uniform monolithic policy was promulgated, and the servants of the Third International slavishly followed it. Thus the dogma of social fascism had prevented an alliance with the Social Democrats at a time when Hitler's rise to power might have been retarded if not prevented. Later, patriotic slogans and social conservatism were encouraged; and frequently the tools of Moscow carried their conciliatory policies to extremes.

POSTWAR

Although the Comintern had been formally dissolved, there was no reason to assume that it had ceased to function. With the change in international conditions, and with the opposition of Western democracies to Soviet expansion into Western Europe, the communist parties have again adopted a revolutionary policy. In the United States the policies of Earl Browder were sharply criticized by Jacques Duclos, the head of the French Communist party, who was evidently chosen by the international communist hierarchy to express its views. It is interesting to observe the effect that this criticism had upon communist policy. The American party transformed itself during the war into the "Communist Political Association" whose function was to act not as a formal political party but as a political educational group. Approved and carried out as a matter of course by all leading party officers and institutions, the Browder policy was unanimously repudiated once it was attacked by Duclos. No better example of control from the top and from abroad is necessary. Instead of defending their old positions, the members and leaders strove with all their energies to repudiate them.

STRUCTURE OF INTERNATIONAL COMMUNISM

Not only do the communist parties differ from other political parties, but the Communist International was unlike all preceding or existing international organizations of labor. In contrast to all such other groups, the Comintern was not made up of national parties, but of a single world party with national sections. Therefore, it should be recognized that communist parties of different countries cannot be regarded as independent political entities, but as subordinate parts of a world movement responding to orders and directives of a central body. A severe but exceptionally well-informed critic has argued that "almost all communist parties are largely dependent upon money from Moscow, money which comes in rather irregularly, according to the good or bad position an individual party holds at Moscow, according to the political importance Moscow considers a given party to have at a given moment." [21] The same author is, however, quick to point out that "it is not money," which determines the attitude of communists and communist political parties, for "there are hundreds and thousands of communists who are prepared to sacrifice their lives" for the "mythical authority of the Russian revolution." [22]

All communist parties are highly centralized and resemble in structure the Russian Communist party. They are directed by a political bureau, the politburo, which in fact carries out the monolithic opinion of the one party leader and his few close co-workers on this bureau. Little influence is exercised upon policy by the rank and file. In addition to the leader of a communist party, the Comintern usually sends one of its representatives —"Rep"—to supervise the carrying out of the "party line," and to offer direction and advice. Obedient and disciplined, the rank-and-file communist activists regard changes in policy and leadership as necessary adaptations and deviations, and accept them without question. The road to the millenium is tortuous, and the communist partisan has neither the time nor the inclination to reflect upon where he is going; nevertheless, he is certain that he is on the way. Reflection is unnecessary, for the professional revolutionary is soon transformed into a plastic instrument of the bureaucracy of international communism. The professional revolutionary was developed in the midst of Czarist autocracy, against which is carried on a relentless war. "The Comintern professional revolutionaries were caricatures of the Russian professional revolutionaries. The westerns who had become professional revolutionaries after the founding of the Comintern had no *Narodnaya Vola* [The People's Will] as precursors. . . . They were not themselves the source from which the current sprang." [23]

21 Borkenau, *op. cit.*, p. 357.
22 *Ibid.*, p. 357.
23 Ypsilon, *Patterns of World Revolution* (Chicago: Ziff-Davis Publishing Co., 1947), pp. 150–151. (By permission of Ziff-Davis Publishing Company, 185 Wabash Avenue, Chicago 1, Illinois.)

The professional revolutionary passionately devoted to socialism disappeared from the Comintern by 1923.

There was no longer place for apostles and fanatics of the revolutionary faith. Socialism as a purpose of the revolutionary movement was banished from the halls of the Comintern. The place of the professional revolutionary was taken by the revolutionary bureaucrat whose morality was determined by the political requirements of the Soviet Union and whose philosophy was regulated by the military commands of his respective central committee.[24]

Yet closely disciplined organization, loyalty, and tenacity are not to be underestimated as political virtues. The sharp revival of European communism after World War II is based upon the excellence of the communist apparatus, and the positiveness of the answers it gives to the problems of the time. To the degree that the future is dark and uncertain the communist answer is likely to find support.

THE COMINFORM

The dissolution of the Communist International was a maneuver to quiet opposition within the Western democracies to the Soviet Union. Yet the Soviet Union never surrendered its control of the foreign Communist parties, as is shown by the drastic and simultaneous shifts in the sentiment, thought, and policies of the Communist parties of the world. The secrecy which surrounded the working of the international Communist apparatus was discarded in the fall of 1947, and the Comintern reappeared in a new dress called the Communist Information Bureau (Cominform).

At the end of September, 1947, a conference by representatives of Communist parties from Yugoslavia, Bulgaria, Rumania, Hungary, Poland, France, Czechoslovakia, Italy, and the Soviet Union met in Poland for a discussion of the international situation. It heard a report of Andrei Zhdanov and adopted a declaration on the international question. An information bureau was set up, upon which each of the participating communist parties was given membership. The "Declaration" called attention to the split between the Soviet Union and its satellites on the one side and the Western nations on the other.

Two diametrically opposed political lines took shape; on the one side the policy of the USSR and the other democratic countries directed at undermining

24 *Ibid.,* pp. 157–158.

imperialism and consolidating democracy, and on the other side, the policy of the United States and Britain directed at strengthening imperialism and stifling democracy . . . . Thus two camps were formed—the imperialist and anti-democratic camp, having as its basic aim the establishment of world domination of American imperialism and the smashing of democracy, and the anti-imperialist and democratic camp, having as its basic aim the undermining of imperialism, the consolidation of democracy, and the eradication of the remnants of fascism.[25]

The declaration denounced the Western powers and charged European socialists with treachery. Communist parties were urged to unite against this menace. The Information Bureau was set up for purposes of spreading information on the international situation.

Unity of the communist parties was broken by the rebellion of Yugoslavia, which sought to cast off its role of a satellite and act as an independent power. At a meeting of all members of the Cominform except Yugoslavia, the latter country was charged with pursuing "an incorrect line on the main questions of home and foreign policy, a line which represents a departure from Marxism-Leninism." [26] The leaders of Yugoslavia were charged with hostility toward the Soviet Union and with treating it similarly to its treatment of other countries. In addition, the Yugoslavs were accused of adopting an incorrect agrarian policy, one which encouraged the growth of capitalistic elements in the countryside. The Yugoslav leaders had violated correct principles in setting up a bureaucracy within the party, and had acted in violation of Communist principles in expelling Comrades Djuivoc and Hebrang because they dared criticize the anti-Soviet attitude of the leaders of the Yugoslav Communist party. The Yugoslavs, in turn, refused to accept this criticism of the Central Committee of the Communist party of the Soviet Union. This refusal placed them outside the cooperating group of communist parties. After the break between the Cominform and the Yugoslav Communist party, the official organ of the Cominform was banned in Belgrade.[27]

The attack upon Tito and the Yugoslav Communists was also conducted on a more substantial plane than the ideological. On March 18, 1948, the Soviet Union withdrew its military and civilian specialists from Yugoslavia. Marshal Tito also objected to Soviet officers in Yugoslavia

[25] *For a Lasting Peace, for a People's Democracy* (Belgrade), November 10, 1947, p. 1.
[26] *Ibid.* (Bucharest), July 1, 1948.
[27] *Ibid.*, July 11, 1948.

seeking economic information from nongovernment sources.[28] The answer to Tito was given by the Central Committee of the All-Union Communist party (Bolshevik), in which the Yugoslav government was charged with shadowing the Soviet representatives. The Yugoslavs were also accused of circulating statements "that the 'A.-U.C.P. (B) is decadent,' and that 'in the U.S.S.R. there prevails a Great Power chauvinism,' that 'the Cominform is a means of conquest of other parties by the A.-U.C.P. (B)' and similar things." The letter added that the Yugoslavs were emulating Trotsky and following policies out of harmony with Marxism and Leninism.

Although the letters between the Central Committees of the Communist parties of the Soviet Union and Yugoslavia concern whether or not the Yugoslav party is following correct principles, the differences between the two countries obviously stemmed from the refusal of Yugoslavia to subordinate its economic and political interests to those of the Soviet Union. In a letter addressed to Stalin and Molotov, Marshal Tito and Kardelj explained that regardless of the amount of "affection any of us may cherish towards the country of Socialism, the U.S.S.R., in no way should he have less affection for his own country in which Socialism is being built . . . and this is to say for the Federal Republic of the Peoples of Jugoslavia." Tito and Kardelj also complain of the interference of the Soviet ambassador in the internal affairs of Yugoslavia. In another letter to Stalin and Molotov, Tito and Kardelj argued that "the Soviet Ambassador, being an ambassador has no right to ask for reports on the work of our Party from whomsoever he wishes; this being not his job." This attitude is condemned by the leaders of the Soviet Union, who maintain that the Soviet ambassador occupies a special place, for "the Soviet Ambassador, a responsible Communist, the representative of a friendly country which freed Jugoslavia from the German occupation, has the right, and more so the duty of entering from time to time into conversations with Communists in Jugoslavia to discuss with them all sorts of questions of interest to them."

The Russians defended their intervention in the internal affairs of Yugoslavia and denied Tito's charge that Yugoslavs were being taken into the Soviet intelligence service, adding that it "would be strange in-

28 "Letter to V. M. Molotov," *The Correspondence between the Central Committee of the Communist Party of Jugoslavia and the Central Committee of the All-Union Communist Party* (Bolshevik) (Belgrade: Jugoslav Book, 1948), pp. 21–22.

deed to demand that Soviet people who work in Jugoslavia should keep their mouths shut and never talk to anybody or exchange ideas with anybody." We can see emerging in this dispute a new form of imperialism. Of course, the leaders of the Soviet Union do not talk of the "white man's burden," but rather of the need to correct deviations from Marxism-Leninism. The right of the Soviet ambassador and of Soviet specialists to interfere in the affairs of an independent nation is explicitly stated. Nor is the Soviet Union above using economic pressure to compel compliance with its will. Trade with Yugoslavia has been sharply curtailed, and the Soviet Union and its satellites have sought to stimulate active revolt within the borders of a country also dedicated to achieving communism. The Cominform, like its predecessor, appears to be an instrument of Soviet foreign policy.[29]

[29] *Ibid.*, pp. 24, 29–30, 45–46, 51.

30. *LABOR INTERNATIONALISM*

The followers of Trotsky were everywhere expelled from the communist parties. Setting up on their own, they organized in September, 1938, the Fourth International. Its aims and philosophy were similar to those of the Comintern; it differed only in that it was weaker organizationally and financially than its hated rival.

INTERNATIONAL TRADE SECRETARIAT

In addition to the revolutionary internationals, the trade unions sought to bring the central organizations of the different countries together for mutual aid and cooperation. Beginning in 1889, international federations were set up in specific crafts and industries. The leather workers, the first, were followed by miners, glass workers, clothing workers, printers, metal workers, transport workers, and others. These organizations were called International Trade Secretariats; they were concerned with disseminating information on trade conditions, supporting financially affiliated unions in serious difficulties with employers, preventing the recruiting of strikebreakers in one country for service in another, and promoting unions of their craft or industry in unorganized areas.[1]

INTERNATIONAL FEDERATION OF TRADE UNIONS

The trade-union centers were not linked up internationally until the turn of the century. In part the delay was due to a widely held belief among European trade-union leaders that international questions fell within the province of the international socialist congresses which many

[1] J. Sassenbach, *Twenty-Five Years of International Trade Unionism* (Amsterdam: International Federation of Trade Unions, 1926), pp. 5, 97–116.

trade-union leaders attended as delegates. An attempt in 1888 to launch an international organization of trade-union centers by the Parliamentary Committee of the British Trades-Union Congress ended in failure. Finally, in 1901, the major European trade-union leaders agreed on the need for regular international conferences, the first one being held at Copenhagen. When the president of the Central Committee of the German trade unions, Karl Legien, opened the conference, he observed that the discussion of general questions was the job of the regular congresses of the Labor and Socialist International. Leaders of national trade-union centers could meet to discuss only trade-union problems. This view was accepted by the delegates.

At a second conference held in Stuttgart in 1902, Germany was chosen as the home of the international center and was allowed to bear temporarily the cost of its upkeep. It was agreed that the Bureau was to form a permanent connection between the trade-union centers of the different countries, to act as a distributor of important information, books, periodicals, and documents, to make available translations of laws, legal regulations, and court decisions of interest to workers of other countries, to start accumulating trade-union statistics, and to arrange for mutual assistance in industrial disputes. As can be seen, the conferences sought to limit their activities to strictly trade-union problems. At the conference of 1903, an International Secretariat of National Trade Union Centers was set up. Legien continued to act as international secretary, and a system of dues was initiated.

Before the Amsterdam conference in 1905, a long correspondence in regard to the issues to be discussed took place between the international secretary and the French C.G.T. The French demanded that the questions of antimilitarism, the general strike, and the eight-hour day be discussed. Legien answered that these issues did not come within the scope of the conference, and refused to place them on the agenda. Legien's views were approved by the national centers.

Samuel Gompers, the president of the American Federation of Labor, who was invited to the conference, suggested that it be made up of elected delegates rather than of secretaries, and that it be arranged so that the American delegates to the British Trades-Union Congress might attend without too much additional expense or loss of time. Gompers's suggestions were accepted by the Amsterdam conference, but the American Federation of Labor was not represented until 1909. To avoid interfering in the internal policies of the affiliated national organizations, the conference of 1905 adopted the following declaration: "All theoretical questions and questions affecting the tendencies and tactics of the trade union movement in the various countries shall be excluded from treatment by the conference." [2]

The leaders of the world trade-union movement were content, before World War I, to pursue limited objectives. Political and theoretical issues were left to the labor and socialist parties. The International Federation of Trade Unions sought to discourage division in the ranks, and did not permit the affiliation of more than one national center from each country.

Faced by the threat of war, both the socialist parties and the trade unions found themselves helpless before the gathering storm. Although they supported their governments in war, the trade-union leaders of Germany were eager to retain their connections with their colleagues in the Allied countries. For a time they exchanged letters with the heads of the Allied trade unions, but as the war went on, relations became more difficult. Allied trade-union leaders sought to have the Bureau of the International Federation of Trade Unions transferred from Berlin to a neutral country, but since Legien, the German leader, would not agree, the French set up an International Correspondence Bureau at Paris. In July, 1916, Allied trade unionists met at Leeds, England, and agreed to urge that special labor clauses be incorporated in the coming peace treaty. Later, a trade-union conference representing the Central Powers and several neutral nations met at Stockholm in June, 1917, took note of the proposals drawn up at Leeds, and called for a meeting of the trade unions of all countries at Berne, Switzerland, for the following September. In a telegram to the head of French labor, the Stockholm trade-union conference declared that "it welcomes the resolutions of the Leeds Conference of July 1916 as an important move in the interests of the organized workers of all countries, and as a pleasing sign of the intention to remove the divisions wrought among the workers by the war." [3] Only the French among the Allied trade unionists were willing to attend the Berne conference but they were not allowed to do so by their government.

The ties that bound the European trade unions together were never completely broken during World War I. In February, 1919, the first meeting of trade-union representatives from Allied, Central, and neutral countries was held at Berne. Fifty-three delegates from sixteen countries

2 Quotation in Sassenbach, op. cit., p. 17.
3 Quotation, ibid., p. 57.

were present. An international labor charter embodying the principles promulgated at the earlier Berne and Leeds conferences was drawn up, and the re-establishment of the International Federation of Trade Unions was planned. A proposal by the French to consider labor's relation to the League of Nations was opposed by several on the ground that such a question was outside the trade-union sphere, but one of the French delegates answered "that a time had set in that compelled them also to deal with political questions which were after all human questions." A conference for winding up the business of the old International and for the re-establishment of international trade union unity was set for some time later in that year.

This conference in the latter part of July, 1919, was preceded by a preliminary meeting at which the head of the Belgian delegation, upon instructions from his organization, presented a bill of complaint against the German labor movement for its conduct during the war. His views were vigorously seconded by Samuel Gompers. Finally, the German delegation admitted "that great injustice was done to Belgium"—a statement accepted as proof of repentance.[4] Differences arose over other issues. Many of the delegates from European countries were socialists who were critical of the peace treaty and of the League of Nations. The British and American delegations, however, believed that the international labor convention represented real progress in behalf of labor. Nevertheless, the congress, with the American and British delegates opposed, declared it was unable to accept the Charter of Labor in the Treaty of Versailles as embodying the demands of the workers of the world. Headquarters were set up at Amsterdam, with the direction placed in the hands of a bureau of five made up of a president, two vice-presidents, and two secretaries. An English trade unionist, W. A. Appleton, was chosen president; when Karl Legien, the head of the German unions, was denied the post of vice-president, he refused all offices.

In contrast to the period following World War II, there was no decisive break in the relations of the world trade unions. Despite the rebuffs administered to the German delegations, German labor was welcomed into the international family as an equal. In fact, trade-union leaders, under the intellectual influence of socialism, doubted the unique responsibility of the Germans for the war. The international trade-union movement became a supporter of lenient treatment for Germany. World labor insisted upon the admission of German and Austrian delegates to

4 American Federation of Labor, *Proceedings*, 1920, pp. 148–150.

the first annual conference of the International Labor Organization, in 1919, upon terms of equality. In addition, the I.F.T.U. was active in lifting the embargo against Soviet Russia, in boycotting the reactionary government of Hungary, and in urging a program of socialization.

Although European trade unionism was united almost immediately after World War I, a permanent division arose in the political segment of labor and socialism; moreover, the Communist International attempted to introduce the same split into the trade-union movement. As its economic arm, the Third International organized the Red Trade Union International in 1921 with the hope of winning the trade unions to a more militant policy. In the summer of 1923, the Soviet unions sought to gain admission to the I.F.T.U. No agreement on conditions was reached, and the negotiations were abandoned. Independently the British Trades-Union Congress then tried to devise a cooperative program with the Soviet unions. The Anglo-Russian Trade Union Committee was set up in 1925 to bring the workers of the two countries into closer contact. Differences soon arose following a sharp attack upon the British trade-union leadership by the All-Russian Central Council of Trade Unions as a result of the latter's disapproval of the direction of the British general strike. Eventually the tenuous bond between the two groups was dissolved.[5]

In the 1920's and 1930's the labor movement of Western Europe was dominated by the Amsterdam International and its socialist allies. In this organization, the German trade unions and socialists played a dominating role, for the differences that had arisen during World War I had been quickly forgotten. In contrast, the Soviet trade unions had no important allies among the trade unions, and the American labor movement, then completely represented by the A.F. of L., followed an isolationist course.

The onset of the great depression placed a serious challenge before the Western European labor movement. An exponent of gradualism and slow change, it found itself seriously threatened by the rise of fascism and Hitlerism. It was against the trade unions and their political allies, the socialist and labor parties, that the fascists directed much of their propaganda fire. With the rise of Hitler to power, a major bastion of the I.F.T.U., the German labor movement, was ruthlessly destroyed. The I.F.T.U.'s membership of 23,170,006 in 1919 fell to 8,145,780 by 1934. Part

5 *Report of Proceedings of the 59th Annual Trades' Union Congress,* 1927, pp. 200–214.

of the loss was due to declining trade-union membership, common in depressions, but the serious loss was mostly due to the spread of the fascist plague throughout Europe.[6]

As a result, the A.F. of L. began to reconsider its formal relation to world labor. At its convention in 1935, the Executive Council called attention to the spread of fascism and to the danger of war. It was suggested that the A.F. of L. join world labor in meeting this threat to peace. Additional benefits would be gained from membership in the I.F.T.U. because the latter aided the workers' delegates with the agenda of the International Labor Office. In 1937 the A.F. of L. joined the I.F.T.U.[7]

With the outbreak of World War II the leaders of European labor were forced to flee from the Hitler terror. An independent labor movement ceased to exist on the European continent, the leaders of the I.F.T.U. became refugees, and the organization found it difficult to carry on any of its functions.

WORLD FEDERATION OF TRADE UNIONS

A new phase in the relations between the trade unions of Soviet Russia and the West was opened soon after Hitler's attack upon the U.S.S.R. The General Council of the British Trades-Union Congress proposed the establishment of an Anglo-Soviet Trade Union Committee, a proposal which the Edinburgh congress in 1941 unanimously endorsed. The committee was made up of an equal number of representatives of the All-Union Central Council of Trade Unions of the U.S.S.R. and the General Council of the British Trades-Union Congress. Its purpose was to help mobilize the full power of labor of both countries in the fight against the common enemy. At a meeting of this committee held in Moscow in October, 1941, an agreement was reached upon the objectives. It affirmed that the separate trade unions would preserve their autonomy and that each would abstain from interfering in the internal affairs of the other. In the spring of 1942, the secretary of the British Trades-Union Congress, Sir Walter Citrine, approached the Executive Council of the American Federation of Labor on the subject of enlarging the committee so as to include representatives of the three countries. He emphasized that the tripartite committee would be consultative and advisory, and that each would obligate itself not to meddle in the internal affairs of the

6 American Federation of Labor, *Proceedings*, 1935, p. 160.
7 *Ibid.*, 1937, pp. 196–197.

others. Moreover, it was Citrine's idea that membership in the committee would in no sense constitute an endorsement of the political or ideological tenets of the other nations; the committee would exist only to promote the war efforts of the trade unions of the member nations, to discuss issues of mutual concern, and to establish a medium for the exchange of information. Citrine hoped to carry the program of cooperation into the period of postwar reconstruction.

The American Federation of Labor refused to join the committee on the ground that the Soviet trade unions could not be regarded as labor organizations in the Western sense. In addition, leaders of the A.F. of L. feared that recognition of the Soviet unions might help to strengthen communist influence in other countries, including the United States. Having failed to win the American Federation of Labor, the British unionists approached the heads of the Congress of Industrial Organizations and several of the railway unions unaffiliated with either.

In the meantime exploratory steps were taken to transform the Anglo-Soviet Trade Union Committee into a world conference of trade unions. In November, 1943, invitations to such a conference were issued to seventy-one union organizations in thirty-one countries. The conference was to devise means of promoting the war effort and of securing representation for the trade unions at the peace conference and on the preparatory commissions working upon problems of the war and the postwar periods.

After some postponements, the World Trade Union Congress opened in London on February 6, 1945, with the British Trades-Union Congress as host. A total of 204 delegates representing about 60,000,000 members attended. Also present were observers from a number of organizations. Organized labor in the United States was represented by a group of top officials from the C.I.O. led by Sidney Hillman and R. J. Thomas of the United Automobile Workers.

A large number of issues came before the conference. It endorsed the decisions made at Yalta—the placing under the control of the United Nations, German industry, transportation, money and credit, and large agricultural estates; and full compensation for war damage to the Allied nations with priority for those who had suffered most. Requests were made for labor representation upon all committees dealing with the peace, the occupation of Germany, collective security, and international economic planning. The world security organization was endorsed and an end of colonies and colonial exploitation urged; punishment for

German and Japanese war criminals, including the emperor, was advocated. Proposals for raising the standards of living of all people and the expansion of social security and the protection of labor were made,[8] and an Administrative Committee was appointed.

PARIS CONGRESS

In September, 1945, 187 delegates and 65 observers from 65 national and 85 international organizations representing more than 66,000,000 workers in 56 countries assembled to launch another trade-union international. The International Federation of Trade Unions (Amsterdam International) was liquidated and its general secretary, Walter Schevenels, given a post in the new organization. An Executive Committee of 26 was chosen, and Paris was selected as the headquarters.

From the beginning, the World Federation of Trade Unions was dominated by the communists. Its attacks upon the Marshall plan finally forced its American and British affiliates to think of withdrawal. In 1948, the conventions of the Congress of Industrial Organizations and the British Trades-Union Congress authorized their officers to take such steps if necessary, and the refusal of the communist union heads to compromise led to the withdrawal of the American, British, and Dutch affiliates. Others have followed. The World Federation of Trade Unions is now the "open economic arm" of international communism.

As one examines the history of the attempts to evolve international organizations of socialism and labor, it is obvious that internationalism has not succeeded in preventing war, although it does make for greater understanding among the peoples of the world and for a measure of mutual aid and cooperation. Communist "internationalism" is a new phenomenon, for while it speaks in the name of common humanity it is actually a movement directed for the benefit of the Soviet Union. The unquestioning support of the Soviet Union by communists throughout the world and the announced readiness of communists to fight against their government without even examining the issues in a particular conflict show that communism is not an international movement in the sense that the communists of each country have an equal voice in the determination of decisions. On the contrary, communists outside the Soviet Union are political "quislings"—colonials—ready to do the bidding of a foreign power. Although the early internationals were unable to enforce disci-

[8] *Labour Monthly* (World Trade Union Conference Number), March, 1945.

pline upon the constituent units because each unit was independent, the Comintern and its successor, the Cominform, have destroyed internationalism by converting every other communist party into a willing and pliable servant of the Soviet Union. Communists outside the Soviet Union can no more be regarded as internationalists than can any other national working for a foreign country.

31. *ECONOMIC PLANNING*

The growth of partial or complete collectivism has raised the question of the efficacy of economic planning and socialization as a means of achieving maximum welfare. Socialists have not shown much concern with this issue. In part this indifference has been due to the type of problems faced by them. As a minority movement devoted to immediate reform and with long-run objectives as an ideal, the classical socialist writers were too busy examining capitalism critically to work out an exact blueprint of the future society. Moreover, the socialists, at least those in the Marxist school, reject most of the assumptions and conclusions of equilibrium economics; therefore the problem of planning would not appear to them in the same light. Individual consumer choices and the distribution of resources are not regarded by Marxist critics of capitalism either as effective or as the most rational method of allocating goods and factors of production. For these reasons the debate on economic planning has been largely a tussle among academic economists who accepted, in the main, the same fundamental economic doctrines. With few exceptions, the Marxists and most other socialists stood on the side lines, unmoved by the arguments that a planned economy would not function. Moreover, as socialists have never accepted their opponents' basic definitions of social efficiency, they have remained unconcerned by the charge that a planned economy will lead to misdirection of resources.

A considerable amount of the discussion with respect to planning fails to recognize that socialism has always been implicitly equalitarian,[1] and is more concerned with achieving what it regards as justice than with economic efficiency as defined by price economists.

Those who attack planning assume that it is an ineffective method for distributing resources. In contrast to a capitalist economy, where the price system distributes resources in accordance with the demand of

---

[1] Stalin has characterized equalitarianism as a petty bourgeois notion.

consumers, no mechanism, it is claimed, for effecting this objective exists in a socialist economy. The essential point in the criticsm of planning is "that an economic use of the available resources was only possible if . . . pricing was applied not only to the final product but also to all the intermediate products and factors of production, and that no other process was conceivable which would take in the same way into account. . . . all the relevant facts as did the pricing powers of the competitive market." [2]

Absence of consumer sovereignty, which means the consumer's inability to determine through the process of demand the type of goods that will be produced, implies that no basis exists for deciding on the quantities and qualities of goods to be produced. If such is the case, it follows that a socialist society is likely to concentrate effort on producing the wrong kinds of goods, since a single small group of official planners can never have sufficient knowledge to evaluate correctly consumer demand. Therefore, the conclusion runs, a great waste of resources would be inevitable in a socialist economic system.

Some writers raise objections to such reasoning. They begin by indicating that consumer choice is influenced by income. The type of consumer goods sought and the division of income between savings and consumption are both influenced by the income level. Moreover, the specific content of demand in any society living above bare subsistence is to some degree conditioned by emulation and socially influenced taste. Propaganda, which in a price economy is designated as advertising, and emulation of the leaders of society certainly influence consumer taste. Conspicuous waste is another determinant of demand in a society where "keeping up with the Joneses" and material wealth are indexes of social importance. H. D. Dickinson has drawn a distinction between needs and wants. "Needs are what we really require for life, efficiency and enjoyment; wants are what we *think* we require." [3]

Although there is considerable truth in these distinctions, they scarcely answer the basic issues involved. Many needs arising in one type of society are absent in another. A society of sybarites has different needs from a society of self-flagellating ascetics. Once technical efficiency makes possible life above a subsistence level, many goods are not indispensable to the survival of the individual, although life would be more dull and uninter-

2 *Collectivist Economic Planning*. Edited by F. A. von Hayek (London: Routledge and Kegan Paul, Ltd., 1935), p. 33.
3 H. D. Dickinson, *Economics of Socialism* (London: Oxford University Press, 1939), p. 31.

esting without them. It is true that tastes are frequently crude and that the worse is often in greater demand than the better. Yet there is no way of changing the situation except by educating the individual. The basic issue remains: in a free market the consumer, no matter how his "wants" and "needs" are shaped, gets what he wants in a planned economy he does not.

As a matter of fact, taste is a social product. The mere fact that the tastes of people residing in one area differ from those of people living elsewhere is proof of that. Demand for specific goods is not transmitted through the germ plasm, but is conditioned by society, income, social position, and cultural outlook. Ostentation may be regarded differently in different societies.

In a planned economy the area of choice will be narrowed. "Economic planning is the making of major economic decisions—what and how much is to be produced, how and where it is to be produced, and to whom it is to be allocated, by the conscious decision of a determinate authority, on the basis of a comprehensive survey of the economic system as a whole." [4] This definition underlines the conscious planning of economic decisions, central control, and the reaching of decisions on the basis of analyzing the "needs" of the entire economy. Economic planning differs from decision making in a competitive market economy in that decisions in the latter emerge as a result of many independent units and are not the outcome of the conscious direction of a central agency.

Certain critics of socialism deny the very possibility of rational economic calculation in a planned economy. Professor Ludwig von Mises has maintained that socialism will provide no mechanism for rational economic decisions, for no means of estimating the cost of instrumental goods will exist.[5] According to von Mises, economic activity is rational when it seeks to achieve the most satisfaction for the individual. What gives the highest pleasure is not always determinable in advance, and the choice made by the individual often fails to meet the earlier expectations. Consequently, the question revolves itself into freedom of choice. A socialist economy, certainly the complete and partial ones we have known, allows consumer choice for the members of the community receive wages and salaries which can be freely spent. It is, of course, within

4 Dickinson, *op. cit.*, p. 14.
5 Ludwig von Mises, "Economic Calculation in the Socialist Commonwealth," in *Collectivist Economic Planning.*

the power of the government to withhold certain types of goods from the market; but a democratic socialist government will within limits be responsive to the desires of its constituents; moreover, price cannot be the ultimate determinant in a planned economy.

It is a question whether the failure to put out the multiplicity of brands of variants of an article would entail any social loss. Many goods are produced and sold whose nonexistence would have aroused no feeling of positive loss. It is true that to the prospective purchaser of such goods, failure to produce them might entail some reduction in satisfaction. However, the social cost of producing numerous unnecessary varieties of a product is frequently high, and the movement for product standardization is based upon the assumption that the benefits of variety are less than the cost of diversity. In fact, choice is frequently made as a result of momentary fancy or some other fortuitous event, and the absence of the numerous varieties developed for competitive purposes would not be felt. Consumer goods will still be transferred to consumers in a market, and the citizen will still show his preference or lack of preference by buying or refusing to buy restricted varieties at existing prices. As in a competitive market, adjustments in prices will take place on the basis of trial and error, and a constant attempt will be made to set prices at a point where they equate supply and demand, a point at which they clear the market, although many equations will have to be solved.

So much for the operation of consumers' choice; there remains the problem of valuing the factors of production. In a competitive economy, factor prices are determined on the market and reflect the relative significance placed upon them on the basis of their marginal productivity in value terms. With the ending of a competitive market for capital goods, valuation and rational distribution of resources, some claim, become impossible. Professor von Hayek believes that although a theoretical solution of this problem is possible through the setting up of a series of simultaneous equations, in practice it would be necessary to draw up innumerable equations based on an unmanageable amount of statistical data.[6] The problem in this connection is more complicated than that raised by the distribution of consumers' goods, for a rational distribution of the factors of production means "to produce the goods in such proportions that the prices which clear the market of them also represent their cost to the community as expressed in other goods which might have

6 F. A. von Hayek, "The Present State of the Debate," *ibid.*, p. 212.

been made instead." [7] If a given number of factors are employed in producing goods which consumers prefer less than those that are not being produced, it is to the advantage of consumers that the former goods be decreased and the latter goods increased. The existence of a factor market in a competitive economy means that prices oscillate around factor value. The value of the factors is derived from the value of the goods produced with their aid, and "where the same production can be secured by substituting a cheaper for a dearer factor, the substitution will be carried out by the alert entrepreneur." [8] In a collectivist planned economy, the argument runs, producers' land and capital will be owned by the community; there will be no bidding, and hence no valuation of the factors.

Instead of decisions being made by individual entrepreneurs as under capitalism, responsibility for production would be lodged with a planning board whose task would be to discover the combination of factors that would hold cost to a minimum. Scale and level of output would be influenced by the same consideration as under competition—the attainment of lowest unit cost. Moreover, believers in central planning contend that the planning board would have available a much greater amount of information than could ever be known by the single entrepreneur.[9] Still, this does not remove the many difficulties involved. As Hall says:

When it is realized that all these members of the class "factors of production" have to be compared with one another—and this not with respect to their power of satisfying the consumer, nor even with respect to their power of producing in their present uses goods which satisfy him, but with respect to their power of producing *all* the goods which satisfy him—the formidable nature of the . . . step will be realized.[10]

Lange has suggested three steps in the approach to this whole problem: (1) the elaboration of a preference scale; (2) knowledge of the terms and alternatives offered; (3) information of the amount of resources available. If conditions (1) and (3) are known, the " 'terms on which alternatives' are offered are determined ultimately by the technical possibilities of transformation of one commodity into another—by the pro-

[7] R. L. Hall, *The Economic System in a Socialist State* (London: Macmillan & Co., 1937), p. 66.

[8] *Ibid.*, p. 67.

[9] Oskar Lange and Fred M. Taylor, *On the Economic Theory of Socialism,* (ed.) B. E. Lippincott (Minneapolis: The University of Minnesota Press, 1938), p. 60.

[10] Hall, *op. cit.*, p. 79.

duction function," [11] which means the relationship between inputs of productive services in a given time period and outputs of product in a given time period. If the factors are divisible, preference will be given to the combination which yields the highest value returns. It is not unlikely that the heads of plants in a socialistic economy would, by adding and subtracting units of a factor, arrive at the most economical combination. The head of a Soviet plant has the problem of discovering the most effective methods of production, and reaches his conclusions in approximately the same manner as the capitalistic entrepreneur—by trial and error.

There remains the question of determining the effective importance of a factor which has alternate uses. Professor Taylor has outlined the following procedure: construction of factor-valuation tables which approximate correct valuation as closely as it can be ascertained. Enterprise managers would then follow a policy as if the valuations were correct, keep a close check on results, and make whatever corrections were warranted by experience. They would thus lower the valuations that were shown to be too high and raise those that appeared low.[12]

What Lange calls the "parametric function of prices" will be retained in a socialist economy.

On a competitive market the parametric function of prices results from a number of competing individuals being too large to enable anyone to influence prices by his own action. In a socialist economy, production and ownership of the productive resources, outside of labor, being centralized, the managers certainly can and do influence prices by their decisions. Therefore the parametric function of prices must be imposed upon them as an accounting rule.[13]

Lange argues that the Central Planning Board will fix prices to which managers of enterprises will have to adhere.

The prices established by the planning authority on the basis of the factor-valuation tables will be costed to the industries in the form of bookkeeping entries; this is simply a statement that the terms on which alternatives are offered must be established for all users of the factors.[14]

If supply and demand are equal at the price set, the accuracy of the valuation tables will be indicated.

11 Lange, op. cit., pp. 60–61.
12 Fred M. Taylor, "The Guidance of Production in a Socialist State," ibid., p. 52.
13 Lange, op. cit., pp. 80, 81.
14 Claude David Baldwin, Economic Planning (Urbana: The University of Illinois Press, 1942), p. 128.

If in regulating producing processes, the authorities were actually using for any particular factor a valuation which was too high or low, the fact would soon disclose itself in unmistakable ways. . . . A too-high valuation of any factor would cause the stock of the factor to show a surplus at the end of the production period . . . . a too low valuation of any factor in the tables would be certain to cause a deficit in the stock of that factor.[15]

Of course, any program of this kind would depend on the ability and honesty of the administrators, who would face problems similar to those faced by an entrepreneur operating in a competitive market. By small variations at the margin and by observing the effect of these variations, the problem of the combination of factors to be used will be solved. We must remember that a socialist society does not start production in a vacuum. An approximation of previous prices of goods or factors may serve as a frame of reference; adjustments can then be made by trial and error, to produce the desired results.

Another question that arises with reference to the socialist economy involves the rate of saving or capital accumulation. Dr. Lange believes that the rate of capital accumulation can be better determined by a central planning agency than by consumers. Although this opinion may be challenged, the actual rate of capital accumulation is scarcely determined in a modern capitalist economy by independent decisions of the individual consumers. Managed currencies, deficit financing, and government influence on interest rates exercise an effect on capital accumulation. Certainly in a high-income economy, where the government is subjected to the pressure of public opinion, a higher rate of savings than that intended by the community would not be possible, for the short-run effects would be immediately visible in a lower standard of living. Therefore, even though the actual decision rested with the planning board, the decisions would in general reflect community will.

It can be admitted, however, that a socialist economy, while allowing choice, will not reflect it as sensitively as will a competitive society; and our society is not purely competitive; it has many monopolistic elements. It can be said, however, that socialists have never been impressed with the arguments presented by such critics as Professors von Mises and von Hayek, and with the exception of a number of socialists holding academic posts, the issue has never aroused much interest. This fact is not due to intellectual obtuseness, but to a feeling that the issues are not real or important. Socialists do not regard the competitive mechanism as an

[15] Taylor, *op. cit.*, p. 53.

effective means of allocating resources. On the contrary, they hold it to be wasteful and inefficient. Socialists cannot be unaware that in a capitalist economy, resources are often devoted to industries satisfying the whim of the rich rather than the needs of the poor. Yet such distribution of resources shows the sovereignty of the consumer, for voting is based on one's power in money on the market. Consumer sovereignty in a capitalist economy is for the socialist an economic "rotten borough" system.[16] The evil involved in lessening choice seems to the socialist minor as compared with the social waste of unemployment. The waste of cyclical unemployment, the most serious of all, could be mitigated if not ended.

If this waste were a cost necessary to the attainment of some more than equivalent advantage, as the waste entailed in movement is a necessary condition of transfer from a less to a more favorable situation, a socialist State, equally with a capitalist one, while doing its best to mitigate individual hardship must needs accept it. There would be no reason to expect any more strenuous attack on industrial fluctuations and, through them, on unemployment under one system than under the other. But the facts are not thus. . . . [When the capitalist] dismisses a workman it makes no difference to his earnings whether the workman finds work elsewhere or is thrown into idleness. The social costs entailed by industrial fluctuations are not weighed up against benefits and accepted as price, which, for the sake of these benefits, it is worth while to pay. They are simply ignored. Under socialist central planning they would, of course, not be ignored.[17]

It is axiomatic that any plan drawn up by a central planning authority will be far from faultless. Mistakes will be made, as they are under capitalism. Losses to the individual and to society that follow from the misdirection of effort under capitalism, and that do not appear on a balance sheet, are not taken into account by those seeking to determine the optimum allocation of resources. If one considers the real rather than the monetary effects of decisions leading to incorrect allocation of resources, the results in a capitalist and a socialist economy are not much different. If an entrepreneur in a capitalist economy invests one million dollars in an enterprise using specialized factors and the enterprise fails, and if we assume that these factors are not now used in other industries, the entrepreneur has lost one million dollars, and society has lost resources of a value that might have been used in other directions. Similar results would take place in a socialist society if a wrong decision were made by the planning board. In real terms, the results are not different,

16 A. C. Pigou, *Socialism versus Capitalism* (London: Macmillan & Co., 1937), p. 32.
17 *Ibid.*, pp. 55–56. Reprinted by permission of The Macmillan Company.

although the penalties imposed upon the individual in a capitalistic society may exercise greater restraint upon him. Although central planning will also emphasize efficiency, the penalties for faulty guessing will be less than under capitalism. Mistakes will not be as severely "punished," and while some regard this as a criticism, it does create a "possibility that economic relationships may more closely conform to the idea of the brotherhood of man, and that gain and loss may more often depend on personal merits or faults." [18]

THE NEW SLAVERY

An even stronger argument against a collectivist economy than the difficulty of allocating resources has recently been made. Socialism and other forms of collectivism have been held to be a danger to freedom. One cannot ignore the towering importance of this issue; irrespective of the merit of the argument, it is both needed and salutary.

To "the great apostles of political freedom the word has meant freedom from coercion, freedom from the arbitrary power of other men, release from the ties which left the individual no choice but obedience to the orders of a superior to whom he was attached." [19] This statement would be accepted by the most extreme Marxist socialist, who would argue that political freedom, while important, is only a halfway house, and that the individual is not free so long as he is by necessity forced to submit to the will of another. Socialists have always proclaimed that their objective was to enlarge the area of freedom, and dictatorship as an important concept in socialist ideology actually dates from the October Revolution. Even though the phrase "dictatorship of the proletariat" can be found in the works of Marx, it never was regarded as of significance by many leading socialists, although Lenin placed much emphasis upon that idea.

Professor von Hayek attributes the growth of science and invention "to the march of individual liberty from Italy to England and beyond." [20] Socialists from Marx to the present day have recognized the progressive character of capitalism in relation to the preceding social and economic systems. The argument that earlier periods had failed to make economic

18 Carl Landauer, *Theory of National Planning* (Berkeley: University of California Press, 1944), p. 113.

19 F. A. von Hayek, *The Road to Serfdom* (Chicago: University of Chicago Press, 1944), p. 25.

20 *Ibid.*, p. 15.

advances because of hampering restrictions is only partially true; the slowness of their economic growth was due in part to the absence of extensive markets, to capital accumulation, and to political separatism.

These remarks are, of course, incidental to the principal objection that is raised. Professor von Hayek believes that the competitive system not only is the most efficient in allocating resources, but is also the most reliable in assuring the greatest amount of freedom for the individual. He does believe that wherever "it is impracticable to make the enjoyment of certain services dependent on the payment of a price, competition will not produce the service; and the price system becomes similarly ineffective when the damage caused to others by certain uses of property cannot be effectively charged to the owner of that property."[21] He believes that governments have gone beyond creating a suitable environment for competition, and that socialism and central planning are inherently hostile to it. This assumption is undoubtedly correct, for socialists believe that competition under capitalism has very harmful features which society should abolish. Socialists approve of competition among workers for higher output and better quality, but they eschew competition in the disposition of products. An attempt is made to plan production so that the clearing of the market at given prices is almost inevitable.

MORAL RULE AND PLANNING

It is maintained that a system of central planning requires some common goal or purpose, and the "welfare of a people, like the happiness of a man, depends on a great many things that can be provided in an infinite variety of combinations. It cannot be adequately expressed as a single end, but only as a hierarchy of ends, a comprehensive scale of values in which every need of every person is given its place."[22] This is actually meaningless. Is the need of every person given its place or is it determined by the weight each exercises in the market? Has the need of a southern share cropper the same attention as the desires of a café society playboy? Moreover, no detailed agreement as to common ends is needed in a planned economy. In a democratic planned society the planning authorities can respond to changes in taste approximately in the same manner as can a nonplanned society. The individual may have a hierarchy of needs, but in a nonplanned economy the satisfaction of a lower or less impor-

21 *Ibid.*, p. 38.
22 *Ibid.*, p. 57.

tant need by one person is possible at the same time that another cannot meet an imperative need, provided, of course, the former has greater purchasing power than the latter. Socialists argue that a planned economy might not allow the printing of more than a million copies of *Forever Amber* at the time when there is a shortage of paper to supply war veterans with college textbooks. Moreover, the English Labour government has, up to now, shown that, irrespective of the doctrinaire pronouncements of socialists and nonsocialists, central direction of the economy is possible without encroachment upon personal liberty.

Yet a planned economy is likely to find the allocation of the factors, especially labor, most difficult. In democratic countries, emphasis is rightly placed on free collective bargaining between labor and employers as the method of settling wages and other conditions of employment. However, as soon as the unions become strong enough to imperil some vital interest or service, steps limiting their right to strike in given industries are urged by some groups in the community. A well-organized labor movement brings with it statutory wage fixing and voluntary and "semi-voluntary arbitrators, and effective strikes in large industries sooner or later become rare or are restrained. This is true in democratic free enterprise economies, and therefore the right to strike is neither absolute nor a major exercise of freedom." [23]

Problems of distributing labor in a socialist society are likely to be serious, as England's shortage of miners in 1947 has shown. This condition was, however, due to long-run causes, but its possible occurrence in a socialist economy cannot be denied. If at a given level, wages are unlikely to attract sufficient workers into a vital industry, it is clear that the utility of the wage is below the expected disutility of the work, or that the wages offered are not high enough to attract labor from other industries. Incentives in the form of more favorable hours and wages will have to be devised, and to argue that a socialist society cannot normally meet such a test without forceful allocation of labor seems unwarranted. England in 1947 was, however, unable to distribute labor by pecuniary inducements. This inability was not the result of the introduction of socialism, but was due to historical causes and to the loss of foreign investments and many other losses occasioned by two wars. The deterioration of the mining industry is caused by the lack of public concern in the past by the former

[23] See Barbara Wooton, *Freedom under Planning* (Chapel Hill: The University of North Carolina Press, 1945), pp. 102–121.

private investors, who allowed the wasting of one of the nation's principal resources; it was not caused by the Labour government.

There is no evidence that a planned economy cannot guarantee certain individual rights, such as free speech, press, and assembly; protection against search and seizure; and assurance of a fair trial in open court. So long as a parliamentary system exists, there is no reason why all these rights as well as others cannot be guaranteed.

The thesis that economic planning breeds dictatorship seems to be based exclusively on economic determinism. While he deplores Marxism and all its works, Professor von Hayek seemingly has accepted one of Marx's basic dogmas that productive relations determine the political superstructure. To neglect the cultural and intellectual influences that have shaped the institutions of a nation like England or the United States and to concentrate upon economic change is to make the cardinal error of the Marxists. Moreover, the Soviet dictatorship did not arise as a result of economic planning, but as a result of the seizure of political power. An even more serious error is the coupling of the Nazis with historical socialism.[24] Although the Nazis urged certain forms of socialization, their anticosmopolitanism, their racism, had deep roots in feudal conservatism. To hold the socialists responsible for the Nazis is as logical as to attribute the excesses of some religious cult to the founder of Christianity rather than to the peculiarities of the particular sect. All forms of historical socialism are basically opposed to Nazism, whose roots are in German history. Not a single important Nazi came from the Marxist camp. As a matter of fact, the urban workers who were raised in the socialist tradition showed the greatest resistance to the Nazi virus, far greater than did the neoliberals, and the Nazis gained few followers among labor.[25] Failure to recognize this explicitly invalidates much of Professor von Hayek's argument. The living reality is more significant than any theory. The English are carrying out a program of socialization without secret police or concentration camps; the Soviets and Nazis have used both. Such differences illustrates that doctrinaire economic interpretations do not necessarily conform to the facts of life. English freedom is rooted in several centuries of history, and changes in economic forms cannot wipe out long-cherished institutions. The roots of Soviet and Nazi tyranny can be found in their history. On these points Professor von

24 *Ibid.*, p. 30.
25 Evelyn Anderson, *Hammer or Anvil* (London: Victor Gollancz, Ltd., 1945), p. 141.

Hayek is not altogether consistent. His thesis is that freedom is the result of liberal economic relations; but, on the other hand, he maintains that the growth of collectivism is due to the growing belief in its desirability.

Nevertheless warning of the dangers of the concentration of power is higly desirable. The libertarian (anarchist) writers were concerned over statism throughout the nineteenth century, and history shows that they understood the power problem. In contrast to the neoliberal school, they were also critical of capitalism and aspired for a society in which the individual not only enjoyed freedom from governmental tyranny, but also was not exposed to economic oppression and inequality.

32. COOPERATION

The cooperative movement was, at the beginning, a response of labor to the evils of industrialism. "The decade in which the Pioneers of Rochdale founded their Co-operative store is known to historians as 'The Hungry Forties.' " [1] Many writers have described the misery and squalor of the early factory town, and the cooperative movement was an attempt to overcome some of the hardships facing the workers in the new industrialism.

Consumers' cooperation was introduced by twenty-eight flannel weavers of Rochdale, who, in 1844, combined their funds to purchase the necessities of life. Cooperation itself is an older movement; it was designed to free the individual in order to permit him to escape from competitive industrialism and build a cooperative society. "The ideal proclaimed by the Rochdale pioneers in their original statement of their objects, had been preached for a generation by Robert Owen to the people of Great Britain, and in a rather different form, by Fourier and others to the people of France." [2] Largely because of Owen's influence, the London Co-Operative and Economical Society was founded with the object of uniting those groups interested in communal living and associated labor. Although an elaborate scheme was devised, the program started and ended with the opening of a store.

Cooperative communities were founded or planned in the 1820's at London, Edinburgh, Exeter, Dublin, Wigan, and Orbiston. All failed.[3] The Brighton Co-operative Trading Association was not more successful, but beginning May 1, 1828, its leader, Dr. William King, issued a

---

[1] G. D. H. Cole, *A Century of Cooperation* (Manchester: Co-operative Union, Ltd., 1944), p. 1.

[2] *Ibid.*, p. 13.

[3] F. Hall and W. P. Watkins, *Co-operation* (Manchester: Co-operative Union, Ltd., 1937), p. 61.

monthly journal, the *Co-operator,* which helped to spread the cooperative gospel.[4] By 1844, the experiments in producer and village cooperation had ended in failure. "Thus ended the Owenite Movement, as a movement for the establishment of 'Villages of Co-operation' where the faithful could escape from the tribulations of the 'old immoral World' into the purer atmosphere of the New Society."[5]

The early cooperative movement had plenty of enthusiasm, and many risked their savings in these ventures. Its weakness was the absence of "unity and cohesion." No national organization was set up, and the movement was a series of "loosely connected regional groups." Workers were unaccustomed to joint action. Only recently freed from the hampering effects of the Combination Acts, the workers did not yet trust one another or their leaders. In addition, they had not yet developed the moral fortitude and faith which enables members to have confidence in the future in the face of present adversity. Moreover, the pioneer cooperatives "were philanthropic movements of patronage, almost of charity. They were created out of a feeling of pity, because of a desire to relieve the miseries of the working classes caused by the terribly low wages in the first half of the nineteenth century, when machinery was taking the place of manual labor, and aggravated by the high price of bread, which the protective duties continued to increase for the benefit of the landlords."[6] Early cooperatives also suffered from lack of good business management. Frequently the accounting system left much to be desired. Fraud and embezzlement were not unknown, and dissipation of profits was sometimes practiced.[7]

ROCHDALE PIONEERS

A more successful formula was devised in Rochdale, a textile community of about twenty-five thousand people, with forty thousand more living in surrounding villages. An important center of the woolen industry, Rochdale had experienced strikes and clashes between workers and employers. The Chartist and Anti-Corn Law agitations also affected the community. In 1844, the town was the scene of a serious strike of weavers

[4] T. W. Mercer, *Co-operation's Prophet* (Manchester: Co-operative Union Ltd., 1947), pp. 21, 51 .

[5] Cole, *op. cit.,* p. 36.

[6] Charles Gide, *Consumers' Cooperative Societies* (New York: Alfred A. Knopf, Inc., 1922), p. 33.

[7] Hall and Watkins, *op. cit.,* pp. 68–73.

which spurred some thought on social and economic problems. At a meeting held on August 11, 1844, the cooperative society was formed, with Miles Ashworth appointed as president. It was decided to open a store, flour, sugar, butter, and oatmeal being the first commodities handled.

The most important principle elaborated by the Pioneers was "dividend on purchases." It is the view of G. D. H. Cole that the Rochdale Pioneers had combined several ideas "none of them individually novel, but making up a total that was essentially new." [8] Perhaps the most noteworthy ingredient of consumers' cooperation is its democratic control, which gives to each member one vote irrespective of the number of shares he owns. Seven additional principles were enunciated: (1) goods were to be sold at existing local prices; (2) a fixed rate of interest was to be paid on shares, and this payment was to have first claim on profits; (3) after profits had been paid, the surplus was to be distributed among members in accordance with purchases; (4) trade was to be conducted on a strictly cash basis and no credit was to be given; (5) membership was open to all regardless of sex; (6) members were to be educated on cooperative principles; (7) accounts were to be regularly kept and audited. These points constituted the charter of consumers' cooperation.

In their original rules adopted in 1844, the Rochdale Society of Equitable Pioneers defined their purposes an an "arrangement for the pecuniary benefit and improvement of the social and domestic condition of its members." Shares were to be sold for one pound each. A store was opened and then before the manufacturing "of such articles as the Society may determine upon, for the employment of such members as may be without employment, or who may be suffering in consequence of repeated reductions in their wages." [9] At the beginning the Pioneers had no notion of the difference between producers' and consumers' cooperation.

Progress was slow but steady. At first the store was opened two nights a week and then, in 1845, every night. In the first full year of operation, the gross sales were £710; by 1850, £13,180; and in 1860, £152,000. The large increase in sales, capital, and membership was in part due to the improved conditions experienced by English labor in the decades following "The Hungry Forties." With success came expansion. New departments and activities were begun, and the gospel of cooperation was spread through preaching and education. A cooperative manufacturing

8 Cole, *op. cit.*, p. 63.
9 Quotation in Cole, *op. cit.*, p. 75.

concern was organized, but after a time those more interested in profit making than in cooperation gained the upper hand, and the producers' cooperative was converted into an ordinary stock company.

Although not successful as a producers' cooperative, the Pioneers marched to success on the consumers' front. However, not all was quiet even there. Disputes over dividends developed, and in 1869 a split in the society led to the setting up of a rival group, which remained independent until 1933.

CHRISTIAN SOCIALISTS

Despite its immediate success, the cooperative movement faced a number of difficulties because of the absence of legal protection. The Christian Socialists[10] who came on the English scene in the 1850's were mainly concerned with promoting producers' cooperation. They did not succeed in their major objective, but their efforts led to the enactment of the Industrial and Provident Societies Act of 1852, which gave cooperatives adequate legal protection and security for their funds. In addition, they bequeathed to the cooperative movement a number of earnest and devoted workers who were extremely helpful after Christian Socialism had ceased to be of much importance.

WHOLESALE COOPERATION

Once retail cooperatives had spread sufficiently and had acquired a large membership and volume of trade, the formation of wholesale cooperative societies was inevitable. According to Cole, the Rochdale Pioneers had established a wholesale department in 1850. "It is clear that the . . . wholesale department was meant from the first to be merely a step towards the creation of a federal Wholesale Society." Nevertheless, the attempts to set up such a society were, for a time, unsuccessful. The launching of *The Co-Operator* was an important move, for it furnished a medium of opinion, a source of information on the place and number of cooperatives, and a means whereby new views could be presented. In 1862 the law was amended so as to allow one cooperative society to invest in another. At a conference in Manchester in April, 1863, it was agreed to set up The North of England Co-operative Wholesale Agency and Depot Society Limited. After approval of the rules, 48 cooperatives

10 See chapter 13.

agreed to join, and by 1867, there were 250 member societies. Removal, in 1867, of the limitation on the £200 that could be invested by one society in another enabled the wholesale cooperatives to furnish an outlet for the surplus funds of the retail society, and also strengthened the financial position of the former. In 1868 the Scottish Co-operative Wholesale Society was founded.

NATIONAL UNITY

After the founding of wholesale societies, and some experience in their successful operation, there was still a need for consultation between the various groups. The leaders believed that cooperation would be advanced if technical and legal advice could be readily obtained, if experiences were freely exchanged, and if the relation of the movement to labor, government, and society were defined. For a short time the Society for Promoting Workingmen's Associations, set up by the Christian Socialists, performed this service for the cooperative movement. The need for legal and technical help was recognized by the leaders, but it required several years of agitation before a national movement could be inaugurated. Finally, in 1869, a national congress was held; it appointed a "consultative committee in London for legal and legislative action and general counsel." In addition the conference sought to amalgamate societies where necessary, and aid in the forming of federations. The congress selected a Central Board and decided on annual meetings. In 1873, the Central Board was reorganized. A number of sectional boards were set up with authority to act in their own areas. This marked the beginning of the Co-operative Union, which allowed any genuine cooperative society to affiliate with it. Between annual congresses, the Central Board and the National Executive, a smaller group chosen from the Central Board, acted for the movement. By the 1870's the foundation of the English cooperative movement had been laid. The Rochdale system was widely accepted, and membership, capital, and trade had steadily risen.

In 1917 the English cooperative movement took another important step. Up to then, it had avoided partisan politics. Regarding the government's treatment of the cooperative movement as unfair, the Co-operative Congress in 1917 embarked on political action. Two years later, an attempt to form a political alliance between labor and the cooperative movement was rejected by the latter. However, members of Parliament elected with cooperative support worked closely with labor, but only in

1927 did the two movements agree to limited voluntary cooperation in politics. Finally the cooperators joined the National Council of Labour, "the central body established by the Labour Party Executive, the Parliamentary Labour Party and Trades-Union Congress General Council to consult about vital matters of policy and to issue from time to time agreed pronouncements on behalf of the entire Labour movement." [11]

UNIT OF OPERATION

"A Co-operative Society is an association which usually begins by the recruiting of a hundred or so members who promise to deal at the new store, and to take one or more shares of a pound each which they may pay for by small installments." [12] As soon as adequate capital is procured, a limited stock of groceries is purchased and a hired manager put in charge of operating the store. Goods are sold at market prices, and income above cost of goods is used to pay for store expenses, including wages of the personnel, depreciation of plant, setting up of a reserve, interest on capital, and a dividend to members proportionate to their purchases.

Whenever a member makes a purchase at the cooperative store, he obtains a receipt giving the amount of the purchase. At the close of each half year, the surplus set aside for distribution among the members is dividend on the basis of purchases made. The manager and other store officers are responsible to a committee selected to supervise the management of the store. Fixing of prices and purchasing tasks which require technical competence are delegated to the trained executives charged with the operation of the store.

REASONS FOR POLICIES

Retail cooperatives sell at prices current in the neighborhood. Consequently members do not save in their daily purchases, but receive instead an annual or semiannual dividend. In England and Belgium "a good number of societies raise the prices of their goods higher than the current market price in order to augment their dividends." [13] This may be regarded as "compulsory savings," for the purpose of the higher prices is to

11 Cole, *op. cit.*, p. 330.
12 Sidney and Beatrice Webb, *The Co-operative Movement in Great Britain* (London: Swan Sonnenschein, 1899), p. 4.
13 Gide, *op. cit.*, p. 67.

encourage a higher dividend payment. Sales for cash are required, for a percentage of lapses is inevitable wherever sales are made on a credit basis. Moreover, an enterprise which sells on credit will have to buy on credit from its suppliers and on less favorable terms.

Profits of consumers' cooperatives are returned to each member in proportion to his purchases. For example, if a cooperative sold $1,000,-000 worth of goods, and made a profit of $150,000, a member who bought $100 worth of goods would receive $15 in dividends. The sum available for dividends depends upon the management of the society; and the amount due each member is determined by his purchases. In the English cooperative movement, the meaning of a good dividend has often been debated. Professor Gide has maintained that only if it is caused by competent management can a dividend be regarded as good; if the dividend is the result of high prices, low wages paid to employees, or the reduction in amounts due for reserve and depreciation, it cannot be so regarded.[14]

Cooperative societies are organized on a principle different from that applying to corporations. Each member, no matter how many shares he owns, exercises only one vote. In corporations, votes are generally proportionate to shares. Moreover, the number of shares that can be sold by a cooperative is unlimited, and late-comers in the society enjoy all the rights exercised by older members. If the member leaves the society, he can withdraw his capital.

Capital for cooperatives is secured by subscriptions. Some consumer cooperatives have started without capital or with very little, but have increased it by new subscriptions, by dividends left on deposit or converted into shares, and by loans from members. However, consumers' cooperatives have relatively low capital requirements, and, on occasion, they have shown a fear of being dominated by large capital groups.

TYPES OF COOPERATIVES

The cooperative principle has been applied to fields other than retail distribution. Cooperative enterprises are of several types. A government study of those in Europe classifies them as follows: (1) farmers' purchasing societies; (2) farmers' marketing societies; (3) general-purpose farm societies; (4) producer cooperatives; (5) consumers' cooperative; (6)

14 *Ibid.,* p. 88.

housing cooperatives; (7) utilities; (8) special service; (9) credit and banking; and (10) insurance.[15]

Farmers purchasing cooperatives are made up of farmers combined for the purpose of buying supplies. A number of local societies may federate into a wholesale cooperative to carry on large-scale buying and even manufacturing. In contrast, marketing cooperatives are organized to market the products of their members. A general-purpose farm cooperative may both buy supplies and equipment for its members and sell their products. Cooperative housing societies build and finance houses and apartment buildings; utility cooperatives operate telephone and power lines, buying or generating power. Special service cooperatives supply their members with burial and medical service. Credit and banking societies invest funds for their members and lend them money. Insurance cooperatives insure members against every contingency, depending upon their purpose.

The extent and importance of the cooperative movement differs from one country to another. In some countries cooperatives are a considerable segment of the economy; in others its significance is small. In England, in 1935, the distributive societies had £159,000,000 of capital and paid a wage bill to 200,000 employees of over £26,000,000. In addition they owned 66,000 acres of farm land and rented 9,000 acres. "They are the largest dealers in butter, sugar, bacon, and dried fruits, as well as tea, in the Empire." [16] More than half of the families in Scotland belong to cooperatives.

In Belgium the cooperative movement embraces 300,000 families, and is dominated by the socialist and labor movement. France, which has had an extensive cooperative movement for many years, has about 4,000 cooperatives with a membership of almost 2,500,000. The consumers' cooperative movement did not take wide hold in Germany until the last decade of the nineteenth century. After the revolution of 1918, cooperation increased sharply. In Austria more than one third of the population belonged to a cooperative. The movement was under the guidance of the Austrian Social Democratic party.

Before World War I, Czechoslovakia had about 17,000 cooperatives of different types. Annual business of consumer and agricultural coopera-

---

15 *Report of the Inquiry on Cooperative Enterprise in Europe* (Washington, D. C.: U. S. Government Printing Office, 1937), p. 6.

16 James Peter Warbasse, *Cooperative Democracy* (New York: Harper & Brothers, 1936), p. 31.

tives amounted to about $100,000,000, which represented about 3 per cent of the total retail trade. Some rural electrification societies were also active.

Danish cooperatives, best known for their excellent organization of the farmers, have engaged in processing and the export trade as well as in the purchase of supplies. In 1937, producer cooperatives controlled 85 per cent of the export of bacon, 49 per cent of the export of butter, and 83 per cent of the expert of fodder. In addition, they operated slaughter-houses, bacon factories, dairies and other food-processing plants. In 1937, between 25 per cent and 30 per cent of Finland's retail trade was done by cooperatives. There match factories, sawmills, flour mills, and other enterprises were operated cooperatively. In addition, 95 per cent of the butter supply and 38 per cent of the egg export were in the hands of cooperatives.

Cooperation is widely practiced in Sweden and Norway. Swiss cooperatives serve about one fourth of the population and handle from 10 to 12 per cent of the national retail trade. Italy, before the advent of fascism, had more than 40,000 cooperatives with a total membership of 500,000. Those groups that were under socialist influence were dissolved. Later many cooperatives were reorganized under fascist control.

COOPERATIVES IN THE UNITED STATES

Consumers' cooperation was tried in the United States during the 1840's. The movement failed to gain much headway, nor did the co-operatives organized by the Grangers after the Civil War fare any better. A successful cooperative movement was launched by the Finns who settled in Wisconsin and Minnesota; in 1917, a wholesale society, now known as the Central Cooperative Wholesale Society, was set up. In 1945, the total volume of business of 178 affiliated local societies was $6,690,000.[17]

The spread of the cooperative movement was especially marked in the 1930's. The Cooperative League, organized in 1916, carried an educational propaganda for the movement. In 1945, 15 wholesale cooperatives in the United States and 5 in Canada did a total business of $178,467,747 in serving 4,101 societies and 1,359,714 members. Mr. Cowling estimated

[17] Ellis Cowling, *A Short Introduction to Consumers' Cooperation* (New York: National Cooperatives, Inc., 1946), p. 27.

that a total of more than 2,500,000 families are affiliated with cooperatives in the United States, exclusive of members of credit unions and rural electrification cooperatives.[18]

Although the movement is by no means insignificant, it has not achieved the same place in the United States as it has abroad. "The strenuous competition among private tradesmen and the allurements of advertising have won the people to a habit of shopping and bargain hunting until these have become prevalent forms of American recreation." [19] Moreover, the chain stores that operate in the United States and the high mobility of the population have placed the cooperative movement under serious handicaps in many parts of the United States. It has made considerable headway in the last few years, but it is far from a mass movement.

COOPERATIVE COLONIES

On the whole, producers' cooperation has not been successful. Lack of funds and lack of managerial skill have usually militated against these experiments. A variant of producers' cooperation, the cooperative colony, has also been tried, but only where these efforts have been motivated by religious or nationalistic ideals have they been successful. Cooperative communities have been established by philanthropic reformers and by religious groups seeking to build a community based on secular or Christian principles. Shakers, Rappists or Harmonites, Transcendentalists, Perfectionists, and others have formed colonies. However, with the passing of the founders and with increasing contact with the outside world, the faith of the original builders withered and the old ideals lost their power. After a time the colonists usually returned to more conventional economic arrangements.[20]

COLLECTIVE VILLAGES IN PALESTINE

In Palestine, the cooperative village has played an important role in economic development. The *Kvutzsot,* or communal village, was first established there in 1909. Some of the inspiration for these projects came

18 *Ibid.,* pp. 30–31.
19 Warbasse, *op. cit.,* p. 57.
20 See William Alfred Hinds, *American Communities* (Chicago: Charles H. Kerr & Company, 1908); and John Humphrey Noyes, *History of American Socialism* (Philadelphia: J. B. Lippincott Company, 1870).

from European socialism through the influence of the General Jewish Labor Alliance of Russia, Poland, and Lithuania, known as the *Bund;* but necessity also played a role. The Bund, at its organization in Vilna, Poland, in 1897, was a typically Marxist group. Yet the peculiar conditions of the Jews in Russia and Poland could not be ignored. In 1895, Martov, the future leader of the Menshevik faction, urged the creation of a separate Jewish labor movement which would fight for the political economic and cultural liberty of the Jewish people.[21] The Bund at the beginning showed no concern for the special problems of the Jews, but under the influence of Vladimir Medem, it became a spokesman not only for socialism, but also for the social and political aspirations of Jewish life. Socialism was needed as well as a system where a majority national group would not possess more rights than a minority, where the former would not oppress the latter.[22]

At its meeting at Bialystok in May, 1900, the Bund came out for a multinational state and Jewish national autonomy.[23] A year after the Bund was organized, the Zionist Socialist party was founded. It was a Marxist party, but it also accepted the views of Theodore Hertzel—who had summoned the first Zionist Congress at Basle, Switzerland, in 1897—that the economic position of Jews in the Diaspora was abnormal and that only by acquiring a land of their own could this pathological situation be overcome. A collectivist system was the remedy, but on a soil owned and governed by Jews. The views of the Zionist Socialists as well as those of the members of the Bund undoubtedly played a role in making the cooperative ideal more acceptable.

The Zionist organization founded by Hertzel recognized the need for establishing an agricultural basis for the Jewish homeland. The early settlers in Palestine had no funds or experience in agriculture, and the communal village or Kvutzsot was a means of surmounting the difficulties of living and working in a new occupation in a foreign land. For the settlers, many of whom were acquainted with the socialist concepts of the Bund, collectivization did not represent an undesirable ideal. The first communal village was started in 1909, and the 120 now functioning

21 N. E. Buchbinder, *Die Geschichte von der Yiddischer Arbeiter-Bewegung in Russland* (Vilna: 1931), p. 78.
22 V. Medem, "Die Sozial-Demokratie und die Nationale Frage," *Vladimir Medem* (New York: American Representation of the General Workers' Union of Poland, 1943), p. 207.
23 A. L. Patkin, *The Origin of the Russian-Jewish Labour Movement* (Melbourne: F. W. Cheshire, Ltd., 1947), p. 145.

contain a membership of 44,000, or one fourth of the inhabitants of rural Palestine.[24]

The communal village is made up of a group varying from 50 to 800 members employed on a large farm. No social distinctions are allowed. All property and income belong to the members of the commune collectively. Every member receives an equal share of goods and services, and cash is furnished only on special occasions. In fact, no wages are paid to members, and personal income is distributed in the form of food, clothing, and shelter directly. Members are free to obtain for the asking and without charge the goods available at the communal store. No money passes over the counter; a good is requested and it is given if available. Food is served in communal kitchens for all members.

Children are wards of the community and spend their time in houses especially set aside for them, but parents are allowed to visit their youngsters several times during the day. Surplus products are sold in the villages, and any needed manufactured products are purchased. The villages offer occasional entertainment and lectures, and each member is allowed week ends and vacations away from the Kvutzsot. On these occasions the member receives a sum of money to care for his expenses. The villages are operated by annually elected management committees whose chief is a manager or "concentrator." Major economic decisions on allocation and expansion of capital and crop rotation are made by the entire membership. Jobs except those requiring expert training are rotated as far as such practice is feasible. Women are treated on the same basis as men in the allocation of jobs, although they may be exempt from the heavier types of labor.

Although the first Kvutzsot is forty years old, one cannot really tell whether this institution could survive a period of prosperous stability. There are, of course, advantages in this form of life: relief from tension, uncertainty, and competition; and the sense of security which every member gains. Yet only time can reveal whether this cooperative enterprise can withstand prosperity and survive the burning out of the fiery idealism of the older generation.

[24] Edwin Samuel, "The Jewish Communal Village in Palestine," *The Political Quarterly*, April–June, 1947, p. 144.

33. CONCLUSION

As one surveys the different movements for social organization, it is clear that the hope for a social millennium has been long and persistent. Man has always sought the promised land, but it is almost inevitable that such hopes should never be fully realized. The confidence of the eighteenth- and nineteenth-century social philosophers that peace, happiness, and abundance would inevitably follow, once an individualist society was abolished, seems to have been an illusion. Neither the Soviet system nor the one introduced in England has, so far, overcome the problem of scarcity which has haunted humanity through the ages. Moreover, the fears of the anarchists that the state in a socialist society might enslave and swallow up the individual have, unfortunately, been demonstrated to be no idle dream. It may be true that the unique history of Russia and its revolutionary movement can more easily account for the contempt for individual freedom found in the Soviet Union than can socialist philosophy. Nevertheless, the results in Russia cannot be ignored, especially when we note that the organizational forms and philosophic attitudes of Bolshevism are being diffused and widely accepted in countries with more democratic traditions. Marx, by excluding the moral factors in social change and arguing that his predictions were historically necessary and inevitable, is, to some extent, responsible for the amoralism of present-day communism. Yet his doctrines could not entirely blot out the beliefs and practices of European socialists, whose passion for social change was based upon humanistic and ethical considerations. It was not possible to convince English and Continental socialists that democracy and welfare legislation were of no importance. Therefore, even when they accepted Marx's doctrines, they frequently behaved as reformers, for they were unwilling to erase from their consciousness their everyday experiences with regard to forms of government and social policy.

Russia had a different tradition. Its autocratic government was scarcely

547

touched by the democratic movements that poured over the West after the French Revolution. Her reformers were forced into conspiracies and exile. At best democracy was a vague concept, and revolutionaries from Pisarev to Lenin emphasized the special place assigned to the intellectual elite. Lenin himself failed to understand the mechanics of power—that a party of revolutionary idealists once in control undergoes a significant transformation. Idealists who are unable to adapt themselves to the new political realities are either pushed into the background or liquidated. Those who enjoy and know the uses of power remain, and the recruits to the party follow in their steps. Those governing a totalitarian nation have no place for anyone highly sensitized to injustice. Instead, obedience and ruthlessness are the qualities most needed, qualities most often found in the careerist and bureaucrat.

Throughout the nineteenth century, and especially in the latter half, the more violent revolutionaries have assumed that once capitalistic production is changed, most of the social problems that bedevil mankind will disappear; and usually they have scoffed at the reformer who argued that a slow rate of change is the pace at which mankind can obtain optimum welfare. In most instances, neither people nor actual conditions have been carefully considered. Man must work with the physical and emotional equipment—including natural resources—he has inherited from the past. Although an ideal society can eliminate inequity and injustice, it cannot immediately overcome sloth, ignorance, and low productivity. Grandiose schemes for industrialization can, of course, be undertaken, but they involve high cost for the existing generation; moreover, it is a real question whether optimum welfare can be obtained by a ruthless policy of forced saving which imposes backbreaking burdens upon people. Programs of "excessive" capital investment are justified by the ultimate results, but that ultimate point of time may be in the vague and distant future. The Soviet Union is now carrying out its fourth Five-Year Plan, but a society of abundance still seems remote despite the sacrifices and deprivations endured by its people.

The single and final solution is attractive to certain people, but they refuse to recognize the stubborn and inexorable fact that there are no ultimate answers to human problems. Moreover, it is a mistake to assume that moderate and steady gains are unreal. If we examine the demands and even the aspirations of radical groups in the late nineteenth or early twentieth centuries, we can measure the real progress that has been made by the democratic societies of the Western world. Our work day is shorter

than the revolutionaries of the time demanded, our consumption standards are higher than the level they hoped to achieve, and our educational facilities for the masses are more impressive than those they envisaged. Even the supposedly chimerical demand for the six-hour work
day is on the verge of becoming a reality. These improvements were
achieved, certainly not without strife and turmoil, but at a cost much
lower than that being paid under the Soviet system.

Although democratic society has solved many problems and has greatly
raised the level of general welfare, the search for the one sudden and
final solution retains its appeal. The danger from this direction would be
small, were it not supported by a powerful government behind the
"Iron Curtain" which controls an international political apparatus. Not
only moral but financial assistance can be furnished to foreign political
groups willing to accept the doctrines and policies of that government.
Although its satellites are ready to defend every action of the Soviet government—irrespective of its effect on the masses of the people of their
own countries—these governments derive their strength in a large measure from other sources. Ruthlessness and command of funds are, of
course, important resources for influencing opinion. Yet there are more
substantial advantages enjoyed by communists outside the Soviet Union.
Their affiliation with historic radicalism, whose more extreme slogans
they have appropriated, is a great advantage for the continuance and
spread of communist influence. It is extremely difficult to convince social-
ist-minded workers in France and Italy that communism is no longer a
philosophy for liberating the individual from political and economic injustice but a device for mobilizing support for a brutal and expanding
dictatorship. Not only do the communists and their camp followers—the
fellow travelers—speak in the historic language of socialism, but outside
the Soviet Union they seek to capitalize on injustice and the discontent
of the masses with their government and with the operation of their
economy. That similar abuses may exist in the Soviet Union on a magnified scale is of no consequence, for such abuses are either denied or ra-
tionalized on the ground that a condition onerous in the United States
ceases to be onerous when established in the Soviet Union. Harsh conditions in the Soviet Union are sometimes justified by the claim that the
country needed to industrialize rapidly, World War II being given as one
of the proofs of the superhuman sacrifices exacted from the people to
build a heavy industry.

Of course no one can outline with assurance the probable history of a

period had crucial events taken a different turn. There is reasonable pre-
sumption that without the existence of the Soviet Union certain other
situations might not have developed. It is reasonably certain, for example, that the bifurcation of the European labor movement into a
communist and noncommunist strand might never have taken place, and
as a consequence Hitler might never have been able to achieve power.
Even if he had, under those circumstances a democratic Russia would not
as easily have signed a nonaggression pact and given the green light to a
world war. The hatred and distrust of democracy so strongly imbedded in
the consciousness of the Soviet leadership would have been absent, and
some plan might have been worked out with the Western nations that
would have stopped the aggressive expansion of a militant Germany.
There is no basis for assuming that a democratic Russia would not have
had the power to resist a German attack successfully. In fact, a democratic Russia might have so changed the balance of forces in Europe and
the world as to have perhaps even prevented World War II.

Yet one cannot underestimate the power of contemporary communism,
or Stalinism. Armed with tremendous physical and ideological resources,
it feeds on the difficulties and tensions of the modern world. The inter-
war years have clearly demonstrated that communism loses most of its
potency in a relatively stable world. Even though the current version of
communism—Stalinist imperialism—is much stronger in numbers and
territory than in the 1920's, this observation is still true. The countries
forced into the Soviet orbit seem to be there permanently. Only if the
Soviet system were shaken by an unsuccessful war could these governments be dislodged. The question arises whether a communist regime
independent of Moscow—Titoism—may develop in the different satellite
countries. Undoubtedly there are elements within them which resent the
economic exploitation and political dominance of Moscow. The insistence of Moscow through the Cominform that its dependencies solve the
agrarian and other problems in accordance with prescribed formulas
creates political difficulties and sometimes forces a policy upon the dependent regimes which arouses passive opposition of groups within the
countries. In addition, having achieved power at home, the native communists may resent the strict tutelage of their masters at the Kremlin.
National pride as well as the desire for power may play a role. Yet
Titoism is a fortuitous phenomenon, and its spread depends upon the
power of the Soviet Union within a particular country as well as upon the
strength and loyalty of individual leaders to the Kremlin. Certainly a

possibility that nationalist trends may develop is not to be overlooked, but it cannot be accepted as inevitable. Active Titoism may be limited to Yugoslavia, and those who harbor deviationist or nationalist views may be limited. Even if Titoism were to spread, the democratic forces would not find any new recruits. Such a development would weaken Moscow, for it would reduce the legions it controls. It would also lessen the dictatorship within the satellite countries, for it would allow them to develop more closely in accordance with their economic and social requirements, and thus decrease the need for Draconian measures. Finally, although the democratic front would not gain new recruits, decentralization would reduce the power of Moscow and make possible friendlier political and economic relations between the Western democracies and the Eastern countries. It would help revive trade between the areas and thus make it easier to attain economic prosperity and thereby reduce the threat from the extreme wing.

In Western Europe it is likely that the communist influence among the masses will recede if a reasonable basis for existence can be found. As in the period after World War I, the communist wave rose in France and Italy, but later it receded in both countries. The evidence is already clear that the peak of communist influence in Western Europe has been passed. The rise of the "Third Force," which seeks to combine economic progress and retention of individual freedom, is a hopeful sign. However, the Third Force contains within it groups that over the years have developed suspicion of each other. The groups that comprise it believe in common that freedom must not be sacrificed, and that means do not justify ends. Freedom cannot be obtained by putting millions into chains. As Dostoyevsky observed through Ivan Karamazov, "If he could enter paradise only through the tears of a child he would respectfully refuse to accept the entrance conditions." Improper means distort and destroy the end, and it is not possible to attain freedom by putting millions in chains.

Although the peak of Communist influence has passed, it is yet too early to assume that political stability has been achieved. In France the Popular Republican Movement (Christian Democrats) seems to be losing its hold on the electorate, because "politics and religion are too closely associated . . . to suit the taste of most Frenchmen." [1] The several wings of the Socialist party have kept the party divided. Granted his great virtues and matchless service to humanity and democracy, its leader, Léon Blum, is too old at seventy-seven to give the kind of leader-

[1] André Geraud, "France Gets to Her Feet," *Foreign Affairs*, April, 1949, p. 396.

ship French socialism needs. Despite its setbacks, the French Confederation of Labor (C.G.T.) headed by the Communist Benoît Franchon, retains its influence over the largest segment of the working class, its membership being concentrated in key industries—mines, docks, and steel mills. It is true that membership in the C.G.T. has been reduced to about two million, a third of its peak strength, but its capacity for evil and its passion for carrying out Moscow-dictated strikes have not been entirely eliminated.[2]

Communist control and direction of the C.G.T. has led to the formation of the Labor Force (*Force Ouvrier*) by the old syndicalists and socialists who desire to free themselves of communist influence. Led by the former head of the C.G.T., Léon Jouhaux, the Labor Force has rallied over a million workers to its ranks, but it has been handicapped by its closeness to the government. Although the Communists have sought to use the labor movement in behalf of the Soviet Union, the support they have received has been due to the failure of the numerous postliberation governments to introduce drastic and much-needed reform. Throughout the postwar period, taxes have been too low; yet evasion has been widespread and a monetary inflation rampant. "The worst feature has been the outrunning of wage rates by prices; this is definitely an inflation at the expense of the poor."[3] Until prices are brought down, profiteering is curbed, and an equitable tax system established, the appeal of communism is not likely to wane. France needs domestic reform, and until she gets it there will be scant hope of destroying the influence of the Communists.

Italy's dilemma is, if anything, more serious. Land reform and emigration are her two great needs, but the government is timid about tackling the former, and restrictions upon movement and settlement thwart any program to solve the latter. In Italy, as in France, the trade-union center, the Italian General Labor Federation established in 1944, was captured by the Communists. It has been used for political purposes, and the Labor leaders affiliated with the Christian Democratic party have withdrawn and set up the Free Italian General Confederation of Workers, whose primary goal is to break the strangle hold of the Communists upon the trade unions by drawing into its ranks the trade unionists who oppose the use of their organizations for political purposes. Unlike the situation

[2] Jules Moch, "Le Communisme et La France." Speech delivered before the National Assembly on November 16, 1948.

[3] John H. Williams, "Europe after 1952," *Foreign Affairs*, April, 1949, p. 434.

in France, the Italian Socialist party is closely allied to the Communists, and the efforts of the moderate Socialists to win a following among labor groups have been only partially successful.

Resolute action by the French Minister of Interior Jules Moch and his Italian counterpart Mario Scelba has prevented the success of the insurrectionary strikes in both countries. We must, however, recognize that the hard core of the communist apparatus is as strong as ever. Moscow-dominated parties are very resilient and are today both relatively and absolutely stronger in all Continental European countries than they were before World War II. The Communists face oppositions which are uncertain and disunited and which have no common policy or program. Through the Marshall plan, the United States has played a major constructive role in stabilizing the European economic and political systems. This aid will expire in 1952, when Europe will be faced with balancing its payments with the other hemispheres, especially with the dollar area. The loss of income from investments and the disruption of intra-European trade between East and West make it doubtful whether Europe can achieve a position that will enable her to do without outside help. A drastic cut in living standards is not a politically feasible alternative. Consequently, the West will face another danger point, and the United States will have to consider the consequences of withdrawal of aid upon European stability.

We must regard the communist danger realistically. The danger recedes with stability, but not because the inner core of communist strength is reduced. To devitalize the communist movement in France and Italy would require years of reasonable prosperity and proof to the ordinary man that a viable existence is possible. Western Europe faces danger from two sources; the false belief that the Communists have been mortally weakened; or a severe economic depression in the United States. The former assumption, based upon an erroneous understanding of the nature of the communist movement, attracts those who feel that the United States cannot continue to support Europe. Large expenditures for other people are not a pleasant prospect, but unless Europe can find a means of increasing its trade and raising its output we may have to continue them. A program as vast as the one we have undertaken and as vital to our safety cannot be cast aside because the estimates of the date of European self-sufficiency prove incorrect. It must be emphasized that the communist apparatus will be weakened only in time. In the short run, the number adhering to the party may wax or wane. The policies pursued and the risks undertaken depend upon the numbers that are rallied behind the communist program. The short-run ebb and flow do not, however, seriously affect the hard core. This can be reduced only by a long-run demonstration that a communist *Putsch* or a parliamentary victory of communism and its allies is impossible.

Of all countries in Europe, England has shown herself the most disciplined and able to cope with the problems that followed World War II. Credit for this achievement belongs in the first instance to the magnificent will to survive of the British people. Readiness to face up to reality and to belie the forebodings of the prophets of doom seems to be the destiny of the British people in the twentieth century. In part the British policy of austerity has affected adversely the economics of Continental European countries, but the English have been willing to tighten their belts and to tax themselves. Their recovery has been made under the leadership of the Labour party, and those who criticize the policies pursued must always remember that no other political group could have commanded the confidence and loyalty of the laboring people whose sacrifices and cooperation were essential to the success of this program. England is demonstrating that peaceful fundamental change is possible, a truth that needs demonstrating whether or not one approves of the policies instituted. It is not likely that the nationalization program will be reversed by a non-Labour government. When and if the Tories return to power, the nationalization program would, for the time perhaps, not be carried further, but little or no "denationalization" is likely. The policies of the Scandinavian countries resemble those of England. Norway has followed British austerity most closely, but Denmark and Sweden both have socialist governments and their policies of gradualism are in harmony with the reformist tendencies. A high level of discipline is essential, especially among the workers, if such a program is to be instituted, much less succeed. England and Scandinavia seem to possess peoples willing to undergo the sacrifices involved.

Europe, if it is to revive economically and regain its strength and initiative, must solve the problem of Germany. The suffering that this country brought upon the world is beyond calculation, its bestiality and ruthlessness beyond understanding. Yet Germany cannot be held permanently in subjection. The crucial question is whether the lust for domination and for the subjection of others has been extirpated by the fire of war. The answer is not easy to find, and any policy with respect to Germany is not without risks. While the Western Powers must not forget the past, they must be concerned for the future. Germany, with her human and physical resources, cannot be allowed to fall into the Eastern orbit. Instead, adequate steps must be taken against a resurgence of militarism, her socialist and labor groups must be encouraged to assume leadership so that a democratic Germany, tied to the West both morally and economically, will arise from the destruction and suffering of the war.

The unification of Europe, a slow and difficult process, is hindered by the desire of the several nations to control their domestic economies. Yet the Continent must be more united, not because of a doctrinaire plan but because unification is necessary for survival. Nations have regional problems of adjustment and vested interests that demand protection. On an international scale these problems are more difficult of solution but are not basically different. The most serious obstacles to union are social and political, the animosities of hundreds of years. Union in Europe, which has long been a utopian's dream, is now on the plane of practical policies. Unfortunately the process of unity cannot be speeded up, but the prospect of success changes with the degrees of danger that confronts the West. Resistance to such a program is great, but the need may slowly overcome the cultural and racial obstacles. However, while we should hope for unity, we ought to recognize that it can be achieved only in the uncertain and distant future. In the meantime, increased cooperation on every level needs encouragement.

In all European countries, a high degree of direction of economic life has been introduced since World War II: prices are controlled, scarce materials are allocated, foreign trade is directed, and manpower is distributed, the amount of control depending on the country. Major attention is given to investment control either by the government's financing of capital expansion directly or through control over the capital market. Comprehensive planning is widespread, and the liberal economies of the prewar years are, at least for the time being, gone. The meaning of these changes upon economic welfare and human freedom is not entirely clear. Yet it is obvious that nations with a large measure of central planning need not necessarily develop common political forms. The history of a nation and its political traditions will undoubtedly influence the political forms that emerge from these changes. With the expansion of central planning and control of economic processes, greater vigilance is still needed against tyranny, for power is concentrated in fewer hands as a result of the merging of economic and political power.

It is not likely that Europe will return to the free type of economics that prevailed before World War I. Either Socialist or mixed economies are inevitable. The entire trend of political change has been in the direction of collectivism, and even an American entrepreneur who had passed away at the turn of the century would scarcely recognize our own society as capitalistic. The numerous controls upon business and the protection and benefits to other groups would certainly be unlike the purer capitalism of his own time. Modern man demands more of government, and the technical levels achieved even in Western Europe and certainly the United States make possible fairly high minimum guarantees of welfare. Moreover, the citizen has been increasingly conditioned to look toward government for solutions and, in some countries, toward some collective ownership as a desirable ideal.

On general grounds we must expect social institutions as well as other departments of life to undergo continual change. So far no economic system has been permanent, and Professor Schumpeter has enumerated a number of reasons for the possible decline of capitalism. The entrepreneurial function, which is for him of central significance in a capitalist economy, is declining in importance, and "innovation itself is being reduced to a routine." Technological progress is increasingly becoming the business of teams "of trained specialists who turn out what is required and make it work in predictable ways." [4] The romance of commercial adventure is becoming extinct, and the innovator will soon be reduced to a salaried employee. Progress becomes automatic and independent of the inspired entrepreneur, so that when "capitalist enterprise," by its very achievements, "tends to automatize progress, we conclude that it tends to make itself superfluous." [5]

Capitalism has also lost the moral force it once commanded. Although new efforts are now being made to show that capitalism can be justified not only by its efficiency but for the greater freedom and individual development it allows, its gospel can no longer fire the souls of people living one hundred years after the publication of *The Communist Manifesto*. An efficient functioning of capitalism also demands a willingness to pay the cost of technical and cyclical adjustments, a cost that modern man is not willing to bear. The average man, unschooled in theoretical economics, cannot understand the paradox of poverty amidst plenty, and

---

4 Joseph Schumpeter, *Capitalism, Socialism and Democracy* (New York: Harpers & Brothers, 1942), p. 132.
5 *Ibid.*, p. 134.

he demands steps to abolish what he regards as an irrational situation. Nor ought we to ignore the distortions and evils of monopoly, unearned incomes, and great inequality of wealth.

Institutions are as impermanent as life itself. Perhaps one of the driving forces toward social change is that man's idea of perfection can never be realized in the actual world, and that the harsh social reality can never conform to the perfect patterns evolved by the imagination. Certainly the constant reappearance of models of perfect societies and the elaboration of theories to explain their inevitability show man's everlasting dissatisfaction with what exists and his aspiration for something better. Yet it is imprudent to discard the benefits we have today for the possibility of greater returns in the future. Revolutionaries implicitly assume that once power is given to them, all uncertainties as to the future will vanish. As the Soviet system demonstrates, the possession of complete power is not enough to sweep aside all obstacles, and the perfect society remains there, as elsewhere, a mirage. Man is too limited, stubborn, fallible, and intractable to solve all the problems of living in two or in an infinite number of generations; nor is he wise enough to realize all the limits of his program. Yet a feeling of smugness and certainty that this is the best of all possible worlds is also dangerous, for such an attitude hampers the slow and peaceful adjustments which give the lie to the doctrines of the inevitability of violent change.

Theories and movements of reform, whether they be Christian, democratic, or totalitarian, are all critical of competition and self-seeking. All of them believe in the subordination of individual interest to collective welfare. However, the Christian and democratic movements emphasize education and persuasion, and are convinced that individual rights and freedom are precious gifts whose destruction would reduce the magnitude of human welfare and would make possible tyranny and other evils that would be worse than those that afflict mankind under capitalism. In contrast, the reform movements that accept dictatorship are based, as we have seen, upon a doctrinaire interpretation of institutions, and the movements themselves stand ready to destroy the gains in freedom and protection the individual has won in many centuries of struggle. Nor is their assurance convincing that a dictatorship will be only a temporary and transitional device. If proof were ever needed, the Soviet government demonstrates that freedom cannot be reached through dictatorship; that once absolute power is attained, it is not willingly surrendered.

More extreme proponents of reform point to the slowness and uncertainty of step-by-step measures, and the tardy and imperfect eradication of evils. Yet revolutionary overturns create problems of perhaps greater magnitude. Repression and dislocation, the lack of adaptability of the community, and the danger of permanent Caesarism are some of the sour fruits of violent social change. People living in a democratic society have too much at stake to gamble on one throw of the political dice. If we are to retain faith in democracy and reasonable progress, doctrinaire revolutionism as well as doctrinaire reaction must be avoided. The thoroughgoing laissez-faire economist is a brother under the skin of the Marxian dogmatist, and both by their irrationality, unrealism, and stubbornness are the bellwethers of disaster. Orderly progress depends upon tolerance and the recognition that man can never give the final answer to the problem of the universe or of society, and that there is no a priori reason to assume that the truths of the eighteenth century are eternal. The multifariousness of doctrines and movements shows that man has always sought and is still seeking something better. Only patience, tolerance, healthy skepticism, an experimental attitude, and the willingness to analyze carefully will enable us to escape from the dangers of reaction and the perils of revolution.

APPENDIX

1. BELGIAN REFORMISM

Before World War II, the Belgian Labor party was an important segment of the world socialist movement. Its history resembled that of other socialist groups: its struggle with the anarchists and the emergence of reformist policies were common phenomena in socialist history. Through the influence of Henri De Man, the Belgian Labor party did present a trenchant criticism of Marxist views, and even though De Man collaborated with the Nazis during World War II, his views on this question deserve consideration.

The development of socialist views in Belgium was strongly influenced by reactions to changes in other countries. Filippo-Michele Buonarroti, a participant in Babeuf's conspiracy and its historian, settled in Belgium in 1823, and was instrumental in disseminating socialist ideas.[1] A group of Saint-Simonian missionaries, including Hippolite Carnot and Pierre Leroux, visited Brussels in 1831, and organized a propaganda campaign in behalf of their gospel. *L'Organisateur Belge* became the official organ.

ADOLPHE BARTELS (1799–1862)

Although Belgian radicalism was strongly influenced by the thinking of leading French socialists, indigenous views also appeared. Adolphe Bartels, who had been a leader of the opposition to the Holland government before the creation of an independent Belgium in 1830, founded a number of short-lived journals which advocated a republic, the universal franchise, and the right of each worker to receive the full fruits of his labor. According to Bartels, two stages were needed to realize socialism: the stage of repurchase by the state of all industrial and landed

[1] Louis Bertrand, *Histoire de la democratie et du socialisme depuis 1830* (Paris: Dechenne, 1906), I, 93–95.

property, and one in which each individual receives the full product of his toil.

Like Saint-Simon, Charles Fourier exercised a widespread influence over early Belgian socialist thought. One of his more eloquent followers, Victor Considérant, carried on missionary activity for Fourier's doctrine. Considérant emphasized that the "societary" order could be achieved without violence.

In 1849, a central propaganda committee for democratic socialism was set up in Belgium. It issued a program demanding universal suffrage, the right to work, the establishment of producers' cooperatives with government assistance, government-supported credit, and the encouragement of direct relation between producer and consumer so as to eliminate the middleman. In addition, it advocated state ownership of mines, railroads, and insurance companies, the introduction of a progressive tax on income, and reforms in government and in the army.[2]

Because of its greater political freedom, Belgium was host to many other refugees. Marx, Proudhon, Herzen, and Bakunin found refuge there at some time. Although they were not as a rule in direct contact with the workers, the *émigrées* did exercise some influence on socialist and democratic writers. Beginning in 1848, democratic and socialist organizations appeared in Belgium.

THE FIRST INTERNATIONAL IN BELGIUM

A year after the establishment of the International Workingmen's Association (the First International) a call for the organization of a Belgian section was issued. Caesar De Paepe represented the section at the London conference. Although this section stimulated organizing activity among the workers and a number of trade unions,[3] Belgian socialism suffered from the conflict between the Marxist and the Anarchists. Many socialist groups disintegrated, and a number of labor unions left the First International and became purely economic organizations devoted to the day-to-day interests of labor. Scattered labor and socialist groups had arisen throughout the country, and attempts to unite them into a single party began. On the one side were those who wanted a party similar to that established by the Gotha congress in Germany; on the other side were those who opposed political activity.

2 *Ibid.*, pp. 141–143, 319–329.
3 *Ibid.*, II, 160–240.

Failure to reach agreement on these issues led the Flemish socialists, in 1877, to organize the Flemish Socialist party. The party declared that social freedom was inseparable from political emancipation; it also recognized the need for forming an independent political party of labor.[4] Subsequently the socialists of Brussels organized the Brabant Socialist party. Its statement of principles demanded a large number of political reforms: public ownership of railroads, mines, and large corporations; the abolition of monopolies; and a progressive income tax. Political action and peaceful agitation were recommended as the means to be used for achieving this program. The union of the socialist parties, Flemish and Walloon, was consummated in January, 1879, by the establishment of the Belgian Socialist party. It declared itself collectivist and internationalist. Trade unions, cooperatives, and study or propaganda circles were eligible for membership. A defense fund for the support of strikers was set up, and a campaign for universal suffrage inaugurated.

A further step toward uniting the Belgian workers' movement was taken in 1885, when the Belgian Labor party was organized. It sought to operate on the political and economic planes: trade unions were organized for advancing the day-to-day interests of the workers; on the political plane the party sought influence in Parliament.

The Belgian Labor party is made up of three types of organization: political organizations, trade unions, and socialist cooperatives. The socialist unions are headed by a Trade Union Commission, made up of the unions affiliated with the Belgian Labor party and independent trade unions which accept the principle of the class struggle. From its beginning, the Belgian Labor party directed its energies toward reforming the franchise and improving the conditions of work. The socialist agitation, in April, 1893, achieved the first objective, which enabled the socialists to increase their parliamentary representation.

WORLD WAR I

The Belgian Labor party supported the government in World War I and several of its members entered the cabinet. Socialists were also members of the first postwar cabinet. Some who had in the past opposed participation in a nonsocialist cabinet now favored it.[5]

---

[4] *Ibid.*, p. 305.
[5] Emile Vandervelde, *Le Parti ouvrier belge* (Brussels: L'Eglantine, 1925), pp. 95–96.

PLANNISM

Between the two world wars, Henri De Man, a leading Belgian, developed a general criticism of Marxist orthodoxy and a program for avoiding the dangers of reformism. He had started as an extreme radical, but gradually lost faith in leftist opinions. His observations in the United States and Germany fortified his belief that Marxism was outmoded and not suited to modern times. Moreover, De Man maintained that socialism is not dependent upon proletarians, and that its ideas can be traced back to great thinkers of antiquity and of modern times. Socialism in origin, he holds, "is less a doctrine of the proletariat than a doctrine for the proletariat." Moreover, the entire analysis of Marxism as to the motivation of capitalists and the aspirations of labor is rejected. De Man argued that "in the days before Marx, socialism was utopian; the motive for establishing socialism was to be found in a recognition of the moral superiority of a socialist commonwealth. Marx wanted to escape the uncertainties involved in this dependence upon visions of the future by proving economic laws make the coming of socialism inevitable." [6] De Man, however, held that there is no necessary connection between the class struggle and the liberation of man. He cited improvements in the conditions of labor, and the increased reformist and middle-class outlook of the workers as proof of the invalidity of the view that socialism must depend upon the worsening in the conditions of labor. Moreover, "the undoubted fact that the originators of socialist doctrines have almost invariably been bourgeois intellectuals, shows that psychological motives are at work, motives which have nothing whatever to do with class interests." [7] He denied Marx's view that the growing solidarity of labor reflects the cooperative character of capitalism, which draws an increasing number of workers together and compels them to cooperate in the performing of their labor. This view was dismissed as materialist mysticism, for labor technically cooperates only when the management of the factory is authoritarian. De Man challenged the notion of increasing misery as forecast by Marx. On the contrary, he held that the real position of labor has been improving under capitalism. However, needs have grown to a greater degree than have the means of satisfying them. Class antagonism arises not as a result of a feeling by workers that they are being

---

6 Henri De Man, *The Psychology of Socialism.* Translated by Eden and Cedar Paul (New York: Henry Holt and Company, 1927), p. 25.

7 *Ibid.*, pp. 26–27.

exploited, but as a result of the belief that they belong to a class regarded as socially inferior. The absence of equality and the recognition by labor that it holds an inferior position stimulate class feeling. The equalitarian basis means that socialism is part of democracy, and aims at its extension. Democracy is thus not an administrative technique, but a moral principle based on the view that man is most protected against tyranny and violence when he himself has a voice in his government.

THESES OF PONTIGNY

After Hitler's rise to power, De Man tried to discover a substitute for fascism, one freed from the romanticism of the left and the sterility of the right. He worked out what has been called the Plan of Work (*Plan du Travail*), intended to attract middle-class and professional people as well as workers. The Plan was not regarded as reformist, but it differed also from the insurrectionary movements of communism and syndicalism. The Plan was evolved as a result of the belief that the economic crisis of the 1930's would convince many of the need for structural changes in the system. Designed to rally all who were suffering from the economic blizzard, it was an attempt to work out an answer to the rise of Hitler.

De Man believed that reformism can yield returns only in prosperity, and that it has no answer to a permanent crisis. A constructive policy is needed, "a programme of action designed not merely to redistribute wealth, but to enlarge its total amount, and not merely to promote the revival of capitalist industry, but to inaugurate fundamental changes in economic structure by removing whole sectors of the economy out of capitalist control and reconstructing them on the basis of complete socialization." [8] The Plan called for nationalization of credit, of basic industries, and of transport services. Private ownership would be allowed in other sectors of the economy. "The Theses of Pontigny," another name for the Plan, declared the crisis of the 1930's as a crisis of the system due to the fact that the formerly progressive system of capitalism had become regressive. The change shows itself in the predominance of finance capitalism, the growth of monopolies, and the replacement of cosmopolitanism by nationalism. Reformism, which has dominated the labor movement, is no longer practical. Structural change rather than a redistribution of wealth is the need of the hour. A passive attitude toward the crisis should be rejected in favor of economic planning based

[8] Henri De Man, *Planned Socialism* (London: Victor Gollancz, Ltd., 1935), p. 14.

upon nationalization of certain basic industries. Nationalized state-owned enterprises were to be placed under autonomous corporations to eliminate bureaucracy.

Socialism should cease to be mainly proletarian, for the increase in the number and proportion of manual workers had ceased, and the support of the majority is needed to effectuate reform. Action should be directed against the monopolist and not against every form of capitalism.[9]

De Man's program created widespread enthusiasm in the ranks of Belgian socialism. Some hoped that such a program would attract workers who shied away from socialism because of religious scruples. However, the failure of the Belgian Workers' Bank in which the labor organizations had some of their funds, plus the need for currency depreciation due to events outside the country, forced a revision of the government. De Man and several other socialists entered the cabinet, and although some success in combating unemployment was achieved, the full objectives of the Plan were not realized.[10]

POSTWAR

After Hitler overran the country, the Socialist party went underground to take part in the clandestine resistance to the Nazis. With liberation, Belgium made a spectacular economic recovery. She had benefited from the quick ousting of the Nazi invaders, which prevented large-scale destruction of plant and equipment. She also profited from the presence of thousands of British and American troops which enabled her to acquire sterling and dollars. Controls were removed and stiff taxes on wartime profits introduced. Indeed, Belgium's recovery was so rapid that, for a time, she served as an example of what an antirestriction policy might achieve. The Socialists have participated in a number of coalition cabinets, several of which were headed by one of their members.

Although they cooperated in several coalition cabinets, the Socialists not only differ with the Catholics on the return of King Leopold to the throne, but are skeptical of the liberal policies pursued since the end of the war. As a result of changes that have also affected other nations, Belgium lost, in 1948, some of its export markets. Unemployment increased until it reached 300,000. The Socialists have argued that restrictive

9 *Ibid.*, pp. 24–25.
10 Adolf Sturmthal, *The Tragedy of European Labor* (New York: Columbia University Press, 1943), pp. 228–229.

policies should be avoided in a period of unemployment, and have demanded an expanded public works program.

Social security legislation made significant strides in the postwar period. Under the leadership of a Socialist prime minister, Achille van Acker, an extensive social security program has been put into effect. All forms of insurance against loss of income have been made compulsory. Employer and employee contributions of 23.5 per cent of all wages and salaries under 4,000 francs support the program. One third is paid by the employee and two thirds come by the employer.

More than ever, the Socialist party is convinced that economic and political democracy are desirable goals and that the abolition of capitalism by peaceful means and through planning is the best way to achieve them. Parliamentary means may be unspectacular and slow, but Belgian socialists believe they are more certain and less costly than force and dictatorship.

2. SPANISH ANARCHOSYNDICALISM

Marxism never gained intellectual dominance over the Spanish revolutionary movement. Spanish radicalism was made up of two opposing movements, anarchist and socialist, the former obviously more in harmony with the Spanish temperament and exercising the steadier influence upon Spanish labor and peasantry. In the 1820's, Sebastian Abreu, a member of the Cortes, tried to propagate the views of Fourier. He was forced to emigrate to France, and upon his return to Spain he attempted to establish a *phalanstère*, but it met with failure. Fernando Garrido tried to start a socialist journal, *Atracción*, in Madrid; the journal was founded in 1845, but lack of support forced its closing after three months.[1] For a time Spanish socialism was devoted largely to mutualism and cooperation. Not until the late 1860's were revolutionary ideas established in Spain.[2]

FIRST INTERNATIONAL AND ANARCHISTS

Under the influence of Bakunin, the modern revolutionary movement began. A close co-worker of Bakunin, Giuseppi Fannelli, an Italian, established a section of the International in Madrid and in Barcelona, the members of which helped to organize groups in other communities. Fannelli's success was instantaneous, and within the "space of less than three months, without knowing a word of Spanish or meeting more than an occasional Spaniard who understood his French or Italian, he had launched a movement that was to endure with wave-like advances and

[1] Angel Marvaud, *La Question sociale en Espagne* (Paris: Félix Alcan: 1910), pp. 27–29.
[2] Marie Oswald, "Le Socialisme en Espagne," *Le Révue socialiste,* May, 1896, pp. 591–593.

recessions for the next seventy years and to affect profoundly the destinies of Spain." [3] Not proletarians but artisans and an occasional schoolteacher were the first recruits. A journal, *Solidaridad,* was established.[4]

In June of the following year a congress met at Barcelona and set up a federal center of revolutionary labor. Each local group received the right to embrace any political opinion it chose. A section of the International, *Federación Regional Española de los Trabajadores,* was organized, with an executive committee to keep the locals in contact with one another. The movement was antipolitical and antiauthoritarian. In a manifesto the Federation declared that the workers who produced the wealth of the world would find the means to realize their own emancipation.[5] Progress was very rapid, and the Spanish International became numerically the largest in the world. Alarmed by its steady gains, the government sought to suppress the International in 1872. The movement fought back, but internal difficulties also appeared. Under the influence of Bakunin, the Spanish revolutionary movement had acquired an anarchist outlook. Opposition from political or authoritarian socialists led the latter to set up a federation in Madrid in which Paul Lafargue, Marx's son-in-law and a leading French socialist, then an exile, participated. Each group established its own publication: the Marxists, *La Emancipación,* and the Bakunists, *El Condenado,* whose slogan was "atheism, anarchy and collectivism."

The anarchists looked toward establishing free and independent communes voluntarily federated together and reciprocally providing public services. They opposed participation in politics and, in contrast to the Marxists, opposed the domination of production by the state.[6] Decentralized, lacking a bureaucracy, the anarchist movement launched at the Cordova congress sought to organize the poor laborers and to lead them into battle for immediate demands. After winning the confidence of the workers, it would be easy to spread the anarchist gospel of hatred of church and state. In harmony with its general outlook, each regional and local group had the right to follow its own political wishes.

The Spanish section of the International participated in the revolts of

3 Gerald Brenan, *The Spanish Labyrinth* (Cambridge: Cambridge University Press, 1943), p. 140.
4 Federica Montsen, *Los Precursores,* (*Anselmo Lorenzo*) (Barcelona: Ediciónes Españoles, 1938), p. 7–8.
5 Marvaud, *op. cit.,* p. 33.
6 *Ibid.,* pp. 34–37.

1874, and although its role was not great, much of the odium and persecution that followed fell upon it. Despite the persecution by the government, the anarchist movement continued. It was at Barcelona, the anarchist stronghold, that an Italian anarchist, Alfredo Baccherini, preached the doctrine of "propaganda by the deed." It consequently became a city of frequent violence, numerous clashes, and bitter labor struggles. A relaxation of the repression followed the coming to power of a liberal government; and in September, 1881, delegates representing about 50,000 members in 209 local and regional federations formed the Regional Labor Federation. A federal committee was to keep the sections together.[7]

A split between communists and collectivists soon followed. Communists envisaged social ownership of the means of production and communal enjoyment of the annual social product. The other group, while favoring common ownership of the means of production, wished each to enjoy the fruits of his own efforts. Perhaps a more significant difference was the fact that the communists repudiated all forms of authority, while the collectivists favored free producers' cooperative federations. The communist view carried at the congress of 1883, where it was decided to allow each individual and each group to evolve its own interpretation of anarchism. The Central Committee was empowered to maintain communication between the affiliated groups and members, but it was not given any power.[8]

This organization went on until 1889, when it was recast into the Alliance of Solidarity and Assistance. Affiliates had to regard themselves as anarchists who opposed all government. The object was the abolition of government, the expropriation of the means of production, and the organization of society on the basis of labor. The exclusiveness of the Catalans was said to have been the cause of the death of the Alliance. Following the breakup of the Regional Labor Federation, Spanish labor was split into local and regional groupings. The Catalans organized, in 1907, the *Federación Regional Catalona,* with which numerous organizations throughout the country affiliated.

In the meantime, Spain was in the throes of serious discontent; the

7 Manuel Buenacasa, *El Movimiento Obrero Español, 1886–1926* (Barcelona: Impresos Costa, 1926), pp. 161–162.
8 Marvaud, *op. cit.,* pp. 50–52.

shooting of Francisco Ferrer was one manifestation of the government's repressive policy. This incident led to the movement for national unity on the part of all radicals. In September, 1911, at the congress of Bellas Artes the *Confederación Nacional del Trabajo* (C.N.T.) was organized, representing about 30,000 workers.[9] A national committee was set up to handle matters, with regional federations and locals in subordinate groups.

Its officers were subjected to governmental persecution, but the C.N.T. grew rapidly. It was anarchist in outlook and shunned all political activity. Its views on social organization was federalist and localist. At the Madrid congress in 1919, the C.N.T. favored the complete and absolute moral, economic, and political liberation of humanity, and claimed that these objectives could be obtained only by socializing the land and other means of production and exchange, and by the elimination of the state. All this could be achieved only by communist anarchism. The relative prosperity of the Catalonian industrial areas enabled the movement to sink deep roots there. Led by the militant anarchists, Angel Pestagna and Salvador Segui, the C.N.T. won the adherence of the majority of labor. Terror by the government and employers was used against the leaders. Hired gunmen, *Pistoleros,* assassinated Pestagna in August, 1922, and Segui the following March.[10]

In contrast to European trade-union movements, the C.N.T did not establish a strike fund, but relied upon support from nonstrikers, with the result that strikes had to be short and were usually violent. No agreements with employers were made, as the C.N.T. looked upon the ending of a strike as a pause in a never-ceasing war. Through the C.N.T. Spanish anarchism became anarchosyndicalism.[11] Absolute local autonomy prevailed, and each group was free to make its own rules. The general attitude showed a primitive revolutionism which, in fact, reflected the backwardness of Spanish labor. In some respects the C.N.T. resembled the American Industrial Workers of the World; the latter also refused to make agreements or build up a defense fund. Such an attitude, which usually shows itself among groups not easily subjected to discipline, makes it very difficult to build a permanent and disciplined organization willing to work out some basis for getting along with the employer and society.

9 Buenacasa, *op. cit.,* pp. 51–53.
10 *Crapouillot,* January, 1938, pp. 46–47.
11 Franz Borkenau, *The Spanish Cockpit* (London: Faber and Faber, 1937), pp. 34–35.

IBERIAN ANARCHIST FEDERATION

The Iberian Anarchist Federation (*Federación Anarqista Iberica*) was set up in the middle 1920's by a number of anarchist groups. Its aim was to keep the C.N.T. from becoming too reformist in outlook and action. The Anarchist Federation was made up of the anarchist elite. Its leaders believed in the possibilities of immediate revolution, and were able to overcome the more cautious elements in the C.N.T. Led by the Iberian Anarchist Federation, whose members dominated the C.N.T., insurrections were started after 1931, but were brutally repressed by the republican government. Anarchism in Spain showed itself as a manifestation of the resistance of the Spanish worker and peasant to capitalism. "Were there no capitalist intrusion whatever, there would be no anarchism. Had the spirit of capitalism permeated the nation, anarchism would be at an end." [12]

The attraction of anarchism for the Spanish people is explained by the fact that its spirit coincides with the feeling of the Spanish masses. A revolutionary spirit could be found only among resolute primitives who had not yet been affected by capitalism. People are revolutionaries out of moral conviction and not because of intellectual agitation. It is not from the ranks of respecters of civilized living and the blessings of property that revolutionary cadres are recruited. Anarchism stresses moral regeneration rather than material reconstruction. Anarchosyndicalism not only had its roots in the idealism of the Spanish people, but was a "natural reaction to intolerable conditions and whenever these conditions cease to be intolerable—whenever that is, one finds peasants owning or renting sufficient land to support them—anarchism ceases." [13]

Spanish anarchists resisted the encroachment of capitalism upon a primitive economic society. They gave the finest examples of solidarity and sacrifice but, in contrast to the socialists, little evidence of the creativeness needed for permanent building.

The Anarcho-Syndicalists, through their spirit, their organization, their natural contrariness, were incapable of making a wide and concerted effort of this sort. Though they might frighten the more timid among the bourgeoisie, no government ever regarded them, in spite of their huge numbers, which mounted in

[12] *Ibid.*, p. 24.
[13] Brenan, *op. cit.*, p. 185.

times of excitement to a million or a million and a half, as anything more than a problem for the provincial governor or police.[14]

Although not as important politically as its large numbers might have made it, Spanish anarchism has expressed the search for a higher moral state. The movement is itself politically unsophisticated, being driven by an inner urge to construct a moral and just society. Averse to subordinating principle to expediency, the anarchists use only right and justice as guides to conduct. This principle leads them to neglect the political effect of their policies. Such lack of political finesse may stamp them as poor politicians, but the anarchists are perhaps alone in regulating their conduct on the basis of principles rather than of political necessity. However, as Gerald Brenan points out, although the Spanish anarchists are sincere devotees of justice, their emphasis upon violence and their intolerance of the church would lead to forms of force and tyranny.

Another root of Spanish anarchism is to be found in the desire of many peasants and factory workers to return to simpler economic and social forms. Modern finance and industry are repugnant, and many Spaniards wish to return to the simpler life of the past, the free peasant commune. Spanish anarchism has lingered because Spain is a nation of small business, independent artisans, and exploited peasants. The discipline of industry which politicizes a nation is absent. As defined by a left-wing critic, anarchism "is a species of courageous, unplanned, unscientific and sporadic action on the part of men who are easily made drunk by glowing phrases, the political content of which they never trouble to analyze." [15]

SOCIALISTS

Originally a small group of Marxists refused to go along with the anarchists. During this time a union of typographical workers was established in Madrid in 1871, and two years later, Pablo Iglesias (1850–1925) was elected president. He recommended the setting up of a defense fund and the extension of the movement. The printers' organization gave many leaders to the Socialist party, the outstanding one being Iglesias himself. The nucleus for the Socialist party was, however, the few

14 *Ibid.*, p. 187.
15 Bertram D. Wolfe, *Civil War in Spain* (New York: Workers Age Publishers, 1937), p. 76.

authoritarians or socialists who could not accept the antipolitical views of the anarchists. Keeping in personal touch with each other, members of this group met in 1879 and worked out a program based upon a recog- nition of the class conflict in modern society. They declared that the basis of class conflict was the possession of the instruments of production which enabled the few to exploit the many, and to assemble vast fortunes. Jus- tice and equity demanded a change.

The Socialist Labor party, which they launched, declared its hope of abolishing class differences, transforming individual into collective prop- erty, and placing political power in the hands of the workers. As a means of obtaining this ideal, the party demanded political freedom, the right of labor to organize and to strike, reduction of the hours of labor by law, prohibition of the labor of children under nine years of age and of women in occupations injurious to health, protection of health and safety of industrial labor, establishment of supervisory commissions elected by labor, establishment of primary and professional schools based on nonreligious instruction, and government ownership of ships and rail- roads. An executive committee with Pablo Iglesias as secretary was chosen.[16]

The movement spread beyond Madrid, and the program underwent slight modifications. However, there was agreement upon the need of labor to achieve political power and upon the complete emancipation of the working class. The accession of the liberal Sagasta to power led to the legalizing of socialist activity, and the party could now come from under- ground. A more liberal attitude by the authorities enabled socialist labor groups to hold a congress at which a resolution urging workers to form an independent political party for the conquest of political power was approved and a program urging immediate reforms adopted.[17] Although the proposal for a national federation was accepted, such a group was not immediately set up. However, it did lead to the diffusion of socialist ideas among workers and to the widening and the strengthening of personal relationships among leading socialist trade unionists, eventually culminating in the formation of the General Union of Labor (*Unión General de Trabajadores de España*) in 1888.

In most countries the socialist and trade-union movements, while

[16] Juan José Morato, *El Partido Socialista* (Madrid: Biblioteca Nueva, 1919), pp. 109–111.
[17] *Ibid.*, pp. 125, 126.

closely tied together, were led by different individuals. The Spanish socialist movement deviated from this rule inasmuch as Pablo Iglesias was not only the head of the national executive of the Socialist Labor party, but also the head of the General Union of Labor. The purpose of the latter was to unite and extend the economic organizations of labor so as to improve wages and working conditions. The workers of all political faiths were eligible, but the General Union of Labor was dominated by socialists. In time it became a powerful labor center and competed with the anarchosyndicalists for the hegemony of the economic movement of labor.

Iglesias came into contact with the anarchist movement in 1870 and joined a Bakuninist group in Madrid. In the controversy between the adherents of Bakunin and of Marx, Iglesias sided with the latter. With Paul Lafargue, then a refugee from the Commune, he tried to establish a Marxist movement and he helped to found the Spanish Social Democratic Labor party in 1878. Two years later the party approved the following program: political power for the workers; transformation of personal property into social property; and the organization of society on the basis of economic federalism, so that the products of social labor would be appropriated by society to guarantee to each the full product of his work. In sum, the party stood for the complete emancipation of labor, the abolition of classes, and the creation of a free and equal society founded on labor.[18]

Political socialism did not progress too rapidly. Hampered by the anarchist tradition, the General Union of Labor was most influential among the more advanced industrial workers in Castile. In 1909 the socialists cooperated with the anarchists and republicans in a general strike. As a consequence, they gained widespread popularity and made extensive gains in the elections that followed. Only in Barcelona did the anarchists retain their hold on labor.

Following World War I new men came to the front. Francis Largo Caballero, a worker in the Madrid building trades, took over from Iglesias the leadership of the General Union of Labor. Indalecio Prieto, a leading socialist orator and executive, occupied an important place in the Socialist party. A struggle between the orthdox Marxist Caballero and the reformist Prieto confronted Spanish socialism. The former was usually in the ascendency, but Prieto was not without influence. After

[18] Julian Zugazagoitia, *Pablo Iglesias* (Madrid: Eddiciónes Españoles, 1938), pp. 27–28.

World War I, strong sentiment existed for joining the Third International, and only the forceful pleas of Iglesias prevented the Spanish party from affiliating.

The advent of the dictatorship of Primo de Rivera presented another problem for Spanish socialism. The liberal and reformist Prieto was opposed to any cooperation with the dictator. In contrast, the Marxist Caballero favored accepting the overtures of the authoritarian government, for he thought he could thus strengthen the position of his group at the expense of the anarchosyndicalists. As a good Marxist, he regarded the anarchosyndicalists as dangerous sentimentalists who prevented the unification of the proletariat.[19]

THE DICTATORSHIP OF PRIMO DE RIVERA

The dictatorship of Primo de Rivera was the immediate cause of the subsequent collapse of the monarchy, which tied its fortunes to the dictator. An atmosphere was created which daily became more and more charged with discontent and revolt. At first the dictator was successful in introducing a certain amount of material improvement and in ending the war in Morocco. On the other hand, he abolished free speech and press and introduced censorship and suppression.[20] His regime was at the beginning to last but ninety days, but it continued year after year. Mounting tension and difficulties led to his resignation in 1931. The opposition to Primo de Rivera was accompanied by strong anti-monarchical feeling and restlessness which manifested itself in strikes. A republican-socialist coalition was set up and a Revolutionary Committee chosen by the antimonarchical groups. For issuing a manifesto calling for a republic, six members of the Revolutionary Committee were arrested. The nominal sentences they received showed the power of revolutionary sentiment rather than the leniency of the government. In the municipal elections in the spring of 1931 the attitude of the republicans was confirmed. An overwhelming republican majority was responsible for Alfonso XIII's abdication. The Revolutionary Committee became the Provisional Government.

---

[19] Francisco Largo Caballero, *Presente y Future de la Unión de Trabajadores de España* (Madrid: Javier Morata Pedreño, 1925), pp. 160–184.

[20] Alfred Mendizabel, *The Martyrdom of Spain* (New York: Charles Scribners' Sons, 1938), p. 37; E. Allison Peers, *The Spanish Tragedy* (New York: Oxford University Press, 1936), pp. 4–6.

THE LEFT IN POWER

At a meeting of the Constituent Assembly in July, 1931, the left had a decisive majority, with 116 socialists representing the largest party. Don Julian Besteiro was chosen president of the Assembly. A majority of members of the Assembly had little or no experience with parliamentary procedures, "and a considerable number of them were men with a doctrinaire turn of mind. . . . The chief defects of the Constitution were the weakness of the Executive, the lack of a Senate and the disestablishment of the Church." [21] The republic made a serious blunder with respect to the church. "Priests were deprived of their salaries, although the clerical proletariat, in opposition to the wealthy bishops, might have been won over to the Republic." [22] The consequence was the withdrawal of Alcale Zamora, the President, and Miguel Maura, the Home Secretary, from the Provisional Government. The constitution was ratified in December, 1931, and Zamora became president and Manuel Azana, a leading anticlerical, prime minister. The policy of extreme anticlericalism aroused many who were not overly sympathetic to the church. The left government lost the confidence of the voters, and in the elections of 1933 the right parties obtained a majority. Repression and the undoing of many reforms were followed by a "Popular Front" coalition for the February, 1936, elections at which the left won a clear majority, with the right parties running a poor third. In the strikes and violence that followed, the right showed renewed vigor. Spanish fascism was manifesting daring and determination in challenging the leftists. Political assassinations became a daily occurrence.

COUNTERREVOLUTION

In reprisal for the assassination of a republican police officer, a group of armed men killed Calvo Sotelo, who was to have led the rightist revolt. Sure of immediate victory, a number of generals decided to strike, and rose on July 17 and 18, 1936. The easy conquest they anticipated proved to have been born of overconfidence. Armed battalions of workers were too much for them, and the principal Spanish cities remained in government hands. [23] The workers closed ranks, and their political and economic

21 Salvador Madriaga, *Spain* (New York: Creative Age Press, 1943), p. 301.
22 *Ibid.*, p. 302.
23 Peers, *op. cit.*, pp. 210–211.

organizations became the real governors. After a time the Popular Front government of Caballero came to power. Factories and estates were taken over by workers' committees, with the anarchists most active in collectiviz-ing. For the anarchists, the Spanish Civil War "was the first and most important step in social revolution. Far from regarding the war as a mere defence against fascism, they saw in it the opportunity for which they had long been waiting to create a new type of society, and were perfectly aware that if they failed to set up a *fait accompli* in the first days of the struggle, they would be overcome and defeated by events." The anarchists believed that an example must be set and that the greatest devotion could be aroused only by tangible proof that a more desirable social system was in the making. Consequently, the anarchists collectivized many under-takings; moreover, they were fairly successful.[24]

Foreign intervention and not the social program was decisive in de-termining the outcome of the Spanish Civil War. Hitler and Mussolini saw in Francisco Franco a useful tool for their contemplated attack on the democracies. Fascist intervention on Franco's side was followed by Soviet intervention on the side of the Loyalists. The Spanish Civil War became the first campaign of World War II. However, the left not only lacked the wholehearted support of the Western democracies, but was it-self rent apart by personal and ideological differences. As the Civil War continued, their prestige raised by Soviet arms, Spanish communists gained an increasingly important role in the management and direction of the Loyalist cause. In addition, the communists had the firmness, energy, and ruthlessness vital in the waging of successful military cam-paigns. Although they excelled in battle,

it was not easy for other parties to get along with them. They suffered from a fixed belief in their own superior knowledge and capacity. They were incapable of rational discussion. From every pore they exuded a rigid totalitarian spirit. Their appetite for power was insatiable and they were completely unscrupulous. To them the winning of the war meant winning it for the Communist Party and they were always ready to sacrifice military advantage to prevent a rival party on their own side from strengthening its position.[25]

Lacking all moral and political integrity, the communists, as is their wont, were ready to pursue any policy that would redound to their party's advantage. For a time the communist influence was very great, but

24 Brenan, *op. cit.,* pp. 319, 321–322.
25 *Ibid.,* p. 326.

it gradually weakened. In the meantime, the Loyalists, despite the valor of the troops, were unable to overcome the forces supported by Hitler and Mussolini. France was unable to help because of Chamberlain's appeasement policy. Nevertheless, the Loyalists held out until March, 1939. General Franco, whose victory was made possible by foreign aid, herded hundreds of thousands of his countrymen into prisons and concentration camps where thousands were executed.

The international importance which this war came to acquire and the active intervention in it of two fascist and one communist states, have tended to obscure the fact that in its inception and in its essence the Civil War was above all Spanish. The Spanish origin and aspects of the Civil War must be stressed in order to understand it adequately even as an episode in the European civil war of which it was the prologue.[26]

In contrast to the European left, except the Austrians, the Spaniards fought heroically. They were weak in the theoretical jargon of modern revolutionary movements, but their heroism was unsurpassed and their valor beyond question. The most impressive characteristic of the Spanish Civil War was the bitter courage displayed by the armed legions of proletarians and peasants. Nevertheless, the "creative political power in which both the French and the Russian revolution has been so rich was conspicuously absent in Spain." [27] Spanish revolutionaries were inhospitable to European political forms, and unadaptable to European military methods; yet the courage of the Loyalist troops shone with a bright glow in a decade when free men surrendered easily to the forces of evil.

[26] Madriaga, *op. cit.*, p. 296.
[27] Borkenau, *op. cit.*, p. 285.

INDEXES

REFERENCE INDEX

583

SUBJECT INDEX

587